Theological Lexicon of the Old Testament

Theological Lexicon of the Old Testament

Volume 1

אָב *ʾāb*

חנף *ḥnp*

ERNST JENNI
CLAUS WESTERMANN

Translated by MARK E. BIDDLE

HENDRICKSON
PUBLISHERS

P. O. Box 3473
Peabody, Massachusetts 01961–3473

Printed in the United States of America

ISBN 1–56563–133–1

Translated from the *Theologisches Handwörterbuch zum Alten Testament*, edited by Ernst Jenni, with assistance from Claus Westermann, 2 volumes; ©1971, 1976, Chr. Kaiser Verlag, Munich, and Theologischer Verlag, Zurich.

First Printing — September 1997

Library of Congress Cataloging-in-Publication Data

Theologisches Handwörterbuch zum Alten Testament. English.
Theological lexicon of the Old Testament / edited by Ernst Jenni with assistance from Claus Westermann; translated by Mark E. Biddle.
Includes bibliographical references and indexes.
ISBN 1–56563–133–1 (cloth)
1. Bible. O.T.—Dictionaries—Hebrew. 2. Bible O.T.—Dictionaries—Aramaic. 3. Hebrew language—Dictionaries—English. 4. Aramaic language—Dictionaries—English. I. Jenni, Ernst. II. Westermann, Claus. III. Title
BS440.T4813 1997
221.4′47—dc21 97–5604
CIP

Table of Contents

VOLUME ONE

חנף - אָב

VOLUME TWO

צִיּוֹן - חֶסֶד

VOLUME THREE

תְּרָפִים - צלח

Preface to the German Edition

I am deeply indebted to my honored colleague Prof. Dr. C. Westermann, Heidelberg, who has also given impetus to the project and has established contact with the publisher, for the enlistment of a great portion of the approximately forty contributors to this first volume of the *THAT.* That the assembly of the contributors has resulted in two geographical centers, one in Heidelberg and the other in Switzerland, should be understood in terms of personal relationships, yet contributions to the first volume originate from about ten different countries.

I have translated the manuscripts of non-German-speaking authors and have subjected all articles to revision with a view to formalities and to the creation of a degree of uniformity. Frequent use has been made of a stipulated right to alter content as well (in the more significant cases, following discussions with the author), less in deletions than in additions. A number of revisions, if sufficiently distinctive thematically or the result of the needs of the structure of the lexicon as a whole (e.g., the placement of semantically related words) and consequently not to be taken as criticism of an author's contribution, are indicated by means of an asterisk (*) as the addition of the editor (* beside section numbers or letters indicates the entire section in question; * after a paragraph indicates only the paragraph in question). The most substantive interventions were necessary in the first two major sections; for the verification of statistical details, I alone bear responsibility. Only the long articles have been submitted to the authors for proofreading; hence I must bear more than usual responsibility for oversights and typographical errors.

Particular thanks are due Prof. Dr. Theol. Thomas Willi (Eichberg, St. Gallen), Prof. Dr. Theol. Gerhard Wehmeier (Dharwar, St. Mysore, India), and Matthius Suter, who, as the editor's assistants from the end of 1968 on, have undertaken the troublesome task of checking references and citations, as well as finally of proofreading.

Basel, April 1971, Ernst Jenni

Preface to the English Edition

A. History of the Volumes

The *Theologisches Handwörterbuch zum Alten Testament*, edited by Ernst Jenni with assistance from Claus Westermann (Munich: Chr. Kaiser; Zurich: Theologischer Verlag) has displayed the longevity of an incomparable reference work. It was originally published as two volumes in the 1970s (volume 1, *ʾalep–mem*, in 1971; volume 2, *nun–taw*, in 1976) and was reissued in 1984. A Spanish translation by J. Antonio Mugica appeared in 1978 (*Diccionario teologico manual del Antiguo Testamento*, Madrid: Ediciones Cristiandad). This present three-volume translation makes accessible for the first time in English a wealth of theological insight that, as the introduction to the German edition promises, "intends to offer a reliable aid for the academic study of the Old Testament but also for the church's teaching and preaching."

B. Features of the Translation

The publisher has sought to make this an easily accessible and valuable resource for students of any level. Toward this end, the entries have been comprehensively updated to reflect new editions and English translations of the bibliographic references. Furthermore, all Hebrew and Aramaic words have been fully transliterated into English forms. For ready reference, a new feature has been added: a resource list has been included with each new entry. This list keys the terms in the main entries (and all cross-referenced words) to the corresponding page locations in *The Brown-Driver-Briggs Hebrew and English Lexicon* (BDB), the *Theological Dictionary of the Old Testament (TDOT)*, and the English edition of Koehler and Baumgartner's *Hebrew and Aramaic Lexicon of the Old Testament (HALOT)*, and to the word numbers in *Strong's Exhaustive Concordance of the Bible* (S), the *Theological Wordbook of the Old Testament (TWOT)*, and the *New International Dictionary of Old Testament Theology and Exegesis (NIDOTTE)*. The English translations of *TDOT* and *HALOT* were not complete upon publication: in these cases, where the English resources ended, we have cited the original German volumes (*ThWAT* and *HAL*, respectively). Some of these lexical aids will be useful to the scholar, some to the student and pastor, and some to the layperson.

This English edition has modified the German *Einleitung* in four places. (1) Section D, "Explanation of the Hebrew Transliteration," represents the conventions we have adopted here, which are those generally used among English-speaking scholars. (2) Section E, "Concordance of Divergent Versification," compares references in the Hebrew text tradition (MT) and in standard English translations (e.g., NRSV). (3) Section F, which contained

Jenni's concluding remarks at the publication of the first volume, has been removed from the introduction and retitled "Preface to the German Edition." (4) Because the English edition comprises three volumes, we have relocated the original *Vorwort* to the second volume to immediately following the foreword to the German edition (p. xii).

The content of these volumes has been altered very little from the German original. In general, the updating of the bibliographic entries extends only to revised editions and English translations. Some exceptions occur. For example, Ugaritic texts are cited according to *Die keilalphabetischen Texte aus Ugarit (KTU),* which appeared too late to be used by the authors of the original edition. In rare cases, the translator has explained nuances and semantic ranges using English analogues rather than strict translations of the original German examples. Direct quotations have also been translated, even when no English-language edition exists. References to Qumran literature have occasionally been modified to indicate that the author worked only with material that was available at the original publication, and some concordance additions have been added to supplement K. G. Kuhn's *Konkordanz zu den Qumrantexten.* We have differed from the German in not setting transliterated proper names with an initial uppercase character.

The translator and the publisher of the English edition have not updated the text to reflect recent discussion. This approach was intentional, since the individual entries are, in effect, lexical essays. They represent clear methodological approaches and interact with the bibliography cited. To update the discussion, which the bibliography reflects, would be to misrepresent the efforts and viewpoints of the contributing scholars. The reader should pursue further inquiry with the tools cited in the resource key, some of which contain subsequent scholarly discussion.

The statistical tables and indexes in the final volume closely reproduce the German originals. The reader should note the following changes. (1) The English edition includes a Scripture index. (2) The English word index is based on the definitions used in the main headings. (3) In the place of separate Hebrew and Aramaic indexes, we have provided one index that alphabetizes the main entries and includes an alphabetical list of the derivatives discussed under each main entry, and a second index that fully alphabetizes all significant words discussed and keys these words to Strong's numbers.

The publisher is confident that the individual studies in the *Theological Lexicon of the Old Testament* remain fundamental to biblical scholars, theologians, pastors, and laypersons. Their careful attention to the history and context of the biblical text has not been superseded, and their theological insights will remain significant to anyone interested in either historical or constructive theology. The rigor of their search for meaning within the historical and linguistic contexts of particular passages stands as an example to another generation of scholars and students.

Foreword to the German Edition

A. Volume 1

This is the first volume of a lexicon that intends to offer a reliable aid for the academic study of the OT but also for the church's teaching and preaching. The contributor's concern has been to set the treatment of the meaning and usage of individual vocabulary entries on the broadest possible methodological basis. In recent decades the consensus in OT research has become to avoid all methodological limitations in questions concerning the meaning of a word (particularly concerning the theological meaning); only the determined application of as many different approaches as possible can lead to a convincing result. These limitations include attempts to explain a word on the basis of grammatical-philological viewpoints alone, to derive the full richness of a word from a postulated basic meaning in every case, and to reconstruct a linear history of a concept that leaves no room for the parallel existence of differentiated categories of usage. Finally, a mechanical differentiation between profane and religious usages, wherein eo ipso the profane usage is frequently seen as the older, should also be regarded as restrictive.

In contrast to all such linear explanations, this lexicon strives to attribute absolute authority to no individual method of linguistic research. Rather, in accordance with the current status of OT studies and of general linguistics, it seeks to establish and maintain as broad an approach as possible.

In contrast to previous OT lexicons, the results of a plethora of form-critical and tradition-critical investigations in particular are incorporated here. In many cases a substantial correction in the objective groupings as well as in the temporal stratification of word usages is required. On the one hand, it is now possible to assess with certainty the context against which a given verb or noun should be exegeted by means of firm and unequivocal categorization of a particular usage of a verb or a noun, perhaps to a particular legal form, to a prophetic speech form, to a psalm genre, or to a particular narrative or report tradition. On the other hand, one is much less likely to speak of "early" and "late" usages of a particular word; and, confronted with a strongly divergent word usage, one is as likely to think of parallel as of subsequent developments.

An essential result of recent linguistics merits particular attention: that the basic unit of speech communication is not the word but the sentence. This result corresponds with those of form criticism and tradition criticism. In contrast to literary-critical methods of research for which the usage of an isolated word can be decisive for the determination of the temporal stratification, it has become ever more apparent in recent research that only the sentence, or a construct of several sentences, characterizes a tradition. This observation has one essential consequence for the treatment of the content of a word: the categorization of the occurrences of a word must result from the sentences in which they occur and from their function in the larger context.

The work of the lexicon is affected by a further important correction offered by so-called semantic-field research, whose usefulness for the determination of the meanings of words that seem very closely related or synonymous, as well as for the translation into other languages where the semantic fields are often structured otherwise, can only be alluded to here.

In conclusion attention must be called to the fact that the powerful expansion of the corpus of texts in Semitic languages, advances in research in Hebrew grammar and syntax, the differentiation and refinement of philological methods, and the many new efforts in general linguistics have truly not made the preparation of an OT lexicon easier, even if they have made possible many advances. One must admit that in many cases uncertainties remain with regard to the determination of the general as well as the theological usage of a Hebrew word. The main emphasis of this lexicon lies in an awareness of continuing difficulties with regard to the careful evaluation of the function of a Hebrew word in a given context. At this point the work of the lexicon spills over into the work of the exegesis that the lexicon seeks to serve.

Basel and Heidelberg, April 1971, E. Jenni and C. Westermann

B. Volume 2

Four years after the appearance of the first volume, work on *THAT* can now be concluded. The preparation of the second volume followed the same principles elucidated in the first volume. The number of contributors has risen to a total of fifty. I thank them all, from those who submitted early contributions to those who stepped into the breach at the end, for their efforts and patience, and especially Prof. Dr. C. Westermann, who once again willingly assisted through word and deed. The Rev. Mr. Matthias Suter (Lauterbrunnen, Canton Bern) and the Rev. Mr. Thomas Hartmann (Basel) deserve thanks for their assistance with the task of proofreading and editing. Furthermore, Mr. Hartmann produced the index of German words.

Because typesetting required more than two years, all articles were not able to take account of the most recent literature. This delay did permit me, however, to expand the statistical appendix to its current scope. We were more concerned with the practical usefulness of the indices of Hebrew and German words than with concordancelike thoroughness. For the same reason, we chose, after careful consideration, to forego additional word, topic, and passage indices, which would have necessarily been capricious in choice of material to be indexed or useful only for specialists. In contrast, the index of authors, which includes all but the most common reference works, will be helpful for bibliographical work.

Basel, November 1975, Ernst Jenni

Introduction

A. Goal of the Lexicon

Relatively good OT lexicons have been available to the Hebraist for some time: GB, BDB, KBL, Zorrel, and more recently *HAL* and *HALOT* merit mention as those used most often. Nevertheless, these lexicons, with their conventional arrangement as lists of possible German and English translations of a Hebrew word (some with thorough etymological introductions, which are, however, useful only to the specialist) without explication and discussion of the problems in complete sentences, undeniably cannot provide information concerning the use and life of OT words corresponding to the state of current knowledge, if only for reasons of space. In addition, alongside traditional philological inquiry, semantics and form- and tradition-critical methods have gained significance in recent years; their results and approaches are rarely dealt with adequately in the normal scope of a lexicon. It is increasingly difficult, particularly with respect to theologically significant words, to take into account the work undertaken by international OT studies in the area of linguistic research. Consequently, the attempt to create a specialized lexicon certainly reflects a need, as formulated in the guidelines for contributors to *TLOT* as a result of project planning in the course of the year 1966, to "present, as a supplement to extant Hebrew lexicons and on a strict linguistic basis with particular attention to semantics and form- and tradition-critical methodology, the theologically relevant words of the OT with a view to their usage, their history, and their significance for OT theology in the most concise and complete manner and with reference to the extant literature."

That the result corresponds in every respect to the envisioned ideal should certainly not be maintained. But it will serve the necessary clarity when it will have been said from the outset what has not been the aim of *TLOT:*

1. Although the index in the third volume indicates that a significant portion of OT vocabulary has been treated, *TLOT* cannot replace the extant lexicons, if only because of the selection of the words to be treated. Rather it supplements these lexicons. Even with respect to the roots and words treated, the rich lexical, grammatical, text-critical, and bibliographical citations of, for example, *HAL* have been far from exhaustively treated.

2. With a complete openness for new developments in linguistics (cf. e.g., the inclusive treatment in the *Encyclopedie de la Pléiade: Le langage*, ed. A. Martinet [1968], or the more specialized introduction of O. Reichmann, *Deutsche Wortforschung* [1969]) and in exegesis (cf. among others K. Koch, *The Growth of the Biblical Tradition: The Form-Critical Method* [1969]), the task of such a community effort cannot be the uniform application of a particular theory and method in order to create something revolutionarily new. Most OT scholars are not linguists, nor is there to this point a unified linguistic

and exegetical method upon which one could establish contributors from various backgrounds. The specialist will likely also be able implicitly to translate into precise terminology many careless expressions found here and there ("basic meaning," "semantic field," etc.). To one person form criticism or some other viewpoint may seem overemphasized; to another it may seem underemphasized. Here also the editors could not, and would not, reduce everything to a common denominator.

3. Although theological usages stand at the center of interest, *TLOT* cannot be concerned with a presentation of OT theology arranged according to lexical entries. Without considering that the contributors to this lexicon may in no way be assigned to a particular theological school or movement, and that the editors also have intruded least with respect to theological issues, it is not possible on the basis of word study alone to construct a theology (cf. J. Barr, *Semantics of Biblical Language* [1961]). *TLOT* starts with words and their usage, which certainly can also lead to explicitly theological concepts, but not with theological ideas and concepts as such ("omnipotence," "sin," "monotheism," etc.), which serve as the building blocks of a system. Although the difference between word meaning and intended referent is frequently effaced, especially with respect to abstract concepts (cf. here also the remarks of H. H. Schmid, *Gerechtigkeit als Weltordnung* [1968], 4ff., concerning the Hebrew language and the Israelite understanding of reality), and semantics can also be rightly supplemented by the onomasiological approach, *TLOT* remains, true to its intention, a lexicon. It does not replace a theological encyclopedia, which would treat "sin in the OT," "OT anthropology," "Israelite covenant ideas," etc., and certainly not a complete representation of OT theology, for which it constitutes only an aid.

4. The envisioned readers and users of this specialized lexicon are primarily theologians and pastors with a minimal knowledge of Hebrew and OT studies. Nevertheless, the lexicon has still been made as accessible as possible to non-Hebraists by means of regular translation of Hebrew words and texts, by means of the transliteration of the Hebrew script, and by means of the index. Indeed, *TLOT* has striven thereby to assemble an overview of the knowledge offered by specialists in widely scattered publications, and to make it more readily available to a larger audience, and it is to be hoped that this work will bear fruit for understanding the OT and for preaching it. At the same time one must recognize definite limits of the lexicon: It ought not to relieve the pastor from the exegesis of the text, nor, for that matter, its translation into today's language. Instead, it remains here, too, simply an aid to exegesis.

B. Arrangement of the Lexicon

With respect to the selection of the "theologically relevant words," one may not entirely avoid subjective criteria. One cannot precisely distinguish "theological usage" from a "general" or "profane usage." On the whole, the widest possible conception of "theological usage" seemed to be appropriate: an evaluation not only of texts with verbs having God as subject or object, or with nouns that refer to God; instead, if possible, of every case in which something of the interchange between God and his people or between God and humans comes to expression. It is precisely then, however, that it is impossible to avoid situations in which in one person's view all sorts of things have been overlooked while to another the scope seems rather to be too widely conceived.

On the one hand, in order to document the distinction from Bible dictionaries or handbooks, individual articles have also dealt with other parts of speech in addition to the mass of nouns and verbs, such as pronouns (→ *ᵓᵃnî* "I," → *kōl* "all"), adverbs (→ *ᵓûlay* "perhaps," → *ᵓayyēh* "where?" → *mātay* "when?"), prepositions (→ *ᶜim* "with"), and even interjections (→ *ᵓᵃhāh* "ah," → *hôy* "woe," → *hinnēh* "behold").

On the other hand, a series of words that one would perhaps expect here have not been treated in individual articles. The same is also true of a few frequently occurring substantives (*har* "mountain," *mayim* "water") or verbs (*yšb* "to sit, dwell," *ktb* "to write"), as well as many institutions, in particular many cultic institutions, concerning which one can refer to Bible dictionaries. *TLOT* has consciously not been planned as a reference work for comparative religion or archaeology, because the latter would shift the major emphasis (similar to that of a theological dictionary) too heavily from the semantic function of words to the description of the referent and its history. Thus those who seek archaeological or religio-historical information concerning the sanctuary, sacrifice, or the priesthood will not find this information here in the guise of a word study of *ᵓᵃrôn* "ark," *zbḥ* "to slaughter, offer," or *kōhēn* "priest." Such words have been excluded here, as have been words such as *ᵓēzôb* "hyssop," *ᵓēpôd* "ephod," *ᵓᵃrîᵓēl* "sacrificial altar hearth," *bāmâ* "high place," etc., with a few exceptions, because otherwise the scope of a concise theological lexicon would have been too greatly expanded.

The same is true also for personal names, which, with the exception of the designations of God, Yahweh, and Shaddai, and the names Zion and Israel, which had become religious honorifics, have not been treated in their own articles. It is certainly true that Abraham and the Abraham tradition, David and the David tradition, Jerusalem, and indeed also Canaan and Babel are theologically relevant concepts; but they may not be incorporated in the scope of a semantically oriented lexicon.

One should note that numerous words not treated individually are discussed in the context of other words, as synonyms, antonyms, or as words that belong in some other manner to the semantic field of the word under scrutiny. Thus, for example, *har* "mountain" in theological contexts may be treated under *ṣiyyôn* "Zion," *mayim* "water" and *yām* "sea" in their mythical meanings under *tᵉhôm* "deep," *yšb* "to sit, dwell" under *škn* "to dwell." In the case of a few frequently occurring words, a reference to the corresponding article in which the word is treated has been set in the alphabetical sequence of main entries; in many other cases the index at the end of the second volume facilitates location.

One could conceive of various possibilities for the arrangement of the words treated. First, it would have seemed appealing to proceed according to a content-oriented ordering principle. Both theoretical and, above all, practical grounds have influenced us to hold to a formal alphabetical ordering principle and to treat the necessary content relationships in the presentation itself and by means of cross references. Thus, as seems appropriate for a Semitic language, words of the same root are treated together in a single article, which naturally does not mean that the semantic autonomy of the words must be sacrificed to a "root fallacy" (cf. Barr, op. cit. 100ff.) or that their meaning must be subjugated to etymology. Such distortions are admittedly not automatically excluded even from strictly alphabetical arrangements of individual words; but the varied treatments of nominal forms and the verb stems of the same root in the extant lexicons, in which *ṣedeq* and *s^e dāqâ* are considered distinct lemmata but *ṣiddēq* and *hiṣdîq* are not, are also not above criticism. Here again practical considerations of presentation have been determinative over against purely theoretical principles. Hence one must permit some freedom and elasticity in the arrangement of the individual articles (cf. e.g., → *ʾbh*, where *ʾebyôn* would have been treated as an independent word, and → *ʾmn*, where the most significant derivatives receive separate treatment in subarticles in the major sections 3–4).

Finally, the scope that one allows the individual articles presents an additional subjective format issue. As one might expect, the original division into short, normal, long, and extralong articles has been disturbed in the practical execution. Many terms could certainly have been treated more concisely and others more extensively. Still, differences in diction do not likely surpass that which can be expected in such a community effort. For the most part, thanks to the discipline of the contributors, the danger known to every editor that the contributions may evolve into self-contained studies has been successfully avoided.

C. Arrangement of the Articles

In distinction from normal lexicons, every article here is a summary of the results of word studies and hence should offer, as much as possible, statements in complete sentences, in concise and short lexicon style. Instead of subheadings and a footnote apparatus, the enumeration of sections and the division into normal and small print stand as the most significant arrangement techniques; parentheses are used rather frequently for secondary issues, citations, bibliographical references, and so forth.

The article heading offers a single Hebrew entry, most often a (verbal) root or a primary substantive, in special cases even the most significant representative of the word group in question (e.g., → *tôrâ*), in addition to the primary meaning in English translation. Because the heading functions at the same time as a column title, it must be kept short. It serves only the practical goal of identifying the article and cannot foreshadow its content. For the roots → *ʾḥr* and → *ʾmn*, which have no representative qal usage and which have numerous equally plausible though semantically divergent derivations, brief approximations of the roots' meanings have been chosen ("after," "firm, certain"). The article itself normally exhibits five set sections, of which the third and the fourth are the most expansive. The enumeration of the major sections occurs by means of arabic numbers, and in some longer articles by means of roman numerals. The hierarchy of the section symbols is as follows: I.II. . . . 1.2. . . . (a) (b) . . . (1) (2) . . . ; confusion concerning the arabic numbers that mark both subsections of the five major sections (which are, as well, indicated by roman numerals) and, normally, the five major sections of an article certainly need not be feared.

With respect to the standard major sections one should note the following:

1. Root and Derivation. The first major section is intended to communicate essential information concerning the root. In addition, it lists the derivatives that the article in question treats, often with information concerning the type of derivation (function of the verb stem, noun-formation class, etc.), if conclusions concerning the meaning can be drawn from this information (cf. D. Michel, *Archiv für Begriffsgeschichte* 12 [1968]: 32ff.). This function of the first major section as a table of contents presenting the word groups to be treated—not as an overevaluation of etymology for the determination of the contemporary meaning of the words in the OT—motivates the placement at the beginning of the article (not at the end, as modern lexicography often emphatically recommends) of materials concerning occurrences of the root in other Semitic languages, considerations of the common "basic meaning" *(Grundbedeutung)* of the word groups, and any other information concerning etymology. Many cases call attention, then, to the limitations of the etymological methods in vogue especially among theologians and issue a warning against speculation. Besides, OT specialists are indeed interested in the distribution of a word group in the other Semitic languages, perhaps also their representation by other roots in particular spheres. Understandably, one can give little weight to the completeness of the information, in distinction from an etymological lexicon. For the most part only the Semitic languages that, in relation to the OT, are older or contemporary—Akkadian, Ugaritic, Phoenician-Punic, and older Aramaic—could receive particular attention.

2. Statistics. A second, likewise relatively short, section gives statistical details concerning the occurrences of a word in the OT and in its individual portions, in some cases in the form of a table. In addition to the pure inventory, particulars of the distribution can be emphasized here. In recent linguistics, statistical analyses are also beginning slowly to achieve their place; if—as is the case with all statistics—all sorts of misuse can also be made of them, it seems nevertheless proper to prepare a reliable basis for the statistical study of OT vocabulary, because, in contrast to the situation in NT studies (R. Morgenthaler, *Statistik des neutestamentlichen Wortschatzes* [1958]), little of substance is yet available.

As is the case with all statistics, the first commandment here, too, is the careful description of the corpus to be counted. The figures in *TLOT* are based on the Masoretic text of *Biblia Hebraica*[3] (without emendation) and count every occurrence of a given word in its different grammatical forms as a unit. For example, according to this principle, the infinitive absolute with a finite verb counts as (a bipartite) two occurrences. The different thought units or verses that contain the word (in each case in multiples) are not counted, therefore, but each individual occurrence of the word. Although small errors or approximations are practically meaningless for the value of the conclusions that one may draw from the numbers, attention has been paid to the greatest possible exactness in these figures. Consequently, the two independent and differently arranged concordances of Mandelkern (including the appendices by S. Herner) and Lisowsky were individually tabulated according to biblical books and the results, when different, evaluated by collation. Whenever the choice was to be made between different grammatical interpretations and parsings, the choice, as far as necessary, has been briefly noted, because a statistic is verifiable only for a precisely defined corpus. The corrections for Lisowsky's concordance that have resulted as by-products have arisen in this manner and are certainly not intended as criticism of the great contribution that this work represents. Wherever the literature offers divergent statistical citations, the reason often lies in a different method of counting that can be in itself as justified as the one used here, presuming that it is recognizable and consistently carried out.

The value of the statistics would naturally be significantly greater for the history of language if they could have been ordered not mechanically according to biblical books but according to the time of the composition of individual literary complexes. But because the literary analysis and dating of many texts is disputed or impossible, this avenue for word statistics could not be traveled except in a few cases. Even the regular special treatment, say, of Deutero-Isaiah (and Trito-Isaiah?), could already have greatly complicated the undertaking. For the individual case such refinements may be acquired, indeed at any time, without too great difficulty.

In order to be able to measure the relative frequency of a word in a particular biblical book, whether statistically significant or not, a comparison table of the total inventory of the individual biblical books is required. The following table of the scope of the books of the OT in (approximated) parts-per-thousand serves as a preliminary aid (based on the statistical material in vol. 3):

Gen	68	Isa	55	Psa	64
Exod	55	Jer	71	Job	27
Lev	39	Ezek	61	Prov	23
Num	54	Hos	8	Ruth	4
Deut	47	Joel	3	Song Sol	4
Pentateuch	263	Amos	7	Eccl	10
		Obad	1	Lam	5
Josh	33	Jonah	2	Esth	10
Judg	32	Mic	5	Dan	20
1 Sam	43	Nah	2	Ezra	12
2 Sam	36	Hab	2	Neh	17
1 Kgs	43	Zeph	3	1 Chron	35
2 Kgs	40	Hag	2	2 Chron	44
Josh–2 Kgs	227	Zech	10	Writings	275
		Mal	3		
Gen–2 Kgs	490	Prophets	235	OT	1000

(Aram. 16: Dan 12 of 20, Ezra 4 of 12).

3. Meaning and History of Meaning. In the third major section the presentation follows the general usage of the word or word group in the OT. The scope is limited to the books of the Hebrew canon; the portions of the book of Sirach extant in Hebrew are also included occasionally, although not regularly. Postbiblical Hebrew and the intertestamental literature extant only in Greek translation have not been taken into account; the concluding portion of the article may touch on the more significant points.

Great freedom has been allowed the authors in presentation. The arrangement can be undertaken according to semasiological (main meaning, expansions, metaphorical usages, etc.), grammatical-syntactical (sg./pl., various constructions of the verbs, etc.), or historical criteria. As a rule, details—omitted for the most part from lexicons to conserve space—concerning series, word fields, antonyms, distinctions with respect to near-synonyms, reasons for changes in meaning, and meanings that do not occur in the OT are also taken into account here. In contrast, sociological or exegetical excurses that transcend word studies are avoided as much as possible. If necessary, references to the literature (handbooks, commentaries, monographs) suffice on these issues.

Because a regular bibliographical section seems to offer no necessary advantage, references have been introduced at the appropriate juncture, in some cases also in the form of a short overview of the history of research. With respect to controversial theses, the contrary position should be at least briefly mentioned; even though streamlined, the articles should provide objective orientation concerning the current state of discussion.

4. Theological Usage. With the background of the more universal third section, the more specific theological usage can then be presented. A strict distinction between "profane" and "theological" is possible with respect to the meaning of the word only in a few cases. But on the basis of form-critical and tradition-critical investigation one can often clarify some gradation in the use of various words—of unequal significance—in theologically more-or-less relevant contexts. The appearance that sharp boundaries may always be drawn everywhere is not intended: as a rule the third section offers general overviews (with the exclusion of particular theological usages). Special problems of a theological nature are treated in the fourth section. Sections three and four may also be combined (e.g., → *ṭmʾ*); a few articles simply treat two different words or word groups in separate sections (→ *ʾbh*, → *ʾḥr*).

The arrangement of the fourth section has also been loosely regulated. One finds here semasiological, historical, and theological criteria according to the free discretion of the author.

Of the extrabiblical comparative material, application is naturally made almost exclusively only of the texts, older or contemporary to the OT, in Akkadian, Northwest Semitic, and sometimes Egyptian; regular sections dealing with the usage of equivalent words from Mesopotamia to Egypt or religio-historical excurses have been omitted in order not to violate the scope of the lexicon, but also considering the given possibilities.

5. Postbiblical Usage. The conclusion concisely treats whether and where the history of the theological usage continues into early Judaism and into

the NT or early Christianity. Concise references to the literature must usually suffice here. Citations of the most important Greek equivalents of the Hebrew words in the Septuagint and the NT are generally correlated by means of references to the corresponding articles in *Theological Dictionary of the New Testament (TDNT)*. On the whole, as is the case with other marginal areas, exhaustive statements are not possible here either. No all-encompassing biblical-theological summa is offered here; instead, only a concise reference to the necessary point of connection to the neighboring discipline is given for theologians.

D. Explanation of the Hebrew Transliteration

Except for article headings and in the few places where Masoretic details are described, this lexicon does not use the Hebrew characters—to the discomfort of many Hebraists, who miss the familiar script and who are not accustomed to transliteration. A glance at contemporary academic publications indicates that the use of transliteration is becoming increasingly popular; although it fails to be sufficient in more precise application for every justified requirement, it is better than the technical compromise of using only the unvocalized Hebrew characters.

Consonants

א	(*ʾalep*)	ʾ
ב	(*bet*)	*b*
ג	(*gimel*)	*g*
ד	(*dalet*)	*d*
ה	(*he*)	*h*
ו	(*waw*)	*w*
ז	(*zayin*)	*z*
ח	(*ḥet*)	*ḥ*
ט	(*ṭet*)	*ṭ*
י	(*yod*)	*y*
כ, ך	(*kap*)	*k*
ל	(*lamed*)	*l*
מ, ם	(*mem*)	*m*
נ, ן	(*nun*)	*n*
ס	(*samek*)	*s*
ע	(*ʿayin*)	ʿ
פ, ף	(*pe*)	*p*
צ, ץ	(*ṣade*)	*ṣ*
ק	(*qop*)	*q*
ר	(*reš*)	*r*
שׂ	(*śin*)	*ś*
שׁ	(*šin*)	*š*
ת	(*taw*)	*t*

Vowels

◌ַ	(*pataḥ*)	*a*
◌ַ	(furtive *pataḥ*)	*a*
◌ָ	(*qāmeṣ*)	*ā*
◌ָה	(final *qāmeṣ he*)	*â*
◌ֶ	(*s^{e}gōl*)	*e*
◌ֵ	(*ṣērê*)	*ē*
◌ֵי	(*ṣērê yod*)	*ê*
◌ִ	(short *ḥîreq*)	*i*
◌ִ	(long *ḥîreq*)	*ī*
◌ִי	(*ḥîreq yod*)	*î*
◌ָ	(*qāmeṣ ḥāṭûp*)	*o*
◌ֹ	(*ḥōlem*)	*ō*
וֹ	(full *ḥōlem*)	*ô*
◌ֻ	(short *qibbûṣ*)	*u*
◌ֻ	(long *qibbûṣ*)	*ū*
וּ	(*šûreq*)	*û*
◌ֲ	(*ḥāṭēp pataḥ*)	^{a}
◌ֳ	(*ḥāṭēp qāmeṣ*)	^{o}
◌ֱ	(*ḥāṭēp s^{e}gōl*)	^{e}
◌ְ	(vocal *š^{e}wâ*)	^{e}

The system of transliteration used here should be understood as a practical aid for the realization of Masoretic Hebrew according to the common tradition of pronunciation in modern universities. It is not meant to reproduce an exact transliteration of all the details of Tiberian orthography; it serves neither purely phonemic goals nor the attempt to reach behind the common grammatical traditions to linguistically more adequate forms. The following explanation of details is primarily for the nonspecialist; the necessary practical decisions encountered in the publication of the lexicon, including printing possibilities, claim no absolute normativity.

Concerning the pronunciation of the consonants (for the details, cf. the grammars, e.g., Meyer 1:41ff.) it should be noted that ʾ and ʿ are conventionally pronounced as firm pre-vocalics (as in the English theatre), *z* as a vocalized sibilant (like French *z*), *ḥ* like German *ch* (as in *ach*), *ṣ* like English *ts*, *ś* like *s*, *š* like English *sh*. Transliteration does not reflect the difference in the pronunciation of the so-called begadkephat letters, *b, g, d, k, p,* and *t*, pronounced after vowels not as stops but as fricatives. The widely practiced pronunciation of the *b* after vowels as *v*, of the *k* after vowels as (German) *ch*, and of the *p* after vowels as *f* need not be represented in transliteration.

The consonants *he, waw,* and *yod,* used to indicate long vowels (vowel letters, *matres lectionis*), are transliterated as a circumflex over the vowel (i.e., *â, ê, î, ô, û*); they are also taken into account when a transliteration reproduces an unpointed text (extrabiblical inscriptions, Qumran texts, Kethib, etc.) and for the purposes of alphabetization. It should be noted that here the present edition has followed standard English academic usage and so differs from the original German, which indicated both full and defective spellings by a macron over the vowel (i.e., *ā, ē, ī, ō, ū*). The German system offered greater consistency, providing a single form for words that exhibit variations or historical changes in spelling (e.g., *ʾōtôt* and *ʾōtōt*; *ṭôbâ* and *ṭōbâ*); but the present system provides a more exact correspondence with the Hebrew of the MT, which the reader can easily reconstruct from the transliteration.

A final *h* represents (1) a consonantal *he* in a nominal form, (2) a weak third radical (III *w/y*) in the standard dictionary form (3d masc. sg. pf.) of a verb, or (3) the fem. sg. poss. ending (*malkāh*, "her king"; compare the fem. ending *-â* in *malkâ*, "queen").

Verb transliterations in article headings in this lexicon represent only unvocalized root consonants (e.g., *ʾbd, ʾbh, ʾbl,* to be pronounced *ʾābad, ʾābāh, ʾābal,* with the accent on the second syllable; in other cases with a long *ē* instead of *a* in the second syllable [e.g., *ḥpṣ* = *ḥāpēṣ;* see also *ṭhr, yrʾ, kbd, lbš*]). An exception is that verbs with a long middle vowel are vocalized (inf. cs. *bôʾ, bîn, gûr*). The only case in these volumes in which *h* as a weak third radical might be confused with *h* as a real root consonant is *gbh* (= *gābah*). The text itself, however, calls attention to the proper pronunciation.

The present edition always transliterates quiescent *ʾalep* (using ʾ; e.g., *lōʾ*, "not," *hûʾ*, "he," *rōʾš*, "head," Aram. *malkāʾ*, "the king").

In Hebrew, stress falls regularly on the final syllable, but readers should note that the present edition generally does not indicate accents, even for exceptions to this rule, such as segholate nouns. However, if stress is relevant to a particular linguistic point, the discussion may retain the accent.

Proper names are not transliterated with capital letters.

For the transliteration of related Semitic languages, one should consult the pertinent grammars and dictionaries; for example, the transliteration of Akkadian follows von Soden (in *GAG* and *AHw*) or *CAD*, and that of Ugaritic follows Gordon (in *UT*; it should be noted here that *a*, *i*, and *u* indicate not vowels but the variously vocalized consonantal ʾ). Egyptian transliteration follows A. Gardiner (*Egyptian Grammar*, 3d ed. [London: Oxford University Press, 1957], p. 18).

Greek transliterations are according to the following table:

α	=	a	ξ	=	x
β	=	b	ο	=	o
γ	=	g	π	=	p
γ	=	n (before γ, κ, ξ, χ)	ρ	=	r
δ	=	d	ῥ	=	rh
ϵ	=	e	σ, ς	=	s
ζ	=	z	τ	=	t
η	=	ē	υ	=	y
θ	=	th	υ	=	u (in diphthongs: au, eu, ou, ui)
ι	=	i	φ	=	ph
κ	=	k	χ	=	ch
λ	=	l	ψ	=	ps
μ	=	m	ω	=	ō
ν	=	n	῾	=	h (with vowel or diphthong)

E. Concordance of Divergent Versification

TLOT follows the chapter and verse enumeration of the Hebrew Bible, which does not always agree with that of the Septuagint, Vulgate, and other translations. In order to facilitate the location of passages for users of the popular New Revised Standard Version (1989), the differences are compiled here in a table. (Other popular English translations, such as the Catholic NAB and the Jewish JPSV, follow the versification of the Hebrew Bible.)

Hebrew Bible		**NRSV**	
Gen	32:1	Gen	31:55
	32:2–33		32:1–32
Exod	7:26–29	Exod	8:1–4
	8:1–28		8:5–32
	21:37		22:1
	22:1–30		22:2–31
Lev	5:20–26	Lev	6:1–7
Num	17:1–15	Num	16:36–50
	17:16–28		17:1–13
	25:19		26:1 (first clause)
	30:1		29:40

Hebrew Bible		**NRSV**	
Num	30:2–17	Num	30:1–16
Deut	13:1	Deut	12:32
	13:2–19		13:1–18
	23:1		22:30
	23:2–26		23:1–25
	28:69		29:1
	29:1–28		29:2–29
1 Sam	21:1	1 Sam	20:42 (last clause)
	21:2–16		21:1–15
	24:1		23:29
	24:2–23		24:1–22
2 Sam	19:1	2 Sam	18:33
	19:2–44		19:1–43
1 Kgs	5:1–14	1 Kgs	4:21–34
	5:15–32		5:1–18
	18:34 (first half)		18:33 (last half)
	20:3 (first half)		20:2 (last half)
	22:21 (last clause)		22:22 (first clause)
	22:44		22:43 (last half)
	22:45–54		22:44–53
2 Kgs	12:1	2 Kgs	11:21
	12:2–22		12:1–21
Isa	8:23	Isa	9:1
	9:1–20		9:2–21
	63:19a		63:19
	63:19b		64:1
	64:1–11		64:2–12
Jer	8:23	Jer	9:1
	9:1–25		9:2–26
Ezek	21:1–5	Ezek	20:45–49
	21:6–37		21:1–32
Hos	2:1–2	Hos	1:10–11
	2:3–25		2:1–23
	12:1		11:12
	12:2–15		12:1–14
	14:1		13:16
	14:2–10		14:1–9
Joel	3:1–5	Joel	2:28–32
	4:1–21		3:1–21
Jonah	2:1	Jonah	1:17
	2:2–11		2:1–10
Mic	4:14	Mic	5:1
	5:1–14		5:2–15
Nah	2:1	Nah	1:15
	2:2–14		2:1–13
Zech	2:1–4	Zech	1:18–21
	2:5–17		2:1–13
Mal	3:19–24	Mal	4:1–6
Psa	3:1	Psa	3:title

Hebrew Bible		NRSV	
Psa	3:2–9	Psa	3:1–8
	4:1		4:title
	4:2–9		4:1–8
	5:1		5:title
	5:2–13		5:1–12
	6:1		6:title
	6:2–11		6:1–10
	7:1		7:title
	7:2–18		7:1–17
	8:1		8:title
	8:2–10		8:1–9
	9:1		9:title
	9:2–21		9:1–20
	11:1 (first clause)		11:title
	12:1		12:title
	12:2–9		12:1–8
	13:1		13:title
	13:2–6		13:1–5
	13:6 (last half)		13:6
	14:1 (first clause)		14:title
	15:1 (first clause)		15:title
	16:1 (first clause)		16:title
	17:1 (first clause)		17:title
	18:1–2 (first clause)		18:title
	18:2–51		18:1–50
	19:1		19:title
	19:2–15		19:1–14
	20:1		20:title
	20:2–10		20:1–9
	21:1		21:title
	21:2–14		21:1–13
	22:1		22:title
	22:2–32		22:1–31
	23:1 (first clause)		23:title
	24–28:1 (first clause)		24–28:title
	29:1 (first clause)		29:title
	30:1		30:title
	30:2–13		30:1–12
	31:1		31:title
	31:2–25		31:1–24
	32:1 (first clause)		32:title
	34:1		34:title
	34:2–23		34:1–22
	35:1 (first word)		35:title
	36:1		36:title
	36:2–13		36:1–12
	37:1 (first word)		37:title
	38:1		38:title
	38:2–23		38:1–22

Hebrew Bible		NRSV	
Psa	39:1	Psa	39:title
	39:2–14		39:1–13
	40:1		40:title
	40:2–18		40:1–17
	41:1		41:title
	41:2–14		41:1–13
	42:1		42:title
	42:2–12		42:1–11
	44:1		44:title
	44:2–27		44:1–26
	45:1		45:title
	45:2–18		45:1–17
	46:1		46:title
	46:2–12		46:1–11
	47:1		47:title
	47:2–10		47:1–9
	48:1		48:title
	48:2–15		48:1–14
	49:1		49:title
	49:2–21		49:1–20
	50:1 (first clause)		50:title
	51:1–2		51:title
	51:2–21		51:1–19
	52:1–2 (first clause)		52:title
	52:2–11		52:1–9
	53:1		53:title
	53:2–7		53:1–6
	54:1–2		54:title
	54:2–9		54:1–7
	55:1		55:title
	55:2–24		55:1–23
	56:1		56:title
	56:2–24		56:1–23
	57:1		57:title
	57:2–12		57:1–11
	58:1		58:title
	58:2–12		58:1–11
	59:1		59:title
	59:2–18		59:1–17
	60:1–2		60:title
	60:3–14		60:1–12
	61:1		61:title
	61:2–9		61:1–8
	62:1		62:title
	62:2–13		62:1–12
	63:1		63:title
	63:2–12		63:1–11
	64:1		64:title
	64:2–11		64:1–10

Hebrew Bible		**NRSV**	
Psa	65:1	Psa	65:title
	65:2–14		65:1–13
	66:1 (first clause)		66:title
	67:1		67:title
	67:2–8		67:1–7
	68:1		68:title
	68:2–36		68:1–35
	69:1		69:title
	69:2–37		69:1–36
	70:1		70:title
	70:2–6		70:1–5
	72:1 (first word)		72:title
	73:1 (first clause)		73:title
	74:1 (first clause)		74:title
	74:2–11		74:1–10
	76:1		76:title
	76:2–13		76:1–12
	77:1		77:title
	77:2–21		77:1–20
	78:1 (first clause)		78:title
	79:1 (first clause)		79:title
	80:1		80:title
	80:2–20		80:1–19
	81:1		81:title
	81:2–17		81:1–16
	82:1 (first clause)		82:title
	83:1		83:title
	83:2–19		83:1–18
	84:1		84:title
	84:2–13		84:1–12
	85:1		85:title
	85:2–14		85:1–13
	86:1 (first clause)		86:title
	87:1 (first clause)		87:title
	88:1		88:title
	88:2–19		88:1–18
	89:1		89:title
	89:2–53		89:1–52
	90:1 (first clause)		90:title
	92:1		92:title
	92:2–16		92:1–15
	98:1 (first word)		98:title
	100:1 (first clause)		100:title
	101:1 (first clause)		101:title
	102:1		102:title
	102:2–29		102:1–28
	103:1 (first word)		103:title
	108:1		108:title
	108:2–14		108:1–13

Hebrew Bible		NRSV	
Psa	109, 110, 120–134, 138, 139:1 (first clause)	Psa	109, 110, 120–134, 138, 139:title
	140:1		140:title
	140:2–14		140:1–13
	141:1 (first clause)		141:title
	142:1		142:title
	142:2–7		142:1–6
	143:1 (first clause)		143:title
	144:1 (first word)		144:title
	145:1 (first clause)		145:title
Job	40:25–32	Job	41:1–8
	41:1–26		41:9–34
Song Sol	7:1	Song Sol	6:13
	7:2–14		7:1–13
Eccl	4:17	Eccl	5:1
	5:1–19		5:2–20
Dan	3:31–33	Dan	4:1–3
	4:1–34		4:4–37
	6:1		5:31
	6:2–29		6:1–28
Neh	3:33–38	Neh	4:1–6
	4:1–17		4:7–23
	10:1		9:38
	10:2–40		10:1–39
1 Chron	5:27–41	1 Chron	6:1–15
	6:1–66		6:16–81
	12:4–5		12:4
	12:6–41		12:5–40
2 Chron	1:18	2 Chron	2:1
	2:1–17		2:2–18
	13:23		14:1
	14:1–14		14:2–15

Abbreviations

A. Biblical Books

Hebrew Bible

Gen	Genesis
Exod	Exodus
Lev	Leviticus
Num	Numbers
Deut	Deuteronomy
Josh	Joshua
Judg	Judges
1–2 Sam	1–2 Samuel
1–2 Kgs	1–2 Kings
Isa	Isaiah
Jer	Jeremiah
Ezek	Ezekiel
Hos	Hosea
Joel	Joel
Amos	Amos
Obad	Obadiah
Jonah	Jonah
Mic	Micah
Nah	Nahum
Hab	Habakkuk
Zeph	Zephaniah
Hag	Haggai
Zech	Zechariah
Mal	Malachi
Psa	Psalms
Job	Job
Prov	Proverbs
Ruth	Ruth
Song Sol	Song of Solomon
Eccl	Ecclesiastes
Lam	Lamentations
Esth	Esther
Dan	Daniel
Ezra	Ezra
Neh	Nehemiah
1–2 Chron	1–2 Chronicles

New Testament

Matt	Matthew
Mark	Mark
Luke	Luke
John	John
Acts	Acts
Rom	Romans
1–2 Cor	1–2 Corinthians
Gal	Galatians
Eph	Ephesians
Phil	Philippians
Col	Colossians
1–2 Thess	1–2 Thessalonians
1–2 Tim	1–2 Timothy
Titus	Titus
Phlm	Philemon
Heb	Hebrews
Jas	James
1–2 Pet	1–2 Peter
1–2–3 John	1–2–3 John
Jude	Jude
Rev	Revelation

Apocryphal and Deuterocanonical Titles

1–2–3–4 Kgdms	1–2–3–4 Kingdoms
1–2 Esd	1–2 Esdras
Add Esth	Additions to Esther
Bar	Baruch
Jdt	Judith
Ep Jer	Epistle of Jeremiah
1–2–3–4 Macc	1–2–3–4 Maccabees
Pr Azar	Prayer of Azariah
Pr Man	Prayer of Manasseh
Sir	Sirach
Sir Prol	Prologue to Sirach
Sus	Susanna
Tob	Tobit
Wis	Wisdom of Solomon
4 Ezra	4 Ezra
Bel	Bel and the Dragon
Sg TYM	Song of Three Young Men

B. Old Testament Pseudepigrapha

Adam and Eve	*Books of Adam and Eve*
2–3 Bar.	*Syriac, Greek Apocalypse of Baruch*

Apoc. Mos.	*Apocalypse of Moses*
As. Mos.	*Assumption of Moses*
1–2–3 Enoch	*Ethiopic, Slavic, Hebrew Enoch*
Ep. Arist.	*Epistle of Aristeas*
Jub.	*Jubilees*
Mart. Isa.	*Martyrdom of Isaiah*
Odes Sol.	*Odes of Solomon*
Pss. Sol.	*Psalms of Solomon*
T. 12 Patr.	*Testament of Twelve Patriarchs*
T. Levi	*Testament of Levi*

C. Rabbinic Literature

TALMUDIC TEXTS

Abbreviations distinguish the versions of the Talmudic tractates: *y.* for Jerusalem and *b.* for Babylonian. A prefixed *t.* denotes the tractates of the Tosephta and an *m.* those of the Mishnah.

ʾAbot	*ʾAbot*
ʿArak.	*ʿArakin*
ʿAbod. Zar.	*ʿAboda Zara*
B. Bat.	*Baba Bathra*
Bek.	*Bekorot*
Ber.	*Berakot*
Beṣa	*Beṣa (= Yom Ṭob)*
Bik.	*Bikkurim*
B. Meṣiʿa	*Baba Meṣiʿa*
B. Qam.	*Baba Qamma*
Demai	*Demai*
ʿErub.	*ʿErubin*
Ed.	*Eduyyot*
Giṭ.	*Giṭṭin*
Ḥag.	*Ḥagigah*
Ḥal.	*Ḥallah*
Hor.	*Horayot*
Ḥul.	*Ḥullin*
Kelim	*Kelim*
Ker.	*Kerithot*
Ketub.	*Ketubot*
Kil.	*Kilʿayim*
Maʿaś.	*Maʿaśerot*
Maʿaś. Š.	*Maʿaśer Šeni*
Mak.	*Makkot*
Makš.	*Makširin*
Meg.	*Megillah*
Meʿil.	*Meʿilah*
Menaḥ.	*Menaḥot*
Mid.	*Middot*
Miqw.	*Miqwaʾot*
Moʾed	*Moʾed*
Moʾed Qaṭ.	*Moʾed Qaṭan*
Naš.	*Našim*
Naz.	*Nazir*
Ned.	*Nedarim*
Neg.	*Negaʿim*
Nez.	*Neziqin*
Nid.	*Niddah*
Ohol.	*Oholot*
ʿOr.	*ʿOrla*
Para	*Para*
Peʾa	*Peʾa*
Pesaḥ.	*Pesaḥim*
Qinnim	*Qinnim*
Qidd.	*Qiddušin*
Qod.	*Qodašin*
Roš Haš.	*Roš Haššana*
Sanh.	*Sanhedrin*
Šabb.	*Šabbat*
Šeb.	*Šebiʿit*
Šebu.	*Šebuʿot*
Šeqal.	*Šeqalim*
Soḥa	*Soḥa*
Sukka	*Sukka*
Taʿan.	*Taʿanit*
Tamid	*Tamid*
Tem.	*Temura*
Ter.	*Terumot*
Ṭohar.	*Ṭoharot*
Ṭ. Yom	*Ṭebul Yom*
ʿUq.	*ʿUqšin*
Yad.	*Yadayim*
Yebam.	*Yebamot*
Yoma	*Yoma (= Kippurim)*
Zabim	*Zabim*
Zebaḥ.	*Zebaḥim*
Zera.	*Zeraʿim*

TARGUMIC TEXTS

Tg. Onq.	*Targum Onqelos*
Tg. Neb.	*Targum of the Prophets*
Tg. Ket.	*Targum of the Writings*
Frg. Tg.	*Fragmentary Targum*
Sam. Tg.	*Samaritan Targum*
Tg. Isa.	*Targum Isaiah*

Tg. Neof.	*Targum Neofiti I*
Tg. Ps.-J.	*Targum Pseudo-Jonathan*
Tg. Yer.	*Targum Yerušalmi*
Yem. Tg.	*Yemenite Targum*
Tg. Esth. I, II	*First or Second Targum of Esther*

OTHER JEWISH TEXTS

ʾAbot R. Nat.	*ʾAbot de Rabbi Nathan*
ʾAg. Ber.	*ʾAggadat Berešit*
Bab.	*Babylonian* (used alone)
Bar.	*Baraita*
Der. Er. Rab.	*Derek Ereṣ Rabba*
Der. Er. Zuṭ.	*Derek Ereṣ Zuṭa*
Gem.	*Gemara*
Kalla	*Kalla*
Mek.	*Mekilta*
Midr.	*Midrash* (+ biblical book)
Pal.	*Palestinian* (used alone)
Pesiq. Rab.	*Pesiqta Rabbati*
Pesiq. Rab Kah.	*Pesiqta de Rab Kahana*
Pirqe R. El.	*Pirqe Rabbi Eliezer*
Rab.	*Rabbah* (+ biblical book)
Ṣem.	*Ṣemaḥot*
Sipra	*Sipra*
Sipre	*Sipre*
Sop.	*Soperim*
S. ʿolam. Rab.	*Seder ʿolam Rabbah*
Yal.	*Yalquṭ*

D. Qumran Texts

Qumran citations are according to J. A. Fitzmyer, S. J., *The Dead Sea Scrolls: Major Publications and Tools for Study* (rev. ed. 1990). The following list of abbreviations is selective.

1QapGen	Genesis Apocryphon from Cave 1
1QH	Hodayot (Thanksgiving Hymns) from Cave 1
1QM	Milḥamah (War Scroll) from Cave 1
1QpHab	Pesher on Habakkuk from Cave 1
1QS	Serek Hayyaḥad (Rule of the Community, Manual of Discipline) from Cave 1
1QSa	Appendix A (Rule of the Congregation) to 1QS from Cave 1
1QSb	Appendix B (Blessings) to 1QS from Cave 1
4QFlor	Florilegium (or Eschatological Midrashim) from Cave 4
CD	Cairo Geniza text of the Damascus Document
p	pesher
Q	Number preceding Q indicates cave

E. Ugaritic Texts

Citations of Qumran texts follow M. Dietrich, O. Loretz, and J. Sanmartín, *Die keilalphabetischen Texte aus Ugarit* (AOAT 24, 1976). Abbreviation = *KTU.*

F. Symbols

→ = see (referring to another entry)
* (before an isolated lexical form) = conjectural, not a documented form
* (before or after a paragraph) = written by the editor (see above p. vii)
> = develops into
< = formed from

G. Common and Reference Abbreviations

AANLR	*Atti della Accademia Nazionale dei Lincei. Rendiconti*
Aḥ.	Aḥiqar text
AbB	Altbabylonische Briefe in Umschrift und Übersetzung. Ed. by F. R. Kraus. Books 1ff., 1964ff.
ABC	Anchor Bible Commentary. Ed. by D. N. Freedman
ABR	*Australian Bible Review*
abs.	absolute, absolutely
acc.	accusative
AcOr	*Acta Orientalia*
act.	active
adj.	adjective, adjectival
adv.	adverb
AfO	*Archiv für Orientforschung*
äg.	ägyptisch
AHw	W. von Soden, *Akkadisches Handwörterbuch.* Vols. 1–3, 1965–81
AION	*Annali dell'Istituto Universitario Orientale de Napoli*
AIPHOS	*Annuaire de l'Institut de Philologie et d'Histoire Orientales et Slaves*
AJSL	*American Journal of Semitic Languages and Literatures*
Akk.	Akkadian
ALBO	Analecta Lovaniensia Biblica et Orientalia
altaram.	altaramäisch
altbab.	altbabylonisch
Alt, *EOTHR*	A. Alt, *Essays on Old Testament History and Religion.* Transl. R. A. Wilson. 1967
Alt, *KS*	A. Alt, *Kleine Schriften.* Vol. 1, 1963^3; vol. 2, 1964^3; vol. 3, 1959
ALUOS	*Annual of the Leeds University Oriental Society*
Amor.	Amorite
ANEP	*The Ancient Near East in Pictures Relating to the Old Testament.* Ed. by J. B. Pritchard. 1954
ANET	*Ancient Near Eastern Texts Relating to the Old Testament.* Ed. by J. B. Pritchard. 1969^3
AnOr	Analecta orientalia
AO	*Der Alte Orient*
AOAT	Alter Orient und Altes Testament
AOB	*Altorientalische Bilder zum Alten Testament.* Ed. by H. Gressmann. 1927^2
AOT	*Altorientalische Texte zum Alten Testament.* Ed. by H. Gressmann. 1926^2
ap.	apʿel
Arab.	Arabic
Aram.	Aramaic
ARM	Archives royales de Mari
ArOr	*Archiv Orientální*
ARW	*Archiv für Religionswissenschaft*
art.	article

Assyr.	Assyrian
ASTI	*Annual of the Swedish Theological Institute*
AT	Altes Testament; Ancien Testament
ATD	Das Alte Testament Deutsch. Ed. by V. Herntrich and A. Weiser
atl.	alttestamentlich
ATR	*Anglican Theological Review*
AV	Authorized Version
BA	*Biblical Archaeologist*
bab.	babylonisch
Bab.	Babylonian
BAGD	W. Bauer, W. F. Arndt, F. W. Gingrich, and F. W. Danker, *Greek-English Lexicon of the New Testament.* 1979^2
Barth	J. Barth, *Die Nominalbildung in den semitischen Sprachen.* 1894^2
BASOR	*Bulletin of the American Schools of Oriental Research*
Bd.	Band
BDB	F. Brown, S. R. Driver, and C. A. Briggs, *A Hebrew and English Lexicon of the Old Testament.* 1907
BCE	Before the Common Era
Begrich, *GS*	J. Begrich, *Gesammelte Studien zum Alten Testament.* 1964
Ben-Yehuda	E. Ben-Yehuda, *Thesaurus totius Hebraitatis et veteris et recentioris.* Vols. 1–16, 1908–59
Benz	F. L. Benz, *Personal Names in the Phoenician and Punic Inscriptions.* 1972
BeO	*Bibbia e Oriente*
Berg. *HG*	G. Bergsträsser, *Hebräische Grammatik.* Vol. 1, 1918; vol. 2, 1929
Berg. *Intro.*	G. Bergsträsser, *Introduction to the Semitic Languages.* Transl. with notes and bibliog. and an appendix on the scripts by P. T. Daniels. 1983
BETL	*Bibliotheca Ephemeridum Theologicarum Lovaniensium*
BFCT	*Beiträge zur Förderung christlicher Theologie*
BFPS	C. Westermann, *Basic Forms of Prophetic Speech.* Transl. by H. C. White. 1967
BH^3	*Biblia Hebraica.* Ed. by R. Kittel, P. Kahle, A. Alt, and O. Eissfeldt. 1937^3
BHH	*Biblisch-Historisches Handwörterbuch.* Ed. by B. Reicke and L. Rost. Vols. 1–3, 1962–66
BHS	*Biblia Hebraica Stuttgartensia.* Ed. by K. Elliger and W. Rudolph. 1968–1977
Bib	*Biblica*
bibl.	biblical
Bibl. Aram.	Biblical Aramaic
bibliog.	bibliography
$BLex^2$	*Bibel-Lexikon.* Ed. by H. Haag. 1968^2
BO	*Bibliotheca Orientalis*
bis	2 occurrences
BJRL	*Bulletin of the John Rylands Library*
BK	Biblischer Kommentar. Altes Testament. Ed. by M. Noth and H. W. Wolff

BL	H. Bauer and P. Leander, *Historische Grammatik der hebräischen Sprache.* I, 1922
BLA	H. Bauer and P. Leander, *Grammatik des Biblisch-Aramäischen.* 1927
BM	G. Beer, and R. Meyer, *Hebräische Grammatik.* Vol. 1, 1952[2]; vol. 2, 1955[2]; vol. 3, 1960[2] (see also Meyer)
BMAP	E. G. Kraeling, *The Brooklyn Museum Aramaic Papyri.* 1953
Böhl	F. M. Th. de Liagre Böhl, *Opera Minora.* 1953
Bousset-Gressmann	W. Bousset and H. Gressmann, *Die Religion des Judentums im späthellenistischen Zeitalter.* 1926[3]
Bresciani-Kamil	see Hermop.
BRL	K. Galling, *Biblisches Reallexikon.* HAT 1, 1937
Brønno	E. Brønno, *Studien über hebräische Morphologie und Vokalismus.* 1943
BrSynt	C. Brockelmann, *Hebräische Syntax.* 1956
BS	See Nöldeke, *BS*
BSOAS	*Bulletin of the School of Oriental and African Studies*
Buccellati	G. Buccellati, *The Amorites of the Ur III Period.* 1966
Burchardt	M. Burchardt, *Die altkanaanäischen Fremdworte und Eigennamen im Ägyptischen.* Vols. 1-2, 1909–10
BWAT	Beiträge zum Wissenschaft vom Alten Testament
BWL	W. G. Lambert, *Babylonian Wisdom Literature.* 1960
BZ	*Biblische Zeitschrift*
BZAW	*Beiheft zur Zeitschrift für die alttestamentliche Wissenschaft*
BZNW	*Beiheft zur Zeitschrift für die neutestamentliche Wissenschaft*
ca.	circa
CAD	*The Assyrian Dictionary of the Oriental Institute of the University of Chicago.* 1956ff.
Calice	F. Calice, *Grundlagen der ägyptisch-semitischen Wortvergleichung.* 1936
Can.	Canaanite
CBQ	*Catholic Biblical Quarterly*
CC	Continental Commentaries
CE	Common Era
cent.	century
cf.	confer, compare
ch(s).	chapter(s)
Chr	Chronicler
Christ.-Pal.	Christian-Palestinian, a late Aramaic dialect
CIS	*Corpus Inscriptionum Semiticarum.* 1881ff.
cj.	conjecture (regarding an uncertain reading)
CML[1], *CML*[2]	G. R. Driver, *Canaanite Myths and Legends.* 1956; 1978[2]
cod.	codex
col.	column
comm(s).	commentary, commentaries
cons.	consecutive
Conti Rossini	K. Conti Rossini, *Chrestomathia Arabica Meridionalis Epigraphica.* 1931
Cooke	G. A. Cooke, *A Text-Book of North-Semitic Inscriptions.* 1903
Copt.	Coptic

Cowley	A. Cowley, *Aramaic Papyri of the Fifth Century B.C.* 1923
CPT	J. Barr, *Comparative Philology and the Text of the Old Testament.* 1968
CRAIBL	*Comptes Rendus de l'Académie des Inscriptions et Belles-Lettres*
cs.	construct
CV	*Communio Viatorum*
D	D (doubling)-stem in Akkadian
DAFA	R. Blachère, M. Chouémi, C. Denizeau, *Dictionnaire arabe-français-anglais (langue classique et moderne).* 1963ff.
Dalman	G. Dalman, *Aramäisch-Neuhebräisches Handwörterbuch.* 1938^3
Dalman, *AuS*	G. Dalman, *Arbeit und Sitte in Palästina.* Vols. 1–7, 1928–42
Delitzsch	F. Delitzsch, *Die Lese- und Schreibfehler im Alten Testament.* 1920
Deutero-Isa	Deutero-Isaiah or Second-Isaiah
Dhorme	E. Dhorme, *L'emploi métaphorique des noms de parties du corps en hébreu et en akkadien.* 1923
Dillmann	A. Dillmann, *Lexicon Linguae Aethiopicae.* 1865
Diringer	D. Diringer, *Le iscrizioni antico-ebraiche Palestinesi.* 1934
DISO	Ch. F. Jean and J. Hoftijzer, *Dictionnaire des inscriptions sémitiques de l'ouest.* 1965
diss.	dissertation
DJD	Discoveries in the Judaean Desert. Vol. 1ff., 1955ff.
DNTT	*The New International Dictionary of New Testament Theology.* Ed. by C. Brown. Vol. 1, 1975; vol. 2, 1976; vol. 3, 1978
DOTT	D. W. Thomas, *Documents from Old Testament Times.* 1958
Drower-Macuch	E. S. Drower and R. Macuch, *A Mandaic Dictionary.* 1963
Driver, *AD*	G. R. Driver, *Aramaic Documents of the Fifth Century B.C.* 1957
Driver-Miles	G. R. Driver and J. C. Miles, *Babylonian Laws.* Vols. 1–2, 1952–55
dt.	deutsch
Dtn	Deuteronomic (history, writer)
Dtr	Deuteronomistic (history; writer); Deuteronomist
Duden, *Etymologie*	K. Duden, *Etymologie. Herkunftswörterbuch der deutschen Sprache. Bearbeitet von der Dudenredaktion unter Leitung von P. Grebe.* Der Grosse Duden Bd. 7, 1963
Dupont-Sommer	A. Dupont-Sommer, *Les Araméens.* L'Orient ancien illustré 2. 1949
Dyn.	Dynasty
E	Elohist source (of the Pentateuch)
EA	El-Amarna tablets. According to the edition of J. A. Knudtzon, *Die el-Amarna-Tafeln.* 1915. Continued in A. F. Rainey, *El Amarna Tablets* 359–379. 1970
ed.	edited; edition; editor
EEA	S. Moscati, *L'epigrafia ebraica antica.* Biblica et Orientalia 15, 1951
e.g.	exempli gratia, for example

Eg.	Egyptian
Eichrodt	W. Eichrodt, *Theology of the Old Testament.* Vol. 1, 1961; vol. 2, 1967
Eissfeldt, *Intro.*	O. Eissfeldt, *The Old Testament. An Introduction.* Transl. by P. R. Ackroyd. 1965
Eissfeldt, *KS*	O. Eissfeldt, *Kleine Schriften.* Vols. 1ff., 1962ff.
EKL	*Evangelisches Kirchenlexikon.* Ed. by H. Brunotte and O. Weber. 3 Vols. 1962^{2}
Ellenbogen	M. Ellenbogen, *Foreign Words in the Old Testament.* 1962
ELKZ	*Evangelisch-Lutherische Kirchenzeitung*
emph.	emphatic
Eng.	English
Erman-Grapow	A. Erman and H. Grapow, *Wörterbuch der ägyptischen Sprache.* Vols. 1–7, 1926–63
ESem.	East Semitic (language group)
esp.	especially
ET	*Expository Times*
etc.	et cetera
Eth.	Ethiopic
ETL	*Ephemerides Theologicae Lovanienses*
etpa.	etpaʿal
etpe.	etpeʿel
excl.	excluding
extrabibl.	extrabiblical
EvT	*Evangelische Theologie*
f(f).	following page(s)
FF	*Forschungen und Fortschritte*
fem.	feminine
FGH	*Die Fragmente der griechischen Historiker.* Ed. by F. Jacoby. 1923ff.
fig.	figurative, figuratively
Fitzmyer, *Gen.Ap.*	J. A. Fitzmyer, *The Genesis Apocryphon of Qumran Cave I. A Commentary.* Biblical et Orientalia 18A, 1971^{2}
Fitzmyer, *Sef.*	J. A. Fitzmyer, *The Aramaic Inscriptions of Sefîre.* Biblica et Orientalia 19, 1967
Fr.	French
Fraenkel	S. Fraenkel, *Die aramäischen Fremdwörter im Arabischen.* 1886
frg.	fragment
Friedrich	J. Friedrich, *Phönizisch-punische Grammatik.* 1951
Friedrich-Röllig	J. Friedrich and W. Röllig, *Phönizisch-Punische Grammatik.* 1970^{2}
FS	Festschrift
FS Albright (1961)	*The Bible and the Ancient Near East: Essays in Honor of W. F. Albright.* 1961
FS Albright (1971)	*Near Eastern Studies in Honor of W. F. Albright.* 1971
FS Alleman	*Biblical Studies in Memory of H. C. Alleman.* 1960
FS Alt	*Geschichte und Altes Testament.* 1953
FS Baetke	*Festschrift W. Baetke. Dargebracht zu seinem 80. Geburtstag am 28. März 1964.* Ed. by K. Rudolph, R. Heller, and E. Walter. 1966

FS Bardtke	*Bibel und Qumran.* 1968
FS Barth (1936)	*Theologische Aufsätze, Karl Barth zum 50. Geburtstag.* 1936
FS Barth (1956)	*Antwort. Festschrift zum 70. Geburtstag von Karl Barth.* 1956
FS Basset	*Mémorial H. Basset.* 1928
FS Baudissin	*Abhandlungen zur semitischen Religionskunde und Sprachwissenschaft.* 1918
FS Baumgärtel	*Festschrift F. Baumgärtel zum 70. Geburtstag.* 1959
FS Baumgartner	*Hebräische Wortforschung. Festschrift zum 80. Geburtstag von W. Baumgartner. SVT* 16, 1967
FS Beer	*Festschrift für G. Beer zum 70. Geburtstag.* 1933
FS Bertholet	*Festschrift für A. Bertholet.* 1950
FS Browne	*Oriental Studies.* 1922
FS Christian	*Vorderasiatische Studien. Festschrift für V. Christian.* 1956
FS Coppens	*De Mari à Qumran. Hommage à J. Coppens.* 1969
FS Davies	*Proclamation and Presence. Old Testament Essays in Honour of G. H. Davies.* 1970
FS Delekat	*Libertas Christiana. F. Delekat zum 65. Geburtstag.* 1957
FS Driver	*Hebrew and Semitic Studies Presented to G. R. Driver.* 1963
FS Dupont-Sommer	*Hommages à André Dupont-Sommer.* 1971
FS Dussaud	*Mélanges syriens offerts à R. Dussaud.* 1939
FS Eichrodt	*Wort—Gebot—Glaube. W. Eichrodt zum 80. Geburtstag.* 1970
FS Eilers	*Festschrift für W. Eilers.* 1967
FS Eissfeldt (1947)	*Festschrift O. Eissfeldt zum 60. Geburtstag.* 1947
FS Eissfeldt (1958)	*Von Ugarit nach Qumran. Beiträge . . . O. Eissfeldt zum 1. September 1957 dargebracht.* 1958
FS Elliger	*Wort und Geschichte. Festschrift für Karl Elliger zum 70. Geburtstag.* 1973
FS Faulhaber	*Festschrift für Kardinal Faulhaber.* 1949
FS Friedrich	*Festschrift für J. Friedrich.* 1959
FS Frings	*Festgabe J. Kardinal Frings.* 1960
FS Galling	*Archäologie und Altes Testament. Festschrift für K. Galling.* 1970
FS Gaster	*M. Gaster Anniversary Volume.* 1936
FS Gelin	*A la rencontre de Dieu. Mémorial A. Gelin.* 1961
FS Gispen	*Schrift en uitleg. Studies . . . W. H. Gispen.* 1970
FS Glueck	*Near Eastern Archaeology in the Twentieth Century. Essays in Honor of Nelson Glueck.* 1970
FS Grapow	*Ägyptologische Studien H. Grapow.* 1955
FS Haupt	*Oriental Studies, Published in Commemoration . . . of P. Haupt.* 1926
FS Heim	*Theologie als Glaubenswagnis.* 1954
FS Hermann	*Solange es Heute heisst. Festgabe für Rudolf Hermann.* 1957
FS Herrmann	*Hommage à L. Herrmann.* Collection Latomus 44, 1960
FS Hertzberg	*Gottes Wort und Gottes Land.* 1965
FS Herwegen	*Heilige Überlieferung. I. Herwegen zum silbernen Abtsjubiläum dargebracht.* 1938
FS Irwin	*A Stubborn Faith. Papers . . . Presented to Honor W. A. Irwin.* Ed. by E. C. Hobbs. 1956
FS Jacob	*Festchrift G. Jacob.* 1932

FS Jepsen	*Schalom. Studien zu Glaube und Geschichte Israels. Alfred Jepsen zum 70. Geburtstag.* 1971
FS Junker	*Lex tua veritas. Festschrift für H. Junker.* 1961
FS Kahle	*In memoriam P. Kahle. BZAW* 103, 1968
FS Kittel	*Alttestamentliche Studien, R. Kittel dargebracht.* BWAT 13, 1913
FS Kohut	*Semitic Studies in Memory of A. Kohut.* 1897
FS Kopp	*Charisteria I. Kopp octogenario oblata.* 1954
FS Koschaker	*Symbolae P. Koschaker dedicatae.* Studia et documenta ad iura Orientis Antiqui pertinentia 2, 1939
FS Krüger	*Imago Dei. Festschrift Gustav Krüger.* 1932
FS Landsberger	*Studies in Honor of B. Landsberger on His Seventy-Fifth Birthday.* 1965
FS Lévy	*Mélanges I. Lévy.* 1955
FS de Liagre Böhl	*Symbolae Biblicae et Mesopotamicae Francisco Mario Theodoro de Liagre Böhl dedicatae.* 1973
FS Manson	*New Testament Essays. Studies in Memory of T. W. Manson.* 1959
FS Marti	*Vom Alten Testament. Marti-Festschrift.* 1925
FS May	*Translating and Understanding the Old Testament. Essays in Honor of H. G. May.* 1970
FS Meiser	*Viva Vox Evangelii, Festschrift Bischof Meiser.* 1951
FS Michel	*Abraham unser Vater. Festschrift für Otto Michel zum 60. Geburtstag.* 1963
FS Mowinckel	*Interpretationes ad Vetus Testamentum pertinentes S. Mowinckel septuagenario missae.* 1955
FS Muilenburg	*Israel's Prophetic Heritage. Essays in Honor of James Muilenburg.* 1962
FS Neuman	*Studies and Essays in Honor of A. A. Neuman.* 1962
FS Nötscher	*Alttestamentliche Studien. F. Nötscher zum 60. Geburtstag gewidmet.* 1950
FS Pedersen	*Studia Orientalia J. Pedersen dicata.* 1953
FS Procksch	*Festschrift O. Procksch.* 1934
FS von Rad (1961)	*Studien zur Theologie der alttestamentlichen Überlieferungen.* 1961
FS von Rad (1971)	*Probleme biblischer Theologie. Gerhard von Rad zum 70. Geburtstag.* 1971
FS Rinaldi	*Studi sull' Oriente e la Bibbia, offerti al P. G. Rinaldi.* 1967
FS Robert	*Mélanges bibliques. Rédigés en l'honneur de A. Robert.* 1957
FS Robinson	*Studies in Old Testament Prophecy. Presented to Th. H. Robinson.* 1950
FS Rost	*Das ferne und das nahe Wort. Festschrift L. Rost zur Vollendung seines 70. Lebensjahres am 30 November 1966 gewidmet. BZAW* 105, 1967
FS Rudolph	*Verbannung und Heimkehr.* 1961
FS Sachau	*Festschrift W. Sachau zum siebzigsten Geburtstage gewidmet.* 1915
FS Schmaus	*Wahrheit und Verkündigung. M. Schmaus zum 70. Geburtstag.* 1967
FS Schmidt	*Festschrift Eberhardt Schmidt.* Ed. by P. Brockelmann et al. 1961

FS Sellin	*Beiträge zur Religionsgeschichte und Archäologie Palästinas.* 1927
FS van Selms	*De fructu oris sui. Essays in Honour of Adrianus van Selms.* 1971
FS Söhngen	*Einsicht und Glaube. G. Söhngen zum 70. Geburtstag.* 1962
FS Thomas	*Words and Meanings. Essays Presented to D. W. Thomas.* 1968
FS Thomsen	*Festschrift V. Thomsen zur Vollendung des 70. Lebensjahres.* 1912
FS Vischer	*Hommage à W. Vischer.* 1960
FS Vogel	*Vom Herrengeheimnis der Wahrheit.* 1962
FS Vriezen	*Studia biblica et semitica. Th. C. Vriezen . . . dedicata.* 1966
FS Wedemeyer	*Sino–Japonica. Festschrift A. Wedemeyer zum 80. Geburtstag.* 1956
FS Weiser	*Tradition und Situation. A. Weiser zum 70. Geburtstag.* 1963
FS Wellhausen	*Studien . . . J. Wellhausen gewidmet. BZAW* 27, 1914
G	Grundstamm, Akkadian basic stem
GAG	W. von Soden, *Grundriss der akkadischen Grammatik samt Ergänzungsheft.* AnOr 33/47, 1969
GB	W. Gesenius and F. Buhl, *Hebräisches und aramäisches Handwörterbuch über das Alte Testament.* 1915^{17}
GCDS	J. H. Charlesworth et al., *Graphic Concordance to the Dead Sea Scrolls.* 1991
gen.	genitive, genitival
Ger.	German
Gesenius, *Thesaurus*	W. Gesenius, *Thesaurus . . . Linguae Hebraicae et Chaldaicae.* Vols. 1–3, 1835–58
Gilg.	Gilgamesh Epic (see also Schott)
Gk.	Greek, referring to lexical forms, not translation
Grapow	H. Grapow, *Wie die alten Ägypter sich anredeten, wie sie sich grüssten und wie sie miteinander sprachen.* 1960^{2}
GKC	*Gesenius' Hebrew Grammar.* Ed. by E. Kautzsch. Transl. A. E. Cowley. 1910^{2}
Gray, *Legacy*	J. Gray, *The Legacy of Canaan.* 1965^{2}
Gröndahl	F. Gröndahl, *Die Personennamen der Texte aus Ugarit.* 1967
GS	*Gesammelte Studien*
Gt, Gtn	G-stem in Akkadian, with *-ta-* and *-tan-* infix, respectively
GTT	*Gereformeerd Theologisch Tijdschrift*
Gulkowitsch	L. Gulkowitsch, *Die Bildung von Abstraktbegriffen in der hebräischen Sprachgeschichte.* 1931
Gunkel, *Gen*	H. Gunkel, *Genesis.* HKAT I/1, 1966^{7}
Gunkel-Begrich	H. Gunkel and J. Begrich, *Einleitung in die Psalmen.* 1933
GVG	C. Brockelmann, *Grundriss der vergleichenden Grammatik der semitischen Sprachen.* Vols. 1–2, 1908–13
H	Holiness Code (Lev 17–26)
ha.	hapᶜel
HAL	L. Koehler, W. Baumgartner, and J. J. Stamm, *Hebräisches und aramäisches Lexikon zum Alten Testament.* Fascicles 1–5, 1967–1995 (= KBL^{3}). Eng. transl. *HALOT*

HALOT	L. Koehler, W. Baumgartner, and J. J. Stamm, *The Hebrew and Aramaic Lexicon of the Old Testament.* Transl. and ed. under the supervision of M. E. J. Richardson, Vols. 1–4, 1994–1997
Harris	Z. S. Harris, *A Grammar of the Phoenician Language.* 1936
HAT	Handbuch zum Alten Testament. Ed. by O. Eissfeldt
Haussig	*Wörterbuch der Mythologie.* Ed. by H. W. Haussig. Part 1, 1961
hebr.	hebräisch
Hebr.	Hebrew
Herdner, *CTA*	A. Herdner, *Corpus des tablettes en cunéiformes alphabétiques découvertes à Ras Shamra-Ugarit de 1929 à 1939.* Mission de Ras Shamra X, 1963
Herm	Hermeneia
Hermop.	Hermopolis Papyri. According to the edition of E. Besciani and M. Kamil, *Atti della Accademia Nazionale dei Lincei.* Memorie, ser. VIII, vol. 12, 1966
hi.	hipᶜil
hišt.	hištapᶜal
hitp.	hitpaᶜel
hitpa.	hitpaᶜal (Aramaic stem)
hitpe.	hitpeᶜel
hitpo.	hitpoᶜlel
Hitt.	Hittite
HKAT	Handkommentar zum Alten Testament
HO	Handbuch der Orientalistik. Ed. by B. Spuler
ho.	hopᶜal
HP	E. Jenni, *Das hebräische Piᶜel.* 1968
HSAT	Die Heilige Schrift des Alten Testaments. Ed. by E. Kautzsch and A. Bertholet. 1922/23[4]
HTR	*Harvard Theological Review*
HUCA	*Hebrew Union College Annual*
Huffmon	H. B. Huffmon, *Amorite Personal Names in the Mari Texts.* 1965
ibid.	ibidem, in the same place
id.	idem, the same
IDB	*The Interpreter's Dictionary of the Bible.* Ed. by G. Buttrick. 4 vols, 1962. *Supplementary Volume.* Ed. by K. Crim. 1976
IEJ	*Israel Exploration Journal*
ICC	International Critical Commentary
ILC	J. Pedersen, *Israel, Its Life and Culture.* Vols. 1–2, 1926; vols. 3–4, 1934
Imp. Aram.	Imperial Aramaic
imper.	impersonal
impf.	imperfect, imperfective
impf. cons.	imperfectum consecutivum
impv.	imperative
incl.	including
inf.	infinitive
inscr.	inscription

Int	*Interpretation*
intrans.	intransitive
IP	M. Noth, *Die israelitischen Personennamen im Rahmen der gemeinsemitischen Namengebung.* 1928
isr.	israelitisch
Isr.	Israelite
išt.	ištapᶜal
itp.	itpeᶜel
itpa.	itpaᶜal
J	Jahwist source (of the Pentateuch)
Jacob	E. Jacob, *Théologie de l'Ancien Testament.* 1955
Jahnow	J. Jahnow, *Das hebräische Leichenlied im Rahmen der Völkerdichtung.* 1923
JANES	*The Journal of the Ancient Near East Society of Columbia University*
JAOS	*Journal of the American Oriental Society*
Jastrow	M. Jastrow, *A Dictionary of the Targumim, the Talmud Babli and Yerushalmi, and the Midrashic Literature.* 1950^2
JBL	*Journal of Biblical Literature*
JCS	*Journal of Cuneiform Studies*
JE	*The Jewish Encyclopedia.* Ed. by J. Singer. Vols. 1–12, 1901–6
JEOL	*Jaarbericht van het Vooraziatisch-Egyptisch Gezelschap (Genootschap) Ex Oriente Lux*
Jew.	Jewish
JJS	*Journal of Jewish Studies*
JNES	*Journal of Near Eastern Studies*
Joüon	P. Joüon, *A Grammar of Biblical Hebrew.* 2 vols. Transl. and revised by T. Muraoka. Subsidia Biblica 14/1–2, 1991
JPSV	Jewish Publication Society Version
JSS	*Journal of Semitic Studies*
JTS	*Journal of Theological Studies*
juss.	jussive
K	Kethib
KAI	H. Donner and W. Röllig, *Kanaanäische und aramäische Inschriften.* Vol. I, Texte, 1966^2; vol. II, Kommentar, 1968^2; vol. III, Glossare etc., 1969^2
Kaiser, *Intro.*	O. Kaiser, *Introduction to the Old Testament.* Transl. by J. Sturdy. 1975
KAT	Kommentar zum Alten Testament. Ed. by W. Rudolph, K. Elliger, and F. Hesse
KBL	L. Koehler and W. Baumgartner, *Lexicon in Veteris Testamenti libros.* 1958^2
KD	C. F. Keil and F. Delitzsch, *Biblical Commentary on the Old Testament.* 1866–91
KerD	*Kerygma and Dogma*
KHC	Kurzer Hand-Commentar zum Alten Testament
KI	M. Lidzbarski, *Kanaanäische Inschriften.* 1907
Kluge	F. Kluge and W. Mitzka, *Etymologisches Wörterbuch der deutschen Sprache.* 1963^{11}
Köhler, *Theol.*	L. Köhler, *Old Testament Theology.* Transl. by A. S. Todd. 1957

König	E. König, *Hebräisches und aramäisches Wörterbuch zum Alten Testament.* 1936^{6,7}
König, *Syntax*	E. König, *Historisch-kritisches Lehrgebäude der hebräischen Sprache mit steter Beziehung auf Qimchi und dei anderen Auctoritäten.* Bd. II/2: *Historisch-comparative Syntax der hebräischen Sprache.* 1897
KS	Kleine Schriften
KTU	M. Dietrich, O. Loretz, and J. Sanmartín, *Die keilalphabetischen Texte aus Ugarit.* 1976
Kuhn, *Konk.*	K. G. Kuhn, *Konkordanz au den Qumrantexten.* 1960
L	"lay source" of the Pentateuch
l(l).	line(s)
Lande	I. Lande, *Formelhafte Wendungen der Umgangssprache im Alten Testament.* 1949
Lane	E. W. Lane, *Al-Qamūsu, an Arabic-English Lexicon.* Vols. 1–8, 1863–93
Lat.	Latin
van der Leeuw	G. van der Leeuw, *Religion in Essence and Manifestation.* Transl. by J. E. Turner, with appendices incorporating the additions of the 2d German ed. by Hans H. Penner. 2 vols, 1967
Leander	P. Leander, *Laut- und Formenlehre des Ägyptisch-Aramäischen.* 1928
Leslau	W. Leslau, *Ethiopic and South Arabic Contributions to the Hebrew Lexicon.* 1958
Levy	M. A. Levy, *Siegel und Gemmen mit aramäischen, phoenizischen, althebräischen . . . Inschriften.* 1869
de Liagre Böhl	see Böhl
Lis.	G. Lisowsky, *Konkordanz zum hebräischen Alten Testament.* 1958
lit.	literally
Littmann-Höfner	E. Littmann and M. Höfner, *Wörterbuch der Tigre-Sprache.* 1962
LS	C. Brockelmann, *Lexicon Syriacum.* 1928
LXX	Septuagint
LXX^{A} etc.	Cod. Alexandrinus etc.
Mand.	Mandean
Mandl.	S. Mandelkern, *Veteris Testamenti concordantiae hebraicae atque chaldaicae.* 1926^{2}
MAOG	Mitteilungen der Altorientalischen Gesellschaft
masc.	masculine
MDAI	*Mitteilungen des Deutschen Archäologischen Instituts*
Meyer	R. Meyer, *Hebräische Grammatik.* Vol. 1, 1966^{3}; vol. 2, 1969^{3}
Mid. Assyr.	Middle Assyrian
Mid. Hebr.	Middle Hebrew
Midr.	Midrash
Min. Pr.	Twelve Minor Prophets (Hos, Joel, Amos, Obad, Jonah, Mic, Nah, Hab, Zeph, Hag, Zech, Mal)
MIO	*Mitteilungen des Instituts für Orientforschung.*
Moab.	Moabite

Montgomery, *Dan*	J. A. Montgomery, *A Critical and Exegetical Commentary on the Book of Daniel.* International Critical Commentary, 1950^2
Moscati, *Intro.*	*An Introduction to the Comparative Grammar of Semitic Languages.* Ed. by S. Moscati. 1964
Muséon	*Le Muséon. Revue d'Etudes Orientales*
MS(S)	Manuscript(s)
MT	Mas(s)oretic Text (textus receptus)
MUSJ	*Mélanges de l'Université Saint-Joseph*
N	Northern (source)
n.	note
NAB	New American Bible
Nab.	Nabatean
NASB	New American Standard Bible
NAWG	*Nachrichten (von) der Akademie der Wissenschaften in Göttingen*
NB	see Nöldeke, *NB*
NCBC	New Century Bible Commentary
NE	M. Lidzbarski, *Handbuch der nordsemitischen Epigraphik.* 1898
NEB	New English Bible
NedGTT	*Nederduitse Gereformeerde Teologiese Tydskrif*
NedTT	*Nederlands Theologisch Tijdschrift*
ni.	nipᶜal
NIDOTTE	*New International Dictionary of Old Testament Theology and Exegesis.* Ed. by W. A. VanGemeren. 5 vols., 1997
nitp.	nitpaᶜel
NIV	New International Version
NKZ	*Neue Kirchliche Zeitschrift*
Nöldeke, *BS*	T. Nöldeke, *Beiträge zur semitischen Sprachwissenschaft.* 1904
Nöldeke, *NB*	T. Nöldeke, *Neue Beiträge zur semitischen Sprachwissenschaft.* 1910
nom.	nominal, nominative
no(s).	number(s)
Noth, *GS*	M. Noth, *Gesammelte Studien zum Alten Testament.* Vol. 1, 1966^3; vol. 2, 1969
NRSV	New Revised Standard Version
NRT	*La nouvelle revue théologique*
NS	new series
NT	New Testament
NTS	*Nieuwe Theologische Studiën*
NTT	*Norsk Teologisk Tidsskrift*
NWSem.	Northwest Semitic (language group)
Nyberg	H. S. Nyberg, *Hebreisk Grammatik.* 1952
obj.	object
OLZ	*Orientalistische Literaturzeitung*
op. cit.	opere citato, in the work cited
Or	*Orientalia* (NS)
OrAnt	Oriens Antiquus
OT	Old Testament

OTL	Old Testament Library
OTS	*Oudtestamentische Studiën*
OuTWP	*Die Ou Testamentiese Werkgemeenskap in Suid-Afrika Pretoria*
P	Priestly source (of the Pentateuch)
p(p).	page(s)
P^s	see H
pa.	paᶜel
Pal.	Palestinian
Palm.	Palmyrene
pap.	papyrus
par.	parallel
pass.	passive
Payne-Smith	R. Payne Smith, *Thesaurus Syriacus.* Vols. 1–2, 1868–97
pe.	Aramaic stem peᶜal (= Heb. qal in German edition)
PEQ	*Palestine Exploration Quarterly*
per.	person, persons, personal
Pers.	Persia, Persian
pf.	perfect, perfective
PHOE	G. von Rad, *The Problem of the Hexateuch and Other Essays.* Transl. by E. W. Trueman Dicken. 1966
Phoen.	Phoenician
pi.	piᶜel
pil.	pilpel
PJB	*Palästinajahrbuch*
PLP	C. Westermann, *The Praise of God in the Psalms.* Transl. K. R. Crim and R. N. Soulen. 1981
pl.	plural
PN	personal name
PNSP	M. Dahood, *Proverbs and Northwest Semitic Philology.* 1963
po.	poᶜlel
Poen.	Plautus, *Poenulus* (see also Sznycer)
poss.	possessive
postbibl.	postbiblical
POT	De Prediking van het Oude Testament
prep.	preposition, prepositional
pron.	pronoun
PRU	*Le Palais Royal d'Ugarit.* Vols. 2–6, 1955–70
ptcp.	participle
pu.	puᶜal
Pun.	Punic
Q	Qere
R	Redactor
RA	*Revue d'Assyriologie et d'Archéologie Orientale*
RAC	*Reallexikon für Antike und Christentum.* 1950ff.
von Rad, *Gottesvolk*	G. von Rad, *Das Gottesvolk im Deuteronomium.* 1929
von Rad, *GS*	G. von Rad, *Gesammelte Studien zum Alten Testament.* 1965^3
von Rad, *Theol.*	G. von Rad, *Old Testament Theology.* Transl. by D. M. G. Stalker. Vol. 1, 1963; vol. 2, 1965

RB	*Revue Biblique*
re	regarding
reg.	register
REJ	*Revue des Etudes Juives*
RES	*Répertoire d'épigraphie sémitique*
resp.	respectively
rev.	reverse
RGG	*Religion in Geschichte und Gegenwart.* Ed. by K. Galling. Vols. 1–6, 1957^3–62
RHPR	*Revue d'Histoire et de Philosophie religieuses*
RHR	*Revue de l'Histoire des Religions*
RivB	*Rivista Biblica Italiana*
Rost, *KC*	L. Rost, *Das kleine Credo und andere Studien zum Alten Testament.* 1965
RQ	*Revue de Qumrân*
RS	Ras Shamra. Texts given according to the excavation numbers; see also *PRU*
RSO	Rivista degli Studi Orientali
RSP	*Ras Shamra Parallels*
RSPT	*Revue des Sciences Philosphiques et Théologiques*
RSV	Revised Standard Version
RTP	*Revue de Théologie et de Philosophie*
S	J. Strong, *Strong's Exhaustive Concordance of the Bible,* 1890
Š	Š-stem in Akkadian
šap.	šapᶜel
SAHG	A. Falkenstein and W. von Soden, *Sumerische und akkadische Hymnen und Gebete.* 1953
Sam.	Samaritan
SArab.	South Arabic (language group)
SBL	J. Barr, *Semantics of Biblical Language.* 1961
SCan	South Canaanite (language group)
Schott	*Das Gilgamesch-Epos.* Neu übersetzt und mit Anmerkungen versehen von A. Schott. Durschgesehen und ergänzt von W. von Soden. 1958
SDAW	*Sitzungsberichte der Deutschen Akademie der Wissenschaften zu Berlin*
Sef.	Sefire stelae (see Fitzmyer, *Sef.*)
Sellin-Fohrer	*Introduction to the Old Testament.* Initiated by E. Sellin. Completely revised by G. Fohrer. 1968
Semit	*Semitica*
Sem.	Semitic
ser.	series
Seux	M.-J. Seux, *Epithètes royales akkadiennes et sumériennes.* 1967
sg.	singular
SNHL	J. L. Palache, *Semantic Notes on the Hebrew Lexicon,* 1959
SSem.	South Semitic (language group)
st.	state
ST	*Studia Theologica*
Stamm, *AN*	J. J. Stamm, *Die akkadische Namengebung.* 1968

Stamm, *HEN*	J. J. Stamm, *Hebräische Ersatznamen,* FS Landsberger, 413–424
Stark	J. K. Stark, *Personal Names in Palmyrene Inscriptions.* 1971
SThU	*Schweizerische Theologische Umschau*
SThZ	*Schweizerische theologische Zeitschrift*
StrB	H. L. Strack and P. Billerbeck, *Kommentar zum Neuen Testament aus Talmud und Midrasch.* Vols. 1–6, 1922–61
StudOr	*Studia Orientalia*
subj.	subject
subst.	substantive, substantival
suf.	suffix
Sum.	Sumerian
suppl.	supplement
s.v.	sub voce
SVT	*Supplements to Vetus Testamentum*
SWSem.	Southwest Semitic (language group)
Syr.	Syriac
Sznycer	M. Sznycer, *Les passages puniques en transcription latine dans le "Poenulus" de Plaute.* 1967
Tallqvist	K. Tallqvist, *Akkadische Götterepitheta.* 1938
TBl	*Theologische Blätter*
TDNT	*Theological Dictionary of the New Testament.* Ed. by G. Kittel and G. Friedrich. Transl. by G. W. Bromiley. Vols. 1–10, 1964–76
TDOT	*Theological Dictionary of the Old Testament.* Ed. by G. J. Botterweck, H. Ringgren, and H. J. Fabry. Transl. by J. T. Willis, G. W. Bromiley, and D. E. Green. Vols. 1ff., 1974ff.
Tg(s).	Targum(s); Targumic
TGI^1; *TGI*^{2}	*Textbook zur Geschichte Israels.* Ed. by K. Galling. 1950^1; 1968^2
TGUOS	*Transactions of the Glasgow University Oriental Society*
THAT	*Theologisches Handwörterbuch zum Alten Testament.* Ed. by E. Jenni, with assistance from C. Westermann. 2 vols., 1971–76. Eng. transl. *TLOT*
theol.	theology; Theologie, theologisch
ThStud	*Theological Studies*
ThT	*Theologisch Tijdschrift*
ThWAT	*Theologisches Wörterbuch zum Alten Testament.* Ed. by G. J. Botterweck, H. Ringgren, and H. J. Fabry. Vols. 1ff., 1970ff. Eng. transl. *TDOT*
TLOT	*Theological Lexicon of the Old Testament.* Ed. by E. Jenni, with assistance from C. Westermann. Transl. by M. E. Biddle. 3 vols., 1997
TLZ	*Theologische Literaturzeitung*
TQ	*Theologische Quartalschrift*
trans.	transitive
transl.	translated (by); translation
Trip.	Tripolitana. Enumeration according to G. Levi della Vida, see *DISO* XXVIII

TRu	*Theologische Rundschau*
TS	*Theologische Studien*
TSK	*Theologische Studien und Kritiken*
TWOT	*Theological Wordbook of the Old Testament.* Ed. by R. L. Harris, G. L. Archer, Jr., and B. K. Waltke. 2 vols., 1980
txt?	problematic or corrupted text
txt em	textual emendation
TZ	*Theologische Zeitschrift*
UF	*Ugarit-Forschungen*
Ug.	Ugaritic
Ugaritica 5	J. Nougayrol, E. Laroche, C. Virolleaud, C. F. A. Schaeffer, *Ugaritica V.* 1968
UHP	M. Dahood, *Ugaritic-Hebrew Philology.* 1965
UJE	*The Universal Jewish Encylopedia.* Ed. by L. Landman. 1948
UT	C. H. Gordon, *Ugaritic Textbook.* AnOr 38, 1965. Number indicates entries in the glossary. Text indicates the texts in transliteration
v(v)	verse(s)
VAB	Vorderasiatische Bibliothek
de Vaux	R. de Vaux, *Ancient Israel: Its Life and Institutions.* Transl. by J McHugh. 2 vols., 1961
VD	*Verbum Domini*
Vers.	version(s)
Vg.	Vulgate
Vriezen, *Theol.*	T. C. Vriezen, *An Outline of Old Testament Theology.* 1970^2
VT	*Vetus Testamentum*
Wagner	M. Wagner, *Die lexikalischen und grammatikalischen Aramaismen im alttestamentlichen Hebräisch.* 1966
WD	*Wort und Dienst* (Jahrbuch der Theologischen Schule Bethel)
Wehr	H. Wehr, *Dictionary of Modern Written Arabic.* 1961
Westermann, *PLP*	See *PLP*
WKAS	*Wörterbuch der klassischen arabischen Sprache.* Ed. by M. Ullmann. 1957ff.
WO	*Welt des Orients*
Wolff, *GS*	H. W. Wolff, *Gesammelte Studien zum Alten Testament.* 1964
WSem.	West Semitic
WTM	J. Levy, *Wörterbuch über die Talmudim und Midraschim.* 1924^2
WUS	J. Aistleitner, *Wörterbuch der ugaritischen Sprache.* Ed. by O. Eissfeldt. 1967^3
WZ	*Wissenschaftliche Zeitschrift*
WZKM	*Wiener Zeitschrift für die Kunde des Morgenlandes*
x	no. of times a form occurs
Yadin	Y. Yadin, *The Scroll of the War.* 1962
yi.	yipᶜil
ZA	*Zeitschrift für Assyriologie*
ZÄS	*Zeitschrift für Ägyptische Sprache und Altertumskunde*
ZAW	*Zeitschrift für die alttestamentliche Wissenschaft*

ZB	Zürcher Bibel
ZBK	Zürcher Bibelkommentare
ZDMG	*Zeitschrift der Deutschen Morgenländischen Gesellschaft*
ZDPV	*Zeitschrift des Deutschen Palästina-Vereins*
ZEE	*Zeitschrift für evangelische Ethik*
Zimmerli, *GO*	W. Zimmerli, *Gottes Offenbarung. Gessamelte Aufsätze zum Alten Testament.* 1963
Zimmern	H. Zimmern, *Akkadische Fremdwörter.* 1917²
ZKG	*Zeitschrift für Kirchengeschichte*
ZNW	*Zeitschrift für neutestamentliche Wissenschaft*
Zorell	F. Zorell, *Lexicon Hebraicum et Aramaicum Veteris Testamenti.* 1968
ZRGG	*Zeitschfift für Religions- und Geistesgeschichte*
ZS	*Zeitschrift für Semitistik*
ZTK	*Zeitschrift für Theologie und Kirche*

Table of Words in Volume 1

אמר	*ʾmr*	**to say**	*H. H. Schmid*	159
אֱנוֹשׁ	*ʾᵉnôš*	**person** → אָדָם *ʾādām*		162
אֲנִי	*ʾᵃnî*	**I**	*K. Günther*	162
אסף	*ʾsp*	**to collect** → קבץ *qbṣ*		166
אַף	*ʾap*	**anger**	*G. Sauer*	166
אֵפֶר	*ʾēper*	**dust** → עָפָר *ʿāpār*		170
אֹרַח	*ʾōraḥ*	**way** → דֶּרֶךְ *derek*		170
אֲרִי	*ʾᵃrî*	**lion**	*F. Stolz*	170
אֶרֶץ	*ʾereṣ*	**earth, land**	*H. H. Schmid*	172
ארר	*ʾrr*	**to curse**	*C. A. Keller*	179
ארשׂ	*ʾrś* pi.	**to betroth**	*J. Kühlewein*	182
אֵשׁ	*ʾēš*	**fire**	*F. Stolz*	183
אִשָּׁה	*ʾiššâ*	**woman**	*J. Kühlewein*	187
אָשָׁם	*ʾāšām*	**guilt**	*R. Knierim*	191
אשׁר	*ʾšr* pi.	**to call blessed**	*M. Sæbø*	195
אֵת	*ʾēt*	**with** → עִם *ʿim*		197
אתה	*ʾth*	**to come** → בוא *bôʾ*		197
בגד	*bgd*	**to act faithlessly**	*M. A. Klopfenstein*	198
בַּד	*bad*	**solitariness** → אֶחָד *ʾeḥād*		200
בוא	*bôʾ*	**to come**	*E. Jenni*	201
בושׁ	*bôš*	**to be ashamed**	*F. Stolz*	204
בחן	*bḥn*	**to test**	*E. Jenni*	207
בחר	*bḥr*	**to choose**	*H. Wildberger*	209
בטח	*bṭḥ*	**to trust**	*E. Gerstenberger*	226
בין	*bîn*	**to understand**	*H. H. Schmid*	230
בַּיִת	*bayit*	**house**	*E. Jenni*	232
בכה	*bkh*	**to cry**	*F. Stolz*	236
בֵּן	*bēn*	**son**	*J. Kühlewein*	238
בנה	*bnh*	**to build**	*A. R. Hulst*	245
בַּעַל	*baʿal*	**owner**	*J. Kühlewein*	247
בקשׁ	*bqš* pi.	**to seek**	*G. Gerleman*	251
ברא	*brʾ*	**to create**	*W. H. Schmidt*	253
ברח	*brḥ*	**to flee** → נוס *nûs*		256
בְּרִית	*bᵉrît*	**obligation**	*E. Kutsch*	256
ברך	*brk* pi.	**to bless**	*C. A. Keller (I–III)/ G. Wehmeier (IV–V)*	266
בשׂר	*bśr* pi.	**to bring a message** → מַלְאָךְ *malʾāk*		282
בָּשָׂר	*bāśār*	**flesh**	*G. Gerleman*	283
בַּת	*bat*	**daughter** → בֵּן *bēn*		285
גאה	*gʾh*	**to be high**	*H.-P. Stähli*	285
גאל	*gʾl*	**to redeem**	*J. J. Stamm*	288
גבה	*gbh*	**to be high**	*H.-P. Stähli*	296
גבר	*gbr*	**to be superior**	*J. Kühlewein*	299
גָּדוֹל	*gādôl*	**great**	*E. Jenni*	302
גּוֹי	*gôy*	**people** → עַם *ʿam*		307
גור	*gûr*	**to sojourn**	*R. Martin-Achard*	307

אָב ʾ*āb* father

S 1; BDB 3a; *HALOT* 1:1b; *TDOT* 1:1–19; *TWOT* 4; *NIDOTTE* 3

I. The biradical *ʾ*ab-* "father" is common Sem. (*GVG* 1:331; BL 450, 524), like the other significant kinship terms (→ ʾ*ēm* "mother," → *bēn* "son," → ʾ*āḥ* "brother"). Like ʾ*ēm* "mother" and pars. in numerous languages, it derives from infant babbling (L. Köhler, *ZAW* 55 [1937]: 169–72; id., *JSS* 1 [1956]: 12f.); derivation from a verbal root (e.g., → ʾ*bh* "to wish") is therefore unsuccessful.

Derivatives from the root form (abstract and adj. forms, diminutives, esp. vocatives) are lacking in OT Hebr.; in contrast, cf. Akk. *abbūtu* "fatherhood" (*AHw* 6a; *CAD* A/1:50f.), mostly in a fig. sense ("fatherly attitude"; *abbūta epēšu/ṣabātu/aḫāzu* "to intercede"), which also occurs in family law documents, e.g., at Nuzi, of the transfer of the family leadership to the wife following the death of the adopter (P. Koschaker, *OLZ* 35 [1932]: 400).

The abstract form is also attested in Phoen.: Karatepe inscription I.12f. (*KAI* no. 26), "Indeed, every king chose me for fatherhood (*b*ʾ*bt p*ʿ*ln*), my justice and my wisdom and the goodness of my heart" (Friedrich 91, 130; *KAI* 2:40; *DISO* 3; cf. *ANET* 654a); contra, although uncertain, M. Dahood, *Bib* 44 [1963]: 70, 291; *HAL* 2a: ʾ*ābôt* as a pl. excellentiae is also to be understood as a sg. in Isa 14:21 and Psa 109:14.

In Syr. (C. Brockelmann, *ZA* 17 [1903]: 251f.; *LS* 1a) ʾ*ḥd* ʾ*bwt*ʾ appears borrowed from Akk. *abbūta aḫāzu* "to intercede" (*CAD* A/1:178), and as a "celque" from Aram. in the Hebr. of Qumran: 1QS 2:9: ʾ*ôḥ*ᵃ*zê* ʾ*ābôt* "intercessor" (P. Wernberg-Møller, *VT* 3 [1953]: 196f.; id., *Manual of Discipline* [1957], 53f.; E. Y. Kutscher, *Tarbiz* 33 [1963/64]: 125f.).

II. With over 1,200 occurrences ʾ*āb* stands after *dābār* and before ʿ*îr* in eleventh place among the substs. ordered according to frequency.

The following statistics do not include ʾ*ābî* as an interjection (1 Sam 24:12; 2 Kgs 5:13; Job 34:6) and the addition of Bombergiana in 2 Chron 10:14; ʾ*ābî(w)* in conjunction with the PN *ḥûrām* (2 Chron 2:12; 4:16) is included; Lis. overlooks Gen 46:34.

	sg.	pl.	total
Hebr.			
Gen	198	10	208
Exod	10	14	24
Lev	22	3	25
Num	28	57	85
Deut	20	51	71
Josh	17	18	35
Judg	44	10	54
1 Sam	48	5	53
2 Sam	27	1	28
1 Kgs	64	31	95
2 Kgs	31	38	69
Isa	16	5	21
Jer	15	48	63
Ezek	13	14	27
Hos	–	1	1
Jonah	–	1	1
Amos	1	1	2

	sg.	pl.	total
Mic	1	1	2
Zech	2	5	7
Mal	3	4	7
Psa	5	14	19
Job	6	3	9
Prov	23	3	26
Ruth	3	–	3
Lam	1	1	2
Esth	3	–	3
Dan	–	8	8
Ezra	–	14	14
Neh	1	19	20
1 Chron	60	46	106
2 Chron	58	65	123
Aram.			
Dan	4	1	5
Ezra	–	2	2
total			
Hebr.	720	491	1,211
Aram.	4	3	7

III. 1. The correlation to son/daughter/child or their pls. is already established in the basic meaning "(natural) father (of his children)"; the word is never used in the OT, then, without this implicit or explicit juxtaposition except in some fig. usages (honorifics, "founder," etc.). A devaluation to a simple correlative term, as occurs to a degree with Arab. *kunja* (e.g., "father of the desert" = ostrich), does not occur in the OT (for *ʾᵃbîʿad* Isa 9:5, see 3).

As a term of interfamilial relationship, the sg. is used in the vast majority of cases (14/15) with a gen. or poss. suf.; consequently it stands only 3x with a (definite) art.

Denoting the male parent, "father" stands in a complementary relationship to "mother," a relationship that constitutes a second, less pronounced semantic dichotomy. Consequently, the two terms will often be bound together in nom. series; the sequence father-mother is determined by the primary position of the father in the patriarchal family (G. Quell, *TDNT* 5:961ff.).

"Father" and "mother" stand in parallelism (parallelismus membrorum) in Psa 109:14; Job 17:14; 31:18; Prov 1:8; 4:3; 6:20; 19:26; 23:22; 30:11, 17; Mic 7:6; cf. further, without strict formal congruity and with rearrangement of the elements determined partly by content, Jer 16:3; 20:14f.; Ezek 16:3, 45.

Of 52 nom. series (lists in B. Hartmann, *Die nominalen Aufreihungen im AT* [1953], 7, with them add Lev 20:9b; Judg 14:6; 1 Kgs 22:53; 2 Kgs 3:13; delete Jer 6:21), three exhibit the sequence mother-father (Lev 19:3; 20:19; 21:2; for the reasons, see Elliger, HAT 4, 256n.5).

In some of these texts one could paraphrase "father and mother" accurately with "parents" (Gen 2:24; 28:7; Deut 21:13; Judg 14:2ff.; 1 Sam 22:3; 2 Sam 19:38; Zech 13:3bis with *yōlᵉdāyw* "who begot him"; Ruth 2:11; Esth 2:7bis; cf. LXX and GNB for Esth 2:7). The usage of the pl. *ʾābôt* for "parents" first occurs postbibl.; cf. also Akk. *abbū* (*AHw* 7b, infrequent), Syr. *ʾabāhē*, and Arab. dual *ʾabawāni*.

In its basic meaning, *ʾāb* has no synonyms.

Alongside the more common *ab*, Ug. also has *ad, adn*, and *ḥtk* as designations for father. In this regard, *ad* (in *KTU* 1.23.32ff. *ad ad* par. *um um;* and *mt mt* respectively) appears to be a term of endearment (cf. *CML*[1] 123a, 135a; *CML*[2] 125, 141: "dad[dy]"; *UT* no. 71; *WUS* no. 73; see further Huffmon 130, 156), which represents the normal vocative expression within the family unit. In contrast, *adn* "lord, master" replaces the designation "father" in polite address (*KTU* 1.16.I.44, 57, 60; 1.24.33; A. van Selms, *Marriage and Family Life in Ug. Literature* [1954], 62, 113). The simple equation of → *ʾādôn* with "father" does not follow, however (contra M. Dahood, *CBQ* 23 [1961]: 463f. on Jer 22:18; 34:5; Prov 27:18; cf. e.g., Gen 31:35, "then she said to her father: 'My lord' "). With respect to *ḥtk* (ptcp. or action noun) the basic verbal meaning (*UT* no. 911; *WUS* no. 985; Arab. *ḥataka* "to cut off") is no longer clearly discernible (cf. E. Ullendorff, *JSS* 7 [1962]: 341: "circumciser"; Gray, *Legacy* 71n.2). The root is probably not represented in Psa 52:7 (A. F. Scharf, *VD* 38 [1960]: 213–22; *UHP* 58: pi. privative "to unfather").

In contrast to *ʾēm* (Exod 22:29, a mother animal of cattle and sheep; Deut 22:6, mother bird), *ʾāb* is not applied to animals.

2. Extended usage of the word is common Sem. and is apparent (a) on the one hand, in the extension of the concept to the ancestors, and (b) on the other, in the inclusion of nonbiological paternity through adoption or other means.

(a) As in Indo-Germanic, Hebr. has no individual word for "grandfather," which may be connected with sociological circumstances: in the extended family the patriarch rules not only over the sons but also over the grandchildren and great-grandchildren (E. Risch, *Museum Helveticum* 1 [1944]: 115–22).

For the paternal grandfather, a simple *ʾāb* suffices in the OT (Gen 28:13, Jacob-Abraham; 2 Sam 9:7 and 16:3, Meribaal-Saul); the maternal grandfather is called *ʾᵃbî-ʾimmᵉkā* "father of your mother" (Gen 28:2, Jacob-Bethuel).

In Akk. *abi-abi* or with sandhi *ababi* also occurs (*CAD* A/1:70; *AHw* 7b), as a (substitute) PN (Stamm, *AN* 302; id., *HEN* 422); cf. in addition the PN *ababouis* at Dura (F. Rosenthal, *Die aramaistische Forschung* [1939], 99n.1) and Syr. *ʾbbwy* (J. B. Segal, *BSOAS* 16 [1954]: 23).

The LXX uses *pappos* "grandfather" (Sir Prol 7) and *propappos* "(great-)grandfather" once each (Exod 10:6, where, however, according to the context, *ʾᵃbôt ʾᵃbōteykā* signifies "your ancestors").

Modern Hebr. makes use of *ʾāb zāqēn* "old father" (cf. Gen 43:27 and 44:20, "aged father").

The extension of the concept to the ancestors takes place first in the pl. *ʾābôt*, which includes the father proper, the grandfather (Gen 48:15f., Isaac and Abraham as the "fathers" of Jacob), and the great-grandfather (2 Kgs 12:19, Jehoshaphat, Joram, and Ahaziah as "fathers" of Joash), or an undetermined number of generations.

In this extended meaning "ancestors" (cf. *ʾᵃbôtām hāriʾšōnîm*, Jer 11:10), the word also acquires synonyms: *riʾšōnîm* (Lev 26:45; Deut 19:14, LXX *pateres*, LXX[a] *proteroi;* Isa 61:4; Psa 79:8) and *haqqadmōnî* (1 Sam 24:14, collectively, provided that one does not read the suf. *-nîm*), also *ʿammîm* in the expression *ʾsp* ni. *ʾel-ʿammeykā/ʿammāyw* "to be gathered to your/his people" (Gen 25:8, 17; 35:29; 49:29 txt em, 33; Num 20:24; 27:13; 31:2; Deut 32:50; → *ʿam*).

The pl. of the basic meaning ("fathers of various families") also occurs in the OT (Judg 21:22, the fathers or brothers of the stolen daughters of Shiloh; Jer 16:3, "your fathers who begot you"; in addition to perhaps two dozen other texts with a general juxtaposition of the older and the younger generations), but is significantly rarer than the meaning "ancestors," which is the only possible meaning of the word with a sg. suf. ("my fathers") on biological grounds.

Whether the fem. pl. form with *-ôt* results from the fact that *ʾāb* is essentially a sg. tantum (L. Köhler, *ZAW* 55 [1937]: 172) is uncertain. Nöldeke (*BS* 69) postulated a formation analogous to the polar concept *ʾimmôt* "mothers" (so also *GVG* 1:449; BL 515, 615; Meyer 2:45; G. Rinaldi, *BeO* 10 [1968]: 24).

DISO 1 and *CAD* A/1:72 give references for the pl. "ancestors" in NWSem. inscriptions and in Akk. (alongside *abbū* in regions of WSem. influence, also *abbūtu*).

The potent expression, "neither your fathers nor your fathers' fathers" (Exod 10:6 of Pharaoh; Dan 11:24 of Antiochus IV), in a negative clause, signifies nothing less than the total series of ancestors.

The sg. can also assume the meaning "ancestor" (80x), but in these cases it always indicates ancestors par excellence (cf. Isa 43:27 *ʾābîkā hāriʾšôn*), namely the patriarchs of a clan (Rechabites, Jer 35:6–18), a tribe (Dan, Josh 19:47 and Judg 18:29; Levi, Num 18:2), an occupational group (Gen 4:21f. txt em; Aaronites, 1 Chron 24:19), a dynasty (David, 1 Kgs 15:3b, 11, 24, etc., 14x), or a people (Israel: Abraham, Josh 24:3 and Isa 51:2; Jacob, Deut 26:5 and Isa 58:14; all three patriarchs, 1 Chron 29:18). Although the eponymous hero can still be called "father" in accordance with this function (Ham-Canaan, Gen 9:18, 22; Kemuel-Aram, Gen 22:21; Hamor-Shechem, Gen 33:19; 34:6; Josh 24:32; Judg 9:28; Arba-Anak, Josh 15:13; 21:11; Machir-Gilead, Josh 17:1; 1 Chron 2:21, 23; 7:14; cf. also the metaphor of the personified Jerusalem, Ezek 16:3, 45), it would be better to translate references to peoples with "ancestor" (the sons of Heber, Gen 10:21; Moabites and Ammonites, Gen 19:37f.; Edomites, Gen 36:9, 43).

In 1 Chron 2:24, 42–55; 4:3–21; 7:31; 8:29; 9:35 (31x) the formula "*X*, father of *Y*" (M. Noth, *ZDPV* 55 [1932]: 100; Rudolph, HAT 21, 13f.) contains not only the name of a family but a place-name.

In Gen 17:4f., *ʾab(-)hămôn gôyīm* "father of many nations," the unusual cs. form is influenced by the play on words with Abraham.

(b) The expansion of meaning in the direction of adoptive paternity is facilitated by the fact that the relationship between child and father is by nature less direct than that between child and mother. Bab. law does not distinguish between the legitimation of a father's own child born to a slave mother and outright adoption (Driver-Miles 1:351, 384). Nevertheless, except for the purely fig. usage, *ʾāb* is seldom used with respect to nonbiological paternity, due in part to the fact that adoption in the precise sense, i.e., outside the family, is scarcely attested in the OT (de Vaux 1:51f.; H. Donner, "Adoption oder Legitimation?" *OrAnt* 8 [1969]: 87–119). With respect to Yahweh as "father" of the Davidic kings, see IV/3b.

Akk. distinguishes between *abum murabbīšu* "stepfather" and *abum wālidum* "biological father" (*CAD* A/1:68b).

In Israel, as in Babylonia (Driver-Miles 1:392–94), apprentices and journeymen could also stand in a sort of adoptive relationship to their masters; yet the usage of the terms of relationship "sons" and "father" for the membership and leadership of a guild is determined primarily by the fact that sons normally assumed the occupation of the father. *ʾāb* as founder or leader of a guild may be attested in 1 Chron 4:14 (cf. 4:12, 23; I. Mendelsohn, *BASOR* 80 [1940]: 19).

The leader of a prophetic guild, who was at the same time the "spiritual" father, may have also been called *ʾāb* (L. Dürr, "Heilige Vaterschaft im antiken Orient," FS Herwegen 9ff.; J. Lindblom, *Prophecy in Ancient Israel* [1962], 69f.; J. G. Williams, "Prophetic 'Father,' " *JBL* 85 [1966]: 344–48); at the least one finds the address *ʾābî* "my father" for Elijah and Elisha (2 Kgs 2:12; 13:14; also used by those outside the *bᵉnê hannᵉbîʾîm:* 2 Kgs 6:21; cf. 8:9 "your son"). Yet the transition to *ʾāb* as an honorific (see 3) is underway here (Lande 21f.; K. Galling, *ZTK* 53 [1956]: 130f.; A. Phillips, FS Thomas 183–94).

Occurrences in 1 Sam 24:12 and 2 Kgs 5:13 should probably be regarded as interjections (*GVG* 2:644; Joüon §§105f.; contra *TDNT* 5:971n.141; otherwise one must assume an honorific or address form directed to the father-in-law in 1 Sam 24:12 and a fixed address formula with a sg. suf. on the lips of a group in 2 Kgs 5:13; cf. L. Köhler, *ZAW* 40 [1922]: 39).

Corresponding to the address of a youth as *bᵉnî* "my son," esp. in wisdom literature (→ *bēn*), one would expect that *ʾāb* would also be applied to the wisdom teacher as the spiritual father (cf. for Eg.: Dürr, op. cit. 6ff.; H. Brunner, *Altäg. Erziehung* [1957], 10; for Mesopotamia: *BWL*, 95, 102, 106). No clear distinction from the normal usage is possible in the OT, however (but cf. Prov 4:1; 13:1).

3. The fig. usage of the word (simile and metaphor) accentuates one aspect of the image in particular. In addition to being held in respect, the father is seen esp. as the protective care giver (also in the related languages).

For the Akk. cf. *CAD* A/1:51f., 68a, 71–73, 76; *AHw* 8a; Phoen.: Kilamuwa inscription (*KAI* no. 24) I.10: "I, however, to some I was a father. To some I was a mother. To some I was a brother" (*ANET* 654b); Karatepe inscription (*KAI* no. 26) I.3: "Ba'l made me a father and a mother to the Danunites" (*ANET* 653b; cf. I.12; see I above); J. Zobel, *Der bildliche Gebrauch der Verwandtschaftsnamen im Hebr. mit Berücksichtigung der übrigen sem. Sprachen* [1932], 7ff. (also deals with rabbinic materials).

Apart from the usage in reference to God (see IV/3), the occasional fig. usages in the OT occur only in Job (originator of rain, Job 38:28; care for the poor, Job 29:16; 31:18; cf. BrSynt §97a; close affiliation, Job 17:14, with the child's formula "you are my father"; cf. Fohrer, KAT 16, 295).

Honorifics for priests and political officeholders attested in the various arenas and times develop into fixed usages: Judg 17:10 and 18:19, "father and priest" (cf. Quell, *TDNT* 5:961–63; following Bertholet 256); Isa 22:21, "father of the inhabitants of Jerusalem and of the house of Judah" (of the governor of the palace; cf. de Vaux 1:129–31); probably also the throne name of the Messiah in Isa 9:5, "eternal father" (cf. H. Wildberger, *TZ* 16 [1960]: 317f.); outside Israel, Aḥ. 55, "father of all Asher" (Cowley 213, 221); Esth LXX 3:13f. *deuteros patēr;* 8:12; 1 Macc 11:32.

One may assume Gen 45:8 "as a father to Pharaoh" is a borrowing of the Eg. title *yt-nṯr* in order to mitigate the offensiveness of the divine designation for the king (J. Vergote, *Josèphe en Égypte* [1959], 114f.). For the history of the Eg. titles for vizier and priest, probably originally used for the attendant of the crown prince, cf. A. H. Gardiner, *Ancient Eg. Onomastica* (1947), 1:47*-53*; H. Brunner, *ZÄS* 86 (1961): 90–100; Kees, ibid. 115–25.

According to Rudolph (HAT 21, 200, 208), *ʾābî* or *ʾābîw* (in 2 Chron 2:12 and 4:16) should not be understood as an element in a name, but should be translated as a title, "my/your master" (so also Stamm, *HEN* 422; cf. also *CAD* A/1:73a).

The address *ʾābî* for Elijah and Elisha has already been mentioned (see 2b). Akk. *abu* as honorific address is attested in letters (cf. *CAD* A/1:71).

4. As a nomen rectum, *ʾāb* relates closely to *bayit* "house." *bêt-ʾāb* "paternal house, family" signified "originally the larger family living together in a common house, headed by the patriarch. It comprised, beside the wife or the wives of the patriarch, the sons, whether they are unmarried or have already themselves founded a family, the daughters, so long as they are unmarried or widowed or have left the houses of their husbands, and the wives and children of the married sons" (L. Rost, *Die Vorstufen von Kirche und Synagoge im AT* [1938, 1967^2], 44).

In pre-exilic times the "paternal house" has relevance only for family and inheritance law, but after the catastrophe of 587, which brought with it the collapse of the tribal organization, it replaces the *mišpāḥâ* (→ *ʿam*) as the basic unit in the structure of society. In (the secondary portions of) P and in Chr, the *ʿēdâ* (→ *ʿēd*) "community" (or → *qāhāl*) is divisible into *maṭṭôt* "tribes" and *bêt-ʾābôt* "paternal houses," headed by a *nāśîʾ* "prince" or a *rōš* "chief" (Rost, op. cit. 56–76, 84).

Of 83 texts with the sg. (for the most part pre-exilic: Gen 18x; Judg 12x; 1 Sam 13x), eleven exhibit the post-exilic technical usage (texts in Rost, op. cit. 56).

The pl. *bêt-ʾābôt* (68x, of which 30x are in Num 1–4, 10x in 1 Chron 4–7; texts in Rost, op. cit. 56, to which add 1 Chron 7:40; the oldest text is probably Exod 12:3) is formed by means of the peculiar pluralization of the second element (GKC §124p; Joüon §136n), which suggests a tightly bound word pair (*TDNT* 5:961 is unclear). The abbreviated *rāʾšê ʾᵃbôt* also occurs (e.g., Exod 6:25) without *bêt* (43x; texts in Rost, op. cit. 56; Ezra 8:1 should be included; see also *nᵉśîʾê hāʾābôt* 1 Kgs 8:1; 2 Chron 5:2; *śārê (-) hāʾābôt* Ezra 8:29; 1 Chron 29:6) in the place of doubled cs. relationships such as *rāʾšê bêt-ʾᵃbōtām* (e.g., Exod 6:14), primarily when followed not only by the 3d pl. suf. but also by other qualifiers (this distinction persists in P; in Chr *rāʾšê hāʾābôt* can occur without qualifier and even *ʾābôt* alone [Neh 11:13; 1 Chron 24:31]). Constructions with *ʾᵃḥuzzâ* "property" (Lev 25:41), *naḥᵃlâ* "inheritance" (Num 36:3, 8), and *maṭṭeh* "tribe" (Num 33:54; 36:3, 8) may simply be translated "fathers" (contra Rost, op. cit. 56f.).

A total of 201 texts with *ʾāb* in the meaning "paternal house" result, of which 129 have the later terminological sense.

5. PNs formed with *ʾāb* occur throughout ancient Sem. nomenclature.

Bibliog.: Akk.: Stamm, *AN;* Mari and ECan.: Huffmon; Ug.: Gröndahl; Phoen.: Harris; SArab.: G. Ryckmans, *Les noms propres sud-sémitiques* (1934); Hebr.: *IP;* an older summary of the material by M. Noth, "Gemeinsemitische Erscheinungen in der isr. Namengebung," *ZDMG* 81 (1927): 1–45, with a statistical overview, 14–17; with regard to Aram., see A. Caquot, "Sur l'onomastique religieuse de Palmyre," *Syria* 39 (1962): 236, 240f.

Approximately 40 name-forms in the OT have *ʾāb* as an element, primarily in first position, almost always as subj., and never as cs. Before one can evaluate this material in terms of religiohistorical significance, one should attempt to distinguish between theophoric and profane usages of this term of relationship. Although the older investigations of W. W. Baudissin (*Kyrios als Gottesname im Judentum* [1929], 3:309–79) and M. Noth (see above) reckon almost exclusively with theophoric usages of the terms of relationship as descriptions of the tribal god, Stamm (*HEN* 413–24) considers it likely that more than one-fourth of the forms are profane usages, so-called substitutionary names, i.e., "names that indicate the supplementary reincarnation of a deceased family member in the newborn" (Stamm, *RGG* 4:1301).

Examples of sentence names are *ʾîyôb* "Job" (a lament formed with the interrogative particle, "where is the father?"), *ʾᵃbîšay* "Abishai" ("the father exists again," according to H. Bauer, *ZAW* 48 [1930]: 77); a descriptive name is *ʾaḥʾāb* "Ahab" ("father's brother"). In cases such as *ʾᵃbîʾē*, *ʾᵉlîʾāb*, *ʾᵃbîyâ*, *yôʾāb*, or *ʾᵃbîmelek* (cf. *ʾᵉlîmelek*), *ʾᵃbîdān* (cf. *dānîyēʾl*), among others, the theophoric significance of the element *ʾāb* is still certain.

A religiohistorical assessment must remember, on the one hand, that such names continue to be preserved even when the contemporary situation with respect to name formation has long since evolved (cf. *IP* 141, concerning confessional names such as Joab: originally an equation of the old tribal god with the new covenant god, but still widely used in post-exilic times); and on the other hand, that grammatical-syntactical and metaphorical reinterpretations could take place (H. Bauer, *OLZ* 33 [1930]: 593ff.). Particularly with respect to etymologies of names that trace back to a divinity considered to be a blood relation of the clan, it is "certain that in Israel's historical era the significance of indigenous names was altered by the equation of the divinity identified as father, brother, or uncle with Yahweh" (Stamm, *HEN* 418). According to W. Marchel (*Abba, Père* [1963], 13, 27ff.), the claim to relationship with the deity made in PNs is to be understood as purely fig. from the outset.

IV. 1. Starting from divine designations in the patriarchal and Moses narratives that contain a PN ("the God of Abraham," etc.) as the second element of a gen. construction, and in comparison to Nabatean analogies, A. Alt ("God of the Fathers," *EOTHR* 1–77) has argued for the existence of a "god of the fathers" religion in the early period of Israel's history (so also W. F. Albright, *From the Stone Age to Christianity* [1957²], 248f.; von Rad, *Theol.* 1:6–8; J. Bright, *History of Israel* [1981³], 96–103; V. Maag, *SThU* 28 [1958]: 2–28; H. Ringgren, *Israelite Religion* [1963], 17f.; contra J. Hoftijzer, *Die Verheissungen an die drei Erzväter* [1956], 85ff.; cf. M. Noth, *VT* 7 [1957]: 430–33). The individual *X*, after whom the divinity "god of *X*" is named, functions then as the recipient of revelation and founder of the cult: in the tribe of *X* the divinity continues to be worshiped as the "patriarchal god" (*theos patrōos*). The association of these divinities not with a place but with a group of people and their changing fortunes influences its movement toward social and historical functions and its abandonment of naturalism (W. Eichrodt, *Religionsgeschichte Israels* [1969], 7–11). With a view to the interfusion of the various gods of the fathers with each other and with Yahweh, a process that took place in the early history of Israel, Alt remarks (*EOTHR* 62): "The gods of the Fathers were the παιδαγωγοί leading to the greater God, who later replaced them completely."

In the pertinent J and E texts in Gen, *ʾāb* in the sg. (26:24; 28:13; 31:5, 29, 42, 53[bis]; 32:10[bis]; 43:23; 46:1, 3; 49:25; 50:17, each with per. suf.) reflects the presumed genealogical interrelationships of the patriarchs and refers to Abraham as Isaac's father (26:24), to Isaac as Jacob's (e.g., 46:1), or to Abraham and Isaac (32:10; also a double formula with only a single occurrence of *ʾāb* in 28:13; 31:42; cf. 48:15), to Jacob as the father of the sons of Jacob (50:17), even if, as in the last text, the PN is not stated. With respect to the sg. texts in Exod (3:6; alongside "the God of Abraham, Isaac, and Jacob," the Sam. text assimilates to the pl.; 15:2 par. to "my God"; 18:4), one may ask whether the expression "the God of my/your father" intends the God of the patriarchs specifically or (in a virtually synonymous sense) more generally the God already worshiped by the family of Moses (concerning 3:6 cf. *EOTHR* 15n.33; contra P. Hyatt, *VT* 5 [1955]: 130–36); the later texts, which refer to the God of the ancestor, David (2 Kgs 20:5 = Isa 38:5; 1 Chron 28:9; 2 Chron 17:4; 21:12; 34:3), simply describe the continuity of the worship of God within the family or dynasty. "The God of our father, Israel" in 1 Chron 29:10 (cf. 29:18, 20) is unique.

The pl. formulation "the God of your fathers" occurs in the equation of Yahweh with the God of Abraham, Isaac, and Jacob in Exod 3:13, 15f.; 4:5 (*EOTHR* 10–14). The remaining texts with the "God of the fathers" (Deut 1:11, 21; 4:1; 6:3; 12:1; 26:7; 27:3; 29:24; Josh 18:3; Judg 2:12; 2 Kgs 21:22, and a further 30x in Dan, Ezra, and Chron) depend upon the Dtn usage of the expression "fathers" (see 2b). Dan 11:37 concerns the gods (pl.) of the fathers of the heathen princes (cf. also Ezek 20:24 *gillûlê ʾᵃbôtām* "the idols of your fathers").

2. The pl. *ʾābôt* "fathers" occurs in a series of more-or-less fixed usages of differing theological weights.

(a) First, euphemisms for "to die," such as "to be laid with his fathers," which B. Alfrink (*OTS* 2 [1943]: 106–18; 5 (1948): 118–31) has investigated, are theologically neutral (cf. also O. Schilling, *Der Jenseitsgedanke im AT* [1951], 11–15; M. D. Goldman, *ABR* 1 [1951]: 64f.; 3 [1953]: 51; G. R. Driver, FS Neuman 128–43).

Verbs used are: (1) *škb* "to lie down," Gen 47:30; Deut 31:16; 2 Sam 7:12; 26x in 1 and 2 Kgs; 11x in 2 Chron; total 40x; in 2 Sam 7:12 with the prep. *ʾet-*, otherwise always with *ʿim-*. The expression refers to death, not to burial; as Alfrink has shown, it is used only of peaceful death (for 9 of 18 kings of Israel and 13 of 19 kings of Judah; concerning the problem with respect to Ahab [2 Kgs 22:40], see C. F. Whitley, *VT* 2 [1952]: 148f.); (2) *qbr* "to bury," Gen 49:29 (with *ʾel-*); 1 Kgs 14:31 and a further 13x in Kgs and 2 Chron (with *ʿim-*); (3) *ʾsp* "to gather," Judg 2:10 (with *ʾel-*); 2 Kgs 22:20 = 2 Chron 34:28 (with *ʿal-*); the formula in Judg 2:10 appears to be a confusion of the expression *ʾsp* ni. *ʾel-ʾammāyw* "to be gathered to his people" (Gen 25:8 and a further

9x in the Pentateuch; cf. Alfrink, *OTS* 5 [1948]: 118f.) with formula (1); (4) *bôʾ* "to enter," Gen 15:15 (with *ʾel-*); Psa 49:20 (with *ʿad-*); (5) *hlk* "to go," 1 Chron 17:11 (with *ʿim-;* cf. Rudolph, HAT 21, 131).

Subst. constructions with *ʾābôt* in reference to grave and burial occur in 1 Kgs 13:22; Jer 34:5; Neh 2:3, 5; 2 Chron 21:19; burial in the grave of the father (sg.) is mentioned in Judg 8:32; 16:31; 2 Sam 2:32; 17:23; 21:14. No religious significance in terms of an ancestor cult can be attributed here to the "fathers" (contra G. Hölscher, *Geschichte der isr. und jüd. Religion* [1922], 30f.).

(b) From ca. the 7th cent. onward, the pl. "the fathers" becomes significant theologically; it communicates the salvation-historical dimension in expressions concerning the people Israel as an organic unity of fathers and sons, whether viewed collectively or individually.

In connection with the patriarchal traditions, the promises to the fathers play a particularly significant role in Dtn theology. Then, language dependent upon Deut repeatedly names the fathers as recipients of various salvation gifts (on Deut see O. Bächli, *Israel und die Völker* [1962], 119–21).

"Fathers" already occurs once in Hos, although not in the patriarchal tradition but in a poetical depiction of the discovery in the desert (9:10 "your fathers" par. to "Israel"). The dominant formula in Dtn allusions to the patriarchal promises is "the land that Yahweh swore to give the fathers" or the like. Texts with *šbʿ* ni. "to swear" in Dtn/Dtr literature include Exod 13:5, 11; Num 11:12; 14:23; Deut 1:8, 35; 4:31; 6:10, 18, 23; 7:8, 12f.; 8:1, 18; 9:5; 10:11; 11:9, 21; 13:18; 19:8; 26:3, 15; 28:11; 29:12; 30:20; 31:7, 20f. (secondarily); Josh 1:6; 5:6; 21:43f.; Judg 2:1; Jer 11:5; 32:22; Mic 7:20; with *dbr* pi. "to promise," Deut 19:8; cf. *ʾmr* Neh 9:23. On Yahweh's oath to the patriarchs, cf. von Rad, *Gottesvolk* 5; N. Lohfink, *Das Hauptgebot* [1963], 86–89 with tables on 307f. In addition to the promise of the land, other subjs. are mentioned as gifts to the fathers, e.g., the multiplication of descendants and, derivative of the fathers tradition, election, grace, and covenant (cf. also Deut 4:37; 5:3 with a parenetic application of the covenant to the current generation; 10:15; 30:5, 9). The discussion of the "God of the fathers" in Dtn theology and later is to be understood in the context of these formulas as well (see IV/1). Often Abraham, Isaac, and Jacob are listed by name as patriarchs (Deut 1:8; 6:10; 9:5; 29:12; 30:20; also 1 Chron 29:18); Deut 10:22 speaks of the fathers as 70 souls who descended into Egypt.

Of the multitude of post-Dtn texts that treat the fathers as recipients of salvation gifts, the first to be mentioned are those with the formulaic expression "land that Yahweh gave the fathers," which has affinities with the Dtn oath formula (verb *ntn*): 1 Kgs 8:34, 40, 48 (= 2 Chron 6:25, 31, 38); 14:15; 2 Kgs 21:8 (= 2 Chron 33:8 txt em); Jer 7:7, 14; 16:15; 23:39; 24:10 (authentic Jer?); 25:5; 30:3; 35:15; Ezek 20:42; 36:28; 47:14; Neh 9:36; with *nḥl* hi. Jer 3:18.

Furthermore, mention should be made of the Dtr overviews of history in Josh 24 (the fathers of the Exodus generation, vv 6 and 17, are distinguished from the heathen fathers beyond the river, vv 2, 14f.); Judg 2:17, 19f., 22; 3:4; 1 Sam 12:6–8; 1 Kgs 8:21, 53, 57f.; 9:9; 2 Kgs 17:13, 15; 21:15; other Dtr texts, e.g., Jer 7:22, 25; 11:4, 7, 10; 17:22; 34:13; 44:10; and Psa 78:12, as well as a few scattered texts: Isa 64:10; Ezek 37:25; Mal 2:10; Psa 22:5; 39:13; 1 Chron

29:15. Negative statements (e.g., Deut 9:15), references to particular ancestors (e.g., Num 20:15; 1 Kgs 21:3f.), and other theologically unproductive references to the fathers (e.g., Dan 9:6, 8) will not be treated.

Texts such as Josh 4:21; Judg 6:13; Psa 44:2; 78:3, 5 (cf. without ʾāb Exod 10:1f.; 12:26f.; Deut 6:20ff.) depict the transmission of salvation history from the fathers to the sons; as a Bab. par. cf. the epilogue of Enuma Elish (VII:147).

The fathers are not only the recipients of the promise and the blessing; their sin also encumbers later generations' relationship with God, a problem addressed in various expression of the solidarity of the sons with the fathers; on this issue see J. Scharbert, *Solidarität in Segen und Fluch im AT und in seiner Umwelt*, I: *Väterfluch und Vätersegen* (1958).

Jer is the first to speak of the fall of the fathers (the distinction between authentic and secondary texts is not always clear), in whose wake the later generations also sin (Jer 2:5; 3:25; 7:26; 9:13; 11:10; 14:20; 16:11f.; 23:27; 31:32; 34:14; 44:9, 17, 21; 50:7).

The following post-Jer texts deserve treatment: Lev 26:39f.; 2 Kgs 17:14, 41; 22:13 (= 2 Chron 34:21); Isa 65:7; Ezek 2:3; 20:4, 18, 24, 27, 30, 36; Amos 2:4; Zech 1:2, 4–6; 8:14; Mal 3:7; Psa 78:8, 57 (cf. 79:8 *ᶜᵃwōnōt riʾšōnîm* "the sins of the ancestors"); 95:9; 106:6f.; Lam 5:7; Dan 9:16; Ezra 5:12; 9:7; Neh 9:2, 16; 2 Chron 29:6, 9; 30:7f. J. Scharbert ("Unsere Sünden und die Sünden unserer Väter," *BZ* 2 [1958]: 14–26) outlines the history of the genre of the confession of individual sin and that of the fathers from Jer (3:25; 14:20) on into the postbibl. era (Tob 3:3, 5; Jdt 7:28; Bar 1:15–3:8; 1QS 1:25f.; CD 20:29; 1QH 4:34).

The principal statements concerning the communal responsibility of children and fathers or concerning the removal of this responsibility use the pl. "fathers," not in the sense "ancestors of Israel" treated to this point, but as a more general contrast of fathers-sons. On the old confessional formula "Yahweh . . . , who visits the guilt of the fathers on the children and grandchildren to the third and fourth generation" (Exod 20:5; 34:7; Num 14:18; Deut 5:9; Jer 32:18), cf. J. Scharbert, "Formgeschichte und Exegese von Exod 34, 6f. und seiner Parallelen," *Bib* 38 (1957): 130–50; L. Rost, "Die Schuld der Väter," FS Hermann 229–33; R. Knierim, *Die Hauptbegriffe für Sünde im AT* (1965), 204–7. With respect to the prohibition of community punishment in Deut 24:16; 2 Kgs 14:6; 2 Chron 25:4 cf. Scharbert, *Solidarität*, 114f., 124f., 251; and von Rad, *Deut*, OTL, 152. Regarding proverbs concerning the fathers who have eaten sour grapes and the sons whose teeth are thereby set on edge (Jer 31:29; Ezek 18:2), cf. comms. and Scharbert, *Solidarität*, 218–26.

3. Although "invocation of deity under the name of father is one of the basic phenomena of religious history" (G. Schrenk, *TDNT* 5:951; see G. Mensching, *RGG* 6:1232f.), the OT is very restrained in the application of the father designation for Yahweh (Quell, *TDNT* 5:965–74; H.-J. Kraus, *RGG* 6:1233f.). This restraint is true to the greatest degree (a) of expressions concerning God's physical paternity that are completely absent from the OT, but also (b) of the adoption idea, and (c) of the metaphorical usage of the word as well.

(a) Mythical concepts of deities as begetters and creators of the gods and people are easily traced in the surroundings of the OT in the Ug. texts (on

Eg. and Bab. → *yld*), where the high god of the pantheon is given the epithet "father" in a series of stereotypical formulae.

El appears as *ab bn il* "father of the gods" in an atonement liturgy (*KTU* 1.40.[16], 25, 33; O. Eissfeldt, *El im ug. Pantheon* [1951], 62–66). The disputed *mlk ab šnm* (*KTU* 1.1.III.24; 1.2.III.5 [reconstructed]; 1.3.V.8 [reconstructed]; 1.4.IV.24; 1.6.36; 1.17.VI.49) appears to have a similar meaning, if one does not translate *ab šnm* with Driver (*CML*[1] 109) and others (*CML*[2] 75) as "father of years" or with Eissfeldt (op. cit. 30f.) as "father of the mortals," but with M. H. Pope (*El in the Ug. Texts* [1955], 32f.) as "Father of Exalted Ones" (= the gods) (so also Gray, *Legacy* 114, 155f.; W. Schmidt, *Königtum Gottes in Ugarit und Israel* [1966[2]], 59n.3). Also occurring are *il abh* "El, his/her father" (e.g., *KTU* 1.13.20f. of Anat) and *il abn* "El, our father" (1.12.I.9, in a fragmentary context; cf. Eissfeldt, op. cit. 34). The formula *t̠r il aby/abk/abh* "Bull, El, my/your/his father" is the most frequent (*KTU* 1.2.III.16f., 19, 21; 1.3.[IV.54], V.10, 35 supplemented in 1.1.III.26 and V.22; 1.4.IV.47; 1.6.IV.10, VI.26f.; 1.17.I.23), or in an alternate sequence *t̠r abk/abh il* "Bull, your/his father, El" (1.2.II.16, 33, 36; 1.14.II.6, 23f., IV.6; 1.92.15; in 1.14.I.41 *t̠r abh* omits *il* because of the preceding *ǵlm il*); the per. suf. refers in each case to the gods or goddesses who appear or have been named (also to Krt). Finally one also finds *ab adm* "father of humanity" in the Krt epic (*KTU* 1.14.I.37, 43, III.32, 47, VI.13, 32).

The observation that the formula *t̠r il abh* "Bull El his (i.e., Baal's) father" is accompanied in a few texts by a par. element, *il mlk dyknnh* "El, the king, who established him (*kûn* po.)," is significant to some degree for the interpretation of Deut 32:6b, "Is he not your father who created you (i.e., the people), is it not he who made and established you (*kûn* po.)." Seen in conjunction with Deut 32:18, a trace of Can. mythology may be detected in v 6b, at least in the poetical language strongly avoided elsewhere in the prophetic critique of the vegetation and fertility cult: Jer 2:27, they will become ashamed "who say then to the tree: 'You are my father,' and to the stone: 'You bore me' " (cf. Quell, *TDNT* 5:968; P. Humbert, "Yahvé Dieu Géniteur?" *Asiatische Studien* 18/19 [1965]: 247–51).

On Isa 1:2 LXX *engennēsa*, cf. J. Hempel, *Gott und Mensch im AT* (1936[2]), 170n.6; Wildberger, *Isa 1–12*, CC, 9.

(b) Statements concerning the father-son relationship between Yahweh and the Davidic king involve adoption concepts (2 Sam 7:14, "I will be his father and he will be my son"; Psa 89:27; 1 Chron 17:13; 22:10; 28:6; cf. also the adoption formula in Psa 2:7, "You are my son, today have I begotten you"). The influence of Eg. royal ideology on the Jerusalemite enthronement ceremony is apparent (S. Morenz, *Äg. Religion* [1960], 35–43, 154f.; id., *RGG* 6:118), as is the distinction in the notion of divine sonship that is understood in Egypt as directly physical, but in the OT as adoptive, the result of a prophetic promise of election (Hempel, op. cit. 173ff.; Alt, *EOTHR* 235; id., *KS* [1964[3]], 2:218; von Rad, *PHOE* 226f.; K.-H. Bernhardt, *Das Problem der altorientalischen Königsideologie im AT* [1961], 74–76, 84–86).

The son concept already appears in reference to the relationship between Yahweh and his people in Exod 4:22 (Noth, *Exod*, OTL, 34f., 47: a secondary accretion to J or JE); Hos 11:1 (here in the sense of adoption with an emphasis on the love and rearing ideas; cf. Wolff, *Hos*, Herm, 197–99); Isa 1:2 (protective paternal goodwill for the sons [pl.], perhaps to be understood against the background of spiritual sonship in the sphere of wisdom [see III/2b]; cf. Wildberger, *Isa 1–12*, CC, 12–14) and 30:9 (→ *bēn;* on Deut cf. D. J. McCarthy, *CBQ* 27 [1965]: 144–47). The word *ʾāb*, however, first surfaces in Jer clearly in reference to adoption and in the sense of loving attention: 3:4 (to be seen with Duhm and others as a gloss derived from v 19; cf. Rudolph, HAT 12, 22); 3:19 "my father!" as an address that acknowledges inclusion among the sons (cf. also S. H. Blank, *HUCA* 32 [1961]: 79–82); 31:9 "for I have become Israel's father."

Psa 27:10 features the adoption motif in reference to an individual, without, however, indicating Yahweh directly as father.

(c) Only a few texts remain in which Yahweh is either compared to a father or metaphorically called "father." If they do not deal with a simple comparison to family life (Psa 103:13; Prov 3:12) or common ancient Near Eastern ideals (Psa 68:6), these (post-exilic) statements stand for the most part in the wake of descriptions of Yahweh as the creator of the people in Deutero-Isa (Isa 43:6f., 15, 21; 44:2, 21, 24; 45:10f.).

On the one hand, seen from the son's perspective, the emphasis of the metaphorical depiction lies on the authority of the pater familias and on the obedience due him. In this manner, Yahweh appears, albeit only indirectly, as father in Isa 45:10 (cf. v 11) par. to the picture of the sovereign potter, an image also taken up in Isa 64:7 together with the direct address "you are our father" (twice also in 63:16 in a formulaic manner). In Mal 1:6a "a son honors his father" parallels "a servant fears his master"; in v 6b the demand for respect derives from the concept of God as father, which is also presupposed in 2:10 on the basis of God's status as creator, but in 2:10 the notion of brotherhood among the sons of one father (= God; cf. comms. and Quell, *TDNT* 5:973; contra Horst, HAT 14, 269, who prefers Jacob) is decisive (→ *ʾāḥ* 4c). The father concept does not evolve into a universalistic notion because the statements concerning creation within this tradition relate to the people (contra R. Gyllenberg, "Gott der Vater im AT und in der Predigt Jesu," *StOr* 1 [1925]: 53f.).

On the other hand, if the viewpoint is that of the father toward the child, solidarity and concern receive the greater emphasis. Thus the appeal in Isa 63:16 (cf. v 15 "look down") is directed to the father and redeemer of old (*gōʾ^{a}lēnû,* → *gʾl)* who is far superior to earthly fathers. Finally, loving attention forms the tertium comparationis similarly in the relatively few comparisons of Yahweh with a father (comparable to the copious Bab. material; see *CAD* A/1:69b): Psa 103:13, "As a father shows mercy to his children, so the Lord shows mercy to those who fear him" (cf. Deut 1:31 without *ʾāb*) and Prov 3:12, "For whomever Yahweh loves he punishes, as a father the son in whom he delights" (so MT; according to the LXX, however, *ûk^{e}ʾāb* should be emended to *w^{e}yakʾib;* regarding content, cf. Deut 8:5 without *ʾāb*).

The motif of the "father of the fatherless" in Psa 68:6 is widely attested, although less pointedly, in the OT and in its environment (cf. Deut 10:18; Psa 10:14, 18; 82:3f.; 146:9; also Job 29:16; 31:18; Sir 4:10; and the ancient Near

Eastern materials in Wildberger, *Isa 1–12*, CC, 50f.). It is hardly necessary to posit a specifically Eg. origin (so Quell, *TDNT* 5:966n.118).

The OT does not yet describe God as the father of the individual believer (for the first time in Sir 50:10 [Hebr.] in allusion to Psa 89:27); with respect to intertestamental Jewish literature see Bousset-Gressmann 377 and esp. J. Jeremias, *Prayers of Jesus* (1967), 15–29.

V. NT studies concerning *abba* and *patēr* usually treat the backgrounds of the concepts in the OT, as well as in Palestinian and Hellenistic Judaism. See e.g., G. Kittel, "ἀββᾶ," *TDNT* 1:5–6; G. Schrenk, "πατήρ," *TDNT* 5:974–1022; D. Marin, "Abba, Pater," FS Herrmann 503–8; W. Marchel, *Abba, Père! La prière du Christ et des Chrétiens* (1963); J. Jeremias, "Vatername Gottes, III," *RGG* 6:1234f.; id., *Prayers of Jesus* (1967), 11–65, 108–12.

E. Jenni

אבד *ʾbd* to perish

S 6; BDB 1a; *HALOT* 1:2a; *TDOT* 1:19–23; *TWOT* 2; *NIDOTTE* 6

---

1. *ʾbd* is common Sem. (Berg., *Intro.* 220–21), in the meaning "to lose, be lost, perish," but is active only in NWSem.

Akk. *abātu* (with a dissimilation of *d* > *t;* cf. *GAG* 8** §51d; otherwise *GVG* 1:512; Berg., *HG* 1:109) is trans., "to destroy"; Old Assyr., however, also has intrans., "to run away" (J. Lewy, *Or* 29 [1960]: 22–47; *CAD* A/1:45).

Besides qal, pi. "to destroy," and hi. "to cause to be destroyed" (Aram. pe., ha., and ho.), only the verbal nouns *ʾᵃbēdâ* "a lost thing" and *ʾᵃbaddôn* "destruction" are formed on the root in the OT (in addition to *ʾabdān* and *ʾobdān* "destruction" as Aram. loanwords; see Wagner no. 1).

ᶜᵃdê ʾōbēd "forever" in Num 24:20, 24 may be derived from a second root *ʾbd* "to last" (D. Künstlinger, *OLZ* 34 [1931]: 609–11), which occurs in Arab. and is also suspected in Ug. (J. Gray, *ZAW* 64 [1952]: 51, 55; *UT* no. 17; *WUS* no. 15; contra M. Dietrich and O. Loretz, *WO* 3 [1966]: 221); suggestions regarding Prov 11:7 remain conjectural (J. Reider, *VT* 2 [1952]: 124) and Job 30:2 (G. Rinaldi, *BeO* 5 [1963]: 142).

2. Statistics: qal 117x (Psa 21x, Jer 16x, Deut 13x, Job 13x), Aram. pe. 1x; pi. 41x (Esth 10x); hi. 26x, Aram. ha. 5x, ho. 1x; the verb occurs in Hebr. a total of 184x, in Aram. 7x; *ʾᵃbēdâ* 4x, *ʾᵃbaddôn* 6x, *ʾabdān* 1x, *ʾobdān* 1x. The root is absent from Gen and Chron-Ezra-Neh (cf. 2 Kgs 11:1; 21:3 with 2 Chron 22:10; 33:3; and 2 Kgs 9:8 with 2 Chron 22:7).

Harmonization with the LXX may be assumed in 1 Sam 12:15; Isa 46:12; and Prov 17:5 (cf. *BHS*).

3. Depending upon the subj. (individual things, collective entities, living things) and the usage of preps. *(bᵉ, min)*, Eng. has various translation options for the relatively unified basic meaning of the qal "to be destroyed" ("to be lost, die, be snatched away," etc.; cf. *HAL* 2b). The meanings of the root in

the related Sem. languages (cf. Akk., Arab., and Eth.) may suggest that the original meaning lies in the more specific meanings "to be lost, to wander about, run away" (Deut 26:5; 1 Sam 9:3, 20; Jer 50:6; Ezek 34:4, 16; Psa 2:12; 119:176; cf. Th. Nöldeke, *ZDMG* 40 [1886]: 726).

Because of its unspecific, negative meaning, the verb has no regular antonym; possible opposites are → *ʿmd* "to remain" (Psa 102:27; cf. 112:9f.), → *hyh* "to be" (Jonah 4:10), and *ʾrk* hi. *yāmîm* "to live long" (Deut 4:26; 30:18).

The meaning of *ʾbd* coincides quite precisely with Akk. *ḫalāqu* (*AHw* 310f. "to disappear, be destroyed, flee"; also Ug. and Eth.); cf. EA 288:52 (from Jerusalem): "all of the lands of the king are lost *(ḫal-qa-at)*" with a Can. gloss *a-ba-da-at*. This root *ḫlq* III is also suspected in Psa 17:14; 73:18; Job 21:17; Lam 4:16 (M. Dahood, *Bib* 44 [1963]: 548; 45 [1964]: 408; 47 [1966]: 405; on Isa 57:6 see W. H. Irwin, *CBQ* 29 [1967]: 31–40); on account of its nearness in meaning to *ḥlq* I (*ḥªlāqôt*, Psa 73:18 "slippery places") and II (pi. "to destroy," Gen 49:7 and Psa 17:14; cf. G. R. Driver, *JTS* 15 [1964]: 342), however, it has not been identified with certainty.

In the pi. and hi. "to destroy," *ʾbd* competes primarily with → *krt* and → *šmd*.

On the difference in meaning between pi. "to destroy, eliminate" and hi. "to destroy" (the latter used mostly of persons and with respect to the future), see E. Jenni, "Faktitiv und Kausativ von *ʾbd* 'zugrunde gehen,' " FS Baumgartner 143–57.

On *ʾªbaddôn* "destruction, ruin" → *šᵉʾôl*.

4. In over two-thirds of the texts with qal and hi. (pi. 1/3) Yahweh is the direct or indirect agent of destruction. *ʾbd* here is hardly neutral (cf. Psa 102:27; 146:4); instead it signifies the destruction meted out by God to his enemy. No formulaic usage may be identified, probably because of the very common meaning of the word; it has not stabilized as a theological term.

ʾbd appears only once, in the extirpation formula in Lev 23:30, in the place of the usual and more concrete *krt* (Elliger, HAT 4, 310, 319n.24). The cry of terror (Num 17:27; cf. Num 21:29 par. Jer 48:46, and Matt 8:25 par. Luke 8:24) is also unconnected with *ʾbd* (cf. Isa 6:5; Jer 4:13; G. Wanke, *ZAW* 78 [1966]: 216f.).

ʾbd is pertinent in the following spheres:

(a) Statements concerning the deed-consequence relationship (cf. H. Gese, *Lehre und Wirklichkeit in der alten Weisheit* [1958], 42ff.) in wisdom literature (Psa 1:6; 37:20; 49:11; 73:27; 112:10; Job 4:7, 9; 8:13; 11:20; 18:17; 20:7; Prov 10:28; 11:7[bis], 10; 19:9; 21:28; 28:28); here Yahweh always implicitly or explicitly sees to the destruction of the fool, the fool's name, the fool's hope, etc.

(b) Conditional curse-threats in the blessing/curse formulae that conclude H and the Dtn code (Lev 26:38; Deut 28:20, 22; on cultic-sacral origins, see Elliger, HAT 4, 372) and in the Dtr sermon (Deut 4:26; 8:19, 20; 11:17; 30:18; Josh 23:13, 16; cf. also 1Q22 1:10); they bear some resemblance to curse formulae in NWSem. inscriptions and ancient Near Eastern treaty texts (bibliog. in D. R. Hillers, *Treaty-Curses and the OT Prophets* [1964]). Cf. a 9th-cent. Phoen. burial inscription from Cyprus: "and may thi[s curse(?)] bring [those m]en to destruction (*wyʾbd* yi.)" (*KAI* no. 30.3; cf. Friedrich 127, contra *DISO* 1f.); in 7th-cent. Aram. burial inscriptions from Nerab near Aleppo: "and may his posterity perish (*tʾbd* pe.)" (*ANET* 661b; *KAI* no. 226.10); "may ŠHR, Šamaš, Nikkal, and Nusku . . . annihilate (*yhʾbdw* ha.) your name" (*KAI* no. 225.9–11); on *ḫalāqu* (see 3) in Akk. curse formulae, see F. C. Fensham, *ZAW* 74 (1962): 5f.; 75 (1963): 159.

(c) *ʾbd* occurs relatively infrequently in 8th-cent. prophetic threats of judgment related to (b) (qal in Isa 29:14; Amos 1:8; 2:14; 3:15); pi. and hi. with Yahweh as subj. are used sporadically beginning with the time of Jer (oldest text Mic 5:9, if authentic; pi.: Isa 26:14; Jer 12:17; 15:7; 51:55; Ezek 6:3; 28:16; Zeph 2:13; hi.: Jer 1:10; 18:7; 25:10; 31:28; 49:38; Ezek 25:7, 16; 30:13; 32:13; Obad 8; Mic 5:9; Zeph 2:5).

5. *ʾbd* and *ʾᵃbaddôn* are not yet used in the OT (or in the available texts from Qumran) for an otherworldly, eternal destruction, even when accompanied by expressions for "eternal" (*lāneṣaḥ* Job 4:20; 20:7; cf. also the Mesha inscription *wyśrʾl ʾbd ʾbd ʿlm* "while Israel hath perished for ever," *ANET* 320b; *KAI* no. 181.7).

On the NT cf. A. Oepke, "ἀπόλλυμι," *TDNT* 1:394–97; J. Jeremias, "Ἀβαδδών," *TDNT* 1:4.

E. Jenni

אבה *ʾbh* to want

S 14; BDB 2b; *HALOT* 1:3b; *TDOT* 1:24–26; *TWOT* 3; *NIDOTTE* 14

אֶבְיוֹן *ʾebyôn* **poor**

S 34; BDB 2b; *HALOT* 1:5a; *TDOT* 1:27–41; *TWOT* 3a; *NIDOTTE* 36

---

1. *ʾbh* (*ʾby*) occurs outside Hebr. chiefly in SSem.; there, however, it has a distinctive semantic development (Class. Arab., Eth. "not to want"; Dial. Arab. "to want").

Some relationship to Eg. *ʾby* "to wish" is possible (cf., however, Calice no. 462).

Regarding supposed Akk. pars., see *HAL* 3a.

The root is uncommon in Aram., if one excludes the targumic Hebraism *ʾᵃbâ* (*BS* 66n.7). *htnʾbw* in the Old Aram. Barrakib inscription, *KAI* no. 216.14, is disputed (hittanaphal of *ʾbh* or *yʾb*, *KAI* 2:233f.; cf. G. Garbini, "L'aramaico antico," *AANLR* 8/7 [1956]: 274; cf., however, id., "Note semitiche," *Ricerche Linguistiche* 5 (1962): 181n.28).

Aram. has the verb *yʾb* "to yearn, desire" (*DISO* 103; *LS* 293a), which may be related to *ʾbh* (*ʾby*) and which also occurs once in Hebr. as an Aramaism (Psa 119:131; Wagner no. 119; Garbini, *Ricerche Linguistiche* 180).

A further Hebr. by-form *tʾb* "to require" (Psa 119:40, 174) may be explained not as an Aramaism but as a secondary back-formation from *taʾᵃbâ* "requirement" (Psa 119:20), a nom. form of *ʾbh* with *t*-preformative (A. M. Honeyman, *JAOS* 64 [1944]: 81; Garbini, *Ricerche Linguistiche,* 180f.).

Contrary semantic development in Arab. (Eth.) may be regarded as an internal SSem. phenomenon, wherein several different basic meanings, both positive and negative, may be posited, e.g., "to be decided" (F. Delitzsch, *Prolegomena eines neuen hebr.-aram. Wörterbuchs zum AT* [1886], 111), "to be stubborn" (W. M. Müller, following GB 3a), "psychological movement of the will" (C. Landberg, *Glossaire Datînois* [1920], 1:21ff.), "se flecti sivit" (Zorell 3a), "to be in need" (Honeyman, op. cit. 81f.). Arab. and Eth. should not be adduced (contra *BS* 66: particle of negation simply as a strengthening of the original negative meaning; followed by L. Köhler, *ZS* 4 [1926]: 196f.; contra *GVG* 2:186; BrSynt 53, 158; Honeyman, op. cit. 81) in order to explain the fact that *ʾbh* regularly occurs negated in Hebr. (see 3a).*

The adj. *ʾebyôn* "needy, poor" is also usually derived from the root *ʾbh* (in the accepted meaning "to want to have, be in need" (e.g., GB 4a; BL 500: actually "begging[?]"; A. Kuschke, *ZAW* 57 [1959]: 53; Honeyman, op. cit. 82; P. Humbert, *RHPR* 32 [1952]: 1ff. = *Opuscules d'un hébraḤsant* [1958], 187ff.; *HAL* 5a); the degree to which this etymological origin remains determinative for the meaning of *ʾebyôn* is uncertain (E. Bammel, *TDNT* 6:888–89). Cf. also W. von Soden, "Zur Herkunft von hebr. *ʾebjōn* 'arm,' " *MIO* 15 (1969): 322–26 (from **ʾbî* "to be poor, needy," which derives from an "old Amor." adj. and which appears as a loanword in Ug., Hebr., and in the Akk. of Mari [*abiyānum* "poor, troubled, destitute"]). Consequently, *ʾbh* and *ʾebyôn* will receive special treatment below in 3 and 4–5.

Copt. *EBIHN* may be a loanword from Sem. (cf. W. A. Ward, *JNES* 20 [1961]: 31f.; contra T. O. Lambdin, "Eg. Loan Words in the OT," *JAOS* 73 [1953]: 145f.).

The Ug. *abynm* (*KTU* 4.70.6) and *abynt* (1.17.I.16) are not fruitful (cf. *WUS* nos. 18, 20; *UT* nos. 23f.).

The derivation of *ʾᵃbôy* "woe" (Prov 23:29) from *ʾbh* is questionable (cf. *HAL* 4a with bibliog.), as is that of *ʾābî* "O that" (Job 34:36; cf. 1 Sam 24:12; 2 Kgs 5:13; → *ʾāb* III/2b; cf. Honeyman, op. cit. 82; *HAL* 4a).

2. The verb *ʾbh* is attested 54x in qal forms, with the majority in narrative literature (2 Sam 10x, Deut 7x, Isa 5x, and 4x each in Judg, 1 Sam, 1 Chron, and Prov).

ʾebyôn (61x) is found primarily in cultic texts (Psa 23x, in addition to 1 Sam 2:8; Isa 25:4; Jer 20:13), but is also represented in the prophetic, legal, and wisdom literatures (Deut 7x, Job 6x, 5x each in Isa and Amos).

3. (a) Remarkably, the verb *ʾbh* is almost always negated and means "to refuse, decline, not want"; it falls therefore within the semantic field of the expression *mʾn* pi. "to refuse" (46x; once in Num 22:13 with Yahweh as subj., although no theological usage is recognizable; par. to *ʾbh* in Deut 25:7; 2 Sam 2:21, 23; Isa 1:19f.; Prov 1:24f.), *mnʿ* "to withhold, refuse," → *mʾs* "to reject," etc. The only two sentences in which *ʾbh* has a grammatically positive usage are not entirely positive in terms of meaning (Isa 1:19, in a conditional sentence, par. to → *šmʿ* "to obey"; Job 39:9, in a rhetorical question, practically equal to a negation).

The explanation for this meaning should not proceed from etymological or linguistic-historical inferences, but from considerations of the contemporary word field (cf. E. Jenni, " 'Wollen' und 'Nichtwollen' im Hebr.," FS Dupont-Sommer 201–7). The positive "to be willing, want" is expressed in Hebr. by means of the verb *yʾl* hi. "to decide, touch, begin" (18x), which is never negated. On the one hand, as a so-called inner-causative, inwardly trans., or internal hi. ("to cause oneself to take something, begin something," etc.), this verb, which always expresses an intentional process, can never be negated (cf. *HP* 95ff., 250ff., 256); on the other hand, it is precisely the inner-causative hi. that is more conducive to the expression of the intentional activity of the subj. than a neutral *ʾbh* in the meaning "to be (de facto, perchance) willing." Thus a positive *yʾl* hi. and a negated or conditional *ʾbh* qal complement each other (cf. Judg 19:6–10, where the two verbs coincide).*

(b) The verb exhibits full verbal force ("to want, be willing," etc.) in only a few cases: Prov 1:30, "They would have none of my counsel"; 1:25, "You would have none of my reproof"; Deut 13:9, "You would not yield to him." These cases refer to a specific act of the will in contrast to an expectation or a demand exerted from without, a—thoroughly neutral—unwillingness. Nom. objs. are introduced then either with *l^e* (Deut 13:9; Prov 1:30; cf. Psa 81:12) or stand in the acc. (Prov 1:25). *ʾbh* occurs formulaically in the bipolar expression "not to hear and to be unwilling" (Deut 13:9; 1 Kgs 20:8; Psa 81:12; cf. Isa 1:19; 42:24). In reality, however, any apparently abs. usage of the word is an elliptical idiom. Cf. e.g., Judg 11:17 (LXX); 1 Sam 31:4 = 1 Chron 10:4; 2 Sam 12:17; 1 Kgs 22:50; Isa 30:15; cf. also Prov 1:10; 6:35.

(c) In the majority of cases an action verb accompanies *ʾbh* that forces it into an auxiliary role (e.g., Gen 24:5, 8, "If you do not want to accompany"). Perhaps as an extension of the formula mentioned above, the expression "not to want to hear" established itself in common usage (Lev 26:21; Deut 23:6; Josh 24:10; Judg 19:25; 20:13; 2 Sam 13:14, 16; Isa 28:12; 30:9; Ezek 3:7[bis]; 20:8).

All sorts of other activities could also be unwanted, avoided, refused (Deut 1:26; Judg 19:10; 1 Sam 22:17; 26:23; 2 Sam 2:21; 6:10; 13:25; 14:29[bis]; 23:16f. = 1 Chron 11:18f.; 2 Kgs 8:19 = 2 Chron 21:7; 2 Kgs 24:4; 1 Chron 19:19); the main verb stands for the most part in the inf. with *l^e* (exceptions, Deut 2:30; 10:10; 25:7; 29:19; 1 Sam 15:9; 2 Kgs 13:23; Isa 28:12; 30:9; 42:24; Job 39:9).

(d) Texts in which the lack of desire results from an inner hardening or stubbornness may indicate traces of a technical theological usage of *ʾbh* (Exod 10:27, "Yahweh hardened Pharaoh's heart, therefore he did not want to let them go"; cf. Deut 2:30), which may have led to a formulaic usage in the prophetic judgment or indictment language: "You were not willing!" (Isa 30:15; cf. Matt 23:37 with the verb *thelein,* which translates *ʾbh* in the LXX in approximately half the cases; see G. Schrenk, "βούλομαι," *TDNT* 1:629–37; id., "θέλω," *TDNT* 3:44–62). The hardening can also be viewed in an entirely inward, almost clinical, manner (2 Sam 13:2, 14, 16; see K. L. and M. A. Schmidt, "παχύνω," *TDNT* 5:1022ff.; F. Hesse, *RGG* 6:1383).

4. (a) *ʾebyôn* belongs to a series of OT words describing the socially weak (*dal, miskēn, ʿānî, rāš,* etc.; → *ʿnh* II; cf. A. Kuschke, "Arm und reich im AT," *ZAW* 57 [1939]: 31–57; J. van der Ploeg, "Les pauvres d'Israël et leur piété," *OTS* 7 [1950]: 236–70; P. Humbert, "Le mot biblique *èbyōn,*" *RHPR* 32 [1952]: 1–6 = *Opuscules d'un hébraïsant* [1958], 187–92; F. Hauck, "πένης," *TDNT* 6:37–40; F. Hauck and E. Bammel, "πτωχός," *TDNT* 6:885–915, with bibliog.). The specific meaning of the word, "to have want" (Kuschke, op. cit. 53), "the poor who beg" (Humbert, op. cit. 188), is no longer clearly discernible (Bammel, *TDNT* 6:889n.24). In legal and prophetic texts the *ʾebyôn* is the

exploited (Exod 23:6, 11; Deut 15:1–11; 24:14; Amos 2:6; 4:1; 5:12; 8:4, 6; Jer 2:34; 5:28; 22:16; Ezek 16:49; 18:12; 22:29). Wisdom passages often simply have material suffering in mind in contrast to wealth (Psa 49:3; 112:9; Prov 31:20; cf. *rāš* "poor," → *ʿnh* II).

(b) Everywhere in the ancient Near East the socially weak have a particular relationship to the divinity.

Cf. *BWL* 18n.1 ("the poor of this world, rich in faith," to whom the gods pay particular attention, so that even Nabopolassar recognizes himself as belonging to their number), with a listing of the expressions for "poor" in Akk. (textual citations in *AHw;* see *akû, dunnamû, enšu, katû, lapnu, muškēnu,* etc.). Cf. W. Schwer, *RAC* 1:689ff.; G. Mensching, E. Kutsch, and E. L. Dietrich, *RGG* 1:616ff.; also the hymns to Shamash (*BWL* 121ff.) and Psa 82:3 as a reflection of ancient Near Eastern concepts.

Against this background it is understandable that *ʾebyôn* acquires a religious nuance in the OT. In genres rooted in the cult (above all in laments and thanksgivings), the worshiper appears before Yahweh as poor and needy. One must admit one's inferiority to the mighty and just God; cf. Job 42:2ff. With such an admission, however, the poor simultaneously lay a particular claim to justice: the duties of the powerful, and therefore of God (the covenant idea need not even contribute in this respect), include pity for the suffering (cf. Deut 14:28f.; Isa 58:7; Ezek 18:7; Psa 72:2, 4, 12f.; 82:3; 112:9; Prov 3:27f.; 31:20). Wealth is always a loaned gift. A person is normally poor and unprotected (cf. Gen 3:21; Ezek 16:4ff.; Hos 2:10; Psa 104:14f., 27ff.; etc.); the OT reflects the awareness that Yahweh esp. desires the good of the sufferer. The belief that Yahweh allots privilege and poverty and elevates the poor, reversing the human order, found classical expression in 1 Sam 2:1ff.

(c) The manner in which cultic texts, in particular, use *ʾebyôn* confirms this general impression. The nuances of the various expressions for "poor, needy" are entirely lost; their social significance has faded.

The following count as symptoms of "being poor before God": unfortunate circumstances (Psa 40:13), contempt (69:9, 11ff.), persecution (35:1ff.; 109:2ff.), sickness (109:22ff.), near death (88:4ff.), etc. (cf. S. Mowinckel, *Psalms in Israel's Worship* [1962], 2:91f.). The enemies of the poor are less profiled; there are many accomplices and executors of anti-Yahweh schemes (cf. Mowinckel, op. cit. 5ff.).

The formulaic usage "I am destitute and poor" (Psa 40:18; 70:6; 86:1; 109:22; cf. also Psa 25:16; 69:30; 88:16; 1 Sam 18:23) describes the situation of the worshiper; it is a confession (of guilt), at once a recognition of the towering might of Yahweh and a foundation for prayer. Yahweh is, however, one who "delivers the weak from the one who is too strong and the weak and needy from the one who despoils" (Psa 35:10; cf. similar hymnic predications in Job 5:15; 1 Sam 2:8; Psa 113:7; etc.). The regular use of two or more synonyms for "poor" (mostly *ʿānî w^{e}ʾebyôn* "destitute and poor," Psa 35:10; 37:14; 40:18; 70:6; 74:21; 86:1; 109:16, 22; cf. Deut 24:14; Jer 22:16; Ezek 16:49; 18:12; 22:29; Job 24:14; Prov 31:9) may indicate firm roots in a diction shaped by parallelism. Hymns of thanksgiving (cf. Psa 107:41) and prophetic or priestly promises of salvation (cf. Isa 14:30; 29:19; 41:17; Psa 132:15) attest to the accomplished or guaranteed salvation of the poor.

5. In many intertestamental religious texts, the poor achieve an even greater significance, likely as a result of a more extensive stratification of society. The Qumran community was particularly suspicious of private property and considered poverty and humility preconditions for the spiritual life. This positive conception of poverty continues in the NT (Sermon on the Mount, Luke, Paul), and the Ebionites were neither the only nor the last Christians to give humility before God programmatical significance. Cf. E. Bammel, "πτωχός," *TDNT* 6:894ff.; *RGG* s.v. "Armenpflege," "Armut," "Ebioniten"; L. E. Keck, "The Poor Among the Saints in Jewish Christianity and Qumran," *ZNW* 57 (1964): 54–78; A. Gelin, *The Poor of Yahweh* (1964).

E. Gerstenberger

אֶבְיוֹן *ʾebyôn* **poor** → אבה *ʾbh*

אַבִּיר *ʾabbîr* strong

S 47; BDB 7b; *HALOT* 1:6a; *TDOT* 1:42–44; *TWOT* 13c; *NIDOTTE* 52

---

1. It is clear that *ʾabbîr* "strong, powerful" and *ʾābîr* (with basically the same meaning; see 4) are related; it is unclear whether *ʾēber* and *ʾebrâ* "pinion, wing" (→ *kānāp*) as well as the related denominative verb *ʾbr* hi. "to soar" (Job 39:26) belong to the same root (so GB 4f., 7; contra *HAL* 6a, 9; cf. *AHw* 7a).

Occurrences of the root in other Sem. languages are similarly opaque in many respects.

ʾēber "wing" is related to Akk. *abru* "wing," Ug. *ʾbr* "to fly(?)" (*WUS* no. 33; contra *UT* no. 39), Syr. *ʾebrā* "feather"; this word family lies too far afield with respect to meaning and will not be taken into account here.

ʾabbîr is related to Ug. *ibr* "bull" (*WUS* no. 34; *UT* no. 39; on *i* or *e* in the first syllable as mutated vowels, see W. Vycichl, *AfO* 17 [1954/56]: 357a; on Ug. PNs formed with *ibr*, see Gröndahl 88, 133), and as a Can. loanword, see Eg. *ybr* "stallion" (Burchardt 2:2; W. F. Albright, *BASOR* 62 [1936]: 30).

Of the postulated Akk. words in *AHw* 4b, 7a, *abru* "strong, mighty(?)," *abāru* "embrace, might," and *abāru* "to span," *CAD* A/1:38, 63 recognizes only *abāru* "strength" as valid.

NWSem. forms yet to be mentioned are: a Pun. PN *ʾbrbʿl* (*CIS* 1:1886; W. W. Baudissin, *Kyrios* [1929], 3:85, "Baal is strong"; Harris 73: an error for *ʾdrbʿl*?) and Old Aram. *ʾbrw* "greatness, mightiness" (*DISO* 3; *KAI* no. 214.15, 21; cf. 2:219).

According to E. Y. Kutscher (FS Baumgartner 165) the Middle Hebr. *ʾbr* pi. "to make strong" should be viewed as a secondary formation.

Associations of the root with Gothic *abrs* "strong" and other Old Nordic, Cheremis, and perhaps Celtic pars., as well as with Sum. *ʿb* "cow," which are thought to point back to a common prehistorical cultural situation (see H. Wagner, *Zeitschrift für vergl. Sprachforschung* 75 [1958]: 62–75) are quite unlikely.

2. *ʾabbîr* occurs 17x, distributed across the entire OT from the Song of Deborah to the discourse of Elihu in the poetry of the book of Job. *ʾābîr* is attested 6x, without exception as part of a divine name, once each in the promise to Joseph in the blessing of Jacob, in Isa, in Deutero-Isa, in Trito-Isa, and twice in Psa 132.

3. *ʾabbîr* is used consistently as a subst. and has meanings in the realm of "strong, powerful" (cf. *ischyros* and *dynatos,* the LXX translations in Judg 5:22; Lam 1:15; and Job 24:22). It indicates:

(a) with reference to humans—"those in power, tyrants, heroes, leaders" (1 Sam 21:8; Isa 10:13 K; Job 24:22; 34:20; Lam 1:15; likely also Jer 46:15: Pharaoh, contra LXX Apis), in the construction *ʾabbîrê* → *lēb,* the "brave" (Psa 76:6 par. "heroes of war"; cf. Isa 46:12);

(b) with reference to animals—"horse" (Judg 5:22; Jer 8:16 par. *sûs* "horse," LXX *hippos;* Jer 47:3 alongside *rekeb* "chariot"; 50:11 and 8:16 alongside *ṣhl* "to neigh") and "bull" (Isa 34:7; Psa 22:13; 50:13 par. *ʿattûd* "ram"; LXX in each case *tauros*); Psa 68:31 plays upon the double meaning "strong" and "bull";

(c) Psa 78:25 is on the way to a theological meaning with the expression *leḥem ʾabbîrîm* "bread of angels" (manna; LXX *arton angelōn;* par. *dᵉgan-šāmayim* "the grain of heaven" in v 24; cf. Psa 105:40; Wis 16:20; John 6:31).

The thesis of K. Budde (*ZAW* 39 [1921]: 38f.) that *ʾēpôd* may frequently be a late replacement for *ʾabbîr* "bull image" is unconvincing. H. Torczyner's rebuttal (*ZAW* 39 [1921]: 296–300) overreaches the mark, however, by entirely denying the root any application to "horse" or to "bull" (cf. also W. Caspari, "Hebr. *abīr* als dynamistischer Ausdruck," *ZS* 6 [1928]: 71–75).

The LXX translations of *ʾabbîr* in Job 24:22 and 34:20 with *adynatos* "powerless" (in Job an additional 4x for the orthographically similar *ʾebyôn* "poor"), as well as in Psa 76:6 with *asynetos* "without understanding" (cf. Isa 46:12), in each case in the context of divine intervention, are noteworthy. Does the LXX attempt a theological correction which argues that before God even the mighty are weak?

4. The divine name *ʾᵃbîr yaʿᵃqōb* (Gen 49:24; Isa 49:26; 60:16; Psa 132:2, 5) or *ʾᵃbîr yiśrāʾēl* (Isa 1:24; cf. Wildberger, *Isa 1–12,* CC, 68) "the strength of Jacob/Israel," which used to be commonly translated "bull of Jacob/Israel," was recognized by A. Alt ("God of the Fathers," *EOTHR* 1–77, esp. 25ff.) as an epithet for the God of the fathers. In Gen 49:24 it parallels "shepherd of Israel" and "God of your father" (cf. V. Maag, "Der Hirte Israels," *SThU* 28 [1958]: 2–28, with a thorough presentation of the God-of-the-fathers concepts; an altogether different approach, J. Hoftijzer, *Die Verheissungen an die drei Erzväter* [1956], esp. 95f.). It is generally supposed that the differentiation in the nom. paradigm *(ʾābîr* in contrast to *ʾabbîr)* may have transpired secondarily. But according to Meyer 2:30, the distinction could simply be a grammatical phenomenon (*qattīl* occasionally evolves into *qātīl* in the cs. st.;

1 Sam 21:8 txt?; cf. LXX and *BH*³). The unusual distribution of occurrences has not yet been thoroughly explained.

5. The psalm inserted at Sir 51:12 (Hebr.) mentions the "strength of Jacob" once more (cf. A. A. Di Lella, *Hebrew Text of Sirach* [1966], 101f.); corresponding formulations do not occur in the texts available from Qumran and in the NT.

H. H. Schmid

אבל *ʾbl* to mourn

S 56; BDB 5a; *HALOT* 1:6b; *TDOT* 1:44–48; *TWOT* 6; *NIDOTTE* 61

---

1. The root *ʾbl* occurs in NWSem. and in Akk., although only NWSem. has the meaning "to mourn"; Akk. does not apply the physical aspect (*abālu* "to wither") to the psychological one, as Hebr. seems to do.

Since G. R. Driver (FS Gaster 73–82), the meaning "wither" is also increasingly recognized for the Hebr. (*HAL* 7a lists eight texts in contrast to three in KBL 6b); a division of the root into *ʾbl* I "to mourn" and *ʾbl* II "to wither" is certainly unnecessary (J. Scharbert, *Der Schmerz im AT* [1955], 47–58; E. Kutsch, *ThStud* 78 [1965]: 35f.); see 3a.

A relationship to Arab. *ʾabbana* (so according to Th. Nöldeke, *ZDMG* 40 [1886]: 724; the lexicons) is hardly likely; this word has a rather different sphere of meaning (cf. Scharbert, op. cit. 48n.95; Wehr 2a: "to celebrate, praise, eulogize [a deceased person]").

Another root *ʾbl* (a by-form of *ybl*) occurs in some place-names formed with *ʾābēl* "watercourse" (*HAL* 7; explained in a folk etymology in Gen 50:11 by means of *ʾbl* "to mourn"). It is uncertain to which root *qrt ablm*, the city of the moon god, belongs (*KTU* 1.18.I.30, IV.8; 1.19.IV.1, 3).

It is unnecessary to assume a further root *ʾbl* "to shut" (GB 5b: a denominative from the Akk. *abullu* > Aram. *ʾabûlāʾ* "gate"; *HAL* 7a) for Ezek 31:15 (see 3a).

In addition to the (intrans.) verb, derivatives include the verbal adj. *ʾābēl* "sad" and the subst. *ʾēbel* "mourning," as well as *tēbēl* "terra firma," which is to be understood against the basic meaning "wither" (perhaps a loanword from Akk. *tābalu* "[dry] land," *GAG* §56k; cf. Zimmern 43; Driver, op. cit. 73).

2. Statistics: qal 18x (apart from Job 14:22 only in prophetic texts), hitp. 19x (primarily in narrative texts), hi. 2x; *ʾābēl* 8x, *ʾēbel* 24x, *tēbēl* 36x (only in poetical texts, often par. to → *ʾereṣ* "land").

3. (a) The meaning of *ʾbl* in the qal cannot be reduced to a single Eng. equivalent but ranges from "to be dry" and "to be ruined, lie disconsolate," etc., to "to mourn" (Kutsch, op. cit. 36, construed "to be diminished" as the governing concept).

Subjs. include earth/land, field, meadowland, vineyard, Judah (Isa 24:4; 33:9; Jer 4:28; 12:4, 11; 14:2; 23:10; Hos 4:3; Joel 1:10; Amos 1:2), wine (Isa 24:7; here and in the preceding texts, the translation "to dry, dry up, lay waste" seems appropriate, if one does not take them as metaphors), gates (Isa 3:26), souls (Job 14:22), and persons (Isa 19:8; Hos 10:5; Joel 1:9; Amos 8:8; 9:5; in these passages it should likely be translated "to mourn").

Par. terms are: *ʾumlal* (pulal of *ʾml*) "to wilt, dry up, wither away" (Isa 19:8; 24:4, 7; 33:9; Jer 14:2; Hos 4:3; Joel 1:10), *yābēš* "to dry up" (Jer 12:4; 23:10; Joel 1:10; Amos 1:2), *nābēl* "to wither, fall apart" (Isa 24:4), *šāmam* "to devastate" (Jer 12:11; cf. Lam 1:4), *qdr* "to become dark, gloomy; to mourn" (Jer 4:28; 14:2), *ʾnh* "to lament" (Isa 3:26; 19:8), *ʾnḥ* "to sigh, moan" (Isa 24:7). *ʾbl* with verbs describing dryness need not be limited to nature, nor with verbs of moaning is it limited to people (cf. Isa 19:8 with *ʾbl, ʾnh,* and *ʾumlal* with per. subjs.).

On Job 14:22 cf. Scharbert, op. cit. 56–58; Horst, BK 16, 214.

The two hi. usages (Ezek 31:15; Lam 2:8) should be translated "cause to mourn" (on Ezek 31:15, see Zimmerli, *Ezek,* Herm, 2:145, 152).

For verbs of complaint, groaning, moaning, sighing → *ṣʿq* "to cry"; for antonyms → *nḥm* "to console," → *śmḥ* "to be happy."

The same lack of distinction between physical and psychological conditions may also be observed with respect to *ʾumlal* "to wilt, disappear" (*HAL* 61a) and *šmm* "to be devastated, ruined, frightened, troubled" (N. Lohfink, *VT* 12 [1962]: 267–75).

(b) The semantic content of the hitp. can be rather fully conveyed with "to mourn." In contrast to the purely circumstantial qal, it denotes "to behave [consciously; in 2 Sam 14:2, fictitiously] as *ʾābēl.*"

ʾbl can refer to mourning for the dead (Gen 37:34; 1 Sam 6:19; 2 Sam 13:37; 14:2[bis]; 19:2; 1 Chron 7:22; 2 Chron 35:24), for a serious mishap or for the sins of those closely associated (1 Sam 15:35; 16:1; Ezra 10:6; Neh 1:4). *ʾbl* hitp. can also refer to oneself (Ezek 7:12, the context suggests the meaning "to be angry") or to one's own improper conduct (Exod 33:4; Num 14:39; Neh 8:9, which approaches the meaning "to regret"). Dan 10:2 refers to asceticism in preparation for the reception of revelation (Montgomery, *Dan,* ICC, 406f.; cf. the development of Syr. *ʾabīlā* "sorrowful" and "ascetic, monk" as a loanword also in Mand. [*MG* xxix] and in Arab. [Fraenkel 270]). Ezekiel announces a time of mourning in a verdict (Ezek 7:27); an apocalyptically colored view of the world describes the present with *ʾbl* hitp. (Isa 66:10; the antonym is eschatological joy, *śîś*).

ʾābēl "sorrowful" exhibits similar usages (death: Gen 37:35; Psa 35:14; Job 29:25; misfortune: Esth 4:3; 9:22; the sorrow of the end time: Isa 57:18; 61:2f.); in Lam 1:4 the predicate adj. corresponds to the qal.

Similarly, *ʾēbel* "mourning" applies, for the most part, to mourning for the dead (Gen 47:21; 50:10f.; Deut 34:8; 2 Sam 11:27; 14:2; 19:3; Jer 6:26; 16:7; Ezek 24:17; Amos 5:16; 8:10; Eccl 7:2, 4; Lam 5:15; in general: Mic 1:8; Job 30:31; Esth 4:3; 9:22; a transformation of eschatological sorrow into happiness: Isa 60:20; 61:3; Jer 31:13).

In the hitp. *ʾbl* expresses sorrow primarily in definite behaviors (crying, mourning clothes, laments, abstention, etc.; cf. Gen 37:34; Exod 33:4; 2 Sam 14:2; 19:2; Dan 10:2; Ezra 10:6; Neh 1:4; 8:9; 2 Chron 35:24; cf. *BHH* 3:2021ff. with bibliog.; E. Kutsch, " 'Trauerbräuche' und 'Selbstminderungsriten' im AT," *ThStud* 78 [1965]: 25–42), without, however, requiring that one define the basic meaning of *ʾbl* in terms of external mourning customs (so KBL 6a and V. Maag, *Text, Wortschatz und Begriffswelt des Buches Amos* [1951], 115–17; G. Rinaldi, *Bib* 40 [1959]: 267f.).

On the distinction among *qdr* "to be dark, dirty, sorrowful" (somewhat more narrowly L. Delekat, *VT* 14 [1964]: 55f.), *ʾgm/ʿgm* "to be sorrowful" (Isa 19:10; Job 30:25), and *spd* "to lament" (originally "to smite the breast in lament"; see Kutsch, op. cit. 38f.), see Scharbert, op. cit. 58–62.

4. The lament for the dead has no religious significance in Israel because any form of the cult of the dead is excluded from Israelite worship (cf. von Rad, *Theol.* 1:276ff.; V. Maag, *SThU* 34 [1964]: 17ff.); accordingly *ʾbl* hitp. has no religious significance, except in relation to self-abasement before God (Exod 33:4; Num 14:39; Dan 10:2; Ezra 10:6; Neh 1:4; 8:9; cf. Kutsch, op. cit. 28f., 36; → *ʿnh* II). In contrast, the qal usage and the related semantic field belong to a motif common in prophecy that is primarily at home in the announcement of judgment (Isa 3:26; 19:8; Hos 4:3; Amos 8:8). In Jer the generally recognized formal transition from announcement of judgment to description of catastrophe is clear (Jer 4:28; 12:4, 11; 14:2; 23:10). Finally, in apocalypticism the motif characterizes eschatological terror (Joel 1:9f.; Isa 24:4, 7; 33:9).

Amos 1:2 may give the origin of the motif (see M. Weiss, *TZ* 23 [1967]: 1–25). Judgment, with its effects on nature and people, is a consequence of Yahweh's theophany (allusions to the theophany also in Amos 9:5; Isa 33:9).

As a par. to Amos 1:2, Weiss (op. cit, 19) cites the words of the dog in a Mid. Assyr. fox fable (*BWL* 192f., 334): "I am mighty in strength, . . . a voracious lion . . . before my horrible voice mountains and rivers dry up (*abālu* Gtn)."

5. OT mourning customs are presupposed in the NT, but Jesus negates their significance for humanity (Matt 8:21f.). The apocalyptic concept that the end time is characterized by "mourning" is significant (Matt 24:30, etc.). The beatitude in Matt 5:4 alludes to Isa 61:2. Cf. G. Stählin, "κοπετός," *TDNT* 3:830–60; R. Bultmann, "πένθος," *TDNT* 6:40–43.

F. Stolz

אֶבֶן *ʾeben* **stone** → צוּר *ṣûr*

אָדוֹן *ʾādôn* **lord**

S 113; BDB 10b; *HALOT* 1:12b; *TDOT* 1:59–72; *TWOT* 27b; *NIDOTTE* 123

מָרֵא *mārēʾ* (Aram.) **lord**

S 4756; BDB 1101b; *HAL* 5:1740a; *TWOT* 2839; *NIDOTTE* 10437

I. The word *ʾādôn* "lord," of undetermined origin, is limited to the Can. language family. The other Sem. languages have various designations for "lord": Akk. *bēlu*, Aram. *mārēʾ*, Arab. *rabb*, Eth. *ʾegzīʾ*.

HAL 12b catalogs various still uncertain attempts at etymology (even more extensive suggestions in F. Zimmermann, *VT* 12 [1962]: 194). According to BL 16, 253 *ʾadōnay* may be a non-Sem. loanword with a secondarily derived sg. *ʾādôn*. Derivation from Ug. *ad* "father" (→ *ʾāb* III/1) is also purely hypothetical; a basic meaning "father" for *ʾādôn* (KBL 10b, speculatively) is unattested, even though a father may be addressed respectfully as "lord" (*KTU* 1.24.33; Gen 31:35; see III/3); according to *KTU* 2.14.18f., Ug. *adn* could as easily signify "brother."

Ug. also attests a fem. *adt* "lady" (*WUS* no. 86). PNs from Amarna, Mari, Ugarit, etc., which are significant for the vocalization and derivation of the forms, are cataloged and discussed (inconclusively) in Huffmon 156, 159 and Gröndahl 88–90.

Phoen.-Pun. *ʾdn* "lord" is frequent (*DISO* 5; PNs: Harris 74); the fem. *ʾdt* "lady" exists here too (once also in a Palm. inscription, likely as a Canaanitism; cf. M. Noth, *OLZ* 40 [1937]: 345f.). On the basis of this evidence O. Eissfeldt (*OLZ* 41 [1938]: 489) suspects a miswritten fem. par. to *ʾādôn* in Jer 22:18 behind *hōdō* (contra Rudolph, HAT 12, 142; M. Dahood, *CBQ* 23 [1961]: 462–64).

In extrabibl. Hebr. *ʾdny* "my lord" is common in the Lachish Letters (*KAI* nos. 192–97 passim; *ANET* 322); cf. also *ʾdny hśr* "my lord, the governor" in the Yavneh-Yam ostracon (*KAI* no. 200.1).

The form *ʾᵃdōnāy*, reserved as a designation for Yahweh, is usually understood as a fixed vocative form of the majestic pl. with a per. suf. in (affect-stressed) pause, "my lords = my lord = the lord" (extensive treatment in W. W. Baudissin, *Kyrios* [1929], 2:27ff.), although the grammatical analysis of the ending *-āy* is disputed.

II. The various forms of *ʾādôn* (incl. *ʾᵃdōnay* "my lords" Gen 19:2) and the divine designation *ʾᵃdōnāy* (incl. Gen 19:18) are listed separately in the statistics. Mandl. overlooks 2 Sam 7:22, reflecting the Bombergiana ed.; Lis. omits Ezek 14:20.

	ʾādôn	*ʾᵃdōnāy*	total
Gen	71	9	80
Exod	10	6	16
Lev	–	–	–
Num	6	1	7
Deut	4	2	6
Josh	3	2	5
Judg	7	4	11
1 Sam	38	–	38
2 Sam	52	7	59
1 Kgs	34	5	39
2 Kgs	37	2	39
Isa	16	48	64
Jer	6	14	20
Ezek	–	222	222
Hos	1	–	1
Joel	–	–	–
Amos	1	25	26
Obad	–	1	1
Jonah	–	–	–
Mic	1	2	3
Nah	–	–	–
Hab	–	1	1
Zeph	1	1	2
Hag	–	–	–
Zech	7	2	9
Mal	3	2	5

Psa	13	54	67
Job	1	1	2
Prov	3	–	3
Ruth	1	–	1
Song Sol	–	–	–
Eccl	–	–	–
Lam	–	14	14
Esth	–	–	–
Dan	6	11	17
Ezra	–	1	1
Neh	3	2	5
1 Chron	5	–	5
2 Chron	4	–	4
total	334	439	773

Concentrations of *ʾādôn* (Gen, Sam, Kgs) are topically influenced; concentrations of *ʾ^{a}dōnāy* (Ezek, Amos) are redactionally determined.

Bibl. Aram. *mārēʾ* "lord" is attested in Dan 4x.

III. 1. As a term of social order, *ʾādôn* in its basic meaning "lord, master (over subject persons)" is defined in opposition to terms such as *ʿebed* "servant" (cf. esp. Gen 24:9, 65; Exod 21:4–8; Deut 23:16; Judg 3:25; 1 Sam 25:10; Isa 24:2; Mal 1:6; Psa 123:2; Job 3:19; Prov. 30:10; with *naʿar* "servant," Judg 19:11; 1 Sam 20:38, etc.; with *ʾāmâ* or *šipḥâ* "maid," 1 Sam 25:25, 27f., 41, etc.), which almost always occur or are implied in context; correspondingly, the word occurs almost exclusively with a succeeding gen. or pron. suf. (a circumlocution for the relationship by means of *l^{e}* in Gen 45:8, 9; 1 Kgs 22:17 = 1 Chron 18:16; Psa 12:5; 105:21; by means of special verbal expressions in Isa 19:4; 26:13; an abs. *ʾādôn* occurs only in the formulaic laments for the dead in Jer 22:18; 34:5, as well as perhaps 10x as a description of Yahweh; see IV/2, 4).

ʾādôn distinguishes itself in this manner very clearly from → *baʿal* "lord, owner (of a thing)" (the wife also counts as property with reference to *baʿal* in the meaning "husband").

F. Baethgen's statement (in *Beiträge zur sem. Religionsgeschichte* [1888], 41, cited in *TDNT* 3:1053), "The master in relation to the slave is בעל as the owner of the slave and אדון as the one who can dispose of this possession as he wills"), is therefore not entirely accurate, because the OT does not use *baʿal* in reference to an *ʿebed.*

Ug. contrasts *adn* and *bʿl* less distinctly; cf. *bʿly* "my Lord" in the address to the king in epistolary style (*WUS* no. 544, 3*) corresponding to the Akk. formula; cf. also the poetical parallelism *bʿlkm/adnkm* in *KTU* 1.2.I.17, 33f., and 1.6.6.57f. "Nqmd, king of Ugarit, *adn* of *Yrgb bʿl* of *Ṯrmn.*"

g^{e}bîr "lord, master" occurs infrequently as a synonym for *ʾādôn* (Gen 27:29, 37 in contrast to *ʾ^{a}bādîm* "servants" in v 37); the fem. *g^{e}bîrâ* "lady, mistress" (in contrast to *šipḥâ* "maidservant," Gen 16:4, 8f.; Isa 24:2; Psa 123:2; Prov 30:23; alongside *naʿ^{a}râ* "maiden," 2 Kgs 5:3; → *gbr* 3e) is more common.

2. *ʾādôn* appears only once in the sense of authority over impersonal spheres: 1 Kgs 16:24 *ʾ^{a}dōnê hāhār* "(Shemer,) the (former) owner of the mountain (Samaria)." Reference to the placement of a lord over the house

of Pharaoh (Gen 45:8) or over the land of Egypt (Gen 42:30, 33; 45:9; Isa 19:4; Psa 105:21) indicates nothing other than elevation over the constituents of the house or country in question.

Of the Ug. texts, those cited above (III/1) with *adn Yrgb* should be mentioned; in the Phoen. oath from Arslan Tash (7th cent.) the reading in l. 15 suggested by W. F. Albright (*BASOR* 76 [1939]: 8), which has been taken up in *KAI* (no. 27), *bʿl pn ʾrṣ* "lord of the surface of the earth," is preferable over the reading *[ʾ]dn ʾrṣ* "lord of the earth" (T. H. Gaster, *Or* 11 [1942]: 44, 61; *HAL* 12b; cf. *ANET* 658b).

3. As in numerous languages (e.g., Med. Lat. "senior" followed by Ger. "Herr," originally a comparative form of "hehr" = "old, honorable"; cf. Kluge 305a; Fr. "monsieur" with a fixed usage of the pron.; Eng. "sir" < "sire"; "mister" < "master"), the word is used in address and declaration not only to reflect an actual lord-servant relationship (very frequently, e.g., in the courtly *ʾᵃdōnî hammelek* "my lord, the king"), but also as a polite form for other persons whom one wishes to honor with this designation (L. Köhler, *ZAW* 36 [1916]: 27; 40 [1922]: 39ff.; Lande 28ff., 81); the subordinating self-designation *ʿebed* "slave" corresponds to this usage. Thus the following may be addressed as *ʾādôn:* the father (Gen 31:35, Rachel's address to Laban), the brother (Gen 32:5f., 19; 33:8ff., Jacob-Esau; Exod 32:22; Num 12:11, Aaron-Moses), the uncle (2 Sam 13:32f., Jonabad-David), the spouse (Gen 18:12, Sarah-Abraham; Judg 19:26f., concubine-Levite; Amos 4:1, the "cows of Bashan"; Psa 45:12, the royal bridegroom), as well as total strangers (e.g., on the lips of women: Gen 24:18, Rebekah-servant of Isaac; Judg 4:18, Jael-Sisera; Ruth 2:13, Ruth-Boaz), or those who are actually of equal or lower social status (1 Kgs 18:7, 13, Obadiah-Elijah; 20:4, 9, Ahab-Benhadad; 2 Kgs 8:12, Hazael-Elisha). The transition from "you/your" to "my lord" (e.g., Num 32:25, 27) occurs just as easily as the role change from "I/my" to "your servant" (e.g., 1 Sam 22:15). *ʾᵃdōnî* "my lord" (cf. Fr. "monsieur") is often used in a fixed form instead of "our lord" by a group of people (Gen 23:6; 42:10; 43:20; Num 32:25, 27; 36:2; 2 Sam 4:8; 15:15; 2 Kgs 2:19).

On the formula *bî ʾᵃdōnî* or *bî ʾᵃdōnāy* "with your permission, lord" (7x and 5x, resp.), see L. Köhler, *ZAW* 36 (1916): 26f.; Lande 16–19; *HAL* 117.

IV. 1. (a) The usage of *ʾādôn and ʾᵃdōnāy* in reference to Yahweh (W. W. Baudissin, *Kyrios* [1929], vols. 1–4; Quell, *TDNT* 3:1058ff.; Eichrodt 1:203f.; O. Eissfeldt, *RGG* 1:97) is closely tied to profane practice, because it was used by Israel or individuals or groups in Israel to address Yahweh as the superior, as lord, or to speak of him as the lord in analogy to earthly (actual or fictional) servant-lord relationships, just as it was used by neighboring religious communities to address their prominent divinities; so too was Israel, terminologically at least since Deutero-Isa, described as the servant of Yahweh (W. Zimmerli, *TDNT* 5:662; → *ʿbd*). (b) This usage is relatively rare and atypical. By contrast, frequent and formulaic is (c) the vocative and (d) the formulaic usage as a divine epithet, which develops, in accordance with the uniqueness of this lord, into (e) an absolutely suitable ontological description (lord par excellence, lord of all), and finally even replaces the divine name.

2. *ʾādôn* occurs in a statement with the per. suf. ("his lord") only in the prophetic verdict against Ephraim in Hos 12:15, "Therefore, his Lord will leave his bloodguilt upon him," where the full force of the word probably underscores the paradox of disobedience; Neh 3:5 is similar: "Their leaders, nevertheless, did not bend the necks to the service of their Lord." Cf. further Isa 51:22 "your Lord" in a positive use of the full sense, par. to "who pleads the cause of his people."

In contrast, statements with "our Lord" (Psa 135:5; 147:5; Neh 8:10; 10:30) should probably be regarded as late variations of the formulaic usage of *ʾādôn* as a divine epithet or as a replacement for the divine name.

Mal 1:6 "Am I Lord? Where is the fear of me?" does not represent an actual divine designation, but a comparison with an earthly (father or) lord, in which the meaning of the word has become thematic. In Mal 3:1 "the Lord, whom you seek," the use of *hāʾādôn* is determined through juxtaposition with the messenger who precedes this Lord, although, as in 1:6, the abs. usage for Yahweh that was known at the time may be reflected.

3. *ʾadōnāy* "my Lord" is already attested early in address. In contrast to e.g., *melek* "king," the word does not serve as a description of the being of God as the sovereign Lord or as the mighty master, but as a simple honorific used by the subordinate in conversation with any superior (Eichrodt 1:203; contra Köhler, *Theol.* 30, who evaluates the meaning of *ʾādôn* in the text that is paradigmatic for him, Psa 105:21, with too great an emphasis on the par. but not synonymous *mōšēl* "master"; cf. also Baudissin, op. cit. 2:246). This usage also occurs in texts that will not be listed individually here (concentrated e.g., in the prayer of David, 2 Sam 7:18–22, 28f., 7x *ʾadōnāy yhwh*, otherwise absent in Sam), certainly incl. the old and textually unquestionable formulae *bî ʾadōnāy* "with permission, Lord" (Exod 4:10, 13; Josh 7:8; Judg 6:15; 13:8; cf. Judg 6:13 *bî ʾadōnî*) and *ʾahāh ʾadōnāy yhwh* "Ah! My Lord Yahweh" (Josh 7:7; Judg 6:22; also 8x in Jer and Ezek; → *ʾahāh;* cf. also the usage of *ʾadōnî* with respect to angels in Josh 5:14; Zech 1:9; 4:4f., 13; 6:4; Dan 10:16, 17bis, 19; 12:8).

The group address "Yahweh, our Lord" is limited to Psa 8:2, 10 and seems to approximate the predication of Yahweh treated in the next section.

4. The abs. usage of *ʾādôn* also appears very early as a formulaic divine epithet. The meaning of the word here too does not at first exceed what has been treated so far, as e.g., in the ceremonious title *hāʾādôn yhwh (ʾelōhê yiśrāʾēl)* "the Lord Yahweh (the God of Israel)" in the pilgrimage legislation (Exod 23:17 and 34:23) and also in the formula *hāʾādôn yhwh ṣebāʾôt* used several times by Isa, which probably stems from Jerusalem tradition (Isa 1:24; 3:1; 10:16, 33; 19:4; cf. Wildberger, *Isa 1–12*, CC, 66–68).

In Phoen.-Pun. inscriptions the epithet *ʾdn* "lord" is attested for numerous divinities and occurs frequently (Baudissin, op. cit. 3:52ff.; *DISO* 5, with a list of the pertinent divinities). The transition from title to PN can be recognized in PNs (cf. *ʾšmnʾdn*/*ʾdnʾšmn* "Eshmun is Lord" with *ʾdnplṭ* "Adn has saved") and esp. with respect to the dying and rising vegetation divinity Adonis from Byblos (W. W. Baudissin, *Adonis und Esmun* [1911]; Eissfeldt, *RGG* 1:97f.; G. von Lücken, "Kult und Abkunft des Adonis," *FF* 36 [1962]: 240–45).

In view of the wide distribution of such epithets in the ancient Near East (Eg. *nb*, Sum. EN, Akk. *bēlu*, Aram. *mrʾ*, Hitt. *išḫa-*), the title *ʾādôn* for Yahweh requires no special derivation; nevertheless one can speculate that the Jerusalem cult tradition, to which the specified formulas apparently belong, has been influenced by Can. idiom (cf. also PNs formed with *ʾādôn*, e.g., *ʾadōnîyāhû*, *ʾadōnîṣedeq*, *ʾadōnîqām*, *ʾadōnîrām*, with their Ug. and Phoen. counterparts; see I; *IP* 114ff.).

The age of the expression *ʾadōnāy yhwh*, other than in address, e.g., "the Lord Yahweh" with a nom. usage of the fixed vocative, is disputed. Contrary to the viewpoint represented by Baudissin (*Kyrios* 1:558ff.; 2:81ff.), that *ʾadōnāy* has been secondarily added to or substituted for *yhwh* in each instance, the nom. usage may be quite old according to Eissfeldt (*RGG* 1:97); according to F. Baumgärtel ("Zu den Gottesnamen in den Büchern Jer und Ezek," FS Rudolph 1–29) formulae such as *kōh ʾāmar ʾadōnāy yhwh* and *neʾum ʾadōnāy yhwh* are original in Jer and Ezek (with J. Herrmann, FS Kittel 70ff., contra Baudissin); cf. also the extensive treatment in Zimmerli, *Ezek*, Herm, 2:556–62.

Many texts, incl. the oldest, remain textually disputed (on Amos cf. V. Maag, *Text, Wortschatz und Begriffswelt des Buches Amos* [1951], 118f.; and Wolff, *Amos*, Herm, 101, 130; on 1 Kgs 2:26, cf. comms.).

In particular, it is not always clear why some authors (or redactors) prefer the expression *ʾadōnāy yhwh*. Baumgärtel (op. cit. 27ff.) assumes that Ezek (217x) avoids the divine designation *yhwh ṣebāʾôt* (associated with the ark in the temple on Mt. Zion and still common in Jer) in the exilic situation and replaces it with *ʾadōnāy yhwh* in connection with an old cult name.

5. The association of *ʾādôn* with an accompanying gen. describing the universal sphere of sovereignty mediates the transition from a divine epithet to an essential designation that is also absolutely applicable: *ʾadōnāy* in the sense of "Lord par excellence" or "Lord of all." Such escalating hyperbolic usages are also known in the Bab. repertoire of titles for gods (e.g., *bēl bēlē* "the Lord of lords"; cf. Tallqvist 40–57) and even for kings (in addition to *bēl bēlē*, e.g., also *bēl šarrāni* "the lord of kings," *bēl gimri* and *bēl kiššati* "the Lord of all"; cf. Seux 55–57, 90f.), and are therefore not per se witness to a purely monotheistic belief in God. The Hebr. OT uses the expressions "God of gods and Lord of lords" (Deut 10:17; Psa 136:2f.) and *ʾadôn kol-hāʾāreṣ* "Lord of the whole earth" (Josh 3:11, 13; Mic 4:13; Zech 4:14; 6:5; Psa 97:5; 114:7 txt em, see Kraus, *Psa*, CC, 2:371, 375; a segment of this text may still be pre-exilic; cf. Noth, HAT 7, 25; H.-M. Lutz, *Jahwe, Jerusalem und die Völker* [1968], 94, 96; following Kraus, *Psa*, CC, 1:83, the expression apparently "derived from the cultic tradition of the old Jebusite city").

mārēʾ, the Bibl. Aram. equivalent of *ʾādôn*, occurs 2x in the vocative *mārî* "my Lord" addressed to the king (Dan 4:16, 21) and 2x with an accompanying gen. in reference to God: Dan 2:47, *mārēʾ malkîn* "Lord of kings" and 5:23, *mārēʾ-šemayyāʾ* "Lord of heaven." For pars. in Aram. inscriptions (a title for kings and gods) cf. Baudissin, *Kyrios* 3:57–61; *DISO* 166f. (on Phoen. *ʾdn mlkm* and Aram. *mrʾ mlkn* "the lord of kings" cf. K. Galling, "Eschmunazar und der Herr der Könige," *ZDPV* 79 [1963]: 140–51).

1QapGen has noticeably multiplied the number of these expressions (with the spelling *mrh*); see Fitzmyer, *Gen.Ap.* 77, 83f., 99, 130, 242.

The originality of the texts with freestanding *ʾᵃdōnāy* "the Lord" not addressed to a second party is in doubt (about 70x, principally in Isa, Psa, and Lam: 1 Kgs 3:10, 15; 22:6; 2 Kgs 7:6; 19:23; Isa 3:17f.; 4:4; 6:1, 8; 7:14, 20, etc.; Ezek 18:25, 29; 21:14; 33:17, 20; Amos 5:16; 7:7f.; 9:1; Mic 1:2; Zech 9:4; Mal 1:12, 14; Psa 2:4; 22:31; 37:13; 54:6, etc.; Job 28:28; Lam 1:14f.; 2:1, etc.; Dan 1:2; 9:3, 9; Ezra 10:3, where, however, one should read *ʾᵃdōnî* and regard it as a reference to Ezra; Neh 4:8). Nevertheless, the MT presumes the exclusive meaning "the Lord *kat' exochēn*." *ʾᵃdōnāy* completely loses its original vocative character, becoming clearly paraphrastic, in a trend toward the avoidance of the name Yahweh beginning in the 3rd cent. BCE (Bousset-Gressmann 307ff.), which may also be observed in the Qumran texts (M. Delcor, *Les Hymnes de Qumran* [1962], 195; cf. in the context of an address, 1QH 2:20, etc., with Isa 12:1; Psa 86:12; 1QH 7:28 with Exod 15:11; outside of an address, 1QM 12:8 with Psa 99:9; 1QSb 3:1 with Num 6:26), and which finally leads to the Qere perpetuum *ʾᵃdōnāy* for the tetragrammaton (→ *yhwh*).

V. On the usage of *ʾādôn* or *kyrios* in early Judaism and in the NT, cf. W. Foerster, "κύριος," *TDNT* 3:1081–98; K. H. Rengstorf, "δεσπότης," *TDNT* 2:44–49; K. G. Kuhn, "μαραναθά," *TDNT* 4:466–72; as well as bibliogs. in NT theologies and in treatments of the dominical titles.

E. Jenni

אַדִּיר *ʾaddîr* **powerful**

S 117; BDB 12a; *HALOT* 1:13b; *TDOT* 1:73–74; *TWOT* 28b; *NIDOTTE* 129

---

1. The root *ʾdr* "to be powerful, mighty, majestic" is limited to Can. (Ug.: *UT* no. 92; *WUS* no. 95; Gröndahl no. 90; Phoen.-Pun.: *DISO* 5f.; Harris 74f.).

The qal, "to be mighty," and the pi., "to make mighty, magnify," are attested only in Phoen. (*DISO* 5); the ni. ptcp. "majestic" (Exod 15:6, 11) and the hi. "to show oneself majestic" (Isa 42:21) occur only in Hebr.

The adj. *ʾaddîr* "mighty, powerful, majestic, leading" is the most important derivative. It occurs relatively frequently in Ug. and Phoen.-Pun., even in everyday speech (e.g., Ug. *aṯt adrt* in the list *KTU* 4.102.4, 7, 9, 16, 18, according to *UT* no. 92 "upper-class wife"; cf. A. van Selms, *Marriage and Family Life in Ug. Literature* [1954], 19f., 58f.; Pun. *KAI* no. 65.2 = no. 81.5: "from the largest to the smallest of them [the buildings]"; the root *gdl* "to be large" is lacking in Phoen.-Pun.); in Hebr. it seems rather to be an archaic or archaizing word, judging from nom. formation and usage (Gulkowitsch 95).

The fem. form *ʾadderet* (< **ʾaddirt-*, BL 479) is either an abstract "glory" (Ezek 17:8; Zech 11:3) or in the concrete meaning "coat" (cf. H. W. Hönig, *Die Bekleidung des Hebräers* [1957], 66ff.). A basic meaning "be broad" (GB 12a), to which "glory" and "coat" may be traced, is not demonstrable; rather, if *ʾadderet* "coat" belongs to the root *ʾdr,* the constant attribute may be used representatively for the thing ("the glorious" < "the glorious [article of clothing])."

The subst. *ʾeder* "splendor(?)" (Zech 11:13; Mic 2:8 txt em *ʾadderet* "coat"?) is exegetically and textually quite disputed; cf. comms. and G. W. Ahlström, *VT* 17 (1967): 1–7.

The PN *ʾadrammelek* (2 Kgs 19:37 = Isa 37:38) has a counterpart in Phoen. (*ʾdrmlk* = "*Mlk* is mighty"; Harris 75). In 2 Kgs 17:31 the homophonous divine name, however, has developed from Akk. *adadmilki* ("Adad [is] king") (Eissfeldt, *KS* [1966], 3:335–39; K. Deller, *Or* 34 [1965]: 382f.).

2. Aside from *ʾadderet* in the meaning "coat" (10x), the distribution of the word family is almost entirely limited to poetical texts: ni. 2x, hi. 1x (for the texts, see above); *ʾaddîr* 27x, besides Exod 15:10 (Song of the Sea) and Judg 5:13, 25 (Song of Deborah), 13x in metrical prophetic texts, and 7x in the Psalter; in prose only 1 Sam 4:8 (on the lips of the Philistines) and Neh 3:5; 10:30; 2 Chron 23:20 (in the meaning "nobles"); *ʾadderet* "splendor" 2x (prophetic texts, see above). Incl. *ʾeder* (2x) the root is attested 44x.

Cf. further Sir 36:7 (hi.); 43:11 and 49:13 (ni.); 40:13; 46:17; 50:16 *(ʾaddîr);* on the Qumran texts cf. Kuhn, *Konk.* 2f.; also *GCDS* 5, 117.

3. Power, might, and splendor are attributed (as in Ug. and Phoen.) both to impersonal things (bodies of water: Exod 15:10; Psa 93:4a; cf. Ug. *gšm adr* "heavy rain" in *KTU* 2.38.14; trees: Isa 10:34 txt? [cf. M. Dahood, *Bib* 38 (1957): 65f.]; Ezek 17:8, 23; Zech 11:2; ship: Isa 33:21b; cf. Phoen. *ʾrṣt dgn hʾdrt* "the splendid cornfields," *KAI* no. 14.19; cf. *ANET* 662b, "the mighty lands of Dagon") and to persons (kings: Psa 136:18; cf. Phoen., *KAI* no. 24.5f. = *ANET* 654b, among others; rulers: Jer 30:21; lords of the flocks = shepherds: Jer 25:34–36; leaders: Judg 5:13, 25; Jer 14:3; Nah 2:6; 3:18; Psa 16:3; Neh 3:5; 10:30; 2 Chron 23:20; Ezek 32:18 txt?; Ug. *WUS* no. 92:2*b; Neo-Pun. *KAI* no. 119.4 and no. 126.7: "the mighty of Leptis and the entire people of Leptis," corresponding to Lat. ordo et populus).

The Neh texts cited and the inscriptions exhibit the concept as a socially undifferentiated personal designation, perhaps in the sense "magnates" (E. Meyer, *Die Entstehung des Judentums* [1896], 132f.). Consequently, it serves in 2 Chron 23:20 as a general replacement for the specific and misunderstood *kārî* "Carites" of 2 Kgs 11:19.

Semantically related terms that occur in the context of *ʾdr* include: *gādôl* "great" (Psa 136:18; cf. Isa 42:21), *mōšēl* "ruler" (Jer 30:21; 2 Chron 23:20), *gibbôr* "hero" (Judg 5:13); cf. also Psa 76:5. The antonym *ṣāʿîr* "small, insignificant, young" (Jer 14:3 "servant"; cf. S. E. Loewenstamm, *Tarbiz* 36 [1966–67]: 110–15), which also occurs in the Pun. inscriptions mentioned above (1), is informative as well.

4. Like *gādôl* "great" (→ *gdl*) and other adjs. that express an attitude of awe toward the powerful, *ʾaddîr* without complement also refers to God and the divine (W. W. Baudissin, *Kyrios* [1929], 3:85f., 120).

In Ug. (*KTU* 1.92.7 *adrt* apparently of Astarte) and esp. in Phoen.-Pun., *ʾdr* and the fem. *ʾdrt* are fixed epithets for various divinities: Phoen. *bʿl ʾdr, KAI* no. 9B.5 (Byblos ca. 500 BCE); *ʾskn ʾdr, KAI* no. 58 (Piraeus, 3d cent. BCE); Isis/Astarte, *KAI* no. 48.2 (Memphis 2d–1st cent. BCE); Pun. (and Neo-Pun.) Astarte, *tnt* and *bʿl ʾdr* (*DISO* 5f.;

KAI 2:11, 89; J.-G. Février, *Semit* 2 [1949]: 21–28; A. Berthier and R. Charlier, *Le sanctuaire punique d'El Hofra à Constantine* [1955], 14, 237).

Because the text and interpretation of Isa 10:34 (see 3) and 33:21a are very questionable, the only texts that remain with a theological usage of *ʾaddîr* or *ʾdr* ni./hi. are Exod 15:6, "Your laws Yahweh, majestic in might"; v 11, "Who is like you, glorious in holiness?"; 1 Sam 4:8, "Who will save us from the hand of this mighty God?"; Isa 42:21, "It pleased God for the sake of his faithfulness, to magnify his law and make it glorious"; Psa 8:2, 10, "Yahweh, our Lord, how mighty is your name in the whole earth"; 76:5, "Frightful are you, glorious"; and 93:4, "Mightier than the thunders of many waters, mightier than the waves of the sea, the Lord on high is mighty."

Statements concerning Yahweh's laws, name, instruction, or being do not exhibit formulaic usage. Noteworthy are the comparative-superlative usages in Exod 15:11 and Psa 93:4. A special theological nuance of the word (the Eng. tr. "mighty" or "majestic" is preferable in these cases) is not evident, nor, in view of the degrees of comparison, to be assumed.

Given the Can. background of the word, it is surely no accident that, in reference to Yahweh, it is particularly at home in the older, Can.-influenced Jerusalem tradition (1 Sam 4:8 in the ark narrative; Psa 76:5 in a pre-exilic Zion hymn [cf. H.-M. Lutz, *Jahwe, Jerusalem und die Völker* (1968), 167f.]; 93:4 in a similarly ancient enthronement psalm [cf. Kraus, *Psa*, CC, 2:233ff.]; cf. also the tripartite verses in Exod 15:11 and Psa 93:4 with the climactic parallelism also known from Ug.).

5. Of the numerous options for *ʾaddîr* in the LXX, *thaumastos* (6x in Psa) and *megas* (→ *gdl*) should be esp. emphasized.

The Near Eastern-Hellenistic divine predication *megas* "great" (W. Grundmann, "μέγας," *TDNT* 4:529–44), which appears in the acclamation formula for Artemis of the Ephesians (Acts 19:27f., 34f.) and which is also echoed in Titus 2:13, "of our great God and of (the) Savior Jesus Christ," does not correspond to Sem. *gādôl* but reflects Phoen. *ʾdr,* in addition to Aram. *rab* (Akk. *rabû;* Phoen. has only *rbt* "lady" as a title).

E. Jenni

אָדָם ʾ*ādām* **person**

S 120; BDB 9a; *HALOT* 1:14a; *TDOT* 1:75–87; *TWOT* 25; *NIDOTTE* 132

אֱנוֹשׁ ʾ*ᵉnôš* **person**

S 582; BDB 60b; *HALOT* 1:70b; *TDOT* 1:345–48; *TWOT* 113a; *NIDOTTE* 632

---

1. (a) *ʾādām* "person, people" occurs only in Can. (Hebr. and postbibl. literature, Phoen.-Pun., and Ug.) and occasionally in SSem. (*HAL* 14a).

Ug. *adm* "people" occurs once par. to *lim* (= Hebr. *lᵉʾōm* "people") in the Baal cycle (*KTU* 1.3.II.7f.) and in the expression *ab adm* "the father of humanity" in the Krt epic (→ *ʾāb* IV/3a).

The Phoen.-Pun. pl. *ʾdmm* is formed on *ʾdm*, as well (*DISO* 4).

Old SArab. *ʾdm* has the meaning "servant" (Conti Rossini 100b).

On the Mid. Hebr. form *ʾādān* cf. E. Y. Kutscher, FS Baumgartner 160.

The etymology of the word has not yet been conclusively determined (cf. lexicons, and comms. on Gen 2:7; esp. also Th. C. Vriezen, *Onderzoek naar de Paradijsvoorstelling bij de oude semietische Volken* [1937], 63f., 129–32, 239).

Vriezen (op. cit.) summarizes the attempts to derive the word from the Sum. or Bab.-Assyr., as well as the attempts to explain the figure of Adam on the basis of divine names or mythical figures (as bringer of culture in analogy to Adapa, following de Liagre Böhl), and finds them inconclusive. Because these attempts (cf. also GB 10a; KBL 12f.) do not enjoy wide acceptance or are entirely rejected, they will not be recounted here.

Vriezen asks, then, concerning the relation of *ʾādām* to *ʾᵃdāmâ* (cf. Gen 2:7 with a typical Hebr. play on words) whether this is merely a folk etymology or, indeed, an original linguistic relationship. The answers given to date on this question differ; although the linguistic derivation of *ʾādām* from *ʾᵃdāmâ* appears to Köhler and others to be certain (*Theol.* 243n.60; 246n.102), Th. Nöldeke (*ARW* 8 [1905]: 161) and others reckon that the two words have nothing to do with each other linguistically. Vriezen concludes that the word is to be explained either from the Hebr. alone (in which case the verb *ʾdm* "to be red" would be pertinent) or from various Arab. options. To him H. Bauer's (*ZDMG* 71 [1917]: 413; *ZA* 37 [1927]: 310f.) derivation from Arab. *ʾadam(at)* "skin, surface," is the most likely, which may have assumed the meaning "man" in SArab. and Hebr. as a pars pro toto, while in Arab. the old meaning is preserved. Then a connection between *ʾādām* and *ʾᵃdāmâ* "surface of the earth" is possible, but in a different way than the author of Gen 2–3 presupposes. Cf. also → *ʾᵃdāmâ* 1.

The Arab. meaning "skin, leather," which has been mentioned, is also accepted by G. R. Driver (*JTS* 39 [1938]: 161; *HAL* 14b; cf. *CPT* 154) for Hos 11:4 (par. to *ʾahᵃbâ*, for which the meaning "leather" is also postulated, → *ʾhb* I), but cannot be considered certain (cf. Wolff, *Hos*, Herm, 199f.; Rudolf, KAT 13/1, 210).

(b) In addition to *ʾādām*, the word *ʾᵉnôš*, which goes back to a common Sem. root, occurs rather rarely in Hebr.; in Bibl. Aram. *ʾᵉnāš* is the normal word for "person(s)" (< **ʾunāš*; cf. Wagner nos. 19f.; P. Fronzaroli, *AANLR* 8/19 [1964]: 244, 262, 275; → *ʾîš* I).

2. (a) The word occurs 554x in the OT (incl. Hos 6:7; 11:4; 13:2; excl., however, the PN Adam in Gen 4:25; 5:1bis, 3–5; 1 Chron 1:1). The distribution is noteworthy. It occurs in Ezek 132x (93 in God's address to the prophet: *ben-ʾādām*). The next highest concentration may be found in two places: 49x in Eccl and 46x in Gen 1–11 (by contrast, it does not occur at all in Gen 12–50, apart from Gen 16:12 *pereʾ ʾādām*). A second lesser concentration is noticeable only in Prov (45x) and Psa (62x); otherwise, the distribution is entirely coincidental (Jer 30x, Isa and Job 27x, Num 24x, Lev 15x, Exod 14x, and the other books under 10x; absent in Obad, Nah, Ruth, Song Sol, Esth, and Ezra).

(b) *ʾᵉnôš* occurs 42x but only in poetical texts (Job 18x, Psa 13x, Isa 8x; also Deut 32:26; Jer 20:10; 2 Chron 14:10, a prayer, is no exception). In addition, *ʾᵉnôš* occurs as a PN in Gen 4:26; 5:6–11; 1 Chron 1:1.

Aram. *ʾᵉnāš* appears 25x (Dan 23x, Ezra 2x; the form *ʾᵃnāšāʾ* should be read instead of the Hebr. pl. *ʾᵃnāšîm* in Dan 4:14), either collectively/generally or individualized in the usage *bar* *ʾᵉnāš* (Dan 7:13; cf. C. Colpe, *TDNT* 8:402ff. with bibliog.) or in the pl. *bᵉnê* *ʾᵉnāšāʾ* (Dan 2:38; 5:21), in both poetry and prose.

3. (a) *ʾādām* signifies collectively "the person (generically), humanity, people" and is used (in contrast to → *ʾîš* "man") only in the sg. and in the abs. st., never with sufs. The "individual man" is indicated by *ben-ʾādām*, the pl. "individual men" by *bᵉnê/bᵉnôt (hā)ʾādām* (cf. L. Köhler, *TZ* 1 [1945]: 77f.; id., *Theol.* 129f.; → *bēn*). The meaning of the word is consistent throughout the OT. It can be used in combinations such as "human blood" (Gen 9:6; according to KBL 12b perhaps 40 such phrases), as a gen. replacing an adj. "in human fashion" (2 Sam 7:14; Hos 11:4), and in commonplace usages where it can be translated "someone" (Lev 1:2, etc.), "all" (Psa 64:10), negated "no one" (1 Kgs 8:46; Neh 2:12; see also 4j).

Only *mēʾādām (wᵉ)ʿad-bᵉhēmâ* "the people and the cattle" (Gen 6:7; 7:23; Exod 9:25; 12:12; Num 3:13; Jer 50:3; 51:62; Psa 135:8) occurs as a fixed usage. Other sequences with *bᵉhēmâ* "cattle, animals" are Exod 8:13f.; 9:9f., 19, 22, 25; 13:2, 15; Lev 7:21; 27:28; Num 8:17; 18:15(bis); 31:11, 26, 30, 47; Jer 7:20; 21:6; 27:5; 31:27; 32:43; 33:10, 12; 36:29; Ezek 14:13, 17, 19, 21; 25:13; 29:8; 36:11; Jonah 3:7f.; Zeph 1:3; Hag 1:11; Zech 2:8; Psa 36:7; cf. Eccl 3:19.

The most common par. is → *ʾîš* (III/4c) (2 Kgs 7:10; Isa 2:9; 5:15; 52:14; Psa 49:3; 62:10; with *ʾᵃnāšîm* Isa 2:11, 17, etc.).

(b) *ʾᵉnôš* never takes the art. and occurs only in the sg. It is a collective term in a stricter sense than *ʾādām* and therefore signifies "the people" or "people" exclusively; once it is individualized: *ben-ʾᵉnôš* (Psa 144:3). L. Köhler's characterization of it as "falling into disuse" (KBL 68a) may be putting it too strongly, because it still occurs 18x in the late book of Job. One may well say, however, that it is strongly limited in usage: only in poetical texts, only without the art., and only in a very narrow semantic field. In this respect, one may presuppose the same limitations of usage that characterize the term *ʾādām* (see 4a): the word *ʾᵉnôš* also never occurs in historical texts or in historical or salvation-historical contexts.

The sense of the human being as mortal, frail, and limited predominate in Job and Psa: Psa 103:15, "the days of man are like the grass"; similarly, 73:5; 90:3; 8:5 = 144:3; Job 7:1; 14:19; 25:6; 28:13. A human being cannot be just (pure) before God: Job 4:17; 9:2; 15:14; 25:4; 33:26. Humans in contrast to God are *ʾᵉnôš:* Job 7:17; 10:4f.; 13:9; 32:8; 33:12; 36:25. A few texts also describe enemies in the same way: Psa 9:20f.; 10:18; 56:2; 66:12; cf. 55:14. Psa 9:21 demonstrates this connection: "the pagans should recognize that they are men." Beyond Psa and Job, Isa uses the same meaning 6x (Isa 13:7, 12; 24:6; 33:8; 51:7, 12; in addition, 2 Chron 14:10). Thus 33 of 42 texts constitute a cohesive semantic group (see also 4e-h).

Deut 32:26; Isa 8:1; 56:2; Jer 20:10; Psa 55:14; 104:15(bis); Job 5:17; and 28:4 differ from the usage treated to this point. These few exceptions involve fixed idioms or tight word combinations: *ʾašrê* *ʾᵉnôš* "blessed is the man" (Isa 56:2; Job 5:17); *lᵉbab* *ʾᵉnôš* "the heart of man" (Isa 13:7; Psa 104:15bis); *ḥereṭ* *ʾᵉnôš* "a man's (= in common use among men) stylus" (Isa 8:1; cf., however,

Wildberger, *Isa 1–12*, CC, 330–32); *ʾᵉnôš šᵉlômî* "my confidant" (Jer 20:10; cf. Psa 55:14 *ʾᵉnôš kᵉʿerkî* "a man like me"). If *ʾᵉnôš* retains the neutral meaning in these combinations, it seems to point to an older stage of the language in which *ʾᵉnôš* still had a broader, more general usage. Except for these combinations, the neutral meaning occurs only in Deut 32:26 and Job 28:4; *mēʾᵉnôš* "(from) among the people" may be a fixed usage here.

Texts in which *ʾᵉnôš* is a PN are to be attributed to this common, neutral sense (Gen 4:26; 5:6f., 9–11; 1 Chron 1:1; cf. Westermann, *Gen*, CC, 1:339, on Gen 4:26; see 4j).

4. (a) The OT does not use *ʾādām* for the creature Homo sapiens without differentiation, but primarily for this creature in relation to its creatureliness or to a particular aspect of its creatureliness. *ʾādām* is not the human being in any family, political, everyday, or communal situation; instead *ʾādām* refers to the human being aside from all of these relationships, as simply human. Above all else, however, God's special salvific activity, God's history with his people, does not concern the *ʾādām*. Not only the two literary complexes in which *ʾādām* occurs most frequently (Gen 1–11 and Eccl), but also the topically cohesive groups of usages concern the human being as creature or an aspect of human creatureliness; no fixed literary or thematic complexes or speech forms in historical or prophetical books feature *ʾādām*.

(b) The word *ʾādām* has its proper place in the primeval history, indeed, in those portions of Gen 1–11 that concern humanity in the primeval events: the creation of humanity (1:26–30 and 2:4b–24), the expulsion from paradise (ch. 3), the flood (chs. 6–9), and the dispersal of humanity (11:1–10). Beyond these narratives the word occurs only in 4:1 *(hāʾādām)*, 25, and 5:1(bis); here, however, *ʾādām* has become (or is on the way to becoming) a PN. The concentration of occurrences in the primeval history and their limitation to these texts indicates that in the OT *ʾādām* signifies humanity (in a collective sense) *before* and *beyond* any specification that begins in the names of the genealogies, and before any division of humanity into peoples, which begins in Gen 11 (the table of nations). Narratives that treat humanity in this sense divide into two basic motifs: they treat (c) the creation of humanity and (d) the finitude of human existence in the narratives of guilt and punishment. They result in the two basic statements that the OT makes concerning humanity: a human being is God's creation and has a limited existence in contrast to God.

(c) The narratives of the creation of humanity (cf. E. Lussier, "Adam in Gen 1:1–4:24," *CBQ* 18 [1956]: 137–39) are found in Gen 1:26–30 and 2:4b–24.

The religiohistorical background of the creation narratives indicates that the creation of the world and the creation of humanity originally represented individual streams of tradition. It has been demonstrated, for example, that in primitive cultures creation almost always occurs as the creation of humanity only, and that, to the contrary, in Egypt creation is predominantly the creation of the world, i.e., cosmogony. The cosmogony that predominates in high cultures has, then, assimilated the creation of humanity; thus the two are bound together in Enuma Elish and Gen 1. By contrast, Gen 2 belongs in the tradition of the creation of humanity. It is therefore incorrect to speak of two creation narratives, an older (chs. 2–3) and a younger (ch. 1); rather, one can consider 1:26–30 as a par. only to ch. 2, not to 1:1–2:4a. Tradition-historical exegesis of ch. 1 demonstrates the original independence of 1:26–30 even more clearly (Westermann, *Gen*, CC, 1:143ff.).

Gen 2–3 is a literarily unified narrative inserted by J, behind which, however, two originally independent narratives may still be unmistakably recognized: a narrative of the creation of humanity in 2:4b–24 and a narrative of the expulsion from the garden in 2:9, 16f., 25; 3:1–24. The first belongs to the motif of the creation of humanity, the second explains human finitude. By joining them, J expressed the interrelationship of these two basic motifs.

The two depictions of the creation of humanity in Gen 1:26–30 and 2:4b–24 agree that: (1) a human being has existence from God, (2) a human being should be understood from the outset as a communal being, (3) the provision of humanity with nourishment is tied to its creation, and (4) humanity is charged with dominion over the animals and the other creatures. In addition to these, P has the unique statements that (5) God has blessed humanity and (6) has created them after his likeness (→ *ṣelem*).

(1) Neither of these depictions actually means that God created the first people. The creation of humanity is, rather, a statement concerning primeval history; it lies beyond history that can be experienced and documented. The contention is that humanity (meaning every individual) owes its existence to God—no more and no less. The man created by God first becomes Adam (PN) when the series of families begins (4:1, 25; 5:1); the man fashioned in the creation narratives is not one in a definite series. Thus the narrative of the creation of humanity maintains that humanity is nothing other than God's creation; it is not possible to separate humanity as such from its creatureliness. Humanity is what it is, as God's creation.

(2) The creation of humanity for community is concisely stated in Gen 1:26–30: "as man and woman created he them." This characteristic is the point of the narrative in 2:4b–24: the man formed by God from the earth (2:7) is not yet the creation that God actually intended ("it is not good . . ." 2:18); only with the creation of the woman is the creation of humanity actually successful. J therefore has esp. emphasized this aspect of the creation of humanity, namely that one receives one's individuality only in community (cf. *ILC* 1–2:61f.).

(3) According to both portrayals, humanity is first provided with vegetable nourishment (1:29; 2:8f., 15); animal nourishment is added only in the context of alienation from God. All the texts, particularly in the Psa, that say that God provides his creatures with nourishment belong to this motif.

(4) In contrast, particularly to the Sum.-Bab. portrayal of the creation of humanity, J and P do not describe humanity as created for the service of the gods, i.e., for the cult, but for dominion over the animals (Gen 1:26b, 28b; 2:19f.) and the remaining creatures (1:28), and for tilling the soil (2:15; cf. 2:5b). Agricultural activity, activity on the earth, is grounded therefore in, or together with, the creation of humanity itself. This cultural task is not separable from human existence.

(5) P expressly reports the blessing of humanity in the context of its creation (1:28). What P describes, J narrates: the power of fertility intended in the blessing manifests itself in the sequence of generations, in the

begetting and birth of descendants (4:1f., 25). The human created by God is created as a being that reproduces itself in successive generations.

(6) Scholars have offered a multitude of explanations concerning the statement that God created in his image; cf. Westermann, *Gen*, CC, 1:142ff. On the basis of religiohistorical backgrounds, Westermann interprets this statement as follows: God created humanity as his partner so that creature and creator may interrelate, so that the creature may hear its creator and respond. This more precise definition has an explicative character; it does not expand the notion of the creation of humanity but instead emphasizes the meaning of the creatureliness of humanity (so also e.g., K. Barth, *Church Dogmatics* [1958], III/1:184f.). Even though J does not state this specifically, J expresses the intention through the combination of the creation narrative itself, 2:4b–24, with the narrative of the transgression of the commandment and the expulsion from the garden: God made humanity in order to relate to it.

(d) The narratives of guilt and punishment form a second group. Narratives of the creation of humanity or statements concerning its creatureliness are regularly accompanied by narratives and statements concerning the limitations of humanity. The two are bound together in contrast: Why is a human being, who is indeed a creation of God, so very limited in existence? Answers to this question may vary; in the OT—as elsewhere—the explanation is seen in a crime of humanity.

The narrative of the expulsion from the garden in Gen 3 focuses on the bare events: God places the people he created in an orchard and grants them the fruits of all the trees for nourishment; he forbids them to eat from the fruit of only one tree; but the people eat the fruit of this tree and are therefore banished from the garden. Thus they are alienated from God, and this alienation from God signifies an existence limited in many ways. This central element is woven together with and enriched by a series of other motifs, which belong to other once-independent narratives from the same narrative complex; such is, above all, the tree of life motif, which is also known elsewhere (e.g., the Gilgamesh Epic and the Adapa Myth), and the individual punishments that explicate the limitations on existence, and perhaps also the temptation scene with the serpent. J's intention in this narrative concerning people can be summarized as follows: (1) Not only the creatureliness but also the limitations on human existence are grounded in a primal event between God and humanity. (2) The transgression of God's commandment and the punishment for this transgression are primal events allowed to stand as enigmas, as inexplicable. Guilt and punishment define humanity; all human existence participates in these realities. (3) God affirms the humanity that has sinned against him. Even when he excludes these humans from his presence, and so ordains an existence limited by toil, pain, and death, he allows them to live and provides for the continuation of life.

Only these three statements together represent the narrative's intentions. An exegesis that describes an elysian state of innocence transformed through the fall into a degenerate state does not reflect the text and the sense of the narrative. In the narrative, commandment, transgression, and punishment alike are primal events and may not be equated with historical periods. The designation "fall," which introduces this slightly different nuance (with far-reaching consequences, however) into the exegesis of the narrative, stems from early Judaism (4 Ezra).

The possibility of human failure inherent in the primal event gains an added dimension in the flood narrative in Gen 6–9. While ch. 3 (and 4) treats the transgression of an individual human, chs. 6–9 deal with a human phenomenon that can destroy or ruin a group, an entire human community. The possibility that the creator may again destroy his creation first arises here. This possibility is already implicit in the fact that the world or humanity has a creator: as such, the creator has the power to destroy his work again. For this reason, narratives of the flood (or of the cataclysm) are as equally distributed in the world as creation narratives. The paradigm beginning time–end time is established here: the potential for the destruction of the human race corresponds to the possibility of its ruin. Consequently, the concern in apocalypticism, as in cosmogony, is humanity.

Gen 6–9 contribute the following to an understanding of humanity: (1) Self-propagating humanity faces the possibility of ruin en masse. (2) The creator has the option of destroying the humanity that he has created. (3) The flood and the salvation of the individual from the flood add to human life the dimension of life as a result of salvation or protection from great catastrophes. (4) The promise that the cataclysm would not be repeated "as long as the earth stands" is the basis of human history, which includes the possibilities of the (partial) ruin of an entire group and (partial) catastrophes. This promise means that salvation and protection are also human phenomena.

The narrative of the construction of the tower (11:1–9) depicts a transgression that is particularly dangerous for humanity—human self-elevation in the realms of politics (city and tower) and of technical progress (which as such is affirmed). This gracious punishment, dispersal, and alienation once again permit life.

(e) A series of texts refer to the creation of humanity or allude to creation motifs, e.g., Deut 4:32, "from that day onward, when God created men in the earth"; or Exod 4:11; Isa 17:7; 45:12; Jer 27:5; Zech 12:1; Psa 8:5ff.; 139:13ff.; Job 15:7; 20:4; Prov 8:31 (wisdom at the creation: "and delighting in the sons of men"); also Psa 115:16 (God gave the earth to humanity); Deut 32:8 (an allusion to the division of the nations).

Statements that value humans as creatures who must be preserved or protected also relate closely to the creatureliness of humanity. Human life is protected because humans are God's creatures (Gen 9:5f.). This view is taken up in the law: "Whoever slays a man . . . " (Lev 24:17, 21).

To the extent that the rationale for this respect in Gen 9:6 is humanity's creation in God's image, the inception of the modern concept of human dignity may be said to manifest itself; such respect rests in human creatureliness and is evident in that the life of humans as God's creatures is protected. A concept of human dignity also stands behind statements such as Hab 1:14, "if he (the conqueror) treats men like the fish in the sea." The notion is evident in the fact that "man does not live by bread alone" (Deut 8:9), or in the lament, "I, however, am a worm and no man" (Psa 22:7), and is particularly prominent in the Servant Song, Isa 52:14, "his appearance was marred beyond human semblance." 2 Sam 7:14 and Hos 11:4 also speak similarly of humanity.

This value is not inherent in humanity; it lies in God's care for humanity: "What is man *(ʾᵉnôš)*, that you consider him, and the son of man *(ben-ʾādām)* that you care for him?" (Psa 8:5). A number of texts speak in this manner of God's preservation of humanity: he is the "guardian of men" (Job 7:20); in such protection and preservation he works "his wonders for the children of men" (Psa 107:8, 15, 21, 31; in addition, Psa 36:7f.; 80:18; etc).

(f) The OT sees humanity's true nature particularly in its existence in relation to God, in its distance from him, and in its dependence upon him. This group of usages of *ʾādām* (perhaps 60 texts) has a specific emphasis. The OT's understanding of humanity does not begin with an independent humanity grounded in its own existence that then enters into relationship with God; rather, *ʾādām* signifies a human being in relationship to God. Humanity, as such, cannot be understood unless its existence is seen in juxtaposition to God.

The juxtaposition of God and humanity, which this group of texts sees primarily as a contrast, corresponds consistently to human creatureliness as presented in the primeval history. The limitation inherent in this contrast is definitive of human existence, and its neglect or disregard presents a particular danger to human existence: "No one remains alive who sees me" (Exod 33:20).

This notion receives an esp. pregnant and unique treatment in Isa in a word against political alliance with Egypt: "Even Egypt is a man and not God" (Isa 31:3). Isa 31:8 uses the word again in a similar sense: "Asshur will fall by the sword, not of man; the sword, not of man, will consume it." The statement in Isa 31:3 is taken up by Ezekiel in the address to the prince of Tyre (Ezek 28:2, 9). It is noteworthy that both texts in Isa expand the schema of the prophetic word beyond the extant speech forms as a means for the prophet to express something unique to his message. The actual foundation of the warning against the alliance with Egypt in Isa 31:1–3 is the announcement of the destruction of the "guardian" in v 3b. Isa expands this foundation through the reference to the finitude of all human power, a given of human existence. The same notion stands behind 31:8: Asshur will be destroyed but not by a human sword (e.g., Egypt's); only the nonhuman, the creator, who is also the Lord of history, is at work here. The statement "Egypt is man and not God" is therefore a statement grounded in the createdness of humanity; it is independent of God's special history with Israel.

The refrain in Isa 2:9, 11, 17; 5:15 belongs in the same context: "So man is humbled and men are brought low" (or something to that effect). Wildberger (*Isa 1–12*, CC, 110f.) correctly points out that this statement of the demise of the mighty is not actually a prophetic saying: "Without a doubt, Isaiah is quoting a wisdom saying, which he puts in the form of an impf. cons. in v. 9, but he also uses it in its original form in 2:17." He refers to the same parallelism of *ʾîš* and *ʾādām* in Prov 12:14; 19:22; 24:30; 30:2; Psa 49:3: "In such sayings, bowing down and being brought low are seen as the consequences of prideful arrogance" (cf. also Jer 10:14; 51:17). When Isa announces "the day" that comes upon all the proud and haughty and in which Yahweh alone will be mighty (2:12–17), and when he includes a wisdom saying that juxtaposes humanity and God, he indicates an important contact between prophetic and wisdom speech: the extension of the announcement of judgment, which is properly valid in Israel only for "man and men," is defined by the contrast God-human, which prevents any overstepping of the boundary.

The same contrast occurs elsewhere as well: "God is not man *(ʾîš)* that he should lie; he is not a son of man *(ben-ʾādām)* that he should repent" (Num 23:19; cf. 1 Sam 15:29). Such statements guard against subsuming God into the human sphere; similarly Mal 3:8 "can a man ever deceive God?" Such statements also indicate that the preservation of the boundary between God and humanity does not result in an ontic determination. Abstract statements are not made concerning the being of God or that of humanity. The distinction remains a contrast in phenomena and is never a contrast of existence. For this reason statements that express a different mode of being for God and humanity are entirely absent. The contrast is decisively significant when a person confronts the decision concerning whom to trust and when trust in God is contrasted in great detail with trust in a human being: Jer 17:5; Mic 5:8; Psa 36:8; 118:8; 146:3; "for the help of man is nothing" (Psa 60:13; 108:13); an individual would much rather fall into the hands of God than into the hands of a human being (2 Sam 24:14 = 1 Chron 21:13); if one trusts in God, one need not fear people (Isa 51:12).

The contrast is also evident in that the manufacture of idols is stringently combated: idols are works of human hands (2 Kgs 19:18 = Isa 37:19; Psa 115:4; 135:15; Jer 16:20 "how can a man make gods for himself"; cf. Isa 44:11, 13).

The over 90 occurrences of God's address to the prophet Ezekiel, "you, son of man," belong in the same context. Cf. Zimmerli, *Ezek*, Herm, 1:131: "The emphasis, however, does not lie on the note of individuality, but on the אדם, to which the unexpressed counterpart is אל (Is 31:3; Ezek 28:2)." Thus this address implies the same juxtaposition of God and humanity as in Isa 31:3 and 2:11, 17, with the exception that here the prophet himself, in his bare, finite creatureliness, is contrasted with God.

(g) The creation of humanity establishes that human and animal alike are living creatures. In J the creation of the animals stands in closest relationship to that of people (Gen 2:7, 18–24); in P animals and people receive the blessing of the creator (1:22, 28). Similarly, animals and people appear together in the flood (6:3; 7:23). Human-animal solidarity is expressed in the only apparently firm idiom formed with *ʾādām: mēʾādām ʿad bᵉhēmâ* "the people as well as the cattle" (see 3).

Many other contexts mention people and animals together without the formula: in reference to the redemption of the firstborn of humans and cattle (Exod 12:12; 13:2, 13, 15; Num 3:13; 8:17; 18:15), in reference to war booty (Num 31:11, 26, 35, 40, 46; Josh 11:14), and in reference to the cultic offering of war booty (Num 31:28, 30, 47). As in creation, so in destruction, people and animals are often mentioned together, as in the Egyptian plagues (Exod 8:13f.; 9:9f., 19, 22, 25; 12:12; Psa 135:8); people and animals are destroyed in the fall of Babylon (Jer 50:3). Complete destruction often includes people and animals (Jer 36:29, "and devastate this land and destroy man and animal in it"; also Jer 7:20; 21:6; 27:5f.; 50:3; 51:62; Ezek 14:13, 17, 19, 21; 25:13; 29:8; 38:20; Zeph 1:3; Hag 1:11; people alone, Zech 11:6). People and animals are affected in the confession in the context of the announcement of destruction in Jonah 3:7f.; they also appear together in Habakkuk's accusation against the conquerors (Hab 2:8, 17). It is noteworthy that announcements of the destruction of people and animals first occur in the Egyptian plagues and then for the first time again in the prophets from Jer onward. Animals and people are also often mentioned together in the context of the promise for the time after judgment: Ezek 36:11, "I will make men and cattle numerous for you"; so also Jer 31:27; Zech 2:8; 8:10 (people alone: Jer 51:14; Ezek 36:10, 12, 37f.; Mic 2:12).

(h) People share transience with animals; Qohelet says so once expressly: "For the fate of the children of man is the same as the fate of the animal" (Eccl 3:19; cf. Psa 49:13). This transience, too, is grounded in the primal event (Gen 3:19, 24), as is human imperfection or wickedness (in the narratives of guilt and punishment), often associated with human frailty.

Statements such as Num 16:29 simply declare this frailty: "If these die as all men die, if they encounter what all men encounter" (similarly Ezek 31:14; Psa 73:5; 82:7; cf. also Judg 16:7, 11, 17). Discussion of the transience of humanity has its particular place in the lament of transience, a developed "I- (we-) lament" (Psa 39:6, 12, "man is only a breath"; 49:13, 21; 62:10; 89:48; 90:3; 144:4; Job 14:1, 10; 25:6; 34:15; Isa 2:22). This lament of transience is particularly well developed in Job, above all in 14:1–12. Here too one may not claim that the word "human" is characteristic of the lament per se; rather, *ʾādām* occurs only in expanded forms that extrapolate the particular lament of the sufferer so that the suffer views the self in his/ her particular suffering as one who participates in the transience of all humanity.

This insignificance or frailty stands in close relationship to human imperfection or wickedness in Gen 1–11, in Job 14:1–12 (v 4, "How can a clean thing come from an unclean? Impossible!"), and correspondingly in Psa 90:7–9 (cf. Num 5:6, "Sin as men commit it"). This situation accounts for the remarkable fact that the individual lament psalms in general (and at other points) speak of the enemies, the fools, only as "men" (Psa 140:2, "Save me, Yahweh, from the evil men"; similarly often: Psa 12:2, 9; 57:5; 116:11; 119:134; 124:2; Job 20:29; 27:13; 33:17; 34:30; often in proverbs; cf. Prov 6:12; 11:7; 12:3; 15:20; 17:18; 19:3; 21:20; 23:28; 24:30; 28:17; proverbs discussing the wise or cunning person mention *ʾādām* much less often; cf. Prov 12:23, 27; 16:9; 19:11, 22; 28:2; cf. Job 35:8).

(i) The book of Eccl radicalizes discussion of the transience or frailty of humanity in that it is not simply stated or lamented; rather, discussion results from reflection concerned, in an attitude of fundamental curiosity (1:13), with human existence (2:3). Qohelet also proceeds from the primary event; human frailty stands in tension with human createdness, and at this point guilt enters the discussion: 7:29, "This I have discovered, that God created people upright; they, however, seek many devices"; cf. 9:3. Through such an understanding of humans as creatures, Qohelet preserves a connection with theology despite his skepticism (cf. 3:11; 7:29; 8:17).

The main points of his concept of humanity are: (1) the radical recognition of the nothingness of humanity, its existence-until-death. In its frailty humanity resembles the animals (3:18f., 21). One sees human essence more clearly in the house of mourning than in the banquet hall (7:2). Existence-until-death is sharpened because death has the character of a surprise attack (8:8; 9:12). (2) What then is the meaning of this existence that rushes toward death? Whatever one accomplishes in one's life of work or study one must abandon again (1:3, "What does man profit from all his effort at which he toils under the sun?"; 2:12, 18, 21f.; 6:1f., 10–12; 7:14; 10:14; 12:5). Esp. in view of the effort, emptiness, and frailty of existence, the moment, the present, affirmation of that which simply is, acquires meaning (2:24, "There is nothing better for man than that he eat and drink and enjoy his work"; 3:13, 22; 5:18, "to accept his portion and to be happy"; 7:14; 8:15;

11:8). This affirmation of life's joy and pleasures is repeatedly emphasized as an affirmation of God's creation (2:24; 3:13; 5:18; 7:14; 8:15). Precisely in such affirmation of the moment, in the enjoyment of the good gifts of life, can one affirm one's creator in the recognition of the limitation of one's existence. (3) Qohelet's understanding of humanity is demonstrated most clearly in 8:17, "Then I recognized that it is impossible for man to fathom the whole work of God, everything which happens under the sun; for however man strives to understand, he does not fathom it." Qohelet discovered that a complete knowledge of God is impossible for humanity, as is a knowledge of the totality of events. One must come to grips with this limitation: the finitude of human existence determines an understanding of existence and the knowledge of God. Only within these limits can human existence have meaning; only within these limits can reference to God be meaningful.

(j) In all of the usages treated to this point, a relationship to creatureliness and to that which it signifies has been recognizable, but the OT also knows a neutral usage that does not involve such a relationship; here the word is used as broadly and imprecisely as in our modern languages.

A group of declarative statements in Prov discusses the being and activity of humanity very generally; these sayings offer observations on humanity, e.g., Prov 20:27, "the human breath is a lamp of Yahweh" (similarly 27:19f.), or observations and experiences from social life that deal mostly with human behavior, e.g., 18:16, "gifts make room for a person"; see also 16:1; 19:22; 20:24f.; 24:9; 29:23, 25; cf. Isa 29:21; Psa 58:2; Job 5:7.

Very general, neutral statements concerning humanity also occur elsewhere, e.g., Psa 17:4, "the wages that one receives"; 1 Sam 16:7; 2 Sam 23:3; Isa 44:15; 58:5; Jer 47:2; Psa 104:23; Eccl 8:1; Lam 3:36, 39. Such generalized language may also then treat various aspects of God's involvement with humanity: Job 34:11, "he requites them according to their work"; Ezek 20:11, 13, 21 "statutes and ordinances that a person should observe in order to remain alive" (cf. Neh 9:29); Amos 4:13, "who declares to a person what his thought is." This small group is quite distinct from the other usages; it seems to prepare the way for something like a universal ethic that emerges from liturgical and salvation-historical structures.

ʾādām is a mere category of species in these usage groups that abstract the concept that a human is a creature, and as such is determined in many ways by creatureliness; e.g., clearly in Deut 20:19, "are then the trees of the field people?" (cf. also Ezek 19:3, 6; 36:13f.).

The group of texts in Ezek that compares what the prophet sees to a person involve the usage as a mere designation of species (Ezek 1:5, "they appeared like human figures"; also 1:8, 10, 26; 10:8, 14, 21; 41:19; cf. Isa 44:13; Dan 10:16, 18). Combinations such as "human hand" (Deut 4:28; etc.), "human voice" (Dan 8:16), "human excrement" (Ezek 4:12, 15), "human limbs" (1 Kgs 13:2; 2 Kgs 23:14, 20; Ezek 39:15), "human corpse" (Num 9:6f.; 19:11, 13f., 16; Jer 9:21; 33:5; Ezek 44:25), and "human body" (Exod 30:32) also fit here.

The many texts in which *ʾādām* stands for "someone" (negated "no one, nobody"), "many people," "everyone," or "with respect to, among, in the presence of people," in enumerations (Mic 5:4; Jonah 4:11; 1 Chron 5:21), or in usages such as "blessed *(ʾašrê)* . . . the one who . . . " (Isa 56:2; Psa 32:2; 84:6, 13; Prov 3:13bis; 8:34; 28:14) are then also to be understood in terms of this usage as a mere designation of species. In each of these instances, *ʾādām* is used synonymously with → *ʾîš* (see 3).

(k) In conclusion, Hebr. *ʾādām* corresponds only partially to the word "man" or "human" in modern languages. *ʾādām* denotes neither "man" as exemplar nor primarily the individual; rather, it denotes the category, humanity as a whole, to which the individual belongs. Humanity is defined by its origin, its creatureliness (4b-e). Most usages deal directly or indirectly with creatureliness; one exists in contrast to God (4f), as a living being (4g), in the finitude inherent in creatureliness (4h-i). In addition, "people" can be discussed quite generally, as in modern languages (4j).

5. On the NT usage and understanding of humanity, cf., among others, J. Jeremias, "ἄνθρωπος," *TDNT* 1:364–67; N. A. Dahl, "Mensch III," *RGG* 4:863–67 (with bibliog.); W. Schmithals, "*Mensch,*" *BHH* 2:1189–91 (with bibliog.). Although the figure of Adam is given a distinct salvation-historical significance in the NT (esp. in Paul), this sense does not conform to the common usage of the word in the OT (cf. J. Jeremias, "Ἀδάμ," *TDNT* 1:141–43; J. de Fraine, *Adam und seine Nachkommen* [1962], 129–41).

C. Westermann

אֲדָמָה *ʾᵃdāmâ* ground

S 127; BDB 9b; *HALOT* 1:15a; *TDOT* 1:88–98; *TWOT* 25b; *NIDOTTE* 141

---

1. *ʾᵃdāmâ* very likely belongs to the common Sem. root *ʾdm* "to be red" (in Aram. replaced by *śmq*) and also appears in the meaning "(red) field, earth, land" outside Hebr. in Neo-Pun. (the Maktar inscription, *KAI* no. 145.3, "for your people who dwell in the land"; *DISO* 5) and Aram. (Jew. Aram. and Syr. *ʾadamtāʾ*; perhaps already Old Aram. in *KAI* no. 222A.10, *ʾdm[h]* "farmland"; cf. *KAI* 2:239, 246; otherwise, Fitzmyer, *Sef.* 36).

On the etymology cf. Dalman, *AuS* 1:333; 2:26f.; Rost, *KC* 77; Galling, *BRL* 151; R. Gradwohl, *Die Farben im AT* (1963), 5f.; *HAL* 14f. Hertzberg's position (*BHH* 1:464) that *ʾādōm* "earth tone" may derive from *ʾᵃdāmâ* is somewhat less likely than the opposite development. BL 466 considers the possibility of a derivation of the color term *ʾādōm* "flesh tone" from **ʾadam* "skin" (Arab. *ʾadamat*), assuming "surface" to be the primary meaning of *ʾᵃdāmâ* (cf. also → *ʾādām* I).

Acceptance of the meaning "earth" for some texts with *ʾādām* also merits consideration (M. Dahood, *CBQ* 25 [1963]: 123f.; *PNSP* 57f.; followed also partially by *HAL* 14b) but must nevertheless probably be rejected (in Gen 16:12, "wild ass of the steppe" instead of "wild horse of a man"; "steppe" stands in contrast to "farmland"; for Isa 29:19 and Jer 32:20 the translation is unnecessarily banal; in Prov 30:14 the parallelism to *ʾereṣ* is overvalued; additional hypotheses are necessary for the exegetically difficult texts Job 11:12; 36:28; Zech 9:1; 13:5).*

2. The 225 occurrences, only once (Psa 49:12 "lands") in the pl., are distributed over the entire OT, yet with a significant concentration in Gen (43x; 27x in the primeval history and 12x in Gen 47), Deut (37x), Ezek (28x), and Jer (18x).

Other occurrences are: Isa 16x, Amos 10x, Exod 9x, 1 Kgs 8x, Psa and 2 Chron 6x each, Num and 2 Sam 5x each, 2 Kgs and Neh 4x each, 1 Sam, Zech, and Dan 3x each, Lev, Josh, Joel, Zeph, Job, and Prov 2x each, Hos, Jonah, Hag, Mal, and 1 Chron 1x each.

This list includes *ʾadāmâ* in 1 Kgs 7:46 = 2 Chron 4:17 as an appellative, "earth," not as a place-name (following Noth, BK 9, 164; cf. *ʾadāmâ* Josh 19:36; *ʾādām* Josh 3:16; *ʾadmâ* Gen 10:19; 14:2, 8; Deut 29:22; Hos 11:8; cf. *HAL* 14b, 15b), as well as Deut 32:43 (*HAL* 15b, following Tur-Sinai: "red blood").

3. On the usage of the word in the OT, cf. L. Rost, "Die Bezeichnungen für Land und Volk im AT," FS Procksch 125–48 = *KC* 76–101; A. Schwarzenbach, *Die geographische Terminologie im Hebr. des AT* (1954), 133–36, 174, 187, 200.

(a) In its basic meaning *ʾadāmâ* describes arable farmland, red (see 1) farmland (cf. von Rad, *Theol.* 1:25, 159), in contrast to the steppe and desert (*midbār, ʿarābâ, yešîmôn, šemāmâ;* cf. B. Baentsch, *Die Wüste in den atl. Schriften* (1883); A. Haldar, *The Notion of the Desert in Sumero-Accadian and West Semitic Religions* (1950); Schwarzenbach, op. cit. 93–112; W. L. Reed, *IDB* 1:828f.)

Cain becomes a nomad when he is expelled from the *ʾadāmâ* (Gen 4:11, 14). It can be cultivated (→ *ʿbd:* Gen 2:5; 3:23; 4:12; 2 Sam 9:10; Isa 30:24; Jer 27:11; Prov 12:11; 28:19; cf. 1 Chron 27:26). The farmer is *ʿōbēd hāʾadāmâ* (Gen 4:2; Zech 13:5; cf. *ʾîš hāʾadāmâ* Gen 9:20). Consequently, verbs of sowing (*zrʿ:* Gen 47:23; Isa 30:23) and of germination (*ṣmḥ:* Gen 2:9; Job 5:6; cf. Gen 19:25) belong in the domain of *ʾadāmâ.*

Only when the *ʾadāmâ* is irrigated is life possible (Gen 2:6); work on it must cease if rain ceases (Jer 14:4 txt?). Dew and rain fall on the *ʾadāmâ* (2 Sam 17:12; 1 Kgs 17:14; 18:1). Dung (Jer 8:2; 16:4; 25:33; Psa 83:11), fruit (Gen 4:3; Deut 7:13; 28:4, 11, 18, 42, 51; 30:9; Jer 7:20; Psa 105:35; Mal 3:11), firstfruits (Exod 23:19; 34:26; Deut 26:2, 10; Neh 10:36), harvest (Deut 11:17; Isa 30:23; cf. 1:7), and tithe (Neh 10:38) are mentioned in connection with it.

(b) In the material sense, *ʾadāmâ* describes the "farmland"; the most common synonym is → *ʿāpār* (cf. Schwarzenbach, op. cit. 123–33).

One can smear *ʾadāmâ* on one's head (1 Sam 4:12; 2 Sam 1:2; 15:32; Neh 9:1), take along a "load" of it (2 Kgs 5:17), cast implements in it (1 Kgs 7:46 = 2 Chron 4:17, see 2). From it vessels are formed (Isa 45:9) and an altar can be built (Exod 20:24); from it the animals of the field and the birds are made (Gen 2:19). Cf. the slightly different mode of expression in reference to humanity: the *ʾādām* is taken from the *ʾadāmâ* (Gen 3:19, 23) or formed from the dust of the *ʾadāmâ* (2:7).

(c) In an expanded application, *ʾadāmâ* generally represents the land on which one stands (Exod 3:5; 8:17) and which can open up (Num 16:30f.); cf. the creeping things of the *ʾadāmâ* (Gen 1:25; 6:20; 7:8; 9:2; Lev 20:25; Ezek 38:20; Hos 2:20).

(d) Even more generally, *ʾadāmâ* signifies simply "earth," mostly in the sense of "inhabited earth" (cf. "families of the earth" in Gen 12:3; 28:14;

Amos 3:2), from which one can be eradicated, etc. (*šmd* hi.: Deut 6:15; 1 Kgs 13:34; Amos 9:8).

Constructions used here are still reminiscent of the meaning mentioned under (c) "ground" or "earth's surface": *ʿal-hāʾᵃdāmâ* "on the earth" (1 Sam 20:31; Isa 24:21; etc.); *pᵉnê hāʾᵃdāmâ* "earth's surface" (Gen 8:13); *ʿal-pᵉnê hāʾᵃdāmâ* "on the earth" (Gen 6:1, 7; 7:4, 23; 8:8; Exod 32:12; 33:16; Num 12:3; Deut 6:15; 7:6; 14:2; 1 Sam 20:15; 2 Sam 14:7; 1 Kgs 13:34; Isa 23:17; Jer 25:26; 28:16; Ezek 38:20; Amos 9:8; Zeph 1:2f.).

4. With respect to the theological usage of the word, attention should be directed to some unique formulations such as *ʾadmat (haq)qōdeš* "holy land" (Exod 3:5; Zech 2:16), *ʾadmat yhwh* "land of Yahweh" (Isa 14:2), the divine cursing of the *ʾᵃdāmâ* (Gen 3:17; cf. 5:29; 8:21), which establishes the toil of agriculture (Gen 3:17ff.; 5:29), and esp. to the primarily Dtn-Dtr formula concerning the *ʾᵃdāmâ* that Yahweh has promised the fathers and that he will give or has given to Israel (Exod 20:12; Num 11:12; 32:11; Deut 4:10, 40; 5:16; 7:13; 11:9, 21; 12:1, 19; 21:1; 25:15; 26:15; 28:11; 30:20; 31:20; [cf. 30:18; 31:13; 32:47]; 1 Kgs 8:34, 40 = 2 Chron 6:25, 31; 1 Kgs 9:7; 14:15; 2 Kgs 21:8; 2 Chron 7:20; 33:8). The curse formula of eradication from the *ʾᵃdāmâ* corresponds to it (Deut 28:21, 63; Josh 23:13, 15; 1 Kgs 9:7; 13:34; etc). Israel and Judah will depart the *ʾᵃdāmâ* into exile (2 Kgs 17:23; 25:21 = Jer 52:27) and will return again to it (Isa 14:1f.; Jer 16:15; 23:8; Ezek 28:25; cf. Amos 9:15; etc.).

No difference in content between this usage of *ʾᵃdāmâ* and the corresponding usage of → *ʾereṣ* (4c) may be determined.

J. G. Plöger (*Literarkritische, formgeschichtliche und stilkritische Untersuchungen zum Deuteronomium* [1967], 121–29) has shown that G. Minette de Tillesse's observation (*VT* 12 [1962]: 53n.1) that the Deuteronomist and the 2d-pl. sections of Deut generally prefer *ʾereṣ* in the sense of "promised land," while the 2d-sg. sections prefer *ʾᵃdāmâ* in a much more general meaning, does not stand up to closer scrutiny (a glance at the evidence in the Dtr history points in the same direction), rather that—at least in Deut—the diction relates to fixed constructions. *ʾᵃdāmâ* occurs in Deut in the constructions *pᵉrî hāʾᵃdāmâ* "the fruit of the land," *ḥayyîm ʿal-hāʾᵃdāmâ* "living in the land," and *ʾrk* hi. *yāmîm ʿal-hāʾᵃdāmâ* "to live long in the land" (fixed constructions involving *ʾereṣ* in Plöger, op. cit.). This differentiation is also obscured in post-Dtr usage.

Although the usage of *ʾereṣ* in these contexts refers to land primarily as a geographical, or occasionally as a political, entity, traces of traditiohistorically older expressions are present in the usage of *ʾᵃdāmâ:* The nomads are not originally promised a geographically or politically defined "land," but possession of "farmland" per se. The indiscriminate association of the two concepts throughout the OT indicates that, at least since the time of the Yahwist, the general promise of permanent settlement has simply been identified with the specific promise of the possession of the land of Canaan. The designation *ʾadmat yiśrāʾēl,* which occurs only in Ezek (although as many as 17x) and which characterizes Israel not politically but theologically (cf. Rost, *KC* 78f.; Zimmerli, *Ezek,* Herm, 1:185, 203), also belongs in the same realm of ideas; cf., however, *ʾadmat yᵉhûdâ* in Isa 19:17 as well.

Similarly ancient is the expression in which *ʾᵃdāmâ* is determined by the poss. pron. ("my/your/his land") and which approaches the meaning "homeland" (Gen 28:15; Amos 7:11, 17; Jonah 4:2; Dan 11:9; cf. Psa 137:4 "foreign land").

5. The few occurrences of the word at Qumran are consistent with OT idioms. NT Gk. distinguishes only slightly between *ʾ^{a}dāmâ* and *ʾereṣ*, a circumstance that also holds true for the LXX. Both use *gē*. Cf. H. Sasse, "γῆ," *TDNT* 1:677–81, who overlooks significant aspects, however.

H. H. Schmid

אהב *ʾhb* to love

S 157; BDB 12b; *HALOT* 1:17b; *TDOT* 1:99–118; *TWOT* 29; *NIDOTTE* 170

I. The root *ʾhb* "to love" is distributed only in Can. (Akk. uses *râmum [rʾm]* for the most part, Aram. *ḥbb* and *rḥm*, Arab. *ḥbb* and *wdd*).

The Ug. verb *yuhb* (*UT* no. 105; *WUS* no. 103; A. van Selms, *Marriage and Family Life in Ugaritic Literature* [1954], 47, 67) occurs in *KTU* 1.5.V.18 euphemistically with the subj. Baal and the obj. *ʿglt* "heifer"; the subst. *ʾhbt* "love" occurs in 1.3.III.7 and 1.4.IV.39 par. to *yd* "love" (root *ydd*). *lihbt* in *UT* 1002.46 (= MF V.46) is uncertain.

In a Neo-Pun. grave inscription from Cherchel (Algeria) (NP no. 130 = *NE* 438d = Cooke no. 56), J. G. Février (*RHR* 141 [1952]: 19ff.) suspects a pu. fem. ptcp. *mhbt* "beloved," although, according to J. T. Milik (*Bib* 38 [1957]: 254n.2) this form is better derived from *ḥbb (ḥ > h)*.

Aram. *ʾhbth* in *CIS* 2:150 (= Cowley no. 75.3, a papyrus frg. from Elephantine) is entirely uncertain (cf. *DISO* 6).

D. W. Thomas ("The Root *ʾāhēb* 'love' in Hebr.," *ZAW* 57 [1939]: 57–64; following Schultens, Wünsche, Schwally), assuming a biradical (onomatopoeic) root *hb* "to blow, breathe heavily, demand" (cf. Arab. *habba*) augmented by ʾ, associates the verb with similar roots (*šʾp, nḥm, nšm,* etc.) that combine the concepts of breathing and emotions (so also Wolff, *Hos*, Herm, 35). But one should not draw exegetical consequences from this etymology (Thomas, op. cit. 64).

An etymological relationship to the conjectural *ʾah^{a}bâ* II "leather" (cf. *CML*[1] 133n.2; *HAL* 18a), suggested in Song Sol 3:10 (less likely also in Hos 11:4), should not be assumed (contra H. H. Hirschberg, *VT* 11 [1961]: 373f.).

Of the derivatives, *ʾōhēb* (ptcp. and subst. "friend") and *ʾah^{a}bâ* (inf. and verbal noun "love") are common; by contrast, the action nouns or abstract formations *ʾ^{a}hābîm* "love affairs" (Hos 8:9; cf. Rudolph, KAT 13/1, 159), "loveliness" (Prov 5:19), and *ʾ^{o}hābîm* "love's pleasures" (Prov 7:18) are infrequent.

The root is not attested in the OT in PNs (in contrast to *ydd, ḥpṣ,* or even *ḥnn*); but extrabiblically it occurs at Elephantine in *nʾhbt/nhbt* (ni. fem. ptcp. "beloved," Cowley nos. 1.4; 22.91, 96, 107) and on a Hebr. seal (Levy 46 = Diringer 217); cf. *IP* nos. 924, 937; J. J. Stamm, "Hebr. Frauennamen," FS Baumgartner 325.

II. Statistics: Of the 251 occurrences of the root in the OT, 231 are allotted to the qal (incl. 63x *ʾōhēb* and 53x *ʾahᵃbâ*), 1 to the ni., 16 to the pi., 2 as *ʾᵃhābîm,* and 1 as *ʾᵒhābîm.* The highest concentrations of the verb are in Psa (41x), Prov (32x), Deut (23x), Hos (19x), Song Sol (18x), and Gen (15x). The pi. examples are concentrated in Jer, Ezek, and Hos, those of *ʾōhēb* in Psa and Prov (17x each), those of *ʾahᵃbâ* in Song Sol (11x, incl. 3:10) and Deut (9x).

According to Gerleman (BK 18, 75), 7 of the roughly 30 passages with the verb *ʾhb* as an expression of erotic love fall to Song Sol and 11 to J and the approximately contemporary narratives of David's accession and of the succession.

The absence of *ʾhb* in Job (only 19:19) is noteworthy; → *rēaʿ*.

III. 1. With respect to the breadth of meaning and the related extensive dominance of the word field, *ʾhb* is rather similar to Eng. "to love" (cf. in contrast the coexistence of the Gk. *stergein, eran, philein,* and *agapan*). *ʾhb,* together with other verbs of emotion (→ *ḥpṣ* "to like," → *yrʾ* "to fear," and → *śnʾ* "to hate"), belongs to the few stative verbs with a trans. usage (Berg., *HG* 2:76). A categorization of usages according to the objs. is helpful (III/2 love of man and woman, III/3 of other personal relationships, III/4 of things); general statements involving substantivized *ʾahᵃbâ* without obj. will also be treated. The personal relationship (comprising *eros, philia,* and *agapē* equally) may be semasiologically primary in comparison to the relationship with things, so that one should consider love for things or activities a derived metaphorical usage (Quell, *TDNT* 1:23).

ʾhb is often further refined with respect to content by means of par. concepts: → *dbq* "to cling to" (Gen 34:3 with further par. formulations; 1 Kgs 11:2; Prov 18:24; cf. Eichrodt 1:250; 2:297f.); → *ḥpṣ* "to like, take pleasure in" (1 Sam 18:22; Psa 109:17); *ḥšq* "to be attached to" (→ *dbq*), and → *bḥr* "to choose" (Deut 10:15; cf. Eichrodt, op. cit.; O. Bächli, *Israel und die Völker* [1962], 134ff.). *rēaʿ* "companion, friend" parallels *ʾōhēb* (Psa 38:12; also *qārôb* "neighbor"; 88:19 associated with *mᵉyuddāʿ* "confidant"; cf. *BHS* and Kraus, *Psa,* CC, 2:192). One finds *yrʾ* "to fear," *ʿbd* "to serve," and *leket bᵉkol-dᵉrākāyw* "to walk in all his ways" (Deut 10:12; cf. Eichrodt side by side with 2:297f.; Quell, *TDNT* 1:28n.39) *ʾahᵃbâ,* although only in theological usage with respect to the individual's love for God; with respect to the love of God for his people → *ḥesed* "grace" (Jer 2:2; 31:2; cf. Psa 37:28) and *ḥemlâ* (→ *rḥm*) "mercy" (Isa 63:9).

The following occur in the OT as infrequent synonyms for *ʾhb: ḥbb* "to love," the counterpart of *ʾhb* in Aram. and Arab. (Wagner no. 82a), in Deut 33:3 in a difficult text with God as subj.; also *ʿgb* "to desire (sensually)" (Jer 4:30; Ezek 23:5, 7, 9, 12, 16, 20; Ezek 16:37 txt em; cf. Zimmerli, *Ezek,* Herm, 1:330, 484) with a specialized meaning.

The root *ydd,* widely distributed in Sem. (KBL 363b), is extant only in noms. (*yādîd* "lovely" Psa 84:2; "darling, friend," Isa 5:1bis; Jer 11:15 txt em; for further texts see IV/2; *yᵉdîdût* "darling" Jer 12:7; *šîr yᵉdîdōt* "love song" Psa 45:1) and in PNs (*IP* nos. 571, 576, 577, 843).

rḥm pi. "to take pity" lies farther afield with respect to meaning; the unique Aram.-sounding *rḥm* qal "to love" in Psa 18:2 (obj. Yahweh) is usually set aside by emendation (to *ʾᵃrōmimkā* "I will raise you").

dôd (61x) should be mentioned as a subst. with widely varied meanings corresponding to its suspected origins as a "babble word" (J. J. Stamm, *SVT* 7 [1960]: 174ff.):

(a) "Darling, beloved" (Isa 5:1 and 33x in Song Sol alongside the fem. *raʿyâ* "beloved," → *rēaʿ*; Akk. *dādu*; cf. *AHw* 149a; *CAD* D:20);

(b) In the pl. "love, desire" (9x; Ezek 16:8; 23:17; Prov 7:18; Song Sol 1:2, 4; 4:10bis; 5:1; 7:13; Akk. *dādū* pl. "lovemaking"; *CAD* D:20a; Ug. *dd KTU* 1.3.III.5, 7; 1.4.VI.12; 1.24.23);

(c) "Uncle" (18x; → *ʾāḥ* 3a), a special meaning that Hebr. shares with Arab. and Aram. (Stamm, op. cit. 175ff.).

A regular antonym for *ʾhb* is → *śnʾ* "to hate." The two verbs occur together in more than 30 texts (Gen 29:31f.; 37:4; Exod 20:5f.; Lev 19:17f.; Deut 5:9f.; 21:15f.; Judg 14:16; 2 Sam 13:15, a transformation of love into hate; 19:7; Isa 61:8; Ezek 16:37; Hos 9:15; Amos 5:15; Mic 3:2; Zech 8:17; Mal 1:2f.; Psa 11:5; 45:8; 97:10; 109:3–5; 119:113, 127f., 163; Prov 1:22; 8:36; 9:8; 12:1; 13:24; 14:20; 15:17; Eccl 3:8; 9:6; 2 Chron 19:2). Occasional contrasts, e.g., with *śṭn* "to be at enmity" in Psa 109:4, are insignificant by comparison. Remarkably, the assonance of the antonyms *ʾōhēb* "friend" and *ʾôyēb* "enemy" is almost never fully used stylistically; cf. Judg 5:31 and esp. Lam 1:2.

The derived stems of the verb occur only in ptcp. forms. Ni. *hanneʾᵉhābîm* "the lovely" appears only once in a gerundive meaning as an epithet for Saul and Jonathan in David's lament (2 Sam 1:23 par. *hannᵉʿîmīm* "the darlings"); see I on PNs. The pi. occurs in the pl. ptcp. *mᵉʾahᵃbîm* with the pejorative meaning "lover, paramour" (Jer 22:20, 22; 30:14; Ezek 16:33, 36f.; 23:5, 9, 22; Hos 2:7, 9, 12, 14f.; Zech 13:6; Lam 1:19); the qal ptcp. is used for the normal meaning "friend, lover." The pi. ptcp. "paramour" is to be understood not as an intensive but as a resultative, summarizing successive incidents, "to love (severally, in succession)" (cf. *HP* 158).

A hi. "to make beloved" is extant in Sir 4:7 and Mid. Hebr. The pealal *ʾhbhb* "to flirt," suggested for Hos 4:18 (*HAL* 17b), is uncertain.

2. The primary human love relationship is that between man and woman (in 2 Sam 1:26 termed *ʾahᵃbat nāšîm* "the love of women," in comparison to the love of friends): Isaac-Rebekah (Gen 24:67), Jacob-Rachel (29:18, 20, 30, 32), Shechem-Dinah (34:3), Samson-the Philistine woman (Judg 14:16), Samson-Delilah (16:4, 15), Elkanah-Hannah (1 Sam 1:5), David-Michal (18:20, 28; cf. Gerleman, BK 18, 73: the only text outside Song Sol with a woman as subj.), Amnon-Tamar (2 Sam 13:1, 4, 15), Solomon-many foreign women (stressed as a disqualification; see Quell, *TDNT* 1:24n.20) in addition to Pharaoh's daughter (1 Kgs 11:1f.), Rehoboam-Maachah (2 Chron 11:21; on "harem management" see Rudolph, HAT 21, 233), Ahasuerus-Esther (Esth 2:17). On the special case of Hosea (Hos 3:1) cf. Wolff, *Hos*, Herm, 60, and Rudolph, KAT 13/1, 89. In these cases love is obviously sexually determined.

That love is only partially constitutive of the legal institution of marriage is demonstrated e.g., by comparative statements: Gen 29:30 (with *min*); 1 Sam 1:5 (*ʾhb* "to prefer"); 2 Chron 11:21 and Esth 2:17 (superlatives). In fact, the law of inheritance in Deut 21:15–17 reckons with the coexistence of a mistress (*ʾᵃhûbâ*) and an estranged (→ *śnʾ*) wife.

The statement of Hebr. lyrical (and wisdom) literature concerning love (cf. esp. Gerleman, BK 18, 72–75) follows here. The verbal expression describes the attractiveness of the beloved (Song Sol 1:3f.), who in Song Sol is usually called *dôdî* "my beloved," but also in a poetically varied paraphrase "the one whom my soul loves" (1:7; 3:1–4). In 7:7 *ʾᵃhūbâ* "beloved" should also apparently be read instead of *ʾahᵃbâ* (abstract for concrete; cf., however, Gerleman, BK 18, 201). The noun *ʾahᵃbâ* "love" occurs in 2:4 uniquely objectified as a sign over the wine house and is set in quotation marks by some translators (Rudolph, KAT 17/2, 130f.; Gerleman 117f.); in 2:5 and 5:8 the maiden is "lovesick" (on lovesickness cf. 2 Sam 13:2 and Rudolph 131n.4; Gerleman 119); according to 2:7 (= 3:5) and 8:4 love should not be prematurely awakened or disturbed. The remaining texts with *ʾahᵃbâ* offer general statements, without, however, hypostatizing love: it is strong like death (8:6), much water cannot extinguish it (8:7), it is unquantifiable (8:7).

dōdîm is used in the comparison "better than wine" (Song Sol 1:2, 4; 4:10) and elsewhere specifically for (intoxicating) sexual indulgence (Song Sol 5:1; 7:13; Prov 5:19b txt em; 7:18); in both Prov passages, however, it parallels *ʾahᵃbâ* or *ʾᵒhābîm*.

The root *ʾhb* also occurs in wisdom literature in the erotic sense as a description of the beloved in Prov 5:19a (*ʾayyelet ʾahᵃbâ* "lovely hind"), also Eccl 9:9 *(ʾiššâ ʾᵃšer ʾāhabtā)* of the wife (Hertzberg, KAT 17/4, 172).

On Song Sol 3:10, see I concerning *ʾahᵃbâ* II "leather(?)."

The nonchalant, natural presentation of love and sexuality does not seek to sublimate love intellectually or spiritually, or to judge it moralistically and thereby to repress it psychologically; in this way it is stripped of its numimous character and distanced from the sexual-mythical phenomenon of Israel's religious environment. Song Sol plays a major role in the struggle against the erotic-orgiastic Baal religion (cf. von Rad, *Theol.* 1:27: "Israel did not share in the 'divinisation' of sex").

3. Among other personal relationships, love between parents and children should be mentioned foremost, although narrative literature discusses it only in special cases (uniqueness of the son, biased preference, e.g., for the youngest): Abraham-Isaac (Gen 22:2), Isaac-Esau and Rebekah-Jacob (25:28), Israel-Joseph (37:3f., comparatively in the sense of preference), Jacob-Benjamin (44:20). The foreigner Ruth loves her mother-in-law Naomi (Ruth 4:15). The normal situation is presupposed paradoxically in Prov 13:24 ("whoever loves his son punishes him"); for other situations cf. the more appropriate → *rḥm.*

Lord and servant can also be bound to one another in love, as in the Covenant Code (Exod 21:15, incl. wife and children) and in the Dtn Code (Deut 15:16); also in narrative literature concerning Saul and David (1 Sam 16:21); David's popularity with the people (18:16, 22) belongs here as well.

A special usage of *ʾhb* concerns the friendship of Jonathan and David. Jonathan's soul is bound *(qšr)* to David's soul (1 Sam 18:1); he loves David *kᵉnapšô* "like his life" (18:1, 3; 20:17; against the interpretation of this as homosexuality, see M. A. Cohen, *HUCA* 36 [1965]: 83f.) and makes David swear "by his love" (20:17), while David confesses in his lament: "your love to me was more wonderful than the love of women" (2 Sam 1:26; cf. v 23; tr. of Hertzberg, *Sam*, OTL, 236).

Although this love of friends leads to a covenant agreement (cf. Quell, *TDNT* 2:112; → *bᵉrît*), the emotional basis is not abandoned. Cases such as this one illustrate how the term "to love" could gain entrance also in politicojuridical contract language as an expression for upright loyalty; W. L. Moran (*CBQ* 25 [1963]: 82n.33) and Th. C. Vriezen (*TZ* 22 [1966]: 4–7) call attention to pars. from the vassal treaties of Esarhaddon: "(You swear) that you will love Ashurbanipal . . . as (you do) yourselves *(kī napšātkunu)*," with the verb *râmu* "to love" (D. J. Wiseman, *Vassal-Treaties of Esarhaddon* [= *Iraq* 20/1] [1958], 49, col. 4.266–68). See IV/3.

ʾhb clearly refers to international political relationships in 1 Kgs 5:15, where King Hiram of Tyre appears as *ʾōhēb*, David's friendly covenant partner (Moran, op. cit. 78–81, with analogous usages from EA; Noth, BK 9, 89). According to Moran, *ʾōhēb* also has the political nuance of a subject's loyalty to the king in 1 Sam 18:16 and particularly in 2 Sam 19:7. The word stands in a religiopolitical context in the prophet's accusation in 2 Chron 19:2 that Jehoshaphat has "cultivated friendship with those who hate Yahweh" (Ahab and the northern kingdom are intended). The expression "all your/his friends" in the sense of "partisans" has a derogatory tone in reference to negatively portrayed persons such as Pashhur (Jer 20:4, 6) and Haman (Esth 5:10, 14; 6:13).

Yet to be treated is the usage of *ʾhb* as a description of community relationships in more general statements in Psa and wisdom literature. The psalmist complains about the disruption of the norm: friends turn away (Psa 38:13; similarly Job 19:19), Yahweh has caused them to be alienated (88:19), love is requited only with hostility and hatred (109:4f.). In Prov "friend" and "love" are presumed as known quantities and positive factors in the arrangement of values. In addition to individual observations (Prov 14:20, the rich have many friends; 9:8, the wise loves the one who reproves, similarly 27:5f.; 16:13, the king loves the one who speaks rightly), statements of principle also appear: the (true) friend loves at all times (17:17); some friends are more devoted (→ *dbq*) than a brother (18:24). Gnomic statements concerning love occur in 10:12 (love covers all offenses; similarly 17:9) and in the comparison in 15:17 ("better a meal of herbs with love, than a fatted ox with hate"). Abstractions in the meristic statements in Eccl are the most advanced: there is a time to love and to hate (Eccl 3:8), people recognize neither love nor hate (9:1), love and hate have long since perished (9:6).

Concerning love for neighbor, stranger, and love of self, see IV/1.

4. Secondary to the personal usage, reference to things, circumstances, and activities accentuate the concept's characteristic of the goal-oriented, unilaterally selective affection and ignore the element of reciprocity; personification of the obj. does not occur in this usage (on the love of wisdom and its love in return, see IV/3). Stronger than → *ḥpṣ* and → *rṣh* "to like, be pleased with," *ʾhb* retains a passionate tone. In addition to neutral (e.g., 2 Chron 26:10, Uzziah loved agriculture) or positive entities (e.g., Zech 8:19, truth and peace), despicable things and activities frequently appear as objs. in accusations (e.g., Isa 1:23, bribery; Hos 12:8, oppression).

Other passages with nontheological usages are: Gen 27:4, 9, 14 (savory cuisine); Isa 56:10 (sleep); 57:8 (nuptuals); Jer 5:31; 14:10; Amos 4:5 (*kēn* "so"); Hos 3:1 (raisin cake); 4:18 (disgrace); 9:1 (harlot's hire); 10:1 (threshing); Amos 5:15 (the good); Mic 3:2 (the evil); 6:8 (→ *ḥesed*); Zech 8:17 (false oath); Psa 4:3 (vanity); 11:5 (foolishness); 34:13 (good days); 45:8 (righteousness); 52:5 (the evil more than the good); 52:6 (pernicious speech); 109:17 (curse); Prov 1:22 (simplicity); 12:1 (discipline, perception); 15:12 (reproof); 17:19 (bickering, foolishness); 18:21 (the tongue); 19:8 (one's life); 20:13 (sleep); 20:17 (lustfulness); 21:17 (wine); Eccl 5:9 (gold, riches).

IV. Theologically relevant statements with *ᵓhb* will be treated in the following three sections: (1) love of neighbor (love of others, love of self), (2) God's love for people, (3) people's love for God.

1. Lev 19:18, which the NT cites frequently (Matt 5:43; 19:19; 22:39; Mark 12:31; Luke 10:27; Rom 13:9; Gal 5:14; Jas 2:8), "You shall love your neighbor as yourself" (J. Fichtner, *WD* 4 [1955]: 23–52 = *Gottes Weisheit* [1965], 88–114, esp. 102ff.), is unique in the OT. H advances this love requirement and eclipses external legislative regulations by reshaping, in a universalizing and interiorizing manner, an older series of negative injunctions concerning Israelite behavior in juridical life into positive commandments (cf. Lev 19:17, "You shall not hate your brother in your heart"). In contrast to the NT, the commandment remains limited to the "compatriot" (→ *rēaᶜ*) and does not yet comprehend the whole ethic of communal behavior as a governing principle, as is already the case in the first part of the double commandment of love (Deut 6:5) in relation to behavior toward God.

An appendix in Lev 19:34, "the sojourner *(gēr,* → *gûr)*, who lives among you, shall be to you as a native from your midst, and you shall love him as yourself," includes the sojourner in the commandment (Elliger, HAT 4, 259), but also implicitly excludes the foreigner *(nokrî,* → *nkr)*, for whom other criteria are valid. Positive love for the stranger is also required in Deut 10:19, "and you shall love the stranger," here in relation to the ancient Israelite demand (cf. the negative formulations in Exod 22:20ff.) for mercy toward the weak (v 18, orphans, widows, strangers; → *rḥm*). In each passage the commandment of love for the neighbor or foreigner does not merely express clan morality (*ILC* 1–2:309; contra Th. C. Vriezen, "Bubers Auslegung des Liebesgebots," *TZ* 22 [1966]: 8f.), but is theologically motivated by Yahweh's love for the people or the foreigner, and depends, as do Yahweh's other commandments, on the covenant relationship (Lev 19:18b follows "I am Yahweh," → *ᵓanî;* Exod 22:20b; Lev 19:34b; and Deut 10:19b recall Israel's own sojourn in Egypt). Pars. from ancient Near Eastern politicojuridical language further confirm this interpretation (see III/3), and show at the same time that self-love (Lev 19:18, 34 *kāmôkā* "as yourself"; cf. also 1 Sam 18:1, 3; 20:17 "as his own life"; Deut 13:7 "as your life") is simply presupposed as the norm (H. van Oyen, *Ethik des AT* [1967], 101f.) and is not viewed e.g., as a dangerous temptation one must combat through self-denial (so F. Maass, "Die Selbstliebe nach Lev 19:18," FS Baumgärtel 109–13).

OT passages such as Exod 23:4f. and Prov 25:21, which are claimed for the concept of love for the stranger, do not use *ᵓhb*.

2. Yahweh's love will be addressed below only insofar as *ʾhb* is used (on the wider topic of God's love, see e.g., Eichrodt 1:250–58; Jacob 108–13; J. Deák, *Die Gottesliebe in den alten semitischen Religionen* [1914]; J. Ziegler, *Die Liebe Gottes bei den Propheten* [1930]; → *ḥesed*, → *qnʾ*, → *rḥm*).

The claim that Yahweh loves his people, Israel, is relatively new. It first occurs in the tradition in which Hos, Deut, and Jer stand (von Rad, *Gottesvolk* 78–83; Alt, *KS* [1964³], 2:272), and, in fact, at the point in the theological development of the election doctrine at which questions arise concerning the basis of Israel's divine election (H. Breit, *Die Predigt des Deuteronomisten* [1933], 113ff.; H. Wildberger, *Jahwes Eigentumsvolk* [1960], 110ff.; O. Bächli, *Israel und die Völker* [1962], 134ff.). The basis lies in the love of God as his sovereign act of the will.

Hosea uses the metaphors of fatherly love (11:1, "when Israel was young, I loved him"; v 4, "with bands of love") and marital love (3:1, "love a wife who loves another and who is an adulteress, just as Yahweh loves the Israelites"; see F. Buck, *Die Liebe Gottes beim Propheten Osee* [1953]), but also uses *ʾhb* more generally (9:15, "I will henceforth love them no more"; 14:5, "in free grace *[nᵉdābâ]* I will love them").

In addition to *ʾhb*, the verb *ḥšq* "to cling (to someone)" appears in Deut; both terms occur in close proximity to → *bḥr* "to choose" (4:37, "because he loved your fathers and chose their descendants"; 7:7f., "not because you were more numerous than all peoples did Yahweh turn *[ḥšq]* his heart to you and choose you . . . , but because Yahweh loved you"; 7:13; 10:15, "indeed, Yahweh turned *[ḥšq]* his heart only to your fathers, in that he loved them, and chose you, their descendants"; 23:6). In Jer 31:3 ("I have loved you with eternal love; therefore have I drawn you to me out of goodness"), the term → *ḥesed* parallels *ʾahᵃbâ*, "an indication that the two traditions of election and covenant begin to converge for Jeremiah" (Wildberger, op. cit. 112).

Later developments of these traditions that should be mentioned are 1 Kgs 10:9 (= 2 Chron 2:10 = 9:8); Isa 43:4; 63:9; Zeph 3:17; and Mal 1:2.

ʾhb used of God's love for his people occurs in a relatively limited setting and, properly, only in relation to individuals. Aside from Psa 47:5 ("the pride of Jacob, whom he loves"), where neither the subj. nor the obj. is unequivocal, and statements concerning whole categories of people (foreigners, Deut 10:18; see IV/1; Psa 97:10 txt em, "who hate evil"; 146:8, the righteous; Prov 3:12, "whomever Yahweh loves he reproves"; 15:9, "who seeks after righteousness"; 22:11, "who is pure of heart"), only two royal figures are named as the obj. of Yahweh's loving attention: Solomon (2 Sam 12:24, apparently in relation to the name *yᵉdîdᵉyāh*, "beloved of Yahweh" in v 25; cf. *IP* 149; Neh 13:26, "in that he was a darling *[ʾāhûb]* of his God") and Cyrus (Isa 48:14, "he whom Yahweh loves"). One may assume the language of ancient Near Eastern royal ideology here (Quell, *TDNT* 1:30); cf. Akk. *narāmu/rīmu* "darling" as a royal epithet (Seux 189ff., 251) and in PNs (e.g., Naram-Sin, Rim-Sin); Eg.: H. Ranke, *Die Äg. Personennamen* (1952), 2:226.

Idioms in which *ʾhb* refer to things and situations (cf. III/4) are also common in the ancient Near East: Yahweh loves justice and righteousness

(Isa 61:8; Psa 11:7; 33:5; 37:28; 99:4; *mišpāṭ* → *špṭ*, *ṣᵉdāqâ* → *ṣdq;* cf. the pars. in the Akk. royal inscriptions found in Seux 236f.). Statements of Yahweh's love for his sanctuary on Zion (Mal 2:11; Psa 78:68, par. to *bḥr;* cf. 132:12; also 87:2, "more than all the dwellings of Jacob," which is comparative and which contains the election idea) are colored by Dtr election theology.

Worthy of mention in this context are additional statements with *yādîd* (Deut 33:12, "Benjamin is the darling of Yahweh"; Psa 60:7 = 108:7, "who are dear to you"; 127:2, "his darling"); on *ḥbb* see III/1.

3. The OT addresses love for Yahweh even later than the love of Yahweh; statements of this idea are concentrated once again in Dtn theology (bibliog.: G. Winter, "Die Liebe zu Gott im AT," *ZAW* 9 [1889]: 211–46; H. Breit, op. cit. 156–65; C. Wiéner, *Recherches sur l'amour pour Dieu dans l'AT* [1957]; Eichrodt 2:290–301; J. Coppens, *La doctrine biblique sur l'amour de Dieu et du prochain,* ALBO 4/16 [1964]).

Indicative and impv. usages of the word should be differentiated. The stated substantival usage of *ʾōhēb* (mostly pl.) in the meaning "partisan" (see III/3) in contrast to "hater" (→ *śnʾ*) and "enemy" (→ *ʾôyēb*) may derive from a cultic-liturgical formulation (N. Lohfink, *Das Hauptgebot* [1963], 78). At issue is the formula "of them who love me" in Exod 20:6 and Deut 5:10, additions to the Decalogue that are not datable with certainty and that may be Dtn (similarly Deut 7:9 and later, without antonym, Dan 9:4 and Neh 1:5; on the whole formula cf. J. Scharbert, *Bib* 38 [1957]: 130–50), the conclusion of the Song of Deborah, Judg 5:31, whose antiquity is disputed (cf. A. Weiser, *ZAW* 71 [1959]: 94), and Psa 145:20. In Isa 41:8, *ʾōhᵃbî* "who loved me" refers to Abraham (dependent upon this are 2 Chron 20:7; Jas 2:23; and Koran 4:125 [124], "God took Abraham as friend *[ḫalîl]*"). The oldest text that we can date with certainty is Jer 2:2, "the love *(ʾahᵃbâ)* of your bridal period," which is based on Hoseanic thought (Rudolph, HAT 12, 14f.).

The requirement of love for God begins in Dtn parenesis and directs itself to the entire people (Deut 6:5; 10:12; 11:1, 13, 22; 13:4; 19:9; 30:6, 16, 20; texts dependent on this concept include Josh 22:5; 23:11; 1 Kgs 3:3, where the requirement is fulfilled by Solomon). *ʾhb* is governed now neither by the marriage metaphor nor by the father-son relationship and is not, therefore, influenced by Hos. Love is commanded (elsewhere only in the didactic warning of the thanksgiving psalm, Psa 31:24); it stands in a series with → *yrʾ* "to fear" (R. Sander, *Furcht und Liebe im palästinischen Judentum* [1935]), → *ʿbd* "to serve," and similar verbs of relationship to Yahweh (Lohfink, op. cit. 73ff., tables on 303f.; cf. also → *dbq* "to cling to" in Deut 11:22; 13:5; 30:20; Josh 22:5; 23:12); it is made concrete as responsive love in answer to the love of Yahweh, in faithfulness and obedience within the Yahweh covenant. According to W. L. Moran ("Ancient Near Eastern Background of the Love of God in Deuteronomy," *CBQ* 25 [1963]: 77–87), all of these characteristics point to the backgrounds of Dtn diction in the diplomatic terminology of the ancient Near East (see III/3; examples particularly from EA). *ʾhb* means, therefore, something like "to exercise upright loyalty toward the covenant partner"; and, although the OT uses it in a religious sense, it belongs to the language of the covenant idea. The addition "with your whole heart, your whole soul, and all your might" in Deut 6:5 (a similar formula is found, however, also in 10:12; 11:13 with *ʿbd* "to serve") and reference to circumcision of the heart by Yahweh (30:6) demonstrate the tendency (but also the necessity) of intensifying and interiorizing the easily hackneyed term.

Love for God as a subjective religious feeling rarely appears in the OT, which is not surprising in view of the absence of mystical religiosity. Textually uncertain are Psa 18:2, "I love you, Yahweh, my strength," with *rḥm* qal (Kraus, *Psa*, CC, 1:254; see III/1) and 116:1, "I love, for Yahweh has heard," with *ʾhb* (Kraus, *Psa*, CC, 2:385). Psa 73:25, "if I have you, then I want nothing on earth" with → *ḥpṣ*, but not in direct reference to Yahweh, should probably also be considered.

In keeping with this reluctance to use Yahweh as the obj. of *ʾhb*, the piety of the Psa preferred objective circumlocutions (see III/4). The following objs. occur: the name of Yahweh (→ *šēm*) in Psa 5:12; 69:37; 119:132; also Isa 56:6; his salvation, Psa 40:17 = 70:5; his sanctuary, 26:8; cf. 122:6 and Isa 66:10, Jerusalem; also his law, commandments, etc., Psa 119:47f., 97, 113, 119, 127, 140, 159, 163, 167.

Statements concerning the love of and for wisdom constitute a separate realm of ideas. They may be included here because hypostatized wisdom is nearly identified with Yahweh. In contrast to e.g., Dtn usages, the formulae are all reciprocal: Prov 4:6, "hold it dear, so will it guard you"; 8:17, "I love those who love me"; 8:21, "I give those who love me wealth"; cf. 8:36, "all who hate me love death" (wisdom is not personified in 29:3, "whoever loves wisdom gladdens one's father"; the text should be included in the cases listed in III/4). The Eg. pars., which deal with the love of and for Maat and with the world order given by the god, make it likely that OT statements concerning hypostatized *ḥokmâ* were given impetus from Egypt (Ch. Kayatz, *Studien zu Proverbien 1–9* [1966], 98–102; contrast G. Boström, *Proverbienstudien* [1935], 156ff.; cf. further Prov 7:4, "say to wisdom: you are my sister [→ *ʾāḥ* 3c], and call insight your confidant, that she may preserve you").

Even when *ʾhb* occurs in reference to foreign divinities, it remains within the framework of the usages treated so far: Jer 2:25, "for I love the strangers" (under the influence of Hos; cf. Jer 2:33), and 8:2, "before the sun and the moon and the whole multitude of the heaven, which she loved and served" (with Dtr diction).

ʾahūbat rēaʿ "who is loved by others" in Hos 3:1 (Rudolph, KAT 13/1, 84) and the pl. ptcp. of *ʾhb* pi. "lover, paramour" (see III/1) in Hos 2:7, 9, 12, 14f. in reference to the Baalim, and in Jer 22:20, 22; 30:14; Ezek 16:33, 36f.; 23:5, 9, 22; Lam 1:19 (cf. 1:2) in reference to alleged political allies (Zech 13:6 without metaphorical language) maintain their actual meaning "lover" even in metaphorical language and are not to be understood as technical cultic expressions because of their association with the Can. syncretistic religious figures depicted (contra A. D. Tushingham, *JNES* 12 [1953]: 150ff.).

V. The NT is already closely bound to the OT by means of the use of the key texts Lev 19:18 and Deut 6:4f. and of the subst. *agapē*, which is rarely attested in pre-Christian usage except in the LXX. Preliminary overviews and bibliogs. concerning the rich NT material may be found in the following articles, each of which offers an introductory section on the OT: G. Quell and E. Stauffer, "ἀγαπάω," *TDNT* 1:21–55; W. Zimmerli and N. A. Dahl, *RGG*

4:363–67. See also E. M. Good, "Love in the OT," *IDB* 3:164–68; G. Johnston, "Love in the NT," *IDB* 3:168–78. Of the larger monographs only C. Spicq, *Agapè dans le NT,* 1–3 (1958–60), deserves mention.

E. Jenni

אֲהָהּ *ᵓᵃhāh* ah!

S 162; BDB 13b; *HALOT* 1:18b; *TWOT* 30; *NIDOTTE* 177

---

1. For pure exclamations such as *ᵓᵃhāh* "ah!" and → *hôy* "woe!" derivation from roots is unjustified (otherwise for e.g., *ḥālîlâ* "far be it!" → *ḥll*). Accent pattern and orthography often have some range of variation, so that one must arrange individual forms of the same or similar function into groups. Thus *hāh* (Ezek 30:2) and *ᵓānnāᵓ*/*ᵓānnâ,* apparently a composite of *ᵓāh* plus *nāᵓ* "indeed" (*ᵓānnâ,* BL 652) will also be treated here alongside *ᵓᵃhāh.*

2. *ᵓᵃhāh* occurs 15x, with concentrations in the Elisha narratives, Jer, and Ezek. *ᵓānnâ* is attested 13x.

3. One finds the spontaneous exclamation to ward off fear *ᵓᵃhāh* "ah!" only in legends that use folksy, fairy-tale motifs (cf. P. Grebe, *Duden Grammatik der deutschen Gegenwartssprache* [1959], 324): Judg 11:35 (Jephthah's vow); 2 Kgs 3:10; 6:5, 15 (Elisha tales). The following *ᵓᵃdōnî* "my lord" in 2 Kgs 6:5, 15 refers to the person addressed (Elisha; cf. Judg 11:35 *bittî* "my daughter"), not to God.

ᵓānnāᵓ "ah" as a sign of complaint introducing a request to a superior occurs only in Gen 50:17 in a nontheological usage.

4. The remaining passages with *ᵓᵃhāh* belong almost exclusively to the language of prayer. The formula *ᵓᵃhāh ᵓᵃdōnāy yhwh* "ah, Lord, Yahweh" primarily introduces strongly emotional laments and petitionary prayers, in which the supplicant protests against God's actual or presumed will: Josh 7:7; Judg 6:22; Jer 1:6; 4:10; 14:13; 32:17; Ezek 4:14; 9:8; 11:13; 21:5. F. Baumgärtel (FS Rudolph 2, 9f., 18f., 27) has shown that *ᵓᵃhāh ᵓᵃdōnāy yhwh* is an old fixed formula in cultic petitions.

Wolff (*Joel,* Herm, 22f.) identifies another fixed formula, the cry of terror announcing the day of Yahweh, introduced with *hêlîlû* "wail!": in Ezek 30:2 *hāh layyôm* and Joel 1:15 *ᵓᵃhāh layyôm* "alas for the day" (cf. also Isa 13:6; Zeph 1:11, 14ff.).

ᵓānnāᵓ (Exod 32:31; Psa 118:25bis; Dan 9:4; Nah 1:5, 11) and *ᵓānnâ* (2 Kgs 20:3 = Isa 38:3; Jonah 1:14; 4:2; Psa 116:4, 16) serve 6x each as an introduction or a transition in a petitionary prayer. Except for Exod 32:31, the divine address always follows *(yhwh,* except in Dan 9:4 *ᵓᵃdōnāy).* In accord with to its composition from an interjection of pain and the petitionary particle *nāᵓ*, the cry suggests complaint and request simultaneously.

5. The NT does not use interjections in association with appeals to God (the LXX renders *ᵓᵃhāh* with *ō, a a, oimmoi, mēdamōs,* or *deomai*).

E. Jenni

אֹהֶל ᵓōhel **tent** → בַּיִת *bayit*

אוה ᵓ*wh* pi. **to desire**

S 183; BDB 16a; *HALOT* 1:20a; *TDOT* 1:134–37; *TWOT* 40; *NIDOTTE* 203

1. ᵓ*wh* pi. "to desire, want" has no direct non-Hebr. counterparts.

Arab. (ᵓ*awā* "to betake oneself"; see *NB* 190) and Syr. (ᵓ*ewā* "to agree") have verbs with the consonants ᵓ*wh*(ᵓ*wy*). J. L. Palache (*SNHL* 2–5) would like to extrapolate the common Sem. basic meaning "to fit, agree" (pi. estimative "consider fitting/pretty" > "to desire"); semantically, however, a relationship to *hwh* III (Hebr. *hawwâ* "caprice, lust"; Arab. *hawiya* "to love," *hawan* "craving, caprice") is much more likely.

Pi. and hitp. forms of the verbs are common (the postulated ni. forms "to be pretty, lovely; be seemly" in Isa 52:7; Psa 93:5; Song Sol 1:10 may belong, despite BL 422 and *HAL* 20a, to *n*ᵓ*h*). Three nom. formations may be added: with the preformatives *ma-* (*ma*ᵓᵃ*wayyîm* "desire," only Psa 140:9 "do not grant the wishes of the godless") or *ta-* (*ta*ᵓᵃ*wâ* "wish, craving") and the derivative of the reduplicated stem (ᵓ*awwâ* "desire").

2. With a total of 27 occurrences (pi. 11x, hitp. 16x; see, however, *BHS* on Num 34:10) the verb is distributed among almost all the literary genres of the OT; by contrast, the noun *ta*ᵓᵃ*wâ* (21x, plus 5x in the place-name *qibrôt hatta*ᵓᵃ*wâ*, Num 11:34f.; 33:16f.; Deut 9:22) exhibits a distinct concentration in Psa and Prov (16x, of which Prov 18:1 and 19:22 are textually uncertain). ᵓ*awwâ* (7x) is certainly attested in Deut 12:15, 20f.; 18:6; 1 Sam 23:20; Jer 2:24 (on Hos 10:10 see comms.).

3. ᵓ*wh* pi. and hitp. offers a highly nuanced spectrum of meaning within a limited word field: the two verbal stems describe the wishing, longing, or wanting of people, which varies highly in intensity and object. Elementary and even impulsive needs awaken the desire for specific things: David wants to drink water (2 Sam 23:15); the Israelites want to eat meat (Deut 12:20); the delicacies of the table excite the invited guest (Prov 23:3, 6); one longs for happy days, for the good in general (Isa 26:9; Amos 5:18; Mic 7:1); the bridegroom desires the bride (Psa 45:12). This multifaceted desire is viewed as healthy, normal, and good; the wise one is aware that a fulfilled wish (*ta*ᵓᵃ*wâ bā*ᵓ*â* or *nihyâ*, Prov 13:12, 19) does one good.

Desire can nevertheless exceed the proper limits; it can aim for perverted objects (Prov 21:19, "the godless is desirous of evil"); it can injure the other or ruin one's own prospects (Prov 13:4). Consequently, misdirected, inappropriate desire—covetousness—is condemned (Prov 23:3, 6; 24:1; Deut 5:21).

The word field of ᵓ*wh* has close contact, then, with that of → *ḥmd.* W. L. Moran ("Conclusion of the Decalogue [Exod 20:17 = Deut 5:21]," *CBQ* 29 [1967]: 543ff.)

distinguishes between *ḥmd* as desire aroused by the sight of the attractive (only in Dan 10:3 in association with food), and *ʾwh* as craving arising from an inner need (hunger, thirst, etc.; only in Gen 3:6 mediated by the eyes).

One may further compare → *šʾl* "to ask (for)" (Deut 14:26), → *qwh* pi. "to await" (Isa 26:8), *šḥr* pi. "to seek" (Isa 26:9), *ʾûṣ* "to press for" (Jer 17:16), and → *bḥr* "to choose" (Psa 132:13) as pars. to *ʾwh;* cf. also *ksp* qal/ni. "to yearn," *ʿrg* "to long for," Bibl. Aram. *ṣbh* "to desire, want," and the substs. *ʾᵃrešet* "request" (Psa 21:3), *môrāš* "wish" (Job 17:11), *haqqāšâ* "desire" (Ezra 7:6 and 7x in Esth), *hawwâ* "lust" (Mic 7:3; Prov 10:3; 11:6), *mišʾālâ* "desire" (Psa 20:6; 37:4).

Like the verb, although in varying degrees, the noun *taʾᵃwâ* describes the more or less forceful wish (of the upright: Prov 10:24; 11:23; of the king: Psa 21:3; of the wicked: Psa 10:3; 112:10; of the lazy: Prov 21:25) and—objectified, as is also possible with Eng. "wish"—that which is desirable, the object worth striving after: *ʿēṣ taʾᵃwâ* "a desirable tree" (Gen 3:6), *maʾᵃkal taʾᵃwâ* "desirable food" (Job 33:20).

For an explanation of the place-name *qibrôt hattaʾᵃwâ* "graves of craving" in Num 11:34, see Noth, *Num*, OTL, 84f.

Modifications in the meaning of the two verbal stems pi. and hitp. per se are difficult to discern, although some syntactical peculiarities also have semasiological consequences. The pi. almost always has *nepeš* "soul" as subj., i.e., wanting is seen as a typical expression of the vital force, the self. The noun *ʾawwâ* (a nonaugmented reduplicated stem) occurs in the fixed combination *kol-ʾawwat nepeš* "according to the desires of the heart" (*kol* is lacking only in Jer 2:24, which refers to the heat of the camel; generalizing usages with *ʾwh* pi.: Deut 14:26; 1 Sam 2:16; 3:21; 1 Kgs 11:37; hitp.: Eccl 6:2). The hitp. sometimes takes an obj. (as a rule the per. subj. is expressly named; cf. Deut 5:21; Jer 17:16; Amos 5:18; Psa 45:12; Prov 23:3, 6; 24:1), but it apparently tends toward an abs. usage (e.g., "to lust, be covetous, lascivious"), as in 2 Sam 23:15 (= 1 Chron 11:17) and with an inner obj. (internal acc.): *hitʾawwâ taʾᵃwâ* in Prov 21:26; Num 11:14; Psa 106:14.

4. The last two texts exhibit significant theological language: insatiable desire in itself is directed against Yahweh (wilderness tradition); cf. Psa 78:29f. Otherwise no specific theological meaning may be determined either for the verb or the nouns, not even for Isa 26:8f. (the supplicant longs for Yahweh); Psa 132:13 (Yahweh had the desire to establish himself in Zion); Job 23:13 (God accomplishes what he desires).

5. From OT roots (cf. esp. Num 11:4, 34; Psa 106:14; 78:29f.), Judaism and Christianity develop statements concerning the sinfulness of desire and impulses (cf. 1QS 9:25; 10:19; 1QS 4:9ff.; and 5:5 for the Qumran sect; rabbinical sources in StrB 3:234ff.; on the NT material, cf. F. Büchsel, "ἐπιθυμία," *TDNT* 3:167–72; *RGG* 6:482ff.; P. Wilpert, "Begierde," *RAC* 2:62ff.

E. Gerstenberger

אֱוִיל ʾᵉwîl fool

S 191; BDB 171; *HALOT* 1:21a; *TDOT* 1:137–40; *TWOT* 44; *NIDOTTE* 211

1. The noms. ʾᵉ*wîl* "fool, idiot" (subst. of the form **qitīl;* cf. *GVG* 1:356; BL 471), ʾᵉ*wīlî* "foolish" (adj. with the poss. suf. *-î,* if Zech 11:15 is not a scribal error; cf. Delitzsch §53a), and ʾ*iwwelet* "foolishness" (fem. abstract form; cf. BL 477; Nyberg 215), which occur only in Hebr. (the Neo-SArab. vocabulary in Leslau 10 lies too far afield), are generally derived from a root ʾ*wl,* which is often introduced in etymological discussions (cf. GB 16a and König 7b, with Zorell 21a and *HAL* 21a, which are more cautious) and which is not attested as a verb.

HAL 21a speculates concerning the Arab. etymology: ʾ*wl* "coagulate, become thick" > "to become stupid." One should compare the closely related verb *y*ʾ*l* "to be/act foolish," attested 4x in the ni. (see KBL 358a).

In some cases ʾᵉ*wîl* is understood as an adj., thus 7x by GB, only 3x by Lis. and *HAL* (Jer 4:22; Hos 9:7; Prov 29:9); indeed, only Prov 29:9 is unequivocal, where ʾᵉ*wîl* is an attribute of ʾ*îš* "man"; cf. Barth §29a.

2. If the etymology remains uncertain, the semantics of the words are rather unambiguous. The distribution of the terms is already illuminative in this respect, because the words prove to be primarily wisdom terms of early date.

Apart from ʾᵉ*wīlî,* which is attested only in Zech 11:15 (the word should not be read in v 17; cf. B. Otzen, *Deuterosacharja* [1964], 260), the words occur mostly in Prov: ʾᵉ*wîl* appears here 19x of 26x (70%), while ʾ*iwwelet* occurs here 23x of 25x (92%). The terms are used primarily in the recognizably older collections (see Gemser, HAT 16, 4f., 55ff., 93ff.; U. Skladny, *Die ältesten Spruchsammlungen in Israel* [1962], 6ff.; as well as H. H. Schmid, *Wesen und Geschichte der Weisheit* [1966] 145ff.); in the second collection (10:1–22:16) ʾᵉ*wîl* occurs 13x and ʾ*iwwelet* 16x, in the fifth collection (chs. 25–29) ʾᵉ*wîl* is attested 3x and ʾ*iwwelet* 4x—together, then, 36x (of a total of 42x in Prov).

The word family (in total 52x) is not represented in Eccl; ʾᵉ*wîl* occurs in Job only 2x (5:2f.).

3. The chief meaning of the personally specific ʾᵉ*wîl* is "fool" or "foolish," that of the abstract ʾ*iwwelet,* "foolishness." The synonyms and antonyms are esp. significant because of the profile of their range of meaning (see T. Donald, "Semantic Field of 'Folly' in Proverbs, Job, Psalms and Ecclesiastes," *VT* 13 [1963]: 285–92).

In the older portions of Prov ʾᵉ*wîl* is primarily an important contrast to *(*ʾ*îš) ḥākām,* the "wise" (10:8, 10, 14; 12:15; 14:3; 17:28; 29:9), to *nābôn,* the "insightful" (17:28), and to ʿ*ārûm,* the "cunning" (12:16; cf. 15:5). In contrast to the *ḥᵃkam-lēb* (10:8; 11:29), the fool is *ḥᵃsar-lēb* "one lacking understanding" (10:21), although the synonymous expression does not parallel ʾᵉ*wîl* (neither do other synonyms; see, however, *pōteh* "simple" in Job 5:2 and *bānîm sᵉkālîm* "simple children" in Jer 4:22). Other close synonyms include → *kᵉsîl* (the most important synonym, occurring 70x; on the distinction in meaning from ʾᵉ*wîl* see e.g., Skladny, op. cit. 52n.30), → *nābāl,* and *petî* (→ *pth*); farther removed is *mᵉšuggā*ʿ "crazy" (Hos 9:7).

ʾ*iwwelet* is frequently associated with *k^{e}sîl* (so 3x in the description of the fool, Prov 26:1–12; also 12:23; 13:6; 14:8, 24; 15:2, 14; 17:12), otherwise with ʾ^{e}*wîl* (16:22; 27:22), *p^{e}tāyîm* "simple" (14:18; → *pth*), *ḥ^{a}sar-lēb* "without understanding" (15:21; cf. 10:21), or *q^{e}ṣar-*ʾ*appayim/rûaḥ* "hot-tempered" (14:17, 29). ʾ*iwwelet* parallels *k^{e}limmâ* "shame" (18:13); the most important antonym is *da*ʿ*at* "knowledge, recognition" (12:23; 13:16; 14:18; 15:2, 14); others are *t^{e}bûnâ* "insight" (14:29), *śēkel* "understanding" (16:22), as well as *ḥakmôt* (sic)/*ḥokmâ* "wisdom" (14:1, 8).

As a stereotypical character, the ʾ^{e}*wîl* is consistently portrayed negatively; the fool is the "opposite of the wise" in every respect (Skladny, op. cit. 12). Indeed, the fool's lack of understanding is first of all "stupidity": the fool must be silent in the gate, wisdom is "too high" (24:7); a fool's folly is frequently associated with mouth/lips, i.e., with (insignificant, meaningless) intellectual expression (17:28; also 10:8, 10, 14; 14:3; as well as 12:23; 15:2, 14Q; 18:13). Moral and social aspects, however, also contribute to a fool's foolishness: the fool is hot-tempered (12:16; 27:3; 29:9; cf. 14:17, 29 and Job 5:2) and quarrelsome, lacking *kābôd* "honor" (20:3; 29:9); unlike the wise, the fool thinks he is self-sufficient and does not heed ʿ*ēṣâ* "counsel" (12:15), disregarding *mûsār* "discipline" even more (→ *ysr;* 15:5; as well as 1:7; 5:23; 7:22 without emendation; 14:3; 16:22; see 4). Although ʾ*iwwelet* may be removed from the young by means of "the rod of discipline" (22:15), the ʾ^{e}*wîl* is otherwise inseparably bound to folly (27:22).

4. Because of the inseparability of "fool" and "folly," the fateful conjunction of deed and consequence is inherent in foolishness (K. Koch, *ZTK* 52 [1955]: 2ff.; G. von Rad, *KerD* 2 [1956]: 68f.). Thus the fool's folly becomes the fool's "discipline" (contrasted with wisdom as a "source of life" 16:22; cf. 14:3). Even more: the fool's mouth is an "impending ruin" (10:14; cf. 10:8, 10); fools die because of ignorance (10:21; cf. 19:3; Job 5:2). Folly results in disaster and leads to death; it is disqualifying in a religious sense and becomes equivalent to "godlessness/sacrilege"; thus it is also associated with the death of the "impious" (→ *rš*ʿ) in 5:23 and in the later portion of Prov, and the ʾ^{e}*wîl* is related negatively to "the fear of Yahweh" in 1:7; but already in the older portion (chs. 10ff.) the "righteous" (→ *ṣdq;* 10:21; cf. 14:9) can be the opposite of the fool, as the contrast "wise-fool" generally corresponds here to the contrast "righteous-impious" (see Skladny, op. cit. 7ff.; Gemser, HAT 16, and Ringgren, ATD 16, on chs. 10ff.). In the expressly theological sense, ʾ^{e}*wîl* can also occasionally be applied to Israel in a prophetic reprimand (Jer 4:22); but the word in Hos 9:7 is an ironic citation to be understood as traditionally gnomic in character (cf. further Isa 19:11; otherwise 35:8).

ʾ*iwwelet* can also be used in the lament's confession of sin (Psa 38:6; 69:6; cf. ʾ^{e}*wīlîm* in the thanksgiving psalm, Psa 107:17, where the text is admittedly uncertain).

5. ʾ^{e}*wîl* occurs 1x and ʾ*iwwelet* 5x in the available Qumran corpus (according to Kuhn, *Konk.* 4b). The LXX translates ʾ^{e}*wîl* by 8 different words, primarily *aphrōn* (13x); ʾ*iwwelet* likewise by 8 words, primarily *aphrosynē* (8x) and *aphrōn* (3x) (concerning the LXX and NT concept of foolishness, cf. G. Bertram, "μωρός," *TDNT* 4:832–47; W. Caspari, "Über den bibl. Begriff der Torheit," *NKZ* 39 [1928]: 668–95; U. Wilckens, *Weisheit und Torheit* [1959]).

M. Sæbø

אוּלַי ʾûlay perhaps

S 194; BDB 19b; *HALOT* 1:21b; *TWOT* 46; *NIDOTTE* 218

1. The modal adv. ʾ*ûlay* "perhaps" is usually understood (GB 16a; *HAL* 21a) as a composite of the particle ʾ*ô* "or" and (dissimilated) *lōʾ* "not" (or *lû* "if only"), although the etymology is no longer determinative for usage. More transparent is the fixed usage *mî yôdēaʿ* "who knows?" for "perhaps."

The related Sem. dialects use various formations unique to each (Mid. Hebr. *semmâ;* Syr. *dalmā, kᵉbar,* and *ṭāk* < Gk. *tacha;* on Akk. *piqat, minde* [< *mīn īde* "what do I know?" *AHw* 655a], *assurri, issurre,* cf. W. von Soden, " 'Vielleicht' im Akkadischen," *Or* 18 [1949]: 385–91).

2. ʾ*ûlay* occurs 45x in the OT, primarily in narrative texts (Gen to 2 Kgs and Job 1:5, 30x, prophetic literature and Lam 3:29, 15x, lacking in Psa and the other Ketubim). In Num 22:33 ʾ*ûlay* should be emended to *lûlê* "if not."

mî yôdēaʿ means "perhaps" 4x (2 Sam 12:22; Joel 2:14; Jonah 3:9; Esth 4:14).

W. F. Albright (*JAOS* 67 [1947]: 155n.23) suspects an extrabibl. attestation of ʾ*ûlay (*ʾ*ûlê)* in l. 2 of the Ahiram inscription (cf., however, *DISO* 13).

3. In addition to ʾ*ûlay* in a preterite or present context (Job 1:5, "perhaps my sons have sinned" with pf.; Gen 43:12; Josh 9:7; 1 Kgs 18:27 in nom. clauses; Gen 18:24 and Lam 3:29 with *yēš;* Gen 18:28–32 with impf.), "perhaps" is found primarily with a view to the future (Josh 14:12 in a nom. clause, 32x with impf.). In the negated clauses in Gen 24:5, 39 and in 27:12, it expresses a fear (LXX *mēpote,* also for Gen 43:12; 1 Kgs 18:27; Job 1:5; *mē* Josh 9:7; otherwise *ei/ean [pōs], hina, hopōs, isōs*). Hos 8:7 can be subordinated concessively with "even if." All other texts contain a more or less hesitant or cautious hope (ironically in Isa 47:12bis; Jer 51:8; similarly already in 1 Kgs 18:27, "perhaps he sleeps").

4. In perhaps a dozen texts, the factor of uncertainty expressed by ʾ*ûlay* is attributed to the will of God (Num 23:3, "whether Yahweh will perhaps encounter me"; 23:27, "perhaps it pleases God"; Josh 14:12, "perhaps Yahweh is with me"; 1 Sam 6:5, "perhaps he will then take his heavy hand from you"; 14:6, "perhaps Yahweh will do something for us"; 2 Sam 16:12, "perhaps Yahweh will look upon my distress"; 2 Kgs 19:4 = Isa 37:4, "perhaps Yahweh will hear"; Jer 21:2, "perhaps Yahweh will do a miracle for us, as he has before"; Amos 5:15 [see below]; Jonah 1:6, "perhaps he will take notice of us"; Zeph 2:3 [see below]), just as in three texts with *mî yôdēaʿ* (2 Sam 12:22, "Who knows? Perhaps Yahweh will be gracious to me"; Joel 2:14, "Who knows? Perhaps he will yet repent"; Jonah 3:9, "Who knows? Perhaps God will yet repent"; the fourth text, Esth 4:14, "and who knows whether you have not come to the kingdom for such an opportunity?" refers to an irrational dispensation of fate). Nevertheless, the statement concerning Yahweh is not thereby an expression of one's uncertainty with respect to a moody despot, but a consciously humble attitude of one who takes into account the

sovereign freedom of God. This humility is also particularly true of two very reserved prophetic salvation sayings: Amos 5:15, "perhaps Yahweh will then . . . be gracious to the rest of Joseph"; and Zeph 2:3, "perhaps you will be hidden on the day of Yahweh's wrath" (cf. R. Fey, *Amos und Jesaja* [1963], 53). Wolff (*Joel*, Herm, 50) writes concerning Joel 2:14: "The 'perhaps' of hope is appropriate to the humility of one who prays [2 Sam 12:22; Lam 3:29b]; in the proclamation of the messenger it underscores the fact that the one called to return stands, for the time being, under the message of judgment [Amos 5:15; Zeph 2:3; Jonah 3:9] and has to face up to it. That the faithful and merciful God is also free in relation to his own anger ('slow to anger' ארך אפים) is the foundation of the hope expressed in the 'perhaps.' "

5. Of NT texts with *isōs* (Luke 20:13) and *tacha* (Rom 5:7; Phlm 15), only Phlm 15 is distantly reminiscent of the thought in Esth 4:14.

E. Jenni

אָוֶן *ᵓāwen* harm

S 205; BDB 19b; *HALOT* 1:22a; *TDOT* 1:140–47; *TWOT* 48a; *NIDOTTE* 224

---

1. The Hebr. noun *ᵓāwen* "harm, disaster" usually derived from a root **ᵓwn* "to be strong, powerful" (*HAL* 21b), seems to have cognates only in NWSem.

The word, which occurs only as a noun, may be formed as a segholate with a negative meaning in intentional contrast to the positive *ᵓôn* "manly vigor, vigor, wealth" (*HAL* 22a). The derivative *tᵉᵓūnîm* (Ezek 24:12) is textually very uncertain (cf. Zimmerli, *Ezek*, Herm, 1:495–96). The PNs *ᵓôn* (Num 16:1 txt?), *ᵓônām*, and *ᵓônān* (cf. *IP* 225) probably belong to the same root, but the subst. *ᵓônî* "sorrow" does not (Gen 35:18; Deut 26:14; Hos 9:4; root *ᵓny;* cf. C. Rabin, *Scripta Hierosolymitana* 8 [1961]: 386f.).

The etymology and meaning of Ug. *an* and *un*, suggested as cognates (*WUS* nos. 292, 295; *UT* nos. 238, 240), are difficult; reference should probably be made to *anm* (pl. "power"; 1.6.I.50). The relationship to Aram. *ᵓwyn*, which accompanies *mwt* "death" in *KAI* 222B.30, also remains unclear (cf. *KAI* 2:256; Fitzmyer, *Sef.* 69). *ᵓwn* in Aḥ. 160 (*DISO* 6) is also uncertain.

2. *ᵓāwen* is not a word of narrative/report language. The 80 OT examples (incl. Ezek 30:17, which should be vocalized, however, as the place-name *ᵓôn*) are found with only one exception in poetical texts, whether cultic, wisdom, prophetic, or literary (Job).

Two-thirds of the examples occur in Psa (29x), Job (15x), and Prov (10x). It occurs 24x in various prophetic books (Isa 12x), as well as in Num 23:21 and 1 Sam 15:23.

The oldest examples are 1 Sam 15:23 and Num 23:21. The texts Amos 5:5; Hos 6:8; 10:8; 12:12; Isa 1:13; 10:1; 31:2; Mic 2:1; Hab 1:3(?); 3:7; Psa 7:15; 28:3; 41:7; 59:3, 6; 101:8 are also probably pre-exilic. Some of the others are surely, and some probably, exilic or post-exilic.

The subst. ʾôn "power, wealth" occurs 10x (Gen 49:3; Deut 21:17; Isa 40:26, 29; Hos 12:4, 9; Psa 78:51; 105:36; Job 20:10; 40:16).

3. The chief meaning of the term largely reflects its etymology: destructive power (S. Mowinckel, *Psalmenstudien* [1921], 1:30ff.). Its usage presupposes a dynamistic understanding of existence (a concept of domains of action): disaster is a mighty process, and might, when it assumes a negative form, is disaster.

(a) ʾ*āwen* is connected with various types of unhealthy activities: mental processes (Isa 32:6; Psa 55:4, 11; 66:18) or intentional thoughts (ʾ*āwen* is associated with → *ḥšb* "to scheme" and derivatives in Isa 55:7; 59:7; Jer 4:14; Ezek 11:2; Mic 2:1; Psa 36:5; Prov 6:18); the utterance of words (Isa 58:9; Psa 10:7; 36:4; Job 22:15; 34:36; Prov 17:4; 19:28); deeds of every sort, e.g., cultic (Isa 1:13; Zech 10:2), political (Isa 31:2), legal (Isa 10:1; 29:20), military (Psa 56:8), etc. With respect to this sphere, cf. the characteristic association of ʾ*āwen* with → *pʿl* "to do" (23x *pōʿalê* [ptcp.] ʾ*āwen* "evildoer": Isa 31:2; Hos 6:8; Psa 5:6; 6:9; 14:4; 28:3; 36:13; 53:5; 59:3; 64:3; 92:8, 10; 94:4, 16; 101:8; 125:5; 141:4, 9; Job 31:3; 34:8, 22; Prov 10:29; 21:15; 1x pf.: Prov 30:20). The general applicability of the term to all types of unhealthy activity is frequently attested; cf. Isa 59:4–7; Psa 5:6; 7:15; 55:4, 11; 92:8, 10; Job 5:6; Prov 12:21; esp. Prov 6:12–14; Job 31:3ff.

(b) ʾ*āwen* describes not just unhealthy activities, however, but also their consequences; cf. Num 23:21; Jer 4:15; Amos 5:5; Hab 1:3; 3:7; Psa 90:10; Job 21:19; Prov 22:8; etc. These examples and texts in which the scope of the word encompasses both deed and consequence (Psa 55:4; 56:8; Job 15:35; 18:7, 12; Isa 59:4, 6b, 7; cf. also Job 4:8; Prov 22:8) indicate that the word, in accord with its dynamistic background, essentially always envisions the totality of a catastrophic process.

(c) The observations put forward under (a) and (b) indicate that ʾ*āwen* is not a material concept that refers descriptively to a specific activity or to the realm of a historical process.

As a consequence, an original meaning "magic" or "sorcery" for ʾ*āwen* (Mowinckel, op. cit.) is neither to be expected from its etymology nor recognized in the usage of the term in the OT. This circumstance does not preclude the possibility that the concept could refer to magical activities or their unhealthy consequences (cf. the relationship between Num 23:21 and 23; cf. 1 Sam 15:23; Zech 10:2; Psa 59:3, 8?; 64:3, 6f.?). This reference is present to the extent that magic was the most applicable—but not the only—means for the manipulation of the realm of phenomena. The aforesaid is true also for the ʾ*awen*-doer in Psa (see 3a). The nature of their deeds can be inferred only from the context in which the term is used, not from the term itself (cf. G. W. Anderson, "Enemies and Evildoers in the Book of Psalms," *BJRL* 48 [1965]: 18–30). Moreover, they are not only doers of iniquity but workers of calamity, as the occasional dimension of the completed effect in *pʿl* "to do" indicates. Finally, ʾ*āwen* is neither "a means to the end" (Mowinckel, op. cit. 8, 12, 15, 29, etc.) nor the end of a deed. The description of deeds, consequences, and circumstances as ʾ*āwen* indicates another function of the word.

(d) ʾ*āwen* characterizes an event negatively as a dangerous power for disaster. The word is always used as a condemnation of another's act, never as a description of one's own act. The adulteress in Prov 30:20 does not dispute the adultery, but the accusation that her adultery is a disaster-bringing act. An investigation of the semantic field confirms this analysis: Of roughly 45 close synonyms, the most prominent by far are *raʿ* "bad, evil" (17x), *rāšāʿ* "guilty" (17x), and *ʿāmāl* "hardship" (11x). Antonyms such as *mišpāṭ* "justice," *tôm* "purity," *ṣedeq* "righteousness," and *ʾemûnâ* "faithfulness" confirm the analysis.

(e) The basic meaning "power of disaster" occasionally encounters difficulty in translation because of its foreignness to modern ontology. One no longer calls a deed a "disaster" but a "misdeed," "wrong," "crime" (cf. *HAL* 21f.). Because such a phenomenon connotes invalidity, translation as "deception" or "nothing" (Isa 41:29) may occasionally be justified. Although the term can refer to an "idol cult," it may hardly be so translated (1 Sam 15:23; Zech 10:2; Hos 10:8; cf., however, Isa 66:3 → *ʾelîl* 4). Cf. V. Maag, *Text, Wortschatz und Begriffswelt des Buches Amos* (1951), 120.

4. The fact that in the OT *ʾāwen* negatively designates a disastrous phenomenon and that it is never used for an act of God (in contrast to *rāʿ* "calamity," e.g., Isa 31:2, "indeed he too is wise and brings calamity"; cf. Jer 4:6; 6:19; 11:11, 17, 23; Mic 2:3, etc.) signifies that every type of *ʾāwen-* act or *ʾāwen-* sphere is implicitly or explicitly ungodly and thereby always appears theologically disqualified. Although the life setting in which an act is disqualified (wisdom, seer or prophetic speech, prayer in the temple, etc.) and correspondingly the form of the disqualification (a wisdom saying, a prophetic judgment speech) reflect the situation, the criterion for the disqualification is the notion that that which is called *ʾāwen* is a perversion of the salvation-effecting spheres of power and thereby of the salvation-effecting divine presence.

Thus *ʾāwen* occurs: in oracular usage as an alternative to obedience to Yahweh (1 Sam 15:23; Zech 10:2); in the perversion of the meaning of the sanctuaries (Amos 5:5; Hos 10:8; Isa 1:13); in every act that stands in contrast to the salvific effects of law, justice, and righteousness (Hos 6:8; 12:12; Mic 2:1; Psa 14:4; Prov 12:21; 21:15). The *ʾāwen*-doer is finally revealed as a denier of God (Isa 32:6; Jer 4:14–18; Psa 10:7; 14:4; 53:5; 92:8, 10; Job 22:15; 34:8, 22, 36; Prov 19:28). According to Isa, the *pōʿalê ʾāwen* are people "who do not look to the holy one of Israel and do not consult Yahweh" (31:1f.) Therefore Yahweh is against them (Psa 5:6; 36:4f., 13; Prov 10:29) and commands them to quit *ʾāwen* (Job 36:10, 21). According to Job 5:6f., humanity causes *ʾāwen:* "For disaster does not arise from the dust, trouble does not sprout from the earth; rather, a human begets trouble." Cf. Job 11:11, 14 (quite to the contrary, cf. Psa 90:7–10).

The reason that the acts of evildoers are called *ʾāwen* in Psa seems to consist in the fact that either the calamity that they wish to bring upon the assailed is unjustified, or that they wish to afflict the assailed with calamity on account of the trouble which has befallen them, even though they have trusted in Yahweh's (oracle of) protection. In both cases they act against Yahweh. Thus their characterization as *pōʿalê ʾāwen* implies a specifically theological judgment.

5. The LXX renders *ʾāwen* irregularly with *anomia, kopos, mataios, ponēria, adikia,* etc. The implications of the Hebr. have been lost here. In contrast, they live on in Qumran; cf. the texts in *GCDS* 9.

R. Knierim

אוֹר *ʾôr* light

S 216; BDB 21b; *HALOT* 1:24b; *TDOT* 1:147–67; *TWOT* 52a; *NIDOTTE* 240

1. Terms related to *ʾôr* "light" are attested almost exclusively in Akk. and Can. (Akk. *ūru/urru* "light," mostly "day"; Ug. *ar, WUS* no. 368; cf. nos. 370, 372; *UT* no. 114; Phoen. *ʾr-* in PNs; cf. Harris 73; also Huffmon 169f. and Gröndahl 103), while elsewhere other roots are used for "light" (Akk. *nūru* and Arab. *nūr;* Aram. *nhr,* as in Bibl. Aram. *nᵉhôr* Dan 2:22 Q; cf. KBL 1098b; on Jew. Aram. *ʾûrtāʾ*, see *WTM* 1:46a; also *DISO* 23).

The Hebr. root yields the verb *ʾôr,* which occurs in the qal "to be light," perhaps also in the ni. (uncertain), esp., however, in the hi. (causative "to cause to be light, illuminate" and inner-causative "to light"), as well as the substs. *ʾôr* (masc., although fem. in Jer 13:16 txt? and Job 36:32 txt?) and *ʾôrâ* "light," *ʾûr* "light," and *māʾôr* "light = body of light, lamp."

Various lexicons also explain the nom. *mᵉʾûrâ* in Isa 11:8 as a derivative of this root (e.g., GB 393a, BDB 22b, Zorell 404b), yet KBL 489b (with reference to Perles, *Journal of the Society of Oriental Research* 9 [1925]: 126f.; so also Fohrer, *Jesaja*, ZBK, 1:151; cf. Kaiser, *Isa 1–12*, OTL [1983²], 253n.12) renders it "the young one," following Akk. *mūru* "young animal." *ʾûr* II (in the expression *ʾûrîm wᵉtummîm*) and III (*ʾûr kaśdîm*) are distinct from this root. But it can hardly be justified to explain *ʾôr* in Isa 18:4 and Job 37:11 in the sense of "rain" or "dew" after Arab. *ʾary* and to reckon in this case with a homonymous *ʾôr* (contra I. Eitan, *HUCA* 12/13 [1938]: 65f.).

2. Exact statistics for the noun *ʾôr* are complicated by the fact that the form may be understood in some cases also as a qal inf. (cf. *HAL* 24a, no. 3; Zorell 23b). According to Lis., the verb occurs 41x, 5x in the qal (Mandl. adds Gen 44:3 and 1 Sam 29:10 as well, although he takes 2 Sam 2:32 as a ni.), 2x in the ni. (Psa 76:5 and Job 33:10, both textually uncertain), and 34x in the hi. (15x in Psa). Its distribution is less characteristic than that of the noun *ʾôr,* which is attested 124x (pl. only in Psa 136:7) and seems to be associated primarily with wisdom.

ʾôr is attested 32x in Job, 4x in Prov, and 3x in Eccl. Of 19 occurrences in Psa (in addition to Lam 3:2), several appear in wisdom psalms or in texts influenced by wisdom (36:10; 37:6; 49:20; 89:16; 97:11; 104:2; 112:4; 119:105; 139:11).

Moreover, it is noteworthy that of 47 prophetic occurrences, 27 are in Isa, which is frequently shaped by wisdom (13x in Proto-Isa, primarily later texts; 6x in Deutero-Isa, to which, in the light of 1QIsa[ab], 53:11 must be added; and 8x in Trito-Isa, where 60:1, 3, 19f. are esp. noteworthy); in Jer 5x and in Ezek only 2x (32:7f.). In the Minor Prophets, 13 occurrences are distributed in books close in time to Isa (e.g., Amos 5:18, 20; 8:8 [txt?], 9 [cf. H. W. Wolff, *Amos the Prophet* (1973), 84]; Mic 2:1; 7:8f.), in the so-called disciples of Isa (Hab 3:4, 11; Zeph 3:5), and in the late texts Zech 14:6 (txt?), 7, although the word occurs only 1x in Hos (6:5 txt?).

In narrative literature, *ʾôr* occurs almost exclusively in the formulaic temporal designation *ʿad-ʾôr habbōqer* "until daybreak" (Judg 16:2; 1 Sam 14:36; 25:[22], 34, 36; 2 Sam 17:22; 2 Kgs 7:9; abbreviated Judg 19:26; cf. Gen 44:3; 1 Sam 29:10; Neh 8:3);

otherwise also in Exod 10:23; 2 Sam 23:4; and 6x in Gen 1:3–5, 18 P (on the impact of wisdom on Gen 1, see S. Herrmann, *TLZ* 86 [1961]: 413–24).

The unique pl. form *ʾôrîm* in Psa 136:7 "(great) lights" probably best corresponds to the *meʾôrōt* "lights, luminaries" of Gen 1. *māʾôr* occurs 19x (9x in Exod–Num in a cultic context, 5x in Gen 1 of the stars); *ʾûr* is attested 6x, 5x in the later portions of Isa. The latest form may be the fem. *ʾôrâ* (Psa 139:12; Esth 8:16).

The foregoing statistics do not include *ʾôr* in 1 Sam 25:22 (cf. *BHS*), although Isa 18:4 (in Mandl. under *ʾôr* II) and Amos 8:8 (in Lis. under *yeʾōr*) are included.

3. The basic meaning of the primary noun *ʾôr* is "light"; its proximity to "fire" (most pronounced in *ʾûr,* Isa 31:9; 44:16; 47:14; 50:11; Ezek 5:2; perhaps also Job 38:24; cf. G. R. Driver, *SVT* 3 [1955]: 91f.; *CPT* 260f.) is occasionally apparent (cf. Isa 10:17; Psa 78:14); *nēr* "lamp" also appears frequently as a par. term (Psa 119:105; Job 18:6; 29:3; Prov 6:23; 13:9; cf. Jer 25:10). "Light" in this context refers, first of all, to daylight (cf. the formulaic usage in the narrative literature [see 2], as well as in Mic 2:1; Prov 4:18). Nevertheless, *ʾôr* is not identical with sunlight, for it can also be associated with the light of the moon and stars (Isa 13:10; 30:26; Ezek 32:7), as well as with *šaḥar* "first daylight" (Isa 58:8; Job 3:9; 41:10; Dalman, *AuS* 1:601; contra L. Köhler, *ZAW* 44 [1926]: 56–59; and KBL 962: "dawn"); association with the verbs *zrḥ* and *yṣʾ* in the meaning "to rise" is not in itself "an indication that the rising of the sun is implied" (S. Aalen, *Die Begriffe "Licht" und "Finsternis" im AT, im Spätjudentum und im Rabbinismus* [1951], 39, emphasizes the Israelites' "presolar" worldview and the alternation of day and night as a basic element of the same, op. cit. 10ff.; id., *RGG* 4:357–59; id., *BHH* 2:1082; contrast W. H. Schmidt, *Die Schöpfungsgeschichte der Priesterschrift* [1964], 95–100).

The alternation of day and night itself contributed greatly to a metaphorical and symbolical usage of the word. On the one hand, the dawning morning light (often only *bōqer* "morning") became a symbol of divine deliverance in the sense of military victory (cf. Exod 14:24; 2 Kgs 19:35 = Isa 37:26; Isa 17:14; Psa 46:6), of the pronouncement of judgment in the juristic sense (Zeph 3:5; Psa 37:6; also Hos 6:5; cf. Isa 59:9), and of medical healing and assistance (Psa 56:14; cf. Isa 58:8; in Job 33:28, 30 *šaḥat* "grave" is an antonym; "to see light" = "to live" in Psa 49:20; Job 3:16, cf. v 20; so J. Hempel, "Die Lichtsymbolik im AT," *Studium Generale* 13 [1960]: 352–68; also Aalen, op. cit.; J. Ziegler, "Die Hilfe Gottes 'am Morgen,' " FS Nötscher 281–88).

ʾôr frequently attracts par. expressions in which some word for "darkness" provides the contrary notion, esp. in wisdom texts.

The most important opposite in this respect is *ḥōšek* "darkness" (Gen 1:3–5:18; Isa 5:20, 30; 9:1; 58:10; 59:9; Amos 5:18, 20; Mic 7:8; Psa 112:4; 139:11; Job 12:22, 25; 18:18; 29:3; 38:19; Eccl 2:13; Lam 3:2; the word occurs a total of 80x, 23x in Job and 14x in Isa). *ʾôr* is associated with the verb *ḥšk* qal "to be dark" (11x), hi. "to darken" (6x) in Job 18:6; Eccl. 12:2; cf. Isa 13:10; Amos 5:8; 8:9; Job 3:9. *ḥašēkâ* "darkness" (6x) occurs in Psa 139:12 alongside *ʾôrâ*, *maḥšāk* "dark place" (7x) in Isa 42:16 alongside *ʾôr* (cf. also Bibl. Aram. *ḥašōk* in Dan 2:22 alongside *nehôr*).

Other antonyms are *ʾōpel* "darkness" (9x, 6x in Job) in Job 30:26, *ʾāpēl* "dark" (1x) in Amos 5:20; *ʾᵃpēlâ* "darkness" (10x) in Isa 58:10; 59:9; *ᶜᵃrāpel* "cloudiness" (15x) in Jer 13:16; *ṣalmāwet* "darkness" (18x, 10x in Job) in Isa 9:1; Jer 13:16; Job 12:22 (on the etymology see D. W. Thomas, *JSS* 7 [1962]: 191–200; on wisdom usage, J. L. Crenshaw, *ZAW* 79 [1967]: 50).

Other terms in the semantic field are *ᶜᵃlāṭâ* "darkness" (Gen 15:17; Exod 12:6f., 12), *ᶜêpâ* "darkness" (Amos 4:13; Job 10:22), *mûᶜāp* "darkness" (Isa 8:22 [txt em], 23), *qadrût* "darkening" (Isa 50:3), *qdr* qal "to darken" (Jer 4:28, etc.; hitp. 1 Kgs 18:45; hi. Ezek 32:7f.), *ṣll* qal "to become dark" (Neh 13:19; on *ṣēl* "shadow" → *ᶜûz*), as well as *nešep* "dawn/dusk" (12x, e.g., "darkness" in Isa 59:10). On the whole word group, see Aalen, op. cit.; H. Conzelmann, "σκότος," *TDNT* 7:423–45.

Synonyms of and pars. for *ʾôr* are more ambiguous than its antonyms. In addition to *nēr* "lamp" (see above), *nōgah* "brilliance" (19x, in addition to Aram. *nᵉgah* in Dan 6:20) in Isa 60:3; Amos 5:20; Hab 3:4, 11; Prov 4:18, and *nᵉgōhâ* in Isa 59:9 may be mentioned; *ngh* qal "to light" (3x) is associated with *ʾôr* in Isa 9:1; Job 22:28, hi. "to light up" (3x) in Isa 13:10.

Cf. further → *šemeš* "sun" in Eccl 11:7, → *kᵉbôd yhwh* in Isa 60:1 (cf. v 2b with *zrḥ* "to rise" of Yahweh) and other pars. such as joy, righteousness, salvation, which involve the metaphorical and theological usage of *ʾôr* (e.g., Isa 42:6; Jer 25:10; Mic 7:9; Psa 27:1; 36:10; 97:11).

Additional semantically related terms are the verbs *ʾhl* hi. "to shine" (Job 25:5), *hll* hi. "(to cause) to shine" (Isa 13:10; Job 29:3; 31:26; 41:10), *zhr* hi. "to shine" (Dan 12:3), *zrḥ* "to rise, radiate" (18x, → *šemeš*), *zrq* qal "to be light" (Hos 7:9), *ṣhl* hi. "to cause to shine" (Psa 104:15), the substs. *zōhar* "brightness" (Ezek 8:2; Dan 12:3), *yipᶜâ* "brilliance" (Ezek 28:7, 17), *nēṣaḥ* "brightness" (Lam 3:18; 1 Chron 29:11), and the adjs. *bāhîr* "brilliant(?)" (Job 37:21; cf. Wagner no. 35), *ṣaḥ* and *ṣāḥîaḥ* "brilliant" (Isa 32:4; Song Sol 5:10 and Ezek 24:7f.; 26:4, 14, resp.; cf. also J. A. Soggin, *ZAW* 77 [1965]: 83–86); → *ypᶜ* hi.

nhr qal "to shine" (Isa 60:5; Jer 31:12; Psa 34:6) and *nᵉhārâ* "(day)light" (Job 3:4) are Aramaisms (Wagner nos. 184f.). The Bibl. Aram. word for "brilliance" is *zîw* (Dan 2:31; 4:33).

4. The usual distinction between literal and metaphorical usage of the word *ʾôr* is hardly sufficient to reveal its theological profile, which encompasses both of these. A classification of usages in (a) wisdom cosmological thought and (b) cultic salvation thought may be more appropriate; in addition, usages in (c) eschatological proclamation and (d) statements that relate specifically to God may be investigated separately.

(a) In wisdom concepts of order, the light of God is the first "good" work of creation (Gen 1:3f.). Gen 1 makes no such statement of darkness; it remains theologically ambivalent, for, despite its positive role as night in God's creation, resulting from God's division and naming (Gen 1:4f.; cf. Westermann, *Gen*, CC, 1:113–15) or separation between light and darkness (Job 26:10; cf. 38:19), darkness is the time of crime (Job 24:13ff.), it symbolizes distress and judgment, and it will be eliminated in the eschaton (see c). Light stands in tension, then, with darkness (cf. Aalen, op. cit. 16f.), which can be maintained only by the "pancausality" and might of God (cf. Isa 45:7, "I form light and create darkness"; see d).

As light and darkness are related to one another, so (1) for the individual, are life and death (cf. Job 3:4, 9, 16, 20f. and, in the Elihu speech, 33:28, 30; also Eccl 12:2ff.); (2) for society, are the "righteous" and the "evildoer" (Job 12:25; 18:5f., 18; 22:28; 38:15; Prov 4:18; 13:9; also Psa 97:11; 112:4), concerning which "righteousness as world order" is the issue (cf. H. H. Schmid, *Gerechtigkeit als Weltordnung* [1968]) and the theodicy question arises (cf. Job 24); (3) for cognition (but not without a religio-ethical character), are wisdom and folly (Eccl 2:13; → *ʾᵉwîl*). When the established order is disturbed, Isaiah raises his cry of woe (Isa 5:20).

(b) This pair of opposites also refers to the salvation and judgment of God. In cultic salvation thought, the light of God('s countenance) expresses his gracious attention, as apparent in the priestly blessing in Num 6:25 (*ʾôr* hi.) with older material (in a later framework; cf. Noth, *Num*, OTL, 58; C. Westermann, *Blessing in the Bible and the Life of the Church* [1978], 42–45), often later in Psa (cf. 36:10; otherwise in expressions of confidence, 4:7; 27:1; in the thanksgiving hymn in 56:14 and in the lament 43:3, as well as in the wisdom exhortation in 37:6; cf. 89:16; A. M. Gierlich, *Der Lichtgedanke in den Psalmen* [1940]), and also as echoed in the prophetic literature (Isa 2:5).

Important for salvation history are Psa 78:14, where *ʾôr* is associated with the desert wandering (cf. Exod 13:21f.; Psa 105:39), and Psa 44:4, where it is associated with the conquest. *ʾôr* is also associated with the king who brings salvation (2 Sam 23:4; Prov 16:15).

(c) On the one hand, the prophetic proclamation of imminent judgment transforms the light of salvation into the darkness of approaching catastrophe (Amos 5:18, 20; Isa 13:10; on the day of Yahweh see F. C. Fensham, *ZAW* 75 [1963]: 170f.; elsewhere Amos 8:9; Isa 5:30; Jer 4:23; 25:10; Ezek 32:7f.; Jer 13:16 in the context of prophetic warnings); Lam 3:2 exemplifies a lament in the aftermath of a catastrophe.

On the other hand, the prophetic salvation-eschatology transforms the darkness of distress into the light of dawning salvation (Isa 8:23–9:1; 10:17; 42:16; 58:8, 10; Mic 7:8f.). Salvation will be valid not only for Israel but also for the nations (Isa 51:4); it will be appropriated to them through a special mediator of salvation (Isa 42:6; 49:6).

Later eschatology uniquely presents the coming salvation experience in relationship to an earlier order (cf. Jer 31:35, where the certainty of salvation is emphasized by the certainty of the order of creation, embodying a new cooperation of cosmological thought and salvation thought, also a characteristic of Deutero-Isa; see von Rad, "Theological Problem of the OT Doctrine of Creation," *PHOE* 131–43), in supersession of the extant order (cf. Isa 30:26; as well as 10:17), or in suspension of the created order (Isa 60:19f.; Zech 14:6f.; cf. also Hab 3:11; more texts in Aalen, op. cit. 20ff.; cf. H.-J. Kraus, *ZAW* 78 [1966]: 317–32). In Zech 14:6f., too, the interest of the post-exilic community has shifted, though not so much to a direct suspension of the created order as to the person of God and his majestic final theophany (cf. M. Sæbø, *Sacharja, 9–14* [1969], 298–300).

(d) Because light—as well as the "luminosities" (*mᵉʾōrōt* Gen 1:14ff.; Psa 136:7–9)—is God's creation, it is completely subordinate to him. Light is an aspect not of his being but of his manner of appearance, e.g., in theophany (cf. Isa 60:1ff.; Hab 3:4, 11; also Psa 44:4; cf. Aalen, op. cit. 73ff.; J. Jeremias,

Theophanie [1965], 24ff., etc.; also F. Schnutenhaus, *ZAW* 76 [1964]: 1–22). God surrounds himself with light not only in his coming but also in his heavenly abode (Psa 104:2; one should not conceive of God in solar categories either here or in Ezek 1 or 43; so Aalen, op. cit. 82ff., contra J. Morgenstern, et al.). Just as light "clothes" (→ *lbš*) him, so also is it an attribute of his revealed word and law (Psa 119:105; Prov 6:23). He is the exalted ruler over his creation (Psa 139:11f.; Job 12:22; 28:11); consequently, he alone knows his origins (Job 38:19f.). "All shining stars" praise him (Psa 148:2).

Theophoric PNs formed with words for "light," such as *ᵓûrîᵓēl, ᵓûrîyâ(hû), ᵓᵃbînēr, ᵓabnēr, nērîyâ(hû)*, and probably also the majority of extrabibl. names of this type (Akk.: Stamm, *AN* index s.v. *nūru, namāru*, etc.; Huffmon 169f., 237, 243; Palm.: A. Caquot, *Syria* 39 [1962]: 243 with bibliog.), should be understood metaphorically (light = fortune, salvation; *IP* 167–69), not as witnesses to astral religion.

Thus *ᵓôr* "light" is a very important theological concept that signifies first a work of creation and a mode of God's appearance. From this dual conceptual center, it develops in several directions, particularly with respect to God's salvation—first for Israel and then also for the nations.

5. The LXX renders *ᵓôr* in various ways, most of which occur only once; *phōs* clearly dominates (cf. Gierlich, op. cit. 3, etc.). On early Jewish and rabbinic material, cf. Aalen, op. cit. 96ff., 237ff. In the Qumran documents the usage of *ᵓôr* (according to Kuhn, *Konk.* 4f., the subst. occurs 42x, the verb 17x; cf. *GCDS* 9, 10) agrees largely with the OT (cf. F. Nötscher, *Zur theol. Terminologie der Qumran-Texte* [1956], 76ff.; H. W. Huppenbauer, *Der Mensch zwischen zwei Welten* [1959], 26ff., 71, 80ff.); although the contrast between "light" and "darkness" (socially as well) is more accentuated.

In distinction from the OT and the Qumran corpus, in the NT light refers to the being of God, esp. in Johannine theology (cf. 1 John 1:5; also John 1:1–18; R. Bultmann, *John* [1971], 40ff.; P. Humbert, "Le thème vétérotestamentaire de la lumière," *RTP* 99 [1966]: 1–6).

M. Sæbø

אוֹת *ᵓôt* sign

S 226; BDB 16b; *HALOT* 1:26a; *TDOT* 1:167–88; *TWOT* 41b; *NIDOTTE* 253

---

1. *ᵓôt* occurs in NWSem. (in OT times only in Hebr. and Bibl. Aram. *ᵓāt*) and in Arab.; apparently Akk. *ittu*, whose range of meaning resembles that of the NWSem.-Arab. word, is also related to *ᵓôt* (*AHw* 406; *CAD* I:304–10). The origin is unknown; one may postulate a root *ᵓwy*.

The semantic range of the word in these languages is very broad and encompasses the profane and the religious spheres (on the Arab. see Lane 1:135; on the Syr. see Payne-Smith 412f.). In a Neo-Pun. inscription, *ᵓt* apparently means "memorial" (*KAI* no. 141.4).

2. *ʾôt* occurs in Hebr. 79x, 44x sg. and 35x pl. (Pentateuch 39x, in all narrative strands; with the exception of Job 21:29, the term does not appear in wisdom literature; occurrences are equally distributed in narrative, prophecy, and psalmody; cf. the chronological and topical statistics in C. A. Keller, *Das Wort OTH als "Offenbarungszeichen Gottes"* [1946], 7f.), in addition to 3x in Aram. (Dan 3:32f.; 6:28).

ʾôt should also be read in Num 15:39 and 1 Sam 10:1 (LXX); Joel 2:23 should perhaps be emended (W. Rudolph, FS Baumgartner 249).

ʾôt occurs outside the Bible shortly before the exile in Lachish Letter IV (*KAI* no. 194.10ff.). The text reads (*ANET* 322b): "And let (my lord) know that we are watching for the signals (*mśʾt*, a technical term; cf. Judg 20:38, 40; Jer 6:1) of Lachish, according to all the indications (*ʾtt*) which my lord hath given; for we cannot see Azekah (or, no sign [*ʾt*] from Azeqah is visible)." The translation of the last line is admittedly disputed (for bibliog. see *DISO* 29). *ʾtt* here apparently means "military signals." Similarly, the Arab. equivalent, *ʾāyat*, can have this meaning, otherwise unattested in Hebr. (Lane 1:135).

3. The OT usage of the term *ʾôt* may not be limited a priori to specific areas of life (contra Keller, op. cit., 66ff.; cf. B. O. Long, *Problem of Etiological Narrative in the OT* [1968], 65–86). The basic meaning is "sign" in the senses of "identification" and "indication."

In a very primitive usage of the word, the "sign of Cain" in Gen 4:15 describes a tribal sign tattooed on the forehead that identifies one belonging to the Kenites and to their tribal obligations (sevenfold blood retaliation!). At the hands of the Yahwist, the sign undergoes a theological interpretation in the total context of the primeval history.

The term *ṭôṭāpōt* "mark" (3x par. to *ʾôt*) also apparently had a similar original meaning. The Dtr expression "an *ʾôt* on the hand and *ṭôṭāpōt* between the eyes" (Exod 13:16; Deut 6:8; 11:18; in Exod 13:9 with *zikkārôn* "memorial" instead of *ṭôṭāpōt*, → *zkr*) is surely meant as a spiritualization, but one may trace it back to the concept of a tattoo (cf. further Noth, *Exod*, OTL, 101, "jewelled ornaments. . . . prophylactic amulets").

In the broader development of the term, *ʾôt* also signifies "field signal" in profane contexts (Num 2:2, taken up by the War Scroll from Qumran; apparently also in Psa 74:4; cf. Kraus, *Psa*, CC, 2:95, 98).

degel "field signal, banner > tribal division" (Num 1:52; 2:2–34; 10:14–25; 13x) is associated with the *ʾôt* of Num 2:2; Song Sol 2:4 still seems to offer the basic meaning "sign, flag" or something similar (cf. Rudolph, KAT 17/2, 130f.; Gerleman, BK 18, 117f.); the Elephantine papyri (*DISO* 55; *BMAP* 41f.) and the War Scroll from Qumran (Yadin 38–64) attest only the meaning "military division."

Semantically related terms in military contexts include: *nēs* "standard, signal" (21x, in prophetic literature except for Exod 17:15; Num 21:8f.; 26:10; Psa 60:6; cf. *BRL* 160f.), which acquires the general meaning "warning signal" in Num 26:10 in reference to Korah's deceased band, and *tōren* "mast, signal pole" (Isa 30:17; 33:23; Ezek 27:5, in each case par. to *nēs*).

Job 21:29 and Ezek 14:8 (par. to *māšāl* "proverb") suggest the meaning "memorable occurrence" in the broadest sense; Josh 2:12, "security" (a late gloss according to Noth, HAT 7, 24f.); and Jer 10:2 and Isa 44:25, "astrological portent."

4. (a) The Yahwist already uses *ʾôt* as a religious term too; probably following the tradition, he applies it to the Egypt narrative (Exod 8:19; 10:1f.). The sign consists of a mighty deed through which Yahweh legitimizes the mission of Moses. Occurrences in Exod 3:12 and 4:17, 30 belong to E. The last two texts (as well as the occurrences of *ʾôt* in Exod 4:8f., 28; Num 14:11, which belong to the final redaction) conform to Yahwistic usage; Exod 3:12 has a somewhat different sense: Moses himself is assured of his divine commission (the actual content of the *ʾôt* has been lost; cf. Noth, *Exod*, OTL, 42f.). The text has close affinity with Judg 6:17ff., where the commission of the charismatic Gideon is authenticated to him. *ʾôt* confirms the commission of the designated charismatic.

Similarly, *ʾôt* can mean (even) the (noncultic) oracular sign (1 Sam 14:10; here the content of the *ʾôt* is the enemies' behavior). Cultic oracles—surely one of the duties of the cult prophet—may be echoed in Psa 74:9; 86:17.

nḥš (also Aram. and Arab.; W. von Soden, *WZKM* 53 [1956]: 157; O. Eissfeldt, *JBL* 82 [1963]: 195–200), pi. "to seek an omen, give an oracle; take as a sign" (Gen 44:5, 15; 1 Kgs 20:33; "to learn through a sign" Gen 30:27; contra J. Sperber, *OLZ* 16 [1913]: 389; H. Torczyner, *OLZ* 20 [1917]: 10ff.; subst. *naḥaš* "omen," Num 23:23; 24:1) and more generally "to foretell" (prohibited in Israel: Lev 19:26; Deut 18:10; 2 Kgs 17:17; 21:6; 2 Chron 33:6), occurs as specialized vocabulary for dealing with (good or evil) omens.*

A somewhat altered usage appears in an early prophetic context. The *ʾôt* legitimizes the prophetic word; it arrives, however, only in the future and is predicted by the prophet (formulated generally in Deut 13:2f., with the characteristic verb → *bôʾ* "to arrive," which also appears in 1 Sam 2:34; 10:[1], 7, 9; cf. further 2 Kgs 19:29; 20:8f. = Isa 37:20; 38:7, 22; Jer 44:29; somewhat more subtly in Isa 7:11, 14). The content of the *ʾôt* in these cases bears no direct relationship to the prophetic message. To some extent the sign is the prophet's technical device for gaining recognition and belief from his hearers (→ *ydʿ* together with *ʾôt*, Exod 10:2; Deut 4:35; 11:2f., etc.; cf. Keller, op. cit. 58f.; → *ʾmn* hi. Exod 4:30; Num 14:11; cf. Isa 7:9ff.).

ʾôt can also signify a "marker" or "memorial" pointing to a past saving act of God (Josh 4:6; similarly a few texts in P; see below) or which envisions a future, eschatological phase of divine history (in texts approaching apocalyptic thought forms, Isa 19:20; 55:13; 66:19).

(b) The term *ʾôt* acquires an essentially theological meaning in classical prophecy, in Dtr theology, and in the P document.

In classical prophecy *ʾôt* or *môpēt* can refer to "symbolic acts" (both terms in Isa 8:18 and 20:3; *ʾôt* alone in Ezek 4:3; *môpēt* in Ezek 12:6, 11; 24:24, 27; Zech 3:8). In fact, the other symbolic acts reported in the OT also belong here (cf. G. Fohrer, *ZAW* 64 [1952]: 101–20; id., *Die prophetischen Zeichenhandlungen* [1953]). In contrast to the prophetic signs of confirmation, the content of the *ʾôt* here relates materially to the message of the prophet. It enacts a future event, which is actualized and realized through the symbolic act itself. The "sign" functions, then, in analogy to the prophetic word (cf. Fohrer, *Zeichenhandlungen* 85ff.; von Rad, *Theol.* 2:91–94).

The Deuteronomist summarizes the entire Egyptian experience in a formula incl. the expression *ʾōtôt ûmôpᵉtîm* (together with "leading out with a strong hand and an outstretched arm," Deut 4:34; 6:22; 7:19; 11:2f.; 26:8; 29:2; 34:11; on the whole formula see B. S. Childs, "Deuteronomic Formulae of the Exodus Traditions," FS Baumgartner 30–39). Not only are the "plagues" described as *ʾôt* but so is the whole divine history in Egypt, i.e., the basic datum of Dtr theology; *ʾôt* is, then, the form of Yahweh's revelation that is to be understood in the present. Therefore the question also arises of Israel's capability of recognizing and understanding the *ʾōtôt* (Deut 29:2ff.). The other texts that speak of *ʾōtôt* and *môpᵉtîm* in Egypt (Jer 32:20f.; Psa 78:43; 105:27; 135:9; Neh 9:10; also Exod 7:3 P; only *ʾōtôt* in Num 14:22; Josh 24:17; and, with clear reference to Egypt, Psa 65:9) are dependent upon the Deuteronomist.

The term *ʾôt* is used Deuteronomically in other contexts (on Deut 13:2f., see 4a). According to Exod 13:9, 16, the Passover haggadah is *ʾôt* and *zikkārôn* or *ṭôṭāpōt* (see 3) for Israel; according to Deut 6:8, it is the confession of faith *(šᵉmaᶜ);* according to 11:18, it is the entire Dtn proclamation. The *ʾôt* here too, then, actualizes past salvation history. According to Deut 28:46, promised blessing and threatened curse are "signs" for Israel; the future may also be deduced through the *ʾôt* of the present.

The P document applies *ʾôt* in great breadth: for the "signs and wonders" in Egypt (Exod 7:3), for some memorials of Israel's cultic history (Num 15:39 txt em "mark"; 17:3 "warning sign"; 17:25 "reminder"); the blood of the Passover in Exod 12:13 is a "protective sign"; the Sabbath is a sign of the relationship between Yahweh and Israel (Exod 31:13, 17; cf. indeed Ezek 20:12). The terminology of covenant making also appropriates the term: the Abrahamic and Noachic covenants have their signs (Gen 9:12f., 17, rainbow; 17:11, circumcision). Finally, the stars too are *ʾōtōt* (Gen 1:14, alongside *môᶜᵃdîm* "seasons"; → *yᶜd*).

Here *ʾôt* signifies the appearance of a comprehensive divine order encompassing nature and time, taking shape in Israel's history, and finally reaching completion in the cult.

The term *môpēt* (36x) may not be explained etymologically (Keller, op. cit. 60f., 115; a suspected occurrence in a Phoen. inscription from Cyprus is ambiguous; cf. *KAI* no. 30.1). It first occurs in Isa 8:18 and 20:3, already par. to *ʾôt* as in Dtr usage and a few dependent texts (Exod 7:3 P; Deut 4:34; 6:22; 7:19; 13:2f.; 26:8; 28:46; 29:2; 34:11; Jer 32:20f.; Psa 78:43; 105:27; 135:9; Neh 9:10; a total of 18x, in addition to the Aram.: Dan 3:32f.; 6:28 *ʾātîn wᵉtimhîn* "signs and wonders"). The usage of *môpēt* corresponds essentially to that of *ʾôt*, later perhaps more strongly emphasizing the miraculous (par. to *niplāʾôt* Psa 105:5 = 1 Chron 16:12, → *plʾ*): mighty deeds in Egypt (Exod 4:21 redactional; 7:3, 9 and 11:9f. P; Deut 4:34; 6:22; 7:19; 26:8; 29:2; 34:11; Jer 32:20f.; Psa 78:43; 105:27; 135:9; Neh 9:10), divine terrors or wonders in general (Deut 28:46; Joel 3:3; Psa 71:7 = 1 Chron 16:12), prophetic signs of confirmation (Deut 13:2f.; 1 Kgs 13:3bis, 5; 2 Chron 32:24, 31), prophetic symbolic acts (Isa 8:18; 20:3; Ezek 4:3; 12:6, 11; 24:24, 27; Zech 3:8).*

5. Early Judaism largely continues OT usage (Qumran: see 3; rabbinic literature employs new meanings to a degree and replaces *ʾôt* with *sîmān*, probably < Gk. *sēmeion*). On the NT, cf. K. H. Rengstorf, "σημεῖον," *TDNT* 7:200–69 (209–19 also treat *ʾôt* in the OT extensively).

F. Stolz

אֹזֶן ʾōzen ear

S 241; BDB 23b; *HALOT* 1:27b; *TWOT* 57a; *NIDOTTE* 265

1. The subst. *ʾōzen* "ear" is common Sem. (**ʾuḏn-; HAL* 27a), as well as Eg. *ydn* (Erman-Grapow 1:154; replaced by *mśḏr* "place upon which one sleeps"; cf. W. Helck, *ZÄS* 80 [1955]: 144f.; W. C. Till, "Zum Sprachtabu im Ägyptischen," *Ägyptolog. Studien*, ed. O. Firchow [1955], 327, 335). The verb *ʾzn* hi. "to act with the ears, hear" is a denominative from the fem. subst. anatomical term (GKC §53g).

The name *ʾᵃzanyâ* (Neh 10:10) is based on the qal, *yaʾᵃzanyāhû* (2 Kgs 25:23; Jer 40:8; Ezek 8:11; *yaʾᵃzanyâ* Jer 35:3; Ezek 11:1; abbreviated *yᵉzanyâ[hû]* Jer 40:8; 42:1) is based on the hi., the only form of the verb that occurs otherwise (*IP* 36, 198; the name *yʾznyhw* occurs extrabibl. on a seal [W. F. Badè, *ZAW* 51 (1933): 150–56; *EEA* 70], and in Lachish letter 1:2f. [*TGI*¹ no. 34]; also *yʾznyh* and *yznʾl* occur on seals [Diringer nos. 21, 28]; on the name forms from Elephantine, cf. *IP* 198; L. Delekat, *VT* 8 [1958]: 251f.).

2. The OT contains the subst. 187x, the verb 41x (Psa 15x) in a normal distribution. The subst. occurs largely in the dual (108x, 80x with *bᵉ*), the verb frequently in the impv. (30x).

3. *ʾōzen* rarely describes the human body part without reference to hearing.

The following customs should be mentioned: the wearing of earrings (Gen 35:4; Exod 32:2f.; Ezek 16:12; *BRL* 398–402); the piercing of the ear as a mark of slaves (Exod 21:6; Deut 15:17; J. Horst, *TDNT* 5:546; contra de Vaux 1:84); rituals for the consecration of priests and the cleansing of the leper (*tᵉnûk ʾōzen* "earlobe" in Exod 29:20bis; Lev 8:23f.; 14:14, 17, 25, 28 P; Elliger, HAT 4, 119); amputation of the ears as a form of punishment by mutilation (Ezek 23:25; Zimmerli, *Ezek*, Herm, 1:489). Amos 3:12 (*bᵉdal ʾōzen* "earlobe" of an animal of the flock) and Prov 26:7 (a dog) mention the ears of animals.

Otherwise the ear is always the organ of hearing: it hears (→ *šmʿ*, Ezek 24:26; Psa 92:12; Job 13:1; etc.); it pays attention (→ *qšb* hi., Psa 10:17; Neh 1:6, 11; etc.). With verbs of speaking, esp. with *dbr* pi. (e.g., Gen 20:8) and *qrʾ* (e.g., Exod 24:7) the hearers are often introduced with *bᵉʾōzen*. Thus the hearers are frequently characterized as witnesses (Gen 23:10, 13, 16). *bᵉʾōzen* (instrumental *bᵉ*) also has this function following *šmʿ* (Jer 26:11; 2 Sam 7:22; Psa 44:2). In contrast, *šᵉmaʿ ʾōzen* means "hearsay" (Psa 18:45; Job 42:5). The communication of important matters (frequently of life-and-death significance) is described by the usage → *glh ʾoznô* "to uncover his ear" (1 Sam 20:2, 12f.; 22:8bis, 17; the author of the story of David's rise to power preferred this expression; also Ruth 4:4; with Yahweh as subj., see 4; → *ʿayin*). The wisdom teacher can summon to hear with the expression *nṭh* hi. *ʾōzen* "to bow the ear" (Psa 78:1; Prov 4:20; 5:1, 13; 22:17; similarly Isa 55:3; Psa 45:11; 49:5; see also 4).

Series of various body parts emphasize their appropriate functions: mostly eyes-ears (2 Kgs 19:16 = Isa 37:17; Isa 11:3; 30:20f.; 35:5; 43:8; Jer 5:21; Ezek 8:18; 12:2; Psa 34:16;

92:12; 94:9; Job 13:1; 29:11; 42:5; Prov 20:12; Eccl 1:8; Dan 9:18; Neh 1:6; 2 Chron 6:40; 7:15), hands-eyes-ears (Isa 33:14), heart-ears (Jer 11:8; Ezek 3:10; Prov 2:2; 18:15; 22:17; 23:12), heart-eyes-ears (Deut 29:3; Isa 6:10; 32:3; Ezek 40:4; 44:5), ear-palate (Job 12:11; 34:3), ear-tongue (Isa 50:4f.), hands-neck-nose-ears-head (Ezek 16:11f.), mouth-eyes-ears-nose-hands-feet-throat (Psa 115:5ff.; cf. 135:16ff.). The talion formula (Exod 21:23ff.; Lev 24:19f.) omits the ear.

Terms for the inability and unwillingness to hear include the following: → *ḥrš* qal "to be deaf" (Mic 7:16; Psa 28:1; 35:22; 39:13; 50:3; 83:2; 109:1), *ḥērēš* "deaf" (Exod 4:11; Lev 19:14; Psa 38:14; 58:5; metaphorically, Isa 29:18; 35:5; 42:18f.; 43:8); *ʾṭm* "to stop up" (Isa 33:15; Psa 58:5; Prov 21:13), *kbd* hi. "to make dull" (Isa 6:10; Zech 7:11), *ʿlm* hi. "to conceal" (Lam 3:56).*

The verb *ʾzn* hi. occurs in the impv. as a call to hear, introducing songs (Deut 32:1; Judg 5:3; Gen 4:23), wisdom sayings (Isa 28:23; Psa 49:2; 78:1), legal teachings (Job 33:1; 34:2, 16; 37:14), and prophetic words (Isa 1:2, 10; 32:9; 51:4; Jer 13:15; Hos 5:1; Joel 1:2; cf. Num 23:18). Most often *šmʿ* or *qšb* hi. stands in parallelismus membrorum (Wolff, *Hos*, Herm, 97, "a summons to receive instruction," contra L. Köhler, *Deuterojesaja stilkritisch untersucht* [1923], 112, "a summons of two witnesses"; I. von Loewenclau, *EvT* 26 [1966]: 296ff.). *dᵉbārîm* are usually the content of the audition (words or events, Gen 20:8; 44:18). On the preps. following *ʾzn* hi., see *HAL* 27a.

In addition to hearing, *ʾōzen* is the organ of recognition and understanding, particularly in wisdom (Job 12:11; 13:1; 34:3; Prov 2:2; 5:1, 13; 18:15; 22:17; 23:12; Isa 32:3). It competes here with the heart (cf. Ch. Kayatz, *Studien zu Proverbien 1–9* [1966], 43–47).

On the Akk. *uznu* "ear > discernment" and *ḫasīsu* "ear, hearing < understanding, wisdom" (*AHw* 330b; *CAD* Ḫ:126f.; on *ḫasāsu* "to recollect"), cf. *HAL* 27b as well as Dhorme 89f.

4. Yahweh's ears are mentioned unabashedly (Num 11:1, 18; 14:28; 1 Sam 8:21, etc.; the ears of the angels, 1QM 10:11; on anthropomorphisms see Köhler, *Theol.* 22–25). The request to be heard, with the formula "to bend your ear to me," is typical of individual laments (*nṭh* hi.: Psa 17:6; 31:3; 71:2; 86:1; 88:3; 102:3; 2 Kgs 19:16 = Isa 37:17; cf. Dan 9:18; in praise, Psa 116:2), just as is the impv. of *ʾzn* hi. together with *šmʿ* and *qšb* hi. (Psa 5:2; 17:1; 39:13; 54:4; 55:2; 86:6; 140:7; 141:1; 143:1; in a communal lament, 80:2; in a petition, 84:9). Yahweh hears people (Psa 94:9; Isa 59:1; but Job 9:16) and their insolence also rises to his ears (2 Kgs 19:28 = Isa 37:29). The idols do not hear (Psa 115:6; 135:17; cf. Kraus, *Psa*, CC, 2:380; Zimmerli, *Ezek*, Herm, 1:269f.; contra Weiser, ATD 20, 54).

Yahweh hollows out, plants, and creates the human ear (Psa 40:7; 94:9; Prov 20:12; Deut 29:3; cf. Gen 2:7). He "uncovers the ear" of a person (1 Sam 9:15; 2 Sam 7:27 = 1 Chron 17:25; Job 33:16; 36:10, 15; 1QH 1:21, etc.; cf. Isa 22:14), he awakens (*ʿûr* hi.) and opens *(ptḥ)* the ear of the prophet (Isa 50:4f.; cf. Ezek 9:1; Isa 5:9; Job 4:12). In his commission the prophet is commanded to speak "in the ears" (Exod 11:2; Jer 2:2; 26:15; Deut 31:11; Judg 7:3). The saying about "ringing in the ears" (*ṣll* in 1 Sam 3:11; 2 Kgs 21:12; Jer 19:3) bears a Dtr stamp. Israel hears Yahweh's word and commandments (Exod 24:7; 15:26; 2 Kgs 23:2; Isa 1:10, etc.) Dtn parenesis does not use the stem *ʾzn*

(→ *šmʿ*). Israel closes itself to Yahweh's word; see the formula in the Jer C layer: "They did not hear and they did not bow their ear (and they strayed)" (Jer 7:24, 26; 11:8; 17:23; 25:4; 34:14; 35:15; 44:5; cf. the Chr's negated *ʾzn* hi. in Neh 9:30; 2 Chron 24:19). Although the people have ears, they do not hear (Jer 5:21; Isa 43:8; Ezek 12:2); their ear has a foreskin (Jer 6:10; cf. H.-J. Hermisson, *Sprache und Ritus im altisr. Kult* [1965], 71); Yahweh himself deafens it (Isa 6:9f.; Deut 29:3; cf. von Rad, *Theol.* 2:147ff.). But in the end time the ears of the deaf will be opened *(pqḥ* ni. in Isa 35:5; O. Procksch, *Jesaja*, KAT, 1:435; → *ʿayin).*

5. Qumran follows the theological usage of the OT. On Philo, Josephus, the rabbis, and the NT, see G. Kittel, "ἀκούω," *TDNT* 1:216–25; J. Horst, "οὖς," *TDNT* 5:543–59.

Cf. the apertio aurium of the early church's baptismal liturgy (*RGG* 6:651f.); on Augustine see U. Duchrow, *Sprachverständnis und biblisches Hören bei Augustin* (1965), with bibliog.

G. Liedke

אָח *ʾāḥ* brother

S 251; BDB 26a; *HALOT* 1:29a; *TDOT* 1:188–93; *TWOT* 62a; *NIDOTTE* 278

אָחוֹת *ʾāḥôt* **sister**

S 269; BDB 27b; *HALOT* 1:31b; *TDOT* 1:188–93; *TWOT* 62c; *NIDOTTE* 295

---

1. **ʾaḫ-* "brother" and **ʾaḫat-* "sister" are (like → *ʾāb* "father") common Sem. (Berg., *Intro.* 210) and commonly occur in all language branches in an expanded meaning (see 3b).

The following derive from *ʾāḥ* in the OT: the abstract *ʾaḥᵃwâ* "brotherhood" (between Judah and Israel, Zech 11:14), a diminutive *ʾaḥyān* "little brother" (only as a PN, 1 Chron 7:19; Stamm, *HEN* 422), and perhaps a denominative verb *ʾḥh* ni. "to fraternize" (*nāḥâ* < *neʾᵉḥâ* in Isa 7:2; cf. *HAL* 30a; contra Eissfeldt, *KS* [1966], 3:124–27; L. Delekat, *VT* 8 [1958]: 237–40; H. Donner, *SVT* 11 [1964]: 8); cf. Akk. *aḫû* Gt "to fraternize with one another" (*atḫû* "companion, associate"), Št "to pair up, come together" (*šutāḫû* "standing together in pairs"), N "to fraternize" (*AHw* 22b).

2. *ʾāḥ* "brother" occurs 629x (296x sg. and 333x pl., in addition to 1x Aram. pl. in Ezra 7:18), most frequently in the family narratives of Gen (178x, 100x sg.); 1 Chron (99x, 79x pl., often in lists such as 1 Chron 25:10–31) and Deut (48x), where the term is strongly accentuated (see 4c), follow.

ʾāḥôt "sister" occurs 114x (9x pl.), concentrated in Gen (24x), 2 Sam 13, and Ezek 16 and 23.

3. (a) The starting point is the description of a biological relationship (with respect to full- or stepbrothers, e.g., 2 Sam 13:4; cf. 2 Sam 3:2f.; *ILC* 1–2:58ff.), which is often further specified in order to distinguish it from a broader term: Gen 37:27, "our brothers and our flesh"; 42:13, 32, "brothers, sons of one man/our father"; Deut 13:7, "your brother, the son of your mother"; similarly,

Judg 8:19 and in parallelismus membrorum Gen 27:29; Psa 50:20; 69:9; Song Sol 8:1 (already so in Ug.: *KTU* 1.14.I.8f., "seven brothers" par. to "eight sons of one mother"; 1.6.VI.10f., 14f.).

A more limited meaning occurs both in the restriction of meaning through related concepts in the word field (e.g., in the listing of the closest blood relatives in Lev 21:2f.; 25:48f.; Num 6:7; Ezek 44:25) and in composite descriptions of relationship:

(1) "father's brother" (Lev 18:14, juristically paraphrasing [W. Kornfeld, *Studien zum Heiligkeitsgesetz* (1952), 103] *dôd*, the conventional word for "uncle" in Lev 10:4; 20:20; 25:49bis; Num 36:11; 1 Sam 10:14–16; 14:50; 2 Kgs 24:17; Jer 32:7–9, 12; Amos 6:10; 1 Chron 27:32; Esth 2:7, 15; cf. *HAL* 206b with bibliog. and Fitzmyer, *Gen.Ap.* 135; on → *ʿam* in the meaning "uncle," replaced in Hebr. by *dôd*, cf. L. Rost, FS Procksch 143f. (= *KC* 90f.); J. J. Stamm, *ArOr* 17 [1949]: 379–82; id., *SVT* 7 [1960]: 165–83; id., *HEN* 418f., 422; Huffmon 196f.);

(2) "father's sister" (Lev 18:12; 20:19; cf. *dōdâ* "father's sister" in Exod 6:20, but in Lev 18:14 and 20:20 "wife of father's brother");

(3) "mother's brother" (Gen 28:2; 29:10; the specific Akk./Aram./Arab. word for "mother's brother," **ḫāl-*, is lacking in Hebr.; Huffmon 194);

(4) "mother's sister" (Lev 18:13; 20:19);

(5) "brother's wife" (Lev 18:16, instead of *yᵉbāmâ* "sister-in-law" in Deut 25:7, 9; Ruth 1:15; → *ʾalmānâ*);

(6) "brother's son" (Gen 12:5).

Cf. also G. Ryckmans, "Les noms de parenté en safaïtique," *RB* 58 (1951): 377–92.

(b) As in many languages, incl. non-Sem. languages, transitions to the expanded meanings "near relative, member of the same tribe, compatriot" or "colleague, friend" all the way to the largely empty meaning "the other" in reciprocal relationships ("one another") occur easily in Hebr. (about 45% of the texts with *ʾāḥ* in the OT), by which, on the family model, members of other close communities can also be described as "brothers" or "sisters." In accord with the situation, the element of solidarity, affection, or similarity, or equality of rights can be emphasized as the point of comparison in the metaphorical usage; cf. J. Zobel, *Der bildliche Gebrauch der Verwandtschaftsnamen im Hebräischen* (1932), 35–42.

One may not always sharply distinguish the narrower and the broader senses (Gen 49:5, "Simeon and Levi are brothers," pregnantly contains the term in both meanings); cf. the overview of the Levi texts in Elliger, HAT 4, 137n.12, 259n.37, and of the Deut texts in C. Steuernagel, *Das Deuteronomium*, HKAT (1923[2]), 42; also Fitzmyer, *Sef.* 112 on Sef. (= *KAI* no. 224) 3.9. Verifiable texts with *ʾāḥ* for the uncle-nephew or cousin-cousin relationship are Gen 13:8; 14:16 (nephew in 1QapGen 22:11 emended to *br ʾḥwhy*, Fitzmyer, *Gen.Ap.* 171); 29:12, 15; Lev 10:4 (sons of the cousins); 1 Chron 23:22; "sister" for stepsister in Gen 20:12.

The meaning "relatives" (in the pl.) is unmistakable in Gen 16:12; 25:18; 31:23, 25, 32, 37, 46, 54; Exod 2:11; 4:18; Judg 9:26, 31, 46; etc. (cf. Ezek 11:15, "all of your brothers, your kindred"; Zimmerli, *Ezek*, Herm, 1:229, 261; → *gʾl*), but cannot always be sharply distinguished from the meaning "fellow tribesman, compatriot" (e.g., Num 36:2; Judg 9:18; 2 Sam 19:13; on Amos 1:9 cf. J. Priest, "Covenant of Brothers," *JBL* 84 [1965]: 400–406; in Num 25:18 "[female] compatriot"), and this meaning, in turn, may not always be distinguished from "colleague" (e.g., 2 Kgs 9:2 among soldiers; Isa 41:6

among artisans; Num 8:26; Ezra 3:8; Neh 5:14 and often in the Chr's history of the Levites). The inscriptions from Zinjirli (*KAI* no. 214.27–31; no. 215.3, 12, 17; no. 216.14 = *ANET* 655a; *DISO* 8) suggest a similar situation.

The synonyms of the expanded meaning are treated with → *rēaᶜ*.

(c) As a metaphorical usage, "my brother/sister" is also characteristically addressed to unrelated persons: Gen 19:7; 29:4; Judg 19:23; 1 Sam 30:23; 2 Sam 20:9; 1 Chron 28:2 (cf. Lande 20, 23f., concerning the connotations that readily accompany courtly modes of speech). The usage of *ʾāḥ* among persons of equal rank in messenger speech (Num 20:14; 1 Sam 25:6 txt em), in courtly correspondence style, and in diplomatic communication (1 Kgs 9:13, Hiram-Solomon; 20:32f., Ahab-Benhadad) conforms to this usage.

Extrabibl. attestations for this letter style are numerous: Akk.: *CAD* A/1:200–202; Ug.: *KTU* 2.4.19; 2.14.3, 10, 15, 18; (between father and son); 2.21.3 (queen as sister); 5.9.8, 10 (par. *rᶜ* "friend"); 2.38.2f., 26 (kings of Tyre and Ugarit); 2.41.18, 20, 22; 2.67.4; 2.44.2; cf. A. van Selms, *Marriage and Family Life in Ugaritic Literature* (1954), 113; Phoen. and Aram.: cf. *DISO* 8 and Fitzmyer, *Gen.Ap.* 86.

The formulaic address in the lament for the dead should also be understood similarly (1 Kgs 13:30, "Alas, my brother!"; Jer 22:18, "Alas my brother, alas my sister!"; 2 Sam 1:26 is probably influenced by this usage: "I am sorrowful for you, my brother Jonathan"; cf. Jahnow 61ff.; Lande 25f.).

"My sister (bride)" occurs as a tender metaphor for the beloved (in Song Sol otherwise named *raᶜyâ* "friend"; → *rēaᶜ*) in Song Sol 4:9f., 12; 5:1f., as in Eg. love poetry (Grapow 32; A. Hermann, *Altäg. Liebesdichtung* [1959], 75–78; Rudolph, KAT 17, 150) and in Ug. (*KTU* 1.18.I.24, Anat to Aqhat: "You are my brother, I am your sister"; cf. van Selms, op. cit. 70, 120, 122; M. Dahood, *Bib* 42 [1961]: 236). Cf. further Prov 7:4, "Say to wisdom: you are my sister," of personified wisdom (Ch. Kayatz, *Studien zu Proverbien 1–9* [1966], 98).

Solidarity and similarity are described by *ʾāḥ* in Job 30:29, "I have become a brother of the jackals"; Prov 18:9, "brother of the destroyer," cf. 28:24, "companion of the villain" with *ḥābēr;* with *ʾāḥôt:* Job 17:14, "I say to the worm 'My mother!' and 'My sister!' "

In Akk. see e.g., *CAD* A/1:172a: "the two eyes are sisters"; in Ug. *KTU* 1.16.VI.35, 51: "sickness has become like a sister to you," in the event that *aḫt* is not to be read verbally with Driver (*CML*[1] 47, 133, etc.; also Gibson, *CML*[2] 101f., 141), "you are a brother."

(d) Pron. usage in expressions with *ʾîš ʾāḥîw* ("one . . . the other") refers to persons (Gen 9:5; 13:11; 26:31; 37:19; 42:21, 28; Exod 10:23; 16:15; Lev 7:10; 25:14, 46; 26:37; Num 14:4; Deut 1:16; 25:11; 2 Kgs 7:6; Isa 3:6; 19:2; 41:6; Jer 13:14; 23:35; 25:26; 31:34; 34:17; Ezek 4:17; 24:23; 33:30; 38:21; 47:14; Joel 2:8; Mic 7:2; Hag 2:22; Zech 7:9f.; Mal 2:10; Neh 4:13; 5:7, partially retaining the specific meaning "brother"), but also to things (Exod 25:20 and 37:9, golden cherubim; Job 41:9, crocodile scales); fem. *ʾiššâ—ʾāḥôt* likewise of things (curtains, Exod 26:3, 5f., 17; wings, Ezek 1:9; 3:13).

Pars. in Akk. (*aḫu aḫa, aḫu ana aḫi,* etc.) likewise refer to persons or things (*CAD* A/1:203f.), just as does Hebr. *tōʾᵃmîm/tᵉʾômîm* (R. Köbert, *Bib* 35 [1954]: 139–41) "twins" (Gen 25:24, Jacob and Esau; 38:27, Perez and Serah; Song Sol 4:5 = 7:4, gazelles; but Exod 26:24 and 36:29, boards).

4. (a) Theologically relevant usages of the word do not relate to the more narrow meaning "biological brother" with its family law implications, but to the more general meaning "member (of a community)" or to the metaphorical usage.

Family law: On the prohibition of sexual relations between siblings (Lev 18:9, 11; 20:17; Deut 27:22), cf. W. Kornfeld, *Studien zum Heiligkeitsgesetz* (1952), 110ff.; on the institution of levirate marriage, cf. F. Horst, *RGG* 4:338f.; Rudolph, KAT 17, 60–65 (bibliog.); → *gʾl;* C. H. Gordon (*JBL* 54 [1935]: 223–31) suspects traces of fratriarchy, which can be demonstrated particularly in the Hurrian realm (P. Koschaker, "Fratriarchat, Hausgemeinschaft und Mutterrecht in Keilschrifttexten," *ZA* 41 [1933]: 1–89) but also in the OT: fratronymy (Gen 4:22; 36:22; 1 Chron 2:32, 42; 24:25; also Ug. *KTU* 4.103.5 *ršpab aḫ ubn*) and a few fratriarchal motifs in the patriarchal narratives (e.g., Gen 24, Laban-Rebekah); cf., however, de Vaux 1:19. On Gen 12:13, "say that you are my sister" as a formula of conditional divorce, see L. Rost, FS Hertzberg 186–92.

(b) Ethical reflections concerning proper brotherhood in daily life, both within the Bible and without, accentuate brotherly affection, dependability, willingness to help, etc. In similes "brother" can par. "father," e.g., Akk. in a Mari text: "I am like a father and a brother to you; you, however, are like an opponent and an enemy to me" (G. Dossin, *Syria* 33 [1956]: 65); Phoen.: Kilamuwa 1.10 (→ *ʾāb* III/3). OT examples from wisdom literature juxtapose the brother with the "friend" (→ *rēaʿ*) and the "neighbor," a comparison that can also work to the disadvantage of the brother (Prov 17:17, "A friend loves at all times, and a brother is born for distress"; but 18:24, "A friend sticks closer than a brother"; and 27:10, "Better a close neighbor than a distant brother"). Other wisdom texts on the topic of brotherliness include Psa 133:1, "See how fine and lovely it is when brothers dwell together in unity," and Aram. Aḥ. 49, "There I cared for you, as one treats his brother" (Cowley 221; *ANET* 428a; *AOT* 456). Cf. also the description of the friends Gilgamesh and Enkidu as "brothers" (Gilg. VI:156 = *ANET* 85a; Schott 58).

(c) The term "brother" receives a theological coloring at the earliest in Dtn usage and in the command to love one's neighbor in H (Lev 19:17, → *rēaʿ;* 25:35f., 39, 46–48, → *gʾl*). No new usage of the word is involved in the Dtn description of the member of the people or the community. The religious undertone in the context of the inculcation of the commandment results only through the emphatic usage of the word with a suf., mostly *ʾāḥîkā* "your brother" (in all texts in the Dtn code, Deut 12–26, unless, as in 13:7 and 25:5–9, specific family law regulations are involved: 15:2f., 7, 9, 11f.; 17:15, 20; 18:15, 18; 19:18f.; 20:8; 22:1–4; 23:20f.; 24:7, 14; 25:3,[11]; Levites, 18:2, 7; Edomites, 23:8; cf. O. Bächli, *Israel und die Völker* [1962], 121–23). Jer 34:9, 14, 17 directly reflect the Dtn usage; the Chr history uses "brother" in the metaphorical sense almost exclusively in the pl.; cf. further H. C. M. Vogt, *Studie zur nachexilischen Gemeinde in Esra-Nehemia* (1966), 113–15, esp. on Neh 5.

The suf. form already plays a particular role in Gen 4:9 ("Where is your brother Abel?") in the exemplary presentation of the relationship between God, individual, and neighbor (W. Vischer, *Witness of the OT to Christ* [1949], 72: "Responsibility before God is responsibility for one's brother").

The Dtn usage develops within the Dtn concept of the people of God (von Rad, *Gottesvolk* 13, 50; H. Breit, *Die Predigt des Deuteronomisten* [1933], 179, 185; O. Procksch, *Theol. des AT* [1950], 239). "The people is the family writ large, which forms a unity. The use of 'brother' as a constitutive element of the people concept also equalizes: brothers stand on the same level, they have the same rights and duties and are responsible to one another" (Bächli, op. cit. 123).

The notion of the brotherhood of the Israelites under one father (→ *ʾāb* IV/3c) is admittedly present in Mal 2:10, but it is not terminologically fixed ("Why do we treat each other faithlessly?" cf. 3d).

(d) That which is true of → *ʾāb* "father" is valid mutatis mutandis for the description of the divinity as "brother" in theophoric PNs in ancient Sem. nomenclature (III/5 with bibliog.).

Alongside theophoric names (*ʾaḥîyāhû*/*ʾaḥîyâ, yôʾāḥ* "Yahweh is [my] brother"; *ʾaḥîmelek, ḥîʾēl* < **ʾaḥîʾēl, ḥîrām* < Phoen. *ʾḥrm;* cf. Friedrich §94), a series of substitute names also occurs here, e.g., *ʾaḥîqām* "my brother is risen (again)," *ʾaḥʾāb* "father's brother," *ʾāḥûmay* "brother of my mother" (according to *BS* 95), cf. Stamm, *HEN* 417f., 422; on *dôdô* "his uncle" and *dāwîd* "uncle" see Stamm, *SVT* 7 (1960): 165–83; on *ʿammôn* "little uncle," id., *ArOr* 17 (1949): 379–82.

5. The further development of the OT usage in Judaism and in the NT is closely bound to the concept of the "neighbor" (→ *rēaʿ*); cf. H. von Soden, "ἀδελφός," *TDNT* 1:144–46; H. Greeven and J. Fichtner, "πλησίον," *TDNT* 6:311–18; *RAC* 2:631–46; W. Günther, U. Falkenroth, and D. A. Carson, "Brother," *DNTT* 1:254–60; J. Fichtner, "Der Begriff des 'Nächsten' im AT mit einem Ausblick auf Spätjudentum und NT," *WD* 4 (1955): 23–52 (= *Gottes Weisheit* [1965], 88–114).

E. Jenni

אֶחָד ʾeḥād one

S 259; BDB 25b; *HALOT* 1:29b; *TDOT* 1:193–201; *TWOT* 61; *NIDOTTE* 285

בַּד *bad* **solitariness**

S 905; BDB 94b; *HALOT* 1:108b; *TDOT* 1:473–79; *TWOT* 201a; *NIDOTTE* 963

1. (a) The numeral "one" is common Sem. in its basic triradical form *ʾḥd* (*GVG* 1:484; Berg., *Intro.* 222; Ug.: *UT* no. 126; *WUS* no. 131; NWSem. inscriptions: *DISO* 9; on Aram. *ḥad* with discarded ʾ, cf. *GVG* 1:243, 257; BLA 54, 248f.).

The Akk. root has the form *(w)ēdum* (later *ēdu*) in the meaning "sole, alone" (*GAG §71c; AHw* 184, 186–88; *CAD* E:27f., 33, 36–39, with further derivatives); the word *ištēnum*, also known in Hebr. (*ʿaštê ʿāśār* "eleven," always in conjunction with *ʿāśār* "ten," according to Zimmern 65 and e.g., Meyer 2:87, an Akk. loanword, although it also occurs in Ug.), is available for "one" (*GAG* §69b; *AHw* 400f.; *CAD* I/J:275–79).

In addition to the original form *ʾaḥad* (Gen 48:22; 2 Sam 17:22; Isa 27:12; Ezek 33:30; Zech 11:7; cf. BL 622; Meyer 2:85), *ʾeḥād* occurs regularly with a virtual or secondary reduplication of the middle radical (*GVG* 1:68; BL 219), and the dissimilation of the *qameṣ* before the *ḥ* to *e* (Berg., *HG* 1:152; BL 216).

(b) Hebr. (and Ug.; cf. *UT* §7.8, and no. 126) also uses the pl. *ʾaḥādîm* (Gen 11:1, "one sort of words"; 27:44; 29:20; Dan 11:20, "some days"; Ezek 37:17, "so that they become one"; according to Gordon, *UT* no. 126: "a set, pair"; cf. also BrSynt 74f.).

(c) The root rarely occurs verbally: Hebr. *ʾḥd* hitp. "to unite" only in Ezek 21:21 (a disputed text); Ug. *ʾḥd* D "to unite" (*WUS* no. 131) is likewise highly uncertain.

(d) The PN *ʾēḥûd* (1 Chron 8:6, a member of the tribe of Benjamin) should probably be emended to *ʾēhûd* (*IP* no. 76; Rudolph, HAT 21, 76; *HAL* 30a).

(e) In addition to *ʾḥd*, the related root *wḥd* (NWSem. *yḥd*) occurs in all subfamilies of the Sem. languages: Akk. *wēdum* "sole, alone" (see 1a); Ug. *yḥd* "lonely" (*WUS* no. 1153; *UT* no. 1087); Old Aram. *yḥd* ha. "to unify" (*DISO* 106); for other (post-OT) forms see KBL 376b. The Hebr. verb occurs rarely: *yḥd* qal "to unite" Gen 48:6 (contra M. Dahood, *Bib* 40 [1959]: 169); Isa 14:20; uncertain pi. in Psa 86:11. More common are the subst. *yaḥad* "unification" (common in the Qumran texts; Deut 33:5; 1 Chron 12:18; cf. S. Talmon, *VT* 3 [1953]: 133–40), the advs. *yaḥad* (44x, incl. Jer 48:7 K) and *yaḥdāyw* (94x, excl. Jer 48:7 Q; *-āyw* may be an old, adapted locative ending; cf. *GVG* 1:460, 465; BL 529f.; J. C. de Moor, *VT* 7 [1957]: 350–55; cf. also *yaḫudunni* "together with me" as a Can. loanword in an Amarna letter, *CAD* I/J:321), both in the meaning "together" (for further modal, local, and temporal nuances, see de Moor, op. cit. 354f.; not, however, "alone," as J. Mauchline, *TGUOS* 13 [1951]: 51–53, and M. D. Goldman, *ABR* 1 [1951]: 61–63, assume for some texts), and *yāḥîd* "sole, alone, lonely" (12x; often of the "only son"; in Psa 22:21 and 35:17, "my only = my life").*

2. The numeral, used 970x (in addition to the scribal errors in Ezek 18:10 *ʾāḥ* and 33:30 *ḥad;* cf. Zimmerli, *Ezek,* Herm, 1:371; 2:196; masc. 703x, fem. 267x, with 2 Sam 17:12 Q; 1 Kgs 19:4 Q; Isa 66:17 Q; Song Sol 4:9 K), occurs in almost all books of the OT (lacking in Joel, Mic, Nah, Hab), concentrated esp., of course, in books containing lists, legal sections, descriptions, etc. (Num 180x, 89x in Num 7 alone; Ezek 106x; Exod 99x; 1 Kgs 63x; Josh 60x); Aram. *ḥad* occurs 14x.

3. GB 22f. and *HAL* 29f. detail the usage of the word more thoroughly. The chief meaning is the cardinal "one," which may refer to God (Deut 6:4; cf. Gen 3:22), people, animals, or things. The abs. usage "the one" (1 Sam 13:17f., etc.; occasionally with the art.; cf. *GVG* 2:69) and the distributive usage "each one" (e.g., Deut 1:23) also derive from the chief meaning. The numeral can describe a nondetermined entity in the sense of "anyone," e.g., 1 Sam 26:15, *ʾaḥad hāʿām* "one of the people" (on the use of *min* in this connection, cf. *GVG* 2:84); negated *(lōʾ* or *ʾên)* it means "none, no one." Occasionally *ʾeḥād* can represent the ordinal, e.g., Gen 1:5, "day one = the first day"; so also dates. Otherwise, *riʾšôn* "the first" is used in these cases. *ʾaḥat* occurs in the sense "once," e.g., in Lev 16:34 and 2 Kgs 6:10.

4. (a) The numeral achieves great relevance in theological usage. The intolerance and—relatedly—the intransigence of OT Yahwism categorically excluded any deification of humanity (Gen 3:22) and any worship of gods or powers beside Yahweh. Thus the *one* God assumed a dominant position, as the Decalogue, which juxtaposes the "other gods" (Exod 20:3; Deut 5:7; → *ʾḥr)* with the divine "I" (Exod 20:2; Deut 5:6), already demands. Although other gods have many names, Yahweh has only *one* (Exod 3:14f.; cf. von Rad, *Theol.* 1:185).

The Josianic (Eichrodt 1:226) statement *šᵉmaʿ yiśrāʾēl yhwh ʾᵉlōhênû yhwh ʾeḥād,* "Hear, O Israel, Yahweh, our God, is *one* Yahweh" (Deut 6:4; another possible translation is: "Yahweh is our God, Yahweh is one [alone]") gives classic expression to the concept. Regardless of precisely how its syntactic structure should be interpreted (on this cf., among others, S. R. Driver, *Deut,* ICC [1902³], 89f.; G. Quell, *TDNT* 3:1080f.; von Rad, *Deut,* OTL, 62–64), and how its primary focus (against poly-Yahwism or polytheism) is determined, this statement most clearly expresses Yahweh's unity and exclusivity (cf. E. König, *Theologie des AT* [1922], 129–32, who refers to the martyr Rabbi Akiba, who died with the words of the Shema on his lips; also H. Breit, *Die Predigt des Deuteronomisten* [1933], 60–65; Vriezen, *Theol.,* 311, 323–28; von Rad, *Theol.* 1:227). It does not appear in isolation but is embedded in the commandment to love this unique Lord just as uniquely (Deut 6:5; cf. N. Lohfink, *Das Hauptgebot* [1963], 163f.; id., *Höre Israel* [1965], 63). The demand for the worship of the *one* God at only *one* place (cf. 2 Chron 32:12) derives logically from this commandment (von Rad, *Theol.* 1:227).

The notion of Yahweh's uniqueness is certainly not limited to usages of the word *ʾeḥād* (e.g., Exod 15:11; 2 Sam 7:22; Isa 44:6; cf. C. J. Labuschagne, *Incomparability of Yahweh in the OT* [1966]). In the late text Zech 14:9, *ʾeḥād* occurs once more in a theological usage describing the eschatological fulfillment of the demand of Deut 6:4f. in a universalistic extension: "In that day Yahweh will be one and his name will be one" (cf. G. A. F. Knight, "The Lord Is One," *ExpT* 79 [1967/68]: 8–10).

In another way, *ᵓeḥād* serves the ideal of the people's unity in Mal 2:10, "Do we not all have *one* father? Has not *one* God created us? Why do we then treat one another faithlessly" (cf. also Job 31:15); moreover, the emphatic usage of the word in eschatological contexts, such as Jer 32:39 "*one* heart and *one* way" (Rudolph, HAT 12, 212); Ezek 34:23 and 37:24, "*one* shepherd"; 37:22, "*one* people . . . *one* king"; Hos 2:2, "*one* head"; Zeph 3:9, "serve him with *one* shoulder (= harmoniously)" is noteworthy.*

(b) In this context one should note forms of the root *bdd* that are somewhat related semantically to particular usages of *ᵓeḥād: bad* "separation," adv. *lᵉbad, millᵉbad* "alone, apart" (158x); *bôdēd* "alone" (3x); *bādād* "alone" (11x). Yahweh's uniqueness is often expressed with *lᵉbad:* Deut 4:35, "Yahweh alone is God and no other"; 1 Kgs 8:39 = 2 Chron 6:30, "you alone know the heart of all the children of men"; 2 Kgs 19:15, 19 = Isa 37:16, 20, "you alone are God"; Isa 2:11, 17, "Yahweh alone is exalted in that day"; Isa 44:24 and Job 9:8, "he who spread out the heavens all alone"; also Isa 63:3; Psa 72:18; 83:19; 86:10; 136:4; 148:13; Neh 9:6; with *bādād* Deut 32:12, "Yahweh alone led him, no strange god was with him." A related concept is the exclusivity of the relationship with Yahweh as expressed by *lᵉbad* in Exod 22:19, "whoever sacrifices to other gods and not to Yahweh only"; 1 Sam 7:3f.; Isa 26:13; Psa 51:6; 71:16; with *lᵉbādād* Psa 4:9; the consequences for the people are shown in Num 23:9, "Here is a people living alone, and not reckoning itself among the nations" (NRSV).*

5. In Judaism "the one" can become an alternate designation for God (StrB 2:28).

This very element of God's uniqueness, which challenges people to the same uniqueness, has exercised the most lasting influence on the NT and its thought (Mark 12:29f.; Rom 3:30). God alone deserves devotion and service (Matt 4:10; 6:24). The divine unity is mirrored in the *one* son of God, Jesus (1 Cor 8:6; Eph 4:4–6), who through his *egō eimi* excludes all other possibilities of religious thought and argumentation (John 6:48; 8:12; 11:25; 14:6). Cf. E. Stauffer, "εἷς," *TDNT* 2:434–42; F. Büchsel, "μονογενής," *TDNT* 4:737–41.

The OT adv. *ᵓaḥat* "once and for all" in Psa 89:36 (H. Gunkel, *Die Psalmen* [1926], 394) most nearly approximates the important NT expression *ephapax* (cf. G. Stählin, "ἅπαξ," *TDNT* 1:381–84).

G. Sauer

אָחוֹת ᵓāḥôt **sister** → אָח ᵓāḥ

אחז ʾḥz to grasp

S 270; BDB 28a; *HALOT* 1:31b; *TWOT* 64; *NIDOTTE* 290

1. The root *ʾḫḏ "to grasp" is common Sem. (Berg., *Intro.* 218) and appears, with variations in the 2d and 3d radicals, in Arab. and Old SArab. as ʾḫḏ, in Akk. and Eth. as ʾḫz, in Hebr. (Moab., ?Pun.) and Old Aram. as ʾḥz, in Ug. and Imperial Aram. onward as ʾḥd (NWSem. examples are found in *WUS* no. 135 and *DISO* 9f.).

HAL 31b adds an ʾḥz II "to draw over" (originally identical with ʾḥz I) for the technical usage of ʾḥz qal in 1 Kgs 6:10 (Noth, BK 9, 96, 99 suggests pi. instead of qal), ʾḥz pi. in Job 26:9 and ho. (or pu.) in 2 Chron 9:18 (cf. 1 Kgs 10:9), and, indeed, in a sense borrowed from the Akk. *uḫḫuzu* "to draw over," which is a denominative from *iḫzu* "enclosure" (cf. *tāpûś* "enclosed" in Hab 2:19, from *tpś* "to grasp").

Another borrowed meaning, in this instance from Aram., is present in Neh 7:3 "to bolt" (cf. Wagner no. 7a); probably related are *ḥîdâ* (Aram. pass. ptcp. with discarded ʾ; Bibl. Aram. ʾᵃḥîdâ Dan 5:12) in the meaning ("something grasped, enclosed > something closed" >) "riddle" (17x, 8x in Judg 14:12–19) and, a denominative from it, *ḥûd* qal "to pose a riddle" (Judg 14:12f., 16; Ezek 17:2); cf. Wagner nos. 100f. (somewhat differently, G. Rinaldi, *Bib* 40 [1959]: 274–76; H.-P. Müller, "Der Begriff 'Rätsel' im AT," *VT* 20 [1970]: 465–89).

The verb occurs in the qal and in the ni. (pass. in Gen 22:13; Eccl 9:12; otherwise a denominative from ʾᵃḥuzzâ "property" in the meaning "to be resident"); on the pi. and ho., see above.

In addition, the subst. ʾᵃḥuzzâ "property" derives from the root in a nom. formation common for legal terms. Finally, the OT has a series of PNs that contain the root ʾḥz (see 4).

With regard to the disputed meaning of ʾāḥūz in Song Sol 3:8 (qal ptcp. "containing" or adj. "learned, skilled") cf. *HAL* 31b with bibliog.

2. The Hebr. OT has the qal of the verb 58x, ni. 7x, pi. and ho. 1x each. Occurrences are distributed over the entire OT; the fact that later writings exhibit a slight increase in occurrences may be accidental. The 66 texts that use the subst. ʾᵃḥuzzâ contrast with this distribution; besides Psa 2:8 it occurs only in late texts, primarily in P and in Ezek 44–48.

3. In the vast majority of cases the verb should be translated "to grasp, lay hold of, seize, hold fast," etc. (on additional derivative technical meanings in 1 Kgs 6:6 and Ezek 41:6 see *HAL* 30a, 31a).

Synonyms of ʾḥz are *tpś* "to lay hold of, grasp, have to do with" (qal 49x, ni. 15x, pi. 1x, Prov 30:28 txt?), *tmk* "to grasp, hold" (qal 20x, ni. 1x; also Phoen., Akk.), and *qmṭ* "to lay hold of" (qal Job 16:8; pu. Job 22:16; also Aram. and Arab.); also → *lqḥ* and → *ḥzq* hi. in some forms.

The obj. is introduced with *b*ᵉ or the acc. (occurrences in *HAL* 31a). One may hold fast to: the heels (Gen 25:26), the ram's horns (Gen 22:13 ni.), the snake's tail (Exod 4:4), the doors of the city gate (Judg 16:3), the ark (2 Sam

6:6 = 1 Chron 13:9), the beard (2 Sam 20:9), the horns of the altar (1 Kgs 1:51), the eyelids (Psa 77:5), the ends of the earth (Job 38:13), a mantle (Ruth 3:15), the beloved (Song Sol 3:4), branches (7:9), clothes (Esth 1:6), spear and shield (2 Chron 25:5; cf. Song Sol 3:8); one may grasp the sling (Job 18:9; Eccl 12:9) and the net (Eccl 12:9 ni.); one may fig. grasp or hold one's way (Job 17:9), the trail (Job 23:11), foolishness (Eccl 2:3; cf. 7:18).

The verb very often applies to the hostile or otherwise violent grasping, seizure, or capture of someone (Judg 1:6; 12:6; 16:21; 20:6; 2 Sam 2:21; 4:10; Isa 5:29; Psa 56:1; 137:9; Job 16:12; Song Sol 2:15).

Even somewhat more frequent are fig. expressions of the fact that anxiety, trembling, cramps, weakness, grief, wrath, etc., lay hold of people (Exod 15:14f.; 2 Sam 1:9; Isa 13:8; 21:3; 33:14; Jer 13:21; 49:24; Psa 48:7; 119:53; Job 18:20; 21:6; 30:16).

Finally, the usage in Num 31:30, 47 "one of fifty" (= a chosen one) is very general; similarly 1 Chron 24:6 (cf. Rudolph, HAT 21, 160).

A few ni. texts (Gen 34:10; 47:27; Num 32:30; Josh 22:9, 19) should be translated "to establish oneself (in the land)," "to take possession (of the land)." The subst. *ʾaḥuzzâ*, which consistently means "possession, property," mostly in the sense of land or real estate (Gen 23:4, 9, 20: possession of a grave; Lev 25:45f.: possession of slaves) is related. The noun acquires a fig. meaning specifying that the Levites are to have no real estate, because Yahweh is their "real estate" (Ezek 44:28; cf. Zimmerli, *Ezek*, Herm, 2:461f.; von Rad, *Theol.* 1:403f.). Par. terms for *ʾaḥuzzâ* are *naḥalâ* (→ *nḥl*), *ḥēleq* (→ *ḥlq*), → *gôrāl*, *yeruššâ*/*yerēšâ* (→ *yrš*). On *ʾaḥuzzâ* (and on the distinction from *naḥalâ*), see F. Horst, "Zwei Begriffe für Eigentum (Besitz): *naḥalā* und *ʾaḥuzzā*," FS Rudolph 135–56, esp. 153ff.

4. The word group has no properly theological meaning. Yahweh appears once as the subj. of the verb, however (Psa 73:23, "you hold my right hand"; cf. also the statements concerning Yahweh's salvific grasp with the verb *tmk* in Isa 41:10; 42:1; Psa 16:5; 41:13; 63:9); twice the hand of Yahweh is the subj.: it grasps even the one who settles in the extremities of the sea (Psa 139:10); it seizes in judgment (Deut 32:41). *ʾḥz* does not, however, acquire a specifically theological emphasis.

The same is true for *ʾaḥuzzâ:* just as surely as land and property are understood as Yahweh's gifts (Gen 17:8; 48:4; Lev 14:34; Deut 32:49, etc.), it is also true that this notion is rarely given specific expression with *ʾaḥuzzâ*, not even when one speaks of an *ʾaḥuzzat ʿôlām*, an "eternal possession" (Gen 17:8; 48:4; Lev 25:34) or once even the *ʾaḥuzzat yhwh* (Josh 22:19; cf. H.-J. Hermisson, *Sprache und Ritus im altisr. Kult* [1965], 108).

In this context, PNs formed with *ʾḥz* require comment, because they are all (originally) theophoric names: *yehôʾāḥāz*/*yôʾāḥāz* "Yahweh has (protectively) grasped" (cf. *IP* 21, 62, 179), *ʾaḥazyâ(hû);* furthermore, synonymous by-forms and shortened forms, some of which are also attested on seals and ostraca (*ʾāḥāz*, cuneiform *ya-u-ḫa-zi;* also *ʾaḥzay*, *ʾaḥuzzām*, *ʾaḥuzzat).*

5. The word group seems to have played no distinct role in postbibl. Hebr. Occurrences at Qumran move within the boundaries of the OT idiom (1QH

4:33; CD 2:18; on 1QS 2:9 → ʾāb I; subst. ʾḥzh CD 16:16 and ʾwḥzh 1QS 11:7). No significant NT equivalent may be noted; the LXX already renders the verb with 27 and the noun with 6 different Gk. words (on *krateō* see W. Michaelis, *TDNT* 3:910–12).

H. H. Schmid

אחר ʾḥr after

S 310; BDB 29b; *HALOT* 1:35b; *TDOT* 1:201–3; *TWOT* 68b; *NIDOTTE* 339

---

1. (a) The common Sem. root *ʾḫr expresses a variety of meanings in numerous parts of speech and forms, all derived from the concept of temporal succession. Local meanings are relatively insignificant and are easily explained as applications of a cognitive process in which the temporally later is seen as the spatially later.

The starting point with respect to *ʾaḥar* is not, therefore, with G. R. Driver (*JTS* 34 [1933]: 377f.; *ZDMG* 91 [1937]: 346), an anatomical designation (dual *ʾaḥ^a^rê* "buttocks"), as may be the case for the root **wark-* (Hebr. *yārēk* "hip, bottom, backside," 34x; *yarkâ* "back, remotest part," 28x; cf. Dhorme 98–100). The *-ê* in *ʾaḥ^a^rê* should not be understood as a dual ending, but as an assimilation to the antonym *lipnê* "before" (BL 644f.); the meaning "backside, hind part" for *ʾaḥôr* (2 Kgs 7:25 = 2 Chron 4:4) is abstract.

The local meaning "behind" is represented in Akk. by **(w)ark-* and occurs for the root *ʾḫr* only (under Can. influence? cf. W. von Soden, *Or* 18 [1949]: 391f.) at Mari (*aḫarātum* "back side," *AHw* 18a; *CAD* A/1:170a) and as a Can. gloss in an Amarna letter from Megiddo (EA 245:10 *arki-šu/aḫ-ru-un-ú* "behind him," *CAD* A/1:194b).

Ug. has also so far evidenced only temporal, primarily adv., usages of the root *ʾḫr* (*UT* no. 138; *WUS* no. 150). In Can. inscriptions the root is seldom attested (*ʾḥr ʾby* "after my father" in the Mesha inscription, *KAI* no. 181.3; cf. *DISO* 10).

In Old Aram. (since Sef. III = Fitzmyer, *Sef.* 100f., 119; *KAI* no. 224.24 *ʾḥrn* "another"; often in the Elephantine papyri) adv., prep., and nom. usages (also in the meaning "posterity"; cf. *DISO* 10) are frequent, but verbal usages are not attested. Local "behind" should probably be conjectured only in the Ahiqar narrative (Cowley 214.63 *[ʾ]ḥryn* "[to send] after us"). *bātar* replaces the root in later Aram. (see KBL 1049a).

(b) The verb occurs primarily in the D stem or pi. ("to delay," etc.); the G stem or qal is attested very little in Hebr. or in the other Sem. langauges.

The Akk. G stem *aḫāru* "to be late" is attested only in EA 59:26 (*CAD* A/1:170b).

Hebr. *ʾḥr* qal "to stay, tarry" (Gen 32:5) and hi. "to delay" (2 Sam 20:5 Q, inner-trans. or internal) are hapax legomena. On pi. "to hold back" cf. *HP* 99. *ʾḥr* hitp. "to stay back, do afterward" also occurs at Qumran (1QS 1:14; CD 11:23).

The nom. formation *ʾāḥôr* "hinder side, west" also lends itself readily to an adv. usage: "afterward; rear(ward)"; the infrequent adv. formation *ʾ^a^ḥōrannît* "backward" (BL 633) also occurs. As a verbal adj. (with virtual or secondary intensification of the middle radical in the sg.) *ʾaḥēr* "coming behind, following, different, other" distinguishes itself in meaning as well from the actual adj. formations with afformatives, *ʾaḥ^{a}rôn* "later, future, last; behind, westerly" and *ʾaḥ^{a}rît* "future, end, posterity."

The abstract *ʾaḥ^{a}rît* is probably a substantivized fem. of an adj. form with *-î* (cf. GKC §95t; G. W. Buchanan, *JNES* 20 [1961]: 188; contra BL 505; Meyer 2:77). Related formations are Akk. *aḫrû* (*AHw* 21a) and Ug. *uḫryt* (*KTU* 1.17.VI.35), according to J. Aistleitner (*Untersuchungen zur Grammatik des Ug.* [1954], 21) and *WUS* no. 150: "belonging to a later time = future, later time"; cf. *ANET* 151b: "further life"; *CML*[1] 134a; *CML*[2] 143; Gray, *Legacy* 113; *UT* no. 138: "latter end."

ʾaḥar (with a virtual reduplication of the *ḥ*, not a segholate) and *ʾaḥ^{a}rê* "after, following, behind" are used only as advs. and preps.

In 2 Sam 2:23, *ʾ^{a}ḥōrê haḥ^{a}nît* "back end of the spear" may be read; in Gen 16:13 and Exod 33:8 the prep. "(to glance) back" may be retained (*HAL* 34b: "back side").

In addition to the temporal meaning "after" and the related local meaning "after" with acts of movement, the purely static meaning "behind" (in answer to the question *where* or *whither*) is relatively rare: *ʾaḥar* "behind" in Exod 11:5; Song Sol 2:9; "to the back" Exod 3:1; Gen 22:13 should read *ʾeḥād (BHS)*, 2 Kgs 11:6 *ʾaḥēr* (cf. W. Rudolph, FS Bertholet 474f.); *ʾaḥ^{a}rê* "behind" in Gen 18:10; Num 3:23; Deut 11:30; Judg 18:12 ("to the west"); 1 Sam 21:10; Ezek 41:15 should read *ʾ^{a}ḥôreyhā (BHS)*; "(to throw/look) behind oneself," Gen 19:17; 1 Kgs 14:9; Isa 38:17; Ezek 23:35; Neh 9:26; *mēʾaḥ^{a}rê* "behind," Gen 19:26 (txt?); Exod 14:19bis; Josh 8:2, 4, 14; 2 Sam 2:23; 1 Kgs 10:19; Jer 9:21; *mēʾaḥ^{a}rê l^e* "behind," Neh 4:7.

Secondary meanings proposed for *ʾaḥar*/*ʾaḥ^{a}rê*, such as "at, near, with" (R. B. Y. Scott, *JTS* 50 [1949]: 178f.) or even "correspondingly, on account of, despite" (W. J. P. Boyd, *JTS* NS 12 [1961]: 54–56), concern only the niceties of rendition into Eng. as a result of differences of idiom (Exod 11:5, "behind the hand mill" = "at the hand mill"; "walk behind someone" = "to walk with someone," etc.). These observations may not lead to the conclusion that the Hebr. (or Ug.) prep. could also have the meaning "with" (so M. Dahood, *Bib* 43 [1962]: 363f.; 44 [1963]: 292f.; Ug. *KTU* 1.24.32 *ʾḫr nkl yrḫ ytrḫ* should not be translated par. to *ʿmn nkl ḫtny* "with Nkl . . . " with "with Nikkal will the moon enter into wedlock," but with W. Herrmann, *Yariḫ und Nikkal,* [1968], 19, adv. "thereafter he/she bought for himself/herself . . . "). Eccl 12:2, "before . . . the clouds (always) return after the rain" (Zimmerli, ATD 16/1, 242, 246) is not a "meteorological absurdity" (Scott, *Eccl,* ABC, 255); rather it makes a conscious point in the image of old age in Prov 12:1ff. (H. W. Hertzberg, *ZDPV* 73 [1957]: 115).

māḥār "morning" and *moḥ^{o}rāt* "next day" should also probably be attributed to the root *ʾḥr* (*GVG* 1:241).

A PN *ʾaḥēr* (1 Chron 7:12) would have been understood as a nickname (*HAL* 34b), but should be emended according to Rudolph, HAT 21, 66.

(c) Beyond the usages treated in 1b, the general usage of this word group will not be investigated. Only *ʾaḥēr* "other" and *ʾaḥ^{a}rît* "end" occur in somewhat theologically significant contexts; these two words, widely divergent in meaning, will be treated in sections 3 (*ʾaḥēr*) and 4 (*ʾaḥ^{a}rît*).

2. The root is attested 1140x in the Hebr. OT; *ʾaḥ^{a}rê* 617x (Gen 69x, 2 Sam 58x) and *ʾaḥar* 96x (Gen 16x, Num 10x); *ʾaḥēr* 166x (not counting 1 Chron 7:12; Lis. overlooks 1 Kgs 3:22), most frequently in Deut (25x), Jer (25x), Gen (15x), 2 Chron (10x), and 1/2 Kgs (9x each). In addition, the following occur

(in order of frequency): *ʾaḥarît* 61x, *māḥār* 52x, *ʾaḥarôn* 51x, *ʾaḥôr* 41x, *moḥorāt* 32x, the verb *ʾḥr* 17x (pi. 15x, qal and hi. 1x each), *ʾaḥōrannît* 7x.

The Aram. portions of the OT contain *ʾoḥorān* (fem. *ʾoḥorî*) "other" 11x, *ʾaḥarê* "after" 3x, *ʾaḥarî* "end" 1x, *ʿad ʾḥryn* (with disputed pointing; cf. KBL 1049a) "last" 1x (Dan 4:5); all 16 texts are from Dan.

3. The expressions *ʾēl ʾaḥēr* "another god" (only Exod 34:14) and *ʾelōhîm ʾaḥērîm* "other gods" (63x) first receive theological significance in the context of the first commandment (cf. R. Knierim, "Das erste Gebot," *ZAW* 77 [1965]: 20–39), where *ʾaḥēr* forms the logical contrast to the one permissible God and, within the negatively formulated passages, becomes a fixed term sooner than, say, → *ʾeḥād*, which presupposes a positive statement. Without entering further into the question of the relative and absolute ages of the various formulations of the prohibition against other gods (cf. e.g., von Rad, *Theol.* 1:203f.; Knierim, op. cit. 27ff.), they may be treated together here: Exod 20:3 = Deut 5:7, "you shall have no other gods (the translation with the sg., which A. Jepsen, *ZAW* 79 [1967]: 287, supports, does not substantially alter the negative phrase) beside me" (or "in defiance of me" or "instead of me"; cf. J. J. Stamm, *TRu* 27 [1961]: 237f.; Knierim, op. cit. 24f.); Exod 22:19, "whoever sacrifices to other gods shall be banned" (txt em; cf. *BHS;* somewhat differently Alt, *EOTHR* 112n.73); 23:13, "you shall not call on the names of other gods"; 34:14, "you shall not bow down before another god."

Meanings such as "strange, unknown" can be appropriate in place of *ʾaḥēr* in traditionally related texts, e.g., Hos 13:4, "you know (→ *ydʿ*) no God except me" (cf. Deut 11:28; 13:3, 7, 14, etc.); Psa 81:10 *ʾēl* → *zār* and *ʾēl* → *nēkār* "a strange god."

The prophet Hosea, who demonstrates an acquaintance with the Decalogue in other ways, too, adopts the phrase "other gods" in 3:1, "to turn to other gods" (cf. Wolff, *Hos,* Herm, 60f.). Jer's use of the formula (at least Jer 1:16 may be genuine; cf. Rudolph, HAT 12, 10f.) and that in the Dtn-Dtr theology (cf. O. Bächli, *Israel und die Völker* [1962], 44–47) stand in this tradition.

The concentration of the word in Deut, Jer, and 1/2 Kgs (see 2) depends upon this formulaic usage of the expression "other gods" (Deut, in addition to 5:7, also 6:14; 7:4; 8:19; 11:16, 28; 13:3, 7, 14; 17:3; 18:20; 28:14, 36, 64; 29:25; 30:17; 31:18, 20; Josh 23:16; Judg 2:12, 17, 19; 10:13; 1 Sam 8:8; 1 Kgs 9:6, 9 = 2 Chron 7:19, 22; 1 Kgs 11:4, 10; 14:9; 2 Kgs 17:7, 35, 37f.; 22:17 = 2 Chron 34:25; Jer in addition to 1:16, also 7:6, 9, 18; 11:10; 13:10; 16:11, 13; 19:4, 13; 22:9; 25:6; 32:29; 35:15; 44:3, 5, 8, 15; 2 Chron 28:25).

Josh 24:2, 16 are pre-Dtn (Noth, HAT 7, 139) and reflect the old tradition concerning the assembly at Shechem and its renunciation of strange gods (Alt, *KS* [1963³], 1:79–88; H.-J. Kraus, *Worship in Israel* [1966], 136–41), a tradition very closely related to the first commandment; according to Knierim (op. cit. 35ff.), the very first formulation of the prohibition of strange gods should be located here.

The verbs associated with *ʾelōhîm ʾaḥērîm* are quite varied. → *ʿbd* "to serve" (Deut 7:4; 11:16; 13:7, 14; 17:3; 28:36, 64; 29:25; Josh 23:16; Judg 10:13; 1 Sam 8:8; 1 Kgs 9:6 = 2 Chron 7:19; Jer 44:3; cf. Josh 24:2, 16; 1 Sam 26:19), → *hlk ʾaḥarê* "to follow" (Deut

6:14; 8:19; 11:28; 13:3; 28:14; Judg 2:12, 19; 1 Kgs 11:10; Jer 7:6, 9; 11:10; 13:10; 16:11; 25:6; 35:15), and *qṭr* "to burn incense" (2 Kgs 22:17 = 2 Chron 34:25; Jer 19:4; 44:5, 8, 15; 2 Chron 28:25; cf. Jer 1:16) have a stereotypical effect.

Although most texts with *ᵓᵉlōhîm ᵓᵃḥērîm* relate to the first commandment, "strange gods" are discussed twice more in another context involving the assumption that Yahweh may be worshiped only in his own land (1 Sam 26:19; 2 Kgs 5:17).

ᵓaḥēr "another" (without *ᵓᵉlōhîm*) functions in a monotheistic hymnic statement in Deutero-Isa (Isa 42:8, "I will give my glory to no other, nor my praise to the idols"; similarly 48:11); cf. also Bibl. Aram. *ᵓoḥᵒrān* in Dan 3:29, "for there is no other god who is able so to save."

The expression "from another place" in Esth 4:14 serves as a euphemism for the name of God according to many exegetes (e.g., Ringgren, ATD 16/2, 116, 131; more cautiously Bardtke, KAT 17/5, 332f.).

4. (a) In the Gk. renderings in the LXX, approximately two-thirds are *eschatos* "last," 5 are *enkataleimma* "remainder" or *kataloipos* "remaining" (Psa 37:37f. and Ezek 23:25bis; Amos 9:1, resp.), 6 with *teleutaios* "last," or *teleutē* or *synteleia* "end" (Prov 14:12f.; 16:25; 20:21 [= 9b LXX]; and 24:14 and Deut 11:12, resp.). These are less significant for understanding the word *ᵓaḥᵃrît* (on the eytmology see 1b) than some analogies in related Sem. languages, such as Ug. *uḫryt* (see 1b), and the meaning "posterity" alongside "future" in Akk. (*aḫrâtu/aḫrûtu;* cf. *AHw* 21a; *CAD* A/1:194b, 195a) and in Aram. (*ᵓḥrth* "his posterity" in a 7th-cent. BCE inscription from Nerab, *ANET* 661b; *KAI* no. 226.10; Nab. *ᵓḥr* "posterity"; cf. *DISO* 10). If one also remembers that Hebr. does not differentiate formally between the comparative and the superlative of the adj. and that, as in most languages, it does not offer a distinct abstract time concept of "temporal essence," then the usage of *ᵓaḥᵃrît* in the basic meaning "that which comes afterward" may be easily explained in all OT texts.

The meaning "last, remainder" (e.g., KBL 33b; cf. LXX)—which complements the notion of coming later with the element of being present, remaining—should be discarded in favor of "that which comes afterward" = "posterity" (cf. GB 27a; *HAL* 36b) in Jer 31:17 (par. "children"); Ezek 23:25(bis) (par. "sons and daughters"; the distinction in Zimmerli, *Ezek*, Herm, 1:475f., is unconvincing); Amos 4:2 and 9:1 (in an unclear context); Psa 37:37f. (or "future"); 109:13 (par. "another generation"); Dan 11:4.

Depending upon whether the time period envisioned by the speaker is limitless or limited, *ᵓaḥᵃrît* may acquire a more comparative ("later time = future") or superlative ("last time = close, end") connotation, although an end point in the sense of a simple termination (for which → *qēṣ*, from *qṣṣ* "to cut off") is never intended.

ᵓaḥᵃrît clearly has a nonfinal meaning in Jer 29:11, "future and hope"; Prov 23:18 = 24:14 "future" (par. "hope"); 24:20, "the evil one has no future" (cf. W. Zimmerli, "Concerning the Structure of OT Wisdom," *Studies in Ancient Israelite Wisdom* [1976], 205n.35). *ᵓaḥᵃrît* clearly has a final sense in Deut 11:12, "from the beginning of the year to the end of the year"; Jer 5:31, "when there is an end to it"; Dan 12:8, "what is the end of these things?" as well as in the meaning "last time" (Dan 8:19, 23). Process and end are contained in the meanings "outcome, end (of a thing)" (Isa 41:22; 46:10; 47:7; Amos 8:10; Prov 14:12 = 16:25; 14:13 txt em; 20:21; 25:8; Eccl 7:8, alongside *rēʾšît* "beginning"; 10:13 alongside *tᵉḥillâ* "beginning"; Lam 1:9; cf. Rudolph, KAT 17, 213) and "end of someone's life" (Num 23:10 par. "death"; 24:20; Deut 32:20, 29; Jer 17:11 alongside "midst of his days"; Psa 73:17; Job 8:7 alongside "beginning"; Prov 29:21; Jer 12:4 should probably read *ʾorḥôtēnû* "our paths"). An unequivocal choice between the two options is often impossible for texts best rendered in Eng. by adv. expressions (Deut 8:16, "finally"; Job 42:12 and Prov 23:32, "afterward"; Prov 5:4, 11, "lastly"; the emendation *bᵉʾōrḥōteykā* "in your ways" has been proposed for Prov 19:20, where the choice between "in the future" and "at your end" is difficult).

In connection with an expression of movement (superlative), *ʾaḥᵃrît* "that which comes last" acquires a local meaning in Psa 139:9, "if I were to take the wings of dawn and settle at the extremes of the sea" (cf. on the contrary the purely static *qîṣôn* "outermost" in Exod 26:4, 10; 36:11, 17, "the outermost curtain").

A qualitative meaning "last = worst," widely accepted for Jer 50:12 based on an appeal to *rēʾšît* "first, best" (cf. Num 24:20 and Amos 6:1, "first of the nations"; B. Duhm, *Jer,* KHC, 362; Weiser, ATD 21, 427; KBL 33b, among others), should be rejected with P. Volz (*Jer,* KAT [1928²], 242f.) and W. Rudolph (*ZAW* 48 [1930]: 285) on exegetical grounds (Rudolph, HAT 12, 300: "see, [that is] the end of the heathens"; cf. Jer 17:11).

(b) The much-discussed expression *bᵉʾaḥᵃrît hayyāmîm* (13x: Gen 49:1; Num 24:14; Deut 4:30; 31:29; Isa 2:2 = Mic 4:1; Jer 23:20 = 30:24; 48:47; 49:39; Ezek 38:16; Hos 3:5; Dan 10:14; and Aram. *bᵉʾaḥᵃrît yômayyāʾ* in Dan 2:28), which has so far been treated together with *bᵉʾaḥᵃrît haššānîm* (Ezek 38:8), should be understood against the background of the discussion to this point. The interpretation of the expression was determined for too long by the later usage of the term *eschatos* in apocalypticism, but since the 1960s scholars have offered a more adequate evaluation of the formula in the framework of the givens of the Hebr. language and of the history of OT religion (cf. e.g., G. W. Buchanan, "Eschatology and the 'End of Days,' " *JNES* 20 [1961]: 188–93; A. Kapelrud, *VT* 11 [1961]: 395f.; H. Kosmala, "At the End of the Days," *ASTI* 2 [1963]: 27–37; Wildberger, *Isa 1–12,* CC, 81f.; Zimmerli, *Ezek,* Herm, 2:306f.).

On the older positions cf. Kosmala, op. cit. 27f.: if one translated the expression with W. Staerk (*ZAW* 11 [1891]: 247–53) as "at the end of days" or "in the last days" and understood it as eschatological in the stricter sense, one came necessarily either to an early dating of eschatology (e.g., H. Gressmann, *Der Messias* [1929], 74ff., 82ff.) or to a comprehensive late dating of the texts in question (e.g., S. Mowinckel, *He That Cometh* [1956], 131).

Because the expression *hayyāmîm* "the days" (or *haššānîm* "the years") does not refer to time per se (→ *yôm;* on the lack of the abstract, "empty" concept of time, cf. von Rad, *Theol.* 2:99ff.), nor to a limited period of time (era, present epoch), but to "the time currently transpiring" (with a light demonstrative force of the art.; cf. Kosmala, op. cit. 29), one should not assume the final meaning "end" for *ʾaḥᵃrît,* but, as in Akk. *ina/ana aḫrât ūmī* "in the future," etc. (*AHw* 21a; *CAD* A/1:194), the nonfinal meaning "later time, continuation, sequel, future." From the outset, therefore, no esp. eschatological meaning characterizes the expression *beʾaḥarît hayyāmîm* "in the sequence of time, in future days"; it signifies practically nothing more than the preceding *ʾaḥar* "after this" in Hos 3:5 and the subsequent *ʾaḥarê denâ* "thereafter" in Dan 2:29 (cf. v 45; Buchanan, op. cit. 190; Kosmala, op. cit. 29).

On the age of individual texts, see Wildberger, *Isa 1–12*, CC, 88: in addition to Gen 49:1 (introduction to the prophecies of Jacob's blessing) and Num 24:14 ("what this people will do to your people at a later time"), Isa 2:2 ("it will occur in the days to come"), and Jer 23:20 (Rudolph, HAT 12, 152f.: "it will become clear and meaningful to you afterward") may also be pre-exilic, against which Jer 30:24 (= 23:20); 48:47; and 49:39 ("but afterward I will restore Moab/Edom") should be regarded as post-exilic, as well as Hos 3:5 (closing formula of a promise) and Mic 4:1 (= Isa 2:2).

The secondary Dtn texts Deut 4:30 and 31:29 envision the calamitous present from the standpoint of the author, but an unspecified future from the standpoint of the fictive speaker, Moses, (4:30, "when all of this comes upon you in your distress in the time to come"; 31:29, "after my death . . . then calamity will come upon you in the time to come"; cf. in 4:32, "the earlier days = the past" as a contrast to the future of v 30); a special treatment of these two texts on account of their supposed eschatological content (H. H. Schmid, "Das Verständnis der Geschichte im Dtn.," *ZTK* 64 [1967]: 12n.71) seems unjustified.

Although the late texts Ezek 38:8, 16 and Dan 2:28; 10:14 stand in general contexts that are thoroughly eschatological in the stricter sense, they too are only prophecies concerning the distant future. If one translates "last time" (cf. *ʾaḥarît* in Dan 8:19, 23; 12:8), then the expression, in itself elastic, is colored by the context. Terminologically, the word → *qēṣ*, not quite synonymous with *ʾaḥarît* (Kosmala, op. cit. 30f.), occurs in Dan for the "end" in the actual sense.

Unlike prophetic introductory formulas not far removed from *beʾaḥarît hayyāmîm* in terms of meaning (e.g., *bayyôm hahûʾ* "in that day," *bayyāmîm hāhēm* "in those days," *bāʿēt hahîʾ* "at that time," *hinnēh yāmîm bāʾîm* "behold, days are coming"), no formulaic usage of the expression may be identified (contra Gressmann, op. cit. 84). Only Isa 2:2, "and it will happen in the course of days," may involve such a formulaic usage, but it is a unique introductory formula; otherwise, in terms of distribution and placement within a phrase, the expression is a rather ordinary temporal designation (its frequent placement at the end of the phrase [cf. Gen 49:1; Jer 48:47; 49:39; Hos 3:5] is due to its meaning).

5. On the continuation of the usage treated in 4b in the intertestamental and NT writings, cf. Kosmala, op. cit. 32ff.; G. Kittel, "ἔσχατος," *TDNT* 2:697f. On the exclusion of any other god (see 3) in the NT, cf. H. W. Beyer, "ἕτερος," *TDNT* 2:702–4.

E. Jenni

אֹיֵב ʾōyēb **enemy**

S 341; BDB 33a; *HALOT* 1:38b; *TDOT* 1:212–18; *TWOT* 78; *NIDOTTE* 367

1. The root *ʾyb* "to be hostile to" is extant only in Akk. and Can. In the OT, *ʾyb* qal occurs with only one exception in the ptcp., which is only rarely verbal (1 Sam 18:29; cf. Psa 69:5; Lam 3:52); as a rule it is a substantive. The abstract noun *ʾêbâ* "enmity" is included as a derivative.

Akk. *ayyābu* (and derivatives; cf. *AHw* 23f.; *CAD* A/1:221–24) and Ug. *ib* (*WUS* no. 7: *UT* no. 144; cf. also Can. *ibi* in EA 129:96 and 252:28, according to W. F. Albright, *BASOR* 89 [1943]: 32n.26) are attested only nominally, each in different nom. formations. In *KTU* 1.4.VII.35f., *ib* is par. to *šnu* "hater"; on the par. to Psa 92:10 in *KTU* 1.2.IV.8f., cf. H. Donner, *ZAW* 79 [1967]: 344–46.

Aram. uses primarily the ptcp. of → *śnʾ* "to hate" for "enemy" (e.g., in the Sef. inscriptions, *KAI* nos. 222B.26; 223B.14; 224.10–12; Fitzmyer, *Sef.* 16f., 82f., 89, 98f.; Bibl. Aram. in Dan 4:16 par. *ʿār*, → *ṣrr*) and later, e.g., Syr., *bᵉʿeldᵉbābā* (< Akk. *bēl dabābi*).

The PN *ʾîyôb* (Job) may derive from another source; cf. Stamm, *HEN* 416; → *ʾāb* III/5 and → *ʾayyēh* 1.

2. *ʾōyēb* occurs 282x (incl. 1 Sam 18:29 and fem. *ʾōyebet* in Mic 7:8, 10), 80x in the sg. and 202x in the pl. (2 Sam 19:10 pl. contrary to Mandl. 41c). The term is most frequent in Psa (74x), followed by Deut 25x, 1 Sam 20x, Jer 19x, 2 Sam 16x, Lam 15x, Lev 13x (only in Lev 26:7–44), Josh 11x; concentrations are in the psalms of lament and in the historical books; the word becomes much less frequent in the wisdom literature (and in Isa).

ʾyb qal occurs 1x as a finite verb (Exod 23:22 with a figura etymologica, par. → *ṣrr*), *ʾêbâ* 5x (Gen 3:15; Num 35:21f.; Ezek 25:15; 35:5).

3. (a) The sg. *ʾōyēb* describes the individual, particular enemy only rarely (in legal disputes: Exod 23:4; Num 35:23; Samson: Judg 16:23f.; Saul and David: 1 Sam 18:29; 19:17; 24:5; 26:8; 2 Sam 4:8; Elijah against Ahab: 1 Kgs 21:20; Nebuchadnezzar: Jer 44:30b; Job against God: Job 13:24; 33:10; Haman: Esth 7:6; on Yahweh as enemy, see 4). "The enemy" usually occurs in the general sense of the pl. "the enemies" (cf. e.g., 1 Kgs 8:37, 44 with 2 Chron 6:28, 34 and the alternation of sg. and pl. in Lam).

In most cases politico-military enemies of the people Israel are meant, as in various types of historiography (Num 10:9; 14:42; 32:21; Deut 1:42; 6:19; 12:10; 25:19; 11x in Josh 7:8–23:1; Judg 2:14[bis], 18; 3:28; 8:34; 11:36; 1 Sam 4:3; 12:10f.; 14:30; 29:8; 2 Sam 3:18; 19:10; 2 Kgs 17:39; 21:14[bis]; Esth 8:13; 9:1, 5, 16, 22; Ezra 8:22, 31; 5x in Neh; 2 Chron 20:27, 29; 25:8; 26:13), in community laments (Psa 44:17; 74:3, 10, 18; 80:7), in hymns (Psa 78:53; 81:15; 106:10, 42; cf. Deut 32:27, 31, 42; 33:27), and also in the Dtn war regulations (Deut 20:1, 3f., 14; 21:10; 23:10, 15) and in Solomon's prayer at the temple dedication (6x in 1 Kgs 8:33–48 par. 2 Chron 6:24–36). Concentrations of the word in blessings, cursings, and similar contexts are noteworthy (Gen 22:17;

49:8; Exod 23:22, 27; 13x in Lev 26:7–44; Num 10:35; 23:11; 24:10, 18 txt em; 8x in Deut 28:7–68; 30:7; 33:29; 1 Sam 25:26, 29; 2 Sam 18:32; 1 Kgs 3:11), to which occurrences in prophetic salvation and judgment sayings are topically related (in Isa only 9:10; 62:8; otherwise in all texts the "enemy" is a personified foreign nation, with the exception of Jer 30:14; Nah 1:2, 8 [see 4]; Mic 7:6 [see below]; Mic 7:8, 10).

Outside the Psa (see b), an individual's enemies receive infrequent mention (1 Sam 2:1; 14:24, 47; 18:25; 20:15f.; 24:5; 29:8; 2 Sam 5:20 = 1 Chron 14:11; 2 Sam 7:1, 9, 11 = 1 Chron 17:8, 10; 2 Sam 18:19; Mic 7:6; Psa 127:5 [a wisdom psalm]; Job 27:7; Prov 16:7; 24:17; 1 Chron 21:12; 22:9); the enemies of the kings should for the most part be equated with those of the people (2 Sam 22 = Psa 18:1, 4, 18, 38, 41, 49; Psa 21:9; 45:6; 72:9; 89:23, 43; 110:1f.; 132:18).

On the euphemistic insertion of *ʾōyᵉbê* in 1 Sam 20:16; 25:22; 2 Sam 12:14, cf. *HAL* 37b (with bibliog.) and comms.

The most frequent par. expressions are the qal/pi. ptcps. of → *śnʾ* "hater" (qal: Exod 23:4; Lev 26:17; Deut 30:7; 2 Sam 22:18 = Psa 18:18; Psa 21:9; 35:19; 38:20; 69:5; 106:10; Esth 9:1, 5, 16; pi.: Num 10:35; 2 Sam 22:41 = Psa 18:41; Psa 55:13; 68:2; 83:3) and *ṣār* "oppressor" (→ *ṣrr;* Num 10:9; Deut 32:27; Isa 1:24; 9:10 txt?; Mic 5:8; Nah 1:2; Psa 13:5; 27:2; 74:10; 81:15; 89:43; Lam 1:5; 2:4, 17; 4:12; Esth 7:6; cf. *ṣōrēr* Exod 23:22; Num 10:9; Psa 8:3; 143:12).

Other quasi-synonyms that appear with *ʾōyēb* include *mᵉbaqqēš rāʿâ* or *nepeš* "one who seeks evil" or "who seeks one's life" (→ *bqš;* Num 35:23; 1 Sam 25:26 or Jer 19:7, 9; 21:7; 34:20f.; 44:30bis; 49:37, resp.), *qām* "adversary" (→ *qûm;* Exod 15:6; 2 Sam 22:49 = Psa 18:49; Nah 1:8 txt em; cf. 2 Sam 18:32; *mitqômēm* Psa 59:2; Job 27:7), *mitnaqqēm* "vengeful one" (→ *nqm;* Psa 8:3; 44:17). The synonym *ṣōrēr* "enemy" occurs in general proximity to *ʾōyēb* in Psa 5:9; 27:11; 54:7; 56:3; 59:11. Cf. also → *śṭn* and the lists in Gunkel-Begrich 196f.

On the antonym *ʾōhēb* "friend" → *ʾhb* III/1.

(b) The question of who the individual's enemies in lament and thanksgiving psalms may be has already been much discussed (G. Marschall, *Die "Gottlosen" des ersten Psalmenbuches* [1929]; H. Birkeland, *Die Feinde des Individuums in der isr. Psalmenliteratur* [1933]; id., *Evildoers in the Book of Psalms* [1955],; N. H. Ridderbos, *De "werkers der ongerechtigheid" in de individueele Psalmen* [1939]; A. F. Puukko, "Der Feind in den atl. Psalmen," *OTS* 8 [1950]: 47–65; Westermann, *PLP* 165–213; summaries in J. J. Stamm, *TRu* 23 [1955]: 50–55; Kraus, *Psa,* CC, 1:95–99).

The material is cataloged in Gunkel-Begrich 196f., among others; texts with *ʾōyēb,* all contained in the genres of the individual hymns of lament and thanksgiving (incl. songs of confidence), are, with the sg.: Psa 7:6; 9:7; 13:3, 5; 31:9; 41:12; 42:10; 43:2; 55:4, 13; 61:4; 64:2; 143:3; with the pl.: Psa 3:8; 6:11; 9:4; 17:9; 25:2, 19; 27:2, 6; 30:2; 31:16; 35:19; 38:20; 41:3, 6; 54:9; 56:10; 59:2; 69:5, 19; 71:10; 102:9; 138:7; 139:22; 143:9, 12; cf. 119:98.

For the most part, interpretations involving party conflict (older Psa exegesis), magicians (S. Mowinckel, *Psalmenstudien* 1 [1921]), and enemies from abroad (Birkeland, op. cit.) should be rejected. Statements concerning the individual's enemies (their threatening schemes, their mocking speech, their corruption; cf. *PLP* 188–93) distinguish themselves markedly from those concerning the enemies in community laments. Although the enemies have already smitten Israel in the latter, in the former they threaten only the sick or the one fallen into legal difficulties. They do not cause the conditions of distress; rather, they attack the supplicant because he/she has fallen into misfortune (cf. Psa 71:11). The fact of the break within the existing social relationship greatly magnifies the difficulty (cf. Psa 41:7; 55:22).

The book of Job provides the best background for explanation and illustration. Because Job has fallen into difficulty, his friends consider him guilty and suspect him of secret sin. In 2 Sam 16, David too becomes the object of contempt and even actual attack following his displacement by Absalom. Sudden fall into suffering in the world of the time is still occasion for isolation, reproach, contempt, and animosity. Private conflicts and religious differences sharpen the isolation of the one who is already halfway in the realm of the dead (C. Barth, *Die Errettung vom Tode in den individuellen Klage- und Dankliedern des AT* [1947], 104–7).

4. (a) Texts that treat Yahweh's intervention against the people's or the individual's enemies (e.g., Exod 23:22, "If you . . . do all that I command, then I will be the enemy of your enemies and the oppressor of your oppressors") need not be listed. That Yahweh also hands his people over to the enemies is a possibility exhibited by the prophetic judgment preaching (Hos 8:3; Amos 9:4) and by the blessing-curse chaps. Lev 26 and Deut 28, and is expressed above all in Jer (6:25; 12:7; 15:9, 14; 17:4; 18:17; 19:7, 9; 20:4f.; 21:7; 34:20f.; 44:30; *ʾōyēb* occurs otherwise in Jer only in 15:11 txt?; 30:14 [see b]; 31:16 in a promise of restoration; and 49:37 in an oracle against the nations), in the laments (all texts), and in the Dtr history (Judg 2:14; 1 Kgs 8:33, 37, 46, 48 par.; 2 Kgs 21:14; cf. Neh 9:28).

(b) That Yahweh succeeds against his own enemies is already the theme of the oldest songs, which extol Yahweh as warrior (Exod 15:6, "your right hand, Yahweh, smashes the enemy"; cf. v 9; Num 10:35, in the ark saying, "stand up, Yahweh, so that your enemy may be dispersed"; Judg 5:31, "may all your enemies, Yahweh, perish so"). Similar statements occur in Psa, esp. in hymns with a somewhat archaic tone (Psa 8:3; 66:3; 68:2, 22, 24; 89:11, 52; 92:10bis). In the prophets, Isa 42:13; 59:18; 66:6, 14; and Nah 1:2, 8 continue the practice.

Texts such as 1 Sam 30:26 ("a gift from the plunder of Yahweh's enemies" with a propagandistic nuance, if *ʾōy^{e}bê* is not a secondary insertion; cf. W. Caspari, *Sam*, KAT, 387); Isa 1:24 (Yahweh's enemies within Israel); Psa 37:20 (a wisdom comparison of the godless with the enemies of Yahweh); 83:3 (in a communal lament in a so-called motif of divine intervention, the enemies of the people are presented to Yahweh as "your enemies") are isolated.

(c) Yahweh himself is called Israel's enemy directly only in Isa 63:10 ("therefore, he changed into their enemy"). Jer 30:14 and Lam 2:4f. compare Yahweh's activity with that of an enemy ("like an enemy"). Each states a paradox.

5. In the LXX, *ʾōyēb* is rendered almost exclusively by *echthros*. In the Qumran texts, *ʾōyēb* is frequent in 1QM (Kuhn, *Konk.* 4; also *GCDS* 8, 118). On the NT and its environment, cf. W. Foerster, "ἐχθρός," *TDNT* 2:811–15.

The concept of "love of the enemy" is absent from the OT; although some cite Exod 23:4f., only the fair treatment of the legal opponent with respect to aid in everyday situations is required here (Prov 25:21 uses → *śnʾ*).

E. Jenni

אֵיד *ʾêd* distress

S 343; BDB 15b; *HALOT* 1:39a; *TWOT* 38c; *NIDOTTE* 369

---

1. The root of the noun *ʾêd* "distress" cannot be clearly determined. An unattested verb **ʾûd* is usually assumed as the stem, for which Arab. words such as *ʾāda (ū)* (e.g., Zorell 40; contra P. Humbert, *TZ* 5 [1949]: 88; cf. L. Kopf, *VT* 6 [1956]: 289) are adduced. *HAL* 38a traces the word to **ʾaid* or **ʾayid*.

A verb *ʾûd* would indeed be attested, if one understood *(lᵉ)ʾêd* in Prov 17:5 as a ptcp., as recommended by G. R. Driver (*Bib* 32 [1951]: 182), who emends, however, to *(lā)ʾēd* ("as it ought to be written"!), and as understood by M. Dahood (*PNSP* 38f.) in reference to Ug., without emendation, as "a stative ptcp."; cf. further Gemser, HAT 16, 72f.; *CPT* 266, 321 (on Job 31:23 and 2 Sam 13:16).

Indeed, it may be better to proceed from Akk. *edû(m)* II "(threatening) flood, flood surge" (*AHw* 187b), which refers to "a rare and catastrophic event" (*CAD* E:36a), and assume it to be a Sum.-Akk. loanword (cf. E. A. Speiser, *BASOR* 140 [1955]: 9–11; M. Sæbø, "Die hebr. Nomina *ʾed* und *ʾēd*," *ST* 24 [1970]: 130–141).

2. *ʾêd* occurs 24x: in Job and Prov, 6x each; Jer, 5x, Obad 13, 3x; elsewhere Deut 32:35; Ezek 35:5; 2 Sam 22:19 = Psa 18:19. The texts of Ezek 35:5, as well as Prov 17:5; 27:10; and Job 31:23, have often been disputed. Except for Ezek 35:5, *ʾêd* occurs only in poetry. It never carries the art., although it is further specified 2x by PNs and 17x by sufs.

3. The word represents a relatively fixed term for "distress"; it is difficult to trace its semantic history. Nevertheless, two usages distinguish themselves from each other so clearly that their basic meaning should be differentiated semantically: (a) in a political or military sense in reference to a *people* (2 Sam 22:19 = Psa 18:19 too); (b) of the fate of an *individual* or a smaller group of individuals; the latter category involves the 12 wisdom occurrences in Job and Prov.

In both categories, *ʾêd* is often associated with "day" (Deut 32:35; 2 Sam 22:19 = Psa 18:19; Jer 18:17; 46:21; Obad 13 [3x]; Job 21:30; Prov 27:10) or "time" (*ʿēt*, Ezek 35:5; cf. Jer 46:21; 49:8); with the prep. *bᵉ*, it is a significant temporal and circumstantial determination. It can be said with equal validity of both groups that *ʾêd* comes "suddenly," surely in the sense of humanly "unfathomable" (Deut 32:35; Jer 48:16; Prov 6:15; 24:22; cf. 1:27). The predicate often has *bôʾ*, either in the qal "to come" (Jer 46:21; Prov 6:15; Job 21:17; cf. Jer 48:16 and *ʾātâ* "to come" Prov 1:27) or causatively in the hi. "to bring" (Jer 49:8, 32); in this regard, moreover, it is associated 3x with *ʿal* (Jer 46:21; 49:8; Job 21:17; cf. 30:12; Prov 1:27). Otherwise, in (a) *ʾêd* "is near" (*qārôb;* Deut 32:35; Jer 48:16) or in (b) it "arises" (*qûm;* Prov 24:22) or "stands ready *(nākôn)* for (the evildoer's) fall" (Job 18:12).

The word has several synonyms in both categories, but almost no antonym (cf., however, *nēr* "lamp" in Job 21:17; cf. also 18:5 and Horst, BK 16, 270); but the synonyms too are distributed among (a) and (b).

In (a) one encounters the frequent *rāʿâ* "evil, distress" (Jer 48:16; Obad 13; cf. also e.g., Isa 7:5; Jer 1:14) and expressions that sound the theme, favored by the prophets, of divine punishment (Jer 46:21; 49:8); cf. further Ezek 35:5, "at the time of their final punishment," and Obad 12, 14, "in the day of his misfortune/their fall/distress." By contrast, in (b) one encounters two uncommon words for "distress": *pîd* (Prov 24:22; otherwise only Job 12:5; 30:24; 31:29; cf. KBL 759a and Fohrer, KAT 16, 232, 237: "fall") and *nēker* (Job 31:3; cf. Obad 12; "something strange" = "something disastrous"); then the more frequent *paḥad* "terror" (Prov 1:26f.; cf. Job 31:23, etc.), *yôm ʿᵃbārôt* "day of wrath" (Job 21:30), and *ḥᵃbālîm* "pain" (Job 21:17), whereby *ʾêd* is associated with illness; so also in Job 30, where it is coupled with *ʾorḥôt* "ways" (*HAL* 84a: "dams"); Prov 1:27 compares *ʾêd* to a storm wind (cf. further Jer 18:17).

Over against the prophetic usage of *ʾêd* in (a), which seems to be traditional, the wisdom usage in (b) is more manifold and rich. The word may have had its own life in the wisdom sphere, but was then adopted by (later) prophetic speech.

4. The abstract nom. is, indeed, theologically neutral only in Prov 27:10; otherwise occurrences in Job and Prov express a theologically based (experiential) wisdom. *ʾêd* refers positively to God; even though it is also personified (esp. Job 18:12; cf. Fohrer, KAT 16, 303), it is still never subordinated to a "fate," but to God who brings it about (cf. Job 31:23; Prov 24:22). It is negatively associated with the disastrous destiny of the godless (*ʿawwāl, raʿ, rᵉšāʿîm);* it is "the final ruin which leads to death" (Fohrer, op. cit.). It belongs in the wisdom scheme of "deed and consequence" (cf. K. Koch, *ZTK* 52 [1955]: 2ff.); it can also appear, then, in the theodicy and lament of the embattled pious (Job 21:17, 30); in the final analysis one may trace it to God's righteousness. Indeed, prophetic occurrences, several of which center upon the national and religious crisis of the year 587 (Obad 13; Ezek 35:5; cf. Jer 49:8, 32) also point in the same direction; *ʾêd* expresses God's judicial activity (cf. Jer 18:17; 46:21; 48:16; also Deut 32:35). In the (perhaps late) thanksgiving hymn, Psa 18 and par., *ʾêd* is the polar opposite of divine help and salvation.

5. The word has no equivalent in the LXX; instead it is rendered by no fewer than twelve Gk. words, of which *apōleia* (9x) and *katastrophē* (2x) may be mentioned. Finally, the word is not attested in the available texts from Qumran and appears to have had no significance in the NT.

M. Sæbø

אַיֵּה *ʾayyēh* where?

S 346; BDB 32b; *HALOT* 1:39a; *TWOT* 75a; *NIDOTTE* 372

1. The element **ʾay-*, extant in all Sem. languages, occurs in various interrogative advs. and interrogative prons. (Barth, *Pronominalbildung* 144–49; *GVG* 1:327f.; Moscati, *Intro.* 114f., 120f.), incl. the Hebr. interrogative particles to be treated here: *ʾê, ʾêpōh,* and *ʾayyēh* "where?" (cf. Ug. *iy, WUS* no. 161; *UT* no. 143); also *ʾê mizzeh* and *mēʾayin* "whither?" *ʾān/ʾānâ* "(where), whither?" and *ʾî-* "where is?" in PNs (*HAL* 37b; Stamm, *HEN* 416). The negated statement "there is not" develops from the rhetorical question "where is?" (→ *ʾayin;* cf. *GVG* 1:500; 2:114; BL 633f.; I. Guidi, "Particelle interrogative e negative nelle lingue semitiche," FS Browne 175–78; A. Goetze, "Ugaritic Negations," FS Pedersen 115–23; cf. Akk. *yānu* "is/are not" < *ayyānum* "where?" *GAG* §111b; *CAD* I/J:323f.)

ʾêkâ (Song Sol 1:7bis) and *ʾêkōh* (2 Kgs 6:13) in the meaning "where?" are Aramaisms (Wagner no. 10).

G. R. Driver's (*WO* 1 [1947]: 31) suggestion that *ʾal* in 1 Sam 27:10 (usually emended to *ʾel-mî* or *ʾān*) may be associated with Akk. *ali* "where?" is unlikely.

2. The roughly 90 OT texts with the question "where?" (in addition to 27x "whence?" and 20x "whither?") use an entire series of interrogatives that are all formed with **ʾay-;* the most frequent, and the most important theologically, is *ʾayyēh.*

The following occur in the meaning "where?": (1) *ʾê* 4x (Gen 4:9; Deut 32:37; 1 Sam 26:16; Prov 31:4 Q txt?; cf. Gemser, HAT 16, 108; contra N. M. Sarna, *JNES* 15 [1956]: 118f.; *UT* §6.31 and no. 52: "any liquor");

(2) *ʾê zeh/ʾê-zeh* 17x, sometimes in a pron. usage "which?" (1 Sam 9:18; 1 Kgs 13:12; 22:24 = 2 Chron 18:23 plus *hadderek;* 2 Kgs 3:8; Isa 50:1; 66:1bis; Jer 6:16; Job 28:12, 20; 38:19bis, 24; Eccl 2:3; 11:6; Esth 7:5; cf. further *ʾê mizzeh* "whence?" 9x and *mēʾayin* "whence?" 17x, incl. 2 Kgs 5:25 Q; and *ʾê lāzōʾt* "on what account?" once in Jer 5:7);

(3) *ʾêpōh (ʾyph)* 10x (Gen 37:16; Judg 8:18; 1 Sam 19:22; 2 Sam 9:4; Isa 49:21; Jer 3:2; 36:19; Job 4:7; 38:4; Ruth 2:19; not to be confused with the *ʾēpôʾ* "for, therefore," written *ʾpwʾ* or *ʾpw,* which can accompany interrogatives such as *ʾayyēh* to intensify them);

(4) *ʾêkâ* 2x (Song Sol 1:7bis; otherwise 15x in the meaning "how?" alongside 60x *ʾêk,* 4x *ʾêkākâ,* and 2x *hêk* [Aramaism; cf. Wagner no. 73 and Bibl. Aram. *hēʾ-kᵉdî* "how" in Dan 2:43 < *hêk dî;* KBL 1068a]);

(5) *ʾêkōh* 1x (2 Kgs 6:13);

(6) *ʾānâ* 1x (Ruth 2:19; otherwise 19x "whither?" and 3x *ʾāneh wᵉʾānâ* "hither and thither," as well as 13x "[until] when?" → *mātay*); cf. *ʾān* in *mēʾān* "whence?" 2 Kgs 5:25 K, "whither?" 1 Sam 10:14; "(until) when?" Job 8:2;

(7) *ʾayyēh* 45x (Isa 10x, Jer 6x, Psa and Job 5x each, Gen 4x; in Judg 9:38 and Job 17:15 strengthened by *ʾêpōh* "then," in Psa 115:2 by *nāʾ* "then");

(8) with a pron. suf. with *ʾê* or *ʾayyēh* 8x (Gen 3:9; Exod 2:20; 2 Kgs 19:13; Isa 19:12 with *ʾēpôʾ* "who, then, are . . . ?"; Mic 7:10; Nah 3:17; Job 14:10; 20:7).

Aram. *ʾān* (*DISO* 18) is not attested in Bibl. Aram.

3. Perhaps only half of the *where* questions in the OT are genuine questions. In the majority of the cases *ʾayyēh* (exceptions are Gen 18:9; 19:5; 22:7; 38:21; Exod 2:20; 2 Sam 16:3; 17:20; Jer 2:6, 8; Job 35:10; Lam 2:12; in Nah 3:17 and Job 15:23 the text should be emended), and to a lesser degree *ʾê(-zeh)* and *ʾēpōh* (only Deut 32:37; Isa 50:1 or Jer 3:2; Job 4:7; 38:4, resp.), introduce rhetorical questions that, for various stylistic reasons (hyperbole, irony and derision, expression of lament, perplexity, etc.), expect the answer "nowhere." Examples from profane speech are Judg 9:38, "where is your mouth, now, you who said . . . "; Nah 2:12, "where, now, is the lion's lair . . . "; Job 17:15, "where, then, is there still hope for me?"

Questions with "whence?" and "whither?" are generally genuine questions (even Psa 121:1, "whence comes my help?"), which could sometimes become somewhat formulaic usages to open conversation (e.g., Judg 19:17, "whither are you going and whence are you coming?"; cf. Lande 40f.). Rhetorical questions also express the perplexity of the questioner or the impossibility of exit (with *mēʾayin:* Num 11:13; 2 Kgs 6:27; Nah 3:7; with *ʾānâ:* Gen 37:30; 2 Sam 13:13; Isa 10:3).

4. Psalmic, prophetic, and wisdom diction use the rhetorical question "where, then, is *x*" (= *x* is nowhere) in numerous forms (cf. F. Asensio, "Teologia e historia del pacto en torno a una interrogación bíblica," *Gregorianum* 47 [1966]: 665–84).

Distinct from this usage are cases in which the questioner already knows the answer ("here," etc.) but poses the question nevertheless, in order to appeal urgently to someone's responsibility: Gen 3:9, "Adam, where are you?"; 4:9, "where is your brother, Abel?"; 1 Sam 26:16, "where is the king's spear?"; also 2 Kgs 2:14, "where, now, is Yahweh, the God of Elijah?" as an appeal to Yahweh to manifest himself in a wondrous act.

The rhetorical question "where" in reference to God (in contrast to the authentic concern for God, which is, however, lacking in those mentioned in Jer 2:6, 8; Job 35:10) should be understood in most cases as a malicious denial of the existence and activity of God, less often (in the question concerning God's mighty deeds) as a lament of the embattled and as an appeal to the hidden God to demonstrate his (former) might (Judg 6:13; Isa 63:11[bis], 15; Mal 2:17; Psa 89:50, "where are your former demonstrations of grace?"). Community laments cite the enemies' mocking question: "Where now is their God?" (Joel 2:17; Psa 79:10; 115:2; cf. Mic 7:10; hence also in the individual lament, Psa 42:4, 11, "Where now is your God?"; similarly in the lament-prayer of Jer 17:15, "Where then is the word of Yahweh?"). The Rabshakeh's speech with the question, "Where are the gods of Hamath?" (2 Kgs 18:34 = Isa 36:19; cf. 2 Kgs 19:13 = Isa 37:13), also applies implicitly to the God of Israel. But Yahweh can also scoff at the impotence of the idols (Deut 32:37, "Where are their gods?"; Jer 2:28, "Where are your gods that you have made?").

In the spirited language of the prophetic and wisdom disputation, the rhetorical "where" is also used in the most varied contexts; cf. Isa 19:12; 33:18 (3x); 50:1; 51:13; Jer 3:2; 13:20; 37:19; Ezek 13:12; Hos 13:10, 14(bis) (reading *ʾayyēh* for MT *ʾĕhî*); Zech

1:5; Mal 1:6(bis); Job 4:7; 14:10; 20:7; 21:28(bis); 38:4; unanswerable questions as evidence for the finitude of knowledge: Job 28:12, 20; 38:19(bis), 24.

In view of the broad distribution of the stylistic technique (J. Konopásek, "Les 'questions rhétoriques' dans le NT," *RHPR* 12 [1932]: 47–66, 141–61; BDF §496), rhetorical questions with *pou* "where?" in the NT (Luke 8:25; Rom 3:27; 1 Cor 1:20 quoting Isa 19:11f.; 12:17; 15:55 following Hos 13:14; Gal 4:15; 1 Pet 4:18 quoting Prov 11:31 LXX; 2 Pet 3:4) may derive from OT tradition only in the event of thematic dependence.

E. Jenni

אַיִן *ʾayin* nothing

S 369; BDB 34a; *HALOT* 1:41b; *TWOT* 81; *NIDOTTE* 401

---

1. Hebr. *ʾayin* "nothing, is not" has cognates in Akk. *yānu* (*GAG* §§111b, 190b, Middle and Late Bab.), Ug. *in* (*WUS* no. 294; *UT* nos. 149, 252), Moab. *ʾn* (*KAI* no. 181.24); cf. Pun. *ynny* (*Poen.* 1006; Sznycer 142).

The basis of the word, treated in Hebr. as a segholate, appears to be the same as that of the interrogative → *ʾayyēh* "where." Therefore, *ʾayin* "nothing, is not" is usually derived from this interrogative particle: the rhetorical question "where is *X*?" could develop into a declaration "*X* is not here" (BL 633; cf. *HAL* 40b). The similar development in Akk. (→ *ʾayyēh* 1) supports this explanation.

Extrabibl. Hebr. occurrences are found in the second Silwan inscription (*KAI* no. 191B.1) and in Lachish letter IV (*KAI* no. 194.5, 7).

2. The word occurs in the OT 789x (*ʾayin* 42x, incl. Isa 41:24; Jer 30:7; *ʾên* 747x, 103x with suf.).

The contrary, *yēš* "to exist," occurs 140x (incl. *ʾīš* in 2 Sam 14:19 and Mic 6:10; cf. Wagner no. 28a, b; Gen 21x, Eccl 16x, Prov 13x, Job 12x).

Bibl. Aram. equivalents are *ʾîtay* (8x) and, negated, *lā ʾîtay* (9x).

3. The basic meaning is "nothing, nonexistent" (par. to *b*ᵉ*lî*, *biltî*, *ʾepes*, *tōhû*) as a negation of *yēš* "being, existent" (cf. Isa 44:8). On the usage of the word, see GKC §152i-p, u.

4. Among the various statements concerning God that use *ʾayin*, those which have a particular formulaic character stand out. Major occurrences are in Deutero-Isa; they are also encountered in a few Dtr texts and in Hos.

First, the formula *ʾên k*ᵉ . . . "there is none like . . . ," expresses a person's incomparability (cf. C. J. Labuschagne, *Incomparability of Yahweh in the OT* [1966]). Behind this comparison one must imagine the question "who is like you?" (1 Sam 26:15); the answer is "none is like you." This statement of incomparability does not occur in the OT in reference to a human (in the 3d per.: 1 Sam 10:24; Job 1:8; 2:3; cf. Lande 103); it occurs frequently, however, in prayers addressed to Yahweh (1 Sam 2:2; 2 Sam 7:22 = 1 Chron 17:20;

1 Kgs 8:23 = 2 Chron 6:14; Jer 10:6f.; Psa 86:8). It is also encountered in the 3d per. in the recognition formula in Exod 8:6, in descriptive praise in Deut 33:26, and as Yahweh's statement about himself in Exod 9:14.

In addition to statements concerning incomparability are those concerning uniqueness or exclusivity. The two speech forms in 1 Sam 2:2, "no one is holy like Yahweh, for beside you there is no other," and 2 Sam 7:22 = 1 Chron 17:20, "therefore you are great, O Lord, my God, for none is like you and there is no god except you," stand in this series. The Dtr influenced recognition formula emphasizes exclusivity with *ʾên ʿôd:* "you/all nations should recognize, that Yahweh is God and no other" (Deut 4:35, 39; 1 Kgs 8:60; cf. Deut 32:39). The statement of uniqueness is associated with the self-presentation formula (W. Zimmerli, "I Am Yahweh," *I Am Yahweh* [1982], 1–28) in Hos (Hos 13:4; cf. 5:14). In view of his emphasis upon the exclusive activity of the *one* God, Yahweh, in creation, direction of history, and salvation, it is no wonder that this combination appears often in Deutero-Isa. His preference for this form is probably also influenced by the hymnic self-glorification or self-praise of a divinity in his Bab. surroundings (cf. Westermann, *Isa 40–66*, OTL, 155f.). The simple form appears in the Cyrus oracle, Isa 45:5f., "I am Yahweh and no other," and in the judgment speech, 45:18, 22; supplemented with "and beside me there is no helper" in 43:11, with "and no one seizes out of my hand" in 43:13 (judgment speech), with "there is no true, saving god beside me" in 45:21, and with "I am God and nothing is like me" in 46:9 (disputation speech).

That these usages should not to be understood as "monotheistic formulae" (so B. Hartmann, *ZDMG* 110 [1961]: 229–35) may most clearly be seen from the genre in which they occur: Yahweh finds himself in a judicial process against the other gods. The phrase "and beside me there is no god" (44:6 cf. v 8) is not a declaration, but a claim (Westermann, *Isa 40–66*, OTL, 140f.; cf. 82ff.). Yahweh demands from the gods of the nations evidence of their divinity in the continuing historical process, evidence that they cannot produce. The opposition can only keep silent (41:26, "no one speaks, no one is heard, no one hears a sound from you") and quit the scene (41:28, "yet there is no one, no one knows their counsel"). The disputation speech in 40:12–31, which uses the phrase 6x, already indicates the significance of the word *ʾayin* for Deutero-Isa: twice to declare that the world's riches and powers are "nothing" before Yahweh (v 17; cf. 41:11f.); Yahweh makes them "nought" (v 23; cf. Ezek 26:21; 27:36; 28:19); Lebanon's wood and forests are insufficient for the presentation of sacrifice (v 16); Yahweh's understanding is unfathomable (v 28), he aids the faint (v 29); cf. further 50:2 and 63:3.

The denial of God *ʾên ʾᵉlōhîm* "there is no God" in Psa 10:4; 14:1 = 53:2 should not be understood theoretically but practically, as "God is not present/he does not intervene," the probable sense of 3:3, "he has no aid from God" (→ *ʾᵉlōhîm* IV/5; cf. Kraus, *Psa*, CC, 1:127f., 221, citing Köhler, *Theol.* 19f.). Cf. also positive statements with *yēš* "is present" in Gen 28:16; Exod 17:7; Judg 6:13; 1 Sam 17:46; Isa 44:8 (*yēš* elsewhere in theological contexts: 2 Kgs 3:12; Jer 14:22; 37:17; Psa 73:11; 2 Chron 25:8).

5. In addition to negated phrases, the LXX also often has compounds with α privative for *ʾayin*/*ʾên*. The formulae of incomparability and uniqueness recede in the NT, together with the struggle with strange gods; cf., however, 1 Cor 8:4.

S. Schwertner

אִישׁ ʾîš man

S 376; BDB 35b; *HALOT* 1:43a; *TDOT* 1:222–35; *TWOT* 83; *NIDOTTE* 408

I. Designations for "man" (in contrast to those for "woman" → *ʾiššâ*) diverged in the Sem. languages through various innovations. Therefore, *ʾîš* occurs only in Hebr., Phoen.-Pun., and older Aram. (*DISO* 26), as well as in Old SArab. (W. W. Müller, *ZAW* 75 [1963]: 306); other designations dominate in Akk. *(awīlu, eṭlu, mutu)*, Ug. *(bnš, mt)*, Aram. (→ *gbr*), and Arab. *(marʾ)*.

The etymology is wholly uncertain, even e.g., K. Elliger's attempt (*Studien zum Habakuk-Kommentar vom Toten Meer* [1953], 78f., 189; id., FS Alt 100f.) to derive the word from a root *ʾšš* (KBL 93b: "to be solid, compact"; *HAL* 91b: Arab. *ʾaṯṯa* "to shoot up") on the basis of *ʾšyšym* "men(?)" in 1QpHab 6:11 (thereafter posited also in Isa 16:7; cf. *HAL* 91b).

The pl. is formed regularly in Phoen.-Pun.; elsewhere, as in Hebr. *ʾanāšîm*, a form of the root *ʾnš* (P. Fronzaroli, *AANLR* 8/19 [1964]: 244, 262, 275) replaces it (cf. Hebr. *ʾenôš* "person"; → *ʾiššâ* "woman" < **ʾanṯ-at-* is not based on this root). The rarely attested pl. *ʾîšîm* may be a more recent formation analogous to the sg. (Isa 53:3; Psa 141:4; Prov 8:4; BL 616).

The diminutive *ʾîšôn* "little man (in the eye) = pupil" (Deut 32:10; Psa 17:8; Prov 7:2; for pars. in other languages, see *HAL* 42a) should be mentioned; the verb *ʾšš* hitpo. "to take courage" in Isa 46:8 is textually and grammatically disputed (cf. *HAL* 96b; *Bib* 41 [1960]: 173* no. 2620).

On the PNs *ʾešbaʿal* (1 Chron 8:33; 9:39; tendentiously altered in 2 Sam 2–4 into *ʾîš-bōšet* "man of shame") and *ʾîšhôd* (1 Chron 7:18) cf. *IP* 138, 225, although one must take into account the possibility of folk-etymological reinterpretations of forms that were originally quite different (cf. *HAL* 89b; even for *yiśśākār*, which according to Gen 30:18 is often understood as *ʾîš śākār* "hireling"). On *ʾîš-ṭôb* (2 Sam 10:6, 8), cf. A. Jirku, *ZAW* 62 (1950): 319; *HAL* 43a.

II. The total of 2,183 occurrences (incl. 2 Sam 16:23 Q; 23:21 Q; excl. Prov 18:24) of the sixth most frequent subst. are distributed normally across the entire OT, somewhat more densely in narrative (Gen, Judg, Sam) and legal books (incl. Prov):

	sg.	pl.	total
Gen	107	51	158
Exod	83	13	96
Lev	93	1	94
Num	98	33	131

Deut	76	14	90
Josh	39	33	72
Judg	155	44	199
1 Sam	141	70	211
2 Sam	105	34	139
1 Kgs	69	16	85
2 Kgs	104	23	127
Isa	49	14 +1	64
Jer	114	47	161
Ezek	65	24	89
Hos	10	–	10
Joel	2	2	4
Amos	2	1	3
Obad	1	2	3
Jonah	4	5	9
Mic	7	1	8
Nah	–	1	1
Hab	–	–	–
Zeph	2	2	4
Hag	3	–	3
Zech	20	3	23
Mal	4	–	4
Psa	38	6 +1	45
Job	29	13	42
Prov	84	5 +1	90
Ruth	19	2	21
Song Sol	3	–	3
Eccl	8	2	10
Lam	1	–	1
Esth	20	–	20
Dan	7	1	8
Ezra	4	10	14
Neh	24	20	44
1 Chron	24	17	41
2 Chron	43	13	56
total	1,657	523 +3	2,183*

III. 1. The word's basic meaning is "man" (the mature male in contrast to the woman). This meaning establishes a natural semantic field in which man and woman stand in contrast.

Nom. series such as "man and woman," "men and women" (sg. alongside pl. in Judg 9:49, 51 and 16:27[bis]) are common; in the patriarchally structured society of Israel (→ ʾ*āb* III/1), the male always occupies first position. The usage "man and/or woman" occurs regularly in legal texts in the meaning "anyone, whoever" (Exod 21:28f.; 35:29; 36:6; Lev 13:29, 38; 20:27; Num 5:6; 6:2; Deut 17:2, 5; 29:17; Esth 4:11; cf. 2 Chron 15:13). "Man and woman" or "men and women" can also describe the totality (Josh 6:21; 8:25; 1 Sam 15:3; 22:19; 27:9, 11; 2 Sam 6:19 = 1 Chron 16:3; Jer 6:11; 51:22; Neh 8:2f., some also in longer series). Tripartite series "men-women-children" also occur (Deut 31:12; Jer 40:7; Ezra 10:1; cf. Jer 44:7; with *mᵉtîm* Deut 2:34; 3:6; with *gᵉbārîm* Jer 41:16). The term *bēn* "son" occurs within the word field only in the general sense (e.g., Gen 42:11, 13; Deut 1:31; Ezek 16:45bis; Mal 3:17).

The man seeks sexual union with the woman (Gen 2:24) or, conversely, the woman with him (cf. Jer 29:6).

"To be married" from the woman's perspective is *hāyᵉtâ lᵉʾîš* (Lev 21:3; Ezek 44:25). Conversely a maiden who has known no man can be defined as such (*lōʾ-yādᵉʿâ ʾîš* Judg 11:39; 21:12; cf. Gen 19:8; 24:16). A whole series of issues concerning extramarital sexual relations between man and woman (slave, maiden, fiancée) are legally regulated (Lev 19:20; Deut 22:22–29), as is sexual involvement with a menstruating woman (Lev 15:24, 33), levirate marriage (Deut 25:7), the emission of semen (Lev 15:16ff.), etc.

In its basic meaning *geber* is a synonym, though it is used much less frequently (→ *gbr;* Deut 22:5 in contrast to *ʾiššâ;* often used like *ʾîš:* Num 24:3, 15). *mᵉtîm* "men, people," which occurs only in the pl., is also infrequent (22x, 6x each in Deut and Job; Akk. *mutu,* Ug. *mt,* Eth. *met* "man, husband"; cf. also the PNs *mᵉtûšāʾēl* Gen 4:18 and *mᵉtûšelaḥ,* Gen 5:21–27; 1 Chron 1:3).

zākār "male, man" occurs esp. to indicate gender (82x, 18x each in Lev and Num, 14x in Gen, 12x in Ezra 8; in addition to the old collective *zᵉkûr* "that which is male" in the pilgrimage law, Exod 23:17 = 34:23 = Deut 16:16, and in the holy war commandment, Deut 20:13; the root **d̲akar-* "male" is common Sem.); its regular antonym is *nᵉqēbâ* "feminine" (22x, except for the difficult text Jer 31:22 [cf. Rudolph, HAT 12, 198f.] only in the Pentateuch).

ʾîš in the basic meaning applies to animals only in Gen 7:2(bis) (otherwise *zākār,* Gen 6:19; 7:3, etc).

2. The basic meaning is commonly limited in a more specialized sense:

(a) Often *ʾîš* should simply be translated "husband" (Gen 3:6, 16, etc.). Legal texts dealing with issues of marital law belong particularly in this category (Num 5:12ff., suspected adultery; 30:8ff., vows before marriage; Deut 22:13ff., divorce; 24:1–4, remarriage after divorce; cf. Jer 3:1; Deut 24:5, exemption from military service).

On the description of Yahweh as "husband" see IV/3.

For the meaning "husband," the term → *baʿal* "husband" is a synonym (2 Sam 11:26 par. to *ʾîš*); cf. also → *ʾādôn* (Gen 18:12; Judg 19:26f.; Amos 4:1; Psa 45:12).

(b) In a few texts *ʾîš* specifically characterizes typical masc. properties such as strength, influence, courage (1 Sam 4:9; 26:15; 1 Kgs 2:2; cf. Gen 44:15; Judg 8:21, etc.). *geber* is a synonym, although it is seldom used in this sense (Job 38:3; 40:7).

(c) *ʾîš* seems to be limited in meaning to "father" or "son" only in a few texts where *ʾîš* "one, someone" contrasts with sons or parents in a general sense in place of the more exact term of relationship (father-child, Gen 42:11, 13; Deut 1:31; 8:5; Mal 3:17; son-parents, Gen 2:24; 1 Sam 1:11; Amos 2:7; Isa 66:13; cf. also Gen 4:1).

(d) In accordance with the context, the pl. can also replace more specific designations. Thus the "men" in Gen 12:20 are Pharaoh's escort for Abraham, in Josh 9:14 mediators, in Josh 10:18 watchmen, in 2 Sam 18:28 rebels, etc. "Men" are very often scouts (Num 13f.; Deut 1; Josh 2; 6f.) or escorts, primarily in Sam and Kgs (frequently in the suf. form *ʾanāšāyw* "his men"). As followers of David (about 30x), Saul, Abner, or Joab perform military functions as a rule (contrast e.g., Gen 24:54, 59; 2 Kgs 5:24).

3. The term lends itself readily to a collective usage, at times in association with numerals (e.g., 2 Kgs 4:43; 10:6, 14). This usage is at home in narrative books; cf. also the fixed expression *ʾîš* → *yiśrāʾēl.*

4. *ʾîš* is quite often used in the generalized meaning "person": (a) The tendency toward generalization may be identified particularly in legal texts (e.g., Exod 21:12 "whoever strikes a man"; the same penalty is applicable to those who strike a woman), in wisdom texts (e.g., Prov 12:25; Psa 37:7), and in curses or blessings (Deut 27:15, "cursed is one who"; Psa 1:1; 112:1, 5, etc.).

(b) The general meaning "person" occurs wherever *ʾîš* contrasts with an animal (Exod 11:7; 19:13; Psa 22:7), as well as wherever a person is distinguished from God: markedly in Num 23:19; Judg 9:9, 13; 1 Sam 2:26, etc.; cf. *bᵉšēbeṭ ʾᵃnāšîm* "with a human rod" (2 Sam 7:14); *miṣwat ʾᵃnāšîm* "human commandment" (Isa 29:13; see IV/5b).

(c) Generalization appears primarily in word combinations: *ʾanšê habbayit* "domestics" (Gen 39:11, 14, incl. both male and female), *bᵉʾammat-ʾîš* "according to the customary measure" (Deut 3:11), etc.

In this general meaning → *ʾādām*, a synonymous term occasionally par. to *ʾîš* (Isa 2:9, 11, 17; 5:15; Psa 62:10, etc.), is comparable; cf. also the term *ʾᵉnôš*, used in the later period mostly in the sense of "weak, mortal" (→ *ʾādām*).

(d) The frequent use of *ʾîš* as a pron. in the sense of "any, everyone, anyone," negated "none," may only be mentioned.

5. *ʾîš* occurs in a whole series of phrases, only the most important of which are listed:

(a) In addition to the common *yôšēb* "inhabitant" to describe the inhabitants of a city or a country (inhabitant of a city: either through the phrase *ʾanšê hāʿîr*, e.g., Gen 24:13 or *ʾanšê hammāqôm*, e.g., Gen 26:7, or in conjunction with a place-name, e.g., Josh 7:4f.; citizens of a country: either in the pl. cs. *ʾanšê yiśrāʾēl*, e.g., 1 Sam 7:11, or collective *ʾîš yiśrāʾēl*, *ʾîš yᵉhûdâ*, etc.). An individual inhabitant of a city or country is described as *ʾîš ṣōrî* "man from Tyre" (1 Kgs 7:14), *ʾîš miṣrî* "Egyptian" (Gen 39:1), etc.

(b) Five texts mention *ʾanšê habbayit:* Gen 17:23, 27 (circumcised male household slaves); 39:11, 14 (Potiphar's domestics); Mic 7:6 (residents of the same house).

(c) *ʾîš* appears in many phrases indicating vocations. *ʾîš milḥāmâ* (or pl.) is the "warrior" (Exod 15:3; see IV/1; Josh 17:1; 1 Sam 18:5, etc.; but also "enemy," 2 Sam 8:10 = 1 Chron 18:10; Isa 41:12). In Solomon's time a specific vocational group seems to have been indicated in this manner (1 Kgs 9:22); the term is attested most frequently in the late royal period (as synonyms cf. *mᵉtîm* in Deut 33:6; Isa 3:25; and *baḥûrîm* Isa 9:16). *ʾîš ḥayil* is closely related. It refers to "able men" in the giving of the law (Exod 18:21, 25), suitable overseers for Pharaoh's cattle (Gen 47:6), useful doormen (1 Chron 26:8), etc. Since the period of the judges, the *ʾanšê ḥayil* are "able warriors" (Judg 3:29; 2 Sam 11:16, etc.); cf. *gibbôr ḥayil*, → *gbr*). Further vocational designations are *ʾîš nābîʾ* "prophet" (Judg 6:8), *ʾîš hāʾᵃdāmâ* "farmer" (Gen 9:20), *ʾîš yōdēaʿ ṣayid* "hunter" (25:27), etc. *ʾîš habbēnayim* "champion" (1 Sam 17:4, 23), *ʾîš raglî* "foot soldiers" (2 Sam 8:4 = 1 Chron 18:4; 1 Chron 19:18), etc., should also be mentioned as descriptions of the activity or being of a man.

(d) *ʾîš* serves as a circumlocution for an adj. in e.g., *ʾîš śāʿīr* "hairy" and *ʾîš ḥālāq* (Gen 27:11).

(e) The expression *bᵉnê ʾîš* occurs occasionally (Psa 4:3; Lam 3:33; par. to *bᵉnê ʾādām* in Psa 49:3 and 62:10). This combination is first attested in the exilic period and may best be translated "people"; the translation "aristocrat" may be considered only for Psa 49:3 (cf. *HAL* 42a; Kraus, *Psa*, CC, 1:148, 481).

(f) The expression *kᵉʾîš ʾeḥād* "as *one* man" describes the unity and cohesiveness of a group, e.g., when the community assembles "as *one* man" (Judg 20:1; Ezra 3:1; Neh 8:1) or when it moves out to battle "as *one* man" (1 Sam 11:7, etc.). One can also kill a large number of people "as *one* man" (Num 14:15, etc.); cf. the concept of the ban in holy war (→ *ḥrm*).

(g) Finally, mention should also be made of expressions that generalize the meaning of *ʾîš* to a great degree (see III/4d). In association with → *rēaʿ* and → *ʾāḥ*, the basic meaning fades to "one to another, one another" (e.g., Exod 18:7 and Gen 42:21). Gen 15:10, where the personal reference itself is lost, lies farthest from the original meaning: "Abraham laid each portion (of the dissected animals) over against the other."

IV. 1. Although the OT represents Yahweh as a male, it describes him as *ʾîš* only infrequently and metaphorically.

The descriptive ascription of praise in Exod 15:3 calls Yahweh an *ʾîš milḥāmâ* "warrior." This statement summarizes a discovery Israel made in military conflicts with its neighbors. Deutero-Isa (42:13) takes up this speech form, as well as the term *ʾîš milḥāmôt* "warrior"; nevertheless, Yahweh's activity is compared here only with that of a warrior *(kᵉʾîš milḥāmôt)*.

2. (a) The old promise narrative in Gen 18 discusses Yahweh and the three men in a strange alternation. Because Yahweh is explicitly named as subj. in v 13 (v 1 is later), he may also be meant as subj. in the other verses that require a sg. subj. (3, 10, 14b, 15b). Gen 18 represents Yahweh as one who appears in the form of "three men," although it never explicitly identifies Yahweh with these three men. Cf. the two men in Gen 19 and the "man" in Gen 32:23ff. In connection with pre-Israelite saga materials, Israel's most ancient period apparently had no misgivings about representing Yahweh as a man, who looks like other men, wanders the earth, eats, or fights (a similar concept may also be found in Josh 5:13–15 and Ezek 8:2).

(b) A few post-exilic instances in connection with the prophetic view of the future describe the heavenly being sent to people (the prophets) as *ʾîš;* although these beings are not, in fact, identical with God, they are also not always sharply distinguished from him:

Ezek 9:2ff. ("six men with an implement of destruction," "man with linen clothing"; cf. Exod 12:12 P; 12:23 J, where Yahweh himself, in the form of the angel of death, moves through Egypt); Ezek 40:3–5; 43:6; 47:3 ("man with the measuring device"); Zech 1:8, 10 ("man between the myrtle trees"); Zech 2:5 ("man with the measuring line"); Dan 10:5; 12:6f. ("man in linen clothing").

3. Hos 2:4, 9, 18 describe Yahweh as Israel's husband. In Israel's early days this description would have been impossible, for it adapts a concept from Can. Baalism with its *hieros gamos* and cultic prostitution. Hosea was the first who could dare to use such a picture; however, the adapted picture allows him to criticize precisely those who felt themselves attracted to this Can. sex cult (cf. Wolff, *Hos*, Herm, 49f., and Rudolph, KAT 13/1, 78f.).

Ezek takes up this fig. language again (Ezek 16, clearly in vv 23, 45; cf., however, also vv 8, 20). In terms of content, Jer 3:6ff. and Ezek 23 could be named here too, but the term *ʾîš* is absent.

Other texts also compare Yahweh or his activity directly with that of a person: Exod 33:11 (as a man speaks with his friend, so God with Moses); Deut 1:31; 8:5; Mal 3:17 (as a man carries/disciplines/has mercy on his children).

4. The "man of God" stands unequivocally on the side of the people; he is the commissioned ambassador of God. The term *ʾîš hāʾᵉlōhîm* occurs 76x in the OT, 55x in Kgs alone.

The following are described as men of God: Elisha (29x in 2 Kgs 4:7–13:19); Elijah (7x in 1 Kgs 17:18, 24; 2 Kgs 1:9–13); Moses (6x in Deut 33:1; Josh 14:6; Psa 90:1; Ezra 3:2; 1 Chron 23:14; 2 Chron 30:16); Samuel (4x in 1 Sam 9:6–10); David (3x in Neh 12:24, 36; 2 Chron 8:14); Shemaiah (1 Kgs 12:22; 2 Chron 11:2); Hanan (Jer 35:4); anonymous men of God (24x in Judg 13:6, 8; 1 Sam 2:27; 1 Kgs 13:1–29; 20:28; 2 Kgs 23:16f.; 2 Chron 25:7, 9bis); → *ʾᵉlōhîm* III/6.

Besides *rōʾeh* "seer" (→ *rʾh*) and → *nābîʾ* "prophet," *ʾîš hāʾᵉlōhîm* is one of the most significant terms for Israel's earliest prophets. Despite a few shades of meaning (Elijah and Elisha are "men of God," their students are called "disciples"; in 1 Kgs 13 a "man of God" and a "prophet" stand in direct opposition), the early man of God exercised prophetic functions.

The "word-reception" formula (1 Kgs 12:22; 17:2, 8), the messenger commission (1 Kgs 12:23; 2 Kgs 1:3, 15), and the messenger formula (1 Sam 2:27; 1 Kgs 12:24; 13:2; 17:14; 20:28, etc.) occur in the word field. Like prophets, the men of God of the early prophetic narratives also announce salvation or judgment. "Man of God" and "prophet" are frequently used synonymously (1 Sam 9:8f.; 1 Kgs 13:18, etc.); cf. C. Kuhl, *Israels Propheten* [1956], 14f.; von Rad, *Theol.* 2:6f.

The term never describes the so-called writing prophets of the 8th–6th cents. In the late period it fades to a simple title for great men (Moses, David).

In addition, reports are made concerning men whom Yahweh has entrusted with a special task: "the staff of the man whom I choose" (Num 17:20; cf. 2 Chron 6:5); "man of my plan" (= Cyrus, Isa 46:11); "man who prophesies in the name of Yahweh" (Jer 26:20); "man of your right hand" (Psa 80:18), etc.

5. The occurrences named above that describe God directly as *ʾîš* or that compare his activity with that of an *ʾîš* (IV/3) are rare in comparison to those which present the *ʾîš* as God's creation and thus in clear distinction from God.

(a) The term is rare in Gen 2–3 (2:23f.; 3:6, 16; the leading term is → *ʾādām*).

(b) A few texts emphasize the difference between God and human very precisely: in contrast to God the human is mortal (Psa 39:7; 62:10); unlike the human God does not lie (Num 23:19) and he stands by his word (Hos 11:9). Wisdom literature in particular refers to this contrast: Prov 21:2; 14:12, etc. Cf. also texts such as Gen 32:29; Josh 10:14; Judg 9:9, 13; 2 Sam 7:14; 2 Kgs 5:7; Isa 40:6ff. (→ *bāśār*).

6. As far as the person per se is concerned, human activity, particularly sexual behavior, is regulated by a series of divine commandments, transgression of which summons the wrath and punishment of Yahweh. A few relationships may be noted:

(a) All must assemble for the reading of the law: men, women, children, foreigners (Deut 31:12; cf. Josh 8:35). Reports concerning the assemblies of the people conducted by Ezra and Nehemiah refer to such lists also (Ezra 10:1; Neh 8:2f.).

(b) The holy war commandment effects men, women, and children (cattle, sheep, and asses; Josh 6:21; 8:25; 1 Sam 15:3, etc.). Prophecy adopts similar lists, except that the enemies of Yahweh who will be totally destroyed are now the Israelites themselves (Jer 6:11; 44:7; cf. 51:22).

(c) The marriage of an Israelite to a foreign woman was permitted at times, but with the passing of time was ever more sharply condemned theologically in Israel, for pagan wives meant the introduction of pagan cults (Gen 34:14; above all in post-exilic times: Num 25:6; Ezra 10:17; Neh 13:25).

(d) Israel protected itself with particular vigor against the introduction and acceptance of pagan cults since the time of Deut. For this reason, idolatrous men are also severely punished (Deut 17:2, 5; 29:19; Ezek 8:11, 16; 11:1; 14:3, 8).

(e) Whoever transgresses against these commandments will be punished, for Yahweh "requites man according to his doing" (Job 34:11; cf., among others, 1 Sam 26:23; 1 Kgs 8:39 = 2 Chron 6:30; Jer 31:30; 32:19; Ezek 7:16; Psa 62:13; Prov 24:29; 2 Chron 25:4).

V. The NT makes a distinction between *anēr* "man, person" (A. Oepke, "ἀνήρ," *TDNT* 1:360–63) and *anthrōpos* "person" (J. Jeremias, "ἄνθρωπος," *TDNT* 1:364–67). Individual lines of tradition from the OT are continued here. A clear division is maintained between God and human (Matt 21:25; Acts 5:29 with *anthrōpos;* John 1:13 with *anēr*), while the connection between God and human is seen in Jesus of Nazareth (Mark 14:71; 15:39; John 19:5 with *anthrōpos;* John 1:30; Acts 2:22; 17:31 with *anēr*).

J. Kühlewein

אכל *ʾkl* to eat

S 398; BDB 371; *HALOT* 1:46a; *TDOT* 1:236–41; *TWOT* 85; *NIDOTTE* 430

---

1. The root *ʾkl* is common Sem. (Eth. only as a subst.). It appears in the Hebr. OT in the qal, ni., pu., and hi., in Aram. only in the pe. (see 3a). The relatively numerous nom. derivatives (only Hebr.) with the general meaning "food," the segholate formations *ʾōkel* and fem. *ʾoklâ,* the Aramaizing form *ʾᵃkilâ,* the nouns with preformative *ma-: maʾᵃkāl* and *maʾᵃkōlet* (1 Kgs 5:25 *makkōlet;* see GKC §23f), are differentiated in 3b. *maʾᵃkelet* "knife" appears as an instrumental noun.

Somewhat synonymous is *lḥm* "to dine" (6x, also Ug. alongside *ʾkl;* on Phoen. Kilamuwa 1.6, cf. *DISO* 137 and *KAI* 2:32; Akk. *laʾāmum, laḫāmu, lêmu* "to partake, eat," *AHw* 527b, 543b), with the subst. *leḥem* "bread, nourishment" (299x, incl. Isa 47:14 and Job 30:4 and 1x Aram. in Dan 5:1 "meal"; also Pun., Aram.; on Arab. *laḥm* "flesh" see L. Köhler, *JSS* 1 [1956]: 10; on Eth. see E. Ullendorff, *VT* 6 [1956]: 192), which occurs in theological contexts in statements concerning Yahweh's creative might (Psa 136:25; 146:7; 147:9; on Deut 8:3 cf. von Rad, *Deut*, OTL, 71f.; H. Brunner, *VT* 8 [1958]: 428f.).

ṭʿm "to taste" is semantically related (11x, fig. "to feel, experience" in Psa 34:9; Prov 31:18) with the subst. *ṭaʿam* "taste," fig. "understanding" (12x, in addition to Jonah 3:7 "command," a meaning borrowed from Aram. or Akk.; cf. Wagner no. 117); Bibl. Aram. *ṭʿm* pa. "to give to eat," subst. *ṭaʿam* and *ṭᵉʿēm* "understanding; command, report."

Other terms for eating, sometimes with more specific meanings, include *brh* "to eat an invalid diet" (*biryâ* and *bārût* "invalid, mourning diet"), *gzr* "to devour" (Isa 9:19), *zûn* "to nourish" (Job 36:31 txt em; *māzôn* "nourishment"; Aram. hitpe. "to nourish oneself" and *māzôn*), *ṣyd* hitp. "to supply oneself" (*ṣayid* and *ṣēdâ* "travel provisions"), as well as *ʾᵃrûḥâ* "food allowance (for the trail)" (cf. *HAL* 84b) and *mispôʾ* "feed" (Ug. *spʾ* "to eat"); cf. further the roots beginning, significantly, with the liquid *l*: *lhṭ* "to consume," *lḥk* "to lick up, eat up," *lʿṭ* "to swallow," *lāšād* "pastries" (Num 11:8; Arab. *lsd* "to suck"); on *lʿʿ* "to slurp" and *lqq* "to lap up" → *šth* "to drink."*

2. According to Mandl. and Lis. (cf. 3b), the verb occurs 809x in Hebr. and 7x in Aram. in the OT (qal 739x plus 7x Aram. pe., ni. 45x, pu. 5x, hi. 20x), *ʾōkel* 44x, *ʾoklâ* 18x (only Ezek and P with the exception of Jer 12:9, always with the prep. *lᵉ*), *ʾᵃkîlâ* 1x, *maʾᵃkāl* 30x, *maʾᵃkōlet* 2x, *makkōlet* 1x, *maʾᵃkelet* 4x (except for the last, the nouns occur only in the sg.).

3. (a) In the vast majority of texts, the verb has the lit. sense "to eat, devour" as a description of a basic function of human and animal life. In association with seeing, hearing, and eating, *ʾkl* can serve as evidence of vitality (Deut 4:28). Nevertheless, numerous nouns other than people and animals can appear as the subj. of *ʾkl* in fig. meanings ("to consume," etc.): fire (about 70x), sword (12x), land (Lev 26:38; Num 13:32; Ezek 36:13f.), forest (2 Sam 18:8), heat and cold (Gen 31:40), curse (Isa 24:6), rage (Exod 15:7), hunger and pestilence (Ezek 7:15), illness (Job 18:13). Accordingly, the objs. of the verbs are not limited to the description of various foods: land (Jer 8:16; 2 Chron 7:13), farmland (Gen 3:17; Isa 1:7), ruins (Isa 5:17), inheritance (Deut 18:1; hi. Isa 58:14), property (Gen 31:15; Isa 61:6; Eccl 5:10, 18; 6:2), sin (Hos 4:8), etc. These combinations result in various expansions of meaning: "to make an end," but also "to enjoy, enjoy the use of, bear the consequences" (esp. with the obj. "fruit," Isa 3:10; Prov 1:31, etc.). A dramatic pictorial idiom with a per. obj., e.g., people, nations, the poor, beloved, also occurs (Psa 14:4 = 53:5; Deut 7:16; Jer 10:25, a play on words with *klh* pi. "to destroy"; 30:16, etc.; Hab 3:14; Prov 30:14).

A similar growth of meaning also occurs for Akk. *akālu*, which can appear with the subjs. fire, gods, diseases, pain, distress, etc. As in Hebr., the Akk. verb can have the more general meaning "to use up" or "to enjoy the use of" depending upon the obj. (field, property, money, etc.).

The verb without obj. also occasionally has an expanded meaning, "to exploit" (2 Sam 19:43) or "to feast" (Eccl 10:16). An expansion of meaning with pars. in Akk. occurs in Ezek 42:5, where *ʾkl* should not be emended, but means "to lay claim to space, area" (cf. *AHw* 27a).

The expression *ʾkl qarṣîn* "to slander" (lit. "to eat pinched-off portions"), known from Akk. (*CAD* A/I:255f.; M. Held, *JCS* 15 [1961]: 12) and Aram. (KBL 1121), occurs in Dan 3:8 and 6:25.

On the expression "to eat his flesh" (Eccl 4:5; hi. Isa 49:26), cf. the idiom in the Kilamuwa inscription 1.6–8 concerning the consumption of one's own beard and hand as a symbol of extreme despair (*KAI* 2:31f.; M. Dahood, *CBQ* 22 [1960]: 404f.; cf. *ANET* 654b).

Assyr. pars. to the (reported or threatened in curses) consumption of the flesh of one's own children or relatives in a famine are noteworthy (*CAD* A/I:250b; D. R. Hillers, *Treaty-Curses and the OT Prophets* [1964], 62f.; cf. 2 Kgs 6:28f.; Lev 26:29; Deut 28:53–57; Isa 9:19; Jer 19:9; Ezek 5:10; Zech 11:9; cf. Lam 4:10).

Not eating, even when unrelated to cultic fasting, signifies sadness (1 Sam 1:7; cf. v 18; 20:34; 1 Kgs 21:4f.; cf. v 7; Ezra 10:6). Conversely, eating is frequently associated with joy (1 Sam 30:16; Job 21:25; Eccl 9:7; Isa 22:13; cf. Gilg. X:iii.6ff. = *ANET* 90; Schott 77f.).

(b) L. Köhler (*JSS* 1 [1956]: 20–22) has referred to the problem of the coexistence of 5 or 6 nom. forms for "nourishment, food." Observation of the context permits the following differentiations:

(1) *ʾōkel* is a collective term for the concrete, quantitative entity "nourishment" (often = "grain"; cf. Akk. *ak(a)lu* "bread," Eth. *ʾekel* "grain"; Ug. *akl* also "grain"; see *UHP* 50). Exod 12:4; 16:16, 18, 21 "according to his appetite," and Job 20:21 "for his gluttony," should be considered qal inf. (therefore qal 744x, *ʾōkel* 39x). Ruth 2:14 *ʿēt hāʾōkel* "mealtime" does not argue unequivocally for a verbal abstract.

(2) *ʾoklâ* (except for Jer 12:9, only Ezek and P, always with *l*ᵉ) should be understood as a fem. inf. (preferred in the later period according to Berg., *HG* 2:84) and thus an action noun.

(3) *ʾᵃkîlâ* (1 Kgs 19:8 "wandered on the strength of this food for 40 days") corresponds to a pass. ptcp. and describes the "eaten food."

(4) According to Nyberg 205ff., *maʾᵃkāl* corresponds to a substantivized relative clause ("that which one eats") and indicates food in relation to its consumability and qualitative variety (cf. *maʾᵃkāl* alongside *lᵉʾoklâ* in Gen 6:21).

(5) *maʾᵃkōlet* (Isa 9:4, 18, "food [for the fire]") probably also corresponds to a pass. ptcp. (otherwise *makkōlet* "provision" 1 Kgs 5:25).*

4. In contrast to Assyr.-Bab. or Ug. divinities (cf. G. E. Wright, *OT Against Its Environment* [1950], 102ff.; W. Herrmann, "Götterspeise und Göttertrank in Ugarit und Israel," *ZAW* 72 [1960]: 205–16), Yahweh is the subj. of *ʾkl* only very rarely and then only negated or in comparisons: Deut 4:24 and 9:3, Yahweh as "consuming fire" (on this and on "fire of God" → *ʾēš* 4; → *kābôd*); Hos 13:8, "and I will consume them immediately like a lion" (however, the text should be emended with the comms.: "there the dogs will eat them up"); Psa 50:13 is a polemic against the notion of Yahweh eating: "Shall I eat the flesh of bulls and drink the blood of rams?" (cf. Deut 32:37f., "where are their gods . . . who ate the fat of their sacrifice?"; Eichrodt 1:141–44; de Vaux 2:449–50).

In contrast, Yahweh appears 13x as the subj. of the hi. "to give to eat," whether as the granter of good gifts (Exod 16:32 and Deut 8:3, 16, manna;

further Isa 58:14; Ezek 16:19; Hos 11:4 txt?; Psa 81:17; in Ezek 3:2 a divine scroll at the commissioning) or in the execution of judgment (Isa 49:26; Jer 9:14; 19:9; 23:15; Psa 80:6).

Eating appears primarily as a religious act in the sacrifice regulations (L. Rost, *BHH* 2:1345–50) and food laws (Lev 11; Deut 14; W. Bunte, *BHH* 3:1828), as well as in the ordinances and narratives concerning not eating (and not drinking) as ritual fasting (→ *ṣûm*). In Lev alone *ʾkl* qal appears 82x, in addition to 22x ni. Like profane eating, the cultic meal also has a joyful premise (Deut 14:26, etc.; cf. B. Reicke, *Diakonie, Festfreude und Zelos* [1951], 167ff.).

On the meal as an element of the covenant-making ritual (Gen 26:30; 31:46, 54; Exod 24:11; Josh 9:14f.) → *bᵉrît*. W. Beyerlin (*Origin and History of the Oldest Sinaitic Traditions* [1965], 33–35) suspects that "to eat and to drink" is a technical term for covenant making.

The rites of mourning include eating a special mourning food, Deut 26:14; Jer 16:7 (txt em); Ezek 24:17, 22 (txt em); Hos 9:4 *leḥem ʾônîm;* cf. H. Cazelles, *RB* 55 (1948): 54–71; T. Worden, *VT* 3 (1953): 290f.; J. Scharbert, *Der Schmerz im AT* (1955), 123f.

5. The expanded usage of the verb may also be identified at Qumran; in addition to profane or cultic eating, it can describe an activity of fire or the sword. In the LXX more than 20 terms occur as translations of *ʾkl* expressing the expansion of meaning of the Hebr. (use up, burn up, harvest, etc.). On the NT, cf. J. Behm, "ἐσθίω," *TDNT* 2:689–95; L. Goppelt, "τρώγω," *TDNT* 8:236f.

G. Gerleman

אֵל *ʾēl* God

S 410; BDB 42a; *HALOT* 1:48b; *TDOT* 1:242–61; *TWOT* 93a; *NIDOTTE* 446

I. **ʾil* is an early common (with the exception of Eth.) Sem. word for "god," which is particularly widespread in Akk. (*CAD* I/J:91–103) and NWSem. (*DISO* 13). Its etymology remains disputed despite numerous suggestions.

It has been primarily associated with *ʾûl* "forward, first" or "to be strong," or with *ʾlh* "to be strong," but also—less probably—with the prep. *ʾl* "to, in the direction of" or *ʾly/ʾlh* "to strive after, reach," *ʾll* "to bind," Arab. *ʾill* "relationship," etc. (cf. F. Zimmermann, *VT* 12 [1962]: 190–95; P. Fronzaroli, *AANLR* 8/20 [1965]: 248, 262, 267, and the literature in lexicons).

Clear points of reference may not be established for any etymology. Even the idiom *yeš-lᵉʾēl yādî* "it is in my power" (Gen 31:29; similarly Deut 28:32; Mic 2:1; Prov 3:27; Neh 5:5) does not facilitate a solution, because it too may not be unequivocally explained eytmologically (cf. *HAL* 47a with bibliog.). Perhaps the word *ʾēl* resists derivation because of its antiquity; nevertheless, one may conjecture that its basic meaning expressed power (like similar designations for deity: → *baʿal*, → *ʾādôn* "lord," or → *melek* "king").

II. The word *ʾēl* occurs in the OT (238x) in very early as well as in later times; they are evenly distributed and are concentrated in Psa (77x), Job (55x), Isa (24x, Deutero-Isa 15x), Gen (18x), and Deut (13x). Accordingly, *ʾēl* occurs regularly in metrical texts (cf. also the Balaam sayings, Num 23–24, 8x) and in archaizing language. Whether individual books (Sam, Kgs, Jer, Chron, etc.) wish to avoid the word—for unkown reasons—is therefore questionable. The pl. *ʾēlîm* is rare in the OT (see III/3 and Psa 58:2 txt em); the fem. sg., familiar in the other Sem. languages, is totally absent from Hebr.

III. *ʾēl* is both a PN for a particular deity as well as a pure appellative for "god" (pl. *ʾēlîm*). The manifold usage of the word may be divided crudely into various categories, which may be understood only with great reservation as phases in a historical sequence: from the more marked religiohistorically determined occurrences (III/1, El in the OT environment; III/2, El deities in Gen; III/3, later occurrences; III/4, superlative use), through the description of God's being with adjs. (IV/1) to usages in Deutero-Isa (IV/2), in Job (IV/3), in the contrast of God and human (IV/4), and in address to God (IV/5).

1. The (mythological) texts from Ras Shamra-Ugarit, in particular, exhibit El as a god of special rank. As "king" he stands at the head of the pantheon. He is "father" of the gods, "creator of the creatures" (a cosmology is nevertheless not yet attested), "wise," "friendly," perhaps also "holy," but he is also called "bull, El." He bears signs of age and lives in mythical seclusion (cf. O. Eissfeldt, *El im ugaritischen Pantheon* [1951]; M. H. Pope, *El in the Ugaritic Texts* [1955]; M. J. Mulder, *Kanaänitische Goden in het Oude Testament* [1965], 13ff.).

WSem. inscriptions also know the god El, but no longer name him in deity lists in the first position (cf. W. Röllig, "El als Gottesbezeichnung im Phönizischen," FS Friedrich 403–16; R. Rendtorff, "El, Ba'al und Jahwe," *ZAW* 78 [1966]: 277–92). Although El is still mentioned in later times (e.g., in Philo of Byblos), he apparently recedes (up until Palmyra) behind Baal (cf. further U. Oldenburg, *Conflict Between El and Baal in Canaanite Religion* [1970]).

2. *ʾēl* first occurs in the OT (from Gen 14:18ff. onward) in various phrases for deities, which appear at particular locales.

In contrast to the address "you are *ʾēl r^{o}ʾî*" "god who sees me(?)" (Gen 16:13 J), the probably more ancient name *b^{e}ʾēr laḥay rōʾî* "well of the living one who sees me(?)" does not contain the element *ʾēl*, so that the numen was perhaps not even originally considered an El deity.

The name attested at Beersheba *ʾēl ʿôlām* (Gen 21:33 J) is corroborated to a degree by the "sun god of eternity" known from Ugarit (*špš ʿlm, KTU* 2.42.7) and Karatepe (*šmš ʿlm, KAI* no. 26.AIII.19; *ANET* 654b "Eternal-Sun"), and by the Ulomos mentioned in the cosmogony of Mochos (Damascius, *De principiis* 125; *FGH* 784).

In Gen 35:7 (E) *ʾēl bêt-ʾēl* "the God (of) Bethel" contains the name of a place, although *bêt-ʾēl* is also attested in the surroundings as a name for a locality (and a stone) as well as a divine name (Eissfeldt, *KS* [1962], 1:206–33; H. Donner, "Zu Gen 2822," *ZAW* 74 [1962]: 68–70). That the saying "I am the God (of) Bethel" (31:13 E; cf. 28:10ff.) hardly goes back to ancient tradition is indicated by the use of the art. with the name (cf. 35:1, 3 *ʾēl* with art.), its no longer appearing in its original local connection, and the probably secondary transferral of the self-presentation formula to the divinity. In addition, the text is uncertain in both 35:7 and 31:13 (see LXX).

Following O. Eissfeldt (*KS* [1966], 3:364n.4, 396n.1; cf. M. Weippert, *ZDMG* 111 [1961]: 42–62; R. Bailey, *JBL* 87 [1968]: 434–38), *ᵓēl šadday* (Gen 17:1; 28:3; 35:11; 48:3; Exod 6:3 P) has also been considered a unique local form of the god El, perhaps at Hebron; but the OT does not know such a fixed local association. Only the element → *šadday*—whose meaning is disputed—is attested from ancient times (Num 24:4, 16); Gen 43:14 J/E (secondary assimilation to P) and 49:25 (correction of MT in 3 mss and translations in order to harmonize with the usual names?) are questionable. Only since the 6th cent., then, are trustworthy occurrences of the dual name extant (Ezek 10:5 and P), so that it may represent a later combination, which would explain its peculiarity (place boundedness). Through it P summarizes the various designations of the gods of the fathers and El deities and thus emphasizes the uniqueness of the patriarchal period (Gen 17:1–Exod 6:3).

None of the divine names is attested in present form outside the OT, only some of the individual elements. It remains uncertain, then, how far back their association goes in antiquity. Perhaps the OT mirrors the religiohistorical circumstances in pre-Israelite Palestine only very imperfectly because it has transformed the tradition more thoroughly than is usually assumed. In fact, every divine designation could be related to deities other than Yahweh only in contradiction to their meaning in their present context. Beyond this situation, one may only conjecture how local deities named in Gen relate to the place-bound El mentioned in WSem. texts (local appearances of the high god?). In any case one should not infer from the various by-names that Yahweh was originally an El deity.

Although the formulations appear to go back to early tradition, they endure in Canaan (cf. also place-names such as *pᵉnûᵓēl*). It is difficult to ascertain whether the nomads already knew an El religion. Only the characteristic theophoric PN formations (verbs in the impf. with a divine name), e.g., "Israel," "Ishmael," or abbreviated "Jacob" and "Isaac," provide evidence for this conjecture. Other bases remain unknown.

The age of the expression "*ᵓēl* (is the?) God of Israel" (the name of an altar in Gen 33:20 E?) is disputed. Is the combination original or secondary? Is the "God of Israel" a so-called god of the fathers (cf. R. Smend, *Die Bundesformel* [1963], 15, 35f.; H. Seebass, *Der Erzvater Israel* [1966])? In any case, the dual expression is structured differently from other divine names formed with *ᵓēl* and is therefore without comparison.

The divine self-presentation to Jacob "I am *ᵓēl* (with art.), the God of your father" (Gen 46:3 E), Jacob's blessing, which uniquely promises Joseph aid from the "*ᵓēl* of your father" (Gen 49:25), and the explanation of the PN Eliezer as "the God of my father is my help" probably secondarily associate elements of El religion with the faith in the patriarchal God.

If the nomads already addressed their deities as *ᵓēl*, then they first became acquainted with more precisely defined divine names that shape the narratives of Gen, such as *ᵓēl ᶜôlām*, at sanctuaries in the cultivated land.

3. Some later occurrences of *ᵓēl* are recognizable as foreign influences, some as reinterpretations.

According to Judg 9:46 an *ᵓēl bᵉrît* was worshiped at Shechem; yet the name of the god is not uniformly transmitted. It is also given as *baᶜal bᵉrît* (Judg 8:33; 9:4), although El and Baal are different deities. Furthermore, no covenant (→ *bᵉrît*) between God and a social group among Israel's neighbors has been discovered to this point, so the significance of the name remains unclear.

Whether the title *ʾēl ʿelyôn* "the highest God (or El the Highest), Creator (→ *qnh*) of heaven and earth" (Gen 14:19, 22), which mirrors Jerusalemite tradition, is an original predication of the god El or unifies two originally independent elements is debatable (following G. Levi della Vide and R. Dussaud, see Rendtorff, op. cit.). Texts from Karatepe, Leptis Magna, Palmyra, and perhaps Boghazköy attest *qn ʾrṣ* "Creator of the earth" as an epithet of El, yet there is to this point no counterpart for "Creator of heaven." It is also uncertain whether *ʿelyôn* was originally a distinct deity or an epithet of the god El. At the least, the two gods must have already been associated with each other very early: they stand side by side in an inscription from Sefire (*KAI* no. 222.A11; cf. Fitzmyer, *Sef.* 37f.) and can be equated in the OT in parallelism (Num 24:16; Deut 32:8 txt em; Psa 73:11; 77:10f.; 78:17f.; 107:11; above all, 78:35; cf. 82:1, 6; Isa 14:13f.).

Ancient Near Eastern, esp. Can., concepts resound when, e.g., Psa 82:1 speaks of an "assembly of El" *(ʿadat-ʾēl)*, Psa 19:2 of the "glory of El" (*kebôd ʾēl;* cf. 29:2), or Num 23:22 in a simile of God's wild bull horns (cf. W. H. Schmidt, *Königtum Gottes in Ugarit und Israel* [1966²], 25ff., 40ff., 83). The divine name "Yahweh" is also characteristically avoided in the boasts of the king of Babel, "I will elevate my throne above the stars of El" (Isa 14:13), and of the prince of Tyre, "I am El, I sit in the seat of gods" (Ezek 28:2; cf. also Deut 32:18; Psa 104:21; Job 38:41?). In the strict sense, however, the OT does not retain *ʾēl* as the name of a particular deity; rather it consistently uses *ʾēl* as an appellative, even if the PN character still shines through repeatedly. Interpretations that infer El's superiority over Yahweh from some OT statements (cf. Eissfeldt, *KS* [1966], 3:389ff.) are therefore actually contrary to the meaning of the text.

The OT's modification of the term *ʾēl*, e.g., perhaps in archaizing language by the adj. *ḥay* "living" (Josh 3:10; Hos 2:1; Psa 84:3; in the oath, Job 27:2; cf. Psa 42:3, 9), may have its model not only in the Ug. PN *ḥyil* (*WUS* no. 917) but also in the mythical expression of the "life" of El (*KTU* 1.4.IV.42, etc.), although El is not a dying and rising god.

Just as the *benê ʾēlîm* "sons of gods" (Psa 29:1; 89:7; cf. Deut 32:8 txt em) originally signified the gods subordinate to the high god (cf. Psa 82:1, 6), but in the OT signified only lowlier divine beings (cf. W. Herrmann, "Die Göttersöhne," *ZRGG* 12 [1960]: 242–51; G. Cooke, *ZAW* 76 [1964]: 22–47), so the question with polytheistic origins, "who is like you among the gods?" (Exod 15:11), comes to refer to the heavenly council. Similar comparative questions or statements of incomparability of various kinds, which still provide some insight into religiohistorical backgrounds, contain the word *ʾēl* in the sg. (Deut 3:24; 33:26; 2 Sam 22:32; Isa 40:18; Mic 7:18; Psa 77:14; cf. 89:7f.).

Nonetheless, with the addition *qannāʾ* "jealous," Israel has interpreted the ancient Near Eastern divine designation completely in terms of its own understanding of God; a "jealous God," who demands—instead of just preeminence—exclusivity of relationship and who punishes transgression against it, is unknown to Israel's neighbors. To be sure, Israel only later deduced a divine attribute from the exclusivity of its relationship to God, for the reference to Yahweh's "jealousy" occurs first in later additions to the Decalogue in Deut, etc. (Exod 20:5; 34:14; Deut 4:24; 5:9; 6:15; cf. Josh 24:19; Nah 1:2; → *qn*ʾ), which support the first commandment.

Finally, the peculiar character of Yahwism resulted in a reshaping of the *ʾēl* concept, characterizing it with appositives such as "strange, other" (→ *ʾḥr,* → *zār,* → *nēkār;* Exod 34:14; Psa 44:21; 81:10; cf. Deut 32:12; Mal 2:11). This exclusion can, indeed, grow to negation: apostasy involves the "un-god" (*lōʾ-ʾēl* Deut 32:21). In each case, relationship to God is thus verbally, or at least thematically, conditioned upon the first commandment.

4. Like → *ʾelōhîm* (III/3), *ʾēl* can also be used in an attenuated sense for intensification: "mountains of God" (Psa 36:7; 50:10 txt em) and "cedars of God" (Psa 80:11) are characterized by unusual size (perhaps also Isa 14:13 "stars of God"; Job 41:17 "mighty, heroes" derives from *ʾayil;* cf. Ezek 32:21).

yhwh ʾēl (Psa 10:12; cf. *hāʾēl yhwh* Psa 85:9; Isa 42:5) resembles the remarkable usage *yhwh ʾelōhîm* (→ *ʾelōhîm* IV/5). The repeated designations for God in Psa 50:1 and Josh 22:22 are ceremoniously elevated usages, similar to the gen. construction, a circumlocution for the superlative, *ʾēl ʾelōhîm,* "God of gods," i.e., "the highest God" (*ʾēl ʾēlîm* Dan 11:36).

IV. 1. Although the OT attributes relatively few predicates to God himself, the use of *ʾēl* in connection with adjs. becomes more frequent in later times, from about Deut onward; the word can assume a wide variety of modifiers on account of its generality. The "jealous God" (see III/3) watches over Israel, who trusts in strange gods; the "holy God" (*hāʾēl haqqādôš* Isa 5:16, secondary) proves himself to be holy in judgment. Yet the "great God" (*ʾēl gādôl* Psa 95:3) can intercede for Israel (Deut 7:21; 10:17) and forgive sin just as easily (Jer 32:18; cf. Neh 1:5; 9:32; Dan 9:4). In a manner unusual for the OT, the confession formulae *ʾēl raḥûm weḥannûn* "merciful and gracious God," etc. (Exod 34:6; cf. Deut 4:31; Jonah 4:2; Psa 86:15; Neh 9:31), also attested only late, do not appeal to a historical event; they have origins in wisdom, which makes a basic, universally valid statement concerning God's being, so that one can find here the origins of a doctrine of God's attributes (cf. R. C. Dentan, *VT* 13 [1963]: 34–51).

Descriptions such as "a righteous = true God" (Isa 45:21; cf. 45:15, "a God who hides himself"), "a hidden God" (Psa 99:8), or "the faithful God" (Deut 7:9) are comparable. Construct relations are synonymous: "God of faithfulness" (Deut 32:4 or Psa 31:6; cf. 68:21). "The God of vengeance" (Psa 94:1; cf. Jer 51:56) can be called upon as judge. On other usages, occasionally with *ʾēl* as nomen rectum (e.g., Psa 78:7 "deeds of God"; cf. Job 37:14), see *HAL* 48b.

2. In Deutero-Isaiah's proclamation of Yahweh's uniqueness ("I am God and there is no other") the appellative *ʾēl* (only in Isa 40–46) plays a weighty role (esp. 40:18; 43:12; 45:22; cf. 43:10). Yet this usage does not continue to identify Yahweh with the deity El. *ʾēl* is no longer a PN; rather it is—sometimes par. to (45:14f.; 46:9) or alternating with *ʾelōhîm* (45:5, 18, etc.; cf. Exod

28:2, 9)—exclusively a generic term for "god," to which Yahweh lays sole claim. *ʾēl* also occurs in disputations with foreign deities (Isa 45:20; in secondary sections "to form, to make, a god": 44:10, 15, 17; 46:6).

3. In Job, particularly in the Elihu speeches, *ʾēl* (with and without art.) becomes the most frequent designation for God (followed by *ʾᵉlōah* and *šadday*, which is often par. to *ʾēl*); *ʾᵉlōhîm* disappears almost entirely (cf. Fohrer, KAT 16, 117f.). On the whole, then, the usage is hardly dependent upon the tradition associated with *ʾēl*, but upon the theme of the book of Job (cf. perhaps 8:3, 20; 13:3; 31:14; 34:5, 12).

This circumstance dictates that *ʾēl* appears in Job neither with suf.—thus the difference between God and human stands out more markedly than in the Psalter—nor with an appositional adj., even when the "majesty" of God is emphasized (36:5, 22, 26).

Conceptualizations such as those found in the themes of many Psalms are comparable. Thus, according to Psa 73:11, the godless explicitly dispute that the transcendent God is cognizant of the activity of people of earth (cf. Job 22:13).

The later period favored using *ʾēl* because it no longer needed to distinguish its God as God of the world (cf. *ʾēl* "in heaven": Deut 3:24; Psa 136:26; Lam 3:41) from the other gods.

4. The OT repeatedly juxtaposes *ʾēl* "God" and humans. "God is not a human, that he should lie" (Num 23:19) paraphrases God's trustworthy faithfulness to his word. The prophet Hosea (11:9) supports his interpretation of holiness as forgiving love instead of punishing wrath with the antithesis, "I am God and not a human." Isaiah's word, "Egypt is a human and not God" (31:3), distinguishes between might and weakness. Ezekiel replies to the arrogant prince of Tyre: "You are a human and not God" (28:2, 9). Finally, the difference between God and human becomes a contrast between right and wrong in Job (except for 32:13): "How can a human be right before God?" (9:2; 25:4; cf. 4:17, etc.). The essences of God and people are so different that discourse and interchange between the two, i.e., a legal proceeding, is impossible (cf. 9:32).

5. Otherwise, *ʾēl* lends itself to the expression of close relationship to God (cf. "God of my life" Psa 42:9, etc.); in this usage, as in the address in prayer, one hears an idiom common among Israel's neighbors (on Bab. prayers, see e.g., J. Begrich, *ZAW* 46 [1928]: 236, 242, 244f.). The individual cries, "My God" (2d per., 3d per., and 1st per. pl. sufs. do not occur), both in laments and in songs of thanksgiving: "My God, my God, why have you forsaken me?" (Psa 22:2; also 18:3; 63:2; 102:25; Exod 15:2; by the king, Psa 89:27; cf. 68:25) and the confession "you are my God" expresses confidence (Psa 22:11; 118:28; 140:7; to the idol, Isa 44:17; cf. Eissfeldt, *KS* [1966], 3:35–47). Yet the individual (Psa 16:1; 17:6; cf. 10:12; 31:6) and the community (Psa 83:2; 90:2; Num 16:22; cf. *ʿimmānû ʾēl* Isa 7:14; 8:8, 10 → *ʿim*) can use *ʾēl* without suf. in the vocative.

V. → *ʾᵉlōhîm*.

W. H. Schmidt

אָלָה ʾālâ curse

S 423; BDB 46b; *HALOT* 1:51b; *TDOT* 1:261–66; *TWOT* 94b; *NIDOTTE* 460

1. The root *ʾlh (ʾlw)* "to curse" seems to be used only in Hebr., Phoen., and Arab.

Phoen. *ʾlt* on an amulet from Arslan Tash (*KAI* no. 27) means "covenant" (line 9) and "curse" (lines 13–15) (see *KAI* 2:45, following T. H. Gaster, *Or* 11 [1942]: 65f.; for other interpretations, see *DISO* 14; cf. *ANET* 658b). The Yaudi evidence *ʾlh* "conspiracy(?)" cited in *DISO* 14 from *KAI* no. 215.2 should be disregarded according to *KAI* 2:223, 225.

Arab. *ʾalā* (*ʾlw* IV) means "to swear"; cf. J. Pedersen, *Der Eid bei den Semiten* (1914), 12f.

Akk. *iʾlu* "contract" (*AHw* 373b) belongs to *eʾēlu* "to bind (contractually)" (*AHw* 189a) and is not related to the root of Hebr. *ʾālâ*. Akk. *māmītu* corresponds most closely to the usage of *ʾālâ;* cf. Pedersen, op. cit. 82; H. C. Brichto, *The Problem of "Curse" in the Hebrew Bible* (1963), 16f., 71–76; *AHw* 599f.

The verb *ʾlh* occurs in qal and hi.; the substs. *ʾālâ* and *taʾ^{a}lâ* "(realized) curse" (so J. Scharbert, *Bib* 39 [1958]: 5) are derivatives (cf., however, Brichto, op. cit., 69).

2. The Hebr. OT attests derivatives of the root 43x: qal and hi. 3x each (in 1 Sam 14:24 one should presumably read *wayyaʾal*), *ʾālâ* 36x, *taʾ^{a}lâ* 1x (Lam 3:65).

The relatively infrequent usage in the old narratives (Gen 24:41bis; 26:28; Judg 17:2; 1 Sam 14:24) and the more frequent occurrence in the Prophets (13x) should be emphasized.

3. (a) *ʾālâ* is essentially a judicial term. In contrast to → *ʾrr* "to curse, place under the ban," → *qll* pi. "to insult, wish someone ill," and other expressions for damaging speech (cf. J. Scharbert, " 'Fluchen' und 'Segnen' im AT," *Bib* 39 [1958]: 1–26; Brichto, op. cit.), according to F. Horst (*RGG* 5:1651), *ʾālâ* indicates the curse "as a legal aid for securing an oath (Gen 24:41; Hos 4:2; Neh 10:30), contract (Gen 26:28; Ezek 17:19), or covenant (Deut 29:19f.; 2 Chron 34:24), as an ordeal curse (Num 5:21), and as legal vengeance against unknown thieves, perjurers, and accomplices (Judg 17:2f.; Lev 5:1; Zech 5:3; Prov 29:24)."

In each case the term concerns a conditional curse that the speaker either accepts or places on another. Consequently, arenas of usage are, on the one hand, (b) oath-taking rituals (→ *šbᶜ*), accompanied by a curse sanction, associated with the finalization of a contract or covenant (→ *b^{e}rît*), and, on the other hand, (c) the subjection of other known or unknown persons to a curse (Brichto, op. cit. 41: "adjuration"), in order to ensure the execution of a command or to bring a criminal to punishment. In both cases metonymic word usage must be taken into account from time to time.

(b) In about half the texts, *ʾālâ* stands in a topical relation to oath (→ *šbᶜ* ni./hi., *š^{e}bûᶜâ*) and covenant (→ *b^{e}rît;* also → *tôrâ* as a written, binding law). In view are first, the sanction inherent in any oath taking through a conditional self-curse, the curse released by a violation of oath, and then, metonymically (as part for the whole), also the obligation or the contract itself.

The translation "curse (sanction)" is appropriate for Deut 29:19 (with *rbṣ* "to lie in wait"), 20 (*ʾālôt habbᵉrît* "covenant curses"); 30:7; Isa 24:6 (with *ʾkl* "to consume"; cf. v 5 *bᵉrît;* similarly Jer 23:10 txt? without *bᵉrît*); Dan 9:11 (par. *šᵉbûʿâ,* written in the *tôrâ* of Moses); 2 Chron 34:24 (written in the book). It should be translated "oath" in Gen 24:41(bis) (with → *nqh min* "to be free from"; cf. v 8 *šᵉbûʿâ,* vv 3, 9, 37 *šbʿ*); Ezek 16:59 and 17:16, 18f. (with *bzh* "to despise," par. *prr* hi. *bᵉrît* "to violate covenant"); Hos 10:4 (*ʾlh* inf. *šāwʾ* "to swear false oaths," alongside *bᵉrît);* Neh 10:30 (*ʾālâ* and *šᵉbûʿâ* as a hendiadys). Gen 26:28; Deut 29:11, 13, 18; Ezek 17:13 (in each case par. to *bᵉrît*) refer to the sworn contract.

Jer 29:18; 42:18; 44:12 describe the apostate Judeans as "(an example) for cursing"; this expansion of meaning only occurs here, characteristically, in a series of synonyms with "terror, hissing, or execration *(qᵉlālâ)*, reproach."

(c) Conditional curses placed on other persons occur in very different circumstances but commonly employ *ʾālâ* as a (in proper usage) legal mechanism, namely in public proclamations to insure compliance and in divine judgment procedures; whoever fails to follow the demand, i.e., the guilty, should be affected by the curse.

Saul places his army under an execration (*ʾlh* hi.; not "to cause to swear"; cf. Brichto, op. cit. 45–48) in the event that someone trangresses against the published fast order (1 Sam 14:24); Lev 5:1 discusses the witness who fails to respond to the public call to report to the court, accompanied by a threat of curse in the event of disobedience *(qôl ʾālâ)* (Elliger, HAT 4, 73; cf. Noth, *Lev,* OTL, 44); Prov 29:24 discusses the receiver of stolen goods who will be affected by the public cursing of a thief, against whom one conceivably cannot bring charges; Judg 17:2 treats the confessed thief for whom the curse (*ʾlh* qal) issued earlier is now repealed by a blessing (→ *brk* only here and in Deut 29:18 alongside *ʾālâ*). Zech 5:3 presents the *ʾālâ,* embodied in the scroll seen in a vision, as a curse issued by Yahweh on thieves and perjurers.

In the context of a curse-ordeal (cf. R. Press, *ZAW* 51 [1933]: 122ff.) involving a woman suspected of adultery, Num 5:11–31 does not treat the self-adjuration required of the woman, but a conditional curse by the priest (v 21aα with *šᵉbûʿâ;* v 23 pl.) that takes effect in the event of guilt (Brichto, op. cit. 48–52); the woman then becomes an "(example of a) curse" (vv 21aβ, 27; metonymic use of *ʾālâ;* cf. Scharbert, op. cit. 5, 11f.). *ʾālâ* also appears in 1 Kgs 8:31 (*ʾlh* hi. and twice *ʾālâ* [read *ûbāʾâ* in v 31b]; par. 2 Chron 6:22) and Job 31:30 (so Brichto, op. cit. 52–56; contra Noth, BK 9, 186: purification oath of the accused) as a legal (but dangerous) technique against an enemy.

Because such a conditional curse always contains an accusation, *ʾālâ* can also acquire the broader meaning "accusation" (Hos 4:2 and Psa 59:13 together with → *kḥš;* Psa 10:7 in an illegal use; Brichto, op. cit. 56–59).

4. (a) Insofar as the conditional self-adjuration in the context of interpersonal agreements and the conditional curse upon a third party are legal techniques bound to God's guarantee of the judicial process (Yahweh hears the *ʾālâ,* 1 Kgs 8:31f. = 2 Chron 6:22f., and acts accordingly, Num 5:21; Ezek 17:15–19; he himself proceeds against the misuse of the *ʾālâ,* Hos 4:2 and 10:4, or sets it in motion, Zech 5:3; cf., however, the cancellation of the *ʾālâ* by a blessing in Judg 17:2), their value and significance vary according to

whether God is taken seriously. In crass cases the *ʾālâ* may be abused unscrupulously in contempt of God and thus in disdain of fellow human beings (cf. Hos 4:2; 10:4; Psa 10:7; 59:13; Job 31:30 for private law; Ezek 17:13, 16, 18f. for international law). Examples of *ʾālâ* pronounced legitimately occur in Gen 24:41; 26:28; Judg 17:2; 1 Sam 14:24; Prov 29:24; naturally general references to the institution also belong in this category (Lev 5:1; Num 5:21–27; 1 Kgs 8:31 = 2 Chron 6:22; cf. Zech 5:3).

(b) The *ʾālâ* has a properly theological aspect only as a sanction in the context of a covenant between Yahweh and Israel (15 texts from the time of Jer and Deut). The manifestation of the curse is implied in the moment of the covenant's finalization (Deut 29:11–20; Neh 10:30), but must be acknowledged in the judgment for apostasy (Isa 24:6; Jer 23:10; 29:18; 42:18; 44:12; Ezek 16:59; Dan 9:11; 2 Chron 34:24); if the people repent, the curses will affect not Israel but its enemies (Deut 30:7).

5. In the literature from Qumran, the expression *ʾālôt habbᵉrît* "covenant curses," derived from Deut 29:20, is particuarly popular (1QS 2:16; 5:12; CD 15:2f.; cf. 1:17; also *šᵉbûʿat hāʾālâ* in CD 9:12).

The LXX primarily translates with *ara* and derivatives, less frequently (6x) with *horkos* and its derivatives.

In the NT the concepts associated with *ʾālâ* become markedly less common because of the altered legal circumstances and the rejection of the oath. Cf. L. Brun, *Segen und Fluch im Urchristentum* [1932]; F. Büchsel, "ἀρά," *TDNT* 1:448–51; J. Schneider, "ὅρκος," *TDNT* 5:457–67.

C. A. Keller

אֱלֹהִים ʾᵉ*lōhîm* God

S 430; BDB 43a; *HALOT* 1:53a; *TDOT* 1:267–84; *TWOT* 93c; *NIDOTTE* 466

I. The etymology of *ʾᵉlōhîm*—like that of → *ʾēl*—is contested.

1. With few exceptions the sg. *ʾᵉlôah* occurs in the OT only in post-exilic literature (see II); hence one may assume that the sg. presupposes the pl. The Hebr. alone suggests the conclusion that *ʾᵉlōhîm* (along with *ʾēlîm*) is a pl. form of *ʾēl*, from which a sg. was formed secondarily.

In support one can—with caution given the uncertain textual situation—call attention to the Ug. pl. of *ilt* "goddess," which seems to be *ilht*, and and to *ilhm*, which may also be found alongside the masc. pl. *ilm* (*WUS* no. 182; *UT* no. 163 and §8.8).

Nevertheless, the sg. *ʾilāh* occurs already in Old Aram. (*DISO* 14) and in Arab. (but not in Akk.); thus the derivation of *ʾᵉlōhîm* from *ʾilāh* seems more probable.

In any case one must not assume an etymology for *ʾilāh* distinct from *ʾil*, but a relationship of the two words, probably in the sense that the older root *ʾil* underwent expansion. Derivation from the Arab. *ʾaliha* "to be timid" (e.g.,

König, *Syntax* §263a) is just as improbable as a direct relationship to *ᵓēlâ*/*ᵓēlôn* "tree" (F. Zimmermann, *VT* 12 [1962]: 190–95). *ᵓᵉlōhîm* never appears in place-names and PNs; thus the association of the two divine designations may have still been known to Israel.

2. *ᵓᵉlōhîm* is usually considered an abstract, intensifying, majestic, or dominical pl. (König, *Syntax* §163; GKC §124g). Yet the fact that from the outset the word also apparently indicates the numerical pl. "gods" (see III/1) may be explained only with difficulty in this manner. If one wishes to trace this double usage to a unified origin, one may theorize that an originally genuine pl. was subsequently or simultaneously understood as an abstract pl. Whether the expression should then be interpreted as a summation of the "divine powers" as a unity must remain at least questionable. In any case, the sg. sense of the pl. form is so uncontested for the OT that it used the word throughout without limitation (suspicion of polytheism).

The pl. *ilānī-ya* addressed to the pharaoh in the Amarna correspondence and Phoen. *ᵓlm* as a divine epithet represent some pars. (cf. esp. J. Hehn, *Die biblische und die babylonische Gottesidee* [1913], 168ff.; W. Röllig, FS Friedrich 403–16; and O. Eissfeldt, *El im ugaritischen Pantheon* [1951], 27f.). The degree to which these expressions (pl. form with sg. meaning) reveal monotheistic tendencies must remain undecided. Otherwise, the assumption that Israel adopted *ᵓᵉlōhîm* from the Canaanites with pl. as well as sg. meanings has not yet been demonstrated.

II. 1.* With 2,600 occurrences *ᵓᵉlōhîm* is the second most frequent subst. in the OT following *bēn* "son."

Gen	219	Nah	1
Exod	139	Hab	2
Lev	53	Zeph	5
Num	27	Hag	3
Deut	374	Zech	11
Josh	76	Mal	7
Judg	73	Psa	365
1 Sam	100	Job	17
2 Sam	54	Prov	5
1 Kgs	107	Song Sol	–
2 Kgs	97	Ruth	4
Isa	94	Lam	–
Jer	145	Eccl	40
Ezek	36	Esth	–
Hos	26	Dan	22
Joel	11	Ezra	55
Amos	14	Neh	70
Obad	–	1 Chron	118
Jonah	16	2 Chron	203
Mic	11		

Pentateuch	812
Josh–2 Kgs	507
Prophets	382
Ketubim	899
Hebr. OT total	2,600

2 Kgs 17:31 K is attributed above to ʾᵉlôah. Lis. lists 1 Kgs 1:47 (K/Q) twice, Mandl. lists Gen 21:4; Psa 108:6, 8 twice. The variants in 2 Sam 7:22a and 1 Chron 15:2b, omitted in Cod. Leningradensis, are not counted.

In addition, ʾᵉlôah occurs 58x: 41x in Job 3–40; other scattered occurrences: 4x in Psa and Dan, 2x in Deut and Hab, 1x in 2 Kgs, Isa, Prov, Neh, and 2 Chron.

The Aram. portions of the OT contain ʾᵉlāh 95x (17x pl., 4x sg. in meaning): Jer 10:11 1x, Dan 51x, Ezra 43x.

2. A peculiarity in the distribution of ʾᵉlōhîm need only be noted: The prophets, excl. the Jonah narrative, avoid unmodified ʾᵉlōhîm as the subj. of the sentence (cf. Lis. 97c), probably because the divine designation is too unspecific for them, while the word is found frequently in this position in the Pentateuch and in the Deuteronomistic and Chronicler's histories.

In Job, not counting the framework narrative, ʾēl (see IV/3) and ʾᵉlôah (cf. Fohrer, KAT 16, 117f.) replace ʾᵉlōhîm almost entirely. In the remainder of the OT, the sg. ʾᵉlôah occurs relatively infrequently, and, moreover, almost exclusively in poetical texts (Deut 32:15, 17; Isa 44:8; Hab 3:3; Psa 18:32; 50:22; 139:19; Prov 30:5; Dan 11:37–39). The word never carries the art. (once a suf., Hab 1:11; also in combinations, Psa 114:7; Neh 9:17), a condition that may be determined by a specific feature of elevated, poetical language. As a rule the sg. already presupposes the transition of the generic designation "god" to the PN (cf., however, Dan 11:37ff.).

III. In distinction from ʾēl, ʾᵉlōhîm is originally only a descriptive term, not a divine name; in the course of history, however, it acquires the character of a PN, so that ʾᵉlōhîm can appear without the art. (Gen 1:1; GKC §125f) or can serve in the vocative as an address to "God" (Psa 5:11; 51:3, etc.). Nonetheless, the word does not mean solely "(the) God" but also "(the) gods" (III/1). In the following sections the more grammatical-semasiological and religiohistorical aspects of usage will be treated in III/1–7, the more theological in IV/1–6 (in view of the multitude of occurrences, citations are generally only exemplary).

1. ʾᵉlōhîm is used of strange gods with the gen. of the circle of worshipers: "gods of Egypt" (Exod 12:12; Jer 43:12f.; cf. Judg 10:6; 2 Kgs 17:31 Q; 18:34f.; 2 Chron 28:23). Other usages express the exclusivity and aniconic nature of the worship of Israel's own God: "gods of the foreigners" (Gen 35:2, 4; Judg 10:16; 1 Sam 7:3; cf. Deut 31:16; Jer 5:19), "gods of the nations" (Deut 6:14; Judg 2:12; Psa 96:5; cf. 2 Kgs 19:12, etc.), "gods of the lands" (2 Kgs 18:35; the Assyrians speaking of Yahweh: 17:26f.), "gods of the earth" (Zeph 2:11), "other gods" (Hos 3:1; frequent in Deut, Dtr, Jer—occasionally to be understood as a sg.; cf. III/2?), "all gods" (Exod 18:11; Psa 95:3; 96:4; 97:7, 9; 2 Chron 2:4), and "gods of silver and gold" (Exod 20:23; cf. 34:17; Lev 19:4).

The pl. form is also used for individual foreign deities (Judg 11:24; 2 Kgs 1:2; 19:37; cf. Amos 5:26 "your astral god"; 8:14; Num 25:2; sg.: Dan 11:37ff.; Deut 32:17), and even for the fem. deity Astarte (1 Kgs 11:5, 33; cf. 1 Chron 10:10 with 1 Sam 31:10), because Hebr. has no term for "goddess."

2. As a designation for Israel's God, ʾᵉlōhîm is grammatically construed to be sg. generally (Gen 1:1; Psa 7:10; 2 Kgs 19:4), but can also be accompanied

by a pl. attribute or predicate with no recognizable difference in meaning. Often both possibilities are found in the same body of literature: ᵓ*ᵉlōhîm ḥayyîm* "living God" (Deut 5:26; 1 Sam 17:26, 36; Jer 10:10; 23:36) and ᵓ*ᵉlōhîm ḥay* (2 Kgs 19:4, 16; cf. 2 Sam 2:27), ᵓ*ᵉlōhîm qᵉdōšîm* "holy God" (Josh 24:19) and *hāᵓᵉlōhîm haqqādôš* (1 Sam 6:20); cf. also Deut 4:7; 1 Sam 4:8; 28:13; Psa 58:12 (GKC §132h; König, *Syntax* §263c). Occurrences with a pl. verb (excl. 1 Kgs 19:2; 20:10, where, as in 1 Sam 4:8, non-Israelites speak) are mostly ambiguous: Gen 20:13 E (see H. Strack, *Die Genesis* [1905²], 77); 35:7 E (cf. Gunkel, *Gen* 224); cf. 31:53 J; Exod 22:8; 1 Sam 2:25. The confessional formula in 1 Kgs 12:28 and Exod 32:4, 8 is consciously ambiguous in order to brand the worship of the bull as idolatry. Later the pl. construction is avoided "from fear of misconception" (GKC §145i; cf. Neh 9:18 with Exod 32:4, 8; 1 Chron 17:21 with 2 Sam 7:23). These linguistic peculiarities do not support religio-historical conclusions concerning an original Israelite polytheism, which would have been retained primarily in E.

3. The semantic range of ᵓ*ᵉlōhîm* reaches farther than "god": from patron deities and ghosts all the way to the fig. usage, incl. even the attenuated superlative sense.

According to Exod 21:6 (abbreviated in Deut 15:17) a slave who wishes to remain with his lord is led "before God" or "to the door" to receive a mark. ᵓ*ᵉlōhîm* here are likely the household gods that protect the family (cf. Gen 31:30; also Judg 18:24). The regulations in Exod 22:7f. should be understood similarly: In unresolvable private law situations one turned in ancient times to the household gods (ᵓ*ᵉlōhîm* does not have the meaning "judge" in Exod 18:19; 22:27; 1 Sam 2:25; Psa 82:1; 138:1; cf. A. E. Draffkorn, *JBL* 76 [1957]: 216–24; H. W. Jüngling, *Der Tod der Götter* [1969], 24ff.; W. Beyerlin, *Die Rettung der Bedrängten in den Feindpsalmen der Einzelnen auf institutionelle Zusammenhänge untersucht* [1970], 56f.).

Spirits of the dead can be called ᵓ*ᵉlōhîm* (1 Sam 28:13; Isa 8:19; cf. Mic 3:7?), although they may not intervene in human affairs on their own, they speak only (at night) per inquiry, and (despite 1 Sam 28:14) they have no cult (cf. L. Wächter, *Der Tod im AT* [1967], 192).

In some phrases such as "man of God" or "spirit of God" (see III/6), ᵓ*ᵉlōhîm* may have only the weakened sense of "divine" or even "demonic."

The king is addressed in the controversial text Psa 45:7 as ᵓ*ᵉlōhîm.* Zech 12:8 promises for "that day": even the weakest Jerusalemite will be strengthened "like David, and the house of David like ᵓ*ᵉlōhîm,*" which an addition mitigates to "angel of Yahweh" (conversely, Judg 13:22 describes the "angel of Yahweh" as ᵓ*ᵉlōhîm*).

A metaphorical or fig. meaning of ᵓ*ᵉlōhîm* occurs in the description of the relationship between Moses and Aaron as one between principle and prophetic spokesman: "He will be your mouth and you will become God for him" (Exod 4:16; cf. 7:1).

Like ᵓ*ēl* (III/4), ᵓ*ᵉlōhîm* may also exercise an intensifying function: "mountain of God" (Psa 68:16; cf. 36:7), "a city large for God" (= beyond measure) (Jonah 3:3), "wisdom of God" (1 Kgs 3:28), "panic of God" (1 Sam 14:15; cf. Gen 35:5; 2 Chron 20:29). Nevertheless, ᵓ*ᵉlōhîm* does not completely lose its meaning in this usage; for the intensification results from the fact that the thing (or person) affected is related to God, e.g., "frightful (= sent by God?) thunder" (Exod 9:28; cf. 9:23) or "God's camp" (Gen 32:3; 1 Chron 12:23); cf. also "prince of God" (Gen 23:6), "God's fight" (Gen 30:8), "God's fire" (2 Kgs 1:12; Job 1:16), perhaps "God's breath" (Gen 1:2), "God's grace" (see III/7); see D. W. Thomas, *VT* 3 (1953): 209–24; 18 (1968): 120–24; F. Dexinger, *Sturz der*

Göttersöhne oder Engel vor der Sintflut? [1966], 41ff. The sense of the word ʾᵉlōhîm, then, cannot be established with certainty in most cases; various nuances may be heard. Moreover, the phrases should be explained variously on the basis of their origins; some have religiohistorical bases, some are later formations (cf. also III/5).

4. The oldest traditions in which ʾᵉ*lōhîm* is firmly rooted are the names of the "gods of the fathers" and of the "mountain of God." But the "Yahweh war" tradition seems not to have known the word originally; ʾᵉ*lōhîm* has replaced the Yahweh name or the divine "I" in the expression "people of God" in the summons to arms (Judg 20:2 in contrast to 5:11, 13 "people of Yahweh"; cf. 2 Sam 14:13) and in the cry "God has given the enemies into your hand" (Judg 7:14; 8:3; 18:10; cf. 1 Sam 23:14; cf. G. von Rad, *Holy War in Ancient Israel* [1991], 42ff.).

In the patriarchal tradition (→ ʾ*āb* IV/1), ʾᵉ*lōhîm* occurs in two different expressions: "God of my/your father" (Gen 31:5, 29 txt em; 46:3; cf. Exod 15:2; 18:4, etc.) and "God of Abraham" (Gen 31:42); "God of my father Abraham" (32:10; cf. 26:24, etc.) represents a hybrid form. In the oath that Jacob and Laban take following a border treaty, both partners summon their God as guardian of the agreement: "The God of Abraham and the God of Nahor shall judge between us" (Gen 31:53). One may still perceive here that the two deities were once distinguished; an addition seems to fuse both into the "God of their father." Formulations such as "God of your father, God of Abraham, God of Isaac, God of Jacob" (Exod 3:6) or "God of your fathers" (3:13, 15f.; cf. 4:5), which combine the individual gods of the fathers and equate them with Yahweh, are even more secondary. The OT recognizes only Israel's God under the various designations, so that one must reconstruct an earlier form contrary to the sense of the text, and it is difficult to decide, regarding the particulars, the degree to which the tradition persists in its early form (on the god of the fathers, see Alt, "God of the Fathers," *EOTHR* 1–77; bibliog. in K. T. Andersen, *ST* 16 [1962]: 170–88; M. Haran, *ASTI* 4 [1965]: 30–55; F. M. Cross, *Canaanite Myth and Hebrew Epic* [1973], 3–43).

Later, in the framing sermons of Deut and particularly in the Chronicler, designations such as "God of your/his/our fathers," etc., which express the fusion of tradition and one's own faith, become very popular. But the expression "God of Jacob," whose antiquity (like that of "God of Isaac"; Gen 28:13) is uncertain, also receives greater significance, esp. in worship (2 Sam 23:1; Isa 2:3; Psa 20:2; 46:8, 12; 84:9, etc.; G. Wanke, *Die Zionstheologie der Korachiten in ihrem traditionsgeschichtlichen Zusammenhang* [1966], 54ff.); cf. "God of Abraham" in Psa 47:10 (1 Kgs 18:36). "God of your father, David" (2 Kgs 20:5 = Isa 38:5; 2 Chron 21:12), "God of Elijah" (2 Kgs 2:14), and also "God of Shem" (Gen 9:26) are formed analogously.

If the God of the fathers is associated with people, in accordance with his name, so the "mountain of God" tradition (Exod 3:1; 4:27; 18:5; 24:13, E in part) associates a god with a place that one must seek in order to experience the divine presence. Because reports of "Sinai" and "mountain of God" are distinct (except for Exod 24:13), it is not entirely clear whether the two traditions refer to the same place. Should they have a common origin, the extent of their subsequent divergence is remarkable. The "mountain of God" tradition takes place in the region of the Midianites (cf. the cultic community, Exod 18:12), about whom the Sinai narrative is silent, and offers no theophany corresponding to Exod 19:16ff. (cf. at best Exod 3).

5. Some ancient Near Eastern mythical concepts, indicated by the expressions "city of God" (Psa 46:5; 48:2, 9; 87:3), "stream of God" (Psa 65:10), "mountain of God" (Ezek 28:14, 16; cf. 28:2; Psa 68:16; 1 Kgs 19:8), "garden of God" (Ezek 28:13; 31:8f; cf. Isa 51:3), survive primarily in the Jerusalem tradition; cf. also from the Moses tradition "rod of God" (Exod 4:20; 17:9), "finger of God" (Exod 8:15; 31:18; Deut 9:10), and "writing of God" (Exod 32:16). Like *bᵉnê ʾēlîm*—an expression also attested outside the OT and therefore perhaps an ancient expression—*bᵉnê ʾelōhîm* (Gen 6:2, 4; Job 1:6; 2:1; 38:7; cf. Dan 3:25) are also "sons of gods," i.e., divine beings, subordinate to Yahweh.

The mythical narrative Gen 6:1–4 assigns them even greater self-sufficiency than the framing report of the book of Job, where they still constitute only a subservient heavenly council. Nevertheless, the preexistent concept, according to which the giants originate in the admixture of gods and people, is also annulled in the story of the "angel marriages"; the myth is reshaped by the historical self-understanding of Israel in order to reveal the responsibility and guilt of humanity.

Israel has subordinated strange powers to Yahweh elsewhere as well. Thus in the mythical judgment scene in Psa 82, sentence of death is pronounced upon the "gods" (vv 1, 6 *ʾelōhîm*), because they are unable to create justice for the needy (Psa 58:2ff.).

6. Significantly, the mythically colored usages mentioned and the superlative form (see III/3; cf. also IV/5) are only rarely formed with the Yahweh name and always with the appellative "god." *ʾelōhîm* occurs with remarkable frequency in fixed phrases, sometimes in ancient preformed material (on III/6–7 cf. F. Baumgärtel, *Elohim ausserhalb des Pentateuch* [1914]). Just as the OT has no "sons of Yahweh" formulation analogous to "sons of God" (perhaps in avoidance of the obvious notion of paternity), it also does not occur with Yahweh in a way corresponding to *ʾîš (hā)ʾelōhîm* "man of God." Other phrases are more or less reserved for *ʾelōhîm* or gain a particular emphasis through the generic name.

The title "man of God" (no pl. is attested) is concentrated in the Elijah and particularly the Elisha narratives, which depict the prophets as wonderworkers (from 1 Kgs 17:18 on); it also describes Samuel, among others (1 Sam 9:6ff.), and is applied to Moses (Deut 33:1; Josh 14:6; Psa 90:1; 1 Chron 23:14; 2 Chron 30:16; Ezra 3:2) and in the Chronicler to David (2 Chron 8:14; Neh 12:24, 36; see R. Rendtorff, *TDNT* 6:809). Cf. similar expressions such as "God's devotee" (Judg 13:5, 7; 16:17) or "prince of God" (Gen 23:6).

The general description "ark of God" (1 Sam 3:3; 4:11ff.) may be older than the specifically Israelite name "ark of Yahweh (God Sabaoth)" (1 Sam 4:6; 2 Sam 6:2). Among other names are "ark of the covenant of God" (Judg 20:27) and "ark of the God of Israel" (1 Sam 5:7ff.; cf. J. Maier, *Das altisraelitische Ladeheiligtum* [1965], 82ff.).

"House of God" (Gen 28:17, 22; Judg 9:27; 17:5; 18:31; cf. Jer 43:12f., etc.) becomes a frequent term for the temple in the Chronicler's history (Ezra 1:4; 4:24ff., etc.), although the alternation with "house of Yahweh" (e.g., 2 Chron

28:24) seems to be inconsistent. The title "chief *(nāgîd)* of the house of God" (Neh 11:11; 1 Chron 9:11; 2 Chron 31:13; 35:8) is firmly established, however.

The expression "food of God" (Lev 21:6, 8, 17, 21f.; 22:25) preserves an ancient sacrificial concept, explicated to a degree in the pertinent laws by the neutral expression *ᵓiššê yhwh* "Yahweh's (burnt) offering"; cf. similar designations in Lev 21:12; 23:14; Num 6:7; perhaps Psa 51:19.

Ezek (1:1; 8:3; 40:2; cf. 11:24; 43:3) has "visions of God" as a fixed phrase for the prophetic reception of revelation.

The "spirit of God" (→ *rûaḥ*) comes upon the prophets (Num 24:4; 1 Sam 10:10; 11:6; 19:20, 23; Ezek 11:24; 2 Chron 15:1; 24:20), gives wisdom (Gen 41:38; Exod 31:3; 35:31), and facilitates dream interpretation (cf. Dan 4:6, "spirit of the holy gods," with 2:28, 47), but also represents the human life force (Job 27:3). 1 Sam 16:14–16 (cf. 16:23; 18:10) distinguishes an evil spirit sent by Yahweh, a "spirit of God," from the "spirit of Yahweh." Perhaps *ᵓᵉlōhîm* here has the attenuated sense of the divine-demonic.

Other expressions also seem to be fixed idioms, although they are not limited to formation with *ᵓᵉlōhîm:* "fearful of God" (Gen 22:12; Exod 18:21; Job 1:1; Eccl 7:18; etc.), "to fear God" (Exod 1:17, 21; Job 1:9; etc.), "to curse God" (or, euphemistically, "to bless God") (1 Sam 3:13 txt em; Job 1:5; 2:9; cf. Deut 21:23 "curse of God"), "to ask God" (Judg 18:5; 20:18; 1 Sam 14:36f.), "word of God" (Judg 3:20; 1 Sam 9:27; 2 Sam 16:23; cf. 1 Kgs 12:22; Mic 3:7), or "knowledge of God" (Hos 4:1; 6:6; Prov 2:5). Such phrases sometimes refer intentionally to the "deity" (cf. also the denial of God, IV/5).

7. *ᵓᵉlōhîm* occurs moreover in other less firmly established figures of speech, e.g., "May God do this or that to me" (1 Sam 3:17, etc.; pl. for non-Israelites: 1 Kgs 19:2; 20:10; subj. Yahweh, 1 Sam 20:13; Ruth 1:17), "to curse God and the kings" (or, euphemistically, "bless") (1 Kgs 21:10, 13; cf. Isa 8:21; Exod 22:27; subj. Yahweh, Prov 24:21), perhaps "to show someone the kindness of God" (= loving service) (2 Sam 9:3; cf. 2:5; subj. Yahweh, 1 Sam 20:14), etc. Some of these idioms may also have been common among Israel's neighbors.

The formula "as *ᵓᵉlōhîm* (pl.?) destroyed Sodom and Gomorrah" may be of pre-exilic origin, if it originally referred to another deity (or deities) as the agent of the fall of the two places (Isa 13:19; Jer 50:40; Amos 4:11; cf. Deut 29:22; Isa 1:7 txt em; Jer 49:18); the saga in Gen 18f. already ascribes the deed to Yahweh.

The designation "angel of God" for God's messenger (Gen 21:17; 28:12 pl.; Judg 6:20, etc.) is less common than "angel of Yahweh" (→ *malᵓāk*), but often appears in a proverbial manner in similes (Judg 13:6; 1 Sam 29:9; 2 Sam 14:17, 20; 19:28; "angel of Yahweh," Zech 12:8).

The disaster coming upon someone can be considered to have been sent from "God's hand" (1 Sam 5:11; Job 19:21), while in post-exilic times the expression "God's (good) hand over me" or variants describe God's gracious control (Ezra 7:6, 9, 28; 8:18, 22, 31; Neh 2:8, 18). In each case the organ is understood in terms of its function.

The expression "gods and men" (Judg 9:9, 13) or "to strive with *ᵓᵉlōhîm* and men" (Gen 32:29; cf. Hos 12:4) also deserves mention. The divine name Yahweh is specifically avoided in the latter usage; as a consequence, the meaning of *ᵓᵉlōhîm* remains ambiguous because of the tangled tradition history of the Penuel narrative.

IV. 1. In some phrases or with a suf., *ᵓᵉlōhîm* expresses the relationship between God and people. "God of Israel" is, then, nothing short of a standard expression (all occurrences in C. Steuernagel, FS Wellhausen 329ff.). The earliest trustworthy witness for it is the Song of Deborah from early in the period of the judges (Judg 5:3, 5).

The antiquity of occurrences in Gen 33:20; Josh 8:30; 24:2, 23, from which one could infer the cultic names of a deity worshiped in Shechem (cf. e.g., M. Noth, *Das System der zwölf Stämme Israels* [1930], 93f.), remains unknown because the structure of the formula in Gen 33:20 differs from the other divine names formed with *ᵓēl* (→ *ᵓēl* III/2), and the time of composition of Josh 8 and 24 is disputed. The formula seems even more secondary in the Sinai tradition (Exod 24:10; cf. 5:1; 34:23). Since approximately the time of the exile, the usage became a favorite (introductions to speeches in Jer, Chronicler, etc.). It occurs in very different contexts: in doxology and prayer (1 Kgs 8:15, 23; 2 Kgs 19:15), in the oath (1 Kgs 17:1), etc. The prophet Ezekiel knows the singular "glory of the God of Israel" (8:4; 9:3; 10:19; 43:2) in addition to the usual formulation "glory (→ *kbd*) of Yahweh" (1:28, etc.).

"God of the Hebrews" (Exod 3:18, etc.) or "God of Jacob" (see III/4) are similar phrases.

2. God's relationship with the people is more frequently expressed through *ᵓᵉlōhîm* with a suf.: "your/our God," etc. (e.g., Josh 24:17f., 27; Exod 32:4, 8; Judg 11:24; Mic 4:5; of strange gods: 1 Sam 5:7; Jer 48:35), as is his relationship with an individual (also through "my God").

The meaning of such forms expanded by pronouns (cf. Ruth 1:16) can only be illustrated by some examples here. Thus the alternation of "our/your God" (Exod 8:21ff.; 10:16f., 25f.) often reflects the contrast of Moses and Pharaoh. In the second encounter with Ahaz (Isa 7:10–17), Isaiah offers the king: "Ask a sign of Yahweh *your* God!" When Ahaz hesitates, the prophet asks threateningly: "Is it too little for you to weary men, so that you also weary *my* God?" The refusal of the offer is a rejection of the promise inherent in the phrase "your God." In a time in which the community between God and people appears to be broken according to the message of judgment of his prophetic predecessors, Deutero-Isaiah begins his proclamation with the cry "Comfort, comfort my people, says *your* God!" (Isa 40:1; cf. 40:8 "the word of *our* God"). He may alter the traditional proclamation, "Yahweh has become king," into "*your* God has become king" (52:7) and he allows a messenger to report already: "Behold, *your* God!" (40:9; cf. 35:4). The people's address "my God" in Hosea's promise (2:25) already embraces everything that the era of salvation will bring (similarly Zech 13:9; Isa 25:9 "our God"). Such suf. forms occur with particular frequency in Hos; Deuteronomic-Deuteronomistic literature impresses Israel even more with the fact that Yahweh is "your God."

The cry "my God" in Hos 2:25, conceived as a collective term (cf. Isa 40:27, etc.), is frequently the address of the individual in distress that opens the lament to God, expresses trust, hope, and thanks (Psa 3:8; 5:3; 7:2, 4; 22:3; 25:2; 38:22; 91:2; 1 Kgs 17:20f.; Dan 9:18f., etc.; cf. O. Eissfeldt, " 'Mein Gott' im AT," *ZAW* 61 [1945–48]: 3–16 = *KS* [1966], 3:35–47). The confessional formula "you are my/our God" represents an expansion (Psa 31:15; 86:2; 143:10; Isa 25:1 or 2 Chron 14:10; of the idol: Isa 44:17; cf. Gen 31:30; Judg 18:24).

3. Finally, suf. forms of *ᵓᵉlōhîm* are constitutive for the so-called self-presentation formula, "I am Yahweh, your God," and the so-called covenant formula, "I will be their God, and they will be my people."

The self-presentation formula, well-known in the ancient Near East, "I am . . . ," refers to Yahweh in Israelite usage and is expanded (to the so-called grace formula) by the promise "your God"; it appears in various contexts in the OT with varied meanings (sometimes the translation "I, Yahweh, am your God" is also justified). It frequently points to history, particularly to the experiences in Egypt (Hos 12:10; 13:4; Psa 81:11), and in the Decalogue the ceremonious 1st-per. speech of God forms the preamble from which the individual commandments follow (Exod 20:2; cf. Judg 6:10). The chief occurrence of this idiom belongs once again to the exile; for it is concentrated in P, esp. in H (Lev 18:2, etc.), and in Ezek (20:5, etc.). In conjunction with "to recognize that" (Exod 6:7 P; Ezek 20:20, etc; → *ydᶜ*), the divine "I" becomes the goal of human knowledge; cf. W. Zimmerli, *I Am Yahweh* [1982], 1ff., 29ff., 104; K. Elliger, *Kleine Schriften zum AT* (1966), 211–31.

The covenant formula is found (since around the end of the pre-exilic era) in various forms, on the one hand, in the later Moses tradition (Deut 26:17f.; 29:12; Exod 6:7 P, etc.), and, on the other, in prophetic promises (Jer 31:33; Ezek 11:20, etc.). It announces the existent or—critically—the future identity of Yahweh with his people; cf. R. Smend, *Die Bundesformel* (1963).

4. *ʾᵉlōhîm* is often more closely defined, more frequently through cs. combinations such as "God of heaven," "God of my help" than through adjs.: "the righteous God," "the living God," etc. In every case, God's nature or the means of encountering him are announced.

Except for Gen 24:7 (v 3, "God of heaven and earth"), "God of heaven" occurs from the post-exilic period onward in apposition to or even instead of the name Yahweh, sometimes in conversation with or speeches before foreigners (Jonah 1:9; Ezra 1:2 = 2 Chron 36:23; Neh 1:4f., etc.; Aram.: Dan 2:18f., etc.; cf. Psa 136:26). The designation may have arisen under Persian influence; in any case it serves the dialog with the Persian government (cf. Ezra's title, "Scribe of the law of the God of heaven," Ezra 7:12). The concept that God dwells in heaven (→ *šāmayim*) is already common early in Israel, however, and Mic 6:6 calls Yahweh "God of the heights." Because this expression is unique, it must be left open as to how far it represents a common Jerusalemite designation for God (cf. Psa 92:9; Josh 2:11, etc.).

Other phrases similarly emphasize God's universality or his sphere of activity in various ways, e.g., "God of eternity" (Isa 40:28; cf. Gen 31:33; Deut 33:27; → *ᶜôlām*) or "God of all flesh" (Jer 32:27; cf. Num 16:22; 27:16). The common name "Yahweh (God) Sabaoth" (2 Sam 5:10, etc.; → *ṣābāʾ*; cf. 1 Sam 17:45 "God of the armies of Israel") is surely an accentuation of Yahweh's might, although the particulars of its meaning are disputed.

The expression of trust, "God of my salvation" or the like (Psa 18:47; 24:5; 27:9; 65:6; 79:9; 85:5; Isa 17:10; Mic 7:7, etc.), already sounds formulaic, shaped by either experience or expectation; cf. "God of my help" (Psa 51:16; "Yahweh God of my help," 88:2), "God of faithfulness" (Isa 65:16), etc. Even the name "God of righteousness" (Isa 30:18) can express God's "grace" or "mercy" (contrast Mal 2:17).

Although adj. modifiers do occur (see III/2), cs. combinations often replace them (e.g., Psa 59:11, 18 "God of my grace" = "my gracious God"). Thus the "living God" reveals himself through his saving intervention (1 Sam 17:26,

36; 2 Kgs 19:4, 16; cf. Dan 6:21, 27) as the "true" God (Jer 10:10; cf. 2 Chron 15:3); he is also able to reverse the misfortune of the individual (Psa 42:3).

5. With the aid of the expression *ʾᵉlōhîm*, a few texts treat the themes of God's deity or of his relationship to humanity in a special way. The confession *yhwh hû hāʾᵉlōhîm* "Yahweh is (the true, only) God" (Deut 4:35, 39; 1 Kgs 8:60; 18:39; cf. Deut 7:9; 10:17; Josh 2:11; Psa 100:3, etc.; as address: 2 Sam 7:28 = 1 Chron 17:26; 2 Kgs 19:15, 19; Neh 9:7) reflects Yahweh's controversy with other gods, even though his exclusive claim to worship has triumphed. As in the statement of incomparability (2 Sam 7:22 = 1 Chron 17:20; Isa 44:6, 8; 45:5, 14, 21; 64:3; cf. 2 Kgs 5:15; Deut 32:39, etc.; cf. C. J. Labuschagne, *Incomparability of Yahweh in the OT* [1966]), the truth of God's deity is bolstered against any doubt; the one circumlocution for the superlative expression "God of gods" (Deut 10:17; Psa 136:2; cf. Dan 2:47) has a similar significance.

The remarkable combination *yhwh ʾᵉlōhîm* also occurs frequently outside Gen 2:4b–3:23 (only *ʾᵉlōhîm:* 3:1b, 3, 5; see Exod 9:30; 2 Sam 7:25; Jonah 4:6; Psa 72:18; 84:12; 1 Chron 17:16f.; cf. 22:1, etc.). If the double name in the J creation and paradise narrative depends on the influence of *ʾᵉlōhîm* in the P creation story, then the other occurrences remain basically inexplicable (more likely to be read as "Yahweh the true God" than as "Yahweh of the gods"); cf. O. H. Steck, *Die Paradieserzählung* (1970), 28n.35.

Like *ʾēl* (see IV/4), if not as poignantly, *ʾᵉlōhîm* can also express the difference between God and human (e.g., Gen 30:2; 45:8; 50:19; 2 Kgs 5:7; Psa 82:6; cf. Job 4:17; Mal 3:8) or God and "not God" (Deut 32:17; 2 Chron 13:9, etc.). Effectiveness is the criterion: The strange gods are "good for nothing" (Jer 2:11 *lōʾ ʾᵉlōhîm;* cf. 5:7; 16:20), a "human product" (2 Kgs 19:18 = Isa 37:19; 2 Chron 32:19; cf. Hos 8:6 and the formulation "to make gods" in Exod 20:23; 32:1; Jer 16:20, etc.). Correspondingly, the denial of God ("there is no God," Psa 10:4; 14:1 = 53:2; cf. 10:13; 36:2) disputes not the existence but the effectiveness of God on earth, just as the question "where is your God?" (Psa 42:4, 11; cf. 79:10; 115:2; Joel 2:17) refers to the appearance of his helping power.

Although the serpent in the paradise narrative promises the couple that they may "be like God" (Gen 3:5; the designation remains ambiguous because of the history of the tradition, which goes back to ancient Near Eastern mythical concepts; cf. Ezek 28:2, 9, 13), God confirms this promise only in the weakened form "be like us" (3:22). Equality with God is recognized only as equality with the heavenly beings. Only the LXX (cf. also at Psa 97:7; 138:1) devalues the "image of God" in this way (W. H. Schmidt, *Die Schöpfungsgeschichte der Priesterschrift* [1967²], 141). The OT itself does not limit the statement that the human is created "as God's image" (i.e., as God's representation, representative, viceroy) in any perceptible manner (Gen 1:26f.; 5:1; 9:6 P; → *ṣelem*). Yet, in a similar context, Psa 8 compares people with "God" (v 6) and not with "Yahweh" (v 2), and so seems to make use of the difference between the proper name and the generic term in order to protect the peculiarity of Yahweh. Perhaps the previously stated expression, which like other fixed expressions with *ʾᵉlōhîm* (III/6–7) has the relationship of humans to "God" and not to "Yahweh" in mind, brings about this usage. In any case, this distinction does not apply to the Priestly primeval history because it uses the divine designation ᵓ*ᵉlōhîm* consistently.

6. Various portions of the OT do not predominantly use the Yahweh name as a divine designation, but ᵓ*ᵉlōhîm* (with and without art.): in two sources of the Pentateuch, E and P, in the so-called Elohistic Psalter, in Eccl, and, to a degree, in Chronicles (on Job, see II). Thus Israel's distinctiveness diminishes at times, negatively put, through the use of the general term for "God" and the avoidance of the proper name, but, positively, one may not easily determine a common tendency of the various works of literature, because particular points of reference for the foundation of the usage are lacking. Is God's universality expressed in this way? Because the individual documents stem from such varied times, there must have also been various occasions and reasons for the usage.

The Elohist apparently did not use the word ᵓ*ᵉlōhîm* (Gen 20:3, 6, etc.) exclusively, but only predominantly, and occasionally employs the name Yahweh, esp. after the revelation to Moses in Exod 3:14 (cf. H. Seebass, *Der Erzvater Israel* [1966], 56n.4). The attempt has even been made to distinguish two Elohistic layers with this characteristic as a criterion; this alternation is, however, more likely due to the influence of the common mode of expression or, perhaps, to secondary influence of the other documentary sources. One may not interpret the use of ᵓ*ᵉlōhîm* as a remnant of an old Israelite polytheism (cf. W. Eichrodt, *Die Quellen der Genesis* [1916], 106ff.; E. König, *Die Genesis* [1925³], 62ff.). Because the general designation is still preserved, at least as a rule, after Exod 3:14, E has also not sought to differentiate, like P, between individual epochs of revelation. Perhaps E wished to emphasize God's transcendence (cf. God's appearances in the dream and through the "angel of God"; see III/7), but in the final analysis, the explanation continues to be based on uncertain suppositions.

In contrast, one may infer that P seeks to acknowledge Israel's God as the God of humanity, because it uses the appellative ᵓ*ᵉlōhîm* exclusively (and thereafter in alternation) in the creation and primeval narratives up until the revelation to Abraham in Gen 17:1 (→ ᵓ*ēl* III/1).

In the Elohistic Psalter (Psa 42–83) the phenomenon stands out sharply insofar as the original Yahweh name was replaced secondarily by the general term ᵓ*ᵉlōhîm* (cf. Psa 53 with Psa 14). Chronicles proceeded similarly, although with far less consequence, in the adoption of texts from the Deuteronomistic history (cf. e.g., "house of God" in 2 Chron 4:11 with 1 Kgs 7:40; see III/6 and M. Rehm, *Textkritische Untersuchungen zu den Parallelstellen der Samuel-Königsbücher und der Chronik* [1937], 108f.; on the frequent names "God of Israel" and "God of the fathers," see III/4; IV/1). One may presuppose for this late period that the Yahweh name may have receded because the distinction between proper name and generic term had faded through the confession of Israel's God as the only true Lord of the world. The emergent reluctance to pronounce the name of Yahweh may have contributed to this accentuation of God's transcendence and therewith the distinction between God and people (cf. also the book of Job); nevertheless, 1/2 Chron do not yet avoid it on principle. Finally, it may have been decisive for Qohelet's choice of the divine designation that he was able to emphasize God's omnipotence in view of the vanity of humanity by means of the general term ᵓ*ᵉlōhîm* (usually with art.).

V. On the whole, then, the generic name ᵓ*ᵉlōhîm* aided the Israelites to understand and to proclaim the God of their own history as the God of the world. On the aftereffects of the OT usage in postbibl. Judaism and in the NT, cf. H. Kleinknecht, G. Quell, E. Stauffer, and K. G. Kuhn, "θεός," *TDNT* 3:65–123.

W. H. Schmidt

אֱלִיל ʾᵉ*lîl* nothingness

S 457; BDB 47a; *HALOT* 1:55b; *TDOT* 1:285–87; *TWOT* 99a; *NIDOTTE* 496

---

1. The word ʾᵉ*lîl* "nothingness" is attested only in the OT and in literature dependent upon it; it finds its clearest pars. in Akk., Aram., and Arab. adj. formations of the root ʾ*ll* in the meaning "weak," etc. (cf. *HAL* 54a). Wildberger reviews the numerous but unproductive attempts at etymology (*Isa 1–12*, CC, 109; cf. also J. A. Montgomery, *JAOS* 56 [1936]: 442). On the (Aramaizing?) nom. form of the word, cf. Wagner 122.

A noun **ill* "annihilation" has not been demonstrated in Ug. (*WUS* no. 216; *UT* no. 184; contra *CML*[1] 136a; *CML*[2] 142; Gray, *Legacy* 60; *KTU* reads *ilm* in 1.5.V.16).

2. ʾᵉ*lîl* occurs 20x in the OT, 10x alone in Isa (2:8, 18, 20bis; 10:10f.; 19:1, 3; 31:7bis), 2x in Lev (19:4; 26:1) and Psa (96:5 = 1 Chron 16:26; Psa 97:7), 1x each in Jer 14:14 Q; Ezek 30:13; Hab 2:18; Zech 11:17; Job 13:4. Cf. also Sir 11:3; 1QM 14:1 (cf. Isa 19:1); 1Q22 1:8.

Textual emendations are suggested for Isa 10:10; Ezek 30:13; Zech 11:17 (cf. commentaries).

3. ʾᵉ*lîl* is used uniquely in three texts as the governing noun of a cs. relationship and can be rendered "for nought, insignificant" (Jer 14:14 txt em, "empty divination"; Zech 11:17, "good-for-nothing shepherds"; Job 13:4 "no-account speech"; cf. further Sir 11:3 "the bee is entirely insignificant among flying creatures").

In the other texts (except for Isa 10:10 txt?), the noun appears in the pl. and is a derogatory designation for foreign gods. Psa 96:5 = 1 Chron 16:26 "all gods are nothing" (cf. also Psa 97:7) shows how this pl. usage developed from the sg. abstract. At any rate, the parody of ʾ*ēl*/ʾᵉ*lōhîm* "God" may play a part in the prophetic literature and in H, which is dependent upon it (Lev 19:4; 26:1).

4. The following is said of the ʾᵉ*lîlîm:* They are the product of human hands (Isa 2:8, 20; 31:7; Lev 26:1), and one can therefore discard them (Isa 31:7); they are dumb (Hab 2:18); they quiver before Yahweh (Isa 19:1) and vanish before him (2:18). The expression ʾᵉ*lîlîm* recalls, then, the impotence and the insignificance of the strange gods. The force of the term is probably most clearly seen in Psa 96:5: "for all gods of the peoples are nothing, but Yahweh made the heavens." Wildberger (*Isa 1–12*, CC, 109) has commented on this passage: "The use of this designation in the two God-king-psalms shows that it has its roots in the Jerusalem cult tradition, which is how Isaiah

would have come to know it. It is not just by chance that this designation is used elsewhere only in the Holiness Code (Lev. 19:4; 26:1) and Habakkuk (2:18)."

ᵓᵉlîlîm parallels *pesel/pāsîl* "sculpted image" (Isa 10:10; Lev 26:1; Hab 2:18; Psa 97:7), *ᶜᵃṣabbîm* "carved image" (Isa 10:11), *gillûlîm* "idols" (Ezek 30:13), and *massēkâ* "molten image" (Lev 19:4; Hab 2:18). Eissfeldt (*KS* [1962], 1:271f.) summarizes the OT designations for "idol" in five groups with Scripture references: (1) derogatory terms: *bōšet* "shame" (→ *bôš*), *šiqqûṣ* "horrible thing," *tôᶜēbâ* "abomination" (→ *tᶜb*), *ḥaṭṭāᵓt* "sin" (→ *ḥṭᵓ*), *ᵓēmâ* "horror"; (2) terms that deny the existence of the gods represented by the idols: → *hebel* "vapor," *šeqer* "lie" (→ *šqr*), → *šāwᵓ* "vanity," *ᵓᵉlîl* "nothing," *lōᵓ-ᵓēl* and *lōᵓ-ᵓᵉlōhîm* "not-god" (→ *ᵓēl* III/3; → *ᵓᵉlōhîm* IV/5); (3) terms that deny idols divine dignity and relegate them to the sphere of the lower, evil spirits: *śᵉᶜîrîm* "satyrs," *šēdîm* "demons," → *ᵓāwen* "evil power"; (4) designations that declare them to be foreign and so more or less explicitly describe them as useless: phrases with → *ᵓaḥēr* "other", → *zār* "foreign", → *nēkār* "strange," → *ḥādāš* "new"; (5) designations that identify them with their images and so declare them to be lifeless matter: *massēkâ* and *nesek* "molten image," *pesel* and *pāsîl* "sculpted image," *ᶜōṣeb* and *ᶜāṣāb* "carved image," → *ṣelem* and *semel* "carved image," *gillûlîm* "(hewn) blocks of stone," *ṣîr* "image," *maśkît* "showpiece," and *nᵉśûᵓâ* "processional image."

5. The LXX renders *ᵓᵉlîlîm* variously, most frequently with *cheiropoiēta* "human product" (6x) and *eidōla* "idols" (4x). The NT adopts *eidōlon* as a designation for the pagan gods in the meaning shaped by the LXX and Judaism (cf. F. Büchsel, "εἴδωλον," *TDNT* 2:375–80).

S. Schwertner

אַלְמָנָה *ᵓalmānâ* widow

S 490; BDB 48a; *HALOT* 1:58a; *TDOT* 1:287–91; *TWOT* 105; *NIDOTTE* 530

---

1. *ᵓalmānâ* "widow" is common Sem. (cf. *GVG* 1:220, 227), with variation of the liquid in Aram. and Arab. (*ᵓarmaltāᵓ* and *ᵓarmalat*, resp., in contrast to Akk. *almattu* < **almantu*, Ug. *almnt*, Phoen. *ᵓlmt*).

The etymology is uncertain; cf. the suggested derivations cataloged in *HAL* 56b.

The abstract formations *ᵓalmānût* "widowhood" (*bigdê ᵓalmᵉnûtāh* "her widow's clothing," Gen 38:14, 19; on 2 Sam 20:3 and Isa 54:4 see 3b) and *ᵓalmōn* "widowhood" (Isa 47:9 par. *šᵉkôl* "childlessness"; see 3b) derive from *ᵓalmānâ*; cf. Akk. *almānūtu* (*CAD* A/1:362a) and Ug. *ḫṭ ulmn* "scepter of widowhood" par. *ḫṭ ṯkl* "scepter of childlessness" in the hand of the god Mot (*KTU* 1.23.8–9; Gray, *Legacy* 95f.).

2. The 55 occurrences of *ᵓalmānâ* are distributed as follows: Gen 1x, Exod 2x, Lev 2x, Num 1x, Deut 11x, 2 Sam 1x, 1 Kgs 5x, Isa 5x, Jer 5x, Ezek 6x, (on Ezek 19:7 see Zimmerli, *Ezek*, Herm, 1:389), Zech 1x, Mal 1x, Psa 5x, Job 6x,

Lam 2x, Prov 1x. *ʾalmānût* occurs 4x, *ʾalmōn* and *ʾalmān* 1x each. One-third of the root's occurrences are in legal texts.

Not included here is the occurrence Mandl. lists in Isa 13:22, where *ʾalmᵉnôtāyw* "his palaces" should be understood as a by-form of *ʾarmôn* (see also Ezek 19:7).

3. (a) *ʾalmānâ* should be translated "widow" in all its occurrences; it describes a woman who loses her social and economic support through the death of her husband (to this degree "widow" is not merely a description of the marital status "formerly the wife of the deceased"; cf. L. Köhler, *ZAW* 40 [1922]: 34; van der Leeuw 1:246f.; *CAD* A/1:364). The widow's lot, in any case, is sorrowful, whether she is childless and returns to her paternal home (Gen 38:11, with the possibility of levirate marriage), or she has children (*ʾiššâ ʾalmānâ* in 2 Sam 14:5; 1 Kgs 17:9f.; even 1 Kgs 7:14 [mother of Hiram of Tyre] and 11:26 [mother of Jeroboam]) and the father has died before the birth of the son (cf. the Phoen. Eshmunazar inscription, l. 3 "son of a widow," *KAI* 2.19, 21f.; *ANET* 662a). The most famous widow story, the book of Ruth, does not use the word "widow."

As a rule, widows are mentioned in one breath with those who bear a similarly hard lot: orphans *(yātôm)*, outcasts *(gᵉrûšâ)*, sojourners *(gēr; → gûr)*, poor *(dal)*, destitute (*ʿānî; →* *ʿanh* II), childless *(šakkūlâ)*, as well as Levites and slaves.

Thus the following nom. series result: widows/orphans (Exod 22:21, 23; Deut 10:18; Isa 9:16); widows/orphans/sojourners/destitute (Zech 7:10; cf. Deut 27:19; Mal 3:5); widow/outcast (Lev 22:13; Num 30:10; Ezek 44:22; cf. Lev 21:14); Levite/sojourner/orphan/widow (Deut 14:29; 26:12f.; similarly Deut 16:11, 14; 24:17, 19–21; Jer 7:6; Ezek 22:7).

The following appear in parallelismus membrorum: orphan-widow (Isa 1:17, 23; Jer 49:11; Psa 68:6; Job 22:9; 24:3; Lam 5:3); poor/destitute-widows/orphans (Isa 10:2, cited in CD 6:16); widow-childless (Isa 47:8, with *ʾalmōn* in 47:9; Jer 15:8; 18:21). Other pars. include Psa 94:6; 146:9; Job 24:21; 29:13; 31:16.

As a precisely delineated term for a personal circumstance, well adapted for fixed series, *ʾalmānâ* has no synonym.

(b) *ʾalmānût* occurs in 2 Sam 20:3 in a fig. meaning "widowhood during the life (of the man)" (or, with textual emendation, "widows of a living man" or "widows for life") for the concubines isolated following the rebellion of Sheba. In the Elephantine papyrus, Cowley no. 30.20, "our wives have become like widows," similarly paraphrases the renunciation of marital relations as a mourning rite.

Moreover, a city can be fig. described as a widow: Lam 1:1, "how she has become a widow," describes Jerusalem after the catastrophe. In Isa 47:8 (oracle against Babylon) the haughty Babylon says: "I do not sit as a widow . . ."; this text, however, announces childlessness and widowhood *(ʾalmōn)* for this very city. Isa 54:4 uses *ʾalmānût* for Israel's widowhood.

4. (a) Within the community in which they live, widows are unprotected, poor, and lonely. Since antiquity, therefore, they stand under the legal protection of Yahweh: in the old curse series of the Shechemite Dodecalogue (Deut 27:19, "cursed be whoever perverts the justice of the sojourner, the orphan, and the widow"), in the Covenant Code (Exod 22:21, "you shall not

oppress widows and orphans," where the legal parenesis following in v 23 further strengthens the old law through a talion threat: "your wives will become widows"); in the Dtn Code, cf. Deut 24:17.

The following verbs appear in the word field: (1) *nṭh* hi. with obj. *mišpāṭ* "to pervert justice" (Deut 27:19); (2) *ʿnh* pi. "to oppress" (Exod 22:23); (3) *ḥbl* "to take as a pledge" (Deut 24:17, clothing; cf. Job 24:3, cow); (4) *ʿšq* "to oppress" (Jer 7:6; Zech 7:10; Mal 3:5); (5) *ynh* hi. "to harass" (Jer 22:3; Ezek 22:7).

Ug. texts also sometimes concern the "justice" due the widow (*dn almnt KTU* 1.16.VI.33, 46; 1.17.V.8; cf. A. van Selms, *Marriage and Family Life in Ugaritic Literature* [1954], 142f.).

A second group of legal texts in Deut regulates the rights of the poor and dispossessed, granting widows (and Levites/sojourners/orphans) particular privileges: they may glean during harvest (Deut 24:19–21); they should also celebrate the Feasts of Weeks and Booths (Deut 16:11, 14); and when the tithe is paid, the widows may eat their fill (Deut 14:29; 26:12f.). Compared with other feast regulations (Exod 23:14ff.; 34:18ff.; Lev 23), this group represents a parenetic legal exegesis peculiar to the Dtn Code.

Three isolated laws shed even more light on the legal status of the widow: a high priest may not marry a widow (Lev 21:14; in contrast to a priest, Lev 21:7). If a priest's daughter returns childless to her paternal home, she may once again eat of the sacrificial offering (Lev 22:13); cf. further Num 30:10 (concerning a widow's vow).

To summarize, one could say with Deut 10:18: Yahweh is the God "who creates justice *[ʿōśeh mišpāṭ]* for the orphan and the widow"; cf. below on Psa 68:6; 146:9. F. C. Fensham ("Widow, Orphan, and the Poor in Ancient Near Eastern Legal and Wisdom Literature," *JNES* 21 [1962]: 129–39) and Wildberger (*Isa 1–12*, CC, 50) cite pars. from Israel's environment.

(b) The principles codified in the various regulations were taken up again in prophecy, in the language of prayer, and in the book of Job.

In prophecy, Isa, Jer, and Ezek in particular return to the old laws for the protection of the widow (surprisingly Amos and Mic use neither this term nor the terms "orphan" and "sojourner"). Prophetic accusations address those who are not concerned for the rights (→ *rîb*) of the widow (Isa 1:23), who oppress orphans and widows (Isa 10:2; Ezek 22:7; Mal 3:5), or who make women widows (Ezek 22:25). Yahweh's retrospective lament (Jer 15:8) and Jeremiah's lament (18:21) are just as likely to use the term as is the announcement of judgment (Isa 9:16: Yahweh will not have mercy on the widows). Conversely, the announcement to Babylon in the oracle against the nations in Isa 47:8f. that she will become a widow means salvation for Israel (on Jer 49:11 and Jer 51:5 see Rudolph, HAT 12, 288, 306f.; a description of the fate of the tyrant occurs in Job 27:15 too); cf. the limited announcement of salvation in Jer 7:6 ("if you . . . do not oppress the widow"). The old laws are most clearly taken up in the prophetic Torah: Isa 1:17; Jer 22:3; Zech 7:10. Ezekiel (44:22) modifies Lev 21:14 from his perspective.

The language of prayer can praise Yahweh as the judge *(dayyān)* of widows (Psa 68:6; cf. 146:9); meanwhile, the lament about the enemy complains of those who slaughter widows and sojourners (Psa 94:6 with *hrg*), and enunciates the wish that the wives of such evildoers may become widows (109:9; cf. Jer 18:21). Lam laments that even Jerusalem (1:1) and its mothers (5:3) have become widows.

The book of Job reiterates the language of Psa, e.g., in the lament concerning criminals who oppress widows (24:3, 21; their catastrophe is described in 27:15). The accusation of Job's friends is typical, i.e., that Job may have sent widows away empty-handed (22:9), which Job repudiates in retrospect in the closing lament (29:13; 31:16).

If the legal protection under which widows stand is violated, then the indictment, lament, or even the announcement of judgment is issued, declaring the judgment of God upon the transgressor. Prov 15:25 also expresses this judgment: "Yahweh tears down the house of the proud, but the boundary of the widow he establishes."

5. Qumran (CD 6:16) and esp. the NT continue the traditions outlined above: Mark 12:40, among others. Luke 4:25f. cites 1 Kgs 17, Rev 18:7 cites Isa 47:8f. The warning against "young widows" (1 Tim 5:9ff.) is new.

J. Kühlewein

אֵם ʾ*ēm* mother

S 517; BDB 51b; *HALOT* 1:61a; *TWOT* 115a; *NIDOTTE* 562

---

1. ʾ*ēm* "mother" derives from the common Sem. *ʾ*imm-* (Akk., Ug., and Arab. *ʾ*umm-*, under the influence of the labial; cf. *GVG* 1:199 and → *lēb*). Contrary to earlier etymologies (e.g., F. Delitzsch, *Prolegomena eines neuen hebr.-aram. Wörterbuchs zum AT* [1886], 109), the etymology of L. Köhler (*ZAW* 55 [1937]: 171) is currently preferred: ʾ*ēm* is "entirely underivable from the stock of Sem. roots known to us"; → ʾ*āb* and ʾ*ēm* are "gibberish" from children's language (cf. "papa," "mama").

2. The total of 220 occurrences are distributed as follows: Gen 26x, Exod 7x, Lev 15x, Num 2x, Deut 13x, Josh 3x, Judg 20x, 1 Sam 4x, 2 Sam 3x, 1 Kgs 16x, 2 Kgs 22x, Isa 5x (Deutero-Isa 3x, Trito-Isa 1x), Jer 9x, Ezek 10x, Hos 4x, Mic 1x, Zech 2x, Psa 12x, Job 3x, Prov 14x, Ruth 2x, Song Sol 7x, Eccl 1x, Lam 3x, Esth 2x, 1 Chron 2x, and 2 Chron 12x. Four foci result: in the historical books (Gen, Judg, Kgs, incl. esp. reference to the name of the queen mother, 19x in Kgs, 9x in Chron), in legal regulations (35x), in the language of prayer, and in proverbs.

3. (a) In its basic meaning ʾ*ēm* describes the biological mother of her own children (son/daughter). Thus, a first natural word field within the family is delineated. This intrafamilial relationship is, with few exceptions, expressed by a following gen., or, most frequently, by a poss. suf. Significantly, ʾ*ēm* is attested only 3x with the art. (Deut 22:6[bis], 7), and of 220 occurrences, 189 are suf. forms.

A second, less frequent word field is also established naturally: *ᵓēm* as the maternal parent corresponds to → *ᵓāb* as the paternal parent. *ᵓāb* occurs around 70x in the word field, mostly in nom. series (→ *ᵓāb* III/1) with "father" generally in first position, as one might expect in a patriarchal society such as Israel (cf. W. Plautz, "Zur Frage des Mutterrechts im AT," *ZAW* 74 [1962]: 9–30).

In its basic meaning, *ᵓēm* has no synonymous subst.; yet verbal forms of *hrh* "to be pregnant" and *yld* "to bear" occasionally par. *ᵓēm:* the ptcp. of *hrh* in Hos 2:7; Song Sol 3:4; the form *yōledet* "bearer" in Jer 15:8f.; Prov 23:25; Song Sol 6:9; in Prov 17:25 independently par. to "father"; other verbal forms of *yld* par. *ᵓēm* in Jer 50:12; Song Sol 8:5.

ᵓēm describes the mother animal (cattle, sheep, goats: Exod 22:29; 23:19; 34:26; Lev 22:27; Deut 14:21; birds: Deut 22:6f.).

(b) The term appears in an extensive series of close word combinations to describe kindred relationships (on the substitution of "father and mother" for the term "parents," which is lacking in the OT, → *ᵓāb* III/1; the pl. ptcp. *hôray* "who conceived me" in Gen 49:26 is textually uncertain). "Son of my/your/his mother" and "daughter of my/your/his mother" may replace "brother" or "sister," resp.

Thus "son of my mother" (or pl.) parallels *ᵓāḥ* "brother" in Gen 43:29; Deut 13:7; Judg 8:19; Psa 50:20; 69:9; Song Sol 1:6; similarly "daughter of my mother" parallels *ᵓāḥôt* "sister" in Gen 20:12; Lev 18:9; 20:17; Deut 27:22; cf. Ezek 23:2 "daughters of one mother." The expression describes here the *biological* brother or sister, although *ᵓāḥ* and *ᵓāḥôt* can also signify the stepbrother and stepsister, resp. In contrast, "the sons of your mother" in Gen 27:29 (par. "brothers") indicates a broader kinship.

Additional phrases describing maternal kinship are: "father of your mother" = "grandfather" (Gen 28:2); "brother of your mother" = "uncle" (Gen 28:2; cf. 29:10; Judg 9:1, 3); "sister of your mother" = "aunt" (Lev 18:13; 20:19).

(c) The term *ᵓēm* is occasionally broadened to describe nonbiological maternity. Hebr. has no term for "grandmother" per se (nor for "grandfather"). Hebr. probably resorts here to the simple *ᵓēm* (on 1 Kgs 15:10 cf., nevertheless, Noth, BK 9, 335f.; on the position of the *gᵉbîrâ* "queen mother" → *gbr* and 4b). As one may infer from the context (35:16ff.), in Gen 37:10 *ᵓēm* refers to Joseph's stepmother.

"Mother-in-law" (mother of the husband) is represented by the common Sem. designation *ḥāmôt* (Mic 7:6; Ruth 1:14–3:17 10x; fem. of *ḥām* "father-in-law" = father of the husband, Gen 38:13, 25; 1 Sam 4:19, 21); the mother of the wife is called *ḥōtenet* (Deut 27:23; fem. of *ḥōtēn* "father-in-law" = father of the wife, from the perspective of the *ḥātān* "bridegroom," Exod 3:1; 4:18; 18:1–27, 13x; Num 10:29; Judg 1:16; 4:11, in each case, Moses; Judg 19:4, 7, 9); paraphrased "the woman and her mother" in Lev 20:14.*

The term is broadened even more in Gen 3:20, where Eve (Hebr. *ḥawwâ*) is described in terms of the etymology of her name as "mother of all the living" ("first mother, founding mother"; on Ezek 16:3, 45, see 4c). The expression "mother earth" does not exist in the OT (cf. A. Dietrich, *Mutter Erde* [1925[3]]; L. Franz, *Die Muttergöttin im vorderen Orient* [1937]; Haussig 1:103ff.).

ᵓēm has no pl. corresponding to the term *ᵓābôt* "fathers, forefathers" and its meaning. Psa 109:14 is typical: "May the guilt of his fathers be remembered, and the sin of his mother never be blotted out."

(d) Figuratively, the term serves to personify a people or a city.

The following are described as "mother": the people Israel in Hos 2:4, 7 (*ᵓēm* in Hos 4:5 refers less to the people than to the mother of the priest mentioned; cf. Wolff, *Hos*, Herm, 78; contra Rudolph, KAT 13/1, 97, 102) and in Isa 50:1(bis) (Ezek 19:2, 10, Judah or the royal house; cf. Zimmerli, *Ezek*, Herm, 1:393f.), and Babylon in Jer 50:12.

"Mother in Israel" occurs as an honorary title both for the individual Deborah (Judg 5:7; it is admittedly unclear from the context which function earned her this title) and for the city Abel of Beth-maacah (2 Sam 20:19, mother in comparison to the "daughter cities" of the environs? cf. *ᵓm* "metropolis" on Phoen. coins, *DISO* 15f.); a fixed expression in Hos 10:14 probably refers to normal mothers with their children (similarly in Gen 32:12); cf. Rudolph, KAT 13/1, 206.

In a similar figurative usage, Job calls the vermin of Sheol "my mother and my sister" in his lament (17:14); only here does he find the familial community disrupted for him in earthly life.

(e) *ᵓēm* participates in fixed phrases describing "mother's womb" and "mother's breast": *beṭen ᵓimmî* with prep. *b^e^ or min* "already in/from my mother's womb" or "since my birth" (Judg 16:17; Psa 22:11; 139:13; Job 1:21; 31:18; Eccl 5:14); *m^e^ᶜê ᵓimmî* (Isa 49:1; Psa 71:6) and *reḥem ᵓimmô* (Num 12:12) "my/his mother's womb"; "mother's breast" *š^e^dê ᵓimmî* (Psa 22:10; Song Sol 8:1), *ḥêq ᵓimmōtām* (Lam 2:12). All these terms could also express the same notion without association with *ᵓēm*.

The term is farthest most from its basic meaning in the phrase *ᵓēm hadderek* (Ezek 21:26) lit. "mother of the road," i.e., the place at which a new road is born from the mother-road, a fork in the road (cf. Zimmerli, *Ezek*, Herm, 1:444).

ᵓēm plays no role as a component of Hebr. PNs.

4. (a) The mother (together with the father) enjoys the particular legal protection of Yahweh:

Father and mother should be honored (*kbd* pi.: Exod 20:12; Deut 5:16), feared (*yrᵓ*: Lev 19:3). Whoever disparages father and mother will be cursed (Deut 27:16); whoever smites them or curses them will be killed (Exod 21:15, 17; Lev 20:9; cf. the law concerning the obstinate son in Deut 21:18–21).

The various regulations of the community reflect the divinely sanctioned social order: that no one engage in marital relations with his mother (Lev 18:7), mother-in-law (Lev 20:14), or aunt (Lev 18:13; 20:19); that a prisoner whom one intends to marry should first mourn her parents for one month (Deut 21:13); that one does not leave without first having once more kissed the parents farewell (1 Kgs 19:20); that one buries father and mother after their death (Lev 21:2; Ezek 44:25; contrast Lev 21:11 for the high priest and Num 6:7 for the Nazirite).

The instruction to honor father and mother also certainly had its place from the outset in wisdom's family doctrine: Prov 23:22; 30:17. Whoever despises father and mother is "foolish" (Prov 10:1; 15:20; cf. 19:26; 20:20; 28:24; 30:11). The instruction of the children is, as a rule, the obligation of the fathers (Deut 6:20ff., etc.; → ʾāb IV/2b), but the mother also gives instruction (Prov 1:8; 6:20; 31:1).

The transgression of these commandments properly elicits prophetic indictment (Ezek 22:7; Mic 7:6).

(b) Compared to the "fathers," ʾēm plays no role in the Deuteronomistic view of history. Nevertheless, four occurrences evaluate a king theologically in accordance with whether he walked in the sinful ways of his parents (1 Kgs 22:53; 2 Kgs 3:2) or of his mother (2 Kgs 9:22; 2 Chron 22:3; cf. Psa 51:7; 109:14). In general, the queen mother seems to have had particular influence on the policy and theological stance of the king: cf. the title "mistress" (*gᵉbîrâ)* in 1 Kgs 15:13; 2 Kgs 10:13; Jer 13:18; 29:2; 2 Chron 15:16; in 22:3 as "counselor"; cf. G. Molin, "Die Stellung der Gᵉbira im Staate Juda," *TZ* 10 (1954): 161–75; H. Donner, "Art und Herkunft des Amtes der Königinmutter im AT," FS Friedrich 105–45. The status of Bathsheba in Solomon's court (1 Kgs 1f.) or of Athaliah (1 Kgs 11) is indicative of this influence; the fact that the Deuteronomistic framework of the royal history lists the name of the queen mother almost without exception (1 Kgs 11:26, etc.) is no less indicative.

(c) The prophet Hosea is the first to describe Israel as "mother" (2:4, 7). In a "legal process against an unfaithful wife" (Wolff, *Hos*, Herm, 32), the unfaithful mother is charged with marital infidelity by her husband and the children (v 4) and is described as a harlot in substantiation of the accusation (v 7). The image of marriage, which Hosea adapted from Can. mythology, serves to oppose Israel's inclination to this cult with its prostitution. The image is taken up in Ezek 16, where the term (vv 3, 45) points to the dark past of the city Jerusalem, while the proverb "like mother, like daughter" (v 44) establishes the connection to the present (cf. also Isa 50:1 and Westermann, *Isa 40–66*, OTL, 223f.). On Ezek 19:2, 10, where Judah or the royal house is described as ʾēm, cf. Zimmerli, *Ezek*, Herm, 1:393f.

(d) The phrase "mother's womb" (see 3e) has a particular place in the language of prayer, primarily in statements of confidence such as Psa 22:10f.: "From the womb onward you are my God"; cf. 71:6; 139:13; Job 31:18. It also occurs in the call of the servant in Isa 49:1 (cf. Judg 16:17 and, without ʾēm, Jer 1:5). The reverse of this affirmation appears in the prophetic lament: "Woe is me, mother, that you bore me" (Jer 15:10; 20:14, 17). Finally the phrase continues to occur in the later wisdom literature: Job 1:21, as a statement of confidence; Eccl 5:14, with a strong skeptical undertone.

(e) In contrast to ʾāb "father" and ʾîš "man," the term ʾēm never directly characterizes Yahweh. Yahweh is a male deity according to OT conceptualization. Only once in post-exilic times is this rule violated, when Yahweh's salvific activity is compared to the activity of a mother: Isa 66:13 ("as one is comforted by his mother, so I will comfort you"); cf. 49:15 (without ʾēm).

5. In the NT, the term becomes meaningful primarily because of the special status of Jesus' mother; cf., however, Jesus' word concerning his "true relatives" in Mark 3:31ff. (cf. Deut 33:9).

J. Kühlewein

אָמָה ʾāmâ **maidservant** → עֶבֶד ʿebed

אָמַן ʾmn **firm, secure**

S 539; BDB 52b; *HALOT* 1:63b; *TDOT* 1:292–323; *TWOT* 116; *NIDOTTE* 586

Contents: Sections I (root and derivatives), II (statistics), and V (post-OT) treat the root as a whole. The major sections III and IV (general and theological usage) will be divided into the following subheadings:

A. ʾmn ni.	p. 138
B. ʾmn hi.	p. 142
C. ʾāmēn	p. 146
D. ʾᵉmûnâ	p. 147
E. ʾᵉmet	p. 151

I. 1. The root ʾmn "to be firm, secure, dependable" is not attested in Akk., Ug., Phoen., or Old Aram., but is common, after the admittedly rare occurrences in Imperial or Biblical Aram., in Aram. and the SSem. language family. Therefore, comparative linguistics, which must essentially be based upon post-OT materials, offers only limited elucidation for the OT; in addition, one must reckon with a borrowing of the specialized meaning ʾmn hi. "to believe" from the Hebr. in Syr. (*LS* 175a), Mand. (*MG* 211), and Arab. (J. Horovitz, *Koranische Untersuchungen* [1926], 55f.).

A relationship to the Eg. *mn* "to be firm, to remain" (Erman-Grapow 2:60ff.) is possible (Calice no. 198; M. Cohen, *Essai comparatif sur le vocabulaire Chamito-Sémitique* [1947], 83).

On the presumably Canaanite *imti* "dependability(?)" in EA 71:8, cf. W. F. Albright, *JNES* 5 (1946): 12n.8; *CAD* E:152b (cj. *em-<qu>-ti-ka?*).

The meaning "truly" for Ug. *imt* in *KTU* 1.5.I.18f. (*CML*[1] 102f., 136; *CML*[2] 68, 142; M. Dahood, *CBQ* 22 [1960]: 406) has not been establishd (*WUS* no. 274: "grass, hay[?]").

The only possibility in Phoen. is the PN ʾlʾmn on a seal (Harris 77f.). On the Pun. *emanethi* (*Poen.* 937), see Sznycer 92–94.

Two passages in 8th-cent. Yaudi inscriptions (*KAI* no. 214.11; 215.21) are totally obscure (cf. *DISO* 17).

The oldest Aram. occurrence may be ʾmyn "firm, lasting" in a papyrus from Saqqara (end of 7th cent.; *KAI* no. 266.3, "firm, as long as the heaven stands"). Cf. further *hymnwth* "his dependability" in the proverbs of Ahiqar (Aḥ. 132; Cowley 217, 224; *AOT* 460; cf. *ANET* 429b: "a man's charm is his truthfulness") and ʾš *mhymn* "a dependable man" in Hermop. IV:9 (Bresciani-Kamil 398f.; J. T. Milik, *Bib* 48 [1967]: 583).

Later Aram. and SSem. terms are summarized in *HAL* 61b; *SBL* 185f.

2. Of the verbal forms, the ni. "to be lasting, continue, be dependable, be faithful" and the hi. "to stand fast, trust, have faith, believe" are relatively frequent (see A and B). The qal seems to be represented at least by the ptcps., yet they stand so isolated in meaning alongside the other derivatives of *ʾmn* that the postulation of a root *ʾmn* II is appealing.

The following derive from this root *ʾmn* II (listed in *HAL* 62b in contrast to KBL 60b): *ʾōmēn* "attendant" (Num 11:12; Isa 49:23), "guardian" (2 Kgs 10:1, 5; Esth 2:7); *ʾōmenet* "wet nurse" (2 Sam 4:4; Ruth 4:16); pl. pass. ptcp. *ʾᵉmûnîm* "carried, protected" (Lam 4:5); *ʾomnâ* "custody" (Esth 2:20); *ʾmn* ni. "to be carried, tended" (a child, Isa 60:4). The relationship to Akk. *ummānu* (*HAL* 62a; see 5) remains highly questionable. Cf. Š. Porúbčan, "La radice *ʾmn* nell' A.T.," *RivB* 8 (1960): 324–36; 9 (1961): 173–83, 221–34.

On *neʾᵉmān* in Num 12:7; 1 Sam 3:20 and *ʾᵉmûnâ* in 1 Chron 9:22, 26, 31; 2 Chron 31:18, where derivation from *ʾmn* II is possible, see below A.III and D.III.

3. The most important of the nom. derivatives are the two fem. substs. *ʾᵉmûnâ* "firmness, dependability, faithfulness, honesty" or "official duty" (see D) and *ʾᵉmet* "durability, duration, dependability, faithfulness, truth" (see E). *ʾᵉmet* may derive from **ʾamint-* (BL 608). In this case the word is a fem. subst. from the adj. *ʾāmēn* and relates to it as *ʾᵉmûnâ* does to *ʾēmûn*. The following should also be noted: the "confirmation formula" *ʾāmēn* "surely" (see C); the subst. *ʾōmen* "dependability" (Isa 25:1 in the adv. asyndetic combination *ʾᵉmûnâ ʾōmen*); and the derivative advs. with the ending *-ām* (BL 529), *ʾomnām* "surely, really, truly" and the synonymous *ʾumnām* (always with *he* interrogative); the related fem. *ʾomnâ* is also used adv. (on these adv. usages see D). The ni. ptcp. *neʾᵉmān* "dependable, faithful" functions widely as an adj., in addition to *ʾēmûn*, which occurs as an adj. only in the pl. and as a subst. "faithfulness, dependability" once in the sg. and somewhat more frequently in the pl. *ʾᵉmûnîm* (see A). The subst. *ʾᵃmānâ* "understanding, official agreement" (associated in Neh 10:1 with the verb → *krt*) and "ordinance" (Neh 11:23 par. *miṣwat hammelek* "royal decree") appears relatively late.

It is uncertain whether *ʾōmᵉnôt* (pl.) in 2 Kgs 18:16, normally translated "doorposts" but which may mean the (golden) coating (?) of the doorposts, should be derived from *ʾmn* (cf. *HAL* 63a).

4. A series of PNs are related: *ʾāmôn* (2 Kgs 21:18ff., etc.; the [short] form *ʾāmî* occurs in Neh 7:59 and Ezra 2:57), apparently a hypocoristic of a theophoric name formation (cf. Phoen. *ʾlʾmn;* see I/1), or, as with *ʾamnôn* (2 Sam 3:2; 13:1ff., etc.; in 2 Sam 13:20 *ʾᵃmînôn* is probably a textual error), a description of a spiritual characteristic (*IP* 228: "dependable, faithful"; somewhat differently, J. Lewy, *HUCA* 18 [1944]: 456; cf., however, J.-R. Kupper, *Les nomades* [1957], 71, 76). *ʾᵃmittay* derives from *ʾᵉmet* (2 Kgs 14:25; Jonah 1:1; according to *IP* 162, a short form; cf. *ḥelqay* alongside *ḥilqîyāhû*).

The name of the river *ʾᵃmānâ*, which flows through Damascus (2 Kgs 5:12 Q; K: *ʾᵃbānâ*) may also belong to the root *ʾmn;* it would then describe the dependable, never receding river; cf. *naḥal ʾêtān* "constant (i.e., always running) brook" (Deut 21:4; Amos 5:24) and the antonym *ʾakzāb* "deceitful" par. *mayim lōʾ neʾᵉmānû* "water not trustworthy" (Jer 15:18; cf. Ph. Reymond, *L'eau dans l'AT* [1958], 72, 114).

It is still unclear whether *ʾᵃmānâ* as a name for Anti-Lebanon (Song Sol 4:8) derives from *ʾmn* "to be firm."

The Eg. god *ʾāmôn* (Jer 46:25; *nōʾ ʾāmôn* = Thebes, Nah 3:8) is not related to this root.

5. Contrary to earlier opinions, *ʾommān* (Song Sol 7:2) and *ʾāmôn* (Jer 52:15; Prov 8:30) "manual laborer" have nothing to do with the root *ʾmn*, but go back via Akk. *ummānu* "manual laborer, artisan" to Sum. *ummea* (cf. Wagner no. 18a). On Prov 8:30 (not "pampered child, darling," but "artisan") cf. Ringgren, ATD 16, 40; H. H. Schmid, *Wesen und Geschichte der Weisheit* (1966), 150, both with bibliog.

6. The basic meaning of the root *ʾmn* is disputed. The traditional understanding suggests "to be firm, dependable, certain" (GB 48a; *HAL* 61b; H. Wildberger, " 'Glauben,' Erwägungen zu *hʾmyn*," FS Baumgartner 372–86; also E. Pfeiffer, "Der alttestamentliche Hintergrund der liturgischen Formel 'Amen,' " *KerD* 4 [1958]: 129–41). Zorell 63b proceeds from *ʾōmᵉnôt* in 2 Kgs 18:16 (see 3) to the basic meaning "to hold fast," or from the ptcps. mentioned above (2) to "to bear." Because it is questionable, however, whether these forms belong to *ʾmn* I, one must set them aside for the determination of the basic meaning. A. Weiser ("πιστεύω," *TDNT* 6:182–91, 197f.) thinks that the usual translation "firm, certain, dependable" does not exhaust the basic meaning; on close examination, *ʾmn* may prove to be a formal term, whose content is determined differently in each case by the particular subj.; the word may refer to the relationship between reality and the essence of the subj. in question (p. 184). Porúbčan (op. cit. 232f.; see 2) concludes similarly that the basic meaning may be expressed by "as . . . as"; it signifies the "conformitas intellectus et rei." Despite the sometimes highly differentiated semantic development of individual forms and derivatives, the basic meaning suggested above should be maintained as the common denominator (also in view of the cognates in other Sem. languages). One should nevertheless heed justified objections against an overvaluation of etymological relationships (*SBL* 161–205), esp. for the root *ʾmn* (against the "formal concept" specifically, see *SBL* 179–81).

Numerous detailed observations indicate that the basic meaning was also still known to the authors of the later layers of the OT. The original meaning is still clearly evident in passages such as Job 39:24 (see B.III/2), and in the Qumran documents the subst. *neʾᵉmānût* "security, guarantee" (CD 7:5; 14:2; 19:1), whose meaning stands quite near the basic meaning, even occurs as a new formation.

7. In many respects → *kûn* is surprisingly close to the root *ʾmn* semantically (*kûn* ni. "to stand fast, be assured, endure," with the ptcp. *nākôn* "trustworthy, true" corresponding to *neʾᵉmān*, and *kûn* hi., which can be used intrans. like *ʾmn* hi.: "to stand unmoved"). Semantically, Akk. *kânu* stands even nearer to Hebr. *ʾmn:* G "to endure, be faithful, dependable, true," Gt "to achieve lasting endurance," adj. *kīnu* "lasting, dependable, faithful, honest, true," subst. *kīnūtu* "faithfulness," and *kittu* "constancy, dependability, reality, authenticity, faithfulness, truthfulness" (*AHw* 438–40, 481f., 494f.). This correspondence indicates that one may indeed speak of a Sem. concept of truth in contrast to the Gk. (H. von Soden, "Was ist Wahrheit?" *Urchristentum*

und Geschichte [1951], 1:1–24; W. von Soden, *WO* 4 [1967]: 44; cf. further the bibliog. cited in E.III/8).

II. The distribution of the root ʾ*mn* in the Hebr. OT (330x without the PNs) is shown in the following table:

	ni.	hi.	ʾ*āmēn*	ʾ*emûnâ*	ʾ*emet*	other	total
Gen	1	2	–	–	6	2	11
Exod	–	8	–	1	2	–	11
Lev	–	–	–	–	–	–	–
Num	1	2	2	–	–	1	6
Deut	3	3	12	1	3	1	23
Josh	–	–	–	–	3	1	4
Judg	–	1	–	–	3	–	4
1 Sam	5	1	–	1	1	–	8
2 Sam	1	–	–	–	3	1	5
1 Kgs	2	1	1	–	5	1	10
2 Kgs	–	1	–	2	2	2	7
Isa	9	4	2	4	12	3	34
Jer	2	2	2	4	11	–	21
Ezek	–	–	–	–	2	–	2
Hos	2	–	–	1	1	–	4
Jonah	–	1	–	–	–	–	1
Mic	–	1	–	–	1	–	2
Hab	–	1	–	1	–	–	2
Zech	–	–	–	–	6	–	6
Mal	–	–	–	–	1	–	1
Psa	8	7	7	22	37	3	84
Job	1	9	–	–	–	6	16
Prov	3	2	–	3	12	3	23
Ruth	–	–	–	–	–	1	1
Song Sol	–	–	–	–	–	–	–
Eccl	–	–	–	–	1	–	1
Lam	–	1	–	1	–	–	2
Esth	–	–	–	–	1	–	1
Dan	–	–	–	–	6	–	6
Ezra	–	–	–	–	–	–	–
Neh	2	–	3	–	3	2	10
1 Chron	2	–	1	3	–	–	6
2 Chron	3	4	–	5	5	1	18
total	45	51	30	49	127	28	330*

The ni. ptcp. *ne*ʾ*emān* occurs 32x. Isa 60:4 (see I/2 on ʾ*mn* II) is not included. Hos 12:1 is textually uncertain.

The three occurrences of the Aram. ha. (Dan 2:45; 6:5, 24) should be added to the hi. Judg 11:20 should be read *wayyᵉmāʾēn;* Isa 30:21 and Job 39:24 are also disputed textually.

ʾāmēn ʾāmēn occurs 5x (Num 5:22; Psa 41:14; 72:19; 89:53; Neh 8:6; in each case in the Psalter as a liturgical conclusion of a collection, for which reason the Syr. version supplies the reduplication in Psa 106:48). The reading in Isa 65:16(bis) is uncertain.

ʾᵉmûnâ appears once in the pl. (Prov 28:20 *ʾîš ʾᵉmûnôt*). The text is uncertain in Isa 33:6; Psa 89:9; 119:90; 143:1; 2 Chron 31:18.

ʾᵉmet is textually uncertain in Isa 42:3; Ezek 18:9; Psa 54:7; 111:7. *ʾᵃmittô* may be read for *mēʾittᵉkā* in Psa 22:26, *ʾᵉmet* for *mātay* in 101:2, *ʾᵃmittekā* for *ʾimrātekā* in 138:2b, and *ʾᵉmet śām* for *ʾim-tāśîm* in Isa 53:10 (M. Dahood, *CBQ* 22 [1960]: 406). The pl. does not exist.

The remaining 28 occurrences of the root are: *ʾōmen* 1x (Isa 25:1); *ʾomnām* 9x (2 Kgs 19:17 = Isa 37:18; Ruth 3:12, and 6x in Job); *ʾumnām* 5x (Gen 18:13; Num 22:37; 1 Kgs 8:27; Psa 58:2; 2 Chron 6:18); *ʾomnâ* 2x (Gen 20:12; Josh 7:20; on Esth 2:20, see I/2); *ʾēmûn* 1x (Deut 32:20) and *ʾᵉmûnîm* 7x (adj.: 2 Sam 20:19; Psa 12:2; 31:24; subst.: Isa 26:2; Prov 13:17; 14:5; 20:6); *ʾᵃmānâ* 2x (Neh 10:1; 11:23); *ʾōmᵉnâ* 1x (2 Kgs 18:16).

A. *ʾmn* ni.

III. 1. The ni. can unequivocally describe duration, permanence (Isa 33:16, water that does not dry up in summer; cf. Jer 15:18; Deut 28:59, lasting, protracted plagues and illnesses; 1 Sam 25:28 "lasting house" of a dynasty, 1 Sam 2:35 of a priest; see IV/4; 1 Chron 17:24, a name). It also expresses the notion of firmness and, above all, in an ethicoreligious perspective, the element of dependability and faithfulness (Isa 22:23, 25, a "firm place" suited for driving a nail; Gen 42:20, "so that your words may prove dependable"; 1 Sam 22:14, a dependable servant; Prov 25:13, a dependable messenger; 11:13, *neʾᵉman-rûaḥ* "the trustworthy spirit" in contrast to the gossip, who blabs secrets; Job 12:20, *neʾᵉmānîm* "well-proved" as an honorific for officials; cf. vv 17–19 with the par. *ʾētānîm;* also Neh 13:13 and 1 Sam 2:35; Isa 8:2 → *ʿēd neʾᵉmān* "dependable witness"; cf. Jer 42:5 and Psa 89:38 txt?, of Yahweh).

2. Does *ʾmn* ni. also mean "to be true, become true, prove true"? Because the subst. *ʾᵉmet* has assumed the meaning "truth," at least in late texts (see E.IV/5; on *ʾᵉmûnâ* D.III/6; IV/2), one cannot prematurely exclude a broadening of the verb to include the truth concept, although the LXX, e.g., never uses *alēthēs* to translate *ʾmn* ni. The concept of the lie occasionally appears in the word field of *ʾmn* ni. (*kzb,* etc.; Hos 12:1f. alongside *kaḥaš* "lie" and *mirmâ* "deceit"; Psa 78:36f. alongside *pth* pi. "to delude"; on Jer 15:18 see 4) and in the word field of the adj. *ʾēmûn* (Psa 101:6f. *rᵉmîyâ* "deceit" and *šᵉqārîm* "lies"; 12:2f. *šāwʾ* "falsehood" and *śᵉpat ḥᵃlāqôt* "smooth tongues"). Indeed, these antitheses establish the affinity of *ʾmn* ni. for the truth concept: one may translate "true" in many passages (so ZB in Gen 42:20; 1 Kgs 8:26; 1 Chron 17:23f.; 2 Chron 1:9; 6:17). One must clearly recognize, then, that the concept "truth" should be understood in terms of firmness, dependability, and faithfulness (the same is true of *nākôn* in passages like Psa 5:10; Job 42:7ff.).

3. The adj. *ʾēmûn* "dependable, faithful" resembles the ni. ptcp. *neʾᵉmān* in its adj. usage. The rare occurrence of this ptcp. does not mean that faithfulness is unimpor-

tant to the OT, but is determined by the Hebrews' preference for expressing such characteristics by means of the abstract gen. Thus, both *ṣîr neʾᵉmān* (Prov 25:13) and *ṣîr ʾᵉmûnîm* (Prov 13:17) occur, *ʿēdîm neʾᵉmānîm* (Isa 8:2), *ʿēd ʾᵉmûnîm* (Prov 14:5), and *ʿēd ʾᵉmet wᵉneʾᵉmān* (Jer 42:5), substantivized *neʾᵉmān* (Psa 101:6; Job 12:20), and the phrases *ʾîš ʾᵉmûnîm* (Prov 20:6) and *ʾîš ʾᵉmet* (Neh 7:2). Both *ʾēl neʾᵉmān* (Deut 7:9; cf. Isa 49:7) and *ʾᵉlōhê ʾᵉmet* (2 Chron 15:3) can also be discussed.

Aram. uses the ha. pass. ptcp. *mᵉhēman* "dependable" (Dan 2:45; 6:5; cf. Hermop. 4.9; see I/1) as an adj.

4. Pars. to this usage are: *tāmîm* "unobjectionable, upright" (Psa 19:8; cf. 101:6) and *yāšār* "straight, honest" (Psa 19:8f., 111:7f.). Once *ʾᵉmûnîm* parallels *ḥāsîd* "pious" (Psa 31:24); *ʾᵉmûnâ* and *ʾᵉmet* are often associated with → *ḥesed.* *ʾmn* ni. is even more closely paralleled by → *kûn* ni. (2 Sam 7:16; Psa 89:38; 1 Chron 17:24, cf. 23; cf. also Psa 78:8, 37).

ʾmn ni. has no regular antonym; the negation with *lōʾ* is used (Isa 7:9; Jer 15:18; Psa 78:8, 37; cf. *lōʾ nākôn* Exod 8:22). In a broader sense, several terms express notions contrary to *ʾmn* ni.: → *bgd* "to deal faithlessly" (adj. *bāgôd* "faithless"), → *mʿl* "to act undutifully, be faithless," → *kzb* pi. "to lie," and → *pšʿ* "to rebel."

5. *ʾmn* ni. is employed unusually in Num 12:7: Moses is "entrusted *(neʾᵉmān)* with (the care of) my whole house" (see the christological meditation on this text in Heb 3:1–6). According to 1 Sam 3:20, Samuel is "commissioned" *(neʾᵉmān)* as a prophet for Yahweh. One may ask whether *ʾmn* ni. should not be understood in these two passages as a denominative from *ʾōmēn* "guardian" (see I/2): "to be commissioned as guardian, caretaker."

IV. 1. *ʾmn* ni. has been richly employed in theological statements. Thus Yahweh is "the faithful God" (Deut 7:9; cf. Isa 49:7). One might expect that the expression would occur much more frequently; indeed, it seems wonderfully suited to describe Yahweh's being. But the OT places no value on cataloging God's characteristics. It is therefore certainly no accident that the OT uses not the proper adj. *ʾēmûn* to describe God's faithfulness but the ptcp. *neʾᵉmān,* which, taken precisely, means "he who proves himself faithful." Thus, in Deut 7:9 *hāʾēl hanneʾᵉmān* is similarly interpreted "he who keeps the covenant and who maintains his grace to those who love him," and in Isa 49:7 "Yahweh, who is faithful" is par. to "the holy one of Israel, who chose you," which guards against the misunderstanding that "faithful" describes the divine being. Israel cannot speak of the faithfulness of God unless it speaks of *the* faithfulness, which *manifests* itself now and again in the relationship to his people. One entreats God to *prove* his word to be dependable (1 Kgs 8:26 = 2 Chron 6:17). He has proclaimed to the tribes of Israel a message whose dependability will no doubt come to light (Hos 5:9). The dependability of the proclamation of his will is discussed (Psa 19:8 and 93:5 *ʿēdût* "witness"; 111:7 *piqqûdîm* "commandments"; 1 Chron 17:23 and 2 Chron 1:9 *dābār* "word"). In God's dealings with Israel, Yahweh's name proves to be dependable and great (1 Chron 17:24).

2. Proper human behavior involves proving oneself to be dependable, upright, faithful. Through faithfulness one finds one's proper place in the world order, as well as in the social community. Respect for faithfulness brings life and blessing (cf. Prov 11:13; 25:13). The depth of wisdom's insight into the circumstances of human community is substantiated by the fact that its

faithfulness is no rigid principle: blows from friends may be more a sign of faithfulness than kisses from enemies (Prov 27:6). The cultically pious individual must maintain faithfulness in relationship to God (Psa 78:8), which means, concretely, faithfulness to covenant (78:37; 89:29). Faithfulness to God must not simply be maintained, therefore, in an inner attitude toward God, but must be realized in the orientation of one's life according to the revelation of God's will. The faithful in the land, over whom God is watchful, are those "who travel the upright paths" (Psa 101:6). The faithfulness of God's people must correspond to the dependability of the revelation of the divine will through respect for the regulations established by God.

3. Because *ʾmn* hi. has assumed the special theological meaning "to believe" (see B), the question arises as to whether *neʾᵉmān* or *ʾēmûn* can also mean "believing" or "devout." One might indeed think so, e.g., of Psa 101:6, the passage just treated. To prevent misunderstanding, however, one should strictly maintain that according to the context, the faith of these faithful ones must be preserved in a relationship to fellow human beings that corresponds to wisdom ideals. In a similar context, Psa 12:2 discusses the *ʾᵉmûnîm*, and according to 31:24 they are the *ḥᵃsîdîm*, whom Yahweh loves (cf. also v 25). *ʾēmûn* is apparently on the way to becoming an expression for "devout," just as *ʾᵉmûnâ* tends toward the meaning "faith."

The use of *ʾᵉmûnê yiśrāʾēl* in 2 Sam 20:19 is peculiar: "one may indeed ask in Abel and Dan whether what 'the faithful of Israel' have prescribed is no longer valid" (txt em; see *BH*³). Weiser (*TDNT* 6:190) believes that the expression may have had its setting in the sacral Yahweh confederacy. The passage is too isolated, however, to support such an inference.

4. Of great significance for the history of Israel's faith is the so-called prophecy of Nathan in 2 Sam 7 with the promise: "Your house and your kingdom shall always endure before me" (v 16, which belongs to the fundamental form of the tradition; cf. L. Rost, *Die Überlieferung von der Thronnachfolge Davids* [1926], 47–74 [63]; and A. Weiser, *VT* 16 [1966]: 346ff.; contra M. Tsevat, *HUCA* 34 [1963]: 73; and R. Smend, FS Baumgartner 288).

The motif of the continued existence of the kingdom itself belongs to ancient Near Eastern royal ideology. Esarhaddon prays: "May my government stand as firm as the heaven and the earth" (R. Borger, *Die Inschriften Asarhaddons* [1956], 26f.; further examples: *VAB* 4:78f.; *SAHG* 281; G. W. Ahlström, *Psa 89* [1959], 53ff.).

The Davidic kingdom is religiously sanctioned by the prophecy of Nathan. This promise has found a rich echo in the OT (cf. also 2 Sam 23:5). The narrator of 1 Sam 25:28 already permits Abigail to say that Yahweh will grant David a "lasting house," and in 1 Kgs 11:38 Ahijah promises Jeroboam at Shiloh that Yahweh will build him a "lasting house" like the one he has built for David. The promise seems originally to have been unconditional. But the narrator already knows the fate of the dynasty of Jeroboam and has placed the promise under the requirement of obedience (cf. also 2 Sam 7:14f.). The formulation in Isa 7:9 is similar: "If you do not believe, you will not remain." The prophet undoubtedly alludes to Nathan's prophecy with the verb *ʾmn* ni. (E. Würthwein, FS Heim 61; Wildberger, *Isa 1–12*, CC, 89f.). But, in view of the faithless behavior of the king, the prophet transforms the tradition's promise into a warning by placing it under the condition of faith.

Nabopolassar formulates a statement in one of his inscriptions with a similar play on words (verb *kânu;* see I/7): "Whoever is faithful to Bel, his ground stands firm" (*VAB* 4:68f.).

The author of Psa 89 seems to have raised questions about the prophecy of Nathan in view of the actual course of history. But he does not abandon it: "I will maintain my grace for him forever and my covenant with him shall remain firm" (v 29; cf. v 38). Here, then, the psalmist no longer treats the duration of the house of David but grace *(ḥesed)* and the covenant (cf. also 2 Sam 7:28 and Psa 132:12; A. Caquot, "La prophétie de Nathan et ses échoes lyriques," *SVT* 9 [1963]: 213–24).

Even after the fall of the Davidides, Israel does not abandon the promise. In the (Dtr) dedicatory prayer for the temple, Solomon prays for the actualization of the promise to David (1 Kgs 8:26). The Deuteronomist seems to have hoped for the reestablishment of Davidic dominion (G. von Rad, *Studies in Deut* [1953], 86ff. = *PHOE* 216ff.). For Deutero-Isaiah, the dynasty no longer has a future. Nevertheless, for him the promise to David is still valid, as surely as Yahweh is *neʾemān* (Isa 49:7). So, then, he interprets *neʾemān* in terms of the dependability of divine grace for *Israel* (55:3). With the Chronicler, however, the hope for the Davidides has returned (1 Chron 17:23f.; 2 Chron 1:9; 6:17; cf. von Rad, op. cit. 84–91 = *PHOE* 214–21).

Nathan's prophecy found an even more radical reinterpretation in 1 Sam 2:35: Now a *kōhēn neʾemān* "a dependable priest" is addressed, who will act according to Yahweh's intention (on the age of the passage cf. M. Tsevat, *HUCA* 32 [1961]: 195).

In CD 3:19 the expression *bayit neʾemān* is further developed in a manner characteristic for Qumran. "He built them a lasting house in Israel . . . , those who hold fast to it are (destined) for eternal life." Here, the "lasting house" (like "house of truth" in 1QS 5:6 and "house of the law" in CD 20:10, 13) has become the community's self-designation.

The *neʾemān* of the Davidic promise has become, then, an axiom of the messianic expectation (von Rad, *Theol.* 1:351); on another plane, however, it expresses the certainty of Israel's election and therefore persists with astonishing tenacity throughout all phases of the history of Israel. Both cases are impressive witnesses of Israel's knowledge of the faithfulness of its God.

5. Neh 9:8 refers to Gen 15:6: "You have found his (Abraham's) heart faithful to you and have made a covenant with him" (cf. Weiser, *TDNT* 6:185f.). Abraham's faith is interpreted here as the faithfulness of his attitude toward God. Thus the sense of the Gen passage (see B.IV/2) has certainly been significantly altered.

6. Finally, one should note Isa 1:21, 26, where the propriety of the honorific *qiryâ neʾemānâ* "faithful city" is denied Jerusalem for the present but is promised for the future. Not otherwise applied to Jerusalem, *neʾemān* seems here to replace the *nākôn* (ptcp. of → *kûn* ni. "to be firm") offered by the tradition (Psa 48:9; 87:5; cf. also Isa 2:2). Isaiah chose the par. term *neʾemān* because he was concerned not with the stability of the city of God in the sense of its invincibility, as in the Zion tradition, but with the faithfulness of its inhabitants. In this respect, the par. expression *ʿîr haṣṣedeq*

"city of the righteous" indicates his understanding of faithfulness. In this way, with the aid of *neʾᵉmān*, an essential motif of the Zion tradition is actualized (see Wildberger, *Isa 1–12*, CC, 62ff.).

B. *ʾmn* hi.

III. 1. *ʾmn* hi. has often been investigated on account of its theological relevance in the meaning "to have faith, trust (in), believe":

See L. Bach, "Der Glaube nach der Anschauung des AT," *BFCT* 4 (1900): 1–96 (still definitive); A. Weiser, "Glauben im AT," FS Beer 88–99; J. C. C. van Dorssen, *De derivata van de stam* ʾmn *in het Hebreeuwsch van het Oude Testament* (1951); Th. C. Vriezen, *Geloven en Vertrouwen* (1957); E. Pfeiffer, "Glaube im AT," *ZAW* 71 (1959): 151–64; A. Weiser, "πιστεύω," *TDNT* 6:182–91; *SBL* 164–206; R. Smend, "Zur Geschichte von *hʾmyn*," FS Baumgartner 284–90; H. Wildberger, " 'Glauben': Erwägungen zu *hʾmyn*," ibid. 372–86 (bibliog.); id., " 'Glauben' im AT," *ZTK* 65 (1968): 129–59 (bibliog.).

2. *ʾmn* hi. is an intrans. or inner-trans. hi. (cf. *HP* 43ff., 250ff.), if it is not a so-called pseudo-hi. (cf. Wildberger, FS Baumgartner 384f.n.2). *ʾmn* hi. is constructed uniquely with the acc. in Judg 11:20 (but see II on the text), so that the declarative-estimative understanding (E. Pfeiffer, op. cit. 152) is untenable.

The original, concrete-physical meaning "to stand fast, hold still" (of the war horse) is still present in Job 39:24. The psychological meaning "to have trust, be dependable" is much more frequent: in the profane arena in Hab 1:5 and Job 29:24 (on the understanding of these passages cf. Wildberger, FS Baumgartner 376f.), but also in the cultic language of the Psalms (27:13 and 116:10). As in these passages, *ʾmn* hi. abs. is also used in Isa 7:9 and 28:16 (in total 7x).

3. The same meaning is present in the construction with *bᵉ* (17x with persons, 7x impersonal): in the profane arena in Job 24:22, "he rises up when he no longer trusts in his life" (ZB "when he doubts life"); see also Deut 28:66 and Job 15:31 (cf. Wildberger, FS Baumgartner 379). For *hᵉʾemîn bᵉ* in theological contexts, see Gen 15:6 and Exod 14:31 (see IV/2, 6).

4. Cases of *ʾmn* hi. with *lᵉ*, e.g., Gen 45:26, "then his heart remained cold, for he did not believe them," have different characteristics. One may also not assume an estimative basic meaning for this usage ("to consider some one trustworthy"). The intention is: "to achieve trust with respect to" a person (7x) or thing (7x). The interest of the narrator lies with the subject of the act of trust, not with the personal or impersonal object of trust. Thus Exod 4:9 does not mean: "if you do not believe these two signs," but "if you do not exercise faith in these two signs" (see ZB). Only in a few passages does *heʾᵉmîn lᵉ* mean "to consider true" (1 Kgs 10:7; Isa 53:1). The same development, i.e., the shift of interest from the subject of belief or of trust to the circumstances to be believed, exists when a phrase is appended with *kî* "that" (Exod 4:5; Job 9:16; Lam 4:12) or an inf. construction follows (Job 15:22; cf. also Psa 27:13).

5. Numerous terms are near or approximate pars. to *ʾmn* hi. in the OT.

The cultic song Psa 27 has → *ḥzq*, → *bṭḥ*, *lōʾ* → *yrʾ*, → *qwh* pi., and → *ʾmṣ* pi. *lēb* (cf. also Psa 31:25 and Isa 28:15b, 17b). Instead of saying that he believes, the supplicant can confess that Yahweh is his protection, shield, refuge, rock, and fortress (Psa 27:5). In Isa 7:9 the impvs. "do not be afraid and do not be alarmed" (lit. "do not let your heart become soft") appear in the context of the admonition to faith (v 4). In Isa 30:15 "believe" is paraphrased with "rest, quietness, trust" (see Wildberger, *ZTK* 65 [1968]: 151f.).

It is characteristic of the subtlety of the term *ʾmn* hi., however, that an entirely different group of par. and contrasting terms appear in other contexts (in fact, for the most part in passages where the verb is constructed with *lᵉ*): → *šmᶜ* "to give heed (to someone's voice)" (Exod 4:1–9; Deut 9:23) and → *mrh* hi. "to be rebellious" (Deut 9:23), "to be stiff-necked" (2 Kgs 17:14). The grounds for unbelief in these contexts is not a lack of trust, human failure, skepticism, or doubt of God and his word, but disobedience, opposition, rebellion.

As important as *ʾmn* hi. is in the OT, one must remember that the *object* of faith is by no means discussed only in the relatively few passages with *ʾmn* hi. The most important par. term, at least in the religious domain, is → *bṭḥ* "to trust" (57x in a religious meaning, 37x in Psa). Where we would speak of "believing," the OT can also use the verbs → *yrʾ* "to fear," → *ydᶜ* "to recognize," and → *drš* "to seek," or → *yḥl* "to await" and *ḥkh* pi. "to hope" (→ *qwh*). "The OT . . . addresses what we mean by faith through a multitude of expressions, by whose combined force the thing becomes transparent" (F. Baumgärtel, *RGG* 2:1588; cf. also C. Westermann, *Blessing in the Bible and the Life of the Church* [1978], 11f.).

IV. 1. According to Bach, of 51 passages with *ʾmn* hi., 33 may be classified as "sacred diction" (op. cit. 30f., with tables). The term has become so significant in its theological usage not because of the number but because of the significance of the passages in which it occurs. In addition, the LXX evidently paid it particular attention: it always translates (with the exception of Prov 26:25 *peithomai*) with *pisteuō* and its compounds, and it always reserves *pisteuō* (except Jer 25:8 for *šmᶜ* "to hear") for forms of *ʾmn.*

2. The profane meaning of *ʾmn* hi. *lᵉ* "to believe (a person or a thing)," which passages such as Gen 45:26 (J) and 1 Kgs 10:7 (cf. also Jer 40:14) suggest was already common very early and was also used in wisdom instruction (Prov 14:15; cf. 26:25), was not sustained in ancient times (on the age of passages such as Exod 4:1, 5, 8f. and 19:9, cf. Smend, op. cit. 289).

In contrast, *ʾmn* hi. already seems to have had its *Sitz im Leben* very early on in the salvation oracle, esp. when directed to army commanders. This genre is common in the ancient Near East: even outside Israel it exhibits concepts semantically related to *ʾmn* hi., e.g., "[do not be afraid Esarha]ddon, [I am Ishtar of Arbe]la . . . have confidence (*tazzazma;* cf. *AHw* 410a). . . . Praise me" (*ANET* 450b = IV:rev. 61, col. vi.1f., 12f.; for further examples see Wildberger, *ZTK* 135f.). Gen 15:1–6 is patterned after such an oracle (for an analysis cf., among others, O. Kaiser, *ZAW* 70 [1958]: 107–26; H. Cazelles, *RB* 69 [1962]: 321–49; Wildberger, *ZTK* 142–47). Admittedly, the call to faith itself has not been transmitted; in its place, however, is the concluding report that Abraham believed in Yahweh on the basis of the promise communicated to him and that God reckoned this belief to him as righteousness. Abraham's faith is without doubt understood in response to the admonition of v 1 "do not fear," associated with the promise of great reward, so that *heʾᵉmîn bᵉyhwh* in this context may intend to convey: "he was full of confidence and trust, well founded in Yahweh."

An imitation of such an oracle to a king also occurs in Isa 7:4–9. Isaiah responds to the king's despondency with the cry "do not fear" (v 4), which he repeats at the end of the oracle with the demand to keep faith. In contrast to Gen 15:6, *ʾmn* hi. abs. is used here, certainly by intention. Ahaz's belief in Yahweh is not in question—he was surely no idolater or atheist—nor even his confidence in the prophetic word; rather, the weight of the cry lies solely on the fact that in the threatening situation he should prove himself a man who maintains calm, trust, confidence. Faith is expected of Ahaz because, after all, the promise of continuing existence stands over the house of David (see A.IV/4).

Further examples indicate that *ʾmn* hi. was used in the context of such war oracles, i.e., Exod 4:31 and Deut 1:32 (cf. Wildberger, *ZTK* 134).

It seems that even the salvation oracle, the response in the sanctuary to the individual's lament, includes an admonition to faith. In any case, the supplicant can assert in the lament that he believes, or testify in the song of thanksgiving that even in deep distress he has not abandoned faith (Psa 27:13; 116:10). Pious persons resist external threat and internal opposition with their faith. The salvation oracle in Hab 2:2–4, with the rich conclusion "the righteous will have life on the basis of faith," offers indirect testimony to this usage of *ʾmn* hi. The oracle answers the complaint of 1:12–17; like Isa 7:4ff., it is pronounced in a situation of serious political threat. If *ʾmn* hi. is translated in Isa 7 with "to believe," then *ʾᵉmûnâ* should be rendered with "faith" in this context so similar in terms of situation and genre (so Rom 1:17; cf. van Dorssen, op. cit. 121, 129; Eichrodt 2:284f.).

Both Gen 15:6 and Hab 2:4b, which became so important for the development of the NT concept of faith, relate faith to righteousness. G. von Rad ("Faith Reckoned as Righteousness," *PHOE* 125–30) has called attention to the fact that the cultic term → *ḥšb* "to reckon" describes a sovereign priestly-juridical act in the context of the approval of sacrifices and does not mean the calculation of payment in a commercial context. The pronouncement of *ṣᵉdāqâ* for Abraham recognizes his faith as the behavior appropriate for the human being before God. His faith reveals that his attitude toward God is as it should be. Faith is in no way meritorious; the promise of reward is unconditional and precedes the determination of Abraham's righteousness. The formulation of Hab 2:4b should, however, be understood in terms of the declarative formula encountered in Ezek: "righteous is he, he shall surely live" (18:9; cf. von Rad, op. cit.; and W. Zimmerli, " 'Leben' und 'Tod' im Buch des Propheten Ezechiel," *TZ* 13 [1957]: 494–508 = *GO* 178–91). Although according to the Ezek passage the fulfillment of some cultic-ethical requirements characterizes the righteousness that leads to life, according to Habakkuk it is faith on which the promise of life can shine.

3. The occurrences of *ʾmn* hi. examined above belong form critically to similar contexts in which faith is understood as the maintenance of dependent trust grounded in the knowledge of God and his promise. Isa 28:16 "the one who believes will not waver" (on the translation cf. *HAL* 288a) fits in here

well but also leads further. Isaiah addresses himself to representatives of Jerusalem cultic theology who consider themselves safe in the protection of the temple. He contrasts their complacency with true faith, which has justice as its measuring line and righteousness as its scale. It becomes clear here why the prophets make such little use of the notion of faith. For them, it is suspect because it can so easily become a pious substitute for authentic devotion to Yahweh in the service of righteousness. They protest against the "careless in Zion, the complacent (→ *bṭḥ*) on the mountains of Samaria" (Amos 6:1; cf. Isa 32:9, 11; Jer 7:4). Where they summarize their demands of Yahweh's people, they do not therefore require trust or faith but obedience: seek Yahweh! (Amos 5:14; Hos 10:12; Isa 9:12; 31:1; Jer 10:21; 30:14; cf. also Psa 24:6).

4. An essentially different aspect of the theological usage of ʾ*mn* hi. is present in six passages in Exod 4:1–9, 31a. This difference is already evident formally in that the verb is constructed here with *lᵉ*. As in Exod 19:9, the concern is whether Moses will gain the people's trust. When a par. expression is used, *šmᶜ bᵉ* or *šmᶜ bᵉqōl* appears (vv 1, 9; cf. *šmᶜ* in v 8). This aspect of the faith concept has truly become theologically relevant for the Deuteronomistic historian: Deut 9:23, "There you were rebellious against the commandment of your God and you did not believe him and did not give heed to his voice"; similarly 2 Kgs 17:14, "They did not obey, but were stiff-necked like their fathers, who did not believe Yahweh their God." The latter passage belongs to Dtr's basic reflection concerning the fall of Israel. The cause is Israel's unbelief as rebellion against God—not just a momentary failure, but Israel's original sin, its murmuring as early as the wilderness wandering period.

5. Neither Isaiah nor Dtr have found much acceptance for their faith concepts in the rest of the OT. Deutero-Isaiah uses ʾ*mn* hi. in a fictive legal speech. Israel should witness for Yahweh in order that the peoples "may gain understanding, believe in him, and come to the awareness that it is he," namely the true God, beside whom there is no helper (Isa 43:10). Surprisingly, entirely different par. terms appear here: → *ydᶜ* and → *bîn* hi. Belief includes a particular knowledge, namely that Yahweh and no other God is lord of history. Belief here means: to know and acknowledge a truth of faith as such (cf. ʾᵉ*met* in v 9).

6. One observes another variation of the faith concept in Psa 78, which already betrays Dtr influence. V 4 reads: "They did not believe in God and did not trust in his help." V 32 indicates how this statement is to be understood: "In all this, they did not have faith in his wonders." This phrase apparently alludes to Num 14:11: "How long will you not believe *in me* despite all the signs that I have done in your midst?" Belief in God has become an acknowledgment of his wonders.

One can observe a similar reconceptualization of faith in Psa 106, which already presupposes the final form of the Pentateuch; see v 12: "Then they believed *in his words* and sang his praise." The allusion is to Exod 14:31. Although the earlier text discusses faith in Yahweh ("and his servant" may be secondary), the Psa treats faith in his words. Similarly, 2 Chron 20:20 alludes to Isa 7:9 (Wildberger, *ZTK* 131f.). The profane usage of ʾ*mn* hi., already encountered in 1 Kgs 10:7, has also become theologically relevant, then, in reflection upon the old texts.

7. A final variation occurs in Psa 119:66 "I believe in your commandments." "Commandments" here seems simply to replace "words." But according to the general tenor of the psalm, this verse means: to be of the conviction that the observance of the commandments offers rich blessing.

8. This overview leads to the conclusion that the theological usage of *ʾmn* hi. is in no way uniform, a conclusion grounded in the fact that the verb, although rather infrequent, is nevertheless at home in various traditions and in the fact that its usage undergoes transformation in the course of the history of Israelite religion.

C. *ʾāmēn*

III. The word *ʾāmēn* occurs in the OT exclusively in theological contexts (cf. A. R. Hulst, "Het woord 'Amen' in het O.T.," *Kerk en Eeredienst* 8 [1953]: 50–58; E. Pfeiffer, "Der atl. Hintergrund der liturgischen Formel 'Amen,' " *KerD* 4 [1958]: 129–41; S. Talmon, "*Amen* as an Introductory Oath Formula," *Textus* 7 [1969]: 124–29). Nonetheless, the word also no doubt belonged to everyday language (Lande 112). Sir 7:22 still knows the original meaning "dependable" (of animals; LXX *chrēsimos*).

In the inscription on an ostracon from Yavneh-yam, a farm worker asserts in a letter of complaint to an official: *ʾmn nqty* "truly, I am innocent," calling on his comrades as witnesses (*KAI* no. 200.11; the reading is disputed; cf. W. F. Albright, *BASOR* 165 [1962]: 45n.49; *KAI* 2:201; Talmon, op. cit. 127).

The LXX translates once each with *alēthōs* (Jer 28[LXX 35]:6) and *alēthinos* (Isa 65:16). Three times it simply transliterates the word, without translating it (Neh 5:13; 8:6; 1 Chron 16:36). In the other passages it translates *genoito* "so be it." The juss. sense is clearly apparent in passages such as Jer 28:6: "Amen, may Yahweh . . . fulfill your words" (Zorell 64 thinks that "is" should perhaps be supplied). In some cases, *ʾāmēn* does actually mean "it stands firm and is valid" (see H. Schlier, *TDNT* 1:335f.). Aquila's rendering with *pepistōmenōs* (Psa 89 [LXX 88]:53) indicates this aspect. These various possibilities of usage are based in the dialectic of the term. *ʾāmēn* intends to indicate that something which has been said stands firm, is "true." But at the same time this truth is recognized as "valid" and therefore also as obligatory for the speaker of the Amen.

IV. 1. *ʾāmēn* is most frequently used in answer to a pronounced curse, e.g., in the series of curses in Deut 27:15–26 (12x). In such contexts one translates "so be it." This *ʾāmēn* does not simply contain a wish. The Israelite concept of curse (and blessing) is still deeply rooted in magical thought (cf. J. Hempel, *Apoxysmata* [1961], 30–113). Because curses have their own power, as a rule they cover crimes that take place in private and thus beyond the scope of human retribution. Whoever pronounces the Amen to them acknowledges awareness of the sentence for the pertinent activities. Thus the speaker judges his/her own guilt in the event such a crime is committed. At the same time the Amen has an apotropaic character (cf. Hempel, op. cit. 103); if spoken by an innocent individual, the curse is diverted to a guilty individual. Whoever does not agree in the Amen against the evildoer is as subject to the curse as the evildoer, because he/she has not denied solidarity with the criminal (cf. *Jub.* 4:5).

Curses are pronounced in oath-taking ceremonies in case someone swears a false oath. Whoever has subjected him- or herself to the ordeal must also say the Amen. This pronouncement also occurs when a covenant is made, because one must swear to a covenant; here, too, the pronouncement of curses in the event of the violation of covenant is an element (Jer 11:1–8; cf. v 5). Regarding the blessings and curses within the covenant tradition (Lev 26; Deut 28), one must therefore think of the *ʾāmēn* of the people as that spoken by the covenant partners. The same is true of Nehemiah's agreement with the leadership (Neh 5:1–13), where the shaking out of the fold of the garment by the official symbolizes the imprecation, here no longer described as a curse (v 13). In Jer 15:11 (txt em) the Amen of the prophet confirms the woe that he has voiced for his mother and thus for himself. Such woes doubtlessly go back form critically to curses (cf. *BFPS* 194ff.).

2. Basically, the complaint of the farm worker in the ostracon from Yavneh-yam is no different: The Amen implies an oath with a corresponding self-imprecation. But the passage indicates how formal language can be devalued, in that the man beseeches the official, in the event that he is found guilty, to give precedence to grace over justice. The Amen here has become a simple particle of assertion.

OT passages also give evidence of a general usage. Thus Benaiah affirms David's word (that Solomon is to be enthroned as his successor) with his Amen in 1 Kgs 1:36. It is clear here that Benaiah also engages himself with his Amen, despite the addition of "may Yahweh do so" (txt em); he commits himself to his role in the execution of the royal decision. Amen is an obligating yes; cf. Neh 8:6.

3. A special usage of the Amen occurs in the (doubtlessly late) doxologies at the conclusion of the divisions of the Psa (41:14; 72:19; 89:53; 106:48, in each case *ʾāmēn ʾāmēn*). 1 Chron 16:36 indicates how this Amen should be understood. It is responsive in character; through it the celebrating community identifies itself with the prayer leader when he has spoken praise. The repetition of the term underscores that one agrees sincerely and joyously. How this new usage came about can still be easily recognized in Neh 8:6. The chapter reports the introduction of the new law. According to the rules of the genre, the people must obligate itself to the law or affirm the curses associated with it through the Amen. But the function of the Amen is new. Tob 8:8 indicates that one can also identify oneself with the word of another in daily life through the Amen.

4. Isa 65:16 requires particular mention: Whoever blesses oneself and, likewise, whoever swears should do so *bēʾlōhê ʾāmēn*. If one accepts the text, then one must interpret, e.g., with Delitzsch, according to 2 Cor 1:20 (cf. also Acts 3:14): "the God of Amen, i.e., the God who turns what He promises into Yea and Amen" (KD, *Isa* 2:487; cf. comms.). *ʾāmēn* may be substantivized here, so that one may translate "God of dependability." The emendation of *ʾāmēn* into the subst. *ʾōmēn* is, however, more likely; cf. *ʾēl neʾemān* (Deut 7:9; Isa 49:7) and *ʾēl ʾemet* (Psa 31:6).

D. *ʾemûnâ* (*ʾēmûn, ʾomnām,* etc.)

III. 1. According to *HAL* 60f., the chief meanings of *ʾemûnâ* are: (a) "firmness," (b) "dependability, faithfulness," (c) "honesty"; to which may be added the special meaning (d) "permanent official duty." Individual nuances are difficult to differentiate; this difficulty is indicated by the fact that other lexicographers classify differently, e.g., Zorell 62f.: (a) firmitas, immobilis stabilitas, (b) firmitas ethica personae, i.e., fidelitas (of God and humans). Porúbčan (op. cit. 230) believes that the richness and diversity of the meanings of *ʾemûnâ* do not permit its derivation from the basic meaning "firmness"; he considers the primary meaning to be "truth" (op. cit. 221). Yet the root's basic meaning "firmness" may also be recognized in this substantive, and it is advisable to proceed from this basic meaning for the subst.

2. One of the most ancient occurrences is Exod 17:12 (J or N): "his (Moses') hands remained firm (*ᵓᵉmûnâ)* until the sun went down." This translation (contra Porúbčan, op. cit. 228f.: "raised in the same position") is supported by the preceding phrase "they supported his arms."

The meaning "security," still close to "firmness," is present in Isa 33:6 (if the text is retained): "will be the security of your times" (cf. H. Gunkel, *ZAW* 42 [1924]: 178).

3. A special meaning "fixed office" or the like seems to occur in 1 Chron 9:22, 26, 31 and 2 Chron 31:18 (here the text is uncertain; cf. Rudolph, HAT 21, 306), although Rudolph (op. cit. 88) translates "dependability" or "durability" (cf. also K. H. Fahlgren, *Sedākā, nahestehende und entgegengesetzte Begriffe im AT* [1932], 145; H. Cazelles, *La Sainte Bible de Jérusalem,* see 2 Chron 31:18). It is not surprising that, on the basis of the fundamental meaning "firm, certain," *ᵓᵉmûnâ* has become a technical term for "fixed position, lasting office." It is also possible, nevertheless, that *ᵓᵉmûnâ* in this meaning does not even belong to *ᵓmn* I but is a derivative of *ᵓōmēn* "guardian" and thus means something like "guardianship" (cf. Num 12:7 and I/2).

4. The meaning "firmness" (in a fig. sense), thus "dependability, faithfulness," corresponding to the ni. of the verb, is most frequent (cf. e.g., 1 Sam 26:23; Isa 11:5; Psa 119:30; also 1QpHab 8:2; moreover, Prov 28:20 *ᵓîš ᵓᵉmûnôt*). Appropriately, → *ḥesed* often appears as a par. term (as well as *ṣᵉdāqâ* and *ṣedeq,* → *ṣdq*).

5. Quite often *šeqer* "deceit" appears as an antonym of *ᵓᵉmûnâ*, indicating that *ᵓᵉmûnâ* must involve the realm we designate as "truthfulness, honesty." One often wonders, however, whether "faithfulness" would be a better translation.

The notion of honesty appears most clearly in a few Jer passages: 5:1 "one who pursues uprightness" (according to M. Klopfenstein, *Die Lüge nach dem AT* [1964], 32f.: "faithfulness"; cf., however, the par. "who practices justice," and in v 2 "they swear falsely"; also 5:5; Isa 59:4; on → *ᶜśh* "to exercise, execute" in such contexts, see R. Bultmann, *ZNW* 27 [1928]: 122f. = *Exegetica* [1967]: 133f.); in Jer 7:28 the prophet complains that *ᵓᵉmûnâ* has disappeared from the mouth of the people; 9:2 is very clear, "They bend their tongue like a bow; deceit, not truthfulness (cf. *BHS*), controls the land" (LXX *pistis;* Klopfenstein, op. cit. 145: "faithfulness," with reference to covenant or marital fidelity; since, however, the first half of the verse mentions the bending of the tongue, "dishonesty" must be intended).

6. In his complaints concerning the lack of honesty, Jeremiah uses concepts that are important to wisdom. The parallelism of the concepts in Prov 12:22, "deceitful lips are an outrage to Yahweh; but those who pursue uprightness are well-pleasing to him," is particularly significant (cf. e.g., the "conversation of the one weary of life with his Ba," H. H. Schmid, *Wesen und Geschichte der Weisheit* [1966], 214; also called "Dispute over Suicide," *ANET* 405ff.). Yet some passages in Prov convey even more, e.g., 12:17 "whoever speaks the truth." Here *ᵓᵉmûnâ* still has the character of a substantivized adj.: "something on which one can depend, what is true" (cf. also Isa 25:1). One must distinguish therefore between *ᵓᵉmûnâ* in a personal sense ("dependability, faithfulness, honesty, truthfulness") and in an objective reference ("something dependable, true"). Passages with this meaning are infrequent,

however, and there is hardly any occasion to translate with the abstract "the truth."

7. The prep. usage *beʾᵉmûnâ* "upright, in good faith" in an adv. function (2 Kgs 12:16; 22:7; 2 Chron 19:9; 31:12, 15; 34:12) frequently expresses the personal, subjective aspect. On the one hand *ʾēmûn*/*ʾᵉmûnîm* "dependability, faithfulness" also represents the personal facet (see II); on the other hand *ʾōmen* "in truth, really" (acc. adv., Isa 25:1) expresses the objective, thing-oriented aspect. *ʾomnâ* "in truth, indeed" (Gen 20:12; Josh 7:20) also occurs in the adv. acc.; the sense is precisely the same as for the proper advs. *ʾomnām* and *ʾumnām* "indeed, really, truly," whether one describes a third-party statement as accurate or underscores the dependability of one's own statement.

8. The following appear as near or more distant pars. to *ʾᵉmûnâ:*

(a) *ʾᵉmet* (Psa 40:11f.; Jer 9:2–5); the spheres of meaning of the two substantives overlap to a great extent (see E);

(b) *ḥesed* appears beside *ʾᵉmûnâ* with noteworthy regularity (Hos 2:21f. alongside *ṣedeq, mišpāṭ,* and *raḥᵃmîm;* particularly in the language of the Psa: 33:4f.; 36:6; 40:11f.; 88:12; 89:2f., 25, 34, 50; 92:3; 98:3; 100:5; 119:75f.; Lam 3:22f.; cf. Psa 31:24; Prov 20:6); the fact that the two terms stand alongside one another so often in cultic poetry is naturally associated with parallelismus membrorum and the pleriphory of cultic language; the two terms are so closely related that they are largely interchangeable;

(c) terms for right and justice such as *ṣedeq, ṣᵉdāqâ,* and *mišpāṭ* occur frequently in the word field of *ʾᵉmûnâ* (Deut 32:4; 1 Sam 26:23; Isa 11:5; 33:5f.; 59:4; Jer 5:1; Hos 2:21f.; Hab 2:4; Psa 33:4f.; 36:6f.; 40:11; 88:12f.; 98:2f.; 119:30, 75, 138; 143:1 txt?; Prov 12:17; cf. Isa 26:2 and Prov 13:17); one can explain this relationship between the terms, which is at first surprising, by the fact that *ṣdq* and its derivatives can be used in the sense of "solidarity, community faithfulness" (cf. H. H. Schmid, *Gerechtigkeit als Weltordnung* [1968], 184f.), as well as by the fact that, like *ṣᵉdāqâ*, *ʾᵉmûnâ* can apparently serve as a circumlocution for orderly behavior (cf. Schmid, op. cit. 68).

IV. 1. The cultic songs of the Psalter favor speaking of Yahweh's *ʾᵉmûnâ.* The lament and thanksgiving songs bear testimony to God's unshakeable, constant faithfulness as the reason for God's past or future helpful attention to people (e.g., Psa 88:12 or 40:11, where the terms used in the context permit only the translation "faithfulness," together with *yᵉšûᶜâ* "aid" perhaps in a hendiadys "your faithful aid"). It manifests itself in all the afflictions brought before God in the laments and mentioned retrospectively in the thanksgivings (illness or deliverance from death, but also in the affliction of enemies as in Psa 92:3 or 143:1). Similarly, the poet of Lam 3:23 clings to Yahweh's *ʾᵉmûnâ,* because of which his demonstrations of grace *(ḥᵃsādîm)* cannot have ended and his great mercy *(raḥᵃmîm)* may be counted on (cf. also Psa 100:5). The enthronement songs also speak of Yahweh's *ʾᵉmûnâ.* Just as Yahweh aids his people on the strength of his *ʾᵉmûnâ* (Psa 98:3), so can he judge the peoples on the strength of the same, realizing his *ṣedeq* in the course of history (96:13, here not with *raḥᵃmîm* or *ḥesed* as parallel terms, but with *ṣedeq,* the "righteousness" through which God ensures that things remain in proper order). *ṣedeq* and *ʾᵉmûnâ* occur together in Psa 119:30 also, although not active in the judgment upon the nations but in the mortification of the pious.

Still, this mortification does not exclude hope in *ḥesed* and *raḥ*ᵃ*mîm* (cf. Psa 119:138).

Psa 89 speaks of Yahweh's ʾᵉ*mûnâ* with intentional frequency (vv 2f., 6, 9, 25, 34, 50); in view of the lamentable situation of the monarchy, the psalm strives for an understanding of the promise of the continuation of the Davidic dynasty. The poet juxtaposes any doubt in the promise with the confession of Yahweh's ʾᵉ*mûnâ*. Because God's ʾᵉ*mûnâ* cannot be doubted, neither can the *ne*ʾᵉ*mān* of Nathan's promise be questioned (cf. vv 29, 38, and *ḥesed* and ʾᵉ*met* in v 15). What may be called the metaphysical foundation of faith in Yahweh's faithfulness (vv 3, 6, 9, 15; similar to the confession in Psa 36:6f.; cf. 57:11; 89:38; 108:5) is interesting in this context.

Even though the OT certainly does not speculate at all about God's essential nature, it still ventures the statement that ʾᵉ*mûnâ* is an aspect of God's being. Correspondingly, Yahweh is described at least once as ʾ*ēl* ʾᵉ*mûnâ* (Deut 32:4; cf. the designations ʾ*ēl* ʾᵉ*met* and ʾ*ēl ne*ʾᵉ*mān*). Nevertheless, the context indicates that the singer of the song wishes to emphasize strongly the elements of uprightness and integrity (in contrast to the perversity of the people). The trait of dependability is not overlooked, however, because the praise of Yahweh as the rock precedes the confession of his faithfulness (v 4a). Isa 65:16 indicates that one may bless oneself or swear by the God of faithfulness (see C.IV/4).

Discussion of God's ʾᵉ*mûnâ* is limited to a rather small segment of the OT tradition: hymns, thanksgivings, and complaint songs. Deut 32 is peculiar insofar as the confession of God's faithfulness is not based on the experience of God's aid in the needs of the day, but in salvation history in which Yahweh has himself born testimony to his people. In view of the infrequency of such passages, one should note that the notion of God's faithfulness is in no way limited to the use of ʾᵉ*mûnâ* or related terms.

2. The ʾᵉ*mûnâ* of God's commandments can be discussed as easily as the ʾᵉ*mûnâ* of God (Psa 119:86). Because the *šeqer* of the impudent is contrasted with it, one may translate it "truth." This translation does not merely mean, however, that they are formally "correct." *šeqer* does not mean "lie," but "deceit"; and, wholly in keeping with this meaning, Yahweh's commandments are "true" because they are dependable. They are the norms of a saving world order; whoever relies on them will not be disappointed, but is assured fullness of life.

3. Psa 89:3 makes clear that one can conceive of ʾᵉ*mûnâ*, prior to realization on earth, as a divine, fundamental principle existent in heaven. According to the royal ideology of the ancient Near East, which also stamped Israel's thinking, the king is administrator of this preestablished harmony praised by the holy ones in heaven (v 6). Every individual can do absolutely nothing better, however, than to incorporate himself/herself consciously into this order, i.e., to become an ʾ*îš* ʾᵉ*mûnâ* (or ʾ*îš ne*ʾᵉ*mān*/ʾᵉ*met*). Such an individual will receive rich blessings (Prov 28:20; cf. the Eg. "Protests of the Eloquent Peasant": "truth, not lies, means wealth, it causes never-ending bloom," F. von Bissing, *Altäg. Lebensweisheit* [1955], 168). The small number of such statements is associated with the strict subordination of this fundamental principle to Yahweh's lordship in Israelite thinking; *he* actualizes the ʾᵉ*mûnâ*

(Isa 25:1). This subordination results in the following formulation: "Lying lips are an abomination to *Yahweh*, but those who practice *ʾᵉmûnâ* are pleasing to him" (Prov 12:22; cf. 12:17). But Psa 119:30 can still say: "I have chosen the path of the (not your) *ʾᵉmûnâ*," although it then conforms to the Yahwistic program: "I strive after your ordinances."

4. The substantivized masc. *ʾēmûn* (mostly in the pl.; see II) appears in addition to *ʾᵉmûnâ*, the substantivized fem. of the adj. A difference in meaning is difficult to ascertain. If God is a God of *ʾᵉmûnâ* (Deut 32:4), then the Israelites are children who do not know *ʾēmûn* (v 20; cf. also v 5). Psa 12:2 "*ʾᵉmûnîm* (honesty, sincerity) has disappeared among human children" is comparable to the Jer passage mentioned above (III/5). Likewise, according to Isa 25:1 and 26:2, divine *ʾᵉmûnâ* and human *ʾᵉmûnîm* ought to correspond to one another (the continuation in 26:3f. mentions reliance upon Yahweh). Just as Hab 2:4 promises life to the righteous because of his/her *ʾᵉmûnâ* (see B.IV/2), so may the righteous, those who keep *ʾᵉmûnîm*, hope for peace, according to Isa 26:2f. One may say that these *šōmᵉrê ʾᵉmûnîm* are the "believers." Israel responds to God's faithfulness, shining in his wondrous deeds, by keeping faith.

E. *ʾᵉmet*

III. 1. The LXX already translated almost half the cases of *ʾᵉmûnâ* with *alētheia;* derivatives of *alēth-* render 100 of 127 occurrences of *ʾᵉmet*, while *pistis* recedes pronouncedly; the relative frequency of *dikaiosynē* (6x) or *dikaios* (5x) is also noteworthy; cf. *SBL* 187ff. This result indicates that *ʾᵉmûnâ* and *ʾᵉmet* are not fully synonymous and that, more than any other derivative of *ʾmn*, *ʾᵉmet* has acquired the meaning "truth." This situation does not change the fact (contra Porúbčan, op. cit. 183) that the meaning "truth" cannot constitute the starting point for the semantics of *ʾᵉmet*, and (contra D. Michel, "'ÄMÄT," *Archiv für Begriffsgeschichte* 12 [1968]: 30–57) that all occurrences of *ʾᵉmet* may not be understood against the concept of correctness or agreement, making a change in meaning for the term imperceptible.

2. The presumed basic meaning "firmness" is still present here only in a fig. sense. But in contrast to *ʾᵉmûnâ*, *ʾᵉmet* has occasionally developed the meaning "permanence, security, duration," in exact correspondence to the ni. of the verb, e.g., in Isa 16:5, "Thus the throne will be established by grace and it will be permanently occupied." If *hûkan* "to be established" corresponds to the *nākôn* "firm" of Nathan's prophecy in 2 Sam 7:16, then *beʾᵉmet*, "constantly," corresponds to *neʾᵉmān* "to have permanence" there. In addition to the element of duration, the word apparently encompasses the element of assuredness in such cases. Thus *śeker ʾᵉmet* in Prov 11:18 may mean "stable, certain reward" (see Klopfenstein, op. cit. 171f.). It is less likely, however, that one may consistently translate the frequent combination *ḥesed weʾᵉmet* as a hendiadys, "lasting mercy" (so *HAL* 66b, 247b, 323a). Admittedly, the dual expression has often become a fixed formula, and the element of constancy, of permanence, certainly belongs to faithfulness (cf. e.g., Josh 2:14; 2 Sam 15:20; Prov 3:3; 14:22; 16:6; 20:28). Passages such as Psa 85:11 "*ḥesed* and *ʾᵉmet* meet" indicate, nevertheless, that the two terms stand entirely on the same level and each can have its own weight. If it still seems appropriate to regard *ʾᵉmet* as a qualifier of *ḥesed* in some cases, it seems best to understand

the phrases as "*ḥesed* (mercy, grace, love) on which one can depend"; the element of duration does not occupy the foreground.

3. *ʾemet* does serve unmistakably as the second member of a cs. combination as a qualifier of a higher concept such as *šālôm* "peace" (Jer 14:13, perhaps "peace of duration, lasting peace," but because of 2 Kgs 20:19 = Isa 39:8 and Jer 33:6 "peace and security," it is still more likely to be read as "peace that guarantees security"), *ʾôt* "sign," etc. One can best approach all these phrases from the notion of dependability (contra Weiser, *TDNT* 6:184: "*ʾmn* is shown to be a formal concept whose content is in each case determined by the specific subj."; it indicates "the relation of the reality to that which is characteristic of the particular subj."; contra *SBL* 179f.).

The following passages should be mentioned here: Gen 24:48 (a dependable and therefore proper path); Exod 18:21 (dependable men who cannot be bribed); Josh 2:12 (a dependable and therefore certain sign); Jer 2:21 (a dependable, i.e., genuine, growth); 14:13 (a dependable, certain peace; see above); 42:5 (a dependable and therefore truthful witness; likewise Prov 14:25 with the antonym "lying witness"); Ezek 18:8 and Zech 7:9 (a legal pronouncement on which one can depend); Prov 22:21 (dependable and therefore true words, par. *qōšṭ* "truth"); Eccl 12:10 (words on which one can depend); Neh 7:2 (a dependable and God-fearing man); 9:13 (dependable instructions).

4. In relation to persons (and God), the meaning of *ʾemet* shifts from dependability to faithfulness, as in the frequent combination *ḥesed weʾemet* "grace and faithfulness": of people: Gen 24:49; 47:29; Josh 2:14; Prov 3:3; of God: Gen 24:27, etc. (see IV/2). The prep. phrase *beʾemet* "in faithfulness" serves as an adv.: "faithfully, uprightly"; it describes the dependability of the person's behavior (not the certainty of a state of affairs like the proper advs. and adverbial acc. mentioned above in D.III/7; but see 6).

The pars. confirm the precise intention: *betāmîm* "uprightly" (Josh 24:14; Judg 9:16, 19); "with the whole heart (and with the whole soul)" (1 Sam 12:24; 1 Kgs 2:4); "in righteousness and with an upright attitude toward you" (1 Kgs 3:6); "with an undivided heart" (2 Kgs 20:3 = Isa 38:3); similarly Isa 10:20; 61:8; Jer 32:41; Psa 111:8; Prov 29:14. Thus *beʾemet* characterizes human presence in terms of integrity and personal engagement.

5. One can "exercise *ʾemet*" (*ʿśh;* cf. *ʿśh ʾemûnâ;* see D III/5): Gen 47:29; Neh 9:33; 2 Chron 31:20. But one can also "speak *ʾemet,*" an expression that refers not to the speaker's dependability but to the pronouncement's dependability. Words are dependable, and therefore trustworthy, if they recount a circumstance accurately, i.e., if they are true: 2 Sam 7:28; 1 Kgs 17:24; 22:16 = 2 Chron 18:15; Jer 9:4 (opposite *tll* hi. "to deceive"); 23:28 "who speaks my word in truth" (so Rudolph, HAT 12, 154; Klopfenstein, op. cit. 103, and others understand *ʾemet* as an adverbial acc. and translate "faithfully"). In fact, one is frequently unable to decide with certainty whether *ʾemet* means "uprightness" in reference to the subj. or "truth" in reference to the obj. Thus one can ask, e.g., regarding the phrase *ʿēd ʾemet,* whether *ʾemet* should be understood as an attitudinal norm ("truthful witness") or whether it confirms the truth of the circumstances attested. If one proceeds from *ʿēd neʾemān* (see A.III/1; cf. Jer 42:5) one will opt for the first possibility, but from

the standpoint of Isa 43:9 or Prov 14:25, one will prefer the second. According to Gen 42:16, Joseph wants to test his brothers, "whether ᵓᵉ*met* is with you"; here one should clearly translate ᵓᵉ*met* not "uprightness" but "truth" (see D.III/6 on ᵓᵉ*mûnâ*). Nevertheless, one may not speak of an abstraction of the specific events (so G. Quell, *TDNT* 1:234), so that one may translate: "whether *the* truth is with you." In the face of great uncertainty in details, surely grounded in the fact that the distinction between (subjective) uprightness and (objective) truth was not so apparent to the Hebrews as to us, the obj.-oriented meaning is still clearly present. This situation is esp. pertinent to the juridical arena, where objective truth, not merely subjective truthfulness, is definitely in view. Witnesses before the court can declare the statement of a litigant ᵓᵉ*met* "it is true," i.e., the relevant statement agrees with reality (Isa 43:9). An accusation can be confirmed as ᵓᵉ*met* (Deut 13:15 and 17:4, made explicit by *nākôn haddābār* "the situation is really so"; cf. 22:20). In Prov 22:21 "words of ᵓᵉ*met*" explicates *qōšṭ* "truth"; *dbr* pi. ᵓᵉ*met* means, if not *the* truth, then still "a true statement" (Zech 8:16; cf. Psa 15:2; Prov 8:7; 12:19 par. "lying tongue"), and *hyh* ᵓᵉ*met* "prove true" (Deut 22:20; 2 Sam 7:28; cf. 1 Kgs 17:24).

6. Finally, one should note passages in which *be*ᵓᵉ*met* does not mean "in faithfulness, uprightly," but "in truth, actually, really" (Judg 9:15; Jer 26:15; 28:9; cf. also the simple ᵓᵉ*met* in Jer 10:10).

7. The most important parallel terms are:

(a) ᵓᵉ*mûnâ* (see D.III/8);

(b) *ḥesed* (see III/2, 4 of people, IV/2 of God);

(c) terms for the totality of the person (see 4);

(d) legal terms: → *ṣedeq* "righteousness" (Psa 15:2; 85:12; Prov 8:7f., etc.; *ṣᵉdāqâ* Isa 48:1; 59:14; Jer 4:2; Zech 8:8, etc.; *ṣaddîq* Neh 9:33); *mišpāṭ* "justice" (→ *špṭ;* Isa 59:14; Jer 4:2, etc.); *mêšārîm* "straightness" (Prov 8:6); *nᵉkōḥâ* "propriety" (Isa 59:14), and others;

(e) *šālôm* (→ *šlm;* 2 Kgs 20:19 = Isa 39:8; Jer 33:6; Zech 8:16, 19; Mal 2:6; Psa 85:11; Esth 9:30).

Antonyms are: *šeqer* "deceit" (Jer 9:4; Zech 8:16; Prov 11:18; 12:19, etc.); *kāzāb* "lie" (Prov 14:25, etc.); *mirmâ* "deceit" (Prov 12:19); *rešaᶜ* "wickedness" (Prov 8:7; cf. 11:18; Neh 9:33).

8. Except for *šālôm* and the one case in which the Aramaism *qōšṭ* "truth" (Wagner no. 274; Bibl. Aram. *qᵉšōṭ*, Dan 4:34) parallels ᵓᵉ*met* (Prov 22:21), the word field surrounding ᵓᵉ*met* coincides quite precisely with that of ᵓᵉ*mûnâ*. ᵓᵉ*met* in the sense of "truth" has no actual par., because Hebr. has no independent word for "truth." This phenomenon does not mean that Hebr. does not have a concept of truth, but that its concept of truth is indissolubly joined with the notion of dependability (cf. W. Pannenberg, "Was ist Wahrheit?" FS Vogel 214–239, esp. 216; H. von Soden, op. cit. [see I/7]; H.-J. Kraus, "Wahrheit in der Geschichte," *Was ist Wahrheit?* [1965], 35–46; K. Koch, "Der hebr. Wahrheitsbegriff im griech. Sprachraum," *Was ist Wahrheit?*, 47–65; M. Landmann, *Ursprungsbild und Schöpfertat* [1966], 213–22). Just as ᵓᵉ*met* in the sense of the dependability of persons means faithfulness and uprightness, understood as truth it means the dependability of a thing or a word. In this

sense, only that which corresponds to reality or is fully appropriate to it can be dependable.

IV. 1. Like the confession of God's ᵓᵉ*mûnâ*, that of his ᵓᵉ*met* becomes prominent primarily in the Psalter. The lament in Psa 31 praises Yahweh as ᵓ*ēl* ᵓᵉ*met* (v 6), just as other texts call him ᵓ*ēl ne*ᵓᵉ*mān* or ᵓ*ēl* ᵓᵉ*mûnâ*. Thus this text simply expresses pregnantly what other laments and thanksgiving songs also attest in reference to Yahweh's ᵓᵉ*met*. No difference between ᵓᵉ*met* and ᵓᵉ*mûnâ* can be ascertained in these contexts.

One may also celebrate Yahweh's ᵓᵉ*met* because one has experienced or would like to experience him as helper. Psa 69:14 implores Yahweh specifically to grant an audience "in the faithfulness of your aid." The hope of aid motivates one to take refuge in Yahweh's faithfulness. The celebration of his faithfulness is designed to move God to intervene before it is too late. To this end, the supplicant can remind him that one cannot praise his faithfulness in the underworld (Psa 30:10; Isa 38:18; cf. Psa 71:22; for ᵓᵉ*mûnâ* see Psa 88:12). Or one can pray that God's light and faithfulness may lead the supplicant to God's holy mountain so that one may there sing his praise with sacrifice (Psa 43:3f.; cf. 138:2). The annihilation of the enemies is frequently an element of the aid that one expects from God's faithfulness (54:7; cf. 22:26 txt em). Psa 91:4b celebrates Yahweh's faithfulness as shield and buckler (didactic poem? cf. Kraus, *Psa*, CC, 2:221).

The hymn in Psa 146 (which also contains elements of the thanksgiving song, however) describes in an especially impressive manner what it means for Israel that Yahweh maintains faithfulness eternally. The poet does not think, as is otherwise the rule, of his personal distress, but praises Yahweh as the helper of all the oppressed. Yahweh himself is, indeed, called the God of Jacob (v 5), but he is described as the creator God and the God of Zion (v 10), who will rule eternally. Here, then, in comparison with the average piety of the Psalms, God's faithfulness (v 6) is placed against a greatly expanded horizon.

2. As in the profane arena, ᵓᵉ*met* is also readily combined with → *ḥesed* (III/1) in reference to God.

Hos 4:1 and Mic 7:20 mention ᵓᵉ*met* before *ḥesed*, but as a rule *ḥesed* stands first. The combination can vary elsewhere also (i.e., Psa 69:14), but for the most part they are joined as closely as possible through the simple *w*ᵉ "and" (Psa 25:10; 40:12; 57:4; 85:11; 89:15; 138:2; beyond the Psalter: Gen 24:27; Exod 34:6; 2 Sam 2:6; 15:20; in a looser combination: Gen 32:11; Hos 4:1; Psa 26:3; 57:11 = 108:5).

One may say that the primary accent lies on *ḥesed* in these phrases. ᵓᵉ*met* modifies *ḥesed* "grace, goodness, love, goodwill" in terms of dependability.

The following occurrences in particular are noteworthy: (a) Psa 89:15. That justice and righteousness are the foundation of Yahweh's throne is thoroughly appropriate to the context, which speaks of God's kingdom. But the statement continues: "*ḥesed* and ᵓᵉ*met* stand in your presence." Here they are seen almost as beings, almost as hypostases. Thus Psa 85:11f. too can say: "*ḥesed* and ᵓᵉ*met* encounter one another, righteousness and peace meet (txt em); faithfulness sprouts from the earth and righteousness blooms from heaven." The exegetes' argument as to whether the text refers to divine or human faithfulness is superfluous: the intention is naturally that *God* causes such faithfulness to sprout. But the formulation also allows for the recognition that *ḥesed* and ᵓᵉ*met* could be envisioned as independent cosmic entities, whose control also guarantees the fertility of the land, because where they come to power, the cosmos must regain harmonious, fertile equilibrium.

(b) Psa 86:15 confesses: "You are a merciful, gracious God, patient and rich in *ḥesed* and *ᵓᵉmet*" (cf. v 5). This statement is apparently an old confessional formula (without *ᵓᵉmet* also in Psa 103:8; 145:8; Joel 2:13 and Jonah 4:2 complemented by "he repents of evil"; with *ᵓᵉmet* in Exod 34:6, but, according to Noth, *Exod*, OTL, 261, the formula here is a secondary insertion). It seems that *ᵓᵉmet* has gained entry into the formula only secondarily, probably by force of the combination *ḥesed weᵓᵉmet*. One sought to establish explicitly the element of faithfulness that continues even in situations that subject the relationship between God and people to a rigorous endurance test. Expansions in Psa 86:5, "rich in mercy" by means of "gracious and forgiving," and references in the passages in Joel and Jonah to Yahweh's preparedness to repent are in the same vein.

(c) The OT speaks of *ḥesed weᵓᵉmet* accompanied by *ᶜśh* "to do" three times beyond the Psa: Gen 24:49; 32:11 *(ḥᵃsādîm)*; 2 Sam 2:6. Each of these refers to God's just guidance of people. Therefore one can also say that Yahweh's paths are *ḥesed weᵓᵉmet* (Psa 25:10; cf. 43:3). The pious individual recognizes that he/she stands under the guidance of divine faithfulness in his/her life.

3. Because *ᵓᵉmet* encompasses the foundations of the cosmic order, the individual must actualize *ᵓᵉmet* just as God does. Naturally, wisdom esp. instructs to this end (Prov 3:3; 14:22; 16:6; 20:28). Gen 24 relates human faithfulness to the divine (vv 27 and 49). Grace and faithfulness, which preserve the king according to Prov 20:28, correspond to the grace and faithfulness that stand in the presence of God (Psa 89:15). Through grace and faithfulness one meets with divine and human approval (Prov 3:3f.). The demand for *ᵓᵉmet* occurs once in the prophets as well: Hos 4:1, "There is no *ᵓᵉmet* and no *ḥesed* and no knowledge of God in the land." Knowledge of God must be realized in the actualization of *ḥesed* and *ᵓᵉmet*. The continuation allows for no doubt that this context envisions not the relationship with God but the relationship with one's neighbors. The OT almost never describes the individual's behavior toward God with *ḥesed weᵓᵉmet* (or *ᵓᵉmet* alone). The response to God's faithfulness can only be faithfulness toward one's fellow human beings. The only exceptions are late passages such as 2 Chron 31:20 and 32:1.

But behavior *beᵓᵉmet* toward God is demanded of Israel, not primarily in the sense of "in faithfulness" (so *HAL* 67a), but "uprightly, genuinely, honestly" (see III/4). Behavior *bᵉtāmîm* and *beᵓᵉmet* legitimately expresses the fear of God (Josh 24:14).

4. As established above (III/5), *ᵓᵉmet* in a profane usage means not only subj.-oriented "dependability, uprightness, faithfulness," but also obj.-oriented "something dependable, truth." Does the OT also speak of the truth of God? Decision between the two options is difficult here too. For example, contrary to many older exegetes (Delitzsch, Duhm, Marti, etc.), one must maintain "faithfulness" in Isa 59:14f. (Klopfenstein, op. cit. 46; Fohrer, *Jesaja*, ZBK, 3:219; cf. Westermann, *Isa 40–66*, OTL, 343, etc.).

The attempt to translate Psa 25:5, "guide me according to your truth *(ᵓᵉmet)*, teach me," is more frequent and the request for instruction seems to justify it. The alphabetic psalm exhibits elements of the lament, however, and laments discuss *ᵓᵉmet* in the sense of "faithfulness." V 6 takes up *ᵓᵉmet* again through *raḥᵃmîm* "mercies" and *ḥesed*. But particularly in view of v 10, one must translate "guide me according to your faithfulness" and not, as is customary, "in your truth." Psa 86:11 should be understood as an exact analogy; "Teach me your way, that I may walk in your faithfulness"; God's faithfulness is the realm in which the individual's journey must be executed if it is to be salvific.

The usage in the two legal psalms, Psa 19 B and 119, is different. In the clause "the commandments of Yahweh are *ʾᵉmet*" (19:10), *ʾᵉmet* is naturally object-oriented. But the rendering "true" is nevertheless problematical. The par. phrase in v 10a states that Yahweh's word (read *ʾimrat* for *yirʾat*) is pure and will stand for eternity. Thus *ʾᵉmet* probably means to attest to the dependability and lasting validity of the divine commandment rather than to its truth. The same situation pertains to statements concerning the law in Psa 119 (vv 43, 142, 151, 160). In each case, the word field indicates that the reference is to the duration or the "eternal" validity of the commandments, as in v 152, "From of old I know from your precepts, that you have established them for eternity." One may wish to translate "true"; but they are true because they are dependable, and this manifests itself, in turn, in the fact that they ensure "life" (vv 40, 116, 144).

Finally, Psa 51:8 is difficult to interpret: "You are pleased with *ʾᵉmet* in secret, and in secret you teach me wisdom." Text and translation are uncertain (cf. Kraus, *Psa*, CC, 1:499, 503f.); but in any case, *ʾᵉmet* here parallels *ḥokmâ* "wisdom," and like *ḥokmâ* it can be taught. Therefore, *ʾᵉmet* must mean truth in the sense of a secret revelation, a deep, not directly accessible knowledge.

5. This usage approaches the meaning of the occurrences in Daniel. Dan 8:26, "the vision that has been revealed is *ʾᵉmet*," can only mean that the vision is true because one can depend upon it, certain that the fulfillment will not fail, just as in 10:1 and 11:2 (txt? cf., however, Plöger, KAT 18, 145f., 150). These Dan passages are sharply distinguished from 1 Kgs 17:24. The latter maintains that Yahweh has really (in truth) spoken to the prophets; the former maintains that he has communicated the truth to the apocalypticist—indeed, in such a way that this revelation is a mirror image of the coming events. These events are recorded in the book of *ʾᵉmet* (Dan 10:21), the "book of truth," which has been understood as a par. to the Babylonian tablets of destiny (cf. comms. by Marti, Bentzen, Porteous on the Dan passage; contra Plöger, KAT 18, 146). But the revelation long familiar in Israel can also be described as "God's truth" (9:13).

This usage leads to 8:12, where *ʾᵉmet* is used in a final, abs. sense. After describing the abominations of the "small horn," the author concludes: "the *ʾᵉmet* was thrown to the ground" (txt em; cf. *BHS*, contra Plöger, op. cit. 120, 122). Here *ʾᵉmet* refers to the truth of Judaism, with its individual legal regulations (K. Marti, *Das Buch Daniel* [1901], 58f.; R. Bultmann, *ZNW* 27 [1928]: 118f. = *Exegetica* [1967]: 129).

The usage of *ʾᵉmet* in Dan is unique. The closest par. to this usage is in Eccl 12:10. Bultmann (op. cit.) suspects the influence of Iranian concepts upon Dan 8:12 and thinks, probably correctly, that the "book of truth," from which the angel communicates revelations concerning the future to the seer (Dan 10:21), also points to foreign influence. In any case, it is clear that Dan initiates a new understanding of *ʾᵉmet*, and thereby a new understanding of truth itself.

V. The continued vitality of the word group or the Gk. equivalents in the Qumran literature, in early Judaism, and in the NT cannot be examined in detail here. The bibliog., too, can offer only a selection:

1. "faith": In addition to A. Weiser and R. Bultmann, "πιστεύω," *TDNT* 6:174–228, and the lexical articles in *RGG, EKL,* etc.:

A. Schlatter, *Der Glaube im* NT (1927); W. G. Kümmel, "Der Glaube im NT, seine katholische und reformatorische Deutung," *TBl* 16 (1937): 209–21 = *Heilsgeschehen und Geschichte* (1965), 67–80; E. Walter, *Glaube, Hoffnung, Liebe im* NT (1940); M. Buber, *Two Types of Faith* (1951); G. Schrenk, "Martin Bubers Beurteilung des Paulus in seiner Schrift 'Zwei Glaubensweisen,' " *Judaica* 8 (1952): 1–25; M. Bonningues, *La Foi dans l'évangile de s. Jean* (1955); G. Ebeling, *Was heisst Glauben?* (1958); id., "Jesus and Faith," *Word and Faith* (1963), 201–46; W. Grundmann, "Verständnis und Bewegung des Glaubens im Johannes-Evangelium," *KerD* 6 (1960): 131–54; F. Neugebauer, *In Christus,* EN ΧΡΙΣΤΩΙ: *Eine Untersuchung zum paulinischen Glaubensverständnis* (1961), 150–81; H. Schlier, "Glauben, Erkennen, Lieben nach dem Johannesevangelium," FS Söhngen 98–111 = *Besinnung auf das* NT (1964), 279–93; H. Ljungman, *Pistis: A Study of Its Presuppositions and Its Meaning in Pauline Use* (1964); H. Conzelmann, "Fragen an Gerhard von Rad," *EvT* 24 (1964): 113–25 (123ff.); E. Grässer, *Der Glaube im Hebräerbrief* (1965); N. Lazure, *Les valeurs morales de la théologie johannique* (1965), 161–204; P. Stuhlmacher, *Gerechtigkeit Gottes bei Paulus* (1966^2), 81–83; H. Conzelmann, *Outline of the Theology of the NT* (1969), 61f., 171ff.; C. A. Keller, "Glaube in der 'Weisheit Salomos,' " FS Eichrodt 11–20.

2. "Amen" in Judaism, the NT, and the early church: H. Schlier, "ἀμήν," *TDNT* 1:335–38; *StrB* 1:242–44; 3:456–61; *RAC* 1:378–80; *BHH* 1:80f.; V. Hasler, *Amen* (1969).

Further: H. W. Hogg, *JQR* 9 (1897): 1–23; G. Dalman, *Words of Jesus* (1909), 226–29; P. Glaue, *ZKG* 44, NS 7 (1925): 184–98; D. Daube, *NT and Rabbinic Judaism* (1956), 388–93.

3. "Truth": In addition to G. Quell and R. Bultmann, "ἀλήθεια," *TDNT* 1:232–51, see *RGG, EKL,* etc.:

R. Bultmann, *ZNW* 27 (1928): 134–63; F. Nötscher, " 'Wahrheit' als theol. Terminus in den Qumrantexten," FS Christian 83–92 = *Vom Alten zum Neuen Testament* (1962), 112–25; H. Kosmala, *Hebräer, Essener, Christen* (1959), 135–73, 192–207; L. J. Kuyper, "Grace and Truth," *Int* 18 (1964): 3–19; O. Böcher, *Der johanneische Dualismus im Zusammenhang des nachbibl. Judentums* (1965); N. Lazure, op. cit. 70–90 (bibliog.); P. Ricca, *Die Eschatologie des vierten Evangeliums* (1966), 111–13.

H. Wildberger

אמץ ʾ*mṣ* to be strong

S 553; BDB 54b; *HALOT* 1:65a; *TDOT* 1:323–27; *TWOT* 117; *NIDOTTE* 599

---

1. The root ʾ*mṣ* "to be strong" occurs only in Hebr. and sporadically in Ug. (cf. *UT* no. 228; *WUS* no. 282).

The description of the horses in Zech 6:3, 7 as *ʾămuṣṣîm* involves a color term that does not belong to this root (cf. *HAL* 63b: "variegated"; A. Guillaume, *Abr-Nahrain* 2 [1962]: 7, "dust-colored"; W. D. McHardy, FS Kahle 174ff.).

In addition to the verb in the qal, pi., hitp., and hi. (cf. *HP* 280), the adj. *ʾammîṣ* "strong" and the substs. *ʾōmeṣ*, *ʾamṣâ* (Zech 12:5 txt?) "strength," and *maʾᵃmāṣ* "exertion" occur.

On the PNs *ʾᵃmaṣyâ(hû)*, *ʾāmôṣ*, *ʾamṣî*, see *IP* 190.

2. The word group is attested 50x in the OT (qal 16x, pi. 19x, hitp. 4x, hi. 2x), *ʾammîṣ* 6x, the substs. 1x each.

The verbal occurrences are located primarily in the Dtr-Chr literature and in Deut (qal 12x, pi. 6x, hitp. 3x), also in the Psa (qal 2x, pi. 3x, hi. 2x), in the wisdom literature (pi. 5x), and in the prophetic corpus (pi. 5x).

3. All meanings of the word group result from the primary meaning "to be strong, mighty." The term occurs only with a personal subj. (God, human). *ʾmṣ* occurs only in the qal (except for the encouragement formula; see 4) in reference to the superior strength of a people (Gen 25:23; 2 Chron 13:18) and in the individual laments in reference to the oppressive might of the psalmist's enemy. The factitive usage of the pi. conveys the idea of the intensification of physical might (often associated with → *kōaḥ:* Amos 2:14; Nah 2:2; cf. Prov 31:17; Isa 35:3; Job 4:4), the hardening of the heart (Deut 2:30; 15:7; 2 Chron 36:13; cf. F. Hesse, *Das Verstockungsproblem im AT* [1955], 16), the encouragement of the distressed (Job 16:5), or of a commissioned individual (see 4), and the restoration of a structure (temple, 2 Chron 24:13; cf. God's establishment of the clouds, Prov 8:28). The hitp. means "to manage to do something by an exertion of might" (1 Kgs 12:18 = 2 Chron 10:18), "to be superior to someone" (2 Chron 13:7), and "to be resolutely decided" (Ruth 1:18). On the hi. see 4.

The most important synonymous roots are → *ḥzq* and → *ʿzz; dll* "to be unimportant" and *rph* "to be limp" can be considered antonyms.

4. In individual laments, the superior strength of the enemy (2 Sam 22:18 = Psa 18:18; Psa 142:7) occasions the request for God's saving intervention, which proves effective against all human might (cf. 2 Chron 13:18). Most remarkable, however, is the stereotypical encouragement formula in Deut and the Dtr-Chr literature: *ḥᵃzaq weʾᵉmaṣ* "to be firm and strong" or (pl.) *ḥizqû wᵉʾimṣû* (cf. N. Lohfink, *Scholastik* 37 [1962]: 32–44). The formula originally belongs to the promise of divine guidance, specifically in the area of war (Deut 31:6; Josh 1:6; 10:25; cf. also Nah 2:2; → *ḥzq*), and is issued to a leader of the people threatened by enemies (Deut 31:7, 23) or to the people prepared for battle (Deut 31:6; Josh 10:25). The relation of the formula to the keeping of the Mosaic commandments or even to the keeping of the commandments of the law code (Josh 1:7ff.; cf. Noth, HAT 7, 28), a relation reflecting Deuteronomic interests, is characteristic. As a divine exhortation that removes fright, the formula is transferred, then, into the cultic sphere (only with *ʾmṣ* hi.: Psa 27:14; 31:25). Similarly based in the cultic salvation oracle, the promise of Yahweh's aid issued to the servant of God also uses *ʾmṣ* (Isa 41:10; cf. Psa 89:22).

The interpretation of Psa 80:16, 18 is disputed; the passage my deal either with the "rearing" of the king based in the ancient concept of the father-son relationship between God and the prince (so Kraus, *Psa*, CC, 2:143) or with that of the entire people (v 16 supports this interpretation, so Weiser, *Psa*, OTL, 550; cf. Hos 10:1ff.; Ezek 16:7).

5. The most important usages of ʾ*mṣ* mentioned above recur at Qumran, as one might expect, in the *War Scroll* (1QM) and the *Hodayot* (1QH) (cf. Kuhn, *Konk.* 17). For the encouragement formula in the NT, see 1 Cor 16:13.

A. S. van der Woude

אמר ʾ*mr* to say

S 559; BDB 55b; *HALOT* 1:65b; *TDOT* 1:328–45; *TWOT* 118; *NIDOTTE* 606

---

1. All Sem. langauges have a root ʾ*mr*, although it means "to say, speak" only in NWSem., i.e., in the various Can. (except for Ug.) and Aram. dialects (cf. *DISO* 17f.). In Arab. and Old SArab., ʾ*mr* means "to command," a meaning also evident in later OT Hebr. In contrast, Akk. *amāru* (and apparently Ug. *amr* Gt; cf. *WUS* no. 283; *UT* no. 229) means "to see"; similarly Eth. ʾ*mr* I/2 "to show."

On the hypothetical development of meaning "to see > to say" cf. S. Moscati, "La radice semitica ʾ*mr*," *Bib* 27 (1946): 115–26; *HAL* 63b with bibliog.; see also H. Kronasser, *Handbuch der Semasiologie* (1952), 93; on the Ger. "sagen/sehen" and "bemerken" [cf. Eng. "say/see" and "observe"—TRANS.] cf. Kluge 698 and Duden, *Etymologie* 633.

The existence of the Akk. meaning "to see" and the etymology of Hebr. ʾ*mr* based on this meaning do not justify M. Dahood's recourse to a so-called basic meaning "to see" in Psa 11:1; 29:9; and 71:10, where direct speech follows in each case (*Bib* 44 [1963]: 295f.).

In addition to the qal, the verb has a ni. (pass.) and a hi. (disputed in meaning, although likely causative; see 3b).

ʾ*mr* hitp. "to act proudly, boast" (Psa 94:4; perhaps also to be assumed in Isa 61:6) and the pertinent substantives ʾ*āmîr* or ʾ*ēmer*, "tree prunings, twig, branch," are treated as a distinct root ʾ*mr* II by *HAL* 61a, 65a in contrast to GB 48a, 51.

In addition to the infrequent *qutl-* form ʾ*ōmer* "saying, information; thing," the related (see 3c) *qitl-* formations ʾ*ēmer*/ʾ*imrâ* "word, pronouncement," as well as the late Aramaizing word *ma*ʾ*ămār* "word, command" (Wagner no. 149) occur as derived noms.; cf. also the Bibl. Aram. substantivized inf. *mē*ʾ*mar* "word, command."

From the related NWSem. langauges, the Ug. *amr* "wish, speech(?)" (*WUS* no. 284) and Yaudi ʾ*mrh* "speech, word, command(?)" (*DISO* 18; *KAI* no. 214.26, 32; cf. 2:221) may also certainly be mentioned.

On the PNs ʾ*ămaryâ(hû)* with the shortened forms ʾ*imrî* and perhaps ʾ*ômār* and ʾ*immēr*, cf. *IP* 173; *HAL* 21b, 65f.; Gröndahl 99; Huffmon 168.

2. *ᵓmr* qal "to say," with its 5,282 occurrences, is the most frequent verb in the OT (followed by → *hyh* "to be," → *ᶜśh* "to do," → *bôᵓ* "to come," → *ntn* "to give," → *hlk* "to go"), "one of the most common words in the language" (O. Procksch, *TDNT* 4:91). The basically equal distribution over the whole OT reflects this commonality, although a greater frequency is naturally encountered in the narrative texts than in legal texts or in poetic pieces.

ᵓmr qal occurs in all the books of the OT: Gen 603x (347x *wayyōᵓmer/wayyōᵓmar,* 81x *lēᵓmōr*), Exod 299x, Lev 80x, Num 244x, Deut 140x, Josh 136x, Judg 269x, 1 Sam 422x, 2 Sam 334x, 1 Kgs 326x, 2 Kgs 343x, Isa 241x, Jer 475x (163x *ᵓāmar,* 49x *wayyōᵓmer,* 114x *lēᵓmōr*), Ezek 362x, Hos 20x, Joel 5x, Amos 52x, Obad 2x, Jonah 22x, Mic 10x, Nah 2x, Hab 3x, Zeph 4x, Hag 26x, Zech 109x, Mal 40x, Psa 99x, Job 97x, Prov 25x, Ruth 54x, Song Sol 2x, Eccl 20x, Lam 10x, Esth 52x, Dan 22x, Ezra 15x, Neh 61x, 1 Chron 72x, 2 Chron 184x. Among the 5,282 forms (Lis. does not take account of 1 Sam 4:16b and 17:10 *wayyōᵓmer;* 2 Kgs 16:7 *lēᵓmōr;* and Ezek 4:14 *wāᵓōmar*), 930x are formulaic *lēᵓmōr* (in addition to 9x *lēᵓmōr* as inf. with *lᵉ*), 2,069x are *wayyōᵓmer* or *wayyōᵓmar,* and 644 others are *waw*-cons. forms (Lis. incorrectly classifies 2 Sam 20:18a *lēᵓmōr;* 2 Kgs 9:17 *wᵉyōᵓmar;* and 1 Chron 16:31 *wᵉyōᵓmᵉrû*).*

ᵓmr ni. occurs 21x, hi. 2x; Aram. *ᵓmr* pe. 71x (Dan 65x, Ezra 5x, Jer 1x).

Of the substantives, *ᵓōmer* occurs 6x, *ᵓēmer* 48x, *ᵓimrâ* 37x, *maᵓᵃmār* 3x (in Esth); Aram. *mēᵓmar* 2x.

3. (a) *ᵓmr* qal means "to say, speak" (in context it is also possible to translate "to ask" or "to answer"; → *šᵓl,* → *ᶜnh* I) and is the normal introduction of direct or (less frequently) indirect speech (BrSynt 140). In contrast to *dbr* pi. (→ *dābār* III/1), *ᵓmr* never means "to speak" without indication of the content of the communication (GB 50; *HAL* 64a, on the apparent exceptions see ibid.; cf. *HP* 165n.192).

With respect to *ᵓmr,* the appearance of the so-called perfectum declarativum pf. (pf. of completion) of the 1st per. sg., a possibility for all verbs of speaking in the broadest sense (→ *qrᵓ*, "to call," → *brk* pi. "to bless," → *šbᶜ* ni. "to swear," also → *ntn* "to give, declare transferred"), expressing the coincidence of statement and behavior: *ᵓāmartî* "I state hereby" (cf. Deut 32:40; Judg 2:3; 2 Sam 19:30; Isa 22:4; Psa 16:2 txt em; 31:15; 75:5; 119:57; 140:7; 142:6; Job 9:22; 32:10; cf. Berg., *HG* 2:27f.; BrSynt 40; D. Michel, *Tempora und Satzstellung in den Psalmen* [1960], 80, 92–95; E. Koschmieder, *Beiträge zur allgemeinen Syntax* [1965], 26–34); the formula *kōh ᵓāmar yhwh* "thus says Yahweh (herewith, through me)" may also belong here.*

God, people, animals (Gen 3:1; Num 22:28, 30), and—in the fable—trees (Judg 9:8ff.) are subjs. of *ᵓmr.* The speech announced by *ᵓmr* is appended in the majority of cases without transition; occasionally *lēᵓmōr* (see below), *kî* (e.g., Gen 29:33; Exod 4:25; Judg 6:16), or *ᵓᵃšer* (Neh 13:19, 22 "to command") stands between introduction and that introduced (cf. Joüon §157c). The addressee is indicated by *ᵓel* or *lᵉ;* the same preps. also describe persons or things about which something is said. The acc. is used in cases such as Psa 41:6, "they speak wickedness against me," with direct speech following, or when the verb should be translated "to mention" or "to name" (*HAL* 64a 3a-c; *lᵉ* may also be used for the latter).

ᵓmr also frequently introduces direct speech following other verbs of speaking, either in the impf. cons. (after *dbr* pi., *ᶜnh,* and *ᵓmr* itself) or, very often, in the inf. with *lᵉ* =

lēʾmōr "in order to say, in that he said, with the words, as follows" (on the form, see BL 223, 370), after *dbr* pi., *šʾl*, *ṣwh* pi., *ʾmr* itself, etc.

In isolated, for the most part relatively late, passages, *ʾmr* can mean "to command," corresponding to the Aram. and Arab. usage. The usage in the sense of "to say to oneself" = "to think" is more frequent, often in the construction *ʾmr bᵉlibbô*/*ʾel-libbô*/*lᵉlibbô* "to say in/to his heart" (cf. N. Bratsiotis, "Der Monolog im AT," *ZAW* 73 [1961]: 30–70, esp. 46f.; on verbs of thinking → *ḥšb*). Instances of this and other features treated in this section are found in GB 50f. and *HAL* 64.

(b) *ʾmr* ni. has a pass. sense ("to be said, to be called") and is often used with an indefinite per. subj. (like Lat. *dicitur* "one says").

On evidence for *ʾmr* hi. "to cause to say" (Deut 26:17f.) cf. R. Smend, *Die Bundesformel* (1963), 7f., 33 ("to proclaim"); Th. C. Vriezen, "Das Hiphil von *ʾāmar* in Deut. 26,17.18," *JEOL* 17 (1963): 207–10; von Rad, *Deut*, OTL, 161f.; GB 51a.

(c) With respect to noms. of the root *ʾmr*, the differentiation of meanings is complicated because of specific passages in which the text is difficult or uncertain (*ʾōmer* in Hab 3:9; Psa 68:12; 77:9; *ʾēmer* in Job 20:29; Prov 19:7; 22:21). But the assessment of the term *ʾēmer* based on the suf. form *ʾimrô* of Job 20:29 is also contested (*GVG* 1:255: dissimilation of *ʾōmrô* to *ʾimrô*; likewise BL 215, where the pl. and fem. forms with *ʾimr-* are explained as analogous formations). Perhaps the following reference points should be observed: *ʾōmer* never precedes a gen. or suf.; correspondingly, it has a very general meaning, in Psa 19:3f. "word" almost in the sense of "speech, language," in Job 22:28 "matter, something" (cf. → *dābār*). *ʾimrâ* always appears (except for Psa 12:7bis) in the sg. and with a following gen. or suf., as a nomen unitatis in the meaning "individual (i.e., individually formed) saying, utterance" (of poetic or prophetic units in Gen 4:23; Deut 32:2; Isa 28:23; 32:9; otherwise, except for Isa 29:4, always of God's word, 19x in Psa 119 as a separate theological entity). The fem. individualizing pls. in Psa 12:7, "the (individual) speeches of Yahweh are (in each instance) pure speeches," conform to this usage; the masc. pl. of *ʾēmer* (the sg. is not attested at all, except for the textually uncertain passage Job 20:29) could form the collective pl. or the pl. of the totality (Nyberg 220; always with gen. or suf., except for Prov 19:7 and 22:21b; the meaning "sayings" is not "individual sayings" but "complete sayings" in all passages, even in Num 24:4, 16; Josh 24:27 "all"; Psa 107:11; Job 6:10, where "words of God" are discussed).*

4. That God speaks is thoroughly obvious to the OT authors; when he keeps quiet, he is disturbed. This is not the place to go into the special problem of the speech and the word of God in the OT (cf. O. Procksch, *TDNT* 4:69f., 91–100; W. Zimmerli, *RGG* 6:1809–12; → *dābār* IV). Nevertheless, a few fixed formulae that discuss God's speech, esp. in the prophetic literature, must be noted.

The usually narrative *wayyōʾmer yhwh*/*ʾᵉlōhîm* "then Yahweh/God said" is very common; it occasionally acquires a somewhat more pregnant sense (e.g., Gen 1; cf. W. H. Schmidt, *Die Schöpfungsgeschichte der Priesterschrift* [1964], 169–77; Westermann, *Gen*, CC, 1:110f.). Particularly significant is the no less frequent formula *kōh ʾāmar yhwh* "thus says Yahweh" (on the translation of the pf., see K. Koch, *Growth of the Biblical Tradition* [1969], 190; see above 3a), the common introduction of the prophetic Yahweh saying. Independently from one another, L. Köhler (*Deuterojesaja stilkritisch untersucht* [1923], 102–5; id., *Kleine Lichter* [1945], 11–17) and J. Lindblom (*Die literarische Gattung der prophetischen Literatur* [1924], 106f.) have recognized the genre introduced with this expression as messenger speech, which has profane precursors. Following them, others have named the expression the "messenger formula" (e.g., H. Wildberger, *Jahwewort und prophetische Rede bei Jeremia* [1942], 46ff.; Westermann, *BFPS* 98ff.). The formula "thus says *X*" finds nontheological usage in Gen 32:4–6; similarly in Babylon and in the Amarna correspondence (cf. Köhler, op. cit.; on pars. from Mari, see M. Noth, "History and Word of God in the OT," *Laws in the Pentateuch and Other Studies* [1966], 179–93). A third formula, simple *ʾāmar yhwh* "says Yahweh," appears rather frequently as an appendix to a messenger saying, occasionally even inserted into it (similar to → *nᵉʾum yhwh;* on the relationship of *(kōh) ʾāmar yhwh* and *nᵉʾum yhwh*, see F. Baumgärtel, *ZAW* 73 [1961]: 278, 284ff.).

These examples make it clear that even the most everyday words could become characteristic of particular literary genres. *dbr* pi. (→ *dābār* IV/1) and more specialized verbs such as → *ṣwh* pi. "to command" are more likely than *ʾmr* to be used to describe a more specific divine discourse in the sense of a command or promise.

5. The usage of *ʾmr* at Qumran corresponds to that in the OT (incl. the usage of *lēʾmōr*). The verb acquires a fixed specialized meaning in 1QpHab and similar commentaries, where the words of Scripture are introduced with *ʾšr ʾmr* "when it says" (cf. K. Elliger, *Studien zum Habakuk-Kommentar vom Toten Meer* [1953], 124f.; E. Osswald, *ZAW* 68 [1956]: 245).

The LXX's use of over 40 different Gk. equivalents to the verb reflects the unspecific nature of *ʾmr*, although *eipein* and *legein* predominate in numbers of occurrences (the distinction of *ʾmr* = *legein* "to say, speak" from *dbr* pi. = *lalein* "to discourse" is maintained with great consistency).

The NT conforms to the OT usage, esp. in the narrative portions of the Gospels. The central meaning of the *logos* in individual NT writings is, at least linguistically, independent of the usage of *ʾmr* in the OT (cf. O. Procksch and G. Kittel, "λέγω," *TDNT* 4:91–143).

H. H. Schmid

אֱנוֹשׁ ʾᵉnôš **person** → אָדָם ʾādām

אֲנִי ʾᵃnî **I**

S 589; BDB 58b; *HALOT* 1:71a; *TWOT* 129; *NIDOTTE* 638

---

1. Sem. languages have a short and a long form for the independent 1st sg. per. pron. An element *-k*, which distinguishes itself in NWSem. from ESem. by means of the final vowel (Akk. *anāku*, Ug. *ank*, Can. glosses in EA

287:66, 69 *a-nu-ki*, Phoen.-Pun. and Old Aram. *ʾnk* and *ʾnky*, Hebr. *ʾānōkî*), is appended in E. and NWSem. to a common Sem. **ʾanā*. Quality and quantity of the final vowel of the short form are not uniform (on Old Bab. *ana* cf. Moscati, *Intro.* 103; *CAD* A/II:110f.; Ug. *an*, Phoen. *ʾn*, Hebr. *ʾᵃnî*, Aram. *ʾᵃnâ*, Arab. *ʾanā*, Eth. *ʾana*).

NWSem. languages (Ug., Phoen.-Pun., and Hebr.) use both the short and the long forms. In Ug. the long form predominates (approximately 5 to 1), appearing in poetic and particularly in prose texts. To date, the short form has been identified only in poetic texts. The short form and the more forceful long form could stand side by side (*KTU* 1.4.IV.59f.). In Phoen.-Pun. the short form is late and infrequent (Friedrich 111; *DISO* 19). In Hebr. the use of the long form has receded, probably under Aram. influence (cf. Wagner 130; see 2). In postbibl. Middle Hebr. the long form continues to appear only in bibl. citations.

2. *ʾānōkî* occurs 358x in the OT (63x bound to *wᵉ*-), and *ʾᵃnî* occurs 870x (177x with *wᵉ*-).

	ʾānōkî	*ʾᵃnî*	total
Gen	56	41	97
Exod	21	39	60
Lev	–	67	67
Num	7	21	28
Deut	56	9	65
Josh	9	4	13
Judg	17	12	29
1 Sam	26	20	46
2 Sam	24	30	54
1 Kgs	7	30	37
2 Kgs	2	16	18
Isa	26	79	105
Jer	37	54	91
Ezek	1	169	170
Hos	11	12	23
Joel	–	4	4
Amos	10	1	11
Obad	–	–	–
Jonah	2	5	7
Mic	1	2	3
Nah	–	–	–
Hab	–	1	1
Zeph	–	2	2
Hag	–	4	4
Zech	5	11	16
Mal	1	8	9
Psa	13	70	83
Job	14	29	43
Prov	2	7	9
Ruth	7	2	9
Song Sol	–	12	12
Eccl	–	29	29
Lam	–	4	4
Esth	–	6	6
Dan	1	23	24

	ʾānōkî	*ʾanî*	total
Ezra	–	2	2
Neh	1	15	16
1 Chron	1	12	13
2 Chron	–	18	18
OT	358	870	1,228

With the exception of Obad and Nah, which have no instances of the independent sg. per. pron., the short form is represented in all OT books. The long form does not occur in Lev, Joel, Hab, Zeph, Hag, Song Sol, Eccl, Lam, Esth, Ezra, 2 Chron, and becomes less prominent in other late books; it predominates over the short form only in Gen, Deut, Josh, Judg, 1 Sam, Amos, and Ruth. The short form is esp. frequent in P, Ezek (long form only in Ezek 36:28), and Deutero-Isa (55:24), as well as in Trito-Isa (15:2). In Gen the ratio of the long to the short form is 39 to 19 in J, 16 to 13 in E, and 1 to 8 in P (source analysis following M. Noth, *History of Pentateuchal Traditions* [1972], 28ff.); cf. *HAL* 70a, which cites older literature on the statistics.

Short form and long form could follow one another (Exod 7:17; 2 Sam 3:13; Job 33:9); the sequence can also be reversed, however (Isa 45:12; Jonah 1:9).

3. The independent 1st sg. per. pron. allows the speaker to inject himself/herself emphatically into the discussion and to represent his/her concerns forcefully. This function of the personal pron. has been almost entirely lost in late texts (Eccl 2:11–13, 15).

The speaker is introduced by name (Gen 27:19; 45:3; Ruth 3:9), by title or profession (Gen 41:44; 1 Kgs 13:18), through reference to heritage or membership (Gen 24:24, 34; 1 Sam 30:13), by origin (2 Sam 1:8; Jonah 1:9), or by legal status (Gen 23:4; 2 Sam 14:5; Amos 7:14). The answer to the question concerning identity is "(it is) I!" (= yes!) (2 Sam 2:20; 20:17; 1 Kgs 18:8). The speaker reports his/her status and condition (1 Sam 1:15; Psa 109:22; 119:141; Job 9:21). To superiors one describes oneself as "slave" (2 Sam 15:34; also used in diplomatic intercourse in cases of political dependence: 2 Kgs 16:7; cf. further L. Köhler, *ZAW* 40 [1922]: 43–45; Lande 30, 68ff.; H. Grapow, *Wie die alten Ägypter sich anredeten* [1960^2], 179–85). Interrogative exclamations express powerlessness, astonishment, and indignation (Gen 4:9; 30:2; 1 Sam 1:8; 2 Sam 3:8), as well as the speaker's self-denigration and humble submission (Exod 3:11; 1 Sam 18:18; 2 Sam 7:18). Uses in the context of the oath (*ḥay ʾānî*, Num 14:21, 28 and a further 20x; *ḥay ʾānōkî*, Deut 32:40, the only passage with the long form; → *ḥyh* 3c) and the statement of one's age (Deut 31:2; Josh 14:7; 2 Sam 19:36) are formulaic. One can identify oneself emphatically with another individual or with a group (Gen 31:44; Judg 7:18; 1 Sam 20:23), or distance oneself from one's surroundings or even oppose them (Job 32:6). The per. pron. bound to *w*^{e}- is often used in contrasts (Gen 27:11; Exod 2:9; Josh 24:15; 1 Sam 17:45; 1 Kgs 12:11; Jer 36:18).

Whether one lends one's words special force by means of repeated usage of the independent 1st sg. per. pron. depends on the concerns addressed, the degree of personal involvement, and the circumstances of the conversation (*ʾānōkî* with the pf.: Josh 7:20; 1 Sam 22:22; with the impf.: Gen 38:17; 1 Kgs

2:18). *kî* often introduces the per. pron. in subordinate clauses, as well as in relative clauses, frequently following a ptcp., in which case no particular force is intended. The preceding particles *gam* (Gen 21:26; 2 Kgs 2:3; Psa 71:22; Prov 1:26) and *ʾap*, preferred in later texts (Gen 40:16; Job 32:10, 17), can heighten the emphasis.

The impv. of → *rʾh* "to see" (2 Sam 7:2), replaced later by the demonstrative particle → *hinnēh* "behold, see," directs the attention of the addressee in a special way to the speaker and his/her statement (Judg 7:17; cf. Gen 25:22).

4. First-per. statements of God appear primarily in the divine speeches of the patriarchal narratives, the legal portions of the Pentateuch, and the prophetic speeches. In post-exilic texts 1st per. statements of God become noticeably less prominent; often they are only citations of older formulae (Hag 1:13; 2:4). The "interpreting angel" replaces God (Zech 1:9; Dan 10:11ff.).

The independent 1st sg. per. pron. is used no differently in the divine speeches than in the human speeches. The presentation formula can begin divine speech that makes statements concerning God's being and his behavior toward individuals or a community. The per. pron. bound to *wᵉ-* is used in contrasts of divine and human behavior and activity (Exod 4:15; 2 Sam 12:12; Isa 65:24; Hos 7:13; Jonah 4:10f.). Subordinate clauses and relative clauses with ptcps. and per. prons. introduced by *kî* appear often in divine speeches. *gam* (Gen 20:6; Lev 26:24; Ezek 8:18) and *ʾap* (Lev 26:16; Psa 89:28) heighten the emphasis. *hinnēh* (Gen 28:15; Exod 4:23; 1 Sam 3:11; Jer 6:19; Ezek 37:5, 12, 19, 21; Amos 2:13) and the more forceful *hinᵉnî* (Gen 6:17; Ezek 5:8; 6:3; 34:11, 20) usually occur in reference to a new undertaking of God.

The self-presentation formula reveals God's name in association with his historical activity. God thus places the addressee under obligation. The revelation of the divine name enables the person to call on God (foundational: W. Zimmerli, "I Am Yahweh," *I Am Yahweh* [1982], 1–28; also K. Elliger, "Ich bin der Herr—euer Gott," FS Heim 9–34 = *KS* [1966], 211–31; R. Rendtorff, "Concept of Revelation in Ancient Israel," in *Revelation as History* [1968], 23–53). The self-presentation formula originates in polytheism and is broadly distributed in the ancient Near East (cf. A. Poebel, *Das appositionell bestimmte Pronomen der 1.Pers. Sg. in den westsemitischen Inschriften und im AT* [1932]). The deity's reference to his own deeds and characteristics lends the self-presentation formula the character of self-praise (in the OT in Deutero-Isa: Isa 44:24; 45:7; also in judgment and disputation speeches; cf. Westermann, *Isa 40–66*, OTL, 154–62; H.-M. Dion, "Le genre littéraire sumérien de l''hymne à soi-même' et quelques passages du Deutéro-Isaïe," *RB* 74 [1957]: 215–34).

The OT self-presentation formula is an independent nom. phrase, both in the short form "I am Yahweh" and in the more complete form "I am Yahweh, your God." Yahweh does not appear as a stranger, but refers, in the context of the announcement of his name, to already well-known things and earlier events (Gen 15:7; 26:24; 28:13; 31:13; Exod 3:6; also Hos 12:10; 13:4). The appended promise speech places the future activity of God in this historical context. The self-presentation formula is not likely to have been originally associated with the proclamation of the law. The short form here, as in the exilic prophets, is a pregnant summary of the divine claim to power that derives from God's self-manifestation in Israel's history (on P cf. Lev 18–19 passim; on Deutero-Isa cf. Isa 45:21; 43:11; 45:22; 48:12).

In association with the verb *ydᶜ*, the self-presentation formula becomes the recognition formula ("know that I am Yahweh!"). Knowledge of Yahweh takes place in the context of his historical self-manifestation (cf. the exodus tradition). The association of the recognition formula with impending events is a characteristic of exilic prophecy (in Ezek predominantly in the context of judgment sayings; in Deutero-Isa in conjunction with grant and call oracles: Isa 49:23, 26; 45:2f., 5f., 7).

5. On Qumran see S. Mowinckel, "Jeg'et i Qumransalmene," *NTT* 62 (1961): 28–46; on the NT see esp. E. Stauffer, "ἐγώ," *TDNT* 2:343–62; also E. Schweizer, *Ego eimi* (1965²), 12ff.; on the milieu: E. Norden, *Agnostos theos* (1960 = 1913), 177ff.

K. Günther

אסף *ᵓsp* **to collect** → קבץ *qbṣ*

אַף *ᵓap* anger

S 639; BDB 60a; *HALOT* 1:76b; *TDOT* 1:348–60; *TWOT* 133a; *NIDOTTE* 678

---

1. The root *ᵓnp* is common Sem. The subst. **ᵓanp-* (> **ᵓapp-*) "nose" derives from it (Berg., *Intro.* 212; P. Fronzaroli, *AANLR* 8/19 [1964]: 269). In turn, the subst. was the occasion for the formation of the denominative verb *ᵓnp* in some Sem. languages.

Except in SSem., the subst., with assimilation of the middle radical and frequently in the dual, occurs regularly in all Sem. dialects in the meaning "nose" (Akk. *appu*, *AHw* 60; *CAD* A/II:184–89; Ug. *ap*, *WUS* no. 344; *UT* no. 264; on the Old Aram., cf. *DISO* 21; Imp. Aram. and Bibl. Aram. *ᵓanpôhî* "his face," Dan 2:46; 3:19, once again written with *n*). It is construed as masc. (K. Albrecht, *ZAW* 18 [1896]: 78).

By contrast, the verb *ᵓnp* "to snort (in anger)," which may be denominative (Mandl. 131; cautiously, O. Grether, *TDNT* 5:392 nn.56f.), is attested only in Hebr. (qal and hitp.), Moab. (*KAI* no. 181.5), Akk. (*AHw* 320a), and Arab. (in the meaning "to disdain, scorn," Wehr 31).

PNs formed on this root are *ᵓappayim* (1 Chron 2:30f.; Nöldeke *BS* 102: "little nose"; *IP* 227: "with a large nose") and *ḥᵃrûmap* (Neh 3:10; *IP* 227: "with a cleft nose").

ᵓᵃnāpâ (Lev 11:19; Deut 14:18), an unclean species of bird with many varieties (unidentified; cf. *HAL* 70b; *IDB* 2:596; *BHH* 3:1578; G. R. Driver, *PEQ* 87 [1955]: 17f.), may be associated with the same root.

2. The verb ʾnp occurs 14x in the OT, 8x in the qal, 6x in the hitp. (the latter always in the Dtn-Dtr linguistic domain).

The use of the word ʾ*ap* is widely attested. The sg. occurs 235x in the OT (excl. Hab 2:15, where the conjunction ʾ*ap* may be attested), 25x in the meaning "nose," 42x with reference to human, and 168x with reference to divine anger.

The dual ʾ*appayim* is attested 42x (1 Sam 1:5 drops out of this group through emendation). The two specimens from the Aram. portions of the OT should also be understood as duals ("countenance"; F. Schulthess, *ZAW* 22 [1902]: 164).

The following list catalogs occurrences of the verb (qal, hitp.), the sg. ʾ*ap* (HA = human anger, DA = divine anger), and the dual ʾ*appayim:*

	qal	hitp.	nose	HA	DA	dual
Gen	–	–	1	6	–	6
Exod	–	–	–	3	5	2
Num	–	–	1	2	10	2
Deut	–	4	1	–	12	–
Josh	–	–	–	–	3	–
Judg	–	–	–	2	5	–
1 Sam	–	–	–	4	1	6
2 Sam	–	–	2	1	2	4
1 Kgs	1	1	–	–	–	2
2 Kgs	–	1	1	–	4	–
Isa	1	–	3	2	20	1
Jer	–	–	–	–	24	–
Ezek	–	–	3	1	11	–
Hos	–	–	–	–	4	–
Joel	–	–	–	–	–	1
Amos	–	–	1	1	–	–
Jonah	–	–	–	–	1	1
Mic	–	–	–	–	2	–
Nah	–	–	–	–	1	1
Hab	–	–	–	–	2	–
Zeph	–	–	–	–	4	–
Zech	–	–	–	–	1	–
Psa	4	–	4	4	24	3
Job	–	–	4	7	11	–
Prov	–	–	2	7	1	6
Song Sol	–	–	2	–	–	–
Lam	–	–	–	–	10	1
Dan	–	–	–	–	1	1
Ezra	1	–	–	–	2	–
Neh	–	–	–	–	–	2
1 Chron	–	–	–	–	1	1
2 Chron	1	–	–	2	6	2
Hebr. OT	8	6	25	42	168	42

3. (a) The starting point is the concrete meaning of the subst. as a designation of the body part "nose." The dual form *ʾappayim* means "the two sides of the nose, the two nostrils" through which the breath of life enters and exits (Gen 2:7; 7:22); this concrete meaning is still fundamental even in Exod 15:8 and Lam 4:20 (perhaps also in *KAI* no. 224.2; cf. *KAI* 2:266; Fitzmyer, *Sef.* 104).

This is also true in Akk., where numerous occurrences demonstrate the original usage of the word to indicate the body part: piercing of the nose, amputation of the nose, etc. (*AHw* 60; *CAD* A/II:184–89).

As a pars pro toto, the dual form indicates the whole countenance (Gen 3:19; Aram. Dan 3:19) and found a firm place in the idiom "to fall on one's face in greeting" (Gen 42:6; 48:12; 1 Sam 20:41; 24:9; 25:41; 28:14; 2 Sam 14:4, 33; 18:28; 24:20 = 1 Chron 21:21; 1 Kgs 1:23, 31; Isa 49:23; cf. Aram. Dan 2:46; before divine messengers, Gen 19:1; Num 22:31; in prayer, Neh 8:6; 2 Chron 7:3; 20:18; cf. also 1 Sam 25:23 *leʾappê* "before"); cf. Akk. *appa labānu* "to prostrate oneself humbly" (*AHw* 522).

The dual is used fig. in the phrase *ʾerek ʾappayim* "patient" to indicate human (Prov 14:29; 15:18; 16:32; *ʾōrek ʾappayim* "patience" 25:15) and divine patience (Exod 34:6; Num 14:18; Jonah 4:2; Nah 1:3; Psa 86:15; 103:8; 145:8; Neh 9:17), and in the phrase *qeṣar-ʾappayim* to indicate impatience (Prov 14:17; cf. 14:29 with *rûaḥ*).

The fig. meaning "anger" occurs in only two (disputed) passages: Prov 30:33b and Dan 11:20 (cf. comms.).

(b) The sg. *ʾap* also indicates the body part, first of all.

Of humans: Num 11:20; Ezek 23:25; Amos 4:10; Prov 30:33a; Song Sol 7:5; as the seat of breath: Isa 2:22; Job 27:3; Song Sol 7:9; rings as ornamentation: Gen 24:47; Isa 3:21; Ezek 16:12; for chastisement: 2 Kgs 19:28 = Isa 37:29; of animals: Job 40:24, 26; Prov 11:22. Cf. also the somewhat more fig. usage *śîm ʾap* "to be determined" (Job 36:13; *HAL* 74b) and *gōbah ʾap* "snobbery" (Psa 10:4). Of gods: Psa 115:6; of God: see 4a.

As in the other Sem. languages, e.g., Akk. *appu* "nose," it is also a term for the highest point or the peak of an object, etc. (*AHw* 60); Ug. *ap zd* "nipple," *ap lb* "breast" (*WUS* no. 344), *ap ṯġr* "gateway" (*UT* no. 264); in NWSem. also "surface" (*KAI* no. 222A.28; no. 228A.14; cf. Fitzmyer, *Sef.* 15 "face"); Arab. *ʾanf* "nose; projection, spur (of a mountain)" (Wehr 31).

(c) Much more frequently *ʾap* indicates "anger," with an easily understood development of meaning from "nose" to the gesture of "snorting" (in anger), which manifests itself in this body part (cf. Dhorme 80f.; Ug.: *WUS* no. 345; ? Aram. Cowley, no. 37.8; cf. *DISO* 21). In almost half the passages that treat human wrath, *ʾap* is associated with the verb → *ḥrh* "to become inflamed" (or the subst. *ḥorî*; primarily in narrative literature: Gen 30:2; 39:19; 44:18; Exod 11:8; Num 22:27; 24:10; Judg 9:30; 14:19; 1 Sam 11:6; 17:28; 20:30, 34; 2 Sam 12:5; Isa 7:4; Psa 124:3; Job 32:2bis, 3, 5; 2 Chron 25:10bis). A holy wrath seizes a person when the Spirit of Yahweh comes over him (Judg 14:19; 1 Sam 11:6). Wrath can turn away (*šûb* Gen 27:45); this is esp. the merit of discerning patterns of behavior (Prov 29:8).

4. (a) That the gods' noses (Psa 115:6), indeed even Yahweh's (Deut 33:10; 2 Sam 22:9, 16 = Psa 18:9, 16; on Ezek 8:17 txt? cf. Zimmerli, *Ezek*, Herm, 1:222, 244f.; the dual in Exod 15:8) can also be mentioned reflects the OT's anthropomorphic conceptualization.

(b) Indeed, most instances of *ʾap* refer to divine anger (168x). All cases of the verb *ʾnp* qal/hitp. describe divine anger, as does the statement in the Mesha inscription (*KAI* no. 181.5; *DISO* 19; *ANET* 320b): the god Chemosh is angy with his people.

The motivation for God's reaction may indeed be understood in terms of similar human patterns of behavior but may not be derived from them; God responds to human deeds that violate his being and commandments (on the ethical motivation, see Vriezen, *Theol.* 303–9). It may not be derived because, according to the OT perspective, divine activity answers to no tribunal, a clear expression that equal partners do not confront one another here, but that the creator confronts his creation, the lawgiver the one obligated to obey, the lord his subjects. The old pentateuchal sources already express the fact that the people can be the object of divine anger (Num 11:1, 10, 33 [J]; Exod 32:10–12, 22 [E]), but the 8th- (Hos 8:5; Isa 5:25, etc.) and 7th-cent. prophets particularly emphasize it. Esp. Jeremiah (all 24 passages exclusively of divine anger, often with other expressions, e.g., 21:5) and after him Ezekiel (11x, except for 7:3 and 43:8, always par. to → *ḥēmâ;* 25:14 and 38:18 are not directed at Israel) speak in oppressive frequency of God's anger.

In addition, it remains palpable throughout the OT that divine anger is, in the final analysis, an unexplainable reaction of a divine Lord, conceived of as a person, who defies clear conceptual definition because this Lord has revealed himself of his own free will to his people in a humanly inconceivable manner. Thus divine anger appears as a necessary correlation to divine love seeking the deliverance of his people (cf. e.g., Exod 4:14; also Psa 30:6).

For the most important expressions associated with or par. to *ʾap*, cf. the articles treating → *ḥrh (ḥārôn)*, → *ḥēmâ*, → *ʿebrâ*, → *qṣp*, → *qnʾ*, also → *šûb* (qal/hi.); further, *zaʿam* "wrath, curse" (Isa 10:5, 25; 30:27, etc.), → *zaʿap* "rage" (Isa 30:30), Aram. *rᵉgaz* "rage" (Dan 3:13).

For orienting overviews and bibliogs. on the theme "God's wrath" cf. Eichrodt 1:258–69; Jacob 114–17; O. Grether and J. Fichtner, "ὀργή," *TDNT* 5:392–412; *RGG* 6:1929–32; *IDB* 4:903–8; *BHH* 3:2246–48; further e.g., R. V. Tasker, *Biblical Doctrine of the Wrath of God* (1951); J. Gray, "Wrath of God in Canaanite and Hebrew Literature," *Journal of the Manchester University Egyptian and Oriental Society* (1947–53): 9–19; H. Ringgren, "Einige Schilderungen des göttlichen Zorns," FS Weiser 107–13.

5. The ambivalent essential characteristics anger and love are also fruitful components for the NT. Cf. F. Büchsel, "θυμός," *TDNT* 3:167–72; G. Stählin, "ὀργή," *TDNT* 5:419–47.

G. Sauer

אֵפֶר ʾēper **dust** → עָפָר ʿāpār

אֹרַח ʾōraḥ **way** → דֶּרֶךְ *derek*

אֲרִי ʾᵃrî lion

S 738; BDB 71b; *HALOT* 1:87a; *TDOT* 1:374–88; *TWOT* 158a; *NIDOTTE* 787

1. In addition to *ʾᵃrî*, Hebr. has *ʾaryēh*, apparently an early Aram. loanword (cf. Wagner no. 28); the OT attests both forms from the very earliest layers of material. In the meaning "lion," the word is otherwise known only in Aram. (*KAI* no. 223A.9; Fitzmyer, *Sef.* 80f., 86; Aḥ. 88f., 110, 117 = *ANET* 428b, 429a; Bibl. Aram. and later: KBL 1053f.; *DISO* 24).

Scholars have conjectured etymological relationships to a common Sem. word for "(large, wild, numinous) animal" (Berg., *Intro.* 210; E. Ullendorff, *VT* 6 [1956]: 192f.; Wagner no. 28; P. Fronzaroli, *AANLR* 8/23 [1968]: 280, 282, 292, 300f.), which has become specialized in individual languages to refer to various animals (Eth. *ʾarwē* still "beast," Dillmann 743; Akk. *a/erû* "eagle," W. von Soden, *AfO* 18 [1957/58]: 393; *AHw* 247; in addition, however, *arwûm* "gazelle," *AHw* 73; Arab. *ʾarwīyat* "ibexes," etc.; cf. *HAL* 84b, 85a). According to L. Köhler (*ZDPV* 62 [1939]: 121–24), the origin of the word, like the animal so designated, should be sought in the Hamitic realm (Eg. *rw*, etc.); J. J. Glück's suggestion (*ZAW* 81 [1969]: 232–35) is purely conjectural.

2. The sg. *ʾᵃrî* occurs 17x (incl. 2 Sam 23:20 Q; Lam 3:10 Q), *ʾaryēh* 45x (excl. 2 Sam 23:20 K; Lam 3:10 K), the pl. *ʾᵃrāyîm* 1x (1 Kgs 10:20; cf. v 19), *ʾᵃrāyôt* 17x; the distribution of the total of 80 occurrences exhibits no peculiarities (1 Kgs 13x, Jer 8x, Isa 7x, Psa 6x).

In addition, Bibl. Aram. *ʾaryēh* occurs 1x (Dan 7:4) and the pl. det. *ʾaryāwātāʾ* 9x (Dan 6:8–28).

3. (a) *ʾᵃrî* indicates the grown (male or female) lion.

The synonyms *lābîʾ* and *layiš* occur only in poetical texts.

lābîʾ occurs 11x in the OT, in addition to the fem. *lᵉbîyâ* 1x and the pls. *lᵉbāʾîm* or *lᵉbāʾôt* 1x each. Cf. Akk. *lābu/labbu* (*AHw* 526); Ug. *lbu*, also in PNs (*WUS* no. 1435; *UT* no. 1347; Gröndahl 154; cf. Huffmon 225); Phoen., among other usages, in PNs *ʿbdlbʾt* (*KAI* no. 21; cf. 2:29); Aram., Aḥ. 117 (Cowley 239); Arab. *lab(u)ʾat* (Wehr 854), etc. There may also be connections with the Gk. *leōn* (KBL 472a; *AHw* 526).

layiš occurs 3x (Isa 30:6; Job 4:11; Prov 30:30) and has counterparts in Akk. *nēšu* (*AHw* 783a), Jew. Aram. *lêtāʾ* (Dalman 217b), and Arab. *layṯ* (Wehr 886).

Other designations for the lion are qualifiers: *gûr* means the suckling lion cub (Gen 49:9; Deut 33:22; Ezek 19:2f., 5; Nah 2:12; also used in Lam 4:3 of the jackal; *gôr* Jer 51:38 and Nah 2:13; cf. *HAL* 177b on the Sem. counterparts), *šaḥal* the weaned youngster (Hos 5:14; 13:7; Psa 91:13; Job 4:10; 10:16; 28:8; Prov 26:13; see Köhler, op. cit.; cf. also S. Mowinckel, FS Driver 95–104), *kᵉpîr* (31x), the young lion already hunting independently (cf. *BS* 70n.10; J. Blau *VT* 5 [1955]: 342). The symbolic value of these expressions is the same; in poetic texts two designations for lion are generally par.

The lion is feared as a predator that threatens people and animals (Amos 3:12; 5:19; Prov 22:13; 26:13; mentioned together with other predators such as the bear and the wolf in 1 Sam 17:34ff.; Jer 5:6; Prov 28:15). It inhabits primarily the Jordan rift (Jer 49:19 = 50:44) and mountainous regions (Song Sol 4:8).

(b) The lion frequently appears in comparisons. Points of comparison are its strength (Judg 14:18; 2 Sam 1:23; Prov 30:30), its ferocity (Gen 49:9; Num 23:24; Isa 5:29; Nah 2:13; Psa 104:21), and its treacherous slyness (Psa 10:9; 17:12).

Because it is the strongest animal, the lion is the symbol of power and courage (2 Sam 17:10; 23:20 = 1 Chron 11:22; 1 Chron 12:9). Its place in the language of blessing should be understood from this perspective: the Balaam oracles describe Israel as a lion (Num 23:24; 24:9); the blessings of Jacob and Moses describe Judah, Gad, and Dan similarly (Gen 49:9; Deut 33:20, 22; alongside *ʾᵃrî* stand *lābîʾ* and *gûr*). Later, the description of Israel as a lion is taken up in other speech forms (Ezek 19:1–9; Mic 5:7).

The ferocity of the lion gives occasion for comparison with the behavior of despotic rulers in prophetic (Ezek 22:25; Zeph 3:3) and wisdom (Prov 28:15; cf. 20:2) texts.

At the same time, the lion, on account of its dangerousness and treachery, is a favorite image for the "enemy" in individual laments (Isa 38:13; Psa 7:3; 10:9; 17:12; 22:14, 17?, 22; Lam 3:10; cf. Jer 12:8; in Psa 35:17 and 58:7 *kᵉpîr*). Prophecy compares threatening powers in the politico-historical sphere, primarily the foreign nations threatening Israel, to the lion (Isa 5:29; 15:9; Jer 2:30; 4:7; 5:6; cf. also Dan 7:4); the image lives on as a description of danger in post-exilic prophecy as well (Joel 1:6). 1 Kgs 13:24ff. and 2 Kgs 17:25f. employ this motif in a popular fashion.

It is not only in Israel that the lion indicates the power that threatens people; cf. e.g., the mention of the lion in a curse formula *KAI* 223A.9 (D. R. Hillers, *Treaty-Curses and the OT Prophets* [1964], 54–56).

Descriptions of the time of salvation speak of the fact that the lion will no longer exist (Isa 35:9) or that it will become a docile animal (Isa 11:6f.; 65:25).

Lion figures are essential in the architectural symbolism of temple and palace (alongside bulls, birdlike creatures, and palms; 1 Kgs 7:29, 36; 10:19f. = 2 Chron 9:18f.).

These animals had religious significance in Canaanite religion. On the one hand, one may think of gods such as El, Baal, and the mother goddess with their holy animals, the bull and the lion; on the other hand, such lions are also imitations of tamed lions with guard functions (cf. B. Brentjes, *WZ Halle-Wittenberg* 11 [1962]: 595ff.).

On the significance of the lion in Egypt, cf. C. de Wit, *Le rôle et le sens du lion dans l'Egypte ancienne* (1951).

The lion figures of Ezekiel's throne-chariot vision are inspired by the images of the temple lions (Ezek 1:10; 10:14).

4. Yahweh's activity is frequently compared with the lion's behavior. As a rule, the image encompasses the frightening and threatening elements of his coming to judge (Jer 50:44 = 49:19; Hos 5:14; 13:7, 8 txt?; Job 10:16; but cf. Fohrer, KAT 16, 200; Lam 3:10; negated in Hos 11:10, provided that v 9 goes with this, cf. Rudolph, KAT 13/1, 213). This imagery is consonant with the fact that portrayals of theophanies use the verb *šʾg*, which probably originally referred only to the roaring of the lion (of thunder in Job 37:4), 5x for the terrifying speech of Yahweh (Jer 25:30 3x; Amos 1:2; Joel 4:16; always with *ntn qôl* "to raise the voice," of the lion Jer 2:15; Amos 3:4; H. Gressmann, FS Baudissin 198f., cites an Eg. par.).

Yet this comparison can also emphasize Yahweh's strength and invincibility in the context of his saving intervention in the history of his people (Isa 31:4; Hos 11:10, which is not Hoseanic; cf. Wolff, *Hos*, Herm, 195, 203); correspondingly, *šʾg* also expresses God's might in these contexts (Hos 11:10[bis]).

Amos compares Yahweh's speech to his prophet with the lion's roar (Amos 3:4, 8). Just as the roar of the lion is a dramatic indication that it has taken prey, so the preaching of the prophet is a consequence of the fact that Yahweh has constrained him.

The OT can use the image of the lion in reference to Yahweh without embarrassment because Israel had no polemic against a lion cult (by contrast, the bull may not be associated with Yahweh); cf. J. Hempel, *ZAW* 42 (1924): 88–101 = *Apoxysmata* (1961), 14–26.

5. In the NT some reminiscences of the function of the lion in the OT are apparent; in particular, the antigod power, now Satan, is compared with the lion: 1 Pet 5:8, citing Psa 22:14; on other passages cf. W. Michaelis, "λέων," *TDNT* 4:251–53.

F. Stolz

אֶרֶץ ʾ*ereṣ* **earth, land**

S 776; BDB 75b; *HALOT* 1:90b; *TDOT* 1:388–405; *TWOT* 167; *NIDOTTE* 824

---

1. ʾ*ereṣ* "earth, land" (root with vocalized emphatic interdental; cf. Moscati, *Intro.* 28–30) is common Sem. (Berg., *Intro.* 214) and is attested in the following forms with an essentially constant meaning: ʾ*rṣ* Ug. (*UT* no. 376; *WUS* no. 420), Phoen., Pun., Moab. (*DISO* 25f.); *erṣetu* Akk., (with a fem.

ending; Old Akk. *arṣatum* in a PN; cf. *CAD* E:311a); *ʾrq* or later *ʾrʿ* Aram. *(DISO* 25f.; on the transition from *q* to *ʿ*, see W. Baumgartner, *ZAW* 45 [1927]: 100f. = *Zum AT und seiner Umwelt* [1959], 88; in Jer 10:11 *ʾarqāʾ* still stands beside *ʾarʿā); ʾrḍ* Arab. and Old SArab.; *ʾarḍ* Tigr. (in Eth. replaced otherwise by *medr*).

The noun consistently appears as a fem.; a reminiscence of the concept of mother earth may have been retained in this form (see 4a).

Job 34:13 and 37:12 (cf. perhaps Isa 8:23 as well) attest to the form *ʾārṣâ*, accented on the first syllable by the Masoretes as a locative, although no locative meaning is present. It is usually suggested, retaining the *-h*, to read *ʾarṣōh* (cf. *BHS* and comms.; cf. also the Mesha inscription, *KAI* no. 181.5–6 *bʾrṣh* "toward his land"; *ANET* 320b "at his land"; BL 252; Meyer 1:95). But one should not judge the variants noted in *BHS* as the older readings, nor is the suf. form in the context of Job 34:13, in particular, very sensible. Should one consider it a weakened acc. or locative ending (so GKC §90f; BL 528), or is it a by-form with an expressly fem. ending (cf. Akk. *erṣetu;* Aram. *ʾrqtʾ*/*ʾrṣtʾ*, KBL 1054b)?

Only Bibl. Aram. *ʾarʿî(t)* "what is beneath, ground" in Dan 6:25 can be noted as a derivative (BLA 197).

The PN *ʾarṣāʾ*, which occurs in 1 Kgs 16:9, has nothing to do with *ʾereṣ*, but, according to *IP* 230, is to be associated with Arab. *ʾaraḍat* "wood-worm" (contra Montgomery and Gehman, *Kings*, ICC, 289; J. Gray, *Kings*, OTL [1970²], 361).

2. *ʾereṣ* is the fourth most common subst. in the OT. The term occurs 2,504x in the Hebr. OT in a regular distribution, 22x in Aram. Only 77 of the Hebr. occurrences offer the pl., which is thoroughly understandable given the meaning of the term: the pl. makes sense only for a small part of the full range of the term's meaning.

The statistics for the individual books are: Gen 311x, Exod 136x, Lev 82x, Num 123x, Deut 197x, Josh 107x, Judg 60x, 1 Sam 52x, 2 Sam 40x, 1 Kgs 56x, 2 Kgs 71x, Isa 190x, Jer 271x, Ezek 198x, Hos 20x, Joel 12x, Amos 23x, Obad 1x, Jonah 2x, Mic 15x, Nah 3x, Hab 10x, Zeph 8x, Hag 5x, Zech 42x, Mal 2x, Psa 190x, Job 57x, Prov 21x, Ruth 4x, Song Sol 2x, Eccl 13x, Lam 11x, Esth 2x, Dan 20x, Ezra 13x, Neh 20x, 1 Chron 39x, 2 Chron 75x; Aram. *ʾᵃraq:* Jer 1x; *ʾᵃraʿ:* Jer 1x, Dan 19x, Ezra 1x; furthermore *ʾarʿî* 1x in Dan. Not included is the variant *ʾāreṣ* (Bombergiana) instead of *ṣedeq (BHS)* in Prov 8:16.*

3. (a) *ʾereṣ* indicates (1) cosmologically: the earth (in contrast to heaven) and the dry land (in contrast to the waters); see 3b; (2) physically: the ground on which one stands (3c); (3) geographically: individual regions and parcels of land (3d); (4) politically: some governed areas and countries (3e).

Which spheres of usage are primary and which secondary may not be deduced from the OT evidence; criteria for a development must be applied to the texts. On the entire problem, cf. L. Rost, "Die Bezeichnungen für Land und Volk im AT," FS Procksch 125–48 = *KC* 76–101.

The meaning "city" for *ʾereṣ* in Prov 29:4; 31:23; and Eccl 10:16 (LXX *polis*) has been suggested (cf. Dahood, *PNSP* 62f.; id., *Bib* 44 [1963]: 297f.; 47 [1966]: 280) with reference to (surely ambivalent) Phoen. pars. (*KAI* no. 14.16, 18 *ṣdn ʾrṣ ym*, "Sidon of the sea-land"; cf. *ANET* 662b: "Sidon-by-the-Sea"; Eissfeldt, *KS* [1963], 2:227ff.).

(b) In its most comprehensive meaning *ʾereṣ* indicates the earth that, together with heaven (→ *šāmayim*), constitutes the entire world, the cosmos. "Heaven and earth" is a common expression for "world" (Gen 1:1; 2:1, 4; 14:19, 22, etc.; cf. B. Hartmann, *Die nominalen Aufreihungen im AT* [1953], 60; in addition to the series noted there, numerous other occurrences appear in parallelism, in all at least 75 examples).

The sequence "heaven-earth," notable in the overwhelming majority of occurrences, still mirrors the mythical conception of the (primary) heavenly and the (secondary) earthly world. The sequence "earth-heaven" appears only either where movement from the earth to heaven is meant (Ezek 8:3; Zech 5:9; 1 Chron 21:16) or where an unequivocally geocentric worldview dominates (Gen 2:4b and Psa 148:13). The proposals of B. Hartmann ("Himmel und Erde im AT," *SThU* 30 [1960]: 221–24) must be modified accordingly. For the Mesopotamian pars., see A. Jeremias, *Handbuch der altorientalischen Geisteskultur* (1929^2), 127.

No proper, specific expression for "world" occurs in the OT; cf. further the paraphrase with → *kōl* "everything, the universe" in Isa 44:24; Jer 10:16; Psa 103:19. The infrequent word *ḥeled* "lifetime" (Psa 39:6; 89:48; Job 11:17; cf. Arab. *ḫalada* "eternal") acquires the meaning "world" in Psa 49:2 (the text of Psa 17:14 is uncertain) in a manner similar to postbibl. → *ʿôlām*, Gk. *aiōn* "aeon," and Ger. *Welt* (originally "era," in imitation of Lat. *saeculum;* cf. Kluge 853b).*

Alongside the bipartite worldview, a tripartite view also occurs, which arises ad hoc, for the most part, e.g., heaven-earth-sea (Exod 20:11; cf. Gen 1:10, 20, etc.), heaven-earth-water under the earth (Exod 20:4; Deut 5:8). A triad heaven-earth-netherworld (→ *ṣ^{e}ʾôl*) seems occasionally to be presupposed; cf. the description of the netherworld as *ʾereṣ taḥtît* or *taḥtîyôt* (Ezek 26:20; 31:14, 16, 18; cf. Zimmerli, *Ezek*, Herm, 2:32, 39) and the related expressions *taḥtît* or *taḥtîyôt (hā)ʾāreṣ* (Isa 44:23; Psa 63:10; 139:15), as well as Psa 115:15–17, among others.

In a few passages, the simple *ʾereṣ* also at least approaches the meaning "netherworld" (cf. Akk. *erṣetu, AHw* 245; *CAD* E:310f.; K. Tallqvist, *Sum.-akk. Namen der Totenwelt* [1934], 8ff.; *HAL* 88a: Exod 15:12; Jer 17:13; Jonah 2:7; Psa 22:30; 71:20; see further M. Dahood, *Bib* 40 [1959]: 164–66; 44 [1963]: 297).

If one conceptualizes the cosmos more precisely (esp. in later texts), one views the earth in dependence on ancient Near Eastern concepts (cf. Jeremias, op. cit. 117ff.) as having arisen through the division of the primal waters (→ *t^{e}hôm;* Gen 1; Prov 8:27–29) and as still resting upon columns in the water (1 Sam 2:8; Psa 24:2; 104:5f.; 136:6; cf. Gen 49:25; Exod 20:4; Deut 5:8; Psa 82:5; Isa 24:18; Jer 31:37; Mic 6:2, among others); the vault of heaven is anchored in the earth (Amos 9:6).

Job 26:7, which says that God spread the earth over the void, preserves another concept, according to which the earth is hung like a piece of cloth. According to Job 38:12f. the dawn grasps the borders of the earth and shakes the evildoers off it. The same concept occurs in the Akk. "Great Hymn to Šamaš" or "Hymn to the Sun-God" (I:22): "Thou (Šamaš) art holding the ends of the earth suspended from the midst of heaven" (*ANET* 387b; cf. *SAHG* 241; *BWL* 126f.).

The earth-water concept envisions the earth as a disk (Isa 40:22 *ḥûg hāʾāreṣ* "circle of the earth"; cf. Prov 8:27; Job 26:10 txt em; also Job 22:14), but the numerous passages that speak of the (four) borders (the cloth image), ends, corners, or points belong to the other conceptual context: *kanpôt hāʾāreṣ* (Isa 11:12; Ezek 7:2; Job 37:3; 38:13; cf. Isa 24:16), *ʾapsê (hā)ʾāreṣ* (Deut 33:17; 1 Sam 2:10; Isa 45:22; 52:10; Jer 16:19; Mic 5:3; Zech 9:10; Psa 2:8; 22:28; 59:14; 67:8; 72:8; 98:3; Prov 30:4), *qᵉṣê hāʾāreṣ* (Deut 13:8; 28:49, 64; Isa 5:26; 42:10; 43:6; 48:20; 49:6; 62:11; Jer 10:13; 12:12; 25:31, 33; 51:16; Psa 46:10; 61:3; 135:7; Prov 17:24), *qᵉṣôt hāʾāreṣ* (Isa 40:28; 41:5, 9; Job 28:24), *qaṣwê ʾereṣ* (Isa 26:15; Psa 48:11; 65:6). On analogous conceptualizations in Mesopotamia, cf. Jeremias, op. cit. 142–48. The two concepts stand side by side without tension in the OT; elements with origins in either of the two notions could—both in Mesopotamia and in Israel—be combined without difficulty (cf. e.g., Job 38:4–13, etc.).

Regardless of whether one speaks of the earth as a disk or of the "ends" of the earth, the question of the center of the earth arises. Ezek 38:12 mentions the *ṭabbûr* "navel" of the world (cf. 5:5 and Judg 9:37; see *HAL* 352b and Zimmerli, *Ezek*, Herm, 2:311, with references to ancient Near Eastern and Gk. pars.).

To be sure, the OT is not concerned with the earth as part of the cosmos so much as with that which fills the earth (*ʾereṣ ûmᵉlōʾāh*, Deut 33:16; Isa 34:1; Jer 8:16, etc.), its inhabitants (Isa 24:1, 5f., 17; Jer 25:29f.; Psa 33:14, etc.), peoples (Gen 18:18; 22:18; 26:4; Deut 28:10, etc.), kingdoms (Deut 28:25; 2 Kgs 19:15, etc.), and the like. Thus the term "earth" in some passages can indicate—as in other languages—both the earth and its inhabitants (Gen 6:11, etc.).

tēbēl "mainland, circle of the earth" (→ *ʾbl* 1, 2) frequently parallels *ʾereṣ* in these contexts.

(c) Physically, *ʾereṣ* indicates the ground on which people and things stand, the dust lies (Exod 8:12f.), creeping things creep (Gen 1:26; 7:14; 8:19, etc.), the slaughtered lie (Lam 2:21), etc. On it fall rain and dew (Gen 2:5; 7:4; Exod 9:33; Job 5:10; 38:26, etc.), captured birds (Amos 3:5), the pebble (Amos 9:9), the toppled evildoer (Ezek 28:17; Psa 147:6), etc. On it sits the mourner (2 Sam 12:17, 20; Ezek 26:16; Job 2:13, etc.), as well as the dejected (Isa 47:1; Obad 3, etc.); one bows down toward it (Exod 34:8, etc.), one prostrates oneself on it before God (Gen 24:52), the king (2 Sam 14:33; 18:28, etc.), one's father (Gen 48:12, etc.), and other superiors. From it structures arise and one measures heights (Ezek 41:16; 43:14, etc.). Passages that mention that the ground or the earth (or its mouth) has opened and swallowed people (Num 16:30–34; 26:10; Deut 11:6; Psa 106:17; cf. Exod 15:12), that the ground or the earth shakes (1 Sam 14:15; Psa 46:7; 97:4, etc.), and that one can descend into the ground or the earth (Jonah 2:7) and sleep there (Psa 22:30), etc., mediate the relationship to the cosmological meaning.

In some of these cases, *ʾereṣ* approaches some usages of → *ʾᵃdāmâ;* → *ʿāpār* can also be used similarly (cf. e.g., 1 Kgs 18:38; Isa 34:7, 9, etc.).

(d) If *ʾereṣ* is modified by a following gen., the term indicates individual regions or tracts of land.

The following random examples could easily be multiplied with many pars.: *ʾereṣ môladtô* "his relatives' land" (Gen 11:28; 24:7; 31:13; Jer 22:10; 46:16; Ezek 23:15; Ruth 2:11), *ʾereṣ ʾābôt* "the fathers' land" (Gen 31:3; 48:21), *ʾereṣ mᵉgûrîm* "land of sojourning" (Gen 17:8; 28:4; 36:7; 37:1; Exod 6:4; all occurrences in P; cf. von Rad, *Gen*, OTL [1972²], 250; *Theol.* 1:168f.; also Ezek 20:38), *ʾereṣ ʾᵃḥuzzātô* "land of his possession" (Gen 36:43; Lev 14:34; 25:24; Num 35:28; Josh 22:4, 9, 19; cf. *ʾereṣ yᵉruššātô* in Deut

2:12; Josh 1:15), *ʾereṣ môšᵉbōtêkem* "land of your dwelling places" (Num 15:2), *ʾereṣ memšaltô* "land of his dominion" (1 Kgs 9:19 = 2 Chron 8:6; Jer 51:28); *ʾereṣ šibyām* (or *šibyâ*) "land of your (or the) deportation" (Jer 30:10; 46:27; 2 Chron 6:37f.; Neh 3:36). Cf. also the frequent usage of "my/your/his land" as a description of the land of origin and the homeland (Gen 12:1; 24:4; Exod 18:27; Num 10:30, etc., often par. to *môledet* "relatives").

(e) Occurrences that speak of the region or "land" of individual tribes stand on the border between geographical and political usages of the term.

Cf. *ʾereṣ ʾeprayim* (Deut 34:2; Judg 12:15; 2 Chron 30:10), *ʾereṣ binyāmin* (Judg 21:21; 1 Sam 9:16; 2 Sam 21:14; Jer 1:1, etc.); *ʾereṣ gād* (1 Sam 13:7), *ʾereṣ gilᶜād* (Num 32:1, 29; Josh 17:5f.; 22:9, 13, 15, 32; Judg 10:4, etc.); also *ʾereṣ zᵉbûlûn/yᵉhûdâ/mᵉnaššeh/naptālî.*

The political meaning dominates where individual states are called the "land X," whether accompanied by the collective name (e.g., *ʾereṣ yiśrāʾēl* in 1 Sam 13:19; 2 Kgs 5:2, 4; 6:23; Ezek 27:17; 40:2; 47:18; 1 Chron 22:2; 2 Chron 2:16; 30:25; 34:7; also with Edom, Asshur, Babel, Canaan, Midian, Moab; on *ʾereṣ miṣrayim* "land of Egypt" in Deut, see J. G. Plöger, *Literarkritische, formgeschichtliche und stilkritische Untersuchungen zum Deuteronomium* [1967], 100–115), the gentilic in the sg. or pl. (e.g., *ʾereṣ hāʾᵉmōrî* "land of the Amorites" in Exod 3:17; 13:5; Num 21:31; Josh 24:8; Judg 10:8; 11:21; Amos 2:10; Neh 9:8; also with reference to the land of the Girgashites, Jebusites, Canaanites, Chaldeans, Hebrews, Philistines, etc.), or as "the land of *X*" accompanied by a reference to the pertinent ruler (e.g., "the land of Sihon" and "the land of Og," Deut 4:46f.; 1 Kgs 4:19; Neh 9:22); cf. also "my/your/his land" with reference to the ruler (e.g., Gen 20:15).

The concept of the *ᶜam hāʾāreṣ* as a collective designation for the political authorities of the land also belongs to the political usage of *ʾereṣ* (cf. E. Würthwein, *Der ᶜamm haʾarez im AT* [1936]; → *ᶜam*).

4. (a) The first theological statement using *ʾereṣ* to be treated here is that God created (→ *brʾ* "to create," Gen 1:1; 2:4a, etc.; → *ᶜśh* "to make" Gen 2:4b; Prov 8:26; Isa 45:12, 18, etc.; → *yṣr* "to form" Isa 45:18; Jer 33:2, etc.; → *qnh* "to create" Gen 14:19, 22) the earth (heaven and earth). Admittedly, interest in Yahweh's creative activity varies in degree in the various circles of tradition in the OT (cf. G. von Rad, "Theological Problem of the OT Doctrine of Creation," *PHOE* 131–43; id., *Theol.* 1:139–53); discussions of the foundation of the earth or of the cosmos, however, attribute it without exception to Yahweh—as a rule either in Psa passages that have affinities with old Canaanite concepts, or in late, priestly materials.

Regarding the Can. origin, cf. esp. the expression *ʾēl ᶜelyôn qōnēh šāmayim wāʾāreṣ* "the most high God, the creator of the heavens and the earth" in Gen 14:19, 22, which has indisputable Can. origins; cf., among others, the Phoen. lower gate inscription of Karatepe (*KAI* no. 26A.III.18; *ANET* 654b: "El-the-Creator-of-the-Earth"), the Neo-Pun. inscription Trip. 13 from Leptis Magna (*KAI* no. 129.1), as well as the name of the god El-kunirsha, attested in Hitt., which may also derive from *ʾl qn ʾrṣ* (cf. H. Otten, *MIO* 1 [1953]: 135–37; W. F. Albright, FS Mowinckel 7f.; *ANET* 519; → *ʾēl* III/3).

In conformity with the worldview, some formulations also maintain that Yahweh established the earth (→ *ysd:* Isa 48:13; 51:13, 16; Zech 12:1; Psa 24:2;

78:69; 102:26; 104:5; Job 38:4; Prov 3:19; → *kûn* po.: Isa 45:18; Psa 24:2; 119:90; hi.: Jer 33:2).

These varied manners of expression agree on one point: the earth is created and is not a god. The OT has no discussion of an earth god or earth goddess; likewise, the notion of "mother earth," so widely distributed in the history of religions, is absent (cf. van der Leeuw 1:91–100; M. Eliade, "Erde," *RGG* 2:548–50). Job 1:21; Eccl 5:14; Psa 139:15 could be allusions to this notion (cf. also Gen 3:19 and Sir 40:1).

On the appeal to heaven and earth as witnesses in Deut 4:26; 30:19; 31:28 and their ancient Near Eastern background, cf. M. Delcor, "Les attaches littéraires, l'origine et la signification de l'expression biblique 'prendre à témoin le ciel et la terre,' " *VT* 16 (1966): 8–25; Fitzmyer, *Sef.* 38.

(b) As Yahweh's creation, the earth is his property (Psa 24:1; cf. 95:4f.). Yahweh is the lord of the whole earth (Josh 3:11, 13; Mic 4:13; Zech 4:14; 6:5; Psa 97:5; 114:7 txt em; → *ʾādôn* IV/5), king of the whole earth (Psa 47:8; Zech 14:9), most high over the whole earth (Psa 97:9), God of the whole earth (Isa 54:5), God in heaven above and on the earth beneath (Deut 4:39). If heaven is Yahweh's throne, the earth is his footstool (Isa 66:1). Yahweh beholds the earth (Gen 6:12; Isa 5:30; cf. Psa 33:14), bestrides the earth (Hab 3:12), terrifies the earth (Isa 2:19, 21); but above all he is the judge of the earth (Psa 82:8; 96:13 = 1 Chron 16:33; Psa 98:9).

(c) The term *ʾereṣ* acquires its specific theological usage in the context of the land promise and its appropriation in the conquest tradition (cf. G. von Rad, "Promised Land and Yahweh's Land in the Hexateuch," *PHOE* 79–93; for Deut, cf. the studies of *ʾrṣ* and *ʾdmh* in Plöger, op. cit. 60–129).

In the event that the so-called short historical creed (G. von Rad, "Form-Critical Problem of the Hexateuch," ibid. 3ff.) of Deut 26:5ff. should actually be understood as an old confessional formula, then the fact that Yahweh gave Israel "this land" was already discussed in a central passage (v 9). On the problems inherent in von Rad's position, however, see Rost, *KC* 11–25.

Nevertheless, it has been generally recognized in one way or the other since Alt (*EOTHR* 64f.) that the land promise (in addition to the promise of progeny) has roots in the patriarchal period. One may regard Gen 15:18 as potentially the oldest formulation (according to O. Procksch, *Die Genesis* [1924], 111, and Alt, *EOTHR* 66n.178, the passage may be a later insertion); 12:7 and 28:18 may indicate that the land promise was handed down later at specific holy places. The double promise stands at the center of J's portrayal of the fathers (12:7; 13:15; 15:7 J?; 15:18; 24:7; cf. the later addition in 26:3f.). That the land promise occupies a minor role in Gen 12:1 has been correctly noted but probably overvalued by H. W. Wolff ("Kerygma of the Yahwist," in W. Brueggemann and Wolff, *Vitality of OT Traditions* [1982^2]: 49f., 61). Gen 15:13 and perhaps also 21:23 indicate that E, too, presupposes the land promise. P has reformulated the promise, with characteristic deviations (Gen 17:8; 28:4; 35:12; 48:4; cf. also P's expression *ʾereṣ mᵉgûrîm* "land of sojourning"; see 3d).

The land promise is of particular importance in Deut:

(1) Yahweh has promised the *ʾereṣ* to the fathers (and their descendants; *šbʿ* ni.: Deut 1:8, 35; 6:10, 18, 23; 8:1; 10:11; 26:3; 31:7; cf. *dbr* pi. in 9:28; 27:3). Par. terms are → *ʾădāmâ* (7:13; 11:9, 21; 26:15; 28:11) and once *gᵉbûl* "region" (19:8).

(2) The *ʾereṣ* is the land given by Yahweh (→ *ntn,* in inf. constructions: 1:8, 35; 4:38; 6:10, 23; 10:11; 26:3; 31:7; with a ptcp. in the relative clause: 1:25; 2:29; 3:20; 4:1; 11:17, 31; 15:7; 16:20, etc.; occasionally the formula is expanded with *lᵉrištāh* "to possess it": 5:31; 9:6; 12:1; 18:2, 14, with → *naḥălâ:* 4:21; 15:4; 19:10; 20:16; 21:23; 24:4;, or both: 25:19; 26:1). Pars. here are *ʾădāmâ* and *naḥălâ.*

(3) Israel takes possession of the land (→ *yrš:* 1:8, 21; 3:18, 20; 4:1, 5, 14, 22, 26; 5:31, 33, etc.).

(4) This land is a "good land" (1:25, 35; 3:25; 4:21, 22; 6:18; etc.; cf. Exod 3:8; Num 14:7; 1 Chron 28:8), a "land where milk and honey flow" (6:3; 11:9; 26:9, 15; 27:3; cf. Exod 3:8, 17; 13:5; 33:3; Lev 20:24; Num 13:27; 14:8; 16:13f.; Josh 5:6; Jer 11:5; 32:33; Ezek 20:6, 15; once with *ʾădāmâ,* Deut 31:20).

(5) The promise of the possession of the *ʾereṣ* is associated most closely in Deut with the proclamation of the commandments. Either the conquest precedes the fulfillment of the commandments ("when you come into the land, which Yahweh, your God, gives you, you shall . . . ," or the like: 12:1; 17:14f.; 18:9; 19:1; 26:1; with *ʾădāmâ,* 21:1), or the fulfillment of the commandments is the condition for the receipt of the land (4:25f.; 6:18; 8:1; 11:8f., 18–21; 16:20; 19:8f.; with *ʾădāmâ,* 28:11; 30:17–20). On the theological significance of this association, cf. H. H. Schmid, "Das Verständnis der Geschichte im Deuteronomium," *ZTK* 64 (1967): 1–15.

Deuteronomic idiom is continued in analogous expressions of Deuteronomistic stamp (Josh 21:43; 23:16; Judg 2:1f., 6). Echoes are found also in prophecy contemporaneous and subsequent to Deut, esp. in Jer (32:22) and Ezek (33:24). At the same time, these two prophets formulate the expectation of a new possession of the land against the background of the exile (Jer 30:3; Ezek 36:28). In a wisdom individualistic form, the promise of the *ʾereṣ* lives on in Psa 37:11, 22, 29, 34; Prov 2:21f.; 10:30; cf. Isa 65:9; and finally Matt 5:5.

(d) Against the background of the land promise and its fulfillment, the land is described as "Yahweh's land" (Hos 9:3) or "my/your/his land" (Jer 2:7; Joel 2:18; Psa 85:2, etc.; cf. *ʾadmat yhwh* in Isa 14:2) in various strands of tradition in the OT. Because the *ʾereṣ* as a region is God's possession, the *ʾereṣ* as ground may never be sold (Lev 25:23ff.; cf. H. Wildberger, "Israel und sein Land," *EvT* 16 [1956]: 404–22). A crime against Yahweh is therefore simultaneously a crime against the land. Israel's abominable behavior desecrates the land (Lev 18:25, 27f.; Num 35:34; Jer 2:7; 3:2, etc.). Thus God's judgment finally includes not only Israel but also his land.

(e) Finally, at the edge of the OT, in the context of the more general apocalypticization of ancient elements, the promise of the creation of a new heaven and a new earth appears (Isa 65:17; 66:22; → *ḥādāš*).

5. The usage at Qumran is consistent with that of the OT. A formulaic manner of expression is particularly apparent in the statement that the community is concerned with the exercise of faithfulness, justice, and righteousness "in the land" (1QS 1:6, similarly 8:3, etc.), or in the discussion focusing on the fact that the council (?) of the community must atone "for the land" (1QS 8:6, 10, etc.).

In NT, Gk. ʾereṣ and ʾ^{a}dāmâ are rendered without distinction by *gē*. Cf. the NT lexicons, esp. H. Sasse, "γῆ," *TDNT* 1:677–81.

H. H. Schmid

ארר ʾ*rr* to curse

S 779; BDB 76b; *HALOT* 1:91a; *TDOT* 1:405–18; *TWOT* 168; *NIDOTTE* 826

---

1. The root ʾ*rr* appears to be common Sem., although it is attested only sporadically (cf. *HAL* 88a; P. Fronzaroli, *AANLR* 8/20 [1965]: 253f., 264; only Akk. *arāru* is in use for "to curse"; cf. *AHw* 65; *CAD* A/II:234–36; Aram. employs *lûṭ*, Arab. *lʿn*, etc.).

Although relatively numerous curse texts are extant from the ancient Near East (cf. the summaries in S. Gevirtz, "West-Semitic Curses and the Problem of the Origins of Hebrew Law," *VT* 11 [1961]: 137–58; F. C. Fensham, "Malediction and Benediction in Ancient Near Eastern Vassal-Treaties and the OT," *ZAW* 74 [1962]: 1–9; D. R. Hillers, *Treaty-Curses and the OT Prophets* [1964]), verbs for "to curse" occur only rarely. Cf. Hebr. ʾ*rwr* "cursed (be the one who opens this)" in a 7th/6th-cent. grave inscription from Silwan, *KAI* no. 191B.2; Aram. *ylwṭyn* "they curse" in the Ahiqar proverbs, line 151 (Cowley 217, 225).

Hebr. ʾ*rr* occurs verbally in the qal, hi., and pi. (cf. *HP* 216), nominally as *m*^{e}ʾ*ērâ* "curse" (BL 492).

2. The root ʾ*rr* is attested a total of 68x in the OT: in the qal 55x (40x in the form of the pass. ptcp. ʾ*ārûr*, the starting point for semantic analysis), in the pi. 7x, in the ni. 1x (Mal 3:9, ptcp.); the noun *m*^{e}ʾ*ērâ* occurs 5x.

Num 22:6 *yûʾār* should be understood with BL 433 as a qal pass. impf.

The distribution is very irregular; the word group occurs with emphatic frequency in some passages: Deut 27:15–28:20 (19x), Num 22–24 (7x), Num 5:18–27 and Mal (6x each), Gen 3–9 (5x).

3. (a) In view of the ancient Near Eastern and OT concepts of blessing and cursing (bibliog. in F. Horst, *RGG* 5:1649–51; C. Westermann, *BHH* 1:487f.; W. Schottroff, *Der altisr. Fluchspruch* [1969]), the meaning of ʾ*rr* as "to curse = cover with misfortune" in distinction from → ʾ*lh*, → *qll* pi., and other verbs of cursing (cf. J. Scharbert, " 'Fluchen' und 'Segnen' im AT," *Bib* 39 [1958]: 1–26; H. C. Brichto, *Problem of "Curse" in the Hebrew Bible* [1963]) results first through semantic opposition to → *brk* "to bless," as expressed particularly in the formulaic usage of ʾ*ārûr* or *bārûk*.

For an understanding of the semantic relationships between ʾ*ārûr* and the other verbal forms, cf. Gen 27:29 and Num 24:9 with Gen 12:3; Gen 3:17 with 5:29. The verb ʾ*rr*, then, means nothing other than "to make ʾ*ārûr*, pronounce ʾ*ārûr*, declare one ʾ*ārûr*."

The restriction on "to bind, hold back" proposed by E. A. Speiser ("An Angelic 'Curse': Exodus 14:20," *JAOS* 80 [1960]: 198–200) is appropriate only for the metonymic usage in the Akk. expression *arrat lā napšuri* "to curse without remission."

ʾ*rr* appears in 12 passages as an antonym for *brk* "to bless": Gen 9:25f.; 12:3; 27:29; Num 22:6, 12; 24:9; Deut 28:16–19; cf. vv 3–6; Judg 5:23f.; Jer 17:5; cf. v 7; 20:14; Mal 2:2; Prov 3:33. An ʾ*ārûr*, then, is the opposite of a *bārûk*, and is thus one stricken by misfortune and afflicted, whose existence is disastrous and whose presence brings misfortune.

Deut 28:15–68 impressively portrays the disastrous existence of an ʾ*ārûr:* in everything that he does, an ʾ*ārûr* harvests only failure. Therefore, Balak wishes to have the people Israel made ʾ*ārûr* by Balaam, in order to be able to drive them out more easily afterward (Num 22:6). ʾ*ᵃrûrîm* must serve others without ever coming "upon a green twig" (Gen 9:25; Josh 9:23). One "rich in *mᵉ*ʾ*ērôt*" is one who must continually suffer want (Prov 28:27). According to Jer 17:5f., an ʾ*ārûr* is like a miserable shrub, laboriously fighting for a meager existence in the steppe, and, according to Jer 20:14–16, like a hopelessly devastated city. Joshua's curse on Jericho is to be realized against the one who restores it, in that he loses his first- and last-born (Josh 6:26); Jonathan, who unknowingly shoulders his father's curse, renders the normal questioning of the oracle impossible because of his ʾ*ārûr* status (1 Sam 14:24–28, 37). The corpse of Jezebel is ʾ*ārûr* (2 Kgs 9:34), first because she stands under prophetic judgment (1 Kgs 21:23), but also because her whole existence has brought disaster to the people. The serpent is ʾ*ārûr* because of its troubled existence and because of the fear it elicits (Gen 3:14); the ground is ʾ*ārûr* because it occasions nothing other than toil and often wasted work (Gen 3:17; 5:29).

By contrast, it is impossible to declare ʾ*ārûr* one who is *bārûk*, i.e., successful and favored with fortune (Num 22:12; cf. 23:8), and one ought not to declare ʾ*ārûr* the prince, upon whose *bārûk* status the well-being of all depends (Exod 22:27).

(b) ʾ*ārûr* is used primarily in the ʾ*ārûr* formula (38x, nonpredicatively only in 2 Kgs 9:34 and Psa 119:21; cf, however, LXX). One says "ʾ*ārûr* is *X*," or "ʾ*ārûr* is the one who. . . . "

The one concerned is described, as a rule, with ʾ*ārûr hā*ʾ*îš* ʾ*ᵃšer* . . . (Deut 27:15; Josh 6:26; 1 Sam 14:24, 28; Jer 11:3; 20:15; cf. 17:5 and *KAI* no. 191B.2) or with a simple ʾ*ᵃšer* (Deut 27:26), often also with a ptcp. (Gen 27:29; Num 24:9; Deut 27:16–25; Judg 21:18; Jer 48:10bis; Mal 1:14), occasionally with direct address: "you are ʾ*ārûr*" (Gen 3:14; 4:11; Deut 28:16bis, 19bis).

The ʾ*ārûr* formula has a double function. First, it designates a particular person, whether known to the speaker or not, as ʾ*ārûr*, i.e., it covers the person with disaster through the medium of the effectual word, in some circumstances through an individual particularly gifted for these purposes (Num 22–24; contra Scharbert, op. cit. 6, it must be maintained that basically everyone is capable of pronouncing the ʾ*ārûr* formula effectively). Presumably, most of the texts that mention only ʾ*rr* "to curse" envision the pronunciation of the ʾ*ārûr* formula. As a rule, the disaster intended for the victim is more precisely described to strengthen the formula (cf. e.g., Josh 9:23; Jer 20:14f.).

One can also describe animals and objects as ʾ*ārûr:* the serpent (Gen 3:14), the ground (Gen 3:17), a day (Jer 20:14; cf. Job 3:8), the "wrath" of a person (in order not to affect the person directly, Gen 49:7).

Second, through an effectual word the ʾ*ārûr* formula as a so-called conditional curse creates a curse zone, i.e., a potential disaster sphere, into which the one who commits the deed named in the formula enters (e.g., Josh

6:26; Judg 21:18; 1 Sam 14:24, 28; Jer 48:10). In some apparently liturgical texts, an entire network of disastrous powers, which become active in the event of transgression, is created through the formation of a series of curses (12 ʾārûr formulae in Deut 27:15–26; 6 ʾārûr formulae in Deut 28:16–19). If the formula is pronounced in the presence of other persons, they answer with ʾāmēn (Deut 27:15–26; Jer 11:5; cf. Num 5:22) and thereby confirm the existence of this potential disaster sphere.

In Num 5:23 the written curse *(ʾālâ)* is dissolved in a liquid; this liquid is therefore called "*ʾārûr*-making water" *(mayim mᵉʾārᵃrîm)*, and it strikes the guilty woman with disaster in the ordeal.

(c) The subst. *mᵉʾērâ* "curse, execration" appears in Deut 28:16–20 and Mal 2:2 in close relationship to *ʾrr* qal ("to send a curse" = "to execrate"), as well as in Mal 3:9 with *ʾrr* ni. In Prov 3:33 *mᵉʾērâ* parallels the verbal expression *yᵉbārēk* "he blesses"; *mᵉʾērâ* indicates, then, not only the result of *ʾrr*, disaster (cf. Deut 28:20 LXX *endeia* "lack"; Prov 28:27 LXX *aporia* "need"), but also *ʾārûr* making or *ʾārûr* declaring as an effective act (contra Scharbert, op. cit. 7).

4. The *ʾrr* word group is doubly significant theologically.

(a) Yahweh is the absolute lord over all *ʾārûr* declaring. He himself makes people and animals *ʾārûr*, if he determines to do so, in that he speaks the fateful word (Gen 3:14, 17; 4:11; 5:29; 12:3; Jer 11:3; Mal 2:2; cf. 3:9), and one knows that his *mᵉʾērâ* pursues some people (Deut 28:20; Prov 3:33). Above all, he can convert the human *bārûk* declaration, even that of the priest, into the opposite (Mal 2:2), or he can even give a magician, preparing to declare *ʾārûr*, the commission to do the opposite (Num 22–24). Therefore, when declaring someone *ʾārûr*, the individual makes the affected one *ʾārûr* "before Yahweh" (1 Sam 26:19).

Yahweh pronounces *ʾārûr* on the criminal (*rāšāʿ*, Prov 3:33), the murderer (Gen 4:11), the one too shrewd (Gen 3:17), the one who violates the commandment (Deut 28:20; Jer 11:3), or—in post-exilic theology—the one who does not exercise his or her holy office properly (Mal 1:14; 2:2; 3:9).

(b) The potential sphere of disaster that one creates by declaring *ʾārûr* is limited by the direction of Yahweh. The one who moves beyond the sphere of activity determined by God's direction, i.e., the one who acts within the realm of that forbidden by Yahweh, is *ʾārûr*, persecuted by disaster. This circumstance is expressed esp. clearly in the juxtaposition of *bārûk* declaration and *ʾārûr* declaration (Deut 27:11–26; ch. 28; *ʾārûr* alone: Jer 11:3): whoever acts within the framework of God's regulations is *bārûk* (favored by good fortune); beyond this framework one is *ʾārûr* (in the grasp of misfortune). The same principle occurs in a more wisdomlike formulation in Jer 17:5, 7: one who builds one's life on the presence of Yahweh is *bārûk;* in contrast, one who trusts every person is *ʾārûr*. According to Jer 48:10, one who conducts Yahweh's work negligently or hinders it is *ʾārûr*. As already seen, Yahweh's own pronouncement of *ʾārûr* is directed at those who do not completely subordinate themselves to him (Gen 3:14, 17; 4:11; Psa 119:21). In Mal the sphere of disaster is primarily activated by improper cultic behavior and, concomitantly, by insulting Yahweh in the cult (Mal 1:14; 3:9).

5. Qumran uses the word group as the OT does: the *ʾārûr* formula is much more frequent than the simple verb (cf. Kuhn, *Konk.* 23; also *GCDS* 35). Conversely, the NT uses *epikataratos* = *ʾārûr* only in an OT quotation (Gal 3:10 = Deut 27:26; the *epikataratos* of Gal 3:13 does not correspond to an *ʾārûr* formula, but to the cs. combination *qilᵉlat ʾᵉlōhîm* in Deut 21:23; cf. L. Brun, *Segen und Fluch im Urchristentum* [1932]; J. Behm, "ἀνατίθημι," *TDNT* 1:353–56; F. Büchsel, "ἀρά," *TDNT* 1:448–51).

C. A. Keller

ארשׂ ʾrś pi. **to betroth**

S 781; BDB 76b; *HALOT* 1:91b; *TWOT* 170; *NIDOTTE* 829

1. *ʾrś* pi. "to betroth a wife" has direct pars. only in postbibl. Hebr. and Aram. (*ʾrs*, also in qal, e.g., Mid. Hebr. pass. ptcp. *ʾārûs* "bridegroom," and in corresponding pass. stem forms).

One may posit connections with Akk. *erēšu* "to demand, request" (*AHw* 239f.; *CAD* E:281–85; infrequent ptcp. *ērišu* "bridegroom," *AHw* 242b; *CAD* E:301a; cf. Ug. *ʾrš* "to desire," *WUS* no. 423; *UT* no. 379; Hebr. *ʾᵃrešet* "desire," Psa 21:3) and with Arab. *ʿarūs* "bridegroom; bride," *ʾaʿrasa* "to arrange a marriage feast" (KBL 90a; P. Wernberg-Møller, *JSS* 11 [1966]: 124), but not with the Akk. *erēšu* "to cultivate" (root *ḥrṯ*, Hebr. *ḥrš* "to plow") in the context of the wife-field metaphor (so A. Sarsowsky, *ZAW* 32 [1912]: 404f.).

2. *ʾrś* occurs 11x in the OT; 6x in the pi. (Deut 20:7; 28:30; 2 Sam 3:14; Hos 2:21bis, 22) and 5x in the pu. (Exod 22:15; Deut 22:23, 25, 27f.).

3. The basic meaning in the pi. (resultative, expressing a juristically comprehensible result; cf. *HP* 248) should be rendered "to betroth a wife"; the freer translation "to betroth (from the man's perspective)" should not be understood, in distinction from contemporary usage, as an indication of a simple engagement with the possibility of withdrawal in contrast to the public legal act of marriage (see below). The verb is constructed with a simple acc.: the *bᵉ* pretii (see GKC 119p) describes the bride-price (2 Sam 3:14, "for the foreskins of one hundred Philistines"; cf. Hos 2:21f.). The man is always the subj. (Yahweh in Hos 2:21f.; see below), the woman is the obj. to whom he betroths himself. The pu. forms indicate the pertinent pass. "to be betrothed (from the woman's perspective)." The virgin (*bᵉtûlâ* or *naᶜᵃrâ bᵉtûlâ*, Exod 22:15; Deut 22:23, 28) or the maiden (*naᶜᵃrâ*, Deut 22:25, 27) is the subj. in these clauses; cf. D. H. Weiss, *JBL* 81 (1962): 67–69.

The determination of the legal meaning (and therefore also the precise translation) of the term is not entirely clear in view of the limited number of examples. First of all, on the one hand, one should distinguish the intention of *ʾrś* from that of the marriage ceremony proper: a man may have betrothed a maiden but not yet have "taken her as wife" (*lqḥ*, Deut 21:11; 22:13f, etc.; cf. also *bᶜl* "to marry," Deut 21:13, etc.; → *baᶜal*; *lqḥ* is directly juxtaposed to ᵓrś in Deut 20:7 and to *hyh* l^eᵓ*iššâ* in Deut 22:29). One should also clearly distinguish ᵓrś from *škb* "to lie with" (Exod 22:15; Deut 22:23, 25, 28; also *šgl* Deut 28:30). Similarly, *šlḥ* pi. "to divorce" is not an antonym for ᵓ*rś*, but for *lqḥ* or *hyh* l^eᵓ*iššâ* (Deut 22:19, 29; 24:1, 3f.).

On the other hand, a *lqḥ* or *škb* obviously follows the ᵓ*rś:* a betrothed man is freed from the military in order to be able to bring his wife home (Deut 20:7); if a betrothed man cannot also live with his wife, he thus stands under a curse (Deut 28:30). Betrothal is a legal relationship protected like marriage; if this relationship is broken, the guilty party receives the death penalty (like an adulterer; cf. Deut 22:23f. with 22:22; Lev 20:10, etc.).

Consequently, it seems appropriate to regard ᵓ*rś* pi. as a description of a publicly binding legal act, which, although not identical with marriage, enacts the marriage legally. This interpretation is confirmed by the fact that the most essential element of the betrothal is the bride-price (*mōhar,* Gen 34:12; Exod 22:16; 1 Sam 18:25), which the bridegroom must give to the bride's father (cf. 1 Sam 18:25 with 2 Sam 3:14; Gen 34:12). If one seduces an unbetrothed virgin, he must still first pay the *mōhar* before he can take her home as wife (Exod 22:15 with the verb *mhr* qal "to acquire through payment of the *mōhar*"; Deut 22:29, "to give fifty shekels of silver").

On marriage in the OT, cf. E. Neufeld, *Ancient Hebrew Marriage Laws* (1944); F. Horst, "Ehe im AT," *RGG* 2:316–18 (with bibliog.); de Vaux 1:24–38 (bibliog. on pp. xxvii-xxviii); on marriage in the ancient Near East and on Jewish marriage law, cf. E. Kutsch, *Salbung als Rechtsakt* (1963), 27–33 (with bibliog.).

4. Hos 2:21f. uses ᵓ*rś* pi. as a metaphor. Yahweh is the subj. of this prophetic salvation message; the woman addressed is Israel according to Hosea's picturesque speech (borrowed from the Canaanite Baal cult). The marriage relationship with Yahweh, which the adulterous Israel had violated (2:4ff.), is to be reestablished, indeed, "forever"; the announced salvation consists in this reestablishment. Yahweh also pays the *mōhar* (cf. the fivefold b^e: "in righteousness, in justice, etc."). That ᵓ*rś* should be a public, "eternally valid" legal act (Rudolph, KAT 13/1, 80; Wolff, *Hos*, Herm, 46, 52, also speaks, therefore, of a "binding, legal act of marriage" and translates ᵓ*rś* with "I will make you my own") is confirmed once again.

5. The LXX uses *lambanein* for ᵓ*rś* in Deut 28:30 and 2 Sam 3:14, otherwise always *mnēsteuein,* which is also used in Matt 1:18; Luke 1:27; 2:5 to characterize the legal status of Mary.

J. Kühlewein

אֵשׁ ᵓ*ēš* fire

S 784; BDB 77a; *HALOT* 1:92a; *TDOT* 1:418–28; *TWOT* 172; *NIDOTTE* 836

---

1. The word occurs in most branches of the Sem. languages (with the exception of Arab.) in the sense of "fire."

In Arab. and partially in Aram., the common Sem. word (*ʾiš-[āt-], cf. P. Fronzaroli, *AANLR* 8/20 [1965]: 145, 149) has been replaced with forms of the root *nûr* "to be bright" (Arab. *nār*, Aram. *nûr*); Syr. *ʾeššātā* means only "fever."

Hebr. *ʾiššeh* "sacrifice" (not necessarily "burnt sacrifice") apparently does not belong etymologically to *ʾēš;* cf. J. Hoftijzer, "Das sogenannte Feueropfer," FS Baumgartner 114–34.

2. Statistics: *ʾēš* occurs 378x in the Hebr. OT (Ezek 47x, Jer 39x, Isa 33x, Lev 32x, Deut 29x, Psa 28x, etc.; Gen only 4x, absent in Jonah, Hag, Ruth, Eccl, Ezra, Esth); in addition, Aram. *ʾeššāʾ* occurs 1x (Dan 7:11; usually regarded as a fem. abs., but could also be masc. emphatic; cf. Fitzmyer, *Sef.* 53) and *nûr* 17x (Dan 3:6–27; 7:9f.).

Jer 51:18 and Hab 2:13 are also included in the statistics above, which *HAL* 89b (following G. R. Driver, *JSS* 4 [1959]: 148) assign to a root *ʾēš* II "trifle."

The pl. is absent from the OT (cf. Sir 48:3); M. Dahood (*Bib* 44 [1963]: 298) posits a dual in Jer 6:29. Num 18:9; Deut 33:2 Q; Ezek 8:2a are excluded through emendation.

3. (a) *ʾēš* concretely indicates fire as a given element of human culture, as used in the household (e.g., Isa 44:16) and handicraft (e.g., Ezek 22:20 in metallurgy; Job 28:5 in mining). In war the enemy is fought with fire (e.g., Isa 50:11 *zîqôt* "flaming arrows"); the rules of holy war, in particular, require that all the enemy's possessions be burned (Deut 13:17; → *ḥrm;* e.g., Josh 6:24; 7:15; 8:8; Judg 20:48; similarly Num 31:10). The death penalty is executed in special cases by fire (Lev 20:14; 21:9; cf. Gen 38:24; in relation to crimes against the holy war laws, Josh 7:15, 25).

Fire is important in the cult because sacrifices are burned (on the rules for various types of sacrifice, cf. Lev 1ff.; on fire as a means of ritual purification, → *ṭhr;* on the incineration of the sacrosanct in order to preserve it from profanation, → *qdš*). Fire is subject to some regulations; if it does not correspond to them, it is *ʾēš zārâ* "illegitimate fire" (→ *zār;* Lev 10:1; Num 3:4; 26:61, the fire of Nadab and Abihu), which brings disaster. The proscription against extinguishing the altar fire belongs to a later layer of priestly laws (Lev 6:1ff.; cf. J. Morgenstern, *Fire on the Altar* [1963]; for the later growth of legends concerning the proscription, see 2 Macc 1:18ff.).

The practice of the "Molech" child sacrifice falls subject to a special prohibition in the OT (R. de Vaux, *Studies in OT Sacrifice* [1964], 73–90; expressions: → *ʿbr* hi. *lammōlek*, Lev 18:21; 2 Kgs 32:10; Jer 32:35; *ʿbr* hi. *bāʾēš* "to cause to go through the fire," Deut 18:10; 2 Kgs 16:3 = 2 Chron 28:3, *bʿr;* 2 Kgs 17:17; 21:6 = 2 Chron 33:6; 2 Kgs 23:10; Ezek 20:31; *śrp bāʾēš* "to incinerate," Deut 12:31; 2 Kgs 17:31; Jer 7:31; 19:5 MT; cf. also Lev 20:2–5; Isa 30:33; Jer 3:24; Ezek 16:21; 23:37; Psa 106:37f.; on *tōpet* "place of fire" see KBL 1038b). The sacrifices are for a god, Melek (contra O. Eissfeldt, *Molk als Opferbegriff im Punischen und Hebräischen und das Ende des Gottes Moloch* [1935]); → *melek* 4e.

*(b) *HAL* 89 offers an extensive list of the verbs and substs. associated with *ʾēš*. Specific verbs of igniting/burning/incineration are mentioned here:

(1) *ʾôr* hi. "to ignite" in Mal 1:10; Isa 27:11, in addition to the normal meaning "to cause to shine," like *ʾûr* "light" > "fire(light)";

(2) *bʿr* qal "to burn" (38x), pi. "to ignite, keep a fire" (13x), pu. "to be ignited" (1x), hi. "to incinerate" (6x); in addition to *beʿērâ* "fuel" (Exod 22:5); cf. *HP* no. 31;

(3) *dlq* qal "to set fire" (Obad 18; Psa 7:14; hi. Ezek 24:10; cf. *HAL* 214b, and J. Blau, *VT* 6 [1956]: 246; L. Kopf, *VT* 8 [1958]: 170f.); in addition, *dalleqet* "heat of fever";

(4) *yṣt* qal "to ignite, incinerate" (4x), ni. "to catch fire, be burnt" (6x), hi. "to set fire, set on fire" (17x); by-form *ṣût* hi. "to ignite" (Isa 27:4);

(5) *yqd* qal "to burn" (34x), ho. "to be ignited" (5x); also *yeqôd* "blaze" (Isa 10:16), *yāqûd* (Isa 30:14) and *môqēd* (Lev 6:2; cf. Elliger, HAT 4, 81; Isa 33:14; Psa 102:4) "furnace";

(6) *kwh* ni. "to be singed" (Isa 43:2; Prov 6:28); also *kewîyâ* (Exod 21:25bis) and *kî* (Isa 3:24) "brand," *mikwâ* "burn wound" (Lev 13:24–28);

(7) *lhṭ* "to consume, singe" (qal Psa 57:5; 104:4; pi. 9x); also *lahaṭ* "flame, blaze" (Gen 3:24);

(8) *nśq* ni. "to catch fire" (Psa 78:21), hi. "to ignite" (Isa 44:15; Ezek 39:9);

(9) *ṣrb* ni. "to be singed" (Ezek 21:3); also **ṣārāb* "scorching" (Prov 16:27) and *ṣārebet* "burn, scar" (Lev 13:23, 28);

(10) *qdḥ* qal "to catch fire, ignite" (5x); also *qaddaḥat* "fever" (Lev 26:16; Deut 28:22), *ʾeqdāḥ* "beryl (fire-stone)" (Isa 54:12);

(11) *śrp* "to incinerate" (qal 102x, ni. 14x, pu. 1x; also *śerēpâ* "that which is consumed or burned, fuel" (13x; see *beʿērâ*, only 2 Chron 16:14; 21:19 "funeral pyre"), *miśrāpôt* "incineration" (Isa 33:12; Jer 34:5).

In Bibl. Aram. *ʾzh* pe. "to heat" (Dan 3:19bis, 22) and *ḥrk* hitpa. "to be singed" (3:27) occur in addition to *dlq* pe. "to burn" (Dan 7:9) and *yqd* pe. "to burn" (Dan 3:6–26; also *yeqēdâ* "flame" 7:11).

Verbs for extinguishing are: *dʿk* qal "to extinguish" (7x), pu. "to be extinguished" (Psa 118:12; ni. "to disappear" Job 6:17) with the by-form *zʿk* ni. "to be extinguished" (Job 17:1), and *kbh* qal "to extinguish" (14x), pi. "to quench" (10x).

The most important semantically related subst. is *lahab/lehābâ* "flame" (12 and 19x, resp., also meaning "blade"; in Exod 3:2 *labbat-ʾēš* should probably be emended to *lahebet-ʾēš; šalhebet* "flame" in Ezek. 21:3; Job 15:30; Song Sol 8:6 txt em is an Aram. loanword; cf. Wagner no. 305); also worthy of mention are *rešep* "flame, blaze" (7x; cf. A. Caquot, *Semit* 6 [1956]: 53–63) and *šābîb* "flame" (Job 18:5; cf. Wagner no. 304; Bibl. Aram. *šebîb* "flame," Dan 3:22; 7:9).

(c) As in other languages, in Hebr. fire is readily used fig. as an image of consuming passions: wrath (Hos 7:6 txt em; on the wrathful fire of Yahweh, see 4), pain (Psa 39:4), love (Song Sol 8:6), adultery (Job 31:12; Prov 6:27f.), contentiousness (Prov 26:20f.), injustice (Isa 9:17), sin in general (Sir 3:30, etc.). The point of comparison is primarily the consuming power, rarely the illuminating function, of fire (Nah 2:4; cf. F. Lang, *TDNT* 6:935; see also his references to proverbial usages).

4. Within the formation of religious tradition, fire has a place in the theophany motif.

The root of the theophany concept in Israel is twofold, reflecting the original significance of fire. A fiery volcano is the original referent in the Sinai theophany (so the J report in Exod 19:18; cf. Noth, *Exod*, OTL, 116f., 156f., 159f.; J. Jeremias, *Theophanie*

[1965], 104ff.). The concept of the thunder theophany with fiery lightning stems from Canaanite religion (e.g., Psa 18:8ff.; 29; 97:2ff.; non-Israelite parallels in Jeremias, op. cit. 75ff.; P. D. Miller, "Fire in the Mythology of Canaan and Israel," *CBQ* [1965]: 256ff.; E also describes the Sinai theophany, inappropriately for the context, as a thunderstorm; cf. Noth, op. cit. 159f.). The two concepts became intermingled very early (e.g., Hab 3:3ff.). The concept of Yahweh's *kābôd* (→ *kbd*) is very closely linked with the theophany tradition and, therefore, with fire (Psa 29; 97:6; Isa 10:16; cf. Ezek 10; cf. von Rad, *Theol.* 1:239f.).

Unique, antiquated concepts occur singly as phenomena accompanying a divine encounter in Gen 15:17 ("torch") and Exod 3:2 ("flame of fire from the thorn bush"; cf. Noth, op. cit. 39f.).

The concept of the Sinai fire acquires its own nuance in the conceptual framework of Deut and P. Deut speaks stereotypically of the "mountain that burns in the fire" (Deut 4:11; 5:23; 9:15); the concept of "Yahweh's speech from the fire" (Deut 4:12, 15, 33, 36; 5:4f., 22, 24–26; 9:10; 10:4; 18:16) is more essential: All elements of the theophany are subordinated to the speech of Yahweh. P speaks of the "pillar of fire" (*ʿammûd ʾēš)* by night and the "cloud" (→ *ʿānān*) by day, appearances that are not linked with Sinai but that lead Israel (Exod 13:21f.; 14:24; 40:38; Num 9:15f.; 14:14; cf. Neh 9:12, 19; associated with Sinai and with the expression *kābôd* in Exod 24:16f., "like a consuming fire"). Similar concepts are found in Deut 1:33; Isa 4:5; Psa 78:14. In a spiritualizing manner, Deut describes Yahweh himself as "consuming fire" (*ʾēš ʾōkᵉlâ*, Deut 4:24; 9:3; also Isa 33:14 and 30:27, "his tongue"). 1 Kgs 19:12 guards against a literal understanding of such statements (in addition to fire, the other theophany elements are named; cf. Jeremias, op. cit. 112–15; J. J. Stamm, FS Vriezen 327–34).

In the Psalm traditions and dependent prophecy, the theophany refers less to a discourse than to an act of God, so that here the effect of the fire is important. God appears in the "fire of wrath" (→ *ʾap*, → *ḥēmâ*, → *ʿebrâ;* Deut 32:22; Isa 30:27, 30; Jer 4:4; 15:14; 17:4; 21:12; Ezek 21:36f.; 22:21, 31; 38:19; Nah 1:6; Psa 89:47; Lam 2:4; → *qinʾâ* "zeal" also occurs in Ezek 36:5; Zeph 1:18; 3:8; Psa 79:5) in order to move against mythical or historical enemies (chaos powers, foreign nations, sinners, even Israel itself: Psa 46:10; 68:3; Isa 9:4, 18; 66:15f.; Amos 1f., etc.; also frequently in Jer, e.g., 11:16; 17:27). Freed from the context of the theophany, fire becomes the fire of judgment, which apocalypticism places at the end of time (Isa 66:24; Zech 9:4; Dan 7:9ff., etc.).

R. Mayer (*Die biblische Vorstellung vom Weltenbrand* [1956], 79ff.) offers a thorough overview of the passages in the OT that treat fire, either literally or (not always an easy distinction) figuratively, as a medium of the execution of judgment.

Although the image of the metalworker also occurs elsewhere in the proclamation of judgment (cf. Isa 1:25; Jer 6:27–30; 9:6; Ezek 22:17–22), one can speak of an actual "refining judgment" by fire only in Zech 13:9 and Mal 3:2f (Mayer, op. cit. 113f.; cf. also G. Rinaldi, "La preparazione dell'argento e il fuoco purificatore," *BeO* 5 [1963]: 53–59).

In a folktale manner the theophany fire becomes a miraculous "fire of God" (2 Kgs 1:9ff.; Job 1:16, etc.). Angelic beings also participate in this fire of God (Ezek 10:2, 6f.; 28:14; 2 Kgs 6:17).

5. Early Judaism and the NT follow apocalyptic usage (not to mention the aftereffects of some OT texts). Cf. F. Lang, "Das Feuer im Sprachgebrauch der Bibel" (diss., Tübingen, 1951); id., "πῦρ," *TDNT* 6:928–952.

F. Stolz

אִשָּׁה *ʾiššâ* **woman**

S 802; BDB 61a; *HALOT* 1:93b; *TDOT* 1:222–35; *TWOT* 137a; *NIDOTTE* 851

---

1. The word *ʾiššâ* "woman" corresponds to the common Sem. **ʾanṯ-at-* (P. Fronzaroli, *AANLR* 8/19 [1964]: 162f., 166, 245, 262): Akk. *aššatu* "wife" (in addition to the infrequent Can. loanword *iššu* "woman, wife," *AHw* 399a; *CAD* I/J:267b); Ug. *aṯt* "wife"; Aram. *ʾintᵉtâ*/*ʾittᵉtâ* "woman"; Arab. *ʾunṯā* "female"; Eth. *ʾanest* "woman."

Because the root has *ṯ*, it may not be derived from Hebr. *ʾîš* "man" (contrary to the folk etymology in Gen 2:23); no etymology can be given. The vocalization of the Akk. *enēšu* "to be weak," which presupposes a harsh laryngeal as the first radical, speaks against the derivations from a root **ʾnṯ* "to be weak" (e.g., *CML*[1] 152n.17); Arab. *ʾanuṯa* may be a denominative (cf. Fronzaroli, op. cit. 162f.).

On the irregular forms *ʾēšet* (sg. cs.) and *nāšîm* (pl.), possibly as harmonizations to *ʾîš* "man" or *ʾᵃnāšîm* "men," resp., see BL 617.

The pl. *ʾiššôt*, a new formation from the sg., is attested only in Ezek 23:44 (txt?; cf. Zimmerli, *Ezek*, Herm, 1:479).

*2. Like *ʾîš*, *ʾiššâ* is most frequent in the narrative books (Gen, Judg, Sam):

	sg.	pl.	total
Gen	125	27	152
Exod	32	6	38
Lev	34	1	35
Num	30	11	41
Deut	33	8	41
Josh	8	2	10
Judg	55	14	69
1 Sam	42	12	54
2 Sam	40	9	49
1 Kgs	29	9	38
2 Kgs	16	3	19
Isa	6	6	12
Jer	12	24	36
Ezek	13	8 +1	22
Hos	5	–	5
Amos	2	–	2
Mic	–	1	1
Nah	–	1	1
Zech	2	7	9
Mal	3	–	3

	sg.	pl.	total
Psa	3	–	3
Job	7	1	8
Prov	23	2	25
Ruth	13	2	15
Song Sol	–	3	3
Eccl	3	–	3
Lam	–	3	3
Esth	5	16	21
Dan	–	2	2
Ezra	1	11	12
Neh	2	8	10
1 Chron	16	4	20
2 Chron	8	11	19
OT total	568	212 +1	781

Lis. does not list 1 Kgs 14:5f.

The pl. *nᵉšêhôn* "your women" occurs 1x in Bibl. Aram. (Dan 6:25; *ʾ*antâ*/*ʾantᵉtâ*, the sg. of **nᵉšîn*, is not attested, but occurs in Imp. Aram.; cf. *DISO* 26f.).

3. (a) Naturally, the basic meaning "woman" (the female person) already implies a correlation to *ʾîš* "man" (the Hebr. words indicate this correlation even more clearly; cf. Gen 2:23).

In the vast majority of occurrences, a marital or extramarital juxtaposition to the man characterizes the term. Nominal series also occur in which the sexual aspect recedes. The expression "man or woman" can be used to mean "anyone, whoever"; "men and women" can also mean "all"; for texts with these usages and the series "men-women-children," etc. → *ʾîš* III/1.

A broader natural word field includes the terms "son/daughter/child" or their pls., also generally in nominal series.

Examples are: "woman-sons-daughters-in-law" (Gen 8:16; cf. 6:18; 7:7, 13; 8:18); in the context of births, "woman-son/daughter" (Gen 18:10, etc.); "women-sons" (Gen 32:23); "woman-daughters" (Gen 19:15f.); "women-daughters" (Isa 32:9 in parallelism); quite often "women-children" (Gen 30:26; Num 14:3, etc.; Psa 128:3 in parallelism).

Moreover, a veritable multitude of verbs characterize the word field of the term. Only the most important may be presented:

hrh "to be pregnant" (Gen 25:21; Exod 2:2; 21:22; Judg 13:3, etc.); → *yld* "to bear" (Gen 3:16, etc., *hrh* and *yld* often stand in close conjunction); → *lqḥ* "to take as wife, marry" (Gen 4:19; Deut 23:1; Judg 14:2, etc.); *hyh lᵉʾiššâ* "to marry" (Gen 24:67, etc.); *ntn lᵉʾiššâ* "to give as wife" (Gen 16:3; Judg 21:1, 7, etc.). An entire series of expressions serve to indicate sexual intercourse: *škb* "sleep (with)" (Gen 26:10, etc.); → *ydʿ* "to know" (Gen 4:1, 17, etc.); *bôʾ ʾel* "to go in to" (Gen 38:8f., etc.); → *glh* pi. *ʿerwat ʾiššâ* "to uncover a woman's nakedness" (Lev 18:6ff.; 20:11, 17–21); → *qrb* "to approach" (Lev 18:14, etc.); *ʿnh* pi. "to rape" (Gen 34:2, etc.); *šgl* "to sleep (with)" (Deut 28:30, etc.). The following may also be mentioned: → *ʾhb* "to love," →*ḥmd* "to desire," → *ʾrś* "to betroth," *zûb* "to menstruate"; *ynq* hi. "to suckle," → *qnʾ* pi. "to be jealous," *nʾp* "to commit adultery," → *šlḥ* "to divorce," → *bgd* "to break faith." For the late period the following may also be mentioned: *yšb* hi. "to marry = to live with a woman" (Ezra 10:2ff.; Neh 13:23, 27); → *yṣʾ* hi. "to divorce" (Ezra 10:3, 19).

No substantives are synonymous with *ʾiššâ* in its basic meaning.

The term is used only once of animals (Gen 7:2; cf. also Ezek 1:9).

(b) Like ʾîš "man/husband" (→ ʾîš III/2a), ʾiššâ is often used in the more specific meaning "wife" (Gen 12:5; 2 Sam 11:27, etc.). Frequent expressions are *X ʾēšet Y*, "X, the wife of *Y*" (e.g., Gen 11:31), and *šēm ʾištô X*, "his wife's name is *X*" (e.g., Ruth 1:2).

On the status of the wife in the OT, cf. F. Horst, "Frau II," *RGG* 2:1067f., and the literature cited there.

The common word for "concubine" is *pîlegeš* (36x, of non-Sem. origins; cf. Ellenbogen 134); *ṣārâ* " rival wife" occurs in 1 Sam 1:6. Further designations specifically for the wife of the king or the members of the royal harem are *šēgal* (Psa 45:10; Neh 2:6; Bibl. Aram., Dan 5:2f., 23) and Bibl. Aram. *lᵉḥēnâ* (in each instance in Dan 5 alongside *šēgal*).

The context of Lam 2:20 limits ʾiššâ to the meaning "mother," that of Gen 29:21 and Deut 22:24 to the meaning "bride." In Eccl 7:26, *hāʾiššâ* appears as a generalization ("the woman" = "the female gender").

(c) The term is occasionally used figuratively to describe a cowardly man, although only in the prophetic oracles against foreign nations, where it applies exclusively to the warriors or heroes of a foreign nation who have become women or like women (Isa 19:16; Jer 48:41; 49:22; 50:37; 51:30; Nah 3:13).

Otherwise ʾiššâ occasionally stands figuratively for Israel or Jerusalem: Hos 2:4; Jer 3:1, 3, 20; Isa 54:6; Ezek 16:30, 32; 23:2ff. (see 4f).

(d) In comparison to ʾîš, ʾiššâ is rarely generalized to mean "anyone" (Exod 3:22; Amos 4:3; Ruth 1:8f.). Expressions for "the one . . . the other" are formed with *ʾāḥôt* (→ *ʾāḥ* 3d) and *rᵉʿût* (Jer 9:19; of animals, Isa 34:15f.; Zech 11:9).

4. The usages of words in more or less theological contexts are suitably diverse:

(a) In the patriarchal narratives the promise to the matriarch that she will have a son forms a narrative motif that is certainly very old. In response to the complaint of the childless woman, God (or his messenger) promises this woman a son: Gen 17:19 (cf. 16:11); 18:10; 24:36; 25:21 (cf. C. Westermann, *Promises to the Fathers* [1980], 10ff.; on the issue of polygamy, cf. W. Plautz, "Monogamie und Polygynie im AT," *ZAW* 75 [1963]: 3–27).

(b) ʾiššâ occurs 17x in Gen 2–3 alone. The etiology of the word in 2:23 (*mēʾîš;* "she is taken from the man"), the special function of the woman in the story of the fall, and the special punishment in 3:16 are emphasized.

(c) Some situations apply to series like "men-women-children (-cattle-sheep-donkeys)," such as the execution of the ban in the Yahweh wars (Num 31:9, 17; Deut 2:34; 3:6; Josh 6:21; Judg 21:10f.; 1 Sam 15:3; 22:19; 27:9, 11). Similar series occur in the prophetic judgment proclamation (Yahweh's enemies are now the Israelites: Jer 6:11f.; 14:16; 38:23; Ezek 9:6; in the wish against the enemies: Jer 18:21).

A second life setting is apparently the act of the public reading of the law, for which "men-women-children (-foreigners)" are assembled (Deut 31:12; Josh 8:35). This usage is taken up in the assemblies that Ezra and Nehemiah hold (Ezra 10:1; Neh 8:2f.).

(d) Foreign women represent a special theological motif. In older times a marriage between an Israelite and a Canaanite was hardly objectionable (Gen 34; Exod 2:21; 4:20; cf. Deut 21:11, 13). The Deuteronomistic theology in Judg and Kgs unequivocally evaluates such a marriage with neighbors negatively: foreign women mean the importation of foreign gods and consequently apostasy from Yahweh (Judg 3:6; 1 Kgs 11:1ff.; 16:31; 21:25; 2 Kgs 8:18). The issue was particularly acute in early post-exilic times: in P (Gen 27:46; 28:1f., 6, 9; closely associated with P, Num 25:6ff.) and in Ezra 10:2ff.; Neh 13:23ff.

(e) To violate a woman is an "abomination in Israel" (*nᵉbālâ,* → *nābāl),* which summons the wrath and punishment of God (Judg 19f.; cf. Gen 34). Consequently, a whole series of laws regulate the sexual relationship between man and woman:

One should not covet his neighbor's wife (Exod 20:17; Deut 5:21). If one lies with a betrothed (Deut 22:23f.) or married woman (Deut 22:22), both parties merit the death penalty. Adultery carries the death penalty (Lev 20:10; Num 5:11ff.). A woman who has sexual intercourse with an animal merits the same punishment (Lev 20:16). An entire series of intrafamilial sexual relationships are regulated in Lev 18, the woman's menstruation in Lev 15. Further laws concerning woman are in Exod 19:15; 21:22; Lev 12:1–8; Num 6:2; 30:4ff.; 36:3ff.; Deut 17:2, 5; 22:19; 24:1ff.; 25:5.

Prophecy occasionally reprises such laws, in part in accusations against those who transgress the commandments (sexual commandments: Hos 2:4; Jer 3:1ff.; 5:8; 29:23, etc.; idolatry: Jer 7:18; 44:15; Ezek 8:14), in part in the prophetic proclamation of judgment (2 Sam 12:11; cf. Isa 13:16; Jer 8:10; Zech 14:2). Finally, reference should be made to the Torah sentences in Ezek 18:6, 11, 15.

The wisdom literature handles these sexual problems in another manner: good judgment "protects you from the wife of another" (Prov 2:16; 6:24; 7:5; cf. 6:29). Otherwise, a good and wise wife is a gift from Yahweh (Prov 19:14; cf. the praise of the worthy wife in Prov 31:10–31).

(f) Israel or Jerusalem is occasionally described as Yahweh's wife in prophecy, first in Hos (2:4; the metaphorical treatment in Hos 1:2ff.; 3:1ff. does not belong in this context). In a "legal process against an unfaithful wife" (Wolff, *Hos,* Herm, 32), the unfaithful wife (Israel) is accused of adultery. The image of marriage, which Hosea borrowed from Canaanite mythology, serves to oppose Israel's attraction to precisely this Canaanite Baal cult with its cultic prostitution. The image is taken up again in the accusations of Jer (3:1, 3, 20) and Ezek (16:30, 32; 23:44). The salvation message of Deutero-Isa (Isa 54:6) treats the image differently: Israel is the abandoned "wife of youth" whom Yahweh will call anew.

(g) The saving activity of Yahweh toward Israel is loosely compared to the act of a woman with respect to her child in Isa 49:15, "A woman will also forget her child" (cf. Isa 66:13; → *ʾēm* 4e).

5. The NT takes up the following aspects again: (a) discussion of an infertile woman to whom God promises a son (Luke 1); (b) Gen 2–3 in Mark 10:7 pars., etc.; (c) the theme of "foreign women" is modified in 1 Cor 7:12ff. into the theme of "non-Christian marriage partners"; (d) as in the OT, marriage is esp. defended, although the many sexual regulations are lacking;

(e) for fig. usages, cf. Acts 21:2, 9; 22:17. Cf. also A. Oepke, "γυνή," *TDNT* 1:776–89.

J. Kühlewein

אָשָׁם *ʾāšām* **guilt**

S 817; BDB 79b; *HALOT* 1:96a; *TDOT* 1:429–37; *TWOT* 180b; *NIDOTTE* 871

---

1. The root *ʾšm* or (according to the evidence of Arab. *ʾaṯima* "to commit an offense") **ʾṯm* has not yet been identified in Sem. prior to Hebr. or contemporary with the OT (on Ug., cf. D. Kellermann, "*ʾāšām* in Ugarit?" *ZAW* 76 [1964]: 319–22; on Pun., cf. Sznycer 143). On Arab. (and possibly Eth.) equivalents, cf. *HAL* 92.

Hebr. forms the following from the root *ʾšm:* the verb in qal, ni., and hi.; the abstract noun *ʾāšām,* which indicates a circumstance (GKC §84f; BL 462f.); the abstract noun *ʾašmâ,* originally a fem. inf. (BL 317, 463; clearly still so in Lev 4:3; 5:24, 26); the verbal adj. *ʾāšēm.*

2. The verb is attested 33x in qal, in addition to once each in ni. and hi., the nom. *ʾāšām* 46x, *ʾašmâ* 19x, the adj. 3x.

Of the total of 103 occurrences of the root in all forms, 49 appear in P portions of Lev and Num, 9 in Chron, 8 in Ezek, and 7 in Ezra. In the legal sections of Exod and Deut, the root does not occur at all, and it is rare in wisdom literature (Prov 2x). The historical books also use the word rarely: Gen 2x, Judg 1x, 1 Sam 4x (all in ch. 6), 2 Sam 1x, 2 Kgs 1x. The same is true for the language of the prophets: Ezek 8x and Hos 5x (verbal forms) are conspicuous; there remain only Jer 3x, Amos, Hab, Deutero-Isa, Deutero-Zech, Joel, and Isa 24 with one text each. Thus around 70% of the corpus belongs to the cultico-theologically stamped texts of the exilic and post-exilic periods.

The oldest occurrences of the nom. are in Gen 26:10 (L/J) and 1 Sam 6:3f., 8, 17, and of the adj. *ʾāšēm* in 2 Sam 14:13. The verb occurs first then in Judg 21:22, followed by *ʾāšām* in 2 Kgs 12:17, *ʾašmâ* in Amos 8:14, *ʾāšēm* in Gen 42:21 (E), and finally the verb in Hos 4:15; 5:15; 10:2; 13:1; 14:1; and Hab 1:11.

The nom. form *ʾašmâ* is used only in the post-exilic period, apart from Amos 8:14 and Psa 69:6, first alongside *ʾāšām* (Lev 4:3; 5:24, 26; 22:16). In Ezra and Chron, where, on the one hand, the remaining 13 occurrences are located, while, on the other hand, *ʾāšām* no longer occurs, *ʾašmâ* has displaced the older form *ʾāšām.* This development is confirmed in the available Qumran texts, where *ʾāšām* occurs only 2x, *ʾašmâ,* in contrast, 37x (according to Kuhn, *Konk.* 23f.; cf. *GCDS* 37f.).

Textual difficulties exist in Judg 21:22 Isa 24:6; Ezek 6:6; Hos 4:15; Hab 1:11; Prov 14:9; Ezra 10:19.

3. (a) Context, formulaic usages, and phrases indicate two foci in the OT usage of the term: (1) a situation of guilt obligation, in which someone gives something.

Cf. e.g., "bring (*bôʾ* hi.) something as *ʾāšām* to Yahweh" (Lev 5:15b, 18, 25; Num 6:12), "present (*qrb* hi.) something before Yahweh" (Lev 14:12), "place (*śîm*) his life (as) *ʾāšām*" (Isa 53:10); further, the means: "*ʾāšām*-goat" (Lev 5:16; 19:21b, 22), "*ʾāšām*-lamb"

(Lev 14:21, 24f.), "ʾāšām-silver" (2 Kgs 12:17). Cf. also the "day of the ʾašmâ" (Lev 5:24; cf. Hos 5:15), and finally the introduction formulae in Lev 6:10; 7:1, 7, 37; Num 18:9, as well as Hos 5:15; Isa 24:6; Zech 11:5.

(2) A situation in which someone is or becomes obligated to discharge guilt by giving something.

This situation is expressed (a) by the verb in a judgment formula in genres dealing with the declaration of guilt (in these cases with the root ʾšm also probably including a formal declaration of the consequences of the judgment): Hos 10:2; 13:1; 14:1; Jer 2:3; Ezek 22:4; 25:12; Prov 30:10; Psa 34:23; cf. Jer 50:7; Psa 5:11; almost all these occurrences have a tripartite structure, with the declaration of guilt located exactly between the accusation and the specific announcement of punishment; cf. also Lev 5:17, 21–23; Num 5:6f.; (b) also by the verb in a judgment formula in instruction in cultic law: Lev 4:13f., 22f.; 5:17, 19b, 23; Num 5:6f.; (c) by ʾāšām in declaratory formulae : Lev 5:19a; 7:5; 14:13; (d) in exhortative communication of Torah: Hos 4:15; 2 Chron 19:10b; (e) in confession: 2 Chron 28:13b; (f) in all occurrences of ʾašmâ (except for Lev 5:24); (g) cf. finally Jer 50:7; 51:5; Psa 68:22; Gen 26:10; also Amos 8:14, "they swear by that by which Samaria has become guilty."

(b) This state of affairs indicates the viewpoints to be excluded for the determination of the meaning of the term:

(1) ʾšm is not a term for "transgression, offense." Accordingly, the texts markedly distinguish ʾšm from terms for "transgression" (e.g., *mʿl*, Lev 5:15, 21; *ḥṭʾ*, Lev 4:2f., 13f.; 5:1f.; cf. also Ezra 9:13). Although the transgression may be of entirely different varieties (Lev 4:13; 5:2, 17–19; Num 5:6f.) and ʾšm can presuppose all varieties (Lev 5:21–23, 26; 2 Chron 19:10), ʾšm itself always refers only to a *particular type of consequence* of offenses.

(2) It is equally impossible to demonstrate that ʾšm means a particular type of punishment (T. H. Gaster, *IDB* 4:152: "simply a mulct," "a fine"). The fulfillment of the obligation could vary; cf. 1 Sam 6:3f., 8, 17; Gen 42:21; 2 Kgs 12:17; Hos 14:1; Jer 51:5; Isa 53:10; also Lev 5:15ff.; Ezek 40:39; 44:29; 46:20; Ezra 10:19, etc.

(3) ʾāšām as fulfillment of obligation cannot be understood originally as "sacrifice," even if the institution appears later alongside the various sacrificial rites; cf. Lev 6:10; 7:7, 37; Num 18:9; 2 Kgs 12:17; Ezek 40:39; 42:13; 44:29; 46:20 (cf. R. Rendtorff, *Studien zur Geschichte des Opfers im Alten Israel* [1967], 227f.; Elliger, HAT 4, 73ff.).

(4) Although ʾāšām and ʿāwōn (the two most nearly synonymous terms) refer to the same situation in Jer 51:5f.; Lev 5:17; 22:16; Ezra 9:6, they still express something distinct: → ʿāwōn addresses the element of the weight, the burdening, the burden (of guilt); in contrast, ʾāšām expresses the element of obligation (with respect to the resolution of guilt). *ʿᵃwōn ʾašmâ* in Lev 22:16 means, then, "the burden of guilt-obligation."

(5) Finally, functional aspects such as "reparation" or "restitution" do not appear to be the primary referent of ʾšm. The primary viewpoint is the situation of obligation that follows a judgment, the state of being obligated, and its fulfillment. Functional aspects appear to belong more to the presupposed sense of the situation of obligation than to be expressed in the word itself. Thus according to Lev 5:14–16, ʾāšām is not "compensation" (contra Elliger, HAT 4, 76; with Gaster, op. cit.: "not an indemnification . . . not

compensatory"), but serves to restore (contra Gaster, op. cit.); cf. → *kpr* pi. *ʿal* and → *slḥ*. Cf. also Lev 5:21–26 and Num 5:6f. Gen 42:21 seems to imply an understanding of compensation. The old text 1 Sam 6:3f., 8, 17 refers to rehabilitation and restitution, Isa 53:10 to restitution; cf. Judg 21:22.

(c) The double usage—from a modern perspective—of the one root *ʾšm* (see 3a) apparently relates to a common foundation assumed in all aspects from judgment of guilt to resolution of guilt: it is *the obligation, the duty, the liability, that results from incurring guilt.* In this respect "obligation" always aims at fulfillment, even if not yet completed; the fulfillment is always characterized according to its nature, namely "liability or punishment for guilt." This situation occurs, above all, in the case of the sentence of liability for guilt (see 3a[1]), during the period of obligation for guilt (adj. forms; cf. Prov 14:9, "fools scoff at liability for guilt"; Psa 68:22, "(he) who walks in his guilt-obligatedness"; Jer 51:5, "the land is full of guilt-liability"), and in the event of fulfillment (see 3a[2]).

In this sense, then, the nominal forms (incl. the adjs.) signify guilt-obligated*ness*, the verb forms, *incurring* guilt-obligation. The reason that the noun is used only in the sg. (exceptions: Psa 69:6; 2 Chron 28:10, both from *ʾašmâ*) may be that "guilt-obligation," with a view to judgment and atonement, is always seen as one. In contrast, the pl. forms of verbs and adjs. refer to the plurality of the obligated persons.

This common basic situation and basic meaning seem, then, to continue to dominate even in texts that do not require a choice between "guilt" and "atonement": Gen 26:10; 42:21 (cf. v 22c); Judg 21:22; 2 Sam 14:13; Hos 5:15 (cf. Wolff, *Hos*, Herm, 105, and Gen 42:21); 10:2; 14:1; Isa 53:10; Prov 14:9; 30:10; Ezra 10:19 MT: "and those under guilt-obligation, a goat for their guilt-obligation (penance? punishment?)"; contrast LXX: "and as their punishment (act of penance?) a lamb for their guilt-obligation." Cf. the double perspective in the contexts of Psa 34:22f.; Lev 5:24, 26, as well.

(d) On the basis, then, of the application of the basic meaning to the various aspects of the guilt-obligation situation, the perspectival usage of the term arises. Finally, in addition to the already mentioned perspectives of being/becoming obligated by guilt and of guilt-*resolution*, the usage of *ʾāšām* as a means of guilt-resolution may be mentioned.

This usage is expressed grammatically by *ʾāšām* as either an acc. obj. or nomen rectum in a gen. construction: "to slaughter *ʾāšām*" (Lev 7:2, an animal is intended); "to bring *ʾāšām*" (Lev 5:6f., 15b, 25a; 19:21a); "to return *ʾāšām*" (1 Sam 6:3f., 8, 17; Num 5:7f.); "the blood of the *ʾāšām* (-animal)" (Lev 14:14, 17, 25b, 28). According to Ezek 40:39; 42:13; 44:29; 46:20, *ʾāšām*, among others, belongs to the holy offerings reserved for the priests.

The alteration of perspectives is indicated clearly in Lev 5:15f.: (1) "*ʾāšām* for Yahweh," (2) "a goat as *ʾāšām* (*lᵉʾāšām*)," (3) "the goat of the *(hā-)ʾāšām*." In (1) *ʾāšām* is the subj., in (2) and (3) the goat is the subj. While (2) and (3) explicate the relationship between *ʾāšām* and the goat, this explication is implied in *ʾāšām*. This shows that even where the word must be understood instrumentally, it expresses more the significance, the function of the means, than the means itself. The contexts indicate that one also had the means itself in view, and stated it.

(e) The modern translation problem consists in the fact that we see primarily the different perspectives and express the distinctions and do not see and express the commonalities that are true of *ʾšm* despite the distinctions. With attention to the basic intention of the Hebr. term, one should consequently translate: *ʾšm* qal "to be/become guilt-obligated or liabilty-obligated"; *ʾšm* ni. "to suffer guilt-obligation, guilt-liability" (Joel 1:18); *ʾšm* hi. "to make obligated due to guilt, liable due to guilt" (Psa 5:11); *ʾāšēm* "obligated due to guilt, liable due to guilt"; *ʾāšām* and *ʾašmâ* "guilt-obligation, guilt-liability, guilt-responsibility" (both nouns so far as possible with a view to the unity of situation and resolution). Where the element of resolution predominates or the instrumental element cannot be set aside, one may translate "resolution of guilt," "reparation." Alternatives include: "guilt/restitution" (Buber); "culpability/punishment" (Wolff; clear linguistically and with respect to content); "to be guilty/to do penance" (ZB; not entirely precise with respect to content and linguistically inconsistent). The following proposals are incorrect or problematic: "to become guilty, guilt" (because this is aimed at the act of the offense); "to do wrong" (ZB, e.g., at Lev 5:17); "to burden with guilt" *(HAL* 93a; cf. KBL 94b; because "to burden" is more appropriate for *ʿāwōn);* "guilt sacrifice" (because "sacrifice" implies something other than the punitive character of the guilt offering).

4. The understanding assumed in an *ʾšm* situation is apparently that guilt-obligation and resolution of liability for injury will create the prerequisite for the restoration of a disturbed situation. The word has a theological character insofar as human liability is the expression, cause, or result of divine judgment or activity and is related to this divine involvement as a human situation or resolution. This relationship is directly visible where Yahweh's privileges (e.g., in the cultic sphere) are violated. And it is implicitly the case where Yahweh's jurisdiction is violated through the infringement of civil rights or of people. The reason for this theological quality of *ʾšm* lies in the view that human guilt-liability involves God basically and entirely. As a consequence, every resolution of guilt simultaneously signifies a realization of liability before God. Thus one may not distinguish between a religious and a secular understanding of *ʾšm*- situations here either.

Correspondingly, God requests or announces *ʾšm* on account of the oppression of the righteous (Psa 5:11; 32:22f.) or on account of the violence done to the law that Yahweh oversees (Ezek 22:4; 2 Chron 19:10; cf. vv 5–9). Or the guilt-obligation of God's enemies results in divine intervention (Psa 68:22). According to Num 5:6f, one is liable to the injured person or to his/her relative, or, if there is no relative, to God, because of the notion that a legal offense against people is an offense against God. Lev 5:14–16, 21–26 declares, as broadly as possible, that one who commits a legal offense against another is liable to God—in addition to being responsible for making restitution to the injured party.

Joseph's brothers understand their situation as a guilt-burden for their crime against Joseph (Gen 42:21). According to 1 Sam 6:3, *ʾšm* is supposed to bring about healing and the recognition of the reason for Yahweh's judgment.

In this sense, *ʾšm* is a consequence, then, of the violation of covenant (Isa 24:6) or of apostasy from Yahweh (Hos, esp. 14:1; Jer 51:5). Guilt-obligation becomes directly visible when one assaults Yahweh's privileges, those dedicated to Yahweh, whether

Israel (Ezek 25:12; Jer 50:7; Zech 11:5), a compatriot (2 Chron 28:13), the property of the sanctuary or of the priests (Ezek 40:39; 42:13; 44:29; 46:20), or a specific religious law (Ezra 10:19).

5. The LXX translated *ʾšm* with no less than 16 different terms. In the lead, with about half the occurrences (mostly from Lev, Num, and related texts) stands *plēmmeleia* "offense" (*plēmmeleō*, etc., is not attested in the NT), followed by *hamartia (hamartanō)*, *agnoia*, and other words for "error." The LXX, then, abandoned the unified basic meaning of *ʾšm* in principle and replaced it with a number of meanings mostly of quite distinct and widely varied backgrounds. This observation applies even to the various layers of tradition noted in the LXX and despite the predominance of *plēmmeleia*. Furthermore, the LXX is not consistent in translation—with only the partial exception of relatively closed text groups (Lev, Num)—not even in the rendering of the major perspectives. These very perspectives have fallen prey to an understanding of deeds implicit in the Gk. terms. With the transition into the Greek-speaking world, then, the specific content of *ʾšm* was basically lost.

R. Knierim

אשׁר *ʾšr* pi. **to call blessed**

S 833; BDB 80b; *HALOT* 1:97b; *TDOT* 1:445–48; *TWOT* 183; *NIDOTTE* 887

---

1. The nominal form *ʾašrê*, usually understood as the pl. cs. of an assumed *ʾešer* "luck, fortune" (cf., however, Joüon §89l; J. A. Soggin, *TZ* 23 [1967]: 82), presents the most important form of the word family *ʾšr* II, with some counterparts in neighboring languages, although they do not sufficiently explain the etymology of the root (cf. *HAL* 94–96; Zorell 87; W. Janzen, *HTR* 58 [1965]: 216; *SBL* 116). The derivative *ʾōšer* "luck" is attested once (Gen 30:13; cf. *HAL* 95b; also *WUS* no. 458; Neo-Pun. *ʾšr lb* "joy of the heart(?)," *KAI* no. 145.11). Verbal manifestations of the root occur only in *ʾšr* pi. and pu. and are commonly perceived as denominatives of *ʾašrê* (cf. D. R. Hillers, "Delocutive Verbs in Biblical Hebrew," *JBL* 86 [1967]: 320–24).

2. Although the distribution of verbs is not very characteristic (pi. 7x, pu. 2x), some tendencies are perceptible for *ʾašrê*. The word is attested a total of 45x (Psa 26x, Prov 8x; also Deut 33:29; 1 Kgs 10:8[bis] = 2 Chron 9:7bis; Isa 30:18; 32:20; 56:2; Job 5:17; Eccl 10:17; Dan 12:12; in addition to *ʾōšer* 1x; see above), 38x in the form *ʾašrê*, 6x with pl. suf. and 1x with sg. suf. (Prov 29:18).

In view of the rather high number of Psa occurrences, the genre of the psalms in question should be examined because the question (controversial in some research) of the origin and nature of the *ʾašrê* statements essentially depends on this evidence.

This investigation indicates that the stereotypical *ʾašrê* formula characterizes known wisdom Psalms (Psa 1; 32; 34; 106; 112; 127; 128; cf. Gunkel-Begrich 392; S. Mowinckel, *SVT* 3 [1955]: 213; Sellin-Fohrer 285ff.) or can occur in wisdom-influenced elements of other Psalms (cf. Psa 94; 119; also Psa 2:12b alongside v 10). Three of nine verbs exhibit wisdom influence (Job 29:11; Prov 3:18; 31:28; cf. Psa 41:3 Q). The extensive attempt of E. Lipiński, ("Macarismes et psaumes de congratulation," *RB* 75 [1968]: 321–67) to demonstrate a cultic origin for the *ʾašrê* formula, first on the basis of the Psalm passages, is already of limited value because of this association with wisdom (see further 4).

3. (a) The basic meaning of the pi., to be understood as an estimative-declarative, is "call blessed" (with e.g., GB 73; *HAL* 94a; *HP* 41, 270). *ʿûd* hi. "give (complimentary) testimony" (Job 29:11) and *hll* pi. "praise" (Prov 31:28; Song Sol 6:9) are occasionally par. The verb, which—like the nominal forms—refers only to persons (but never to God; see G. Bertram, *TDNT* 4:365), expresses a predicative description with positive content, a description further modified and given foundation by the context or by assertions of various types (e.g., a *kî* clause, Mal 3:12).

(b) The nominal beatitude using suf. forms and, above all, the more frequent *ʾašrê*, confirms the verbal evidence, but exhibits at the same time a broader application, still markedly formulaic.

The form with the simple *ʾašrê* is always in first position; so, too, usually the suf. forms (in Prov 14:21; 16:20; 29:18, however, post-positive). Par. allusions occur in 1 Kgs 10:8 = 2 Chron 9:7; Psa 144:15; doublets in Psa 32:1f.; 84:5f.; 119:1f.; 137:8f.; Prov 8:32, 34 (cf. K. Koch, *Growth of the Biblical Tradition* [1969], 7, 95), which give rise to series (these series dominate, however, only later; cf. C. A. Keller, FS Vischer 89). The syntactic extension of the form often occurs through a noun: *ʾādām* (Psa 32:2; 84:6, 13; Prov 3:13; 8:34; 28:14) and *ʾᵉnôš* (Isa 56:2; Job 5:17) "person," *ʾîš* (sg.: Psa 1:1; 112:1; pl.: 1 Kgs 10:8 = 2 Chron 9:7) and *geber* (Psa 34:9; 40:5; 94:12; 127:5) "man," *gôy* (Psa 33:12) and *ʿam* (Psa 89:16; 144:15bis) "people," "his sons" (Prov 20:7), "your servants" (1 Kgs 10:8 = 2 Chron 9:7), and "those who walk blamelessly" (Psa 119:1), then through a ptcp. (sg.: Psa 32:1; 41:2; 128:1; Dan 12:12; pl.: Isa 30:18; Psa 2:12; 84:5; 106:3; 119:2), or through a relative clause formed either asyndetically with an impf. (Psa 65:5; Prov 8:32; cf. BrSynt 144) or with *še-* and an impf. (Psa 137:8f.) or nom. clause (Psa 146:5). This extension characterizes or grounds the beatification of the person (or group) in question.

There are occasionally address forms (Deut 33:29; Isa 32:20; Psa 128:2; Eccl 10:17, with suf. forms; cf. Mal 3:12 with the verb). In some circumstances a congratulatory act can also be presupposed (cf. Gen 30:13; also Psa 127:3–5; 128; cf. *TDNT* 4:367), so that the beatitude may hardly be described generally as a greeting or felicitation (cf. H. Schmidt, *TSK* 103 [1931]: 141–50; Gemser's characterization of them as "a hymnically elevated mid-form between statement and exhortation" (HAT 16, 29) may be too imprecise, according to W. Zimmerli, "Concerning the Structure of OT Wisdom," *Studies in Ancient Israelite Wisdom* [1976], 202n.16). It should more likely be understood as a predicative salvation saying (cf. Fohrer, KAT 16, 152; also Kraus, *Psa*, CC, 1:115, with reference to M. Buber), which focuses praise on a person (or group) for his/her beneficent well-being and establishes the person as exemplary—with a particular exhortative character—and which may be issued primarily in a wisdom context, but also with a more limited religious interest.

4. Of theological significance is the fact that one does not contrast these interests so that "wisdom" is essentially equated with "empirical wisdom," but that one emphasizes the religious character of wisdom (cf. Zimmerli, "Place and Limit of the Wisdom in the Framework of the OT Theology," *Studies in Ancient Israelite Wisdom* 316; Ch. Kayatz, *Studien zu Proverbien 1–9* [1966], 51f., who adduces Eg. material, as does, esp., J. Dupont, " 'Béatitudes' égyptiennes," *Bib* 47 [1966]: 185–222). Thus felicitous good fortune can be of various types and can refer e.g., to the possession of children, beauty, and honor, to the discovery of wisdom, as well as to the forgiveness of sin and trust in God (more precise references in Bertram, *TDNT* 4:365), yet it is generally true that the person congratulated does not violate God's established order but conforms to it (cf. Wildberger, *Isa 1–12*, CC, 196), and that, at the same time, well-being can be an observable expression of the manifest or expected blessing of God (so Janzen, op. cit. 218ff., contra S. Mowinckel, *Psalmenstudien* [1924], 5:1f., 54, and others, who, in the interests of the cult, understand *ʾašrê* as a kind of blessing very near to the word stem → *brk*, which seems inappropriate, however; cf. also J. Dupont, *Les Béatitudes* [1958^2], 321ff.). "Theological wisdom" and piety could also be given a nomistic turn (so, above all, in Psa 1; cf. also Psa 119:1f.; Prov 29:18b). Like the apocalyptic expression of Dan 12:12, Psa 1 deals with salvation as a contrast to ruin under God's power.

5. In the LXX, which continues to remain basically true to the conceptual model of the OT, as well as in the NT, where the term "refers overwhelmingly to the distinctive religious joy which accrues to man from his share in the salvation of the kingdom of God" (F. Hauck, *TDNT* 4:367), the Gk. equivalents to the word stem *ʾšr* are formed almost exclusively from the word group *makarios, makarizō,* and *makarismos.* Otherwise, the series (makarisms) are formally characteristic esp. of later literature (cf. Sir 25:7–11; Matt 5:3–12; Luke 6:20–23; → *hôy*). Cf. F. Hauck and G. Bertram, "μακάριος," *TDNT* 4:362–70; J. Dupont, *Les Béatitudes* (1958^2); A. George, FS Robert 398–403; K. Koch, *Growth of the Biblical Tradition* (1969), 6–8, 39–44, 59–62; W. Käser, *ZAW* 82 (1970): 225–50.

M. Sæbø

אֵת *ʾēt* **with** → עִם *ʿim*

אתה *ʾth* **to come** → בוא *bôʾ*

בגד *bgd* to act faithlessly

S 898; BDB 93b; *HALOT* 1:108a; *TDOT* 1:470–73; *TWOT* 198; *NIDOTTE* 953

1. The root *bgd* "to act faithlessly" has so far been identified outside Hebr. only in the Arab. dialect of the Datinah (C. Landberg, *Etudes sur les dialectes de l'Arabie Méridionale* [1905], 2:365f.; *Glossaire Datînois* [1920], 1:135), where *bajada* means "to mislead, to deceive."

Concerning the relationship of the root to *beged* "garment, covering" (215x in the OT) or Arab. *bijād/bujd* posited by Gesenius (*Thesaurus* 177), Landberg (op. cit.), etc., which would result in a basic meaning "tecte agere," one must abide by the caution of P. Joüon (*Mélanges de la faculté orientale de Beyrouth* 6 [1913]: 171). It is more likely that *beged* "garment" is a primary noun and can be disregarded in the following.

Derivatives include the noun *beged* "unfaithfulness" (Isa 24:16; Jer 12:1 in the cognate acc. *bgd beged*), the abstract pl. ptcp. *bōgᵉdôt* "faithlessness" (Zeph 3:4, in the phrase *ʾanšê bōgᵉdôt* "men of faithlessness"; according to Gemser, HAT 16, 113, also in Prov 23:28 *bôgᵉdîm* "deceit"), and the adj. *bāgôd* "faithless" (Jer 3:7, 10, interchangeable with the act. ptcp. *bôgēd*).

2. The verb occurs 49x in the OT, only in the qal. Thirty occurrences fall in the prophetic corpus (post-exilic additions in Isa 10x, Deutero-Isa 2x, Jer 9x, Hos 2x, Hab 2x, Mal 5x), 9 in Prov, 5 in Psa, and once each in Job, Lam, Exod, Judg, and 1 Sam. Together with the five occurrences of the noun mentioned above, the whole word group occurs a total of 54x; 35x or approximately 65% in prophecy.

The verb appears abs. 35x (23x in the ptcp.) and 14x (in addition to Psa 73:15 txt em) with *bᵉ* and the person (Yahweh in Jer 3:20; 5:11; Hos 5:7; 6:7; otherwise people: woman 4x, compatriot 3x, foreign nation 2x, king 1x). It is incorrect to assume a construction with *min* in Jer 3:20; *min* here should be translated "on account of" (contra S. Porúbčan, *Sin in the OT* [1963], 61, who also incorrectly cites a construction with *ʾēt*).

3. (a) The semantics of *bgd* must be derived from the OT itself, because the Arab. pars. mentioned under 1 are hardly productive. If one begins with the three presumably oldest attestations in Exod 21:8; Judg 9:23; 1 Sam 14:33, one derives, first of all, three categories of usage for the root, the first of which may be its original setting in life, while the second and third probably represent primarily transitional areas. Two secondary areas of expansion, one pretheological and one specifically theological, are appended; this differentiation is undertaken for the sake of overview and may not signify a strict distinction in subject matter.

The following categorization results: marriage law (3b), politico-diplomatic law (3c), cultico-sacral law (3d), social (3e), and specifically theological (4a-d) spheres.

(b) Exod 21:8 relates *bgd bᵉ* strictly to a legal status within slave law, a status established through a marital relationship. A slave designated for marital relations thereby attains "at least to a certain extent—the rights of a wife" (Noth, *Exod*, OTL, 179); if she displeases her husband, she may not be sold to a foreigner. Accordingly, the verb means: "to act contrary to the duty required by law or established by a relationship of loyalty into which the parties have entered." The translation "to act faithlessly" must bear in mind that the reference is less to an offensive attitude than to an objectively measurable offensive behavior.

If one extends the marriage law line from this passage, the following may be treated: Mal 2:14f. (on vv 10f., 16, see 3e), where *bgd* concerns divorce (v 16 *šlḥ* pi.) and is juridically qualified by *ʾēšet bᵉrîtekā* "wife of your marital contract" (Horst, HAT 14, 268), whose "witness" is Yahweh (v 14); Prov 23:28, where, in context with "whore" and "stranger" (= the wife of a strange man), *bôgᵉdîm* specifically means "adulterer"; Lam 1:2, where the faithlessly abandoned woman is a picture of Jerusalem abandoned by its allies, which established the transition to the political context (see c).

(c) Judg 9:23 exhibits *bgd* in the realm of politico-diplomatic law; it refers to the Shechemite defection from Abimelek.

In addition to Lam 1:2 (see b), Isa 21:2 (crime of the Babylonian vassals against Babel); 33:1; Hab 1:13; 2:5 lie in the same vein. In the last three passages, *bgd* has admittedly been applied, in an unusual expansion and at the same time an inversion, to the power politics of the foreign superpowers who scoffed at all limits of international law and in which "the godless *(rāšāʿ)* devours the righteous *(ṣaddîq)*" (Hab 1:13). It is noteworthy that Isa 33:1, "woe to the faithless, on whom faithlessness has not been practiced," is interpreted in v 8 precisely with "he has broken the contract *(bᵉrît)*." "Human power must be seen as . . . dissolved by God when it attacks the law, when it commits, as it were, a faithless contract *(bgd)* by brutally oppressing in order to elevate its own might" (Horst, HAT 14, 177).

(d) In 1 Sam 14:33, *bgd* qualifies the transgression of the ritual law of Lev 7:26f.; 17:10ff. (the prohibition against the consumption of blood) in par. to → *ḥṭʾ* "to err" as a cultico-sacral offense.

Such a usage also appears in Psa 78:57, as the comparison with v 58 ("high places," "idols") shows. In the probable event that this passage reprimands cult prophets, *ʾanšê bōgᵉdôt* "men of faithlessness," it belongs in this category too.

(e) *bgd* appears in Jer 12:6 (family); Job 6:15 (compatriots); Mal 2:10f., 16 (kinship of God's children); and in the proverbs applied to the still pre-theological realm of the community faithfulness demanded by created or natural social structures. In Psa 73:15 it means betrayal of the community of the "pious" (v 1), who, as "those who hope in Yahweh," oppose the *bôgᵉdîm rêqām*, the "senselessly faithless" in Psa 25:3. Prov 25:19 associates the *bôgēd* with false testimony (v 18).

4. (a) The specifically theological usage appears in the phrase *bgd bᵉ* with Yahweh (Jer 3:20; 5:11; Hos 5:7; 6:7), and in the usage of the verbs with direct reference to the relationship with God, often the ptcp. without obj. (or with a cognate acc.) (1 Sam 14:33; Isa 24:16; 48:8; Jer 3:8, 11; 12:1; Psa 25:3; 78:57; 119:158), and in the similar usage of the adj. *bāgôd* (Jer 3:7, 10).

(b) The application of marriage law concepts to the relationship with God occurs in Jer and Hos. Corresponding to the covenant ideology underlying this application, par. expressions here are *šûb mēʾaḥᵃrê* "to turn aside from," *znh* "to commit harlotry," *nʾp* "to commit adultery," and the antonyms *šûb ʾel* "to return to," *ʾth lᵉ* "to come (back) to," and *ydᶜ ʾet-yhwh* "to (ac)know(ledge) Yahweh." When Mal 2:10–16 uses the interrelated key words *bgd* and *bᵉrît* for both marriage and the covenant with Yahweh (vv 10, 14), it has long been anticipated, as shown by Hos 6:7 (*bgd bᵉyhwh* and *ᶜbr bᵉrît* "to transgress the covenant" elucidate each other) and Jer 3:8 (the "decree of divorcement" presupposes the concept of the "marriage contract").

(c) In the remaining passages, *bgd* is measured more in terms of norms and regulations of righteousness and community loyalty: in terms of *mišpāṭ* (→ *špṭ;* Isa 33:1, 5; Hos 5:1, 7; 6:5, 7; Hab 1:12f.), of *ṣᵉdāqâ* (→ *ṣdq;* Isa 33:1, 5; cf. the antonym *ṣaddîq* in Isa 24:16; Hab 1:13; 2:4f.), of *ʾᵉmûnâ* (→ *ʾmn;* Jer 9:1f.; Hab 2:4f.), and of → *ḥesed* (Hos 6:4, 6f.; Job 6:14f.). The adj. *rāšāᶜ* (→ *ršᶜ*) parallels the ptcp. *bôgēd* in Jer 12:1; Hab 1:13. Another important par. is the root *pšᶜ* "to break with" (R. Knierim, *Die Hauptbegriffe für Sünde im AT* [1965], 113ff.), which explicates the *bāgôd tibgôd* of Isa 48:8a in v 8b and the *bōgᵉdîm bāgādû ûbeged bôgᵉdîm bāgādû* of Isa 24:16 in v 20. The assumption that the political strain, in particular, found application to the relationship with God in the passages named in 4c is supported by this proximity to *pšᶜ*, which often indicates political apostasy.

(d) It is form-critically noteworthy that most passages appear in the accusation of prophetic judgment speech, also in the threat and in the lament. Elements of lament and accusation also carry the term in Psa and Lam. The legal home of the root *bgd* required that the prophets use it for the accusatory indictment of apostasy.

5. The stereotypical usage of the ptcp. of *bgd* at Qumran to describe the "sons of darkness" = "*the* disloyal" is foreshadowed in the OT. The par. *ᶜdt bwgdym* (CD 1:2; 6Q 3:13 = DJD 3:140) to *ᶜᵃṣeret bōgᵉdîm* in Jer 9:1, both of which may mean "assembly of the faithless," is interesting.

Because *atheteō* and *asyntheteō* are the most analogous translations of *bgd* in the LXX (in addition to the sporadic *anomeō, enkataleipō,* and the somewhat more frequent *paranomeō*), one probably reencounters the *bōgᵉdîm* in the *asynthetoi* of Rom 1:31 and the primitive Christian interpretation of the OT concept of *bgd bᵉyhwh* in Luke 10:16, "but whoever rejects *(athetōn)* me, rejects *(athetei)* him who sent me."

M. A. Klopfenstein

בַּד *bad* **solitariness** → אֶחָד *ʾeḥād*

בוא *bô*ʾ to come

S 935; BDB 97b; *HALOT* 1:112b; *TDOT* 2:20–49; *TWOT* 212; *NIDOTTE* 995

אתה *ʾth* **to come**

S 857; BDB 87a; *HALOT* 1:102a; *TWOT* 188; *NIDOTTE* 910

1. The verb *bô*ʾ "to enter, come" has cognates in most Sem. languages, although sometimes with somewhat divergent meanings (Akk. *bâʾu* "to go along," etc.; Arab. *bāʾa* "to return"); Aram. uses *ʾth* for "to come," *ʿll* for "to enter" (both occur as Aramaisms in Hebr.; see Wagner nos. 31f., 219f.).

In Mari, Akk. *bâʾu* is attested in the West Sem. meaning "to come" (*AHw* 117b; *CAD* B:181).

Ug. *ba* corresponds to Hebr. *bô*ʾ in meaning (*WUS* no. 487; *UT* no. 453). In Phoen.-Pun. the yi. (*KAI* nos. 5.1; 81.4) also seems to occur alongside the qal (*DISO* 32), as well as the subst. *mb*ʾ "setting (of the sun)" (*DISO* 141).

*môbā*ʾ and *mābô*ʾ "entrance," *tᵉbûʾâ* "produce," and once *biʾâ* "entrance," perhaps as an Akk. loanword (*HAL* 102a), occur as nom. forms in Hebr.

2. *bô*ʾ is the fourth most frequent verb in the OT, after *ʾmr* "to say," *hyh* "to be," and *ʿśh* "to do, make," and thus the most frequent verb of movement (*hlk* "to go" is sixth after *ntn* "to give"):

	qal	hi.	ho.	total
Gen	168	46	3	217
Exod	78	45	1	124
Lev	30	44	7	81
Num	69	22	–	91
Deut	84	22	–	106
Josh	54	5	–	59
Judg	87	8	–	95
1 Sam	143	27	–	170
2 Sam	133	15	–	148
1 Kgs	96	18	–	114
2 Kgs	128	19	5	152
Isa	102	21	–	123
Jer	159	52	2	213
Ezek	131	57	3	191
Hos	11	–	–	11
Joel	7	1	–	8
Amos	10	3	–	13
Obad	4	–	–	4
Jonah	5	–	–	5
Mic	10	1	–	11
Nah	1	–	–	1
Hab	6	–	–	6
Zeph	2	1	–	3
Hag	5	3	–	8
Zech	18	4	–	22
Mal	7	3	–	10
Psa	70	8	1	79
Job	47	4	–	51

	qal	hi.	ho.	total
Prov	31	3	–	34
Ruth	18	–	–	18
Song Sol	5	5	–	10
Eccl	12	3	–	15
Lam	7	3	–	10
Esth	29	8	–	37
Dan	33	10	–	43
Ezra	13	4	–	17
Neh	29	20	–	49
1 Chron	46	16	–	62
2 Chron	109	48	2	159
OT	1,997	549	24	2,570

The table includes passages with the place designation *lᵉbô*ʾ *ḥᵃmāt* ("where one enters Hamath") (11x; cf. M. Noth, *Num*, OTL, 104f., 250; id., BK 9, 192; K. Elliger, *BHH* 2:630), as well as Gen 30:11 Q, but not Job 22:21.

Of the nouns, *mābô*ʾ occurs 23x (Ezek 5x), *môbā*ʾ 2x (2 Sam 3:25 Q; Ezek 43:11), *tᵉbû*ʾ*â* 43x (incl. Job 22:21; 11x in Lev, 9x in Lev 25; 8x in Prov, 6x in Deut) and *bi*ʾ*â* 1x (Ezek 8:5).

3. The numerous usages of the verb cannot be exhaustively treated here. The lexicons (cf. GB 86–88; Zorell 98–100; *HAL* 108–10) categorize these usages by the two major meanings "to enter" (antonymn → *yṣ*ʾ "to exit") and "to come" (antonym → *hlk* "to go") and append rarer meanings ("to go," "to come back," etc.) together with the many idiomatic expressions.

The usage with the subject → *šemeš* in the meaning "go down" should be added to the meaning "to enter" in *HAL* 109a (Gen 15:12, 17; 28:11; Exod 17:12; 22:25; Lev 22:7; Deut 16:6; 23:12; 24:13, 15; Josh 8:29; 10:27; Judg 19:14; 2 Sam 2:24; 3:35; 1 Kgs 22:36; Isa 60:20; Jer 15:9; Mic 3:6; Eccl 1:5; 2 Chron 18:34; cf. hi. "to cause to go down," Amos 8:9; *mᵉbô haššemeš* "sunset, west," Deut 11:30; Josh 1:4; 23:4; Zech 8:7; cf. Mal 1:11; Psa 50:1; 104:19; 113:3; ʿ*rb* IV, with the subst. *maʿᵃrāb*, also occurs in the same meaning; cf. Akk. *erēbu*).

The common meaning adapts itself well to euphemistic language, e.g., in Gen 15:15 "to go to the fathers" = "to die" and frequently in the meaning "to go in to a woman" = "to live together" (Gen 6:4; 16:2, 4; 19:31; 29:21, 23, 30; 30:3f., 16; 38:2, 8f., 16, 18; Deut 21:13; 22:13; 25:5; Judg 16:1; 2 Sam 3:7; 12:24; 16:21f.; Ezek 17:44; Psa 51:2; Prov 6:29; 1 Chron 2:21; 7:23; similarly also in Arab. and Ug.; see *WUS* no. 487 on *KTU* 1.10.II.21f.).

The meaning "to come" is developed in several directions. J. G. Plöger (*Literarkritische, formgeschichtliche und stilkritische Untersuchungen zum Deut* [1967], 174–84) investigated the formulaic combination of *bô*ʾ and *yṣ*ʾ ("to come and go," "exit and entrance"), and concluded that no specific life setting may be found for the combination (cf. Deut 28:6, 19; 31:2; Josh 6:1; 14:11; 1 Sam 18:13, 16; 29:6; 1 Kgs 3:7; 15:17 = 2 Chron 16:1; 2 Kgs 11:8 = 2 Chron 23:7; 2 Kgs 19:27 = Isa 37:28; Psa 121:8; 2 Chron 15:5; cf. Akk. *erēbu* and *aṣû*, *CAD* E:263; *HAL* 109b with bibliog.).

In addition to the spatial, the temporal usage of "to come" also occurs quite often, not only with temporal expressions (e.g., → *yôm* "day," in the prophetic introductory formula *hinnēh yāmîm bā*ʾ*îm* "behold, days are coming" in 1 Sam 2:31; 2 Kgs 20:17 = Isa 39:6; Jer 7:32; 9:24; 16:14; 19:6; 23:5, 7;

30:3; 31:27, 31, 38 Q; 33:14; 48:12; 49:2; 51:47, 52; Amos 4:2; 8:11; 9:13), but also with reference to announced events, which "arrive, come to pass" (cf. Deut 13:3; 18:22; 28:2, 15, 45; 30:1; Josh 21:45; 23:14f.; Judg 9:57; 13:12, 17; 1 Sam 9:6; 10:7, 9; Isa 5:19; 42:9; 48:3, 5; Jer 17:15; 28:9; Hab 2:3; Psa 105:19; Prov 26:2). *habbāʾôt* "the coming events" (Isa 41:22; cf. *hāʾōtîyôt*, Isa 41:23; 44:7, from *ʾth* "to come") is substantivized.

The Aramaizing equivalent *ʾth* qal "to come" (19x) and the hi. "to bring" (2x) occur occasionally in poetical texts as synonyms for *bô*ʾ, with concentrations in Deutero-Isa and Job. On Isa 21:12, see C. Rabin, FS Rinaldi 303–9.

Aram. *ʾth* "to come" occurs in the pe. 7x, in the ha. 7x in the meaning "to bring" and 2x in the meaning "to be brought."

4. (a) Approximately 40 passages mention a "coming" of God quite distinctly (cf. G. Pidoux, *Le Dieu qui vient* [1947]; F. Schnutenhaus, "Das Kommen und Erscheinen Gottes im AT," *ZAW* 76 [1964]: 1–22; E. Jenni, FS Eichrodt 251–61). One may best differentiate the coming of God in revelation in the old narratives, the coming conditioned by the cult or temple, and the hymnic or prophetic-eschatological descriptions of theophany.

Passages in the old narratives form a group in themselves. They describe not only the more modest coming of God's messenger (Judg 6:11; 13:6, 8–10; cf. Josh 5:14), but also of God himself, if even, as in E, only in a dream by night (Gen 20:3 to Abimelek; 31:24 to Laban; Num 22:9, 20 to Balaam; similarly in the story of Samuel's youth, 1 Sam 3:10) or in a rather indefinite usage in Exod 20:20 ("to come to test you"; cf. Deut 4:34, where *bô*ʾ also serves only as the basis for the following verb), or, as in J, in the cloud (Exod 19:9, J according to W. Beyerlin, *Origin and History of the Oldest Sinaitic Traditions* [1965], 10; according to Noth, *History of Pentateuchal Traditions* [1972], 31n.112, this is an addition in Dtr style).

The second group is very disparate: the altar law in Exod 20:24 ("to come to you and bless you") presupposes the drawing near of God to a cultic act. In the Philistines' thinking, God came into the camp with the ark (1 Sam 4:7). A cultically conditioned coming or entry of God is also probable in Psa 24:7, 9 in the context of the procession of the ark. Finally, God also returns to the new temple according to Ezek 43:2, 4; 44:2.

Depictions of epiphany or theophany, in which *bô*ʾ occurs often, although not as a key term (cf. → *yṣ*ʾ, → *yrd*, → *yp*ʿ hi.), form the most important group theologically (Westermann, *PLP* 93–101; J. Jeremias, *Theophanie* [1965]). According to Jeremias (op. cit. 136–46), the broadly varied genre of the theophany portrayal is independent of extrabiblical motifs (contra Schnutenhaus, op. cit. 4, 6) in its initial element, the depiction of Yahweh's arrival from his dwelling place (Deut 33:2 from Sinai; cf. Psa 68:18b txt em; Hab 3:3 from Teman); it has its original setting in the victory celebrations of the Israelite summons to arms, which celebrated the arrival of Yahweh to aid his people in the Yahweh war. From there the motif also spread widely beyond the hymnic sphere into the prophetic announcements of judgment and salvation, which could no longer announce Yahweh's coming only from Sinai, but, reflecting the prevalent notion of the dwelling place of Yahweh, also from Zion (Psa 50:3; cf. v 2), from afar (Isa 30:27, the name of Yahweh), even from the north (Ezek 1:4; cf. Zimmerli, *Ezek,* Herm, 1:119f.; cf. also Job 37:22 txt em, *ʾth* of the glory of God), or without reference to place of origin (Isa 40:10; 59:19f.; 66:15; Zech 14:5, cf. 2:14; Mal 3:1f., 24; cf. also Isa 19:1, Yahweh comes to Egypt). Psa 96:13 = 1 Chron 16:33; Psa 98:9 associate theophany, present only in overtones, with the motif of coming in judgment. These passages all share the fact that in them *bô*ʾ testifies to the God who intervenes in history.

Isa 3:14 (*bô*ʾ *b*ᵉ*mišpāṭ* ʿ*im,* "to enter judgment with"; cf. Psa 143:2; Job 9:32; 22:4; H. J. Boecker, *Redeformen des Rechtslebens im AT* [1964], 85) and Isa 50:2 ("why have I come and no one is here?"; cf. Isa 41:28) do not concern coming in the full sense of theophany, but involve *bô*ʾ in a fixed legal expression; cf. *ʾth* in Dan 7:22.

In Hos 6:3, "he will come to us like the rain," the verb is governed by the comparison. In Hos 10:12 *bô*ʾ functions only as an auxiliary verb introducing the subsequent action, as is the case in Zech 2:14 (cf. above on Exod 20:20; Deut 4:34).

(b) The verb *bô*ʾ plays a distinct role, moreover, in the messianic prophecy in Zech 9:9, "behold, your king comes to you"; Gen 49:10 ("until the *šîlōh* comes [?]") and Ezek 21:32 ("until he comes to whom the claim/judgment belongs") remain difficult and disputed. Cf. also Dan 7:13, the coming *(ʾth)* of the "man" in the clouds of heaven.

→ *qēṣ* "end" (Amos 8:2; Ezek 7:2–6 is probably dependent; cf. Gen 6:13; Lam 4:18), → *yôm yhwh* "the day of Yahweh," and similar expressions (Isa 13:6, 9, 22; cf. 63:4; Jer 50:27, 31; cf. 51:33; Ezek 7:10, 12; cf. vv 25f.; 21:30, 34; 22:3f.; Joel 1:15; 2:1; 3:4; Zeph 2:2; Zech 14:1; Mal 3:19, 23) are chief among the coming eschatological realities (e.g., fall, Isa 30:13; vengeance and recompense, Isa 35:4; sword, Ezek 33:3f., 6; days of vengeance and revenge, Hos 9:7; affliction, Mic 7:4; but also positively, light and salvation, Isa 56:1; 60:1; 62:11; the former dominion, Mic 4:8; with *ʾth:* Cyrus, Isa 41:25).

5. Of the very numerous translation options for *bô*ʾ in the LXX, the most frequent are *erchesthai, eiserchesthai,* and *ēkein.* On *bô*ʾ in the context of the messianic expectation at Qumran (1QS 9:11; CD 19:10f.), see A. S. van der Woude, *Die messianischen Vorstellungen der Gemeinde von Qumran* (1957), 58, 76f. On the coming of God (Acts 1:4, 8; 4:8), Christ, and the kingdom in the NT, cf. J. Schneider, "ἔρχομαι," *TDNT* 2:666–84; id., "ἥκω," *TDNT* 2:926–28; K. G. Kuhn, "μαραναθά," *TDNT* 4:466–72; A. Oepke, "παρουσία," *TDNT* 5:858–71.

E. Jenni

בושׁ *bôš* to be ashamed

S 954; BDB 101b; *HALOT* 1:116b; *TDOT* 2:50–60; *TWOT* 222; *NIDOTTE* 1017

1. The verb *bôš,* formed on the biradical base **bṯ* with a long vowel *(ā > ō),* occurs primarily in ESem. and NWSem., in Aram., with a triliteral

resolution of the hollow root to *bht;* cf. the infrequent Arab. *bhṯ* (Th. Nöldeke, *ZDMG* 40 [1886]: 157, 741).

One should distinguish *bôš* I from *bôš* II, used in the po. (Exod 32:1; Judg 5:28) in the meaning "to delay, hesitate" (N. H. Torczyner, *ZDMG* 70 [1916]: 557; cf. *HAL* 112f.; the meanings of Ug. *bš* and *bṯ* are disputed; cf. *WUS* nos. 597, 609f.; *UT* nos. 532, 544; Ezra 8:22 in the qal, cited as a possibility in *HAL* 113a, hardly belongs to *bôš* II).

That a double formation is possible in the hi. deserves mention as a grammatical peculiarity of *bôš* I: in addition to the normal *hēbîš,* the more frequent form *hôbîš* is to be explained as confusion with *ybš* hi. (BL 402); see 3b.

The following are derivatives: *bōšet* and *bûšâ* "shame," *mᵉbûšîm* "private parts"; *bošnâ* in Hos 10:6 appears to be a textual corruption (cf. Barth 346).

2. The verb occurs 129x (qal 95x, hi. 33x [*hēbîš* 11x, *hôbîš* 22x, incl. Isa 30:5 Q; Joel 1:12a, under *ybš* in Lis.], hitpo. 1x). It is absent from the Pentateuch except for Gen 2:25 (hitpo.), very rare in prose, little used in wisdom texts (Prov 6x hi.), and frequent in the Prophets (esp. Jer, 36x) and in Psa (34x).

The MT of Hos 13:15; Psa 25:3b *(BHS)* is not applicable; on Isa 30:5 Q/K, cf. comms.; Ezek 7:26 txt em *(BHS)* should be included.

Of the derivatives, *bōšet* occurs 30x, *bûšâ* 4x, *bošnâ* (Hos 10:6) and *mᵉbûšîm* (Deut 25:11) once each.

3. (a) The basic meaning in the qal is apparently "to be ashamed," in two senses: first, objectively establishing the fact ("to come to nothing"), but at the same time, subjectively characterizing the feeling of the one come to nothing ("to feel ashamed").

The expression *ʿad-bôš* (Judg 3:25; 2 Kgs 2:17; 8:11) is a stereotypical formula with the sense "(to the point of) embarrassment," etc.; cf. similar formulations in Eng. (Torczyner, op. cit. assumes *bôš* II here).

The verb's range of meaning becomes apparent in the par. expressions, sometimes with an objective and sometimes with a subjective character:

(1) *klm* ni., ho. "to be humiliated" (originally "to be injured"; cf. L. Kopf, *VT* 8 [1958]: 179), Isa 41:11; 45:16f.; Jer 14:3; 17:13 txt em *(BHS);* 22:22; 31:19; Ezek 36:32; Psa 35:4; 69:7; Ezra 9:6; more remotely, Isa 54:4;

(2) *ḥpr* "to feel shame," Isa 1:29; 24:23; 54:4 (hi.); Jer 15:9; 50:12; Mic 3:7; Psa 35:26; 40:15; 71:24; more remotely, Psa 35:4; 83:18;

(3) *ḥtt* "to be shattered, dismayed," 2 Kgs 19:26 = Isa 37:27; Isa 20:5; Jer 17:18 (ni.);

(4) *ḥwr* "to turn pale," Isa 19:9 txt em *(BHS);* 29:22;

(5) *sûg* ni. "to withdraw," Isa 42:17; Psa 35:4; 40:15; 129:5;

(6) *bhl* ni. "to be terrified," Psa 6:11; 83:18.

pḥd "to terrify" (Isa 44:11), *šdd* pu. or qal pass. "be destroyed" (Jer 9:18), *ʾumlal* "to wither, mourn" (Jer 15:9), *ʾbd* "to perish" (Psa 83:18), *kšl* "to stumble" (Jer 20:11) occur once each; cf. also expressions of mourning such as *ḥph rôʾš* "to cover the head" (Jer 14:3) and *npḥ nepeš* "to exhale life" (Jer 15:9).

The subjective or objective aspect may be isolated only in a few cases, e.g., in the diction of the individual lament, the language is of shame, remorse

(Jer 31:19; 51:51; otherwise Job 19:3), or, by contrast, the enemy's ruin (Psa 6:11; 31:18, etc.; see 4). *śmḥ* "to be happy" (Isa 65:13; Psa 109:28; cf. Isa 66:5) appears as the antonymn of the subjective aspect.

(b) The regular hi. has the causative meaning "to cause to be ashamed" (Psa 44:8; 119:31, 116; 14:6 and 53:6 txt?; Prov 29:15, in each case with obj.); the ptcp. occurs without obj. in Prov 10:5; 12:4; 14:35; 17:2; 19:26 as a characterization of the unwise fool, primarily in contrast to the wise (*maśkîl*, Prov 10:5; 14:35; 17:2; *ʾēšet ḥayil* "worthy wife" Prov 12:4; cf. the par. expression *maḥpîr* "disgraceful" Prov 19:26).

The second form, constructed on the analogy of the initial *waw/yod* verbs, almost exclusively has an inner-transitive meaning and thus approaches the qal (in Joel 1:10, 12a the distinction from *ybš* "to wither" is difficult), although a causative meaning also occurs rarely: "to shame" 2 Sam 19:6; cf. "to treat disgracefully" Hos 2:7.

(c) The hitpo., perhaps originally used by J in Gen 2:25, moves entirely in the personal-subjective realm ("to be ashamed before one another").

(d) Like the verb, the derivatives embrace both aspects, from disgrace, worthless(ness), to shame (Deut 25:11 *mᵉbûšîm*, specialized in the meaning "private parts"). Parallel terms are *kᵉlimmâ* "humiliation" (Isa 30:3; 61:7; Jer 3:25; Psa 35:26; 44:16; 69:20; 109:29) and *ḥerpâ* "disgrace" (Isa 30:5; 54:4; Psa 69:20). The expression *bōšet pānîm* (Jer 7:19; Psa 44:16; Dan 9:7f.; Ezra 9:7; 2 Chron 32:21), lit. "shame of the face," perhaps "blush," is common. *bōšet* is used synonymously with the divine name *baʿal* in Jer 3:24; 11:13; Hos 9:10, as well as in the PNs *ʾîš bōšet* (2 Sam 2:8), *yᵉrubbešet* (11:21), *mᵉpībōšet* (21:8), perhaps also in the Lachish Letter 6:6 for Bel-Marduk (H. Michaud, *Sur la pierre et l'argile* [1958], 101; cf. *HAL* 158b).

The vocalization of the divine name *melek* as *mōlek* may be explained from this perspective; such has been the common opinion since A. Geiger, *Urschrift und Übersetzungen der Bibel* (1857); contra O. Eissfeldt, *Molk als Opferbegriff im Punischen und das Ende des Gottes Moloch* (1935).

4. The subjective aspect plays a minor role in the religious usage of the word, mostly in the plaintiff's description of his/her remorseful attitude. The objective aspect is esp. significant, first in the lament of the enemy (Psa 6:11; 35:4, 26; 40:15; 70:3; 71:13, 24; linguistically dependent, Jer 17:13, 18; Isa 26:11): The plaintiff prays for the annihilation of the enemy, but also for his/her own protection from destruction. This prayer is usually associated with the motif of trust (Psa 22:6; 25:2f., 20; 31:2, 18; 69:7; 71:1). The supplicant, then, lays claim to God's help and protection from destruction; because the enemy cannot expect this aid, he/she is abandoned to annihilation.

The prophets borrowed the verb from the cult; in prophecy it has its place in proclamations of judgment (Isa 1:29; 19:9; 41:11; 65:13; 66:5; Jer 15:9; 20:11; Ezek 16:63; 32:30; 36:32; etc.) directed either at foreign nations or at Israel, but also in promises of salvation for Israel (annihilation of the enemy; esp. since Deutero-Isa, Isa 45:17, 24; 49:23; 54:4; etc.). The concept formulated in the Psa is consistently maintained here too: that which contradicts Yahweh's will must come to naught.

Thus one can finally understand why *baʿal* is called "*bōšet*" and *melek* is vocalized on the same model: These gods are the power deeply hostile to Yahweh, revealed in Yahweh's presence as pernicious nothingness; cf. the designation *beliyaʿal*, which apparently means something similar ("worthless," "negative principle," etc.; cf. V. Maag, "*Belījaʿal* im AT," *TZ* 21 [1965]: 287–99).

5. The NT continues to employ the OT usage, borrowed from the LXX, to a degree; cf. R. Bultmann, "αἰσχύνω," *TDNT* 1:189–91.

F. Stolz

בחן *bḥn* to test

S 974; BDB 103b; *HALOT* 1:119a; *TDOT* 2:69–72; *TWOT* 230; *NIDOTTE* 1043

---

1. *bḥn* "to test" is also represented outside Hebr. in Aram. (although sparsely).

On account of the proximity of meaning, an original connection with Arab. *mḥn* is postulated, as well as with the root → *bḥr* "to choose," Aram. also "to test" (older literature in GB 92a). Yet in the OT, *bḥn* "to test" and *bḥr* "to choose" are distinct (the meaning "to test" for *bḥr* in Isa 48:10; Job 34:4, 33; ni. Prov 10:20 is to be viewed as a borrowing from the Aram.; see Wagner no. 38; id., FS Baumgartner 358f.).

The two citations in *DISO* 33 for Imp. Aram. *bḥn* "to test" on an ostracon from Elephantine and in Aḥ. 203 are rather uncertain; Syr. *bḥn* pa. means "to test, dispute." *bḥr* is apparently not attested in Old Aram.

The verb occurs in the qal and ni. The nomen agentis *bāḥôn* "examiner" occurs as a subst.

L. Köhler (*TZ* 3 [1947]: 390–93) identifies the *bōḥan* stone in Isa 28:16 as an Eg. loanword for a type of rock ("paragneiss"); the traditional translation "proven stone" or "proving stone" assumes derivation from *bḥn* "to test" (cf. *HAL* 115a).

The word *bōḥan* in Ezek 21:18 stands in an entirely uncertain text. *baḥûn* (Isa 23:13) and *baḥan* (Isa 32:14) in the meaning "watchtower" or some such (Eg. loanword; see *HAL* 114a, 115a) do not belong to the root.

2. *bḥn* qal occurs 25x (Psa 9x, Jer 6x, Job 4x, also in Zech 13:9bis; Mal 3:10, 15; Prov 17:3; 1 Chron 29:17), ni. 3x (Gen 42:15f.; Job 34:36), *bāḥôn* 1x (Jer 6:27a, with *bḥn* qal in 6:27b).

3. (a) One may not prove that *bḥn*, like *ṣrp* "to smelt, purify," which acquires the fig., more general meaning "to sort (people)" and "to examine (liver and heart)" (e.g., Judg 7:4; Psa 26:2), had a technical meaning that gave rise to the metaphorical meaning "to test" (*HAL* 114b), even though the word occurs once with the obj. "gold" (Zech 13:9, par. *ṣrp* with the obj. "silver") and the process of the purification of fine metals is readily used as a metaphor for "to purify, test" in the personal arena (*ṣrp* par. to *bḥn* in Jer

6:27–30; 9:6; Zech 13:9; Psa 17:3; 26:2; 66:10; cf. Prov 17:3; also perhaps Isa 48:10 *ṣrp* par. *bḥr* "to test"; other verbs in Mal 3:3; Dan 12:10).

Other par. verbs and usages of *bḥn* point to a rather general meaning "to test = to investigate (critically)."

bḥn appears alongside → *ydᶜ* "to know, recognize" (Jer 6:27; 12:3; Psa 139:23), → *pqd* "to investigate" (Psa 17:3; Job 7:18), → *rʾh* "to see (inspect)" (Jer 12:3; 20:12; cf. Psa 139:24; cf. Akk. *amāru* and *barû* "to see" and "to test," *AHw* 40f.), → *ḥzh* "to see" (Psa 11:4), *ṭᶜm* "to taste" (Job 12:11; 34:3), → *špṭ* "to judge" (Jer 11:20), and → *nsh* pi. "to try" (Psa 26:2; 95:9).

The objs. of testing always belong, with the exception of Zech 13:9 (gold), to the personal realm.

People (12x), their way (Jer 6:27), their words (Job 12:11; 34:3; Gen 42:16, ni.), their heart (Jer 12:3; Psa 17:3; Prov 17:3; 1 Chron 29:17; cf. also Sir 2:5; Wis 3:6; 1 Pet 1:7; → *lēb*), or liver and heart (Jer 11:20; cf. 17:10; Psa 7:10; Jer 20:12 and Psa 26:2). Concerning Yahweh as obj. (Mal 3:10, 15; Psa 81:8 txt em; 95:9), see 4.

(b) Besides the verbs already mentioned (→ *ydᶜ*, → *nsh*, → *pqd*), a few other, less frequent terms with various connotations must be considered as semantically related verbs:

(1) *ʾzn* pi. "to weigh out" (Eccl 12:9; cf. G. Rinaldi, *Bib* 40 [1959]: 268f.) is a denominative from *mōʾzᵉnayim* "scales";

(2) *bûr* (Eccl 9:1 txt?) and *brr* (Eccl 3:18; pi. Dan 11:35; hitp. Dan 12:10; hi. Jer 4:11) mean "to sort, test," proceeding from the concrete notion of cleansing, sorting, purifying (Ezek 20:38 qal; Isa 52:11 ni.);

(3) on *bḥr* "to test" see 1 (in Isa 48:10 1QIsa[a] has *bḥn*);

(4) the pi. ptcp. *mᵉbaṣṣēr* "gold tester" has been suggested for *mibṣār* in Jer 6:27 (*HAL* 142b) as a derivative of *beṣer* "gold ore" (Job 22:24f.; cf. F. Rundgren, *Or* 32 [1963]: 178–83);

(5) *bqr* pi. "to examine, care for, have in mind" (Lev 13:36; 27:33; Ezek 34:11f.; Prov 20:25) could go back to a cultic technical term (2 Kgs 16:15; Psa 27:4; cf. *HAL* 144b with bibliog.; Kraus, *Psa*, CC, 1:334);

(6) *ḥqr* "to investigate, explore" (qal 22x) can also be translated "to test" in some cases (e.g., Job 29:16 of the examination of a legal case; *ḥqr* with Yahweh/God as subj.: Jer 17:10; Psa 44:22; 139:1, 23; Job 13:9; 28:27);

(7) on *ṣrp* see 3a;

(8) *śbr* qal means "to test (walls)" in Neh 2:13, 15; otherwise pi. "to hope, wait" (Wagner no. 292; cf. Lat. *spectare* and *exspectare*);

(9) *tkn* "to test" (Yahweh tests the spirits/hearts/deeds: Prov 16:2; 21:2; 24:12; ni. 1 Sam 2:3) connotes that which is fixed or ordered in other occurrences of the root.

4. (a) More often than people (Jer 6:27; Zech 13:9, in a comparison; Mal 3:10, 15; Psa 95:9; the ear: Job 12:11 and 34:3; cf. Gen 42:15, 16 ni.; through emendation, also in Jer 9:6; cf. Rudolph, HAT 12, 66, and Psa 81:8; cf. Kraus, *Psa*, CC, 2:146), Yahweh is the subj. of the testing (all other passages, Psa 11:4, his eyes [not: "eyelashes"; cf. *UHP* 67]), in Jer 6:27 and 9:6 through the

agency of his prophet. The nation is infrequently the obj. of Yahweh's testing; as a rule it is the individual or people in general.

Jer 6:27; 9:6; Zech 13:9; Psa 66:10 (cf. also Isa 48:10) use the image of the testing and purification of fine metal in the context of Yahweh's history with his people. Part of Jeremiah's prophetic office involves his commission as examiner of the people (6:27); he is to lament over the negative result (6:27–30; 9:6). In the other cases of salvation manifest through judgment (Zech 13:9, the purification of the remaining one-third; Psa 66:10, communal thanksgiving song), the "testing" takes on the sense of a purificatory judgment.

Most cases envision Yahweh's relationship to the individual. In the language of the Psa, also adopted in the confessions of Jer, as well as in wisdom literature, one knows God as the righteous judge who tests heart and liver (Jer 11:20; 12:3; 17:10; 20:12; Psa 7:10; 17:3; 26:2; Prov 17:3; 1 Chron 29:17) and who calls the individual to account (Psa 11:4f.; 139:23; Job 7:18; 23:10). In Job 34:36, Elihu's thought escalates to the level of trial by suffering (cf. Fohrer, KAT 16, 469).

5. The LXX most often uses *dokimazein* to translate *bḥn.* On the Qumran literature and the NT (OT quotations in 1 Thess 2:4; Acts 2:23), cf. Kuhn, *Konk.* 30f. (also *GCDS* 65) and W. Grundmann, "δόκιμος," *TDNT* 2:255–60; G. Delling, "ἐρευνάω," *TDNT* 2:655–57.

E. Jenni

בחר *bḥr* to choose

S 977; BDB 103b; *HALOT* 1:119b; *TDOT* 2:73–87; *TWOT* 231; *NIDOTTE* 1047

I. 1. (a) The root **bḥr* is represented irregularly in the Sem. languages. It occurs in a meaning similar to Hebr. primarily in Akk. and in later Aram. (also in Amor. and Old SArab. in PNs), but is absent (to date) in the NWSem. texts of the OT period. The basic meaning may be preserved most truly in Bedouin Arab.: "to fix one's eyes intently upon" (*HAL* 115a).

Classical Arab. has a *bḥr* V "to penetrate deeply; to study thoroughly" (Wehr 42). J. G. Wetzstein has documented the verb in the meaning "to look around, look up (on the hunt)" or "to look (in a tent)" among the bedouin of the Syrian wilderness in the Damascus area (*ZDMG* 22 [1868]: 75, l. 9, cf. 122; 83, l. 9, cf. 148). Old SArab. seems to know only the theophoric name *ybḥrʾl* (G. Ryckmans, *Les noms propres sud-sémitiques* [1934], 1:221).

Akk. uses the verb *bêru,* which, according to the law of sound changes, corresponds to *bḥr,* in the meaning "to choose" (objs.: men, messengers, fighters, etc., but also things, wares) and, less certainly, "to test" (cf. *AHw* 122f. with *CAD* B:212f.), in addition to the verbal adj. *bēru* "chosen, picked," at Mari also substantivized *beʾrum* (so *AHw* 122b and *CAD* B:211 instead of the older reading *beḫrum,* e.g., in ARM XV:193; cf. *GAG* §23e, f) in the meaning "elite troop" (cf. M. Noth, *Die Ursprünge des alten Israel im Lichte neuer Quellen* [1961], 35; D. O. Edzard, *ZA* 56 [1964]: 144; M. Wagner, FS Baumgartner

358f.). *beḫēru* "to choose, select (troops)" and *biḫirtu* "selection (of soldiers)" occur as Aram. loanwords in Late Bab. (*AHw* 117f, 125b; *CAD* B:186a, 223b).

The root occurs in Amor. PNs (*yabḫarum, bataḫrum, biḫirum, biḫira,* etc.; cf. Huffmon 175).

The root cannot be identified in Old and Bibl. Aram. The later Aram. dialects (Jewish Aram., Christ. Pal., Syr., Mand.) use the verb in both meanings "to test" and "to choose" (Wagner no. 38).

(b) In a few passages in the OT *bḥr* also means "to test" (Isa 48:10; Job 34:4, 33; cf. Sir 4:17; ni. ptcp. "tested" in Prov 10:20; perhaps also pu. "to be tested" in Job 36:21 txt em; cf. Hölscher, HAT 17, 84f.; *HAL* 115b). "To test" is otherwise → *bḥn* in Hebr. (so also in Isa 48:10 according to 1QIsa[a] *bḥntykh*). Aram. influence is possible for both Job passages. The similarity in form and meaning suggests the likelihood that a relationship exists between the roots *bḥr* and *bḥn* (cf. the bibliog. in Wagner no. 38); the variant *bḥr* has established itself almost completely in the meaning "to select, choose," and *bḥn* in the meaning "to test, put to the test."

(c) M. Dahood (*Bib* 43 [1962]: 361) postulates an additional root *bḥr* "to assemble" for 1 Sam 20:30 (where *bōḥēr* is usually emended to *ḥābēr*) and Eccl 9:4 (where Q *y[e]ḥubbar* is read instead of K *y[e]buḥar*) on the basis of Akk. *paḫāru* "to assemble," Ug. *pḫr* and *mpḫrt*, Phoen. *mpḥrt* "assembly." This suggestion may deserve consideration (cf. also *HAL* 115b); otherwise, the emendations cited are to be accepted, so that both passages become irrelevant for *bḥr* "to select."

2. (a) The verb *bḥr* occurs in the qal and the ni. (on the possible pu. in Job 36:21 see 1b; on Eccl 9:4 K see 1c). The pass. ptcp. *bāḥûr* "selected," replaced in religious language by the substantivized adj. *bāḥîr* "chosen," belongs to the qal. Other substantives (in the profane arena) are *mibḥôr* (2 Kgs 3:19; 19:23) and *mibḥār* "choice, best."

(b) In analogy to Akk. *beʾrum* "elite (troop)," Hebr. *bāḥûr* "(fully grown, strong) young man" (Mid. Hebr. also *b[e]ḥûrâ* "maiden"), pl. *baḥûrîm* (GB 91a: "young warriors," Isa 9:16; 31:8; Jer 18:21; Amos 4:10; Lam 1:15; etc.) should not be treated apart from the verb *bḥr* (Noth, op. cit. 35; contra *HAL* 114a, 115a). It contrasts with *zāqēn* "old" (Jer 31:13, etc.) and parallels *b[e]tûlâ* "virgin" (Deut 32:25, etc.); it is used in the military sense in 2 Kgs 8:12; Isa 31:8; Jer 18:21; 48:15; 49:26 = 50:30; Ezek 30:17; Amos 4:10; Psa 78:31; 2 Chron 36:17; cf. also Ezek 23:6, 12, 23. The two abstract pls. *b[e]ḥûrîm* (Num 11:28) and *b[e]ḥûrôt* (Eccl 11:9; 12:1), which mean the "age of the young man" and the "bloom of life," resp., belong to this *bāḥûr.*

Akk. *baḫūlāti* "warriors, troops," which has been seen as evidence for a separate root *bḫr* since J. Barth, *ZA* 3 (1888): 59; and H. Holma, *Die Namen der Körperteile im Assyrisch-babylonischen* (1911), 100n.4 (e.g., P. Joüon, *Bib* 6 [1925]: 314f.; Zorell 103a; KBL 117b), is, according to *AHw* 96b, 117b, only artificially differentiated from *baʾūlātu* "subordinates" for Sargon and Sennacherib; this word belongs, however, to *bêlu* (→ *baʿal*). G. Quell's reference (*TDNT* 4:146n.5) to the Mid. Hebr. *bḥl* pi. "to ripen" is also unproductive (cf. Dalman 51b; *HAL* 114b).

(c) *mibḥār* (probably "selected"; cf. *IP* 224) and *yibḥār* (contra KBL 359a, probably a wish name in hypocoristic abbreviation like Amor. *yabḫarum;* cf.

IP 209) occur as PNs in 1 Chron 11:38 and 2 Sam 5:15; 1 Chron 3:6; 14:5, resp. Here it is testimony to the individual's belief in election. That it does not occur more frequently and that PNs containing Yahweh are altogether absent (cf., in contrast, Amor. *yabḫar-*[d]IM and Old SArab. *ybḥrʾl*) should be considered evidence that in Israel "election" relates primarily to the relationship between God and people (see IV).

baḥûrîm (2 Sam 3:16, etc.; on the location see *BHH* 1:191f.; 2:1342; in addition to *baḥûrīmî*, which is conjecturally a gentilic in 2 Sam 23:31 and 1 Chron 11:33) is possibly so named because young people were accustomed to gathering there.

II. 1. *bḥr* qal occurs in the MT 146x. The following table distinguishes between a profane usage (Pr) and a theological usage with God (TG) or with people (TP) as subj. The following distribution results:

	Pr	TG	TP	total
Gen	2	–	–	2
Exod	2	–	–	2
Num	–	3	–	3
Deut	1	29	1	31
Josh	1	1	2	4
Judg	–	–	2	2
1 Sam	5	5	–	10
2 Sam	5	2	–	7
1 Kgs	2	10	–	12
2 Kgs	–	2	–	2
Isa 1–39	2	1	1	4
Isa 40–55	1	7	1	9
Isa 56–66	–	3	4	7
Jer	–	1	–	1
Ezek	–	1	–	1
Hag	–	1	–	1
Zech	–	3	–	3
Psa	1	9	3	13
Job	7	–	–	7
Prov	–	–	2	2
Neh	–	2	–	2
1 Chron	2	7	–	9
2 Chron	1	11	–	12
OT	32 (22%)	98 (67%)	16 (11%)	146

Contrary to Lis. 208c, Jer 8:3 should be parsed as ni. The passges 1 Sam 20:30 (see I/1c); Psa 84:11; and 2 Chron 34:6 K are excluded from the profane category through textual emendation; Isa 48:10 (see I/1b) should probably be excluded from the TG category. *bḥr* is conjectured in Psa 16:4 and Job 23:13. The verb also occurs in Sir 4:17 in the meaning "to test."

The table suggests that: (a) The theological usage predominates markedly, esp. the usage with God as subject (b) The profane usage already occurs in the old portions of the OT (already in J); the oldest passage, albeit textually uncertain, may be Judg 5:8. The theological usage is later (not yet attested in J and E), and seems therefore to have arisen and prevailed only in the course of Israel's history. (c) The theological usage with people as subj. occurs relatively seldom; it is certain, however, that Israel's or individual Israelites' choice of God (or proper behavior) can be discussed. (d) The distribution, esp. of the theological usage with God as subj., is very irregular; thus it had not become dominant in all circles of Israelite piety. The concentration lies in Deut (29x) and in the Dtr history (20x).

The qal pass. ptcp. *bāḥûr* (19x, not included in the table: 2 Chron 5x; Judg 3x; 1 Sam, 2 Sam, and Jer 2x each; Exod, 1 Kgs, Psa, Song Sol, and 1 Chron, 1x each), the ni. (7x: Prov 6x, and Jer 8:3; cf. also Sir 37:28 and 41:16), and the pu. (1x; see I/1c) are not used in the profane meaning.

2. Among the substantives, *bāḥîr* always refers to the chosen of God (Psa 106:23, Moses; 2 Sam 21:6 txt?, Saul; Psa 89:4, David; Isa 42:1, the servant of God; Isa 43:20 and 45:4, the people; Isa 65:9, 15, 22; Psa 105:6 = 1 Chron 16:13; Psa 105:43; 106:5, the pious individual; cf. also Sir 46:1 and perhaps 49:19 = 50:44 emending *bāḥûr;* 13x in a noteworthy distribution: Psa 5x, Deutero-Isa and Trito-Isa 3x each, 2 Sam and 1 Chron 1x each).

mibḥār and *mibḥôr* occur 12x and 2x, resp., *baḥûr* "young man" 44x (36x are pl.; Jer 11x, Isa, Ezek, and Lam 5x each; Amos and Psa 3x each; Isa 42:22 is to be stricken from Lis. 207a), *b^{e}ḥûrîm*/*b^{e}ḥûrôt* 1x and 2x, resp.

III. 1. Aside from the few passages in which the translation "to test" is likely (see I/1b), *bḥr* in the profane usage means "to choose" or "to select." Thus the historical texts speak frequently of the selection of warriors (cf. Exod 17:9; Josh 8:3; 1 Sam 13:2; 2 Sam 10:9 Q "selection from all the choice ones *[b^{e}ḥûrê]* of Israel"; 17:1; cf. also *mibḥār* in Exod 15:4; Jer 48:15 *mibḥar baḥûrāyw* "his chosen band of young men"). The people choose their king (1 Sam 8:18; 12:13); the priest selects the sacrificial animal (1 Kgs 18:23, 25). But the commoner, too, is repeatedly confronted with a choice in daily life: Gen 13:11; Deut 23:17; 1 Sam 17:40, etc. The meaning of *mibḥār*/*mibḥôr* "choice, the best" reflects this situation; cf. e.g., Gen 23:6; Deut 12:11; Isa 22:7; Jer 22:7.

2. (a) The choice that one makes can be related strictly to an obj.: one chooses the fittest, the most appropriate, the best, and the most beautiful. Because the basic meaning may be "to regard precisely" and the verb can also mean "to test," this value orientation is surely a primary element. The subj. itself is involved, in fact, because it evaluates, but this evaluation arises from a rational consideration. Typical of this aspect are the par. terms → *ḥzh* "to discern" (Exod 18:21 in comparison to v 25), → *yd^c* "to recognize, understand" (Job 34:4; cf. Amos 3:2; Jer 1:5), → *bîn* hi. "to recognize" (Job 34:4 txt em).

(b) The subj.-conditioned, volitional meaning should be distinguished from this obj.-oriented, cognitive meaning: one chooses what one would dearly like to have, what pleases one, what one loves. A strict distinction between the two aspects is impossible. But the second aspect manifests itself very clearly in the translators' rendering of the word in such passages with "to elect" and not simply with "to choose, select," occasionally even with "to choose for oneself," expressing the subj.'s engagement, as well as with "to wish for"

(2 Sam 19:39), "to want" (Gen 6:2), "to have greater desire" (Job 36:21), "to be pleased with" (Prov 1:29), "to prefer" (Job 7:15) and "to determine" (Job 29:25, all examples taken from ZB); cf. also *bḥr l*ᵉ in 2 Sam 24:12 with the corresponding *qbl* pi. *l*ᵉ in 1 Chron 21:11. Par. terms that appear in this sense are → *ḥmd* "to desire" (Isa 1:29), → *š*ʾ*l* "to request" (1 Sam 12:13), → *bqš* pi. "to seek" (Isa 40:20), → ʾ*wh* pi. "to wish for" (Psa 132:13; Job 23:13 txt em), → *ḥpṣ* "to take pleasure" (Isa 56:4; 65:12; 66:3f.). In Hos 5:11 *y*ʾ*l* hi. "to want" appears where one would expect *bḥr;* one chooses for oneself not simply the good, but "what is good in one's eyes" (cf. 2 Sam 19:39). Consistent with this connotation, the ni. ptcp. means "desired, precious" (Prov 8:10, 19; 10:20; cf. also 16:16; 21:3; 22:1). The "choice" transpires in these cases on the basis of a pleasure that is not rationally founded or, indeed, rationally demonstrable.

3. (a) In the profane usage in the OT, the subj. of the act of selection is a prominent personality (the leader of the people, the king, the priest) or the people, collectively; in the wisdom sphere, however, it is the person, the individual.

(b) In wisdom, the obj. of choice shifts too. One is called to make the correct choice between the ways of good and evil (Prov 3:31; cf. also 1:29), between right and wrong (Job 36:21; cf. also Job 9:14; 15:5; 34:33). Here it is assumed, without reflection, that people can freely choose between good and evil, right and wrong. Moral decision is not always intended by the choice of the "good" (→ *ṭôb*). In 2 Sam 19:39, "what is good in your eyes" means the choice of that which pleases. Isa 7:15 may mean Immanuel's capacity to comprehend the external world by the choice of the good and the rejection of the evil (cf. Wildberger, *Isa 1–12*, CC, 315).

4. *m*ʾ*s* "to reject" occurs as the primary antonym of *bḥr*, indeed, apparently for the entire range of its meaning (cf. e.g., 1 Sam 8:7, 18; Isa 7:15; Psa 78:67; Job 34:33).

IV. The word *bḥr* has become a technical term in the OT for "election" (most important studies: K. Galling, *Die Erwählungstraditionen Israels* [1928]; H. H. Rowley, *Biblical Doctrine of Election* [1950]; Th. C. Vriezen, *Die Erwählung Israels nach dem AT* [1953]; K. Koch, "Zur Geschichte der Erwählungsvorstellung in Israel," *ZAW* 67 [1955]: 205–26; R. Martin-Achard, "La signification théologique de l'élection d'Israël," *TZ* 16 [1960]: 333–41; H. Wildberger, *Jahwes Eigentumsvolk* [1960]; P. Altmann, *Erwählungstheologie und Universalismus im AT* [1964]; H. J. Zobel, "Ursprung und Verwurzelung des Erwählungsglaubens Israels," *TLZ* 93 [1968]: 1–12; H. Wildberger, "Die Neuinterpretation des Erwählungsglaubens Israels in der Krise der Exilszeit," FS Eichrodt 307–24; also G. Quell, *TDNT* 4:145–68 [bibliog.]; G. E. Mendenhall, *IDB* 2:76–82 [bibliog.]).

The focus of the theological usage of *bḥr* lies on the discussion of the election of the people by God (IV/2–4, pre-exilic, exilic, and post-exilic periods), while the human choice of God or of the right path fades in significance (IV/5). The concept of God's election of the king is, however, older in Israel than that of the election of the people (IV/1).

1. (a) Among Israel's neighbors the king was generally regarded as the one selected by the deity (cf. S. Morenz, "Die Erwählung zwischen Gott und König

in Ägypten," FS Wedemeyer 118–37; R. Labat, *Le caractère religieux de la royauté assyro-babylonienne* [1939], 40ff.).

On the Nile, as in the Mesopotamian region, the title "son" expresses the special, "select" status of the king with his god, although in varied theological conceptualizations (→ *bēn* IV/3a). In the 18th–20th Dynasties, the formula "Amun, who loves (the pharaoh) *X* more than all other kings" occurs (Morenz, op. cit.; further D. Müller, *ZÄS* 86 [1961]: 134; Quell, op. cit. 157n.64, 158n.68). Mesopotamians say that the deity knows the king (Akk. *edû*, → *ydᶜ*); he is the deity's favorite (Akk. *migru;* cf. Seux 162–68, 448f.), the deity commissions him, calls his name (Akk. *nabû*), etc. The Akk. *(w)atû(m)* (Sum. pà), with the meaning "to see" and the nuances "to discern, choose, call," as well as "to look around, seek," often used to express the election of kings by gods (Seux 368f., 433–36; ibid. 121f. on *itûtu* "election, elect, called"), approximates Hebr. *bḥr* most closely in terms of meaning and usage. The theme "election of the king" is also present when e.g., Zkr of Hamat acknowledges: "Be'elshamayn made me king" (Aram. *mlk* ha.; *ANET* 655b; *KAI* no. 202A.3). For details see H. Frankfort, *Kingship and the Gods* (1948), 238f.; de Vaux 1:100f.

(b) In view of the situation among Israel's neighbors, one should presume that Yahweh's election of the king was a theme from the very beginning of the Israelite monarchy. The question is only the degree to which the term *bḥr* already described the king's special status before Yahweh within the royal ideology. Considering the presence of this usage already in David's succession narrative (2 Sam 16:18; cf. also 2 Sam 6:21; see A. Weiser, *VT* 16 [1966]: 344, 348), the use of *bḥr* may go back as far as the Davidic period (cf. also the admittedly late texts 1 Sam 16:8–10). Even Saul may have already been characterized as Yahweh's chosen (cf. 1 Sam 10:24 and the uncertain text 2 Sam 21:6, which, contrary to most exegetes, should probably be retained), in each case in passages that use older traditions.

(c) Even though Israel shares with its neighbors the notion of the king's election, the unique character of its faith becomes apparent very soon here too. This development becomes evident already in that the Saul tradition addresses not only the election but also the rejection of the king (1 Sam 15:23, 26, admittedly, not in the same layer of tradition, but rejection presupposes election). This duality is all the more remarkable when texts occasionally attribute imperishability to "Yahweh's anointed" (1 Sam 24:7, 11; 26:9, 11, 16, 23; 2 Sam 1:21). The king's failure explains the rejection. Just as the question arises as to how one chosen by Yahweh can fail, it expresses the recognition that election by Yahweh must find response in the proper behavior of the elect. Without an awareness of the responsibility inherent in election, election itself is called into question. That northerners apparently hardly discussed the king's election is related to this insight. Even Deut 17:15 (if 17:14ff. is truly northern, as K. Galling, *TLZ* 76 [1951]: 133–38, assumes, and the statement on election is not to be regarded as secondary with R. P. Merendino, *Das deuteronomische Gesetz* [1969], 179ff.) constitutes less a witness to the notion of the king's election than to the fact that this theme has not been fully developed.

(d) The situation differs in the south. No one ever doubted David's election. Admittedly, 2 Sam 7 does not exhibit the root *bḥr,* but the title *nāgîd* conferred upon David is semantically related to *bāḥîr* (cf. W. Richter, *BZ* 9 [1965]: 77).

The focus of the Nathan promise is not the election of David, however, but of his "house." Indeed, the royal psalms (which doubtlessly belong to the pre-exilic period) have recourse to David's election, but primarily because it implies the election of the current ruler (Psa 78:67; 89:4, 20). It was not easy to maintain belief in the election of the Davidides in the face of the quite often unpleasant reality. Psa 89 is a moving document concerning the struggle about the validity of the election of the Davidic house. The author considers it necessary to conclude from the weakness of the Davidides that Yahweh has rejected *(mʾs)* his "anointed" and has abandoned his covenant with David (vv 39f.). But he cannot and will not believe that election may thus be void. He interprets election as a covenant sworn by Yahweh to David (vv 4, 35, 50; cf. also Psa 132:11), appeals to Yahweh's faithfulness (vv 2f., etc.), and underscores the constancy, duration, even "eternity" of the relationship between Yahweh and king created by election (vv 5, 22, 29f., 37). Election cannot become invalid, even if rejection has become evident.

(e) The tribes apparently exalted Saul to king because of his brave deliverance of Jabesh (1 Sam 11). But the narrative in 1 Sam 10:17–24 has it otherwise: Saul is chosen by lot. He is a shy man who hides. As he is brought forth, it becomes apparent that he "towers over everyone by a head." The parallel David narrative goes deeper: the criterion is not height—Yahweh rejects David's tall brother—"Yahweh regards the heart" (1 Sam 16:7). David's beauty is then, indeed, extolled (v 12). But what proves David as king is neither his physical features nor his spiritual qualities, but it is the Spirit of Yahweh (v 13) that is conferred upon him in the process of election. The qualities of the chosen are therefore not incongruent with those expected of a king; but precisely why one is chosen remains, finally, a contingent, divine secret, not to be revealed.

(f) These texts do not depict the purpose to which the king is chosen. But it is self-evident that Yahweh's anointed is committed to a task among the people. David is "prince over Yahweh's people" (2 Sam 6:21; cf. 7:8 and Psa 78:71). Nathan's prophecy already used the term *ʿebed* to describe the king's relationship to God (→*ʿbd;* 2 Sam 7:5, etc.; Psa 78:70; 89:4, etc.; 132:10). Indeed, *ʿebed yhwh* became a par. term for *bᵉḥîr yhwh* (e.g., Psa 105:6). In this context the word means the "minister" or "vizier" ordained to execute his lord's will among the people, indeed, among the peoples (cf. W. Zimmerli, *TDNT* 5:657f., 663f.).

2. (a) From a particular point of time onward, the OT discusses not only the king's election but also the people's election, embodying a novelty in the history of ancient Near Eastern religion. The idea of Israel's special status before Yahweh is nothing short of constitutive for its faith. It is already expressed in the simple formula that Yahweh is Israel's God. One does not speak of traditions of election without reason (K. Galling, *Die Erwählungstraditionen Israels* [1928]; H. Wildberger, *Jahwes Eigentumsvolk* [1960]; cf. Zobel, op. cit. 6ff.). The notion of Israel's election can be easily expressed, however, without the term *bḥr.* OT research has almost reached a consensus that Israel's election was not explicitly discussed before Deut (von Rad, *Gottesvolk* 28: "The verb *bḥr* [subj., God; obj., people] is an original Dtn coinage"; Vriezen, op. cit. 47; Mendenhall, *IDB* 2:76). This consensus is questionable,

however, because the pertinent statements in Deut already exhibit a molded, stereotypical form. The Psalms provide additional indications. As mentioned above, Psa 78 speaks not only of David's election but also of Judah's (v 68), commenting that Yahweh rejected the tent of Joseph and did not choose the tribe of Ephraim. This psalm gives a clue as to the great distress that the fall of Israel (or an earlier crisis of this political entity) caused proponents of the election idea. Statements concerning election in Psa 33:12; 47:5; and 135:4, usually considered post-exilic, may indeed go back to formulations older than Deut.

(b) In Deut, then, the theologoumenon of Israel's election is present in a comprehensive theological formulation. In 17:15 the book also speaks, however, of the king's election (see IV/1c), and the stereotypical formula "the place that Yahweh your God will choose" occurs most frequently by far in Deut, notably only in the law code (Deut 12:5–26:2, 20x; cf. also 31:11; Josh 9:27; etc.; see 3a). Everything points, however, to the fact that the theory of Zion's election ("in order to cause my name to dwell there," etc.) made its way into Deut only in the context of the Jerusalemite redaction (see Merendino, op. cit. 382ff.). In contrast, Deut speaks of Israel's election primarily in the second preface (7:6f.; 10:15; in addition to 14:2 and 4:37). The notion of the king's election was, without doubt, also alive in the north. But presumably under the weight of the old exodus-election tradition, possibly also as a result of the experience of the monarchy's failure, the term *bḥr* became the terminological expression of Yahweh's devotion to Israel. The concept was thus transferred in the process of this democratization from the realm of myth (election of the king or of the divine mountain) into that of history (exodus from Egypt). According to the evidence of Psa 78:68, people seem to have sincerely struggled, even in Jerusalem after the demise of the north, with the question of the status of the election of the people.

(c) The classical OT text for Israel's election is Deut 7:6–8. The passage is nestled in the parenetic piece 7:1–11, which challenges Israel to separate itself from Canaan; i.e., election is not thematic, but serves as the motivation of the parenesis. The continuation vv 9–11 uses the covenant tradition as a second motif. Israel's election is therefore not treated in isolation, but in order to justify Yahweh's claim on Israel. Indeed, the reference to the election in 10:12 establishes Yahweh's comprehensive demand for obedience: to fear God, to walk in his paths, to love him, and to serve him with the whole heart and soul. The stereotypical formulation "chosen from the peoples" betrays the fact that the theological usage of *bḥr* in this area resulted from interchange with Canaan.

The meaning of election is explicated by association with the two terms *ʿam qādôš* "holy people" and *ʿam* → *sᵉgullâ* "special people," apparently derived from the tradition. Thus the polyvalent term *ʿam qādôš* is simultaneously defined: Israel is not holy because of a special cultic or moral integrity, but by virtue of the fact that it has become Yahweh's own people through election. Because Israel's holiness is accordingly not inherent but rests upon Yahweh's choice, however, Israel must acknowledge its obligation to behave in conformity with this act of Yahweh's free grace. The misunderstanding that Yahweh's choice may rest upon Israel's special merit is resisted vehemently in 7:7f. (probably secondary; cf. the "2d-per.-pl. style"): first, in v 7 through the explication of *bḥr* by *ḥšq* "to cling to, love," in v 8 through the reference to Yahweh's love for Israel (→ *ʾhb* IV/2) and to his faithfulness to his promise to the fathers, but then also through the negation, "not because you were more numerous than the other nations." Deut 9:4–6 extends the notion even more clearly: "not for the sake of your righteousness *(ṣᵉdāqâ)* and the purity *(yōšer)* of your heart"—indeed, even radicalizes it: "for you are a stubborn people." Deut 10:14f. (also secondary) further underscore the irrationality of Yahweh's attention to Israel expressed in election by presenting Yahweh as the lord of heaven and earth.

The contribution of the Deuteronomic author is carefully conceived theologically; because of him "election" prevailed as a terminological expression of Yahweh's attention to Israel. He interpreted election as an absolute act of grace, grounded only in Yahweh's love for Israel, which cannot be further explained. Finally, he described it as a dialectical process: it attests to Yahweh's love and demands obedience in faithfulness on the part of God's people. The community-founding word proceeds from Yahweh; it demands, however, an unmistakable answer from the addressee, Israel. With this understanding of the relationship between Yahweh and Israel, Deut stands in proximity to pre-exilic prophecy.

(d) In a peculiar disjunction, the election of Zion stands alongside that of the people (12:5, 11, 14, 18, 21, 26; 14:23–25; 15:20; 16:2, 6f., 11, 15f.; 17:8, 10; 18:6; 26:2; 31:11). The even more thoroughly formulaic nature of this material makes it clear that Deut has already incorporated preexistent viewpoints. Koch (op. cit. 215f.; contra Vriezen, op. cit. 46f.) has rightly called attention to this state of affairs. Psa 132, probably early pre-exilic, already speaks of the election of Zion as Yahweh's dwelling place (v 13). Psa 78, from the late royal period, also knows of Yahweh's election of Zion (v 68 "which he loves"). One can even ask whether Jerusalem's election was not already discussed in the Jebusite period. Mesopotamian sources also occasionally mention the election of a sanctuary by a divinity, although this election usually occurs only indirectly, insofar as the king is specifically chosen to build or care for the sanctuary (cf. H. Wildberger, FS Eichrodt 309n.9). But the election of one sanctuary in the exclusive sense of the Jerusalemite cultic centralization called for in Deut is unparalleled.

The election formula, "the place that Yahweh, your God, will choose," can be expanded by "from all your tribes" or "in one of your tribes" (12:5, 14). These expansions reflect Jerusalem's claim to be the central place of worship for all Israel. The formula can also be expanded by the expression "in order to place his name there" (12:5, 21) or "in order to cause his name to dwell there" (12:11; 16:2, 6, 11; cf. also 12:5). In contrast to the statement of Psa 132, which still speaks naively of Yahweh's choice of the temple as his "dwelling place," as a "lasting resting place," these expressions signify a sublimation. "Name" means revealing presence (→ *šēm*).

Occasionally the formula "the place that Yahweh will choose" is, indeed, simply a circumlocution for the name Zion/Jerusalem (arising from the fiction that places Deut on Moses' lips so that Jerusalem's election may not already be anticipated as fact). In general, however, the formula signifies more. The place of Yahweh's presence is the source of blessing, delight, life (e.g., Psa 36:8ff.). Yahweh's choosing this place in the midst of the tribes testifies to his solidarity with Israel; Yahweh manifests himself thus as "your God." But the contrast with Deut's statements concerning Israel's election is even more striking: if Israel realizes its election in Deut by considering its salvation history, it does so here by participating in the cult of the central sanctuary. If election implies the obligation of Israel in Deut, here it implies the facilitation of a life under the protection and blessing of God. A bit of temple theology has thus broken into the amphictyonic world. It is certainly no accident that the formula occurs repeatedly in ch. 12 with its regulations governing cultic centralization and in ch. 16 with its festival calendar. Correspondingly, Deut, although doubtless in a later layer of material, already speaks of the Levites' election "from all your tribes" (18:5; 21:5). The elect priesthood belongs to the elect sanctuary. Like the unity of the temple, the unity of the priestly family also assures the proper function of a mode of worship that grants and assures salvation.

(e) In view of the cultic election doctrine evident here, it is noteworthy that the pre-exilic prophets, both collectively and singly, do not speak of Zion's election, or even of Israel's, using the term *bḥr.* They surely know the *concept* of election (e.g., Amos 3:2), but they also call it into question (e.g., Amos 9:7). One can understand, then, their avoidance of the term *bḥr;* it too easily gave rise to the dangerous illusion that Israel's salvation may be assured through the execution of the cult at holy places, or that Israel is immune to disaster because it is chosen. Even the Jerusalemite Isaiah, who knew the notion of the election of the king and the temple, mentions it only to qualify it theologically by placing both concepts under the condition of faith (7:9; 28:16) and shifting them into the horizon of eschatological events (2:2–4; 9:1–6).

3. (a) The Deuteronomistic history, dating to the exilic period, found it necessary to deal with the realities of the collapse of the Davidic kingdom, the destruction of the temple, and the end of Israel as a nation. If 1 Sam 10:24 spoke of the election of Saul (cf. H. J. Boecker, *Die Beurteilung der Anfänge des Königtums in den deuteronomistischen Abschnitten des 1. Samuelbuches* [1969], 48f.) and later passages of Saul's rejection (see IV/1c), the Dtr passage 8:18 now says that the people themselves chose the king. This choice by Israel is, according to v 8, to be frankly equated with idolatry (cf. Judg 10:14). Yahweh alone can be king over Israel; the people's choice of the king was in fact a rejection of Yahweh (1 Sam 8:7). To be sure, the Deuteronomistic history did not suppress the old traditions sympathetic to the kingdoms of Saul and David, or even Nathan's promise. But the Deuteronomistic writer himself used *bḥr* only of David (1 Kgs 11:34 and perhaps 8:16 txt?). Never does Dtr call one of the Davidides Yahweh's "elect," although the royal psalms do precisely that. It is easier for Dtr to speak of Jerusalem's election (1 Kgs 8:16, 44, 48; 11:13, 32, 36; 14:21; 2 Kgs 21:7 "eternally"; 23:27; as in Deut, "in order to place my name there," etc., can be added). Apart from 1 Kgs 3:8 (not certainly Dtr), Dtr never speaks of Israel's election in Kgs,

apparently simply because the unconditional corollary to election according to Deut, namely, fear of Yahweh and love for him, appears to him to be lacking in the Israel of the royal period. Indeed, he not only brackets out the theme of Israel's election, but in his summary concerning the fall of the north he speaks of its rejection (2 Kgs 17:20), which, according to v 19, includes Judah too. And in 23:27 he speaks expressly of the removal of Judah "from my presence, as I removed Israel." In the same breath he speaks of the rejection of the elect city Jerusalem together with its temple (cf. also 24:20). The picture that he paints is gloomy enough, then: the people have thoroughly wasted the unheard-of possibilities that Yahweh offered Israel through election, and indirectly through the election of the king and the temple site.

But the Deuteronomistic history would indeed be misunderstood if interpreted as a funeral song for the great utopia of Israel's election: the election of the Davidides, in contrast to that of Saul, is not revoked. The conclusion of the entire work, the narrative of the friendly turn in Jehoiachin's destiny, seems to offer the house of David too yet another chance. The "eternally" in 2 Kgs 21:7 indicates that Jerusalem will yet have a future beyond its rejection.

Josh 24 also belongs to the exilic period. It is certainly an old tradition, but the Deuteronomist has redacted it (cf. J. L'Hour, "L'alliance de Sichem," *RB* 69 [1962]: 5–36, 161–84, 350–68), e.g., in vv 15 and 22, which seem to offer Israel the possibility of free choice. But one must interpret the passage from an exilic background. Israel is in danger of transferring allegiance to other gods. The Dtr addresses his historical sermon to this situation. The decision has been made long ago: "You are witnesses against yourselves, that you have chosen Yahweh to serve him" (v 22). The chief image is "Joshua and his house" with his clear Yahwistic position. The author does not speak of Israel's election by Yahweh because for him the question is not whether Yahweh will continue to view Israel as his people, but whether Israel, under the influence of the experience of catastrophe, is willing in the final analysis to abide by the decision for Yahweh.

Dtr speaks once, though rather extensively, of Israel's election: Deut 4:37, "because he loved your fathers and chose their descendants and brought you out of Egypt." The passage, apparently an adaptation of Deut 7:6–10 to a new situation, provides clues as to the kind of test of strength belief in election underwent after the fall of Jerusalem. Here, too, election is anchored in Yahweh's love, but in his love for the fathers. Instead of the statement that Yahweh made Israel his own people in the act of election, it is now emphasized, after possession of the land has become questionable, that the election became manifest in Yahweh's gift of the land to Israel as an inheritance. The corollary to election by Yahweh is no longer just obedience and fear of God, but—after the crisis of 586 had shaken Yahwism to the core—more radically, the recognition that Yahweh alone is God and no other (v 35), in heaven above and on earth below (v 38). Nevertheless, the Deuteronomist continues in the tradition of Deut by incorporating his statement concerning election into a sermon, which has as its theme, however, not only obedience to Yahweh but return to him (v 30).

(b) At approximately the same time as the Deuteronomistic writer, Deutero-Isa must have been written. While the former was presumably active in

Palestine, the latter was in Babylon. But Deutero-Isa belongs to another world, not only geographically but also intellectually. He sees himself in relation to an audience that certainly does not deceive itself concerning the extent of the collapse, but that asks uncertainly whether Israel still has a future. He answers the question by consciously concentrating his preaching on the election notion. It is indicative that he prefers to address the theme in salvation oracles. This usage occurs most impressively in Isa 41:8–13. God's people will be addressed not only as Israel and Jacob, but also as "offspring of Abraham, my friend": election is transposed even further back into history and related to the relationship between Yahweh and Abraham. The title "my servant" for Israel is also a novelty (cf. also 44:21; 45:4). The par. terms *ᶜebed* and *bāḥîr* stem from royal ideology (see IV/1f). The democratization of the concept of the king's election is thus fully realized in Deutero-Isa (cf. e.g., 55:3ff., where the grace promised David is transferred to the people). The fact that 41:9 verifies "I have chosen you" with "and not rejected" indicates that it is combating a radical doubt in the doctrine of election. Deutero-Isa too saw election as realized in a historical act: Yahweh selected Israel "from the ends of the earth." It may be an allusion to the call of Abraham from Mesopotamia rather than to the exodus from Egypt. At other points Deutero-Isa refers even more radically to the beginnings: According to 43:20f., the elect Israel is "the people that I formed for myself"; election is transposed into the act of Israel's creation (cf. also 44:1f.). This radicalization does not mean, however, that election remains an event of the distant past. In 43:18 Deutero-Isa plainly exhorts his reader to cease considering the former things, because Yahweh is creating something new, and, in conjunction with the election statements in 44:2, promises of salvation follow in vv 3f. The knowledge of election opens a future for Israel. For Israel's sake Yahweh entrusts Cyrus with dominion over the nations. Yahweh, who chose Israel, is also a redeemer (*gōʾēl*) and leads Israel, the "horror of the nations," home in a triumphal victory procession.

By contrast, temple theology found only partial reception in Deutero-Isa. Although he hopes for the reconstruction of Jerusalem and its temple (44:26; 49:17–23), he dares not base his faith on Zion's election. The pre-exilic prophets' harsh critique of the absolutization of the election concept had taken effect.

This effectiveness is also true of the Deuteronomistic critique of the throne. Deutero-Isa apparently sees no future at all for the Davidides. But individual elements of the royal ideology are incorporated in his picture of God's servant. The "servant of Yahweh" (surely a reference to an individual) is, like the king, *bāḥîr* (42:1). Like the king, he is equipped with Yahweh's Spirit (1 Sam 16:13; Isa 11:2). As servant he has a mission in the world: he is to carry the truth to the nations, he is to be the light of the nations; through him Yahweh glorifies himself. Whoever the servant of God may be, it cannot be accidental that the titles *ᶜebed* and *bāḥîr* are granted to him, as to Israel itself. He represents the true Israel, and statements about him make it clear that Israel's election cannot be separated from his mission. All previous interpretations of election are transcended, however, by the fact that the election of the servant of God is fulfilled in representative suffering.

One could ask whether the manner in which Deutero-Isa speaks of Israel's election might lead to the false sense of security that caused the pre-exilic prophets to oppose the notion of election so critically. Deutero-Isa avoids the danger by basing Israel's assurance of salvation neither on the temple nor on the king; above all, he excludes the danger through his interpretation of the *ᶜebed* concept. Here, too, election means being placed under obligation, but now as Yahweh's servant among the nations, not only for obedience but even for a witness in apparent failure, in suffering, and in death.

(c) Ezekiel too does not speak of the election of the Davidides or of the temple. He speaks expressly of Israel's election only once (Ezek 20:5). The reason for the obvious reticence lies in the repeatedly expressed awareness that Israel rejected Yahweh's commandments (Ezek 5:6; 20:13, etc.). Significantly, in the one passage where he mentions Israel's election, he does so only in order to accuse the people of failing to draw the implication of election, the abandonment of idols. Like the Dtr he does not want the essential contemplation and repentance to be neglected because of a reversion to election. In view of the extreme incisiveness of his judgment oracles, it is indeed remarkable that he does not speak of Israel's rejection.

(d) Jer 33:23–26 demonstrates that the problem of rejection was posed pointedly by contemporary events. The people discuss the rejection of the "two families that Yahweh chose." The author, who also probably belonged to the exilic period, forcefully resists this abandonment of faith: "As surely as I created day and night . . . , so surely will I not reject the family of Jacob and my servant David." Israel and its royal house remain chosen, not e.g., because they preserved themselves, but because Yahweh alters their fate and has mercy on them.

The author of Isa 14:1 sees it otherwise. For him, rejection has become a fact, but he dares to speak of an additional election of Israel. Just as the foundational election manifested itself in the exodus from Egypt, so now this repetition, which he also sees grounded in Yahweh's mercy, manifests itself in Israel's return to its homeland. Just as "many foreigners" accompanied Israel in the flight from Egypt (Exod 12:38), so many foreigners will join the house of Jacob in the second exodus. A later hand, then, commented rather unhappily on this beautiful notion: the nations that Israel will take along will be its manservants and maidservants.

4. (a) If the text of Jer 49:19 = 50:44 has been correctly transmitted, some circles in the exilic period expected Yahweh to install his "elect" as ruler. The reference can only be to a Davidide, and the passage would then be a further witness to the fact that belief in the election of the Davidides was not extinguished even in the exilic period. In any case, a little later in the post-exilic period Haggai dared to proclaim the Davidide Zerubbabel the elect of Yahweh (2:23). The old par. expression "my servant" is not overlooked, and his supremacy is described with the words: "that you may be to me like a signet ring." Zech 6:9–15 still suggests that Haggai's contemporary Zechariah also hoped for a reestablishment of the kingdom. The prophet also speaks

expressly of Jerusalem's election (3:2). In 1:17 and 2:16 he speaks more precisely of the *re*election of the city. One is prone to judge that statement, like the similar statement in Isa 14:1, to be theologically careless—in the final analysis, destructive of the election notion. But that the statement is possible in the OT realm indicates, nevertheless, that election is not deterministic and that the correlation of divine election and human submission to obligation is taken very seriously. "Yahweh's election does not only mean a blessed destiny. It is a summons which calls for responsibility" (Zimmerli, *Ezek*, Herm, 1:408). From another standpoint, Zechariah goes on like Isa 14:1: Yahweh will indeed continue to reside in Israel's midst, but "many nations will adhere to Yahweh in that day and will be his people." The particularism of the election belief is breached, a circumstance already foreshadowed in Deutero-Isa, without abandoning the special status of Israel.

(b) The post-exilic Psa 33 bears similar testimony. It uses the election concept in a felicitation: "Peace to the nation whose God is Yahweh, to the people he has chosen as an inheritance" (v 12). Israel need not fear because it is Yahweh's own (see also Psa 135:4, where even the old term *s^e gullâ* "special property" [cf. Exod 19:5] is used once more; further Psa 47:5). Nevertheless, Yahweh's choice of Israel as his inheritance does not exclude, but in fact involves, his reign over the whole earth (Psa 47:8). For this reason the psalmist dares the bold statement that the princes of the nations are assembled as "the people of the God of Abraham" (v 10). Even if *ᶜim ᶜam* "with the people" or simply *ᶜim* "with" instead of *ᶜam* "people" should be read (cf. comms.), the universality of God's dominion would still be linked to Israel's election (cf. P. Altmann, *Erwählungstheologie und Universalismus im AT* [1964]; H. Schmidt, "Israel, Zion und die Völker" [diss., Zurich, 1968], 11f., 19ff., 99f.).

(c) Psa 105 and 106 are also post-exilic; they retrace salvation history and already presuppose the closed Pentateuch. Psa 105:6 speaks of the "descendants of Abraham, his servant" par. to the "sons of Jacob, his chosen ones *(b^eḥîrāyw)*." Apparently one should read *b^eḥîrô* "his chosen one" here (cf. *BHS*): the patriarch is chosen, but at the same time, naturally, in him Israel is chosen. Therefore one could speak without difficulty in v 43 as in Psa 106:5 of the people as the chosen of Yahweh. The pl. is nevertheless noteworthy: the people now appears as a collection of individuals. The question arises, however, whether the chosen and the rejected in Israel should not therefore be distinguished.

(d) Trito-Isaiah too speaks of Yahweh's chosen (Isa 65:9, 15). Even old promises, which were associated with Israel's election, are revisited: they will possess the land and, as Yahweh's servants, live there. The chosen is no longer the empirical Israel, however, but the yet-to-be-created people of God of the coming era of salvation. Israel, as it is, has chosen evil in Yahweh's eyes (65:12; cf. 66:3f.). People's perverted choice excludes them from the circle of Yahweh's chosen. But Yahweh must yet create the true Israel: "I will bring forth a second growth from Jacob" (65:9), and this second growth will be "my people, who seek me" (v 10). Thus the boundaries of Israel, as it has been, are totally set aside. Those who keep Yahweh's Sabbath and choose what pleases him are "circumcised"; they are to have a "name and memorial" in Yahweh's house "that is better than sons and daughters" (56:4f.). It is enlightening that the disintegration of the people Israel in the late post-exilic period made it necessary to reformulate the election doctrine. This reformulation redefines the entity of the people of God in individual terms through the required correlation between human and divine choice. But this reconceptualization does not mean a cancellation of belief in Israel's election. The new people of God will continue to be, if not "Jacob's seed," then still "seed come forth from Jacob." Even though the temple too will be "a house of prayer for all peoples" (56:7), the Yahweh-fearers will still be instructed in Jerusalem. Above all, one can fall away from the elect Israel through one's own wrong choice; the new Israel, however, does not constitute itself by means of its own correct choice, but will be Yahweh's eschatological creation.

(e) The election of the tribe of Levi to the priesthood was already attested in a secondary layer of Deut (see IV/2d). It is no surprise that P concerns itself with the question of the legitimate priesthood in three passages where it speaks expressly of election (Num 16:5, 7; 17:20): the priesthood is now limited to the descendants of Aaron. This limitation is not undisputed, however. The narrative of the rebellion of Korah's band (Num 16, P version) is a description of the ordeal that should reveal "who belongs to him and who is holy so that he may draw near to him; whom he chooses, he may draw near to him" (v 5; cf. v 7). Num 17:16ff. (v 20) also speaks of a divine declaration that certifies election. The passages become transparent in meaning only when one ascertains that, besides this election, P speaks neither of the election of the people nor that of the king. The certainty of the election of the priestly house is sufficient. Salvation is assured by the fact that the right men exercise their duty before Yahweh. The priestly perspective can be understood against the struggle to provide Israel's faith in the presence of divine grace with a certain foundation. The disadvantage is, however, that Israel's obligations are limited to cultic correctness. The protest of the pre-exilic prophets against Israel's false security, which thought it possible to base its faith in the salvation-granting presence of Yahweh upon the temple, seems to have died away.

(f) The viewpoint of P found an echo in Psa 105. It too speaks of Aaron's election. But it mentions Moses as Yahweh's servant together with him (v 26; 106:23 does indeed expressly describe Moses as *bāḥîr*). The reason that the same psalm speaks of election of individuals (see IV/4c) and of that of Aaron and Moses is clear: Yahweh has chosen the people in love in order "to see its joy" in its good fortune (106:5). But Israel has proved itself unworthy of this election, as its history illustrates. It was destined to fall had not Moses "stepped into the breach" before Yahweh (106:23). This is an interesting attempt to deal with the problem of the repeated failure of the chosen people and the threat that election will be overturned in rejection; aware of its failure as Yahweh's chosen people, Israel clings to the election of its fathers, leaders, and mediators of salvation: Abraham (cf. also Neh 9:7), Jacob, Aaron, and now Moses too. The powerful spectacle in Isa 53 of the suffering of God's servant, who indeed is also Yahweh's elect, is again illuminating: "he, the righteous, my servant, will create righteousness for many" (v 11). The trial of the one who is elect makes it possible to sustain belief in the election of the many, just as one cannot speak in the NT of the election of God's people apart from Christ, the one *eklektos tou theou* (G. Schrenk, *TDNT* 4:186–92).

(g) The Chr history reworked available tradition. Accordingly, it offers no new election concept but a reformulation of earlier concepts. Its peculiar tendencies are nevertheless visible. In 1 Chron 28:4ff. and 2 Chron 6:5f. it incorporates 1 Kgs 8:16, which speaks of the election of Jerusalem and David. But the Chr expands: David's election presupposes the election of Judah, which is apparently identical with the true Israel. Above all, however, he speaks of Solomon's election too. The repetitions in 1 Chron 28:5f., 10 and 29:1 indicate that this election is of great importance to him. The actual reason for the king's election is that he is to build Yahweh a house (28:10; 29:1). Already according to Sum. and Akk. sources (see IV/2d), the deity selects the king specifically to function as caretaker of sanctuaries. In this way the Chr has associated the election of the king with that of Jerusalem as the place where Yahweh will cause his name to dwell even more closely than in the documents available to him. Elsewhere too he places great weight on Jerusalem's election (2 Chron 6:5f., 34, 38; 7:12, 16; 12:13; 33:7; Neh 1:9), the more so because he must justify an anti-Samaritan stance. Of course, the temple cannot be discussed without mentioning the Levites (1 Chron 15:2; 2 Chron 29:11). This summary indicates that the Chr is indeed interested only in the election of the temple and its priesthood. The king's election is no longer an independent theme; Israel's election is not discussed at all. If the temple worship can be properly celebrated, the problem of Israel's election becomes superfluous (1 Chron 16:13 is a quotation of Psa 105:6; Neh 9:7 too belongs to incorporated traditional material). The old temple ideology (see IV/2d) triumphed in the end, then. At any rate "Israel" is no longer God's people in the ethnic sense, but the cultic community as the band of those assembled at the place of sacrifice and worship, seeking God and praising him.

5. (a) God is not the only one who chooses and elects; people do too. The OT operates on the assumption that they can also choose their God or gods. If the text of Judg 5:8 is original, the oldest OT passage with *bḥr* in any form speaks of the choice of new gods. In the realm of polytheism and in the complex ethnic and religious situation of Canaan, the temptation to seek success with new gods must have been great. The first commandment addresses this very situation. As a rule, *bḥr* was not used of turning to other gods; the word had too much theological significance and too solemn connotations to be used in the polemic against apostasy. At any rate, Isaiah threatens: "Truly, you will be ashamed on account of the trees that you desire *(ḥmd)*, and you will blush on account of the gardens that you chose *(bḥr)*" (Isa 1:29; cf. Wildberger, *Isa 1–12*, CC, 74, 76f.). The Dtr challenges Israel sarcastically: "Go and cry to the gods whom you chose" (Judg 10:14), and in his anti-idol polemic Deutero-Isa calls to them: "See, you are nothing and

your deeds are nothing; the one who chooses you is an abomination!" (Isa 41:24). The same polemic also occurs once again in Trito-Isa (Isa 65:12; 66:3), and Psa 16, approximately contemporaneous, also seems to speak of the selection of other gods (v 4 read *bāḥārû* for *māhārû;* see H. Gunkel, *Psa* [1926⁴], 52). Significantly, this usage does not occur in contexts that simply note that Israel serves other gods, but in ironic polemic: if you believe you will do better with other gods, then, good, try. If you take pleasure (as ZB translates *bḥr* in Isa 66:3) in their paths, and your heart "takes delight *(ḥpṣ)* in their abominations," then also bear the consequences that such a choice brings. The choice of other gods and cults is indeed a possibility, which is given with the freedom of Israel, or its people, and it becomes a reality in this freedom time and again, but a reality that leads to self-destruction. This freedom to choose makes ruin possible.

(b) Whoever chooses a deity not only chooses another name for the divine but prescribes for himself/herself a particular path (Isa 66:3; cf. also Psa 119:30) and chooses particular regulations (Psa 119:173). Whoever denies Yahweh chooses not only what is evil in his eyes but evil per se, because Yahweh is creator and guardian of the moral world order. In this way, the wisdom ideal could be incorporated into the confession of Yahweh. In the final analysis, the choice of Yahweh or the fear of him and the choice of the way of truth (Psa 119:30) or of life are one and the same. The pious trusts in this identity: to the one who fears Yahweh, "he shows the way that he should choose" (Psa 25:12). Conversely, later wisdom, at least, can exhort one to choose the fear of Yahweh (Prov 1:29; cf. 3:31), but can also assure that the one who makes the right choice can expect blessing. His "soul" will "lodge overnight" in the realm of the good, i.e., will find fortune and salvation, "and his descendants will inherit the land" (Psa 25:13). Thus the old blessings and curses that conclude the legal corpus can be summed up in the Deuteronomist's interpretation by the challenge: "So choose now life, so that you may live" (Deut 30:19).

(c) Although the exhortation to choose the good in Yahweh's eyes, the right path, life, etc., can be stated, the final consequence—the summons to choose Yahweh himself—is lacking. This summons would correspond precisely to the complaint that Israel has chosen strange gods. Josh 24:15 at least approximates this conclusion: "If it does not please you to serve Yahweh, then choose today whom you will serve." Israel is apparently confronted here with the choice between Yahweh and the gods. But, aside from the fact that Dtr has in reality obligated Israel to a choice long since made (see IV/3a), the logic of the correlation breaks down even in this passage: the alternative to choosing the gods is not choosing Yahweh, but fear of Yahweh and worship of Yahweh in uprightness and faithfulness (v 14). Joshua contrasts the possibility of the people's faulty decision not with his own decision to choose Yahweh but with his pledge: "But I and my house, we will serve Yahweh." Israel is aware that one cannot choose Yahweh, as one may choose other gods. In the pluralistic history of religion, Yahweh is not one of the many options confronting the pious individual. Israel should not choose Yahweh; rather it should acknowledge that it is chosen by him. Therefore the choice of other gods affects only whether Israel will realize its potential as Yahweh's private possession. Israel is indeed required to choose the right path, but it may also trust that Yahweh will show it this path; it should choose life, but this choice is possible because Yahweh has "placed (life) before it" (Deut 30:19).

V. 1. *bḥr* occurs 30x and *bāḥîr* 20x in the available Qumran literature (according to Kuhn, *Konk.* 30f.). The election idea is closely linked to the Sinai covenant (1Q34bis 3 II:5), more directly than in the OT. The concept is transferred from the Sinai covenant to the "new covenant"; its members are "elect of God" (1QpHab 10:13) or "of Israel" (1Q37 1:3, etc.). Within the Qumran community itself, the Zadokite priests are elect in a specific sense. The *b*^{e}*ḥîrîm* are righteous and lead a perfect life (1QS 4:22f.), and God grants them a portion in the lot of the saints (1QS 11:7). They are chosen from the beginning of the world, which should not be understood, however, as strict determinism, for "before they were created, he knew their works" (CD 2:7f.). The chosen, then, are completely free to decide, and they are therefore also called the "free-willed" (1QS 5:1, etc.); they choose the path themselves (1QS 9:17f.). On Qumran, cf. F. Nötscher, *Zur theologischen Terminologie der Qumran-Texte* (1956), 174f.; id., *BZ* 3 (1959): 220ff.; J. Gnilka, *BZ* 7 (1963): 44–48; J. A. Fitzmyer, "The Aramaic 'Elect of God' Text from Qumran Cave IV," *CBQ* 27 (1965): 348–72.

2. The LXX usually translates *bḥr* with *eklegesthai* (for details, cf. G. Quell, *TDNT* 4:145f.). *bāḥîr* is always translated with *eklektos; eklegesthai* renders other Hebr. roots in only a few cases, which indicates that the word was understood as a theologically stamped term.

3. On the usage of *bḥr* or *eklegesthai* in early Judaism and in the NT, cf. G. Quell and G. Schrenk, "λέγω: ἐκλέγομαι/ἐκλογή/ἐκλεκτός," *TDNT* 4:144–92; G. Nordholt, "Elect, Choose," *DNTT* 1:533–43; further N. A. Dahl, *Das Volk Gottes* (1941), 51ff.; B. W. Helfgott, *Doctrine of Election in Tannaitic Literature* (1954); I. Daumoser, *Berufung und Erwählung bei den Synoptikern* (1955); H. Braun, *Spätjüdisch-häretischer und frühchristlicher Radikalismus* (1957); J. Jocz, *Theology of Election* (1958); U. Luz, *Das Geschichtsverständnis des Paulus* (1968), 64f., 179.

H. Wildberger

בטח *bṭḥ* to trust

S 982; BDB 105a; *HALOT* 1:120a; *TDOT* 2:88–94; *TWOT* 233; *NIDOTTE* 1053

---

1. Only a few, isolated instances of *bṭḥ* "to trust" have been identified so far outside the OT in Can.; it is absent in Aram. (apart from a few borrowings from the Hebr.) and is represented by the roots *rḫṣ/raḫāṣu* and *tkl/takālu* in Akk. Etymologies that attempt to trace *bṭḥ* to a physical-concrete root meaning have not yet produced universally accepted results.

A Can. gloss in EA 147:56 offers *ba-ti-i-ti (baṭīti)* "I am confident" (cf. *CAD* B:177a; *DISO* 33).

bṭḥ appears in a 6th-cent. Phoen. letter (*KAI* no. 50.5) in a damaged, not entirely lucid context ("security, guarantee"?).

On the PN *mbṭḥyh*, "Yahweh is the object of (my) trust," with the by-form *mpṭḥyh* and the abbreviated forms *mb/pṭḥ* in the Aram. Elephantine Papyri (Cowley 295a, 297b; *BMAP* 187), cf. J. J. Stamm, FS Baumgartner 314. Hebr. *mbṭḥyhw* occurs in Lachish Letter 1:4 (cf. *TGI*[1] no. 34).

On the basis of Arab. *bṭḥ* "to throw down" (VII "to lie on one's belly"), the meaning "to fall to the ground" has been postulated for Jer 12:5 and Prov 14:16, whether this may be taken as the basic meaning ("to lie there" > "to depend on" >) "to trust" (G. R. Driver, FS Robinson 59f.; J. Blau, *VT* 6 [1956]: 244; L. Kopf, *VT* 8 [1958]: 165–68), or a root *bṭḥ* II is assumed (*HAL* 116a: qal Jer 12:5; Prov 14:16; *baṭṭūḥâ* "inhabited valley" Job 12:6; denied e.g., by Rudolph, HAT 12, 84; Fohrer, KAT 16, 237), which presumes a different etymology for *bṭḥ* I (L. Köhler, *ZAW* 55 [1937]: 172f.; id., *OTS* 8 [1950]: 144f.; and KBL 118b: following Arab. *bāṭeḥ* "pregnant mare" and Hebr. *ʾabaṭṭīḥîm* "watermelons," he suggests *bṭḥ* "to be taut, firm" > "to be trustworthy, trust, be certain"; otherwise, Ch. Rabin, FS Baumgartner 225–28: Arab. *btʿ* with the basic meaning "to be strong" and a semantic shift from "strength, greatness" > "self-confidence").*

Qal and causative hi. forms are attested for the verb; there are also the nom. derivatives *beṭaḥ* and (traditionally) *baṭṭūḥôt* "security"; *biṭḥâ, mibṭāḥ,* and *biṭṭāḥôn* "trust"; *baṭûaḥ* "trusting."

2. The following statistics include passages attributed to *bṭḥ* II (see above):

	qal	hi.	*beṭaḥ*	other substs.	total
Gen	–	–	1	–	1
Lev	–	–	3	–	3
Deut	1	–	3	–	4
Judg	5	–	2	–	7
1 Sam	–	–	1	–	1
1 Kgs	–	–	1	–	1
2 Kgs	8	1	–	1	10
Isa	18	1	3	4	26
Jer	14	2	4	3	23
Ezek	2	–	11	1	14
Min. Pr.	5	–	4	–	9
Psa	44	1	3	4	52
Job	4	–	2	4	10
Prov	10	–	4	4	18
Eccl	–	–	–	1	1
1 Chron	1	–	–	–	1
2 Chron	1	–	–	–	1
OT	113	5	42	22	182

The column "other substs." consists of *baṭṭūḥôt* 1x (Job 12:6), *biṭḥâ* 1x (Isa 30:15; *biṭḥēk* is counted here, following Mandl. and *HAL* 116a, as qal inf., in Lis. under *beṭaḥ*), *mibṭāḥ* 15x (Prov 4x; Jer, Psa, Job 3x each; Isa and Ezek 1x each), *biṭṭāḥôn* 3x (2 Kgs 18:19 = Isa 36:4; Eccl 9:4), and *baṭûaḥ* 2x (Isa 26:3; Psa 112:7).*

3. (a) The verb occurs most often in the OT in prayer and song formulae: two-fifths of all texts are in the Psalter; moreover, outside Psa, many more texts belong to worship genres (cf. the prayer in Isa 12:2; the song in Isa 26:4) or mirror their themes (cf. the Dtr "discourses" in Jer 7:4ff.; 2 Kgs 18:5ff.). Without implicating the pertinent institutions, reference may be made to curse and blessing formulations, etc. (cf. Jer 17:5, 7; Isa 31:1; Amos 6:1), and prophetic judgment and salvation sayings that speak of trust in a similar manner (Isa 30:12; 42:17; 47:10; 50:10; 59:4; Hos 10:13; Mic 7:5; Zeph 3:2, etc.). Even genuine wisdom passages adopt the "religious" usage of *bṭḥ* (Prov 3:5; 16:20; 28:25; 29:25; cf. Job 11:18); the cultic usage stands, therefore, prominently in the foreground. The nouns are strewn over the literary field; *mibṭāḥ* seems to have arisen only since Judah's exile (Jer 2:37, the earliest text?).

(b) *bṭḥ* can describe secure circumstances or a secure frame of mind; the qal act. ptcp. esp. fulfills this purpose. The inhabitants of pre-Israelite Laish live calmly and peaceably (*šōqēṭ ûbōṭēaḥ*, Judg 18:7, 27) reflecting their good fortune; the word of judgment is directed against the peasant women who consider themselves safe (Isa 32:9ff.). "If a war befalls me, I will remain confident even in it" (*b^{e}zōʾt ʾ^{a}nî bōṭēaḥ*, Psa 27:3). One who feels safe in this manner does not fear (Isa 12:2; Psa 56:5, 12) and is shaken by nothing (Psa 21:8; cf. 25:2; 26:1). The simple qal impf. can also describe this status of security (Prov 28:1). As a rule one states the basis or direction of this feeling of security, esp. through prepositional usages *(bṭḥ b^{e}/ʾel/ʿal)*. One entrusts oneself (cf. the reflexive usage in 2 Kgs 18:24; Jer 7:8) to all sorts of objects, persons, and circumstances (the city walls, Deut 28:52; battle tactics, Judg 20:36; strength? Hos 10:13; treasures, Jer 49:4; beauty, Ezek 16:15), or even to evil (Isa 30:12). The relative clause "in which you trust" is used formulaically (cf. Deut 28:52; 2 Kgs 19:10 = Isa 37:10; Jer 5:17; 7:14; Psa 41:10; 115:8). If external circumstances are ordered and peaceful, one lives "in security" (adv. *beṭaḥ, lābeṭaḥ;* cf. 1 Sam 12:11; Isa 32:17; Mic 2:8; Prov 1:33; Lev 25:18f.; Judg 18:7; 1 Kgs 5:5; Ezek 38:8ff., etc.).

bṭḥ is not just a stative verb, however. It also expresses the beginning of the act of trust, which increases in a secure area of life or which aims at the creation of this area. Challenges to trust and warnings against unjustified security (pure impf.: Jer 17:5, 7; Psa 44:7; 55:24; 56:4f., 12; also impv., juss., and negated: Isa 26:4; 50:10; Jer 7:4; 9:3; 49:11; Mic 7:5; Psa 4:6; 9:11; 37:3; Prov 3:5) refer to a future act of trust; pf. predicates refer to the already proved, significant "entrusting of oneself" (cf. e.g., *bāṭaḥtî* "I trust," Psa 13:6; 25:2; 26:1; 31:7, 15; 41:10; 52:10; 56:5, 12, in addition to the impf. *ʾ^{a}nî ʾebṭaḥ* Psa 55:24 or the ptcp. *ʾ^{a}nî bōṭēaḥ* Psa 27:3). Whether it describes circumstances or states confidence of various durations, frequencies, and magnitudes, it always envisions an object of confidence; *bṭḥ* almost always refers to a process at the foundation of existence (contra A. Weiser, *TDNT* 6:191f.). Whoever trusts, relies on something (cf. *šʿn* "to rely on" and Isa 30:12; 31:1; 50:10; Prov 3:5; → *smk* and 2 Kgs 18:21 = Isa 36:6; Isa 26:3; Psa 71:5f.), and everything depends upon the reliability of the other; one seeks protection (cf. → *ḥsh* and Judg 9:15; 2 Sam 22:3; Isa 30:2; Psa 11:1; 16:1; 31:2; 71:1; 91:4; 118:8f., etc.), and one stands or falls with that on which one relies.

The derivative noun *mibṭāḥ* "basis, object of confidence" (unlike the other substs., it must not be understood as an action noun, but almost always clearly refers to the object of confidence, e.g., Yahweh, Jer 17:7; Psa 40:5; 65:6; 71:5; Bethel, Jer 48:13; cobwebs, Job 8:14; tent 18:14; refined gold, 31:24; in the pl. for several objects of confidence, Isa 32:18; Jer 2:37; also Prov 22:19, "so that your confidence may be in Yahweh"), *biṭṭāḥôn* "confidence, hope" (only 2 Kgs 18:19 = Isa 36:4 and Eccl 9:4; the nuance expressed by the nom. form cannot be precisely comprehended), *biṭḥâ* "trust" (only Isa 30:15, nomen actionis; cf. the inf. in Jer 48:7), and the adj. *bāṭûaḥ* "trusting" (only Isa 26:3; Psa 112:7) fit this linguistic model very well.

4. A specifically theological usage occurs in OT passages that assume that one can successfully place confidence only in Yahweh, that no other entity can be an ultimate object of trust. This restriction applies to almost all texts in which *bṭḥ* occurs; it is thus an eminently theological term, its meaning approximating the synonyms → *ʾmn* hi. "to believe," → *ḥsh* "to seek refuge" (cf. A. Weiser, *TDNT* 6:191ff.; R. Bultmann, *TDNT* 6:4f.).

There are sufficient programmatic declarations concerning trust in Yahweh: wisdom (Jer 17:5 "cursed be the man who relies on men"; v 7 "blessed the man, who relies on Yahweh"; Prov 16:20 "whoever relies on Yahweh finds happiness"), prophetic (cf. Isa 30:12 "you trust in oppression and perverseness and rely on them"; v 15 "you will be helped through returning and resting, you will become strong through waiting and trusting"), and theological illustrations.

The tradition-critically complex Hezekiah narrative of the Assyrian siege of Jerusalem (2 Kgs 18f. = Isa 36f.; cf. the revised version in 2 Chron 32 woven into another context) reads like a paradigm of the theme: "Yahweh is the only God (2 Kgs 19:15, 19), trust only in him!" 2 Kgs 18ff. emphasizes Hezekiah's special virtue; the besiegers provoke the king: "In what, then, do you trust?" (18:19f.; 19:10) and draw out the logical absurdities of his faith. The unreliability of the allies, historical events, and God's authorization of the Assyrian world ruler (18:19–25; 19:11–13) contradict Hezekiah's trust in Yahweh (cf. esp. 18:22, 25; the climax is in v 30: "Do not let yourselves by misled by Hezekiah to have hope in Yahweh [*bṭḥ* hi.]"). Contrary to every military calculation, Hezekiah's confidence in Yahweh is wondrously confirmed (19:35ff.). On the relationship between the narrative and Isaiah's preaching, cf. von Rad, *Theol.* 2:168f.; B. S. Childs, *Isaiah and the Assyrian Crisis* (1967); R. Deutsch, *Die Hiskiaerzählungen* (1969).

Jeremiah's Temple Sermon (Jer 7:3–15) illustrates, in view of historical events, how even confidence in Yahweh can be falsified if not linked to a genuine, direct obedience.

Both narratives are examples of exilic (Dtr) concerns for a new relationship with Yahweh.

The same theological viewpoints occur in specifically cultic and liturgical passages. Is Yahweh trustworthy? Is he the only dependable one? The song formulae encourage the participants to dare the leap of trust (examples of direct invitations in the impv. are Psa 37:3; 62:9; 115:9ff.); they confess that Yahweh is indeed aid, protection, and sanctuary (cf. Psa 25:2f.; 27:3, 5, 9f.; 28:7; 31:4, 7f.; 71:5; 91:2; cf. Gunkel-Begrich 232ff.) and that he does not disappoint his protégés (cf. the affirmation that often immediately follows a statement of confidence: "I am not afraid," etc., Psa 56:5, 12; 25:2; 21:8), and they raise the expectation that the example of trust will set a precedent

(Psa 40:4). The statement "I (we) trust in Yahweh" is extremely significant, however, in the language of the Psalms.

In the Psalter, 17 of 44 passages with *bṭḥ* qal are such personal confessions; they are often strengthened by means of the 1st sg. or pl. per. pron. (cf. also the synonymous usages with → *ḥsh*, Psa 7:2; 11:1; 16:1; 71:1; etc.; → *qwh* pi. Isa 8:17; 25:9; Psa 25:5, 21; 40:2; 130:5; → *dbq*, Psa 63:9; 119:31; → *smk* ni., Isa 48:2; Psa 71:6; *šʿn* ni., 2 Chron 14:10, etc.). The personal statement of confidence stands occasionally at the end of a psalm (Psa 55:24; 84:13), but as a rule it is the focus of a formal component of the lament, the "declaration of confidence" (cf. Gunkel-Begrich 254ff.; S. Mowinckel, *Psalms in Israel's Worship* [1962], 1:220; see also "confidence" in the index).

This evidence means that Israelite tradition recognizes and demands an absolute, exclusive devotion to Yahweh; this trust in Yahweh includes *hope* of salvation (Job 11:18) and *faith* in the God of the fathers (Psa 22:4f.).

5. Jewish and Christian theologians include the meaning "confidence in God" in their considerations of the total sphere of "faith, obedience, hope." Now and then, trust once again attains the forefront (in the Qumran texts, cf. 1QM 11:2 with 1 Sam 17:45; on the apocryphal and pseudepigraphal, as well as the NT and early Christian literature, cf. R. Bultmann, "πιστεύω," *TDNT* 6:197–230, esp. 200f., 206f.; id., "πείθω," *TDNT* 6:1–11, esp. 4–6). The concept of *pepoithenai epi tō theō* has no special theological meaning in the NT; it is subsumed under *pisteuein*, "confidence takes the form of faith" (Bultmann, *TDNT* 6:7). Cf. also StrB 3:188, 191f.; R. Bultmann, "ἐλπίς," *TDNT* 2:521–23.

E. Gerstenberger

בין *bîn* to understand

S 995; BDB 106b; *HALOT* 1:122a; *TDOT* 2:99–107; *TWOT* 239; *NIDOTTE* 1067

---

1. The root *bîn* "to understand" (< "to distinguish") is attested in almost the entire NWSem. and SSem. language realm (cf. *HAL* 117b; on *bn*, attested prior or contemporaneous to the OT only in Ug., cf. *WUS* no. 531; *UT* no. 461).

Beside the verb (qal, ni., hi., po., hitpo.) are the substs. *bînâ* "insight, understanding" and *tᵉbûnâ* "insight, facility"; cf. also the PN *yābîn*.

The words *bên* "between" and *(ʾîš hab)bēnayim* "champion" (*HAL* 118, 134), usually attributed to the same root, will not be treated here.

2. The verb occurs in the qal and hi. a total of 126x (incl. Jer 49:7 [Lis. lists this under *bên*] and Prov 21:29 Q); almost half of the impfs. cannot be distinguished between the two stems (BL 396; Berg. *HG* 2:149). The ni. occurs 22x (21x as the ptcp. *nābôn*, adj. "insightful"), po. 1x, hitpo. 22x, the substs. *bînâ* 37x (also 1x Aram. in Dan 2:21) and *tᵉbûnâ* 42x.

Most of the 250 Hebr. occurrences are in the Psa and wisdom texts (Prov 67x, Job 36x, Psa 30x), and in Isa (28x), the Chr's history (23x), and Dan (26x, in addition to 1x Aram.).

3. The verb *bîn*, rarely employed without a modifier (on the usage in wisdom literature, see 4), should be translated in both the qal and the hi. mostly with "to notice" or "to observe" (hitpo. often "to pay attention to"; on the difference in meaning between qal and hi., cf. *HP* 254).

Examples: noticing who calls (1 Sam 3:8); that the child is dead (2 Sam 12:19); shortcomings (Psa 19:13); fire (58:10); a misdeed (Neh 13:7); ruin (Job 6:30), abs., *ʾên mēbîn* "no one notices it" (Isa 57:1); paying attention to the reading of the law (Neh 8:8; cf. 8:2f., 12; 10:29); hitpo. "to inspect carefully" (1 Kgs 3:21; cf. Job 31:1, 12).

In Chron it occasionally means "to be able to do something professionally" (→ *ḥkm;* 1 Chron 15:22; 25:7; 27:32; 2 Chron 34:12; cf. Dan 1:4, 17; 8:23; cf. *tᵉbûnâ* in Exod 31:3; 35:31; 36:1; 1 Kgs 7:14).

The hi. occasionally means "to differentiate" (1 Kgs 3:9), "to be clever" (3:11); negated, "to understand nothing" (Isa 29:16 of the potter).

In addition to the inner-transitive (internal) meaning, the hi. is also used about 20x as a normal causative: "to give insight," and thence "to instruct" (e.g., 2 Chron 35:3 Q; ptcp. *mēbîn* "teacher," Ezra 8:16; 1 Chron 25:8).

For the various object and prepositional constructions, cf. *HAL* 117f.

4. Regarding the theological usage of the verbs, attention must first be directed to passages in which Yahweh appears as subject.

Yahweh notices misdeeds (Psa 94:7 par. *rʾh* "to see"), knows people's thoughts (139:2; cf. 1 Chron 28:9), notices sighing (Psa 5:2 par. *ʾzn* hi. "to hear"), pays attention to people's works (33:15), observes his people (Deut 32:10 po.). God's *tᵉbûnâ* is mentioned in Isa 40:14, 28; Jer 10:12 = 51:15; granted to the king, 1 Kgs 5:9; cf. Isa 11:2, *bînâ.*

With the people or the individual as subject, *bîn* frequently deals with attention to Yahweh's activity in nature and history (Deut 32:7 par. *zkr* "to remember"; Psa 28:5; 73:17; hitpo.: Isa 43:18; Job 37:14; 38:18; contrast Isa 52:15 and Jer 2:10).

That in the OT the right relationship to God is frequently formulated exactly with wisdom ideas (cf. H. H. Schmid, *Wesen und Geschichte der Weisheit* [1966], 199–201 with bibliog.) has still received much too little theological consideration.

A number of diverse formulations express the fact that the people or the individual ought to "understand" (often par. to *ydᶜ* "to recognize") something (Isa 6:9f.; 32:4; 40:21; 43:10; 44:18; Jer 23:20 = 30:24; Hos 14:10; Psa 94:8; 107:43; cf. with *bînâ:* Isa 27:11; 33:19), or that this "understanding" is often lacking (Deut 32:28f.; Isa 1:3; Jer 9:11; Hos 4:14; Psa 49:21; cf. Psa 82:5; Dan 11:37).

Later on, when the law assumes centrality in OT religion, it becomes the object or goal of this understanding: Neh 8:2f., 12; 10:29; Psa 119:27, 34, 73, 95, 100, 104, 125, 130, 144, 169; cf. already Deut 4:6 *(bînâ).*

The word group is particularly important in Prov, Job, and Dan.

The proverbs of Solomon serve *lᵉhābîn ʾimrê bînâ* "the understanding (or the learning) of the words of insight" (Prov 1:2), their objective is the *bînâ* or *tᵉbûnâ* (2:3), they are concerned with understanding the *māšāl*, the wisdom saying (1:6), acquiring *ᶜormâ* "cleverness" (8:5a), understanding the way (14:8), becoming insightful (8:5b txt?); *mēbîn* is, then, "the insightful" (8:9; 17:10, 24; 28:2, 7, 11), *bînâ* "insight" (often par. to *ḥokmâ* "wisdom"; 4:1, 5, 7; 7:4; 8:14; 9:6, 10; 16:16; 23:23; 30:2), similar to *tᵉbûnâ* (2:2f., 6, 11; 3:13, 19; 5:1; 8:1; 10:23, etc.), *nābôn* "prudent" (par. *ḥākām* "sage"; antonym: fool, cynic; 10:13; 14:6, 33; 15:14; 16:21; 17:28; 18:15; 19:25). False, purely human *bînâ* is treated in 3:5; 23:4; *tᵉbûnâ:* 21:30.

The word group is used very diversely in the poetry of Job. In addition to "profane" (6:30; 14:21; 18:2; 31:1; 32:12, etc.) and general wisdom usages (28:23; 32:8f.; 34:16; 36:29, etc., as well as most occurrences of *bînâ* and *tᵉbûnâ*), there are several, more specific usages: observing God's injustice (13:1 par. *rʾh* "to see," *šmᶜ* "to hear"; cf. 23:8), Job is unable to see God (9:11 par. *rʾh;* 23:8). He wishes to know how God would answer him (23:5 par. *ydᶜ*); but God pays no attention (30:20 txt em). In his friends' opinion, Job understands nothing (15:9 par. *ydᶜ*); nevertheless, he wishes them to show him his errors (6:24 par. *yrh* hi. "to teach").

In the vision narratives of Dan, *bîn* becomes a technical term for the understanding of visions and auditions (in various constructions: 1:17; 8:5, 15–17, 27; 9:22f.; 10:1, 11f., 14; 11:33; 12:8, 10); cf. the understanding of the scriptures in 9:2 also.

5. The thought of the Qumran sect also participated in the amalgamation of wisdom, apocalypticism, and gnosticism at the turn of the era. On the meaning of wisdom expressions at Qumran, cf. F. Nötscher, *Zur theol. Terminologie der Qumran-Texte* (1956), 38ff. (on *bîn* and *bînâ*, ibid. 54ff.).

For the NT usage of the Gk. verb *ginōskein,* which already represented both *bîn* and → *ydᶜ* in the LXX, see R. Bultmann, "γινώσκω," *TDNT* 1:689–719.

H. H. Schmid

בַּיִת *bayit* **house**

S 1004; BDB 108b; *HALOT* 1:124a; *TDOT* 2:107–16; *TWOT* 241; *NIDOTTE* 1074

אֹהֶל *ʾōhel* **tent**

S 168–169; BDB 13b; *HALOT* 1:19a; *TDOT* 1:118–30; *TWOT* 32a; *NIDOTTE* 185–186

הֵיכָל *hêkāl* **temple**

S 1964; BDB 228a; *HALOT* 1:244b; *TDOT* 3:382–88; *TWOT* 493; *NIDOTTE* 2121

---

1. **bayt-* "house" is common Sem. (Berg., *Intro.* 216); fig. meanings occur in all Sem. languages as in Hebr. (cf. e.g., *AHw* 132–34; *CAD* B:272–77, 282–97; *WUS* no. 600; *UT* no. 463; *DISO* 35f.).

Direct derivatives of *bayit* do not occur in Hebr.; *bîtān* "palace" (Esth 1:5; 7:7f.) may be an Akk. loanword transmitted through Aram. (Wagner no. 42). Bibl. Aram. offers the denominative verb *bît* "to spend the night" (Dan 6:19) in addition to *bayit* (pars. in Akk., Ug., Aram., Arab., and Eth., but not in Hebr., where *lîn* "to spend the night," also more generally "to lodge," performs this function).

In contrast, place-names formed with *bêt-* are quite frequent (*HAL* 120–24: nos. 1–52); *bêt-* often originally indicated the sanctuary of a deity (e.g., *bêt dāgôn, bêt ᶜᵃnāt, bêt šemeš*).

Although not conclusive, a fem. form (Aram.) of *bên* "between" is often assumed (Wagner no. 41; *HAL* 124a; on Ezek 41:9 cf. Zimmerli, *Ezek*, Herm, 2:373; on Job 8:17, cf. Horst, BK 16, 126) for the difficult texts 2 Kgs 11:15 = 2 Chron 23:14 (*ʾel-mibbêt [lᵉ]*; see 3c) and Prov 8:2 (*bêt nᵉtîbôt* "crossroad"?; cf. Gemser, HAT 16, 44). In 2 Kgs 23:7b a plural of *bat* III "woven garment" should probably be conjectured to replace the present pl. of *bayit* (*HAL* 159b).

2. Statistics are complicated for *bayit* because the removal of place-names formed with *bêt-* cannot always be satisfactorily accomplished.

In the following presentation, nos. 5, 30, 46, 51 listed in *HAL* 120–24 will not be counted among the place-names, following Lis. (and Mandl.), although nos. 12, 23, 27 (*bêt haggān* 2 Kgs 9:27; *bêt-hakkerem* Neh 3:14; *bêt millōʾ* Judg 9:6, 20bis; 2 Kgs 12:21) will be (against Lis.). Excluding the approximately 50 place-names with adj. formations (around 240 occurrences) and 2 Chron 34:6 K, but including 2 Kgs 23:7b (see 1) as well as Num 1:22 and 2 Sam 19:12b (the last two omitted in Lis.), the following numbers result:

Gen	109	Hos	15	Prov	38
Exod	59	Joel	6	Ruth	7
Lev	53	Amos	27	Song Sol	5
Num	58	Obad	5	Eccl	11
Deut	45	Jonah	–	Lam	3
Josh	25	Mic	16	Esth	28
Judg	68	Nah	1	Dan	3
1 Sam	61	Hab	3	Ezra	30
2 Sam	115	Zeph	5	Neh	52
1 Kgs	194	Hag	11	1 Chron	112
2 Kgs	151	Zech	31	2 Chron	218
Isa	75	Mal	2		
Jer	146	Psa	53		
Ezek	181	Job	26	Hebr. OT	2,048

bîtān occurs 3x, Bibl. Aram. *bayit* 44x (Dan 9x, Ezra 35x), *bît* pe. 1x.

3. (a) In its basic meaning *bayit* describes the fixed "house" built of any material (*BRL* 266–73, 409–16; *BHH* 2:658f.; 3:1361–65), usually in distinction from *ʾōhel* "tent" (cf. 2 Sam 16:22; Jer 35:7, 9f.; Hos 12:10; but Psa 132:3 *ʾōhel bêtî* "my house-tent"; 1 Chron 9:23 txt? *bêt-hāʾōhel* "tent-house"; cf. Rudolph, HAT 21, 88; *ʾōhel* occurs 435x in the OT [Num 76x, Exod 62x, Lev 44x, Gen 23x, Psa 18x, Prov 14x, Judg 13x], in 60% of the texts in the cultic sense of "tent of Yahweh," "tent of meeting," etc. [→ *yᶜd* 2, 4b]) and *sukkâ* "booth" (cf. Gen 33:17; 31x in the OT); cf. A. Alt, "Zelte und Hütten," FS Nötscher 16–25 = *KS* [1959], 3:233–42; W. Michaelis, "Zelt und Hütten im biblischen Denken," *EvT* 14 (1954): 29–49. On the idiom "to your tents, O Israel!" in reference to the dissolution of the Israelite army and in other passages in which fixed formulae from the nomadic period have not undergone the evolution appropriate to the changed circumstances of settlement in the land (tent > house), see Alt, *KS* 3:240.

Except perhaps for the general abstract *binyān* "building" (→ *bnh* "to build"; an Aram. loanword in Ezek 40:5; 41:12bis, 15; 42:1, 5, 10 [41:13 *binyâ*]; cf. Wagner no. 44), synonyms appear only as descriptions of mansions, palaces, etc.: in addition to the frequent *bêt hammelek* "king's palace," the loanwords *hêkāl* "palace, temple" (Sum. **haikal* [A. Falkenstein, *Genava* NS 8 (1960): 304] > *é-gal*, Akk. *ekallu*, Ug. *hkl*, Bibl. Aram. *hêkal;* in the OT 80x in Hebr. [Jer 7:4 3x] and 13x in Aram., 14x plus 5x resp. in the meaning "palace": 1 Kgs 21:1; 2 Kgs 20:18 = Isa 39:7; Isa 13:22; Hos 8:14; Joel 4:5; Amos 8:3; Nah 2:7; Psa 45:9, 16; 144:12; Prov 30:28; Dan 1:4; 4:21, 26; 5:5; 6:19; Ezra 4:14; 2 Chron 36:7), *ʾappeden* "palace" (< Pers. *apadāna;* cf. Wagner no. 25; Dan 11:45), and *bîtān* "palace" (see 1). The terms *ʾarmôn* (Isa 13:22 *ʾalmôn*) "(fortified) palace" (33x, primarily in the Prophets) and more definitely *bîrâ* "citadel" (18x, only in Esth, Dan, Neh, and Chron; Aram. *bîrâ* Ezra 6:2, an Akk. loanword; cf. Wagner no. 40) emphasize the aspect of fortification (cf. also *migdāl* "tower," → *gdl*).

(b) In conjunction with *ʾᵉlōhîm* "God" or a divine name (less often elliptically free-standing or otherwise modified, e.g., 1 Kgs 13:32 and 2 Kgs 17:29, high places; Amos 7:13, royal sanctuary; Mic 3:12; Hag 1:8), *bayit* usually indicates a "divine house," a "temple" (cf. *BRL* 511–19; *BHH* 3:1940–49). A few cases in the OT deal with sanctuaries of foreign gods (e.g., 1 Sam 5:2, Dagon's temple; cf. also the place-names; see 1) or with Yahweh sanctuaries outside Jerusalem (Judg 18:31, "as long as the house of God was in Shiloh"; 1 Sam 1:7; on *bêt-ʾēl*, see 4b and → *ʾēl* III/2), but by far the majority deal with the temple in Jerusalem (→ *ʾᵉlōhîm* III/6; the phrase *bêt yhwh* "house of Yahweh" occurs 255x in the OT [2 Chron 75x, 2 Kgs 52x, Jer 33x, 1 Kgs 22x, 1 Chron 20x, Psa 9x]; on Hos 8:1, see 3d). Synonyms are *hêkāl* (see 3a), which can also indicate, however, the main hall of the temple in distinction from the foyer and the holy of holies (*HAL* 235a), and the more general expressions *qōdeš* and *miqdāš* "sanctuary" (→ *qdš*).

(c) If we remain in the impersonal sphere without reference to the inhabitants of the house (see 3d), the fig. meanings of *bayit* touch mostly on the concept of the house as an enclosed area. If the habitation of living things plays a role, one may speak of a "resting place" (of people: Job 17:13, "If I hope, then the underworld is my house"; 30:23, "You will bring me to death, to the house where all that lives enters"; of animals: Job 39:6, the steppe as the habitation of the wild donkey; Job 8:14 and 27:18, txt em, cobwebs). The expression for the grave in Eccl 12:5, "eternal house" (*bêt* → *ʿôlām;* cf. Psa 49:12), also attested in Pun., Palm., Gk., and Lat., goes back to a concept of Eg. origin (cf. E. Jenni, *ZAW* 65 [1953]: 27–29). "Clay houses" in which people "live" *(škn)* in Job 4:19 are not references to the grave but metaphorically to frail human bodies (cf. Horst, BK 16, 76).

Some technical usages of *bayit* also minimize the concept of habitation, resulting in a meaning "container" or the like: for bars (Exod 26:29; 36:34) or poles (Exod 25:27; 30:4; 37:14, 27; 38:5); *bāttê nepeš* in Isa 3:20 is traditionally interpreted as "perfume jars," but also as "soul cases" = amulets (cf. Wildberger, *Isa 1–12*, CC, 153f.). Ezek 1:27 "fire that is ringed about," which has, then, a "halo," is also difficult (Zimmerli, *Ezek*, Herm, 1:88f., 122f.). Finally, 1 Kgs 18:32 "area for two measures of seed" recalls the meaning "plot of ground" attested for the Akk. *bītu* (*AHw* 133a).

In the sense of "inner, within" (antonym: *ḥûṣ* "lane, outside"), *bayit* has become a fully adv. or prep. expression in *baytâ* "inward" (Exod 28:26, etc.), *mibbayit* (Gen 6:14, etc.) and *mibbaytâ* (1 Kgs 6:15) "inside," *mibbayit lᵉ* (1 Kgs 6:16), *lᵉmibbêt lᵉ* (Num 18:7) "inside," and *ʾel mibbêt lᵉ* "into the middle" (2 Kgs 11:15; cf. 2 Chron 23:14).

Neh 2:3, "the city where *(bêt)* the graves of my fathers are," recalls the Neo-Assyr. usage of *bīt* as a prep. or subordinating conjuction in a local clause (*GAG* §§116f, 175c; *AHw* 131b).

(d) In Hebr. as in the related languages, the meaning of "house" shifts frequently to the contents of the house ("property, possessions," e.g., Gen 15:2), and particularly to the household living in the house (classically in Josh 24:15: "but I and my house, we will serve Yahweh"). *bayit* thus means "family" (Gen 7:1, etc.; → *bnh*, → *ʿśh*), "clan" (e.g., Jer 35:2, "house" of the Rechabites, for whom the possession of a house in the concrete sense is directly prohibited), also "lineage, descendants" (Exod 2:1, etc.), and, in reference to kings, "(royal) court" or "dynasty" (Isa 7:2, 13, etc.). *bêt-ʾāb* "paternal house, (paternal) family" (e.g., Gen 24:38) becomes a term of tribal organization in the post-exilic period (→ *ʾāb* III/4). The entire tribal and national society could also be described as *bayit* according to the model of family and tribe, thus *bêt ʾeprayim* "house of Ephraim" (Judg 10:9), *bêt yaʿᵃqōb* "house of Jacob" (Exod 19:3, par. "Israelites"; Isa 2:5f., etc.), esp. also in a political meaning for the two kingdoms Judah and Israel (*bêt yᵉhûdâ*, 2 Sam 2:4, 7, 10f., etc., in all 41x; *bêt yiśrāʾēl*, 2 Sam 12:8, etc., in all 146x, 83x in Ezek; on the development of this expression in analogy to *bêt yᵉhûdâ* → *yiśrāʾēl* 2; names for regions such as *bīt-ammānu*, etc., in Assyr.-Bab. sources are also comparable; see *RLA* 2:33ff.). Emulating this usage, Hos 8:1 calls the land (not a temple) "house of Yahweh" (cf. also Hos 9:8, 15; Jer 12:7; Zech 9:8; Wolff, *Hos*, Herm, 137). In Ezek *bêt mᵉrî* "house of rebelliousness" contrasts with *bêt yiśrāʾēl* (→ *mrh* 4c; cf. Zimmerli, *Ezek*, Herm, 1:134).

A more specifically constituted metonymy "house > inhabitant" occurs in the Eg. royal title "pharaoh" (Hebr. *parʿōh*); *pr-ʿʾ* "great house" originally meant the royal palace, but was then applied (since the 16th cent. BCE) to the king (*BHH* 3:1445).

4. (a) J. Hempel offers a review of the religious concepts associated with the house that were theologically significant even for the NT ("Der Symbolismus von Reich, Haus und Stadt in der biblischen Sprache," *WZ Greifswald* 5 [1955/56]: 123–30, under the headings "Einwurzelung," "Eingrenzung," "Ordnung"). Aspects of cultural history and religious history, e.g., the Rechabites, who were obligated to the nomadic ideal, resisted housing construction as an expression of a distinctive faithfulness to Yahweh (Jer 35), and the prophetic polemic against mansions (e.g., Amos 3:15; 5:11), will not be further treated here, because they did not influence the usage of *bayit*.

(b) The numerous texts that discuss a "house of God" or "house of Yahweh" will not be treated further. As with other cultic objects (ark, tent, sacrifice, etc.), the essence and history of cultic institutions will not be examined with respect to the Jerusalem temple; instead, possible special theological usages will only be noted (on the theologically significant concept of the dwelling of God, cf. → *škn* "to dwell"). At just this point, however, the material is not very productive. The OT employs the term "house" without distinction for pagan temples and the temple of Yahweh in Jerusalem; it is also difficult to determine any variations in the usage of the term across time. The intentional contrast between the two meanings of *bayit*, "temple" and "dynasty," is stylistically effective in the rejection of the temple building in 2 Sam 7:5, 11, 29 ("should you build me a house . . . Yahweh will build you a house . . . I will build you a house").

In an ancient tradition, which still shines through in Gen 28:22, *bêt* *ʾᵉlōhîm* can mean not only the constructed house of God, the temple, but also a cultic stone (*maṣṣēbâ* "massebah") "as a representation, resting place, dwelling place of the deity" (H. Donner, *ZAW* 74 [1962]: 68–70, with the Old Aram. par. *bty ʾlhyʾ* "houses of the gods," related to the stele that contains the covenant text in *KAI* no. 223C., lines 2f., 7, 9f.; cf. Fitzmyer, *Sef.* 90 with bibliog.; on the pre-Israelite deity Bethel [Jer 48:13? but cf. Rudolph, HAT 12, 258f.], cf. O. Eissfeldt, *ARW* 28 [1930]: 1–30 = *KS* [1962], 1:206–33; → *ʾēl* III/2).

In addition to the earthly temple, e.g., in Shechem (Judg 9:4), in Shiloh (Judg 18:31; 1 Sam 1:7), and above all in Jerusalem, the OT also mentions a heavenly palace of God (perhaps *bayit* in Psa 36:9 [*HAL* 119b], but uncertain; possibly *hêkāl* in Mic 1:2; Hab 2:20; Psa 11:4; 18:7 = 2 Sam 22:7; cf. also Isa 66:1; → *škn*). The poetic concept in Job 36:29 of heaven as God's *sukkâ* "booth" (actually "leafy canopy") above the clouds (Fohrer, KAT 16, 480) is different.

On the land of Israel as the "house" of God or Yahweh, see 3d.

5. "House" does not yet serve in the OT as a figure for the community, as is the case in Qumran (1QS 5:6; 8:5, 9; 9:6; CD 3:19; cf. J. Maier, *Die Texte vom Toten Meer* 2 [1960], 46f.) and in the NT (1 Tim 3:15; Heb 3:6; 1 Pet 2:5; 4:17). *bayit* in Num 12:7, which compares Moses' position with "that of the chief slave who is at once the confidant of his master and the man to whom his master's whole 'house' is entrusted" (Noth, *Num*, OTL, 96), can refer to Israel as the realm of Yahweh's lordship only if the metaphor is extended (cf. Heb 3:1–6). On the LXX and the NT, cf. O. Michel, "οἶκος," *TDNT* 5:116–59; W. Michaelis, "σκηνή," *TDNT* 7:369–94; J. Goetzmann, "House," *DNTT* 2:247–56, with bibliog.

E. Jenni

בכה *bkh* to cry

S 1058; BDB 113a; *HALOT* 1:129b; *TDOT* 2:116–20; *TWOT* 243; *NIDOTTE* 1134

---

1. The verb **bky* "to cry" is common Sem. (Berg., *Intro.* 218; P. Fronzaroli, *AANLR* 8/19 [1964], 270). Hebr. derivatives are the substantives *bᵉkî*, *bᵉkît*, *bekeh* "crying."

The words *bōkîm* (Judg 2:1, 5 with an etymology of the name, explaining *bōkîm* as the crying of the people) and *bākût* (in the expression *ʾallôn bākût* "lament oak," Gen 35:8, also with a secondary etymology) found in place-names deserve consideration as further derivatives. Was "crying" originally a form of expression of the tree spirit (B. Stade, *Biblische Theologie des AT* [1905], 1:112)?

*bk*ʾ is also probably a by-form of *bkh;* the root occurs in this form in names of a shrub variety *bᵉkāʾîm* (2 Sam 5:23f.; 1 Chron 14:14f.), probably dripping, "crying" shrubs. Psa 84:7 mentions an *ᶜēmeq habbākāʾ*, apparently the PN of a valley with sparse vegetation (with only drops of water); cf. *HAL* 124a. Apparently the place-name *bōkîm* was originally to be similarly understood.

2. The verb occurs 114x (qal 112x, pi. 2x). The distribution exhibits no peculiarities. *bᵉkî* occurs 30x; *bᵉkît* (Gen 50:4), *bekeh* (Ezra 10:1), and *bākût* (Gen 35:8) are hapax legomena.

3. The meaning of *bkh* can be consistently rendered with "to cry, bewail." The word is used for the crying of the child in Gen 21:16; Exod 2:6. The adult cries during the lament for the dead (par. expression: *spd* "to lament," Gen 23:2; 2 Sam 1:12; Ezek 24:16; also in this context: *dmᶜ* "to shed tears," Jer 13:17; cf. *dimᶜâ* "tear," Jer 31:16; Ezek 24:16; Mal 2:13; Lam 1:2; *ṣûm* "to fast," Judg 20:26; 2 Sam 1:12; 12:21f.; *nûd* "to lament," Jer 22:10; brief descriptions of lament practices in Jer 41:6; Ezek 27:31). Women esp. are to perform laments (2 Sam 1:24); it was considered particularly unfortunate if there were no one to lament the dead (Psa 78:64; Job 27:15).

Crying also played a role in the ritual lament, which usually took place in the temple; this lament is described as "crying before Yahweh" (Judg 20:23, 26). Par. expressions here are *ṣûm* "to fast" (Judg 20:26; Psa 69:11), *nzr* hi. "to set oneself apart [through observance of particular rules]" (Zech 7:3). It is known from post-exilic times that the priests were found on occasions of communal lament "between hall and altar" (Joel 2:17); cf. further in this context, 2 Kgs 22:19; Psa 137:1; Lam 1:2, 16. This cultic weeping originally had the purpose of winning the deity's favor (Hos 12:5 should perhaps be so understood; see P. R. Ackroyd, *VT* 13 [1963]: 250f.; but cf. e.g., Wolff, *Hos*, Herm, 212f.), but in the OT is probably simply an indication of the pain of the lamentor. Jeremiah is dependent upon the diction of the individual lament when he describes his suffering (Jer 8:23; 13:17).

The crying of adults is not only determined by custom, but breaks out spontaneously in conditions of strong emotion, sickness (1 Sam 1:7f., 10), sadness over an unfortunate occurrence (Gen 27:38; Judg 11:37; 1 Sam 30:4; 2 Sam 3:16; Neh 1:4 par. to → *ṣûm* "to fast," → *ʾbl* hitp. "to mourn," → *pll* hitp. "to pray"; Isa 33:7 par. → *ṣᶜq* "to cry out"), excitement (2 Kgs 8:11), emotional upset (Gen 42:24; 43:30; 50:17; 1 Sam 24:17; Job 2:12; Ezra 3:12; Neh 8:9). A call to cry occurs in the prophetic reprimand in Mic 1:10 txt em (cf. S. J. Schwantes, *VT* 14 [1964]: 455).

Greeting and farewell (Gen 29:11; 33:4; 45:2 with *bᵉkî;* 45:14f.; 46:29; 1 Sam 20:41; Ruth 1:9, 14, often together with verbs such as "to kiss," "to embrace," "to bow [before someone]") are special cases of emotional upset. Cf. R. Lehmann, "Der Tränengruss im AT," *Baessler-Archiv* 19 (1936), reviewed in *ZAW* 55 (1937): 137.

Weeping to accompany sowing may have been customary in Israel as an echo of Can. mourning for the death of the vegetation deity (allusion in Psa 126:6; later, weeping accompanied the Jewish New Year's Festival; the sounding of the shofar is a symbol of this weeping; cf. F. Hvidberg, *Weeping and Laughter in the OT* [1962]), although this custom has no significance in the context of official Yahwism. On cultic weeping in later Judaism, cf. J. A. Wensinck, FS Sachau 26–35; and J. L. Palache, *ZDMG* 70 (1916): 251–56, who expands earlier treatments.

In poetic diction, *bkh* can be used with a nonhuman subj. (Job 31:38, the ground "cries," par. *zᶜq* "to cry out"; the issue is the proper relationship between human and nature). Eccl 3:4 maintains that, like laughing, weeping has its place in human life (antonymn: *śḥq*).

On the usage of the pi. (Jer 31:15, a picture of the lament for the dead; Ezek 8:14, weeping for Tammuz; cf. Psa 126:6), see *HP* 157.

4. Weeping plays a role in the relationship between God and human in only a few cases (particularly not in mourning for the dead; → *ʾbl;* and certainly not in the context of the vegetation cult, even though here a rather significant folk religion may need to be taken into account), as in the individual and community laments; here it is a sign of human weakness that approaches God in supplication, or an expression of emotional upset when one learns of God's pronouncement of judgment (Judg 2:4; 2 Kgs 8:11ff.).

Weeping has a special place in the motif of the "murmuring in the wilderness" (Num 11:4, 10, 13, 18, 20; 14:1; Deut 1:45). It indicates the attitude of the disobedient people who do not have confidence in divine guidance and therefore complain.

If, then, weeping is a sign of human distress, in later apocalyptically oriented times Israel expected a new era in which such weeping would cease (Isa 30:19).

5. The latter notion, in particular, acquires some significance in the NT in that Jesus promises this end time (cf. Matt 5:4, etc.). On the whole notion in the NT, cf. K. H. Rengstorf, "κλαίω," *TDNT* 3:722–26.

F. Stolz

בֵּן *bēn* son

S 1121; BDB 119b; *HALOT* 1:137a; *TDOT* 2:145–59; *TWOT* 254; *NIDOTTE* 1201

בַּת *bat* **daughter**

S 1323; BDB 123a; *HALOT* 1:165b; *TDOT* 2:332–38; *TWOT* 254b; *NIDOTTE* 1426

I. The word *bēn* (**bin-*) "son," with its fem. counterpart *bat* (**bint-*) "daughter," is common Sem. (Berg., *Intro.* 210); replaced in Eth. by *wald,* in Akk. by *māru*). It should perhaps be associated with **bnw/y* "to build."

The term survives in Akk. only in poetic diction and PNs; *māru/mārtu* takes its place (*AHw* 127a, 138b, 614, 615f.).

The relationship between *bar/bᵉrāʾ (brt),* which replaces the sg. *bēn* in the Aram. realm, and **bin* has not yet been fully explained. Cf. R. Ružička, *Konsonantische Dissimilation in den semitischen Sprachen* (1909), 68f.; contra BLA 179; Wagner no. 46; *HAL* 131b.

II. With around 5,000 occurrences, *bēn* is easily the most frequent substantive in the OT. Concentrations in Gen, Num, and the Chr history may be explained, first of all, on the basis of the genealogies.

	bēn sg.	pl.	total	*bat* sg.	pl.	total
Gen	177	188	365	45	64	109
Exod	39	194	233	13	10	23
Lev	28	132	160	20	2	22
Num	224	387	611	10	16	26
Deut	37	90	127	14	7	21
Josh	44	197	241	2	14	16
Judg	52	152	204	8	19	27
1 Sam	80	58	138	9	7	16
2 Sam	140	67	207	14	6	20
1 Kgs	140	48	188	11	–	11
2 Kgs	163	58	221	16	1	17
Isa	38	46	84	14	9	23
Jer	143	82	225	21	19	40
Ezek	116	75	191	6	31	37
Hos	6	18	24	2	2	4
Joel	1	14	15	–	2	2
Amos	2	9	11	–	1	1
Obad	–	2	2	–	–	–
Jonah	3	–	3	–	–	–
Mic	2	4	6	7	–	7
Nah	–	–	–	–	–	–
Hab	–	–	–	–	–	–
Zeph	5	3	8	3	–	3
Hag	10	–	10	–	–	–
Zech	8	5	13	4	–	4
Mal	2	4	6	1	–	1
Psa	15	88	103	6	6	12
Job	6	30	36	–	5	5
Prov	41	19	60	–	2	2
Ruth	2	6	8	8	3	11
Song Sol	–	2	2	2	10	12
Eccl	5	11	16	–	1	1
Lam	–	4	4	21	1	22
Esth	8	7	15	5	–	5
Dan	2	7	9	2	–	2
Ezra	41	156	197	–	4	4
Neh	115	131	246	1	17	18
1 Chron	338	370	708	10	18	28
2 Chron	127	105	232	14	13	27
OT	2,160	2,769	4,929	289	290	579*

PNs compounded with *ben-*, *bin-*, *bat-* and the expression *bat hayyaᶜᵃnâ*/*bᵉnôt yaᶜᵃnâ* "ostrich" are not included in the figures above, although *bᵉnê* in *rabbat bᵉnê-ᶜammôn* and *bēn*/*ben-* in 1 Chron 4:20a; 7:35; 15:18 (probably a textual error, not a component of a PN) are included; 1 Chron 6:11 K is counted as a sg., 2 Chron 11:18 K is omitted (Q *bat*). Lis. overlooks *bēn* in 2 Kgs 1:17b.*

bar "son" occurs in Bibl. Aram. 19x (sg. 8x, Dan and Ezra 4x each; pl. 11x, Dan 4x, Ezra 7x). *bar* appears (3x) as an Aramaism in Prov 31:2 (cf. Wagner no. 46).

III. 1. In its basic meaning *bēn* means "son," indeed, as a rule, "the biological son of his father or mother." This relationship delineates a primary natural word field within the family.

Usually the family relationship is expressed in the sg. with a following gen. ("son of *X*," esp. frequent in the various genealogies) or through a possessive suf. (cf. e.g., the stereotypical usage in the Dtr framework, "his son *X* ruled in his stead," 1 Kgs 14:20, 31, etc.). Frequently, however, the terms → *ʾāb* "father" (e.g., Gen 22:7; 42:32; 2 Sam 7:14 = 1 Chron 17:13; pl. Exod 20:5; Num 14:18, etc.) and → *ʾēm* "mother" (Gen 27:13; 43:29; Hos 10:14, etc.) occur in the immediate context; the mother can also be further described (Judg 11:1, son of a whore; 1 Kgs 7:14, son of a widow; Gen 25:6, sons of the concubines, Judg 8:31 sg.; Gen 21:10, 13 and Exod 23:12, son of a servant) or simply be described as → *ʾiššâ* "woman" (1 Sam 1:4; 1 Kgs 17:17).

A second, though less frequent word field is also naturally established: *bēn* as the male descendant corresponds to the female *bat* "daughter," usually in nominal series in the pl. (Gen 5:4ff.; 11:11ff., etc.; in parallelismus membrorum, e.g., in Isa 60:4).

Other nominal series associated with *bēn:* woman-children (Exod 4:20, etc.); sons-woman-daughters-in-law (Gen 6:18; 7:3, 13; 8:18; cf. 8:16); women-sons-daughters (Gen 36:6; Exod 32:2, etc.); son-daughter-male slave-female slave-cattle-foreigner (Exod 20:10; cf. Deut 5:14); children-grandchildren (Deut 4:9, 25, etc.); son-daughter-male slave-female slave-Levite (Deut 12:18; 14:11, 14, cf. 12:12); sheep-cattle-sons-daughters (Jer 3:24; cf. 5:17); other series: Josh 7:24; Exod 32:29; 2 Sam 19:6; Jer 16:3.

In the meaning "son," *yeled* occasionally occurs as a synonym for *bēn* (Exod 2:10; 1 Kgs 3:25; Ruth 4:16; in parallelism, Jer 31:20). *yeled* is considerably less frequent, however, and in the meaning "child" also much less specific than *bēn.* The term *ṭap* parallels *bēn* in Deut 1:39, certainly a reference to a small child or infant. Additional parallel terms are *ʿûl* "infant" (Isa 49:15) and *p^erî-beṭen* "fruit of the womb" (Jer 13:18; Psa 127:3); on *b^ekôr* "firstborn" → *rōʾš (riʾšôn).*

The following verbs appear regularly in the word field of *bēn:* (a) *yld* qal of a woman or the mother: "she bore a son" (often in conjunction with the preceding verb *hrh* "to be pregnant"): Gen 4:25; 16:15; 19:37f.; 21:2; 29:32; 1 Sam 1:20; Hos 1:3, etc.; in the promise of a son: Gen 16:11; Judg 13:3; Isa 7:14 (cf. P. Humbert, "Der biblische Verkündigungsstil und seine vermutliche Herkunft," *AfO* 10 [1935]: 77–80); *yld* hi. of the father: "he begot sons and daughters" (Gen 5:4ff.; 11:11ff.; cf. Deut 28:41, etc.); *yld* pu. of the father: "a son was born to him" (Gen 4:26; cf. 10:25; 35:26, etc.); (b) *lqḥ ʾiššâ l^ebēn* "to take a wife for the son" (Gen 24:3ff.; cf. Jer 29:6, etc.); (c) *ntn l^ebēn* "to give (as wife) to the son" (Gen 38:26; cf. Deut 7:3; Judg 3:6, etc.); (d) *lōʾ-hāyû lô bānîm* "he had no sons" (Josh 17:3; cf. Num 3:4; Deut 25:5; 1 Chron 23:17, etc.); (e) a series of verbs describing the transmission of particular traditions from the fathers to the children: *ʾmr* "to say" (Exod 12:26; Deut 6:21); *šʾl* "to ask" (Exod 13:14; Deut 6:20; Josh 4:6, 21); *ngd* hi. "to announce" (Exod 13:8); *ydʿ* hi. "to make known" (Josh 4:22; Psa 78:5); *lmd* pi. "to teach" (Deut 4:10); *šnn* pi. "to inculcate" (Deut 6:7); *spr* pi. "to narrate" (Joel 1:3; Psa 78:6).

bēn quite frequently describes animal offspring. Thus *bēn* in Lev 22:28 means the young of a cow or sheep, in Deut 22:6f. a young bird, in Gen 32:16 a camel foal, in 1 Sam 6:7, 10 calves, and in Job 39:4 a young hind. Still more frequent are phrases with *bēn* to describe young animals, e.g., *ben-ʾātôn* "donkey foal" (Gen 49:11; Zech 9:9), *ben-bāqār* "young cow" (Gen 18:7f.; Lev

4:3, 14; Num 7:15–81, etc.); *b*e*nê (hay)yônâ* "young doves" (Lev 1:14; 5:7, 11; 14:30, etc.); additional phrases, e.g., in Psa 114:4, 6; 147:9. Such a phrase also occurs once with reference to plants: *bēn pōrāt* "young fruit tree" (Gen 49:22).

2. The term is occasionally expanded, on the one hand, to indicate children, grandchildren, descendants; and on the other, in the direction of nonbiological sonship.

(a) The pl. of the word may not always be translated "sons" (in contrast to the "daughters"); rather it sometimes means "children" (sons *and* daughters), e.g., Gen 3:16 "in pain you shall bear children" (2 Kgs 19:3, also of the yet unborn), and, above all, in the usage "children and children's children" (Exod 34:7, etc.). Occasionally *bēn* describes the "grandchild" (beside the more common phrase *ben-b*e*nô;* see 3c), Gen 31:28, 43; 32:1, or even more generally, the descendants (beside the phrase *b*e*nê bāneykā* "your children's children," e.g., Gen 45:10, and the more common phrase *b*e*nê bānîm,* Exod 34:7; Deut 4:25; Judg 12:14, etc.), for instance, 1 Kgs 9:21.

(b) One may distinguish the following spheres of reference for the OT usage of *bēn* in a nonbiological sense:

The address *b*e*nî* "my son" is formulaic; it occurs occasionally in the historical books (Josh 7:19, Joshua to Achan; 1 Sam 3:6, 16, Eli to Samuel; 4:16, Eli to the messenger).

One could ask whether the address "my son" in the wisdom literature (Prov 1:10, 15; 2:1; 3:1, 11, 21, etc.) refers to an intellectual sonship, i.e., a teacher-student or master-disciple relationship. If it is true that such instructions and proverb traditions were transmitted not only at royal courts but also in the clan (cf. H. W. Wolff, *Amos the Prophet* [1973]; with additional bibliog.), however, the *bēn* addressed here may be easily understood as the biological son of his father, at least as a clan member (Prov 1:8 suggests this meaning).

The *b*e*nê hann*e*bî*ʾ*îm* "sons of the prophets" discussed in the Elijah and Elisha narratives (1 Kgs 20:35; 2 Kgs 2:3, 5, 7; 4:1, 38; 5:22; 6:1; 9:1) are not biological but spiritual sons of the prophets in the sense of disciples (→ ʾ*āb* III/2b). Cf. also 2 Kgs 8:9 (Benhadad to Elisha), but also the political usage in the submission formula of King Ahaz to Tiglath-pileser, "I am your slave and your son" (2 Kgs 16:7).

Finally, the group of occurrences that describe a person as "son of Yahweh" belongs in this category (see IV/3).

The meaning of the term has been greatly expanded to describe the inhabitants of a city as "sons" (e.g., Isa 51:18, 20; 66:8; Psa 147:13; Lam 1:16); Jerusalem is figuratively compared with a mother who has borne her children (inhabitants).

3. The term *bēn* is readily combined with other words:

(a) *bēn* in the pl. cs. is combined most frequently with a following ethnic name to indicate members of this people. The expression *b*e*nê yiśrā*ʾ*ēl* (about 630x) should be mentioned first; in addition to the rarer ʾ*îš yiśrā*ʾ*ēl* (50x) or ʾ*anšê yiśrā*ʾ*ēl* (9x), it is *the* expression that refers to the "Israelites"; a distinction in meaning between the three expressions is difficult to determine.

Similar phrases, such as *b^{e}nê y^{e}hûdâ* "Judeans," *b^{e}nê ʿammôn* "Ammonites," etc., and designations for tribal members such as *b^{e}nê lēwî* "Levites," correspond to these ethnic terms. More general phrases, such as *b^{e}nê ʿam* "compatriot" (Gen 23:11; Lev 20:17, etc.; in contrast to *b^{e}nê hāʿām* "common people" in 2 Kgs 23:6; Jer 26:23) and *b^{e}nê qedem* "easterners" (Gen 29:1; Judg 8:10, etc.), also belong in this category.

(b) *ben . . . šānâ* (lit. "a son of . . . years"; Gen 5:32; Num 1:3–47; 7:15–88, etc.) serves as a common expression of age.

(c) In order to specify degrees of relationship, *bēn* is occasionally combined with other terms of relationship:

ben-ʾimmô "son of his mother" = "brother" (Gen 43:29, par. to → *ʾāḥ;* cf. 27:29); *b^{e}nê ʾābîkā* "sons of your father" = "brothers" (Gen 49:8, par. to *ʾaḥeykā* "your brothers"); *b^{e}nê ʾîš-ʾeḥād* "sons of *one* man" = "brothers" (Gen 42:13; cf. v 32).

The daughter-in-law is the "son's wife" (Lev 18:15); the granddaughter, the "son's/daughter's daughter" (Lev 18:10, 17); the nephew, the "brother's/sister's son" (Gen 12:5; 14:12; 29:13); the cousin, the "uncle's son" (Lev 25:49; Num 36:11); and, correspondingly, descendants are the "children's children" (Gen 45:10; Exod 34:7, etc.).

(d) Only the most important of the remaining phrases with *bēn* preceding a gen. will be mentioned:

ben-ʾādām or the pl. *b^{e}nê ʾādām* often indicates the individual (sg. 93x in Ezek; Num 23:19; Isa 51:12, etc.; pl. with art., Gen 11:5; without art., Deut 32:8, etc.; → *ʾādām* 3). *ʾ^{e}nôš* (Isa 51:12; 56:2; Psa 8:5; 90:3; Job 25:6), *ʾîš* (Isa 52:14; Mic 5:6; Psa 80:18; Job 35:8; Prov 8:4), and *geber* (Job 16:21) par. *ben-ʾādām.*

ben-hammelek is the "king's son, prince" (Judg 8:18; 2 Sam 9:11; 13:4, 23, 32). Otherwise phrases with *bēn* readily form adjs., e.g., *ben-šāmen* "fat" (Isa 5:1), *bēn maśkîl* "clever" (Prov 10:5), *ben-māwet* "mortally doomed" (1 Sam 20:31; 26:16; 2 Sam 12:5), *b^{e}nê ʿawlâ* "wicked" (2 Sam 3:34; 7:10 = 1 Chron 17:9, etc.), *b^{e}nê ḥayil* "wealthy, landowners subject to military service, combatants" (Deut 3:18; Judg 18:2, etc.), *b^{e}nê b^{e}lîyaʿal* "worthless fellows" (Deut 13:14; Judg 19:22; 20:13, etc.), *b^{e}nê nēkār* "foreigners" (Exod 12:43; Lev 22:25; 2 Sam 22:45f., etc.).

Phrases such as *bēn zākār* "boy" (Jer 20:15; cf., however, the idiom in the Aram. marriage contract, Cowley no. 15.20: *wbr dkr wnqbh* "be it a male or female child") or *b^{e}nê ʾîš* "men" (Psa 4:3) indicate the degree to which the term *bēn* could be distanced from its basic meaning and could become an individuating expression in collectives and a simple filler. *GVG* 2:242; J. Zobel, *Der bildliche Gebrauch der Verwandtschaftsname im Hebr.* (1932), 25–35; and *WUS* no. 534 (*bn* 2) offer examples from the related Sem. languages of the meaning "belonging to something."

4. The rare PNs composed with *bēn* as the first element should be seen in the context of ancient Near Eastern onomastics (cf. Huffmon 120f., 175f.; Gröndahl 80, 118f.; A. Caquot, *Syria* 39 [1962]: 239f.; on *binyāmîn* cf. K.-D. Schunck, *Benjamin* [1963], 4ff.; also: Alt, *KS* [1959], 3:198–213).

On theophoric names such as *ben-h^{a}dad,* not attested among the Israelites, cf. O. Eissfeldt, FS Baetke 110–17. The Eg. etymology of the name Moses (short form of a theophoric name with *mś* "child"; cf. H. Ranke, *Die äg. Personennamen* [1935], 1:338, 340) is no longer held.

IV. 1. One of the oldest narrative motifs in the patriarchal history is the narrative of the promise of a son and its fulfillment. In response to the complaint of the childless woman, God (or his messenger) promises her a son, e.g., Gen 18:10, 14, "in one year your wife Sarah will have a son"; cf. Gen 16:11; 17:16, 19; 21:2, etc. (C. Westermann, *Promises to the Fathers* [1980], 12ff.). This motif occurs throughout the entire OT (Judg 13:3, 5, 7; 1 Sam 1:20; Isa 7:14; 54:1) and on into the NT (Luke 1–2).

A related significant theological motif in the Gen patriarchal narratives is the transmission of the blessing through the father to his son. Gen 27 preserves the procedure most clearly, climaxing in the pronouncement of blessing in vv 27–29; cf. e.g., Gen 9:25–27; 48:15f.; 49. These texts are significant because they offer a glimpse into an intrafamilial phenomenon between father and son.

The transmission of tradition also originally transpired between father and son in the family.The son questions the significance of an action or an object, the father relates what he has heard himself (see II/1).

2. (a) Sons receive from their fathers not only the blessing; they must also bear their fathers' guilt and they are held responsible for it: Yahweh "visits the guilt of the fathers on the children and children's children to the third and fourth generation" (Exod 20:5; 34:7; Num 14:18; Deut 5:9; cf. Isa 14:21; Jer 32:18; → *ʾāb* IV/2b). This collective responsibility is breached in later times (Jer 31:29; Ezek 18:2, 4, 20; 2 Kgs 14:6 = 2 Chron 25:4; cf. J. Scharbert, *Solidarität in Segen und Fluch im AT und in seiner Umwelt* 1 [1958]; R. Knierim, *Die Hauptbegriffe für Sünde im AT* [1965], 204–7).

(b) The prophetic accusation refers directly to the sons' guilt: children who have forsaken Yahweh (Jer 5:7), children of harlotry (Hos 2:6), and rebellious sons (Ezek 20:21). Guilt binds children, fathers, and wives as a family (Jer 7:18); it manifests itself in the fact that the guilty sacrifice their own sons and daughters to other gods (Hos 9:13; Jer 7:31; 19:5, etc.; cf. Deut 12:31; Psa 106:37f.).

As a result, the announcement of judgment recurs in various prophets in similar phraseology: the fathers together with the sons will stumble (Jer 6:21) and will be smashed (Jer 13:14); sons and daughters will die (Jer 11:22); women and children will be led away (Jer 38:23), etc. Only on the other side of the catastrophe does a voice sound again that speaks of the return of the children (Isa 49:22).

(c) In this context the prophets' actual children and their names are interesting. Thus the names of the two sons (and the daughter) of Hosea already contain a clear pronouncement of judgment: Hos 1:3f. "Jezreel" ("for in a short time I will avenge Jezreel's blood on the house of Jehu"); 1:6 "Not-pitied"; 1:9 "Not-my-people." The same is true of the names of Isaiah's sons: Isa 7:3 Shear-jashub ("a remnant returns") and 8:3 Maher-shalal-hash-baz ("spoil speeds-prey hastens"). The name of Isaiah's first son simultaneously announces judgment (for the majority) and salvation (for the remnant); the same is true of the son announced in Isa 7:14 named "Immanuel" ("God with us"), although it is disputed in this case whether reference is made to a biological son of Isaiah (cf. H. W. Wolff, *Immanuel* [1959]; J. J. Stamm, *TZ* 16

[1960]: 439–55; id., *ZDMG* Suppl. 1 [1969]: 281–90); cf. also Isa 9:5 on the promise of the son.

That Jeremiah is not permitted to have biological sons and daughters is also a sign of the coming judgment (Jer 16:2).

(d) The address of the prophet as *ben-ʾādām*, 93x in Ezek, should be translated "you individual" (Zimmerli, *Ezek*, Herm, 1:131). At any rate, the "son of man" here is not yet a heavenly being of some sort. The expression *ben-ʾādām* in this period still parallels the terms *ʾenôš* and *ʾîš* (see III/3d). *ʾādām* is the person in distinction from God. Num 23:19 is characteristic: "God *(ʾēl)* is not a man *(ʾîš)* that he should lie, nor a son of man *(ben-ʾādām)* that he should repent."

On the figure of the one "like a man" *(kebar ʾenāš)* in Dan 7:13 and of the associated "son of man," a term now distinct from other OT usages, cf. comms. and C. Colpe, "ὁ υἱὸς τοῦ ἀνθρώπου," *TDNT* 8:400–477.

3. The characterization of a person as "son of God" or of a group as "sons of God" occurs rarely in the OT in contrast to other religions.

(a) A few passages regard the Davidic king as a son of Yahweh: 2 Sam 7:14, "I will be his father and he will be my son"; cf. 1 Chron 17:13; 22:10; 28:6; also Psa 2:7, "You are my son, today I have begotten you." In contrast to the old Eg. royal ideology, which represents the current pharaoh as god's son in the physical and mythical sense, the OT offers merely an adoption concept. The conferral of divine sonship implies the special rights and responsibilities of the king (cf. G. von Rad, "Royal Ritual in Judah," *PHOE* 222–31; M. Noth, "God, King, and Nation in the OT," *Laws in the Pentateuch and Other Studies* [1966], 145–78, esp. 171ff.; Kraus, *Psa*, CC, 1:130f.; G. Cooke, "Israelite King as Son of God," *ZAW* 73 [1961]: 202–25; K.-H. Bernhardt, *Das Problem der altorientalischen Königsideologie im AT* [1961], 74ff., 84ff.).

(b) In a few passages the son concept describes the relationship of Yahweh to his people Israel. Hos 2:1 and 11:1 are probably the earliest instances. Again, these texts do not envision a physical sonship, nor likely a spiritual one (wisdom tradition?), notions common in Israel's environment. When Hosea calls Israel "God's sons" (in contrast to the apostate "children of harlotry"), he means "an intimate relationship of care, guidance, and obedience" (Wolff, *Hos*, Herm, 27, 197f.). A later addition to the JE narrative in the Pentateuch, Exod 4:22f., characterizes Israel as Yahweh's "firstborn son," thus foreshadowing the last plague by which Yahweh will avenge the evil committed against his son on "Pharaoh's firstborn son" (v 23; cf. Noth, *Exod*, OTL, 47).

The notion of rearing is prominent (as in Hos 11:1) in the discussion in Isa 1:2 of Israel as "sons" whom Yahweh has reared but who are fallen away from him again (cf. H. Wildberger, *Isa 1–12*, CC, 12f.). Deut 14:1; 32:5, 19f. discuss the "sons of Yahweh" in a similar metaphor (cf. P. Winter, *ZAW* 67 [1955]: 40–48); Jer 3:14, 19, 22; Isa 43:6; 45:11 (→ *ʾāb* IV/3; G. Quell, *TDNT* 5:971ff.).

(c) Heavenly beings, discussed occasionally, are characterized as *benê-hāʾelōhîm* "sons of God" (Gen 6:2, 4; Job 1:6; 2:1; 38:7), *benê ʾēlîm* (Psa 29:1;

89:7), *bᵉnê* *ᶜelyôn* "sons of the Most High" (Psa 82:6), Aram. *bar* *ᵓᵉlāhîn* (Dan 3:25). "The *bēn* ('son') describes them, however, as sons of God, not in the physical, genealogical sense, i.e., mythologically, but generally as belonging to the world of the Elohim" (von Rad, *Gen*, OTL [1972[2]], 114). The significance and the function of these figures is limited in the OT. Cf. W. Herrmann, "Die Göttersöhne," *ZRGG* 12 (1960): 242–51; G. Cooke, "Sons of (the) God(s)," *ZAW* 76 (1964): 22–47.

(d) Finally, a few post-exilic passages that compare Yahweh's activity with people with that of a father toward his son should also be mentioned: as a father carries his child (Deut 1:31), reproves his son (Deut 8:5; Prov 3:12), shows mercy to his children (Psa 103:13) or his son (Mal 3:17), so also Yahweh behaves toward his (cf. Mal 1:6).

V. The term *huios* in the NT reflects the OT *bēn*. Discussion of Jesus as the "son" (cf. the christological titles "son of man," "son of David," and "son of God") gives the term an entirely new accent in the NT. Cf. H. E. Tödt, *Son of Man in the Synoptic Tradition* (1965); F. Hahn, *Titles of Jesus in Christology* (1969); P. Wülfing von Martitz et al., "υἱός," *TDNT* 8: 334–99; C. Colpe, "ὁ υἱὸς τοῦ ἀνθρώπου, *TDNT* 8:400–477; E. Lohse, "υἱὸς Δαυίδ," *TDNT* 8:478–88.

J. Kühlewein

בנה *bnh* to build

S 1129; BDB 124a; *HALOT* 1:139a; *TDOT* 2:166–81; *TWOT* 255; *NIDOTTE* 1215

1. The root **bny* "to build" occurs in all Sem. languages except Eth. (Akk. *banû* and Ug. *bny* also in the meaning "to create, beget"; see 3a).

A close relationship between *bēn* "son" and *bnh*, although possible, remains uncertain; the same is true of an etymological relationship between *bnh* and *brᵓ* "to create" (cf. *HAL* 133).

binyâ, *binyān*, *mibneh* "building," and *tabnît* "building plan, model, image" occur in the OT as nominal derivatives; PNs such as *bᵉnāyâ*, *bᵉnāyāhû*, *binnûy*, *yabnᵉᵓēl*, *yibnᵉyâ*, etc., also derive from the root.

2. In the Hebr. OT the verb occurs 346x in the qal (incl. Ezek 16:31) and 30x in the ni. Although otherwise normally distributed, half of all occurrences of the qal are concentrated in those books that record the construction of the temple or the walls (63x in 1 Kgs, 61x in 2 Chron, 28x in 1 Chron, 23x in Neh).

Of the substantives, *tabnît* is attested 20x, the three others, all limited to Ezek 40–42, 9x (*binyān* 7x).

In Bibl. Aram. the pe. occurs 15x, the hitpe. 7x, in addition to *binyān* 1x.

3. (a) The basic meaning is "to build, erect," occasionally "to fortify" and "to rebuild" (so also in NWSem. inscriptions; see *DISO* 38). Objects are: house, palace, wall, city, altar, temple, etc. A meaning "to create, beget" in Hebr. may not easily be demonstrated, in contrast to Akk. and Ug., if one does not wish to assume them in PNs such as *b^e^nāyāh(û)*.

In Ugaritic there occurs the El epithet *bny bnwt*, which is translated "creator of the creation" (cf. W. H. Schmidt, *Königtum Gottes in Ugarit und Israel* [1966^2], 59). On the Akk., see *AHw* 103.

(b) *bnh bayit* means metaphorically "to found a family, beget descendants" (Deut 25:9; cf. Ruth 4:11), "to found a dynasty" (2 Sam 7:27; 1 Chron 17:25). In Gen 16:2 and 30:3, *bnh* ni. "to be built" is an idiom for "to obtain children." Here too the starting point is the basic meaning, and no independent secondary meaning is present.

If the text of Job 22:23 is in order, one must also assume a fig. meaning (cf. *UHP* 53).

(c) The following parallels to the other meanings of *bnh* may be noted: *kûn* hi. "to establish" (2 Sam 7:13 = 1 Chron 17:12; Psa 89:3, 5); *nṭ*ᶜ "to plant" (Jer 1:10; 31:28; 45:4, etc.); *ᶜśh* "to make" (cf. 2 Sam 7:11, 27). *hrs* "to tear down" serves as an antonym, e.g., Jer 1:10; 45:4; Psa 28:5; Job 12:14; Prov 14:1.

4. (a) Theologically significant are, first of all, passages that discuss Yahweh's building. These passages deal with promises of future salvation: 2 Sam 7:27; 1 Chron 17:10, 25 (David's house; cf. 2 Sam 7:11; Psa 89:5); 1 Kgs 11:38 (Jeroboam's house); Amos 9:11 (the rebuilding of David's booth); Jer 24:6; 31:4, 28; 33:7; 42:10 (Dtr influence, often with the par. *nṭ*ᶜ "to plant," of the reconstruction after judgment); Ezek 28:26; 36:33–36 (addition with an echo of Jer diction; cf. Zimmerli, *Ezek*, Herm, 2:100, 245, 251n.30); Psa 102:17; 147:2 (Zion or Jerusalem; similarly in the request in Psa 51:20; in restrospect, 78:69).

The concept occurs in a negative sense in the announcement of judgment in Jer 45:4 (tearing down that which is built); Mal 1:4 (Edom).

(b) Additional salvation sayings are Isa 58:12; 60:10; 61:4; 65:21f., of the rebuilding after the exilic crisis as a realization of Yahweh's blessing (cf. also Jer 29:5, the task of the exiles). Jeremiah is called as a prophet "to pluck out, to destroy, to plant, and to build up," i.e., to be active as a prophet of doom and salvation (Jer 1:10). Concerning the pairs of terms used here and elsewhere, cf. R. Bach, "Bauen und Pflanzen," FS von Rad 7–32; S. Herrmann, *Die prophetischen Heilserwartungen im AT* (1965), 165–69.

(c) The usage of this verb in the context of salvation history can be traced to the notion that "building houses and living in them" should be considered a blessing; it is an expression of good fortune and full enjoyment of the gifts of the settled land given the people by God, a concept esp. encountered in Deut (6:10f.; 8:12; 20:5; the contrary in 28:30).

5. Of the Qumran texts, 1QS 11:8 (*mabnît qōdeš* "holy building" as a description of God's chosen) merits particular attention. On the NT, cf. O. Michel, "οἰκοδομέω," *TDNT* 5:137ff.

A. R. Hulst

בַּעַל *baʿal* owner

S 1167; BDB 127a; *HALOT* 1:142b; *TDOT* 2:181–200; *TWOT* 262a; *NIDOTTE* 1251

1. The word **baʿl-* "lord, owner," like its fem. equivalent, is common Sem. The transition from appellative to proper name of one or more deities is religiohistorically significant; in other usages the extensive limitation to a purely modal function ("a formal term," *GVG* 2:240f.) should be noted. The related verb is often only a denominative.

Akk. *bēlu*/*bēltu* "lord/lady" (*AHw* 118–20) is thus the base for *bêlu* "to rule, control" (cf. *beʾūlātum* "discretionary or operational capital" *AHw* 124a; *baʾūlātu* "the subordinates" *AHw* 117b). Akk. *bēlu* also includes Hebr. → *ʾādôn* in its range of meaning. On the divine names Bēl (for Enlil and Marduk) and Bēlet (for Ninlil and Ṣarpānītu), cf. Haussig 1:46; *AHw* 118; *bēl* occurs in the OT in Isa 46:1; Jer 50:2; 51:44. Of the numerous expressions composed with *bēl*, the following may be mentioned: *bēl pī/āḫāti* "representative, commissioner" (*AHw* 120a), giving rise to Aram. and Hebr. *peḥâ* "governor" (Alt, *KS* [1964³], 2:333; KBL 757b, 1112a; E. Y. Kutscher, *Tarbiz* 30 [1960/61]: 112–19), and *bēl ṭēmi;* cf. Aram. *beʿel ṭeʿem* as an official designation (Ezra 4:8f., 17; Cowley no. 26.23; KBL 1079b; Driver, *AD* 18).*

The preponderance of NWSem. instances (Ug.: *WUS* nos. 544f.; *UT* no. 493; Gröndahl 114–17; cf. also *DISO* 40; *HAL* 137f.; *LS* 83f.) are of the appellative "lord, owner" (limited in range of meaning by → *ʾādôn* and *mārēʾ* "lord, ruler") and of the various divine names (see 4a). Of great significance here, too, is the usage of the word as a designation for the husband in relation to his wife (Aram., e.g., in the marital contract, Cowley no. 15.23). The verb here has often assumed the meaning "to marry" (cf. e.g., R. Yaron, *JSS* 3 [1958]: 26f.); in contrast, Ug. *bʿl* "to make, work, manufacture" (*WUS* no. 546; *UT* no. 494) should be regarded as a by-form of the root → *pʿl* "to make" (*bʿl* may also occur in this meaning in the OT: on Isa 54:5, cf. *UT* no. 494; *HAL* 136f.; as well as in Isa 1:31; Job 31:39; Prov 1:19; 3:27; Eccl 8:8; cf. M. Dahood, *Bib* 46 [1965]: 320; contrast, however, *CPT* 100f.).*

2. The appellative *baʿal* "owner" occurs 84x in the Hebr. OT (Judg 19x, Exod and Prov 14x, Eccl 7x), the fem. *baʿălâ* 4x; in addition *beʿēl* occurs 3x in Aram. (Ezra 4:8f., 17).

The meaning "husband" occurs 15x (except for Esth 1:17, 20, always sg.).

baʿal appears 36x in the sg. and 48x in the pl., although the 18 pl. forms with the 3d sg. suf. all have a sg. meaning ("his/their lord" as a so-called pl. of majesty: Exod 21:29bis, 34, 36; 22:10f., 13f.; Isa 1:3; Job 31:39; Prov 1:19; 3:27; 16:22; 17:8; Eccl 5:10, 12; 7:12; 8:8).

baʿal occurs as a divine designation or a divine name in the sg. 58x (2 Kgs 24x, 1 Kgs 12x, Jer 11x, Judg 6x, Hos and 2 Chron 2x, Zeph 1x); see also the phrases *baʿal berît* (Judg 8:33; 9:4), *baʿal zebûb* (2 Kgs 1:2f., 6, 16), and *baʿal peʿôr* (Num 25:3, 5; Deut 4:3bis; Hos 9:10; Psa 106:28); the abundant place-names formed with *baʿal*/*baʿălâ* (the classification of Num 22:41 and Hos 9:10 is disputed) and PNs are left aside here. The pl. *beʿālîm* occurs 18x (see 4a).

The verb occurs 10x in qal and 2x in ni.; the fem. pass. ptcp. *b^eʿûlâ* "married" occurs an additional 4x.

3. (a) In its basic meaning "owner (of a thing)," the semantic field of the term exhibits no consistent par. or related terms.

A ptcp. of → *qnh* "to acquire" parallels *baʿal* once (Isa 1:3). The term *ʾādôn*, which can be translated "owner" only in 1 Kgs 16:24, describes more a relationship of dominion than of ownership: e.g., Joseph is *ʾādôn* "ruler" over Egypt and its inhabitants, without being owner of the land (Gen 42:30, 33; → *ʾādôn* III/1).

baʿal (as well as *baʿ^alâ*) is never used absolutely (except in the expression *b^eʿūlat baʿal;* see 3b), but always with an accompanying gen. or pron. suf. The gens. dependent upon *baʿal* vary widely according to context; in the 13 instances in the Covenant Code alone *baʿal* is the owner of a woman (Exod 21:3, 22), a domestic animal (21:34; 22:10f., 13f.; cf. Isa 1:3), esp. of an ox (21:28, 29[bis], 36), a house (22:7; cf. Judg 19:22f.), or a cistern (21:34).

(b) In 15 of the 84 occurrences mentioned, *baʿal* should be understood as the "owner" of a woman, i.e., as "husband"; passages with this meaning are spread over the entire OT (Gen 20:3; Exod 21:3, 22; Lev 21:4 txt em; Deut 22:22; 24:4; 2 Sam 11:26; Hos 2:18, fig.; Joel 1:8; Prov 12:4; 31:11, 23, 28; Esth 1:17, 20). → *ʾiššâ* "wife" occurs in the semantic field without exception as the complementary term (2x in the gen. construction *baʿal (hā)ʾiššâ* "husband," Exod 21:3, 22). *ʾîš* in the meaning "husband" is more neutral than *baʿal,* which connotes ownership (the term → *ʾādôn* used in the meaning "husband" expresses a different nuance of this dependent relationship: Gen 18:12, etc.). 2 Sam 11:26 indicates, however, the close relationship of the two terms: "when the wife of Uriah heard that her husband *(ʾîš)* was dead, she mourned her husband *(baʿal).*"

The verb *bʿl,* in the qal "to marry (from the male perspective)" (with three exceptions: "to rule" in Isa 26:13; Jer 3:14; 31:32; 1 Chron 4:22 is disputed) and in the ni. "to be married" (Isa 62:4; Prov 30:23), also belongs here. The semantic field displays no consistent parallels. *bôʾ ʾel* "to go into" (Deut 21:13), *hyh l^eʾiššâ* "to become wife" (Deut 21:13), and *lqḥ ʾiššâ* "to take a wife" (Deut 24:1) appear as pars. once each. Any of the following may be married, according to context: a woman (Deut 21:13; 24:1), a virgin (Isa 62:5), a daughter of a foreign god (Mal 2:11), a rejected woman (Prov 30:23) or, in the fig. sense, Israel in exile (Isa 54:4), the land (Isa 62:4), or Jerusalem (62:5); in each case in which a community is the obj., Yahweh is the subj. (see 4b).

Although the fem. nom. form *baʿ^alâ* always means "mistress" (1 Sam 28:7bis, *ʾôb* "spirit of the dead"; 1 Kgs 17:17, a house; Nah 3:4, sorcery), the verb forms a pass. ptcp. *b^eʿûlâ* "married" (Gen 20:3 and Deut 22:22 in the set phrase *ʾiššâ b^eʿūlat baʿal* "a married woman with a husband"; Isa 54:1 and 62:4 refer fig. to the Israel of the exilic period or to the land, contrasting *b^eʿûlâ* "the married" and *šômēmâ* "the abandoned").

(c) The pl. cs. followed by a city name indicates, closely dependent upon the basic meaning, the "land owners," the "citizens" of a given city (cf. also Akk. *baʾūlu* as a synonym for *rubû* "prince," *AHw* 117b). Of the total of 21 occurrences of this meaning, 16 are concentrated in Judg 9 alone (citizens of Shechem; in v 51, of the city; in vv 46f., occupants of the fortress of Shechem); the remaining occurrences are closely related: Josh 24:11, Jericho;

Judg 20:5, Gibeah; 1 Sam 23:11f., Keilah; 2 Sam 21:12, Jabesh. In each case, the expression refers to the (mostly Can.) inhabitants of a city who trade and negotiate with outsiders independently, who, probably on the basis of their land ownership, occupy lofty positions in respect to the other "inhabitants" *(yôšᵉbîm)* or "men" (*ʾᵃnašîm;* cf. J. A. Soggin, *Das Königtum in Israel* [1967], 23, with a reference to *KAI* no. 222A.4; cf. Fitzmyer, *Sef.* 28).

(d) Like *bēn* "son" and *ʾîš* "man," *baᶜal* readily combines with other nouns in cs. relationships, describing the "owner" as bearer of a characteristic or as involved with a given thing or activity, e.g., *baᶜal haḥᵃlōmôt* "owner of dreams = dreamer" (Gen 37:19); *baᶜal ʾap* "possessor of wrath = wrathful" (Prov 22:24, par. to *ʾîš ḥēmôt* "man of excitement = hot-tempered"; cf. 29:22, where *ʾîš ʾap* is par. to *baᶜal ḥēmâ*); *baᶜal haqqᵉrānayim* "owner of the two horns = double-horned" (Dan 8:6, 20). Cf. BrSynt 69 and the extensive list of usages with *baᶜal* as a formal term in *HAL* 137.

4. (a) In the OT, *baᶜal* as a divine designation usually refers to the Can. rival of Yahweh.

In the Ug. pantheon, Baal is considered alongside El to be king of the gods (cf. W. H. Schmidt, *Königtum Gottes in Ugarit und Israel* [1966²], 10–21, 29–54); he is worshiped as the god of fertility. When he dies, vanquished by the god of death, Mot, all nature withers; when he returns again to life, nature blossoms again (A. S. Kapelrud, *Baal in the Ras Shamra Texts* [1952]; Haussig 1:253–64).

With reference to the OT, O. Eissfeldt (*ZAW* 57 [1939]: 1–31 = *KS* [1963], 2:171–98) has broken with the formerly common concept that the Baals named there are a number of smaller, insignificant local deities. According to him, they are always forms of *one* god, namely Baᶜalšamēm, the "god of heaven," or the weather god Hadad (cf. *RGG* 1:805f.).

The name *baᶜal* appears in three areas in the OT: (1) In the narrative books, it represents a deity always linked with a particular place and exercising a particular function there.

Several passages (see 2) mention *baᶜal pᵉᶜôr,* who was worshiped at a border sanctuary between Moab and Israel on the mountain *pᵉᶜôr* (Num 23:28) or at *bêt pᵉᶜôr,* about 12 miles east of the northern tip of the Dead Sea (O. Henke, *ZDPV* 75 [1959]: 155–63). *baᶜal bᵉrît* "covenant Baal" (Judg 8:33; 9:4; cf. 9:46) with a temple in Shechem, *baᶜal zᵉbûb* (2 Kgs 1:2–16, designated expressly as the city god of Ekron; cf. *BHH* 1:175f.; F. C. Fensham, *ZAW* 79 [1967]: 361–64), as well as a few deities attested only in place-names such as Baal Zaphon (Exod 14:2, 9; Num 33:7; cf. O. Eissfeldt, *Baal Zaphon, Zeus Kasios und der Durchzug der Israeliten durchs Meer* [1932]; Haussig 1:256–58) and the Baal of Hermon (Judg 3:3; cf. 1 Chron 5:23) also deserve mention.

"The Baal" without complement describes the Baal of Ophrah (Judg 6:25–32), that of Carmel (1 Kgs 18:21ff.; cf. Alt, *KS* [1964³], 2:135–49; O. Eissfeldt, "Der Gott Karmel," *SDAW* [1953], 1; K. Galling, FS Alt 105–25), and the Tyrian god introduced to Samaria (1 Kgs 16:31f.; 18:19; 22:54; 2 Kgs 10:18–28, etc.; cf. Alt, *KS* [1959], 3:258–302). One may ask (contra Eissfeldt) whether these deities, sometimes widely separated geographically, should really be understood as manifestations of one Baᶜalšamēm, rather than as distinct deities.

(2) Of the 20 occurrences of the divine designation *baᶜal* within the prophetic corpus, 13 are in Jer (in a few passages in Dtr formulation), 6 in Hos (on 2:18, see 4b below), and one in Zeph. Hosea and, following him, Jeremiah take up Elijah's struggle against the Baal cult. Hosea uses the image of marriage in his attack on the Baal cult: the faithless wife (= Israel) turns aside from Yahweh and whores after her lovers (Hos 2:7ff.; on the pl. *beᶜālîm* in 2:15, 19; 11:2, cf. Wolff, *Hos*, Herm, 38–40). The judgment announced by Hosea consists in the fact that Yahweh will visit the "days of the Baals" (participation in the Can. cultic festivals) on this faithless wife (2:15); the day of salvation will come when Yahweh removes the "names of the Baals" (2:19). The apostasy to the Baal cult of which Hosea accuses Israel already had roots, according to this prophet, in the early period of Israel, as the historical retrospectives show (9:10; 11:2; 13:1).

In Jer, the accusation against those who turn to the Baal cult broadens: the prophets are accused of prophesying in the name of Baal (Jer 2:8; 23:13), of sacrificing the entire people to the Baals.

The following verbs express the prophetic accusation of apostasy to the Baals: *zbḥ* "to sacrifice" (Hos 11:2), *qṭr* pi./hi. "to burn incense" (Hos 2:15; 11:2; Jer 7:9; 11:13, 17; 19:4f.; 32:29); *nzr* ni. "to dedicate oneself" (Hos 9:10); *ᵓšm* "to incur guilt" (Hos 13:1); *šbᶜ* ni. "to swear" (Jer 12:16), *bnh bāmôt* "to build high places" (Jer 19:5; 32:35). The nouns used in the semantic field as parallels also indicate something of the prophetic assessment of the Baals: *bōšet* "shame" (Hos 9:10); *šiqqûṣîm* "horrors" (Jer 32:34); *ᵓelōhîm ᵓaḥērîm* "other gods" (Jer 7:9; 19:4; cf. 11:13); *pesīlîm* "images" (Hos 11:2).

(3) The third area, which uses most of the pls. of the term, consists of the Dtr and Chr histories closely dependent upon Hos and Jer.

Typical expressions characterizing apostasy to the Baals are: *ᶜbd* "to serve" (Judg 2:11, 13; 3:7; 10:6, 10; 1 Kgs 16:31; 22:54; 2 Kgs 17:16); *hlk ᵓaḥarê* "to follow after" (Deut 4:3; 1 Kgs 18:18; Jer 2:23; 9:13); *znh ᵓaḥarê* "to whore after" (Judg 8:33).

Occasionally fem. counterparts appear alongside the Baals as additional Can. deities: the Ashtaroth (Judg 2:13; 10:6; 1 Sam 7:4; 12:10) and Asherahs (Judg 3:7; as well as the "hosts of heaven": 2 Kgs 17:16; 21:3 = 2 Chron 33:3; 2 Kgs 23:4f.).

(b) One only rarely dared associate the root *bᶜl* with Yahweh in the later periods.

The verb *bᶜl* qal in the meaning "to rule" in Isa 26:13 expresses the people's complaint about a time when Yahweh did not rule over the supplicants but other rulers did. In Jer 3:14 and 31:32 *bᶜl* is constructed with *be*; the context suggests the translation "to be lord." Yahweh, who speaks in the 1st person, is the subj. in each case. In Jer 3:14 the term occurs in the framework of a conditional announcement of salvation: as Lord, Yahweh is mighty enough to bring the "apostate sons" back to Zion. In Jer 31:32 Yahweh proves himself to be the Lord who punished those who had broken his covenant.

baᶜal occurs in Nah 1:2 as a mere formal term: Yahweh is *baᶜal ḥēmâ* "one full of wrath." Isa 1:3 belongs conditionally in this context too; it compares the behavior of a donkey toward his master's crib with the behavior of Israel toward Yahweh.

Yahweh is occasionally compared to a *baᶜal* "husband." In Hos 2:18 *baᶜalî* parallels *ᵓîšî*: "then you will say 'my husband' and you will no longer call 'my *baʿal.*' " As Wolff (*Hos,* Herm, 49) suggests, this salvation oracle treats, on the one hand, the fact that Israel will no longer merely respect Yahweh as the legal husband *(baʿal)* "in that day," but will love him as husband *(ʾîš);* at the same time, however, one must understand (in view of 2:19) that one who calls Yahweh *baʿalî* does not clearly distinguish between Yahweh and the Can. Baal (yet cf. Rudolph, KAT 13/1, 78f.).

Behind the unit Isa 54:1–10 stands the lament of the childless woman (cf. Westermann, *Isa 40–66,* OTL, 269ff.), an image for exilic Israel. The salvation announced by Deutero-Isaiah consists in the fact that Yahweh becomes the husband of this abandoned woman (Isa 54:5).

Trito-Isaiah uses the concept of Yahweh's marriage to the people or to the land of Israel again in Isa 62:4f. The new names "my desire" and "married" *(beʿûlâ)* characterize the era of salvation and contrast with the old names "abandoned" and "alone" (cf. 54:1).

On the problem of PNs with the theophoric element *baʿal* in the period of the judges and the earliest monarchy, cf. *IP* 119–22; Eichrodt 1:200–203.

5. The NT displays no single counterpart to the root *bʿl.* The LXX already translates *bʿl/baʿal* with great variety, e.g., in Exod 21:28 ("owner") with *kyrios,* in Judg 9 ("citizen") with *andres,* in Deut 21:13; 24:1 ("to marry") with *synoikizein;* in 2 Sam 11:26 both *ʾîš* and *baʿal* ("husband") are translated with *anēr,* while the name of the Can. deity Baal is merely transliterated. The divine name continues in the NT only in the name *Beezeboul* (Mark 3:22, etc.; cf. W. Foerster, "Βεεζεβούλ," *TDNT* 1:605f.; L. Gaston, "Beelzebul," *TZ* 18 [1962]: 247–55).

J. Kühlewein

בקשׁ *bqš* pi. **to seek**

S 1245; BDB 134b; *HALOT* 1:152a; *TDOT* 2:229–41; *TWOT* 276; *NIDOTTE* 1335

---

1. The root *bqš* is attested only in Hebr., Ug. (*bqṯ,* cf. *UT* no. 505; *WUS* no. 572), and Phoen. (*DISO* 41).

In addition to the pi. and pu., Hebr. forms a verbal abstract *baqqāšâ* "longing, desire," morphologically an Aram. pa. inf. (GKC §84e; BL 479).

According to C. Brockelmann (*ZS* 5 [1927]: 31f.), *bqš,* which arose from *bqr* "to examine," also extant in Aram. (cf. Wagner no. 45), is a rhymed form patterned after the somewhat synonymous → *drš,* which often accompanies *bqš;* cf., however, Ug. *bqṯ* alongside *drš.*

2. *bqš* appears as a verb in the pi. 222x, in the pu. 3x, esp. frequent in Sam-Kgs (50x), Jer (22x, 1x, resp.), and Psa (27x). The verbal noun *baqqāšâ* occurs 8x, all in Esth except for Ezra 7:6.

3. The basic meaning of *bqš* pi. is the search for something lost or missed (cf. C. Westermann, "Die Begriffe für Fragen und Suchen im AT," *KerD* 6

[1960]: 2–30, for *bqš* esp. 2–9). In perhaps half of all occurrences, the sense is "to search for someone or something (the location of which is unknown)"; cf. Lat. *quaerere.* Objs. are persons or animals (together about 50x) or things (around 60x), e.g., Gen 37:15f.; Josh 2:22; Judg 4:22; 1 Sam 9:3; 23:14; 26:2, 20; 1 Kgs 18:10. The obj. can also be undetermined or anonymous: "to seek out, select someone (from a crowd)" (e.g., 1 Sam 13:14; 16:16; 28:7; 1 Kgs 1:2f.; Isa 40:20; Ezek 22:30; Nah 3:11, to "seek" in vain). 1 Kgs 10:24 = 2 Chron 9:23 and Prov 29:26 speak of seeking the countenance (→ *pānîm*) of a person in the sense of a display of courtesy (see 4).

If the obj. is a quality or ideal and therefore the goal is not to locate but rather to fulfill a wish or to realize a plan, the verb acquires an emotional nuance: "to strive after something, be busy, be concerned," e.g., Jer 2:33; 5:1 (faithfulness); Ezek 7:25 (peace); Zeph 2:3 (justice, humility); Psa 4:3 (lies); 27:4 (dwelling in the house of God); above all Prov 2:4; 11:27; 14:6; 15:14; 17:9, 11; 18:1, 15 (wisdom, or the like); likewise Eccl 7:25; Dan 8:15. It is noteworthy that the cognitive element is very understated. *bqš* pi. occurs only rarely in the sense of "to examine, investigate" (cf. → *drš*). Except for Judg 6:29, where it parallels the preceding *drš* and is indeed colored by it, only a few passages from the wisdom literature with "wisdom" as the obj. merit consideration (e.g., Prov 2:4, where, however, wisdom is personified; 18:15; Eccl 7:25; 8:17).

In the meaning "to be out for something, seek after" with similar ideal objects, *šḥr* pi. (12x, with God as obj. in Isa 26:9; Hos 5:15; Psa 63:2; 78:34; Job 8:5) is largely synonymous with *bqš* pi. (cf. *HP* 222).

On the delimitation of the meanings of *bqš* pi. (obj.-oriented and resultative "to trace something, try to obtain") and *drš* (activity-related "to be concerned for, ask after, be mindful of something") cf. *HP* 248f., and → *drš* 3.

nepeš appears as the obj. around 30x, "to seek someone's life" and *rāʿâ* 9x, "to seek evil for someone." *bqš* pi. is used only twice in the opposite expression "to seek someone's well-being" (Psa 122:9 and Neh 2:10 with *ṭôb* or *ṭôbâ*). In contrast to *drš,* then, *bqš* pi. in this context refers primarily to malicious intent.

About 20x *bqš* pi. refers to an urgent search for a person, thus "to desire, require," also on the basis of a legal claim (cf. Lat. *petere*), e.g., Gen 31:39; 43:9; Num 16:10; Josh 22:23; 1 Sam 20:16; with → *dām* "blood" as obj. in 2 Sam 4:11; Ezek 3:18, 20; 33:8.

bqš pi. is not used as a verb of motion, "to search for a place."

In addition to nom. or pron. objs., an inf., with *lᵉ* 17x, without *lᵉ* 2x (Exod 4:24; Jer 26:21), appears occasionally.

bʿh "to seek" (pe.: Dan 2:13 "one seeks"?; 6:5; pa.: 4:33) and "to request" (9x) appears as a Bibl. Aram. equivalent. For Dan 2:13 the meaning "to be on the verge, be near to, run the risk" is also possible (KBL 1058b with bibliog.); cf. *ḥšb* pi. in Jonah 1:4 and *bqš* pi. in Gen 43:30 (*HAL* 146a, 347b).

Other related verbs worthy of mention are: *ḥpr* "to dig," in Job 3:21 and 39:29 in the fig. meaning "to trace, seek," in Deut 1:2 and Josh 2:2f. "to spy out (a land)" (*HAL*

327a; attributed to two roots in GB 250a); *ḥpś* qal/pi. "to search through" (cf. *HP* 130f.); further *tûr* qal/hi. "to explore, research" (qal 19x, 14x in Num 10:33–15:39; hi. 3x).

4. In the 14 passages in which God searches, the usage conforms to profane usage: "to seek after a lost one" (Ezek 34:16; Psa 119:176; cf. Eccl 3:15), "to choose selectively" (1 Sam 13:14), "to seek, examine" (Ezek 22:30; Job 10:6), "to strive after" (Exod 4:24; Judg 14:4; Zech 12:9), "to require" (Josh 22:23; 1 Sam 20:16; Ezek 3:18, 20; 33:8).

More numerous and also more significant theologically are the passages in which God is sought (perhaps one-fourth of all occurrences). The expression "to seek God" only rarely indicates a one-time event (8x), with no unique theological nuance. *bqš* pi. is used in the sense of "to seek a revelation, an oracle" only in extraordinary cases (→ *drš* 4). The only clear case is Exod 33:7. Cultic roots are also evident in Hos 5:6 (of the vain seeking of sanctuaries) and 2 Chron 20:4. The usage "to seek the face of God" or the like (see 3) occurs in 2 Sam 21:1; Psa 24:6; 27:8; 105:4 = 1 Chron 16:11; 2 Chron 7:14.

A theologically fixed usage does occur in the 30 passages in which *bqš* pi. designates proper behavior before Yahweh, repentance and fear of God. "It intends a state rather than an act" (Westermann, op. cit. 5). *bqš* pi. can parallel *drš* synonymously in these cases (Deut 4:29; Jer 29:13; Zeph 1:6; Psa 105:3f. = 1 Chron 16:10f.; 2 Chron 20:3f.).

5. Kuhn (*Konk.* 35) lists 7 occurrences in Qumran literature (cf. *GCDS* 89). The usage conforms primarily to OT usage (3x with direct obj.: *nepeš, rûaḥ, bînâ;* 2x with *l*ᵉ and inf.). 1QS 5:11, which employs *bqš* (together with *drš*) in the sense of "to search, study in *(b*ᵉ*)* his (God's) commandments," has no exact counterpart in the OT.

In the LXX 17 different verbs occur as translations of *bqš* pi. Despite the variety of equivalents, a strong concentration on *zētein* (175x) and its compounds (*ekzētein* 25x) is recognizable.

On the NT, see H. Greeven, "ζητέω," *TDNT* 2:892–96.

G. Gerleman

ברא *br*ʾ **to create**

S 1254; BDB 135a; *HALOT* 1:153b; *TDOT* 2:242–49; *TWOT* 278; *NIDOTTE* 1343

---

1. Of the many attempts to determine the etymology of the verb, the most likely is the frequently offered association of *br*ʾ I "to create" (qal, ni., in addition to the verbal abstract *b*ᵉ*rîʾâ*) with *br*ʾ III (pi.) "to cut down, clear (a forest)" (Josh 17:15, 18), "to cut in pieces" (Ezek 23:47).

*br*ʾ occurs in a Pun. inscription (*CIS* 1:347.4) as a professional designation, perhaps in the sense of "sculptor" (*DISO* 43 posits "graveur"; cf. *NE* 244).

*br*ʾ I/III could have arisen from a biradical root *br,* perhaps with the meaning "to cut, divide" (cf. also G. J. Botterweck, *Der Triliterismus im Semitischen* [1952], 64f.); yet even this assumption remains questionable.

On the one hand, *br*ʾ III pi. does not exhibit the same characteristics as *br*ʾ I qal (exclusive subj.: God). On the other hand, the basic meaning "to cut," etc., does not echo anywhere in the usage of *br*ʾ qal/ni. The verb is strikingly absent e.g., in the first, original portion of the creation account of Gen 1, which, in accordance with ancient Near Eastern tradition, describes the formation of light and darkness, heavenly and earthly oceans, water and land (Gen 1:4b, 7, 9 LXX) from one preexistent primordial stuff (v 2; cf. also vv 14, 18).

It is no longer possible to trace confidently a development of meaning within the OT, which limited the expression to God's creation; at best, one may identify a growing specialization in the objects of *br*ʾ- creation (see 3c and 4). In the OT, the two verbal stems, if once combined, are kept separate. *br*ʾ I is already characteristically shaped, so that any hypothetical notion related to a specific craft or myth is no longer operative.

On the verb, in addition to the comms. and OT theologies, see: F. M. Th. Böhl, FS Kittel 42–60; W. Foerster, *TDNT* 3:1000–1015; J. van der Ploeg, *Muséon* 59 (1946): 143–57; P. Humbert, *TZ* 3 (1947): 401–21 (= *Opuscules d'un hébraïsant* [1958], 146–65); N. H. Ridderbos, *OTS* 12 (1958): 219–23; E. Dantinne, *Muséon* 74 (1961): 441–51; W. H. Schmidt, *Die Schöpfungsgeschichte der Priesterschrift* (1967²), 164–67; C. Westermann, *Gen,* CC, 1:98–100.

2. (a) The verb (qal 38x, ni. 10x; *bᵉrîʾâ* 1x; cf. the statistics in Humbert, *Opuscules* 146–49) occurs primarily in the exilic prophet Deutero-Isa and (roughly contemporaneously) in P, scattered in the Psa and in other contexts. This distribution suggests that the verb is at home in cultic language; for the message of Deutero-Isa is indeed strongly influenced by the Psa. The expression seems to be foreign to wisdom literature (despite Eccl 12:1); in any case, it is surprisingly absent from Job, which frequently has recourse to the creation theme.

(b) Pre-exilic occurrences are at least very rare; thus the word is not very ancient.

The J creation account (Gen 2:4bff.) does not use the verb. Gen 6:7 J (in both the relative clause constructed with *br*ʾ and the list of living creatures) is redactionally influenced by the language of P. So *br*ʾ occurs in J actually only in Num 16:30 in the more colorless expression *br*ʾ *bᵉrîʾâ* "to produce something new, wonderful"; yet here too later influence may not be excluded on principle (cf. the term *ʿēdâ* "community" in v 26). The promise of wonders such as "have not yet been created" among all the peoples is an addition in Exod 34:10 between the announcement of the covenant and the proclamation of the commandments. Amos 4:13 initiates the doxologies of the book of Amos inserted only later. Isa 4:5 belongs to an "unauthentic" salvation oracle, combining theophany and creation in a highly unusual manner. The parenesis in Deut 4:32 (*br*ʾ in a temporal clause as in Ezek 28:13, 15) derives, at the earliest, from a later (Dtr?) framework of Deut. Psa 102 (v 19), 148 (v 5), as well as 51 (v 12) are hardly pre-exilic. The promise of a new creation of the people in Jer 31:22 may be attributable to the Josianic era.

If one leaves open the question of the age of Psa 89 (vv 13, 48) and 104 (v 30), then the limited attestation is insufficient to support the assumption that the verb *br*ʾ belonged essentially to the pre-exilic witness to Israel's belief in creation. Rather, one must adhere to the judgment of J. Wellhausen: "the word and the notion only coming into use after the Babylonian exile" (*Prolegomena to the History of Ancient Israel* [1957], 305).

3. Some peculiarities characterize the usage of *br*ʾ*:*

(a) God is always the subj. of the expression, indeed, always Israel's God, never a foreign deity (cf. perhaps Ezek 28:13, 15). "The most important point is that a special word is employed, which stands for nothing else than the creative agency of God, and so dissociates it from all analogy with human making and shaping" (Wellhausen, op. cit.). To the extent that the OT reserves the verb exclusively for God, this type of creation has no analogy and is, therefore, beyond conceptualization; divine activity can be perceived only insofar as it remains comparable to human activity. Therefore the verb expresses nothing further concerning the method of creation.

(b) No material from which God "creates" (cf. esp. Gen 1:27) is ever mentioned (in the acc. or with a prep.).

(c) The objs. of *br*ʾ vary often, however; they are special, extraordinary, new:

(1) Heaven and/or earth: Gen 1:1; 2:4; Isa 65:17; 42:5; 45:18; cf. 40:28; Psa 148:5; 89:13 (north and south = the whole);

(2) People: Gen 1:27; 5:1f.; 6:7; Deut 4:32; Isa 43:7; 45:12 (God "made" the earth, "created" humanity); Ezek 28:13, 15; Mal 2:10; Eccl 12:1; Psa 89:48;

(3) The people of Israel: Isa 43:1, 15; Psa 102:19; Ezek 21:35 (Ammon);

(4) Wonders, novelties, etc.: Exod 34:10; Num 16:30; Isa 48:6f.; 65:17; Jer 31:22; cf. Isa 41:20; 45:8; Psa 51:12; 104:30.

In a few passages the specificity of *br*ʾ recedes into the background. Thus Amos 4:13 ("who created the storm") uses various verbs synonymously, or Isa 42:5 adds the "spreading" of the heavens to "creating." *br*ʾ refers here only to an intermediate, not the final, stage of creation.

The review of materials in (3) and (4) indicates that the determinative factor is not that there was "nothing" prior to creation but that God's activity brings about something new, which (as such) did not exist before (also Isa 41:20; Psa 51:12; 102:19). On its own, then, the verb does not describe a creation ex nihilo, but it refers precisely to that which other systems of thought (see 5) seek to ensure through discussions of creation ex nihilo: God's extraordinary, sovereign, both effortless and fully free, unhindered creation.

4. The exilic prophet Deutero-Isaiah uses the verb *br*ʾ to describe not only the past or present (Isa 40:26, 28; 42:5; 45:12, 18; cf. Psa 104:30) but also the future (41:20; 45:8; cf. 65:17f.; Jer 31:22) work of God; just as the world as a whole (cf. 45:7) is God's creation, so is the new salvation. By contrast, P consistently limits the previously varied usage to the creation "at the beginning."

Even with this limitation, the specific character of the verb is still evident (in the context of the originally independent creation by the word also in Psa 148:5). Although Deutero-Isa generally continues to combine the word with various other equally significant expressions, P uses it to indicate a final action that needs no supplement and employs it in emphatic passages that do not belong in this form to the oldest layer of tradition. Superscript (Gen 1:1) and conclusion (2:3f.) together emphasize the fact that God created everything (without precondition). The threefold usage in the creation of humanity (1:27; cf. 5:1f.; but not in the announcement in 1:26) on the one hand demonstrates the peculiarity of this work, and on the other hand permits one to forgo any suggestion as to how people came to be and whence they originate (contra Gen 2:7; Psa 139:15). In the same way, mythical conceptions are excluded even though God creates the playfully free sea monsters (the first living creatures; Gen 1:21).

Despite the tendency to think comprehensively of the whole as God's work (e.g., Gen 1:1; Isa 45:7; 65:17), *br*ʾ can also express God's care for the individual (Isa 43:7; Mal 2:10; Eccl 12:1). For this reason Psa 51:12 "create in me a pure heart," can express the eschatological promise of a new humanity (cf. Ezek 36:26, etc.) as a request.

5. The LXX does not always translate *br*ʾ with *ktizein* (cf. W. Foerster, *TDNT* 3:1000–1035), but rather (in contrast to Aquila, Symmachus, Theodotion) occasionally in Gen with *poiein* (cf. H. Braun, *TDNT* 6:459ff.). The distinctives of the concept are not maintained, then. To the contrary, the Hellenistic notion of creation from nothing (cf. 2 Macc 7:28; Rom 4:17) seeks substantially to maintain by other means—presumably through the augmentation and inversion of the causal principle—the intention of the usage of *br*ʾ.

W. H. Schmidt

ברח *brḥ* **to flee** → נוס *nûs*

בְּרִית *b*ᵉ*rît* obligation

S 1285; BDB 136a; *HALOT* 1:157a; *TDOT* 2:253–79; *TWOT* 282a; *NIDOTTE* 1382

I. 1. The subst. *b*ᵉ*rît* has (so far) been identified only in Hebr. (against the interpretation of TAR *be-ri-ti* in two Akk. texts from Qatna as *krt b*ᵉ*rît* by W. F. Albright, *BASOR* 121 [1951]: 21f.; cf. J. A. Soggin, *VT* 18 [1968]: 210–15); the mention of an ʾ*ēl b*ᵉ*rît* (Judg 9:46) or a *ba*ʿ*al b*ᵉ*rît* (Judg 8:33; 9:4) at Shechem (cf. R. E. Clements, "Baal-*b*ᵉ*rîth* of Shechem," *JSS* 13 [1968]: 21–32) suggests a Can. usage of *b*ᵉ*rît* too.

2. Attempts to explain the etymology of *bᵉrît* are manifold.

(a) Some derive *bᵉrît* from an Akk. subst. *birītu* "fetter." *bᵉrît* would then have meant "first 'band,' . . . then fig. 'binding agreement' " (R. Kraetzschmar, *Die Bundesvorstellung im AT* [1896], 245; cf. P. Karge, *Geschichte des Bundesgedankens im AT* [1910], 228f., etc.). But aside from other difficulties (cf. O. Loretz, "*bᵉrît*—'Band-Bund,' " *VT* 16 [1966]: 239–41), according to this etymology the expression *krt bᵉrît*, lit. "to cut a *bᵉrît*," would mean "to cut (off) a band/fetter," which hardly fits the (generally accepted) meaning "to make a covenant" for *krt bᵉrît* (E. Nielsen, *Shechem* [1959²], 114).

(b) M. Noth ("OT Covenant-Making in the Light of a Text from Mari," *Laws in the Pentateuch and Other Studies* [1966], 108–17) compared *bᵉrît* with the Akk. prep. *birīt* "between" (cs. of *birītu* "space between") on the strength of ARM II:37.13f. But in the Akk. phrase *salīmam birīt . . . u . . . aškun*, "I brought about an agreement between . . . and . . . ," *birīt* corresponds not to the Hebr. *bᵉrît* in the comparable Hebr. expression *(krt) bᵉrît bên . . . ûbên . . .* (Gen 9:17, etc.), but to the prep. *bên*.

(c) If one thinks of a derivation from a verb *brh*, then such a verb with the meaning "cecidit, secuit" (so Gesenius, *Thesaurus* 1:238f.; P. Humbert, *TZ* 6 [1950]: 60) occurs only in Arab., not in Hebr. A semasiological relationship to *brh* I "to eat," so that *bᵉrît* would originally have meant the meal attested in conjunction with the making of covenants (Gen 26:30; cf. 28; 31:46, 54; cf. v 44; E. Meyer, *Die Israeliten und ihre Nachbarstämme* [1906], 558n.1; KBL 152b; L. Köhler, *JSS* 1 [1956]: 4–7; etc.), is out of the question, because this *brh* always indicates the food of the sick and mourning, just as the related substs. *bārût* (Psa 69:22) and *biryâ* (2 Sam 13:5, 7, 10) indicate the food of the unfortunate and ailing.

(d) *bᵉrît* more probably derives from a stem *brh* II (E. Kutsch, "Sehen und Bestimmen: Die Etymologie von *bᵉrît*," FS Galling 165–78; cf. also already GB 114b). This stem occurs in Akk. *(barû)* with the basic meaning "to see, look" (*AHw* 109; *CAD* B:115); earlier attempts to relate *bᵉrît* to this stem (e.g., H. Zimmern, *Beiträge zur Kenntnis der bab. Religion* [1901], 2:50) failed as long as the term was attested only for the "seeing" of the oracle priest. In accord with the Akk., the root *brh* II in the only Hebr. occurrence (1 Sam 17:8 "choose yourselves a man to come down to me") means "to see, choose, select, designate (for a particular task)" (like *rʾh* in Gen 22:8; Deut 12:13; 1 Sam 16:1; 2 Kgs 10:3; Esth 2:9; *ḥzh* in Exod 18:21). *bᵉrît* "determination (to do a particular thing), obligation" is formed on this root.

The process of semantic development is the same as for the substs. *ḥōzeh* and *ḥāzût*, used by Isaiah (Isa 28:15, 18; emendation is excluded) to parallel *bᵉrît*: they are derived from *ḥzh* in the meaning of the verb attested in Exod 18:21; this sense "to see > select > determine > prescribe" also recurs in the Aram. of the Tgs. (e.g., on Lev 5:10; Jer 22:13a; 32:7f.; 1 Chron 15:13) and in Palm. (customs tariff, *CIS* 2:3913; 2:114, 123, 129; cf. 1:7; 2:131; *DISO* 85).

II. The subst. *bᵉrît* occurs 287x in the OT (only in the sg.): Gen 27x, Exod 13x, Lev 10x, Num 5x, Deut 27x, Josh 22x, Judg 7x, 1 Sam 8x, 2 Sam 6x, 1 Kgs 14x, 2 Kgs 12x, Isa 12x (Deutero-Isa 4x, Trito-Isa 4x), Jer 24x, Ezek 18x, Hos 5x, Amos 1x, Obad 1x, Zech 2x, Mal 6x, Psa 21x, Job 3x, Prov 1x, Dan 7x, Ezra 1x, Neh 4x, 1 Chron 13x, 2 Chron 17x.

On account of the stratified nature of OT books, such statistics have only limited usefulness; more suggestive are statistics based on the periods of origin of the texts. The following occurrences may be placed in the pre-Dtr period: Deut 33:9(?); Josh 7:11,

15(?); 9:6f., 11, 15f.; 24:25(?); Judg 8:33; 9:4, 46; 1 Sam 18:3; 20:8; 23:18; 2 Sam 3:12f., 21; 5:3; 23:5; 1 Kgs 5:26; 15:19a, b; 20:34a, b; 2 Kgs 11:4; in J: Gen 15:18; 26:28; in E: Gen 21:27, 32; 31:44; further Exod 24:7, 8(?); Hos 6:7; 8:1(?); 10:4; 12:2; Isa 28:15, 18; from the Psa, possibly Psa 89:4, 29, 35, 40. In all, this is only about 43 occurrences. From the immediate pre-exilic period onward, *bᵉrît* occurs much more often; it acquires greater significance, then, indeed, primarily in the theological arena. Occurrences in Dtn-Dtr literature are particularly numerous. In addition to Deut 4:13 and a further 18x in Deut: Exod 19:5; 23:32; 34:10, 12, 15, 27f.; Josh 23:16; Judg 2:1f., 20; 1 Kgs 8:23; 11:11; 19:10, 14; 2 Kgs 11:17; 17:15, 35, 38; 18:12; 23:2, 3 (3x), 21; Jer 11:2f., 6, 8, 10; 14:21; 22:9; 31:31, 32a, b, 33; 34:8, 10, 13, 15, 18a, b; Amos 1:9 (62 passages, apart from Psa); 42 passages from Num 10:33; 14:44; Deut 10:8, etc., to 2 Chron 5:2, 7 mention the "ark of the *bᵉrît* of Yahweh/God"—either in a secondary expansion of the expression "ark of Yahweh/God" or originally—in which (according to the Dtr concept) the "tablets of the *bᵉrît*" (Deut 9:9, 11, 15; 1 Kgs 8:9 LXX) were stored (1 Kgs 8:9, 21; cf. Deut 10:2). P together with additions and H also constitute a large block, with 39 occurrences (Gen 6:18; 9:9–17 7x; 14:13; 17:2–21 13x; Exod 2:24; 6:4f.; 31:16; Lev 2:13; 24:8; 26:9–45 8x; Num 18:19; 25:12f.).

III. 1. As early as the end of the 19th cent., J. J. P. Valeton, Jr. (*ZAW* 12 [1892]: 1–22, 224–60; 13 [1893]: 245–79) and R. Kraetzschmar (op. cit.; see I/2a) demonstrated that the modern term "covenant" is simply inadequate to render the Hebr. *bᵉrît.* Accordingly, B. Baentsch (*Exodus-Leviticus-Numeri* [1903]), e.g., suggested "covenant" for *bᵉrît* in Exod 2:24, "unbreakable promise" in 6:4f., and "covenant regulation" in 19:5. In contrast to such differentiation, Eichrodt 1:37 (cf. also id., "Bund und Gesetz," FS Hertzberg 30–49) emphasized that in Israel, as with the profane usage, the "religious *bᵉrît* too was always regarded as a bilateral relationship; for even though the burden is most unequally distributed between the two contracting parties, this makes no difference to the fact that the relationship is still essentially two-sided." In a new approach, J. Begrich ("Berit. Ein Beitrag zur Erfassung einer alttestamentlichen Denkform," *ZAW* 60 [1944]: 1–11 = *GS* [1964], 55–66) interpreted *bᵉrît* as "a relationship, in which a more powerful party stands by a weaker party" (op. cit. 4; cf. also e.g., already B. Duhm, *Jesaia*, HKAT, 385, on Isa 55:3), wherein only the powerful party accepts an obligation and the (weaker) recipient plays no active role; only secondarily did *bᵉrît* come to be understood as a contract involving the rights and duties of the partners. A. Jepsen ("Bᵉrith. Ein Beitrag zur Theologie der Exilszeit," FS Rudolph 161–79) also emphasized the unilaterality of the *bᵉrît*, interpreting it as a "solemn pledge, promise, obligation" (op. cit. 165, 178); but he disputed whether *bᵉrît* also means the obligation under which another is placed, at least for the profane arena (op. cit. 165). By way of affirmation and critique of these approaches, the following may be said regarding the meaning of *bᵉrît* (E. Kutsch, "Gesetz und Gnade. Probleme des atl. Bundesbegriffs," *ZAW* 79 [1967]: 18–35; id., "Der Begriff *bᵉrīt* in vordeuteronomischer Zeit," FS Rost 133–43; cf. also G. Fohrer, "Altes Testament—'Amphiktyonie' und 'Bund'?" *Studien zur atl. Theologie und Geschichte* [1969], 84–119, esp. 103ff.), first in the profane arena.

2. *bᵉrît* does not indicate a "relationship," but is the "determination," "obligation," accepted by the subject of the *bᵉrît;* in such contexts *bᵉrît* can even mean the "pledge." The content of such a *bᵉrît* as "self-imposed

obligation" can be seen in the context: "to let (others) live," Josh 9:15a, so also 1 Sam 11:1; Deut 7:2; Exod 23:32f.; 34:12, 15; Judg 2:2; giving a life partnership, 1 Sam 18:3 (Begrich, op. cit. 6; Jepsen, op. cit. 163); protection of the wife, Ezek 16:8, 60a; Mal 2:14; on David's acceptance of obligations in relation to the elders of Israel, 2 Sam 5:3; cf. perhaps Psa 101 (and Jepsen, op. cit. 163f.). Not only the more powerful but also the subordinate, weaker, lowlier can accept such a self-imposed obligation, as the defeated Aramean king Ben-hadad accepted toward Ahab of Israel (1 Kgs 20:34a, b; cf. Jepsen, op. cit. 164f.; on the content cf. v 34a), Israel in relation to Assyria (Hos 12:2b; cf. v 2c), the Jews (Ezra 10:3) or Hezekiah (2 Chron 29:10) toward Yahweh. These passages do not refer to a repayment or reciprocal obligation on the part of the beneficiary of the *b*ᵉ*rît*. Moreover, on the occasion of the "cutting" of a *b*ᵉ*rît* (→ *krt*), i.e., on the assumption of a self-imposed obligation, the subj. of the *b*ᵉ*rît* does not even require a partner. King Josiah "cut the *b*ᵉ*rît* before Yahweh to follow Yahweh," 2 Kgs 23:3a: he assumes the obligation, and the people enter into it in a second act (v 3b); and this occurs "before" Yahweh, not "with" Yahweh. Therefore, there is no covenant agreement with Yahweh or with the people. The same usage also occurs in Exod 34:10; Jer 34:15b, 18b; Hos 10:4; 2 Chron 15:12; 34:31 (cf. also Neh 10:1, 30). Yahweh's enemies in Psa 83:6 obligate themselves to a common action against Yahweh; cf. also 2 Chron 23:16.

The one who assumes this type of self-imposed obligation can strengthen it even more through a ritual of self-deprecation, in which he passes between the parts of a slaughtered animal (Jer 34:15b, 18b, 19; Gen 15:17f.): In the event that he does not fulfill his pledge, he should experience the same fate as this animal.

3. The subject of the *b*ᵉ*rît* places another, the one with whom a *b*ᵉ*rît* is "cut," under obligation. Thus, according to Ezek 17:13ff., Nebuchadnezzar obligates the Jewish king Zedekiah: only he, not the Babylonians, must "enter into a curse" (v 13b), namely in the event he does not "maintain" this *b*ᵉ*rît* (on *krt b*ᵉ*rît [*ʾ*et-]* in Ezek 17:13a cf. Aram. *gzr* ʿ*dn [*ʿ*m]* in *KAI* no. 222A.7; see Fitzmyer, *Sef.* 32f.). Similarly, the Gerarites want to obligate Isaac (Gen 26:28; cf. v 29a), David takes Abner into his service (2 Sam 3:12f.), the Israelites obligate David (as king, 2 Sam 3:21; cf. 2 Chron 23:3), also death (namely to spare them, Isa 28:15, 18), King Zedekiah obligates the Judeans and Jerusalemites (to release their slaves, Jer 34:8), Job obligates the stones of the field (Job 5:23; cf. Horst, BK 16/1, 87f.), also his eyes (Job 31:1), the priest Jehoiada "assembles" the leaders of the palace troops (2 Kgs 11:4). In none of these cases does *b*ᵉ*rît* also include an obligation of those who "cut the *b*ᵉ*rît*."

4. From self-imposed obligation (see 2), the concept can evolve into the assumption of mutual obligations on the part of two or more partners, into a reciprocal *b*ᵉ*rît*. Thus Solomon and King Hiram of Tyre have "both cut a *b*ᵉ*rît*" (1 Kgs 5:26b); between them for continued *šālōm* (v 26b; Eng. 5:11). The *b*ᵉ*rît* between the kings of Damascus and Judah (1 Kgs 15:19a) was also conceived as a nonaggression treaty, as a reciprocal obligation, probably also the one between the Arameans and Basha of Israel (v 19b). According to

1 Sam 23:18 the *b^e^rît* between Jonathan and David was also reciprocal, as was, according to Gen 31:44, the *b^e^rît* between Jacob and Laban. The translation "covenant" for *b^e^rît* is rooted in this secondary and relatively infrequent usage.

5. Finally, a third individual can establish a *b^e^rît* between two parties. No illustration indicating that this *b^e^rît* means obligation for the two parties occurs in the OT (for the model, cf. ARM II:37.6–14, and Noth, op. cit. 108ff.). According to 2 Kgs 11:17b, the *b^e^rît* that the priest Jehoiada established "between the king and the people" may involve the king's obligation to the people in the light of 2 Sam 3:21; 5:3; and 2 Chron 23:3. In 2 Kgs 11:17a, too, the obligation ("to be a people of Yahweh") lies clearly on one side only, namely with the people. The *b^e^rît* that Yahweh will establish with the animals of the field to the benefit of the Israelites (Hos 2:20; see 7c; on the topic cf. Ezek 34:25; Lev 26:6; and H. W. Wolff, "Jahwe als Bundesvermittler," *VT* 6 [1956]: 316–20) also belongs here.

6. Various verbs indicate the (a) establishment, (b) observance, and (c) violation or invalidation of a *b^e^rît* (the following also takes account of the theological usage).

(a) The oldest and most common usage is *krt b^e^rît*, lit. "to cut a *b^e^rît*," to be translated "to reach a settlement, establish an obligation." Contrary to the widely held opinion, the expression is not derived from the dismemberment of animals as in Jer 34:18f.; Gen 15:10, 17 (→ *krt*). Cf. *krt* → *ʾālâ* (Deut 29:11, 13; and Phoen. in *KAI* no. 27.8f.; *ANET* 658b: "An eternal bond has been established"), *krt dābār* (Hag 2:5), *krt ʾ^a^mānâ* (Neh 10:1).

The formula → *qûm* hi. *b^e^rît* "to set up, enact a *b^e^rît*" appears immediately prior to the exile (Ezek 16:60, etc.; cf. 2 Kgs 23:3a); cf. *qûm* hi. with the obj. *š^e^bûʿâ* "oath" (Gen 26:3, etc.), *nēder* "vow" (Num 30:14f.; Jer 44:25), *dābār* "word, promise" (Deut 9:5, etc.), but also "word of the Torah" (Deut 27:26, etc.), *miṣwâ* "commandment" (Jer 35:16, etc.). The other usages are also later: with *b^e^rît* as obj. the verbs *ntn* "to give" (Gen 9:12; 17:2; Num 25:12), *śîm* "to establish" (2 Sam 23:5), *šbʿ* ni. "to swear" (Deut 4:31, etc.), *ngd* ni. "to announce" (Deut 4:13), *ṣwh* pi. "to command" (Deut 4:13, etc.), with *b^e^* "in" preceding *b^e^rît* the verbs *bôʾ* "to enter" (Jer 34:10; Ezek 16:8; 2 Chron 15:12; cf. 1 Kgs 8:31 = 2 Chron 6:22, with *ʾālâ;* Neh 10:30, with *ʾālâ* and *š^e^bûʿâ*), *ʿbr* "to enter" (Deut 29:11), *ʿmd* "to enter (into)" (2 Kgs 23:3b), further *bôʾ* hi. "to cause to enter" (1 Sam 20:8; cf. Ezek 17:13 with *ʾālâ*), *lqḥ* "to take (into)" (2 Chron 23:1; Ezek 17:13b?), *ʾmd* hi. "to cause to enter" (2 Chron 34:32 txt em).

(b) Verbs describing the observance of a *b^e^rît* also occur only from the late monarchy: of profane *b^e^rît: zkr* "to remember" (Amos 1:9) and *šmr* "to keep" (Ezek 17:14); God of his *b^e^rît* = "promise": *zkr* (Gen 9:15 and a further 11x), *šmr* (Deut 7:9 and a further 6x; cf. Deut 7:8; 1 Kgs 2:43, with the obj. *š^e^bûʿâ*); the person of God's *b^e^rît* = "law": *šmr* (Gen 17:9 and a further 5x; cf. 1 Sam 13:13, etc., with the obj. *miṣwâ*), *nṣr* "to keep" (Deut 33:9; Psa 25:10), *ʾmn* ni. "to be faithful" (Psa 78:37), *ḥzq* hi. "to hold fast" (Isa 56:4, 6).

(c) The following describe the violation or invalidation of a *b^e^rît:* profane, a human *b^e^rît* = "promise": *ḥll* pi. "to profane" (Psa 55:21; Mal 2:10), *prr* hi. "to break" (1 Kgs 15:19); God of his *b^e^rît* = "promise": *prr* hi. (Lev 26:44; Judg 2:1), *škḥ* "to forget" (Deut 4:31), *ḥll* pi. "to profane" (Psa 89:35), *nʾr* "to abandon" (Psa 89:40); the person of God's *b^e^rît* = "law": *prr* hi. (Gen 17:14, etc.; cf. Num 15:31 and Ezra 9:14, with *miṣwâ;* Psa 119:126, with *tôrâ;* but also Zech 11:14 with *ʾaḥ^a^wâ* "brotherhood"), *ʿbr* "to transgress"

(Deut 17:2 and a further 7x, as well as Hos 6:7?; cf. Dan 9:11 with *tôrâ;* 2 Chron 24:20 and Sir 10:19 with *miṣwâ;* Num 22:18 and 1 Sam 15:24 with *peh* "utterance, command"), *ᶜzb* "to abandon" (Deut 29:24 and a further 4x; cf. Prov 4:2 with *tôrâ*), *škḥ* "to forget" (Deut 4:23; 2 Kgs 17:38; Prov 2:17; cf. Hos 4:6 with *tôrâ;* Deut 26:13 with *miṣwâ*), *mʾs* "to reject" (2 Kgs 17:15; cf. Isa 5:24 and Amos 2:4 with *tôrâ;* 2 Kgs 17:15 with *ḥuqqîm;* Lev 26:15 and Ezek 20:24 with *ḥuqqôt;* 2 Kgs 17:15 with *ᶜēdōt;* Isa 5:24 with *ʾimrâ;* 1 Sam 15:23, 26 with *dābār*), *šḥt* pi. "to destroy" (Mal 2:8), *ršᶜ* hi. "to be guilty (with respect to)" (Dan 11:32), *šqr bᵉ* "to act deceitfully toward" (Psa 44:18); cf. also *gōʾal* "defilement" (Neh 13:29); the individual to a *bᵉrît* = "promise" to God: *škḥ* "to forget" (Jer 50:5).

7. The classification by usage discussed in III/2–4 finds additional confirmation in many respects.

(a) If *bᵉrît* means a self-imposed obligation, the substantive can parallel *šᵉbûᶜâ* "oath, vow" (Psa 105:9 = 1 Chron 16:16; cf. also *šbᶜ* ni. *šᵉbûᶜâ* in Num 30:3; Josh 9:20 alongside *šbᶜ* ni. *bᵉrît* in Deut 4:31; 8:18) or even *ʾālâ* "curse" (Deut 29:11, 13; Gen 26:28; Ezek 16:59; 17:18f.). If *bᵉrît* indicates the obligation of another party, however, other substantives occur as parallels, namely, those which reflect the character of this usage: *tôrâ* "instruction" (Hos 8:1; Psa 78:10; cf. also e.g., Deut 28:69 with v 58; 2 Kgs 23:3a with v 24; 2 Kgs 23:2, 21 with 22:8, 11), *ḥuqqîm* and *ḥuqqôt* "regulations" (2 Kgs 17:15; Psa 50:16 or 1 Kgs 11:11; cf. also, however, in contrast, *ḥōq* "decree to the benefit of" in Psa 2:7, with *bᵉrît* and *šᵉbûᶜâ* in Psa 105:9f. = 1 Chron 16:16f.), *tôrōt* and *ḥōq* "instructions" and "regulation" (Isa 24:5), *ᶜēdōt* "stipulations" (2 Kgs 17:15; Psa 25:10; 132:12), *piqqûdîm* "directions" (Psa 103:18), *ʾimrâ* "word (of Yahweh)" in the sense of "commandment" (Deut 33:9).

(b) From the perspective of one assuming a self-imposed obligation in the establishment of *bᵉrît*, one can also be said to "swear" (cf. Josh 9:15b with v 15a; 1 Sam 20:17 LXX [!] with 18:3; Ezra 10:5 with v 3; Psa 89:4; cf. also Hos 10:4; Ezek 16:8; 2 Chron 15:12, 14). But if the subj. of the *bᵉrît* obligates another, "one causes another to swear" (2 Kgs 11:4; cf. also Ezek 17:13). In cases of reciprocal *bᵉrît*, one can say that both swear (to one another) (cf. 1 Sam 20:42 with 23:18; Gen 21:31b with v 32a).

(c) The classification outlined in III/2–4 is also mirrored in the use of the preps. that express the manner in which the partner is bound by having *krt bᵉrît*. The prep. *lᵉ* "for" is used in the context of self-obligation; this obligation benefits the other. *ʾet-* and *ᶜim* "with" constitute exceptions here (*ʾet-:* Gen 15:18; Psa 105:8f. = 1 Chron 16:15f.; Zech 11:10; *ᶜim:* Hos 12:2; Job 40:28; Neh 9:8). The obligation of another is usually expressed by *ʾet-* (Jer 34:8; Ezek 17:13; Exod 34:27; Deut 5:3, etc.) or *ᶜim* (Hos 2:20; Exod 24:8, etc.; cf. in Aram. *KAI* no. 222A.1, etc.; Fitzmyer, *Sef.* 12f.), and only as an exception by *lᵉ* (Josh 24:25; 2 Kgs 11:4; Job 31:1). Reciprocal *bᵉrît* exists *bên . . . ûbên . . .* "between . . . and . . . " (1 Kgs 15:19). The same preps. can also appear, however, in later texts in the contexts of self-imposed obligation (Gen 9:12f., 15–17; 17:2, 7), of joint acceptance of the same obligation (2 Chron 23:16), or of the obligation of another party (Gen 17:10f.). If a third person establishes a *bᵉrît* involving two parties, *ᶜim* appears—appropriately—for the obligated individual, *lᵉ* "to the benefit of" for the one benefited by the other's obligation (Hos 2:20: therefore people and animals are not "covenant partners"!). In 2 Kgs 11:17a and, probably also v 17b, cases of the obligation of only one side, both parties are associated with *bên . . . ûbên. . . .*

A special case is the reference to the one involved in the *bᵉrît* in the acc. In this case, *bᵉrît* once again means self-obligation (Lev 26:42, "I remember my *bᵉrît* [promise] to Jacob [Isaac, Abraham]"; cf. Jer 33:21a, b) or "obligation, arrangement, regulation" (Jer 33:20a, "If you could break by *bᵉrît* [arrangement, regulation] concerning the day and my regulation concerning the night," namely that both occur at the proper time, v 22b; cf. v 25 and *ḥōq* "regulation" for stars in Psa 148:6). From this standpoint, the accs. in MT of Isa 59:21; Ezek 16:8, 60; 37:26 should also be considered correct (cf. GKC §118m, q; BrSynt §81e).

IV. 1. In application to the theological realm, *b^erît* contrasts God and human. The subj. of the *b^erît* here is, as a rule, Yahweh; it is "his" *b^erît*, he establishes the *b^erît* (even in 2 Kgs 11:17a; Jer 50:5; Ezra 10:3; 2 Chron 29:10, where the Israelites or Hezekiah enter into a *b^erît* concerning Yahweh, maintain Yahweh's supremacy). *b^erît* here indicates either Yahweh's self-obligation, his promise to do or give a particular thing (IV/2; cf. III/2), or the obligation that Yahweh places upon the individual (IV/3; cf. III/3), but not a reciprocal obligation (IV/4; cf. III/4).

2. The OT speaks of Yahweh's *b^erît* as his "self-obligation, promise" in various contexts. The content of the various *b^erît* varies in reference to the recipient and his/her particular situation.

(a) The OT names primarily the patriarchs as recipients of a *b^erît*. They (or their descendants) receive a *b^erît* in three ways: (1) Yahweh promises Abraham or his descendants the gift of the land of Canaan: already in J, Gen 15:18; then in Exod 6:4 (P); Psa 105:10 = 1 Chron 16:17. (2) Among the promises to the fathers, P also describes the "promise of increase" as *b^erît:* Gen 17:2 + 6, 3–5. (3) Finally, Yahweh's promise to be the God of the patriarchs or of Israel also appears as a *b^erît*, primarily in P and the Dtr sphere: Gen 17:7, (8b); (Lev 26:45). This *b^erît* is also probably intended in the following passages, which speak of Yahweh's remembrance—to Israel's benefit and well-being—of his *b^erît* (Exod 2:24; 6:5 P; Lev 26:42, 44; Jer 14:21; Psa 106:45; 111:5; cf. 2 Kgs 13:23) or of his keeping his *b^erît* and his faithfulness *(ḥesed)* (Deut 7:9, 12; 1 Kgs 8:23; Neh 1:5; 9:32; 2 Chron 6:14); cf. also the *b^erît* that Yahweh swore to Israel's fathers (Deut 4:31; 7:12; 8:18).

In all three cases *b^erît* is the most important form of assurance next to the oath (the land: Gen 24:7 J; 26:3 addition to J; 50:24 E; Deut 1:8, 35, etc.; increase: Gen 22:16f. E; Exod 32:13 Dtr; Deut 13:18; to be their God: Deut 29:12b) and the simple promise via the word (land: Gen 12:7; 13:14f., 17; 28:13 J, etc.; increase: Gen 12:2 J; 22:17 R^JE?; 26:4 addition to J; 26:24 J; 28:3; 48:4 P; Exod 32:13 Dtr; to be their God: Exod 29:45; cf. 25:8; Deut 29:12a; Ezek 34:24a; cf. v 24b; cf. Lev 11:45; 22:33; 25:38; 26:45; Num 15:41). A distinction in the appraisal of Abraham's sons is indicated in that Gen 17 promises blessing and offspring to Ishmael (v 20; cf. Gen 16:10 J), the slave's son, just as to Isaac (cf. 17:16), while Yahweh's *b^erît* (in reference, with some LXX MSS, to the promise to be his God, v 7) is reserved for Isaac alone (vv 19, 21).

(b) The *b^erît* Yahweh established with David includes the promise that David's throne will always exist and will always be possessed by a Davidide (2 Sam 23:5; Psa 89:4, 29, 35, 40; Isa 55:3; Jer 33:21; 2 Chron 13:5; 21:7; once more in addition to the oath, Psa 89:4; 132:11; and the word, 2 Sam 7:11b, 16, 25; 1 Kgs 8:20; Jer 33:17; 1 Chron 22:8; cf. v 10; cf. Psa 89:35).

(c) P also describes Yahweh's assurance to Noah not to punish the earth again with a flood as a *b^erît* (Gen 9:8–17; cf. the simple promise in J Gen 8:21 and the oath, Isa 54:9). As a sign of the *b^erît*, Yahweh's rainbow should be a reminder of this assurance (Gen 9:12–17).

(d) *bᵉrît* also appears as a divine assurance of the continuity of the priestly office for Levi (Mal 2:4f., 8; Jer 33:21b; cf. vv 18, 22) or for Phinehas (Num 25:12f.; cf. Neh 13:29).

(e) The question, which arose following the conquest of Jerusalem and the fall of the Judean state in 587 BCE, of whether, in view of the people's disobedience, Yahweh had rescinded his *bᵉrît*, his promise to the fathers, received a variety of responses. According to one interpretation, Yahweh maintained his *bᵉrît* even in the exilic situation (Lev 26:44, with the Israelites; Jer 33:21, *bᵉrît* with David and Levi), he remembered his *bᵉrît* (Lev 26:42 [patriarchal *bᵉrît*], 45 [exodus *bᵉrît*]). Nonetheless, the prophets announce that Yahweh will —once again—establish a *bᵉrît* with his people: the promise that in the future he will protect Israel from a disaster similar to the contemporary experience (Isa 54:9f.) as he did humanity after the flood, the announcement of a happy future (Isa 61:8), the eschatological era of salvation, in which both war and natural catastrophe will be eliminated (Exod 34:25; Hos 2:20, a secondary text). Above all, however, Yahweh takes responsibility to see that the God-people relationship is never again destroyed by Israel's disobedience. Thus it is his *bᵉrît* = "promise" that his spirit (probably of obedience) and the words (of the law), which he has placed in the mouth of the Israelites, will never again leave them (Isa 59:21). The *bᵉrît* that God will never again cease to do good by them (Jer 32:29f.) stands in the context of the announcement that Yahweh will give them one heart and one way to fear him always (cf. Jer 24:7; Ezek 11:19; 36:26f.; on Jer 31:31–34 see 3d). In relation to such promises of a salvific future (cf. *bᵉrît šālôm* in Isa 54:10; Ezek 34:25; 37:26), reference can also be made to an earlier *bᵉrît* (Ezek 16:60; cf. Isa 55:3).

3. (a) Thematically and explicitly paralleled with *tôrâ* "instruction," *ḥōq* "precept," etc. (see III/7a), *bᵉrît* indicates any act of the divine will in respect to people. The content of the obligation placed by God upon people is not usually further qualified; *bᵉrît* here often constitutes the totality of divine regulations, e.g., Isa 24:5; Hos 8:1; Psa 25:10, etc. Elsewhere the content may be derived from the context, as e.g., in Prov 2:17; cf. Exod 20:14; Deut 5:18 (Lev 20:10).

(b) In the Dtr realm the proclamation of Yahweh's *bᵉrît* = "regulations, obligations" (for Israel) is associated with two places: (1) Horeb and (2) the land of Moab (cf. the juxtaposition in Deut 28:69).

(1) The Horeb *bᵉrît* is associated with the communication of the divine will at Sinai according to JE. Here *bᵉrît* indicates the Decalogue, the "ten words," which are written on two tables (Deut 4:13; 5:2, 22 [vv 6–21 Decalogue!]; 9:9, 11, 15; 1 Kgs 8:21, also LXX v 9), deposited in the ark (1 Kgs 8:9, 21; cf. Deut 10:2; on "ark of Yahweh's *bᵉrît*" see II). In other passages only the the first commandment, namely to worship no gods other than Yahweh, is specifically called *bᵉrît* (Deut 17:2; 29:24f.; 31:16, 20; 1 Kgs 11:11; cf. v 10; 19:10, 14 [here *bᵉrît* in the Dtr sense is inserted secondarily]; 2 Kgs 17:15, 35, 38; Jer 11:3f., 10; 22:9; cf. also 2 Kgs 23:3a, b and 2 Chron 34:32 with 2 Kgs 23:4ff. and 2 Chron 34:33).

(2) The concept of a *bᵉrît* = "obligation" that Moses places upon Israel in the land of Moab is a Dtr "exclusive" (Deut 28:69; 29:8,[11], 13, 20). The content is, to be sure, the Dtn code (cf. also Deut 15:1, 12 with Jer 34:12–14), which as a "Moab *bᵉrît*" is dated back to the Mosaic era, as the so-called "Covenant Book," Exod 20:22–23:19 through Exod 24:3–8.

(c) In the exilic period the concept of a *bᵉrît* imposed on the patriarchs also appears for the first time; the requirement of circumcision according to P in Gen 17:9ff. (through v 10, distinguished markedly from the *bᵉrît* = "promise" in vv 2, 4, 7). Now the observance of the Sabbath is also described as a divine *bᵉrît* (Exod 31:16 P^s; Isa 56:4), and it, like the preparation of the showbread (Gen 17:13; Exod 31:16), is described as an "eternal *bᵉrît*" (Lev 24:8).

(d) In an express contrast to the *bᵉrît* = "obligation" associated with the exodus of the fathers from Egypt (see 3b[1]), which Israel violated, Jer 31:31–34 announces a *bᵉrît ḥᵃdāšâ*, a "new obligation," in which Yahweh will place his instruction in the Israelites' hearts in order to achieve compliance and to ensure the God-people relationship (see 2e).

(e) Nowhere is the act of law-giving, whether at Sinai/Horeb or in the land of Moab, described as *bᵉrît*, but only that which was communicated, established; there is therefore no *bᵉrît* in the sense of a "Sinai covenant." The presentation offered here places polarities such as "Sinai covenant-Davidic covenant" (cf. L. Rost, *TLZ* 72 [1947]: 129–34; M. Sekine, *VT* 9 [1959]: 47–57) and "Sinai covenant-Abrahamic covenant" (cf. W. Zimmerli, *TZ* 16 [1960]: 268–80) in a new light.

4. It is theologically significant that the OT does not know a reciprocal *bᵉrît* that pairs God and people—a *bᵉrît* in which both God and people accept mutually enforceable responsibilities (as e.g., the *bᵉrît* between Solomon and Hiram, 1 Kgs 5:26). The improperly termed "covenant formula" (more apt is: "identification formula") "Yahweh the God of Israel—Israel the people of Yahweh" (cf. R. Smend, *Die Bundesformel* [1963]) describes the relationship between Yahweh and Israel with the terms "God-people," indeed, in the sense of "Lord-servant." In this God-people relationship only God establishes obligations. God can make the execution of his *bᵉrît* = "promise" dependent upon the fulfillment of particular conditions (Deut 7:9; 1 Kgs 8:23), the God-people relationship dependent upon the maintenance of his *bᵉrît* "obligations" (Exod 19:5; cf. Psa 132:12). But the individual cannot obligate God to keep his promise by fulfilling these conditions; the promise is guaranteed only by the fact that God stands by his word. If one understands "partners" as equals in relationship, then it is conceivable from the standpoint of the term *bᵉrît* to speak of a "partnership" between human and God.

V. 1. Postbibl. Hebr. uses *bᵉrît* in the same way as the OT (of *bᵉrît* in early Judaism; see J. Behm, *TDNT* 2:126–29; A. Jaubert, *La notion d'alliance dans le judaïsme* [1963]).

(a) Sir uses *bᵉrît* in the sense of the obligation that one assumes: of people, 41:19 (par. *ʾlh*); 44:12 (cf. P. A. H. de Boer, FS Baumgartner 25–29), 20 (Abraham accepts the circumcision *bᵉrît*); of God in respect to Noah, 44:17f., in respect to the fathers, 44:22, in respect to Aaron, 45:15 (priesthood), and Phinehas, 45:24 (high priesthood), in respect to David, 45:25.

(b) At Qumran *bᵉrît* occurs: (1) in a nontheological usage: as a self-imposed obligation, 1QS 1:16 (cf. 2 Kgs 23:3a), then in the expression *yqym bbryt ʿl npšw*, "he should take it upon himself through a *bᵉrît*" (i.e., "to separate himself from all evildoers"), 1QS 5:10 (cf. 1QH 14:17 as well as CD 16:1, 4, 9). *bᵉrît* should be understood as the obligation of another in the usage *bʾy bryty*, "those who have entered into my (the supplicant's) *b^{e}rît*" = "those obligated to me" (1QH 5:23); cf. in the same sense "the men of their (the priests') *b^{e}rît*," 1QS 5:9; 6:19; 1QSa 1:2.

(2) In the theological realm *b^{e}rît* means God's self-obligation, promise, where God "remembers" his *b^{e}rît* (1Q34 3:2, 5; 6Q15 3:5; CD 1:4; 6:2; 4QDibHam 5:9), "keeps" his *b^{e}rît* (e.g., 1QM 18:7). The "promise" to the fathers (1QM 13:7; 14:8; CD 8:18 = 19:31), to David (4QDibHam 4:6), and to the priests (1QM 17:3) should also be mentioned here. The *b^{e}rît* "to act according to all that he (God) has commanded, and not to turn aside from him" (1QS 1:16f.) and "to separate oneself from all evildoers" (5:10, etc.) appears as an "obligation." It is meant when one enters into the *b^{e}rît* (*bô*ᵓ 1QS 2:12, 18, etc.; ᶜ*br* 1:18, 20, etc.). The *bryt ḥdšh* (CD 6:19; 8:21; 19:33), which, according to CD 20:12 has been placed in effect (*qym* pi.) "in the land of Damascus (= Qumran?)" and into which one enters there, is also understood as an "obligation."

(3) At Qumran *b^{e}rît* can also describe a group of people: as in 1QS 5:11, 18 "(the evildoers) will not be reckoned to his (God's) *b^{e}rît*" (cf. CD 19:35: "(the apostates) will not be reckoned to the assembly of the people"); as in 1QM 14:4, where "his *b^{e}rît*" parallels "people of his redemption" and in 17:7, where "Israel's *b^{e}rît*" parallels "lot/portion (= people) of God." *b^{e}rît* seems to be used in the same manner in Dan 11:22, 28, 30a, b (but not in 9:27 and 11:32). Both cases refer to believers, those who do the will of God.

2. The Aram. of the Tgs. renders *b^{e}rît* (with only 3 exceptions) with *q^{e}yām*, which no more means the "covenant," etc. than does *b^{e}rît*, rather the "arrangement" (cf. *qym* pi. as well as Aram. pa.).

That *q^{e}yām* includes the full range of the meaning of *b^{e}rît* is indicated by the fact that *q^{e}yām* can stand not only for *b^{e}rît* but for Hebr. *š^{e}bû*ᶜ*â* "oath, vow" (e.g., Num 30:3; Deut 7:8; Hab 3:9), *nēder* "vow" (e.g., Gen 28:20; 31:13), and *ḥōq* "regulation" (e.g., Exod 18:16, 20; Psa 99:7; cf. Bibl. Aram. *q^{e}yām* "ordinance," Dan 6:8, 16). The translation *g^{e}zērâ* "decision, law" (2 Kgs 17:15) or ᵓ*ōray^{e}tâ* "doctrine, law" (Lev 26:25; Ezek 16:61) for *b^{e}rît* confirms the notion that the Aram. linguistic awareness could hear the nuance of "law" in *b^{e}rît*.

On this point and on V/3–4, see E. Kutsch, "Von *b^{e}rīt* zu 'Bund,' " *KerD* 14 (1968): 159–82.

3. The shift into the Gk. language and its conceptual world was more problematic. The LXX offers the word *diathēkē* about 267x for *b^{e}rît* in all the possible meanings mentioned under III and IV, in 1 Kgs 11:11 *entolai* (on the other occurrences, cf. Kutsch, op. cit. 166n.27). Here *b^{e}rît* is understood not as "covenant, contract," etc., but properly as "arrangement, settlement"; at any rate, the translation *diathēkē* ("last will") does account for the aspect of "last will" inherent in this subst. (as does Aristophanes, *Aves* 440f.; cf. Kutsch, op. cit. 167n.30).

In accord with this use of *diathēkē*, the LXX also uses it to render *tôrâ* "instruction" (Dan 9:13 LXX), ᶜ*ēdût* "testimony" = Decalogue (Exod 27:21; 31:7; 39:35 (= LXX v 14), *kātûb* "that written (in the [law]book of Moses)" (2 Chron 25:4). The grandson of Jesus Sirach also has *diathēkē* 8x for *b^{e}rît* (Sir 41:19 [Rahlfs: v 20]; 44:12, 18, 20, 22 [23]; 45:15, 24f.), but also 9x for *ḥōq* and in 47:11 for *ḥuqqâ* "regulation."

In contrast to LXX, Aquila offers *synthēkē* "covenant, contract" for *b^{e}rît* in at least 26 instances, with (perhaps) 3 instances of *diathēkē*. Symmachus also prefers *synthēkē* (Exod 24:7); but Theodotion, who has only 4 texts with *synthēkē*, stands closer to the LXX, if *diathēkē* (11x) does not go back to his exemplar here.

4. The Old Lat. version of the OT follows (with only a few exceptions) the LXX reading, translating *testamentum* for *b^e^rît*, but distances itself in this even farther from the Hebr. concept. Jerome's new translation of the Hebr. OT (390–405 CE) renders *b^e^rît* 135x with *foedus* and 96x with *pactum* and thus follows explicitly the understanding of Aquila and Symmachus, but also perhaps of his Hebr. teachers. Occurrences of *testamentum* in the Psa are additional to the few passages with it in the Vg., since an older version of the Psalter was incorporated.

E. Kutsch

ברך *brk* pi. **to bless**

S 1288; BDB 138b; *HALOT* 1:159b; *TDOT* 2:279–308; *TWOT* 285; *NIDOTTE* 1385

I. 1. The root *brk* is attested in NWSem. and SSem. (extensive treatment of the inscriptional material in W. Schottroff, *Der altisraelitische Fluchspruch* [1969], 178–98; and G. Wehmeier, *Der Segen im AT* [1970], 8–66).

In Akk. it is represented by *karābu* "to pray, dedicate, bless, greet" (*ikribu* "prayer, consecration; blessing"). The concept of blessing in the limited sense does not, however, play a significant role among the Babylonians, and the element of greeting dominates the usage of *karābu* (cf. B. Landsberger, *MAOG* 4 [1928/29]: 294–321; *AHw* 369f., 445f.; *CAD* I/J:62–66). An etymological relationship between *brk* and *karābu* is unlikely (cf. Old SArab. *krb* "to consecrate, sacrifice").

The Arab. derivatives, esp. frequent in thanksgiving and greeting formulae, are all based on the ground form *baraka*, defined as a benevolent power proceeding from God, saints, and some animals, plants, or objects and guaranteeing wealth, well-being, health, and good fortune (cf. *DAFA* 1:567; pre-Islamic usage makes no connection with the activity of any gods; but the Koran attributes blessing expressly to God, probably under NWSem. influence; cf. J. Chelhod, *RHR* 148 [1955]: 81f., 87f.; A. Jeffery, *Foreign Vocabulary of the Qur'ān* [1938], 75; in popular belief the two concepts compete with one another).

The relationship of *brk* to Hebr. *berek* "knee," on the one hand (cf. Akk. *birku* "knee," as well as "durability, might" and "lap," euphemistically for the genitals, but also in the context of adoption rites; cf. Dhorme 108, 156f.; *AHw* 129a; M. Cohen, "Genou, famille, force dans le monde chamito-sémitique," FS Basset 203–10), and Hebr. *b^e^rēkâ* "pond," on the other (cf. A. Murtonen, *VT* 9 [1959]: 164), is difficult to determine.

2. The verbal stems qal, pi., pu., hitp., and ni. are attested; *b^e^rākâ* functions as a subst.

Most Sem. languages exhibit only the pass. ptcp. for the qal (Ug.: *KTU* 1.19.IV.32; in Aram. this form occurs almost exclusively; cf. *DISO* 44); Pun., however, also had finite qal forms, in addition to the pi. (*KAI* no. 175.4f.; J. Friedrich, *ZDMG* 107 [1957]: 282–90); pe. forms in late Aram. dialects may, conversely, have been formed secondarily in analogy to the pe. pass. ptcp. (*MG* 215n.2).

Various Arab. forms correspond to the Hebr. pi.: *barraka* (subj. people, not in the Koran) "to pronounce a blessing" (cf. Lane 1:193) and *bāraka* (subj. God) "to impart life-sustaining power"; the 5th stem substantially approximates the ni. in meaning ("to receive blessing"; see III/3), the 10th stem the hitp. ("to request blessing"; see III/2f).

The noun is attested extrabibl. in NWSem. only rarely and in late texts (cf. *DISO* 44).

PNs composed with forms of *brk*, the thanksgiving name *berekyâ(hû)* and *barakʾēl*, the wish name *yᵉberekyāhû*, and the short form *bārûk* (*IP* 183, 195f.), have counterparts esp. in Pun. (Harris 91) and in the later Aram. dialects (A. Caquot, *Syria* 39 [1962]: 246). *bᵉrākâ* in 1 Chron 12:3 should probably be emended to *berekyâ* (Rudolph, HAT 21, 104; contra *HAL* 154b).

II. The verb *brk* and the subst. *bᵉrākâ* occur 398x in the Hebr. OT:

	qal	ni.	pi.	pu.	hitp.	*bᵉrākâ*	total
Gen	8	3	59	–	2	16	88
Exod	1	–	5	–	–	1	7
Lev	–	–	2	–	–	1	3
Num	2	–	14	1	–	–	17
Deut	9	–	28	1	1	12	51
Josh	–	–	8	–	–	2	10
Judg	1	–	3	2	–	1	7
1 Sam	7	–	4	–	–	2	13
2 Sam	3	–	10	1	–	1	15
1 Kgs	6	–	6	–	–	–	12
2 Kgs	–	–	3	–	–	2	5
Isa	2	–	4	–	2	4	12
Jer	2	–	1	–	1	–	4
Ezek	1	–	–	–	–	3	4
Joel	–	–	–	–	–	1	1
Hag	–	–	1	–	–	–	1
Zech	1	–	–	–	–	1	2
Mal	–	–	–	–	–	2	2
Psa	17	–	52	4	1	9	83
Job	–	–	7	1	–	1	9
Prov	1	–	3	2	–	8	14
Ruth	4	–	1	–	–	–	5
Ezra	1	–	–	–	–	–	1
Neh	–	–	4	–	–	2	6
1 Chron	2	–	13	1	–	–	16
2 Chron	3	–	5	–	–	2	10
OT	71	3	233	13	7	71	398

The topographical designation *ʿēmeq bᵉrākâ* (2x in 2 Chron 20:26) is counted among the occurrences of the noun, but the PN *bᵉrākâ* in 1 Chron 12:3 (see I/2) is not. The inf. abs. *bārôk* (Josh 24:10, otherwise *bārēk*) belongs to the pi., not to the qal.

brk occurs in Bibl. Aram. only in Dan (1x pe. pass. ptcp., 3x pa.).

The root occurs with remarkable frequency in the patriarchal narratives of Gen (82x) and in Deut, while it disappears entirely in the legal portions of the Pentateuch (occurrences in Num are limited to the Balaam pericope, 14x, and the Aaronite blessing, 3x). More than half of the occurrences in the Psa concern the praise of God. In the narrative books a relatively high number of forms are used in the context of greetings and good wishes. The noun occurs relatively often in texts influenced by wisdom. In the prophetic literature the root plays a nonessential role (26x).

III. One usually assumes a basic meaning (with reference primarily to the Arab. *baraka*) "benevolent power, health-creating power." *bārûk* (see III/1) would accordingly be "one who is gifted with health-creating power," the pi. (see III/2) would mean "to gift someone with health-creating power or to declare someone so gifted," the ni. (see III/3) "to experience health-creating power," and *b*ᵉ*rākâ* would be the "health-creating power" as such (see III/4).

Cf. Th. Plassmann, *Signification of B*ᵉ*rākā* (1913); S. Mowinckel, *Psalmenstudien* 5 (1924); id., *Psalms in Israel's Worship* (1962), 2:44–48; J. Hempel, "Die israelitischen Anschauungen von Segen und Fluch im Lichte altorientalischer Parallelen," *ZDMG* 79 (1925): 20–110 = *Apoxysmata* (1961), 30–113; *ILC* 1–2:182–212; F. Horst, "Segen und Segenshandlungen in der Bibel," *EvT* 7 (1947/48): 23–37 = *Gottes Recht* (1961), 188–202; id., *RGG* 5:1649–51; J. Scharbert, *Bib* 39 (1958): 17–26; id., *Solidarität in Segen und Fluch im AT und in seiner Umwelt* (1958); A. Murtonen, "Use and Meaning of the Words lebårek and bᵉråkåʰ," *VT* 9 (1959): 158–77; C. Westermann, *Blessing in the Bible and the Life of the Church* (1978); G. Wehmeier, *Der Segen im AT* (1970).

This interpretation is probably basically correct; still it must be emphasized that health-creating power is often associated to a prominent degree with the effective *word*, particularly when people bless others (cf. Horst, op. cit.). Besides, one can ask to what degree the concept of health-creating *power* (alongside divine action) was actually still current (cf. the most probable instance, Isa 65:8).

1. (a) The qal pass. ptcp. *bārûk* indicates the state of possessing the *b*ᵉ*rākâ* (not the result of a preceding act of blessing; this status is expressed by the pu.; see III/2e; cf. *HP* 216f.). As a rule *bārûk* is used as a predicate in a nom. sentence; indicative forms of *hyh* "to demonstrate oneself" are added only twice (Gen 27:33; Deut 7:14; both cases express the nuance "to prove oneself to be truly *bārûk*").

In 63 (of 71) cases, *bārûk* is used in a pronouncedly formulaic manner, indeed, as a rule, emphatically at the beginning of an utterance (58x; also *y*ᵉ*hî* "may he be . . . *bārûk*": 1 Kgs 10:9 = 2 Chron 9:8; Prov 5:18; Ruth 2:19; negated in Jer 20:14). Of these 63 cases, 38 refer to God (also the Aram. *b*ᵉ*rîk* in Dan 3:28) and 25 to people (and things pertaining to them: Deut 28:4, offspring, v 5 basket; 1 Sam 25:33, cleverness; Jer 20:14, day of birth).

On the formal structure of the Israelite blessing and its form-critical development, cf. W. Schottroff, *Die altisraelitische Fluchspruch* (1969), 163–77.

The remaining 8 cases refer to people: 3x in the cs. phrase "blessed of Yahweh" (Gen 24:31; 26:29; pl. Isa 65:23) and 5x in a simple declaration that someone is "blessed" (Gen 27:29 and Num 24:9, "whoever blesses you will be blessed"; Gen 27:33, "he shall remain blessed"; Num 22:12, "you may not curse the people, for they are blessed"; 1 Kgs 2:45, a blessing formula with a prefixed subj., Solomon).

A regular antonym for *bārûk* is *ʾārûr* (→ *ʾrr;* Gen 9:25f.; 27:29; Num 24:9; Deut 28:3–6 par. vv 16–19; Jer 17:7 par. v 5; 20:14).

(b) In reference to people, *bārûk* has largely the same meaning as *ʾašrê* "happy" (→ *ʾšr;* cf. Jer 17:7 with Psa 40:5) and was apparently replaced in later times by this word. *bārûk* (in this sense the LXX generally rendered it by *eulogēmenos*) is, first, an exclamation of thankfulness and admiration, and, at the same time, a felicitation (Gen 14:19; 1 Sam 23:21; 25:33; 26:25; 2 Sam 2:5; Ruth 2:19f.; 3:10; cf. Prov 5:18, "may your fountain [= wife] be *bārûk,*" i.e., a source of joy). The one designated as *bārûk* is the originator of a healthful situation and therefore the object of praise and thanks. The one praised is preferably associated with God: *bārûk ʾattâ lᵉyhwh* "you are, thanks to Yahweh, a doer of good," i.e., equipped by Yahweh with benevolent power (1 Sam 15:13; fem.: Ruth 3:10; pl.: 1 Sam 23:21; 2 Sam 2:5; Psa 115:15; 3d per.: Gen 14:19; Judg 17:2; Ruth 2:20; cf. also the cs. phrase "blessed of Yahweh," see 1a, further Num 22:12; Psa 118:26). In Judg 17:2, the exclamation *bārûk bᵉnî lᵉyhwh* is the mother's protective measure against a curse threatening the son.

The *lᵉ* in the expression *lᵉyhwh* is often interpreted as a *lamed* auctoris and *bārûk* is understood passively as a wish ("may *X* be blessed by Yahweh"). In Aram. burial and memorial inscriptions, however, *bryk l* and *bryk qdm* ("blessed is/may be *X* to") alternate without significant difference in meaning (cf. *RES* 1788 with *KAI* nos. 267, 269; *RES* 608, 960–62, 1366 with *RES* 1364, 1368, 1370, 1376, etc.; cf. also the expression *brk l* "to bless someone to a deity" = "to recommend someone to a particular deity with the request that the deity bless the individual," Phoen. *KAI* no. 50.2; Eg. Aram. *RHR* 130:17:2f.; Hermop. nos. 1–6, with the addition in each case of "that she [the deity] may let me see your face again"; perhaps also in Ug. *KTU* 1.17.I.23; cf. *UT* no. 517; C. H. Gordon, *Ugaritic Literature* [1949], 86; also Hebr. *brk* pi. *lipnê yhwh,* Gen 27:7). This construction may correspond to the OT usage, so that the *lᵉ* should also be understood here in the sense of a *lamed* relationis: "complete blessing with Yahweh" (cf. J. Scharbert, *Bib* 39 [1958]: 21f.: "may *X* be one for Yahweh to bless"). The fact that syntactically analogous curse formulae are formed with *lipnê* supports this interpretation (Josh 6:26; 1 Sam 26:19 pl.; cf. Num 5:16; 1 Kgs 8:13).

Also in relation to people, the formula that begins with *bārûk* in Deut 7:14 and 28:3–6 (v 5 in reference to fruit basket and kneading trough) describes the Israelites and their activity as crowned with success, although only to the degree that they adhere to the instructions of Yahweh. The sixfold repetition of the word in Deut 28:3–6 (cf. the corresponding sixfold *ʾārûr* "cursed" in Deut 28:16–19 and the twelvefold *ʾārûr* in Deut 27:15–26) clearly indicates the character of the effectual, energizing word (cf. the triple repetition of *bārûk* in 1 Sam 25:32f. and the double in Gen 14:19f.; cf. also 1 Kgs 10:8f. = 2 Chron 9:7f. with *bārûk* alongside a double *ʾašrê*). These presumably cultic series concern the creation of a virtual well-being zone (or, for *ʾārûr,* an illness zone), formed in accordance with the behavior of the Israelites. The *bārûk* formula in Jer 17:7 (alongside *ʾārûr*), which resembles wisdom diction (cf. Psa 40:5), also belongs in this context.

(c) In reference to God, *bārûk* (in this sense the LXX generally rendered it with *eulogētos;* Exod 18:9f.; 1 Kgs 5:21; Zech 11:5; cf. J. Hempel, *ZDMG* 79 [1925]: 88f.) is an even more joyous exclamation of thanksgiving and admiration. The basis of joy is as a rule specifically cited, introduced with *ʾᵃšer* (Gen 14:20; 24:27; Exod 18:10; 1 Sam 25:32, 39; 2 Sam 18:28; 1 Kgs 1:48; 5:21;

8:15 = 2 Chron 6:4; 1 Kgs 8:56; 10:9 = 2 Chron 9:8; Psa 66:20; Ruth 4:14; Ezra 7:27; 2 Chron 2:11), *še-* (Psa 124:6), *kî* (Psa 28:6; 31:22), a ptcp. (Psa 72:18; 144:1), or an asyndetic clause (Zech 11:5). One occasionally addresses God directly: "you are *bārûk*" (Psa 119:12; 1 Chron 29:10).

God is *bārûk* because he gives all sorts of beneficial things: a king (1 Kgs 1:48), indeed, a wise king (1 Kgs 5:21; 10:9 = 2 Chron 9:8), rest (1 Kgs 8:56), might (Psa 68:36), good thoughts (Ezra 7:27); because he keeps faith (Gen 24:27; Psa 31:22; 66:20; Ruth 4:14), grants victory (Gen 14:20; 2 Sam 18:28), sends an enraged man a wise woman (1 Sam 25:32), then sees to justice himself (1 Sam 25:39), teaches the art of war (Psa 144:1), hears prayers (Psa 28:6; 66:20), does wonders (Psa 72:18), fulfills promises (1 Kgs 8:15), and, finally, even apparently gives a scoundrel opportunity to become rich (Zech 11:5). All this may be summarized to a degree in the lapidary formula *bārûk šēm kᵉbôdô* (Psa 72:19).

Such an exclamation is not linked solely to a particular cultic situation: it forces itself to the lips whenever the individual suddenly finds himself/herself before a demonstration of the benevolent might of God. One can say, therefore, that one "blesses God (in prayer)" (Gen 24:27; Psa 135:19–21; 1 Chron 29:9f.), or also—typically—that one "blesses people" (Gen 14:19f.; 1 Kgs 1:47f.; 8:14f., 55f.). All cases concern a declaration of God as *bārûk* on the basis of a concrete demonstration of his might. One of the analogous usages of *bārûk* mentioned in 1b above is excluded from usage in reference to God: one cannot call him *bārûk* sub conditione.

2. (a) In the pi. *brk* has various shades of meaning, primarily factitive and declarative-estimative, according to whether God (see 2d) or people (with people as obj., see 2b; with God as obj., see 2c) are subjects; the pu. (see 2e) and the hitp. (see 2f) offer the corresponding pass. and reflexive meanings.

Of the 233 occurrences, 97 concern God's blessing activity (incl. Gen 48:16: angel; Gen 32:27, 30: man; Gen 49:25; txt em *ʾēl šadday*), 136 concern human activity (incl. Psa 103:20–22: heavenly beings, creation). God is the grammatical subj. of finite verbs in 87 cases (in addition to 4x impv., 4x inf. abs., 2x inf. cs.), people are the subj. 85x (incl. Job 31:20: loins of the poor; in addition to 26x impv., 5x inf. abs., 15x inf. cs., 5x ptcp.).

The 6 cases that use *brk* pi. euphemistically for "to curse" (1 Kgs 21:10, 13; Job 1:5, 11; 2:5, 9) may be mentioned first. Regarding the fact that the OT never has God as the obj. of a verb for "to curse," except in prohibitions (cf. the commandment Exod 22:27; Lev 24:15; further Isa 8:21; 1 Sam 3:13 txt?), cf. J. Hempel, *ZDMG* 79 (1925): 91; as well as Schottroff, op. cit. 165.

Outside the OT and the texts under its influence, NWSem. uses the finite verb *brk* almost exclusively with particular deities as the subj. The notion that a person may bless (= pronounce a blessing formula) may, however, be attested in Ug. by *KTU* 1.19.IV.32 (Pǵt asks her father or the gods for the blessing). The meaning "to praise (God)" is entirely absent. Ug. parallels *brk* with *mrr* "to strengthen" (*KTU* 1.15.II.14f., 19f.; 1.19.IV.32f., I.23f., 34f.), clearly demonstrating that the primary meaning is "to equip with life-force." In Pun. *ḥnn* "to demonstrate grace" parallels *brk* once (*CIS* 1:5891.2f.); in *CIS* 1:196.5 this verb replaces the *brk* common in the closing wishes of dedicatory inscriptions.

The content of blessing is usually not distinctly cited; it is already contained in the verb itself. Exceptions use either a double acc. (Gen 49:25;

Deut 12:7; 15:14; Isa 19:25; cf. *KAI* no. 26A.III.2f.) or introduce the content with *b*[e] (Psa 29:11; cf. *KAI* no. 26C.III.16f.; *ANET* 654a); in all other cases this prep. indicates the realm in which the blessing is bestowed (Gen 24:1; Deut 2:7; 14:29; 15:4, 10, 18; 16:15; 23:21; 24:19; 28:8; 30:16; contra J. Scharbert, *Bib* 39 [1958]: 21n.5).

(b) In everyday Israelite speech, *brk* pi. (subj.: people, obj.: people) means, first, quite simply "to greet" (Gen 47:7; 1 Sam 13:10; 25:14; 2 Sam 6:20; 2 Kgs 4:29; 10:15; Prov 27:14; 1 Chron 16:43), "to bid farewell" (Gen 24:60; 28:1; 32:1; 47:10; Josh 22:6f.; 2 Sam 13:25; 19:40; cf. Ug. *KTU* 1.15.III.17), or "to congratulate" (Exod 39:43; 2 Sam 8:10 = 1 Chron 18:10; 1 Kgs 1:47; Neh 11:2; oneself: Psa 49:19), "to wish well" (Josh 14:13), "to thank" (Deut 24:13; 2 Sam 14:22; Job 31:20), or "to honor thankfully" (Prov 30:11). The use of the verbs often seems to have lost much of its vigor; indeed, the most correct usage would be the locution "to pronounce someone *bārûk*" (cf. Arab. *barraka*, further Arab. *kabbara* "to declare Allah *akbar*," *sallama* "to declare someone *salām*"; cf. D. R. Hillers, "Delocutive Verbs in Biblical Hebrew," *JBL* 86 [1967]: 320–24), i.e., originally, to describe one as benevolently active and as possessor of health-creating power. Indeed, one said "*bārûk ʾattâ*" or "*bārûk yhwh*" (cf. 1 Kgs 1:47f.) or also *y*[e]*bārek*[e]*kā yhwh* "Yahweh bless you!" (Jer 31:23) or *yhwh ʿimm*[e]*kā* "May Yahweh be with you!" (Ruth 2:4). Mention is occasionally made of embracing the departing (*nšq* Gen 32:1; 2 Sam 19:40), bowing before superiors (2 Sam 14:22), and perhaps also on parting prior to marriage, offering a lengthy blessing (Gen 24:60).

Such declarations of *bārûk*, "greeting," "bidding farewell," and "congratulating" were also made, naturally, in the realm of cultic encounters or in encounters with "holy" persons. To be mentioned here are e.g., Melchizedek's "greeting" to Abraham (Gen 14:19, with an extended *bārûk* formula), or the "farewell" of the priest Eli to Elkanah (1 Sam 2:20, with a wish formula). At the beginning of cultic assemblies one "greeted" the participants (Josh 8:33; 1 Kgs 8:14f.; in the course of a procession, Psa 118:26), at the end one "dismissed" them with blessing formulae (Lev 9:22; 2 Sam 6:18; 1 Kgs 8:55; Psa 129:8). Examples of the formulae are *bārûk yhwh* (1 Kgs 8:15, 56), *b*[e]*rûkîm ʾattem* (Psa 115:15), *birkat-yhwh ʿ*[a]*lêkem* (Psa 129:8), or *y*[e]*bārek*[e]*kā yhwh* (Num 6:24, with the extended, tripartite formula of the priestly blessing with the doubled appeal to the "face of Yahweh," i.e., his wellness-creating presence). In these cultic contexts the actual wellness-creating character of the *bārûk* pronouncement was probably more vivid than usual.

The one who pronounces the formula "places himself/herself" before the congregation (1 Kgs 8:55; Josh 8:33), "spreads his/her arms over them" (Lev 9:22), and "speaks with a loud voice" (1 Kgs 8:55). Then "one places the name of Yahweh on the people" (Num 6:27). Perhaps the only passage in which a prophet "blesses" a cultic meal (1 Sam 9:13) should be mentioned in this context. Samuel presumably "blesses" not the meat but the participants in the sacrificial meal; cf. J. Scharbert, *Bib* 39 (1958): 24; contra J. Hempel, *ZDMG* 79 (1925): 35; F. Horst, *EvT* 7 (1947/48): 25; A. Murtonen, *VT* 9 (1959): 163.

In the course of the cultic assembly, absentees could also be included in the "congratulation" (Exod 12:32; cf. *pll* hitp. *b*ᵉᶜ*ad* "to make intercession for" par. to *brk* pi. in Psa 72:15).

The Balaam pericope deals with a cultic congratulation of a special kind (Num 22–24). Instead of "cursing" (*ʾrr,* Num 22:6; 24:9; *qbb,* 23:11, 25; 24:10; *z*ᶜ*m,* 23:7f.), the man with access to extraordinary powers must declare Israel *bārûk,* because—as God observes at the very outset—it is already irrevocably *bārûk* (22:12).

Of supreme importance for people in the ancient Near East is one's final "farewell" before death (Gen 27; 48; 49; Deut 33). In the case of such a "farewell" and "well-wishing," *brk* pi. seems to acquire an expressly factitive sense (cf. *HP* 216f.): through the pronouncement of *bārûk* one makes the addressees *bārûk;* this result is at least the original intention of the custom. This intention is the reason for the measures designed to amplify the "power" to be transferred (the meal of Isaac), for the emphasis upon the exact identification of the recipient (Gen 27:24; 48:8f.; cf. the careful naming of the sons and tribes in Gen 49 and Deut 33), for the embrace (Gen 27:26f.), and for the laying on of hands (Gen 48:14). The well-considered choice of the formulae pronounced indicates, however, that these formulae did not simply involve a transferral of power; these formulae refer primarily to fertility, well-being, and victory over the enemies.

(c) 40x (27x in Psa) people (or God's creation, Psa 103:20–22) "bless" God, i.e., declare him *bārûk* (in addition to the Aram. Dan 2:19; 4:31, see also the euphemistic usage of *brk* pi. [see 2a], and Isa 66:3 "to worship an idol"). Par. expressions indicate that the usage deals primarily with a laudatory "thanksgiving": *hll* pi. "to praise" (Psa 145:2; cf. 135:1, 19f.), to proclaim praise (*t*ᵉ*hillâ;* 66:8; 145:21; cf. 34:2), *ydh* hi. "to praise" (100:4; 145:10), to exclaim the name of Yahweh (63:5), *šîr* "to sing" and *bśr* pi. "to proclaim" (96:2), to exalt Yahweh (145:1), to remember his benevolent deeds (103:2).

Since this meaning is to be expected for the declarative pi. ("to designate God as *bārûk*"; cf. Gen 24:27, *bārûk yhwh* with the summary in v 48 "and I blessed Yahweh"), the assumption that this usage of the word described first a process intended to intensify God's power (so e.g., S. Mowinckel, *Psalmenstudien* [1924], 5:27–30; S. H. Blank, *HUCA* 32 [1962]: 85–90) becomes unnecessary, esp. since this usage may not be demonstrated otherwise in Sem. and it apparently rests upon an inner-Hebr. semantic development. Derivatively, *brk* pi. can also accompany other objs. (Psa 10:3 "he praises success," txt em; 49:19 "he praises himself"; Isa 66:3 "he worships an idol").

For such a "blessing" one prostrates oneself before Yahweh (Gen 24:48; Neh 8:6; 1 Chron 29:20), or one stands up (Neh 9:5), positions oneself in the temple (Psa 34:2, anytime; 134:1, at night), in the midst of the assembly (Psa 26:12; 68:27), in unison with the whole creation (Psa 145:10; 103:20–22), while one cries "*bārûk yhwh*" (Gen 24:27; Psa 135:18–21; 1 Chron 29:9f.). Grounds for this laudatory thanksgiving are personal experiences (Gen 24:48), the experience of victory over the enemies (Josh 22:33; Judg 5:2, 9), or—in the Psa—anything at all, for which Israel has God to thank.

(d) In 80 of 97 cases with *brk* pi. and a divine subject, the discussion concerns the fact that God "blesses" or "may bless" people (Gen 25x, Deut

19x, Psa 14x), in 17 cases the blessing of God extends to animals (Gen 1:22; cf. Deut 7:13) and things (Sabbath: Gen 2:3; Exod 20:11; house and field, work and harvest, etc.: Gen 27:27; 39:5; Exod 23:25; Deut 7:13b; 28:12; 33:11; Jer 31:23; Hag 2:19; Psa 28:9; 65:11; 132:15bis; Job 1:10; Prov 3:33): God makes people and things *bārûk*, he furnishes them with the power of fertility and growth, he grants life, happiness, and success.

brk pi. in these texts is often paralleled by a whole series of verbs such as "to make fruitful, to multiply" (Gen 17:20, etc.), "to love, to multiply" (Deut 7:13), "to grant life, to multiply" (Deut 30:16), "to protect, to cause the face to shine, to lift the countenance, to grant *šālôm* (→ *šlm*)" (Num 6:23–27), but esp. → *ntn* "to give" (children and riches, Gen 17:16; 24:34; 28:3f.; 48:3f.; Psa 29:11); also e.g., "to pour out grace" (Psa 45:3), "to help" (Gen 49:25), "to establish the gates" (Psa 147:13), "to be with you" (Gen 26:3, 24), etc. The expression "to grant *šālôm*" summarizes the blessing activity of God (Psa 29:11; cf. Hempel, op. cit. 51ff., but also Westermann, *Blessing* 22).

It is clear that such activity of God often appears as a wish formulated by people, i.e., as a felicitation and benediction, e.g., for Isaac (Gen 28:3), Jacob (Gen 48:16; 49:25), Moses (Deut 1:11; cf. 33:11), or anyone at all in daily life, on greeting (Ruth 2:4), and, finally, also in the cult (Psa 29:11; 67:2, 7f.; 115:12f.; 128:5; 134:3; Num 6:24), occasionally in the form of a prayer addressed directly to God (Psa 5:13; 28:9; 109:28; Deut 26:15; 33:11). This phenomenon indicates a close association between God's "blessing" and human speech: God's activity can be actualized through human speech, it can be ignited by it.

Many texts demonstrate therefore that God's health-creating act can be in response to human deed and speech: the hearing of prayer (Gen 17:20; cf. 32:27, 30) or the fulfillment of the blessing pronounced by the priests (Num 6:27). In addition, God "blesses" those who "bless" his elect (Gen 12:3), and he "blesses" other people for the sake of the chosen (Gen 26:24; 30:27; cf. 39:5), i.e., he creates well-being and success for them. God is certainly the author of beneficial activity; yet the person must also affirm this activity (cf. Psa 109:17).

Deut (cf. already Gen 22:17) esp. emphasizes the close relationship between human action and divine blessing: if Israel fully subjects itself to Yahweh's instructions, he will "bless (it) in all its undertakings," i.e., cause everything to succeed for it, in the city, in the field, at the beginning of work, at its end, etc. (e.g., Deut 7:13; 14:29; 15:10, 18; 23:21; 24:19; 30:16; cf. 27:1–14). Conversely, Yahweh's blessing is a motivation for the joyous fulfillment of his instructions (12:7; 15:4, 6, 14; 16:10, 15, etc.).

In this sense the psalmist confesses: "You bless the righteous" (Psa 5:13), just as Job is richly rewarded for his faithfulness (Job 42:12).

Despite the close interaction between human and divine word and deed, both the old patriarchal tradition (Gen 12:1–3) and the later P (Gen 1:28; 5:2; 9:1; 17:16) teach that in the final analysis all "blessing," i.e., all benevolent power, the source of fertility, victory, and well-being, is based on God's free decision, grounded only in himself, and on his word, which actualizes this decision (cf. H. Junker, *BETL* 12 [1959]: 548–58; C. Westermann, *BHH* 3:1757f.). Perhaps one should add 2 Sam 6:12, where Yahweh "blesses

(Obed-Edom) for the sake of the ark," i.e., bestows well-being (according to 1 Chron 26:4f.: eight sons) on account of his own presence.

(e) The pu. is the pass. conjugation corresponding to the pi. In reference to people (Num 22:6; Psa 37:22; 112:2; 128:4; Prov 20:21; 22:9) or things (Deut 33:13, land; 2 Sam 7:29b = 1 Chron 17:27b, the Davidic dynasty), it means "someone (something) has been blessed." Num 22:6 ("he, whom you bless, is blessed," par. *yûʾār* "he receives a curse") and 1 Chron 17:27 ("for you, Yahweh, have blessed it"; cf. 2 Sam 7:29 "through your blessing") speak, then, expressly of a prior act of blessing. God's authorship of the blessing is otherwise either directly stated (Deut 33:13; Psa 37:22) or implied by the context (Psa 112:2; 128:4; Prov 20:21; 22:9).

The pu. ptcp. appears in Psa 113:2; Job 1:21; Aram. Dan 2:20 in the function that the pi. pl. impv. has otherwise (cf. Psa 113:1 *halᵉlû*): people are summoned to praise God. All three cases employ the juss.: "May the name of Yahweh (God) be praised." The same usage, in reference to a king, should apparently be assumed for Psa 72:17 (txt em according to LXX).

Par. to the call to the cultic curse against Meroz (Judg 5:23; cf. 21:5), Judg 5:24(bis) probably deals with a call to carry out a blessing ritual for Jael.

(f) The hitp. (reflexive pi. with *t*-prefix) means quite generally "to make or call oneself *bārûk*." Deut 29:18 is rather unequivocal in this regard: as a countermeasure against a threatening curse one calls oneself *bārûk* "protected" (cf. Num 22:12; 23:8) by declaring: "I have *šālôm*" (i.e., nothing can happen to me). The formula *brk* hitp. *bᵉ* "to make oneself happy through (mention of another, particularly blessed person, or God in a blessing)" is a favorite appeal to this other person as a model (Gen 22:18; 26:4; Jer 4:2 refers to Israel; cf. Rudolph, HAT 12, 31; Psa 72:17) or source (Isa 65:16[bis], God) of benevolent power (cf. Gen 48:20; Prov 10:7). The translation of A. Murtonen (*VT* 9 [1959]: 172), "to consider oneself fortunate on account of," is much too weak.

3. The ni. occurs only 3x in the partriarchal narratives (Gen 12:3b; 18:18; 28:14). It is often understood as a pass. (e.g., Zorell 130a; cf. von Rad, *Gen*, OTL [1972²], 160) or in the sense of the hitp. ("to wish for blessing for oneself," e.g., *HAL* 153; H. Gunkel, *Gen* [1910³], 165). Yet the usage of this conjugation—in contrast to the pu. and hitp.—probably emphasizes its specific meaning. It indicates an action completed on the subj., without viewing the subj. itself (hitp.) or another person (pu.) as the author of the action (cf. H. Junker, *BETL* 12/13 [1959], 553). *brk* ni. means, then, "to experience blessing, participate in blessing," etc. (cf. J. Schreiner, *BZ* 6 [1962]: 7; O. Procksch, *Gen* [1924³], 96f.).

Gen 12:3b means, then, "by you shall all the families of the earth gain blessing." This is the only meaning possible for Gen 18:18; God's monologue inserted by the Yahwist in the narrative (18:17f.) is meant to explain God's desire to include Abraham in his secrets; he does so because Abraham plays a significant role in his plan of salvation: "through him shall all families of the earth gain blessing." Gen 28:14 renews the same promise for Jacob and his descendants.

4. (a) Like *brk* pi., the subst. *b^erākâ* occurs in a multitude of meanings. The OT seems to use *b^erākâ* only in some relationship to God's action, not simply to indicate the power of growth and increase (corresponding to Arab. *baraka;* see 1a), except perhaps in Isa 65:8.

God's intention not to destroy his whole people is manifest here in an idiom from the language of the vinedresser; the proverb is best understood from the standpoint of the second pruning of the vine (Dalman, *AuS* 4:312f., 330f.) in which infertile vines are removed; the vines that promise to bear fruit should be left uncut: "As is said, when one finds sap in the vine: Do not ruin it, there is life in it."

(b) In approximately 25 cases *b^erākâ* indicates the effective *bārûk*-declaration directed by people to people (Gen 27:12–41, 6x; Deut 11:26f., 29; 23:6 = Neh 13:2; Deut 28:2; 30:1, 19; 33:1; Josh 8:34; Ezek 44:30; Mal 2:2; Job 29:13; Prov 10:6f.; 11:11, 26; 24:25; perhaps also Gen 49:28), i.e., the benevolent word of blessing (cf. the programmatic phrase in Prov 11:11 "through the *bārûk* saying of the righteous the city will be exalted.")

In Gen 27:12 the pair of terms *b^erākâ* and *q^elālâ* indicate both the blessing or curse saying and the resulting success or failure: "Then I brought on myself curse (pronouncement and power) and not blessing (pronouncement and power)." The same double meaning may also be present in the other usages of *b^erākâ* in the context of Gen 27 (vv 35–38, 41). The marked objective character of blessing here (v 35, "your brother has taken your blessing"; cf. v 36a; v 36b, "have you not reserved a blessing for me?") may be largely attributed to the adoption of a pre-Israelite exemplar of the narrative (cf. E. A. Speiser, *JBL* 74 [1955]: 252–56).

2 Kgs 18:31 = Isa 36:16, "make *b^erākâ* with me = let us exchange blessings"—an invitation to an official peace treaty—presumably also belongs here (cf. A. Murtonen, *VT* 9 [1959]: 173f.; according to J. Scharbert, *Bib* 39 [1958]: 19, *b^erākâ* should be understood here as "allegiance"; cf. 2 Sam 14:22; 1 Kgs 1:47).

(c) In 6 or 7 passages *b^erākâ* indicates a gift. At issue here is a *bārûk*-declaration in the form of a gift; derivatives of the root *brk* are often closely associated with the idea of giving.

Caleb bequeaths his daughter a *b^erākâ* (Josh 15:19 = Judg 1:15), Jacob brings Esau a *b^erākâ* (Gen 33:11), just as Abigail brings David (1 Sam 25:27), David, the elders of Judah (1 Sam 30:26), and Naaman, Elisha (2 Kgs 5:15). In Prov 11:25 *nepeš b^erākâ* is presumably a person who gives gifts. 1 Kgs 10:8–10 explicitly links *bārûk*- declarations to gift giving.

(d) In Neh 9:5 and 2 Chron 20:26(bis), *b^erākâ* indicates the people's laudatory thanksgiving of God, the laudatory *bārûk*- declaration (Neh 9:5, "and they praise (*brk* pi.) the majestic name, which is exalted above all glory *(b^erākâ)* and all praise *(t^ehillâ)*"; 2 Chron 20:26 "explains" the place-name *ʿēmeq b^erākâ* with reference to the praise offered there). This usage apparently developed only secondarily from the usage of *brk* pi. in the sense of "to praise" (see 2c). In Judaism this type of usage of the term became the most common: *b^erākâ* = "benediction" (cf. the Mishnah tractate *Berakot*).

(e) In 23 cases *b^erākâ* is associated with Yahweh, particularly as a summary of his health-creating activity ("Yahweh gives blessing," etc., Gen 28:4; Exod 32:29; Lev 25:21; Deut 28:8; Isa 44:3 par. *rûaḥ* "spirit"; Joel 2:14; Mal 3:10; Psa

21:4; 133:3 par. *ḥayyîm* "life"; "from Yahweh" Psa 24:5 par. *ṣ*^e^*dāqâ* "righteousness"; "Yahweh's blessing," etc., Gen 39:5; Deut 12:15; 16:17; 33:23 par. *rāṣôn* "good fortune"; 2 Sam 7:29; Psa 3:9 par. *y*^e^*šûᶜâ* "salvation"; 129:8; Prov 10:22; mediated by various natural powers, Gen 49:25 3x; Ezek 34:26b; Psa 84:7). Many texts deal more emphatically with the transmission of power (*ṣwh* pi. "to regulate," Lev 25:21; Deut 28:8; Psa 133:3; "to pour out," Isa 44:3; cf. Mal 3:10), others focus upon its effects, namely fertility of the fields and well-being among people (Gen 39:5; Deut 12:15; 16:17; 33:23; Joel 2:14; Mal 3:10; Psa 21:4; Prov 10:22), the status of the recipient of the promise (Gen 28:4), and of the priest (Exod 32:29), and the continuation of the dynasty (2 Sam 7:29). The statement made in a few passages that Yahweh "pours" the *b*^e^*rākâ* may be related somehow to the occasional appearance of the *b*^e^*rākâ* as vitalizing rain, dew, etc. (Gen 49:25a; Ezek 34:26b; Psa 84:7). In a land like Israel, God's beneficial rule is understandably experienced, among other ways, in the distribution of the rains; yet this usage should not mislead one to see the central meaning of the word in this element.

(f) Theologically interesting, if not easy to interpret, are the 5 cases (in addition to Ezek 34:26a txt?), where people appear as *b*^e^*rākâ* for others: Gen 12:2; (Abraham for the nations); Isa 19:24 (Israel in the midst of the world); Zech 8:13 (Israel among the nations); Psa 37:26 (the descendants of the righteous for their fellows); Psa 21:7 (pl., the king for his people). In Psa 37:26 *b*^e^*rākâ* status is brought about through God's health-creating word and deed. The people characterized as *b*^e^*rākâ* are truly *b*^e^*rûkîm*, i.e., the essence of benevolence and well-being (cf. Psa 21:7), and are therefore, on the one hand, a source of well-being for others (so H. Junker, *BETL* 12/13 [1959]: 553; contra J. Scharbert, *Bib* 39 [1958]: 25: a proverbial example in blessings), and on the other hand, an incarnate blessing, "through which" one calls others and oneself *bārûk*.

(g) In a few passages *b*^e^*rākâ* (or the pl.) indicates the status of "good fortune," whether the result of human *bārûk*-saying or of divine *bārûk*-making.

According to Prov 28:20, the one who acts faithfully is *rab-b*^e^*rākôt* "rich in well-being" (or "rich in pronouncements of blessing"?; opposite: "whoever seeks to become rich quickly does not avoid injury"; cf. Prov 28:27, where "rich in curses" is the opposite of "without want"). Psa 109:17 uses the word in its double meaning: "Whoever does not love the *b*^e^*rākâ* (= the benediction) distances himself/herself from it (i.e., the *b*^e^*rākâ* as well-being effected by the benediction)." The *b*^e^*rākôt* in Gen 49:26(bis) should also presumably be perceived as well-being resulting from a *bārûk*- declaration (cf. v 25).

IV. The overview of the theological usage of the word group in the individual layers of the OT may be divided, in accordance with the three major categories of usage, into treatments of God's blessing (IV/1; see esp. III/1a, 2a, d, e, 3, 4e), blessing through human agency (IV/2; see III/1a, 2b, f, 4b, c) and the praise of God (IV/3; see III/1c, 2c, e, 4d).

1. OT language concerning God's blessing has *brk* first (a) in the adaptation of pre-Yahwistic traditions, then (b), esp. in the promises to the patriarchs in Gen in J and P, (c) in Deut, and (e) in wisdom, while *brk* fades in significance (d) in the prophetic literature.

(a) A few passages preserve the memory that the blessing is not a specifically Israelite phenomenon, but one that also occurs among the neighbors of God's people (esp. in Num 22–24; cf. particularly 22:6). The OT also unabashedly incorporates materials that show that blessing was originally understood as a substance effective in itself (Gen 27: the dying father transfers his life-force to his son; Gen 32: Jacob wrests the blessing from the numen). Yet such texts are then edited so that no doubt can arise about the OT's contention that Israel's God is the only true source of all blessing (thus the benediction in vv 27–29 interprets the blessing extorted by Jacob in the context of Gen 27 unequivocally as God's gift; according to Gen 32:30 the deity blesses freely; Balaam must act toward Israel in express commission of Yahweh, Num 22:18; 24:13 J; 22:38 E; verbal clauses relate the impersonally formulated benedictions in Deut 7:14; 28:3–6 to God's action; cf. 7:13; 28:7–14). Not only passages that explicitly name Yahweh as giver of blessing, but also all other contexts integrate the discussion of blessing with the faith of Israel: all blessing comes from Yahweh.

Remarkably, very little is said concerning the manner of its mediation. Blessing is experienced in the natural processes of growth and multiplication, in productivity and success. Even in these phenomena, faith sees Yahweh at work, without the necessity of always expressly naming his activity. Above all, the texts do not give evidence that—as often maintained—blessing was traced to the effectiveness of the divine word. The whole OT relates blessing to divine speech only in two contexts: in P's creation account ("God blessed, saying" Gen 1:22, 28; 9:1; cf. 35:9f.; 48:3f) and Isa 19:25 ("whom Yahweh of hosts has blessed, saying"). The first instance subordinates the discussion of blessing to the priestly notion of creation through the word, the second may involve an imitation of a prophetic speech. Nevertheless, these exceptions confirm the rule that the OT understands blessing as a direct act of Yahweh.

(b) The blessing concept, originally naturalistic and then anchored in the narrow realm of the family (cf. e.g., Gen 24:34–36: the blessing of Abraham = "Sarah has born him a son even at his age"), is related to the activity of the God who works in the history of his people, first of all through the adaptation of this word in the promises to the fathers (Gen 12:2f.; 17:16, 20; 22:17; 26:3, 24; 28:14): the God who maintains the life of his people and multiplies them in the cultivated land is no other than he who saved Israel from Egypt (on the distinction between the saving and blessing activity of God, cf. Westermann, *Blessing* 1–14, among others).

That this viewpoint became definitive for the OT may be essentially because of the theological work of the Yahwist (cf. H. W. Wolff, "Kerygma of the Yahwist," in W. Brueggemann and Wolff, *Vitality of OT Traditions* [1982²], 41–66). For J the promise of descendants stands in the foreground in the blessing (Gen 12:2, "I will make you a great nation and I will bless you"; 26:24, "I will be with you and bless you and multiply your descendants"). Yet Yahweh's actual goal is not reached in Israel's growth to a great and mighty people. As the structure of the promise in Gen 12:2f. makes clear (cf. A. Murtonen, *VT* 9 [1959]: 159f.; H. Junker, *BETL* 12/13 [1959]: 554; Wolff, op. cit. 47–49), the actual goal is "that in you all families of the earth shall gain blessing" (Gen 12:3b; cf. 18:18; 28:14). With the call of Abraham, the possibility of God's blessing takes the place of the curse burdening humanity (Gen 3–11, 5x *ʾrr* "to curse").

P relates the blessing to the two most important elements of the promise to the patriarchs, the promises of descendants and of land (cf. Gen 17:4–8; 28:3f.; 35:11f.; 48:3f.). God's blessing applies not just to Israel but to all of humanity from the beginning of creation onward. It consists of God's providing humanity, as all living beings (Gen 1:22), with the power of fertility and multiplication (cf. the frequent combination of *prh* and *rbh* qal: Gen 1:22, 28; 8:17; 9:1, 7; 35:11; 47:27; Exod 1:7; hi.: Gen 17:20; 28:3; 48:4; Lev 26:9; outside P only in Jer 23:3, in reverse order, Jer 3:16; Ezek 36:11); the genealogies characteristic of P clarify the manner in which the blessing appears (cf. Westermann, *Gen*, CC, 1:17f.).

The concept of blessing characteristic for this documentary source may also be consistently maintained in the passage that discusses the Sabbath blessing (Gen 2:3a; God's blessing of things and institutions is mentioned elsewhere in Gen 27:27; 39:5; Exod 20:11; 23:25; Deut 7:13; 28:12; 33:11; Jer 31:23; Psa 65:11; 132:15; Job 1:10; Prov 3:33): since God sets the holy day apart (*qdš* pi.), he furnishes it with a power that makes it "fertile" for humanity (cf. Westermann, *Gen*, CC, 1:167–77).

The gift of the land is, then, in the real sense the "blessing of Abraham" (Gen 28:4; cf. the repetition of the promise to Jacob, Gen 48:4).

(c) Deut does not relate the blessing to the gift of the land itself (regularly associated with Yahweh's "oath"), but to the maintenance and support of life in the cultivated land (cf. the blessing in Deut 7:13; 14:29; 15:4, 10, 18; 16:15; 23:21; 24:19; 28:8, 12; 30:16; cf. Exod 23:25). The commandment to place the blessing on Gerizim and the curse on Ebal on entry into the land (Deut 11:29) signals the beginning of a new epoch in salvation history with the conquest of the land: God's enduring activity in blessing replaces episodic acts of salvation (cf. Josh 5:11f.; the enjoyment of the produce of the land replaces the eating of manna). Israel's relationship to God is also largely determined by its attitude to the land's produce: will they be understood as gifts of the Canaanite fertility gods or do the people recognize Yahweh as the sole grantor of all blessing? The more carefreely Israel enjoys the benefits of blessing (namely the fertility of people, cattle, and field; cf. Deut 7:13; 28:3–6), the more properly it honors Yahweh (cf. von Rad, *Theol.* 1:229f.).

As a result, a close functional relationship between blessing and call to obedience also exists, mirrored in a peculiar duplication of statements: on the one hand, the promise of blessing is issued in an unconditional form (Deut 16:15; 28:8, 12); on the other hand, one encounters statements that call for keeping the commandments "in order that Yahweh, your God, may bless you" (14:29; 23:21; 24:19; cf. 15:10, 18) or which are conditionally phrased "if you . . . , then Yahweh, your God, will bless you" (30:16; cf. 7:12f.; 15:4f.). That Yahweh grants blessing freely demands recognition of his exclusive power to bless.

The whole people receives the blessing. Consequently, the blessing notion contains the actual motivation for the "humanitarian commandments" in Deut: as long as the weakest member of the community does not also participate in the fullness of God's blessing, the promise remains unfulfilled (cf. von Rad, *Gottesvolk* 42–49; Eichrodt 2:336).

Statements concerning the fulfillment of God's blessing correspond to the announcements of it in Gen and Deut (cf. Gen 24:1, 35; 25:11; 26:12; 30:27, 30; 32:30; 35:9; 48:3; Deut 2:7; 12:7; 15:6, 14). Outside these layers, references to God's blessing are more infrequent. A particular concentration may be identified, however, for the confession of confidence, "Yahweh will bless," etc. (cf. Psa 29:11; 67:7f.; 128:5; 134:3a; probably also 115:21a; in prayer style in Psa 5:13; 65:11; 109:28) and for benedictions, "May Yahweh bless," etc. (cf. Num 6:24; Psa 67:2; 115:12b–14; Ruth 2:4 as a greeting). Otherwise, corresponding statements occur in rather diverse contexts (pi.: Exod 20:24; Num 6:27; Josh 17:14; Judg 13:24; 2 Sam 6:11f. = 1 Chron 13:14; 2 Sam 7:29 [cf. 1 Chron 17:27]; Isa 19:25; 51:2; 61:9; Psa 45:3; 107:38; 147:13; Job 42:12; 1 Chron 4:10; 26:5; 2 Chron 31:10; pu.: 2 Sam 7:29 [cf. 1 Chron 17:27]; Psa 37:22; 112:2; 128:4; Prov 20:21; 22:9; on the noun cf. III/4e, less clearly also in Deut 28:2; Isa 19:24; Ezek 34:26a; 44:30; Mal 2:2; Psa 21:7; Prov 10:6; 24:25; 28:20; 1 Chron 5:1f. txt em).

(d) Prophetic books focus much less upon the blessing, since their real interests lie in God's activity in salvation and judgment. The root *brk* does not occur at all in pre-exilic texts. Only since Deutero-Isa does this term describe God's future activity (cf. Isa 44:3; 51:2; Ezek 34:26; Joel 2:14; Hag 2:19; Zech 8:13; Mal 3:10), an activity not exhausted in single acts of salvation but accompanying human life continually and experienced in the natural processes of growth and multiplication (cf., however, already Hos 2:20–25, without *brk*). The language of blessing also governs "descriptions of salvation" (cf. Westermann, *Blessing* 32–34, with bibliog. on 26n.14), although *brk* occurs in such a depiction only in Isa 65:23.

(e) Unlike prophecy, wisdom experiences God's activity not in his great acts in history but in the regular daily phenomena of life, in the realms of the household, the field, and the village, in the sector, then, to which blessing normally pertains. As always in the OT, blessing consists of numerous descendants (Psa 112:2; 128:3f.; Job 42:13), land ownership (Psa 37:22), large herds (Job 1:10; 42:12), wealth (Psa 112:3; Prov 10:22; 24:25; 28:20), long life (Psa 133:3), and a lasting memory (Prov 10:7). Insight into the impermanence of earthly possession surfaces occasionally (e.g., Prov 11:28; 23:4f.); this insight likely leads to the differentiation between those goods seen as God's gift and those the individual acquires for himself/herself; the one who seeks to secure his/her own life in this manner misses good fortune (Prov 10:22; 20:21). Nevertheless, the conviction that the righteous may expect blessing (Psa 37:25f.; 112:2; Prov 3:33; 10:6f.) and the godless may expect misfortune and failure is fundamentally upheld. The criteria for "righteousness" are relationship to God (Psa 112:1f.; 128:4; Prov 28:20) and proper treatment of the fellow human being (Prov 11:26; 22:9; 24:25).

2. The blessing bestowed by people in the public or private cult is not actually dependent upon the spiritual power of the one blessing, upon the receptivity of the one blessed (see e.g., *ILC* 1–2:182f.; S. Mowinckel, *Psalmenstudien* [1924], 5:10f.), or upon the efficacy of the spoken word (e.g., F. Horst,

RGG 5:1649–51; E. J. Bickerman, *RB* 69 [1962]: 524). Rather, the ones who bless function as intermediaries through whom God himself blesses. This point becomes esp. evident in texts that mention a blessing formula in association with *brk* (paternal blessing: Gen 27:27–29; 48:15f., 20; cf. 28:1, 3f.; bridal blessing: Gen 24:60; cf. Ruth 4:11; Tob 10:11; priestly blessing: Num 6:23–27; cf. Psa 67:2; 115:12–15). As a rule, the blessing explicitly claims God as bestower of the blessing. This claim is particularly emphasized in association with the Aaronite blessing: when the priests place the name of Yahweh on the people, i.e., speak the previously cited blessing formula (Num 6:24–26), Yahweh himself blesses his people (v 27). The expression used only for the priestly blessing *brk bᵉšēm yhwh* "to bless by using (invoking) the name of Yahweh" has the same intention (Deut 10:8; 21:5; 2 Sam 6:18 = 1 Chron 16:2, David functions as a priest; Psa 129:8b, concluding blessing—it does not belong to the greeting of the reaper; 1 Chron 23:13; cf. H. A. Brongers, *ZAW* 77 [1965]: 8f.).

The notion that the gift of blessing was a priestly privilege may be supported only for the relatively late layers of the OT (Aaronites: Num 6:23; 1 Chron 23:13; levitical priests: Deut 21:5; 2 Chron 30:27; the tribe of Levi: Deut 10:8; Deut 10:8 and 21:5 are secondary; cf. von Rad, *Deut*, OTL, 79f., 136). The oldest traditions do not mention the priestly blessing at all, probably in order to declare that life and prosperity need not be periodically recreated through the cult, but that they are given to people on the basis of God's free decision (Gen 8:22 J). That Deut, too, does not yet place emphasis on the priestly blessing as a privilege may be elucidated by the fact that, according to 27:12 (cf. 11:29; Josh 8:33), the members of all twelve tribes are commissioned to bless and to curse. Although one must also understand that in such a procedure (in analogy to Deut 27:14–26) the people only answer the recited formulae with "amen" (cf. 1QS 2:1–10; *m. Sota* 7:5), it is still noteworthy that in essence the responsibility of the whole community for the granting of blessing and curse is accented.

Although the primary layer of P does not yet view the bestowal of blessing as a priestly privilege (others who bless: Isaac, Gen 28:1, 6; Jacob, 49:28; Moses, Exod 39:43 [Lev 9:23a is secondary]), blessing still receives a highly significant place in its historiography (cf. K. Elliger, *ZTK* 49 [1952]: 134): according to Lev 9:22 Aaron pronounces the blessing upon the people after the offering of the first sacrifice, and the theophany that follows (v 23b) legitimizes sacrificial practice as well as the institution of the priestly blessing.

The tradition of Gen 14:18–20—closely related to P—could have a similar significance: Melchizedek's blessing on Abraham demonstrates the priestly blessing as an essential component of worship "after the order of Melchizedek" (cf. W. Zimmerli, FS Rost 255–64).

The priestly blessing is applied as a rule to a larger community. 1 Sam 2:20 also discusses the bestowal of blessing upon an individual, however (cf. Psa 91; 121). If, according to 1 Sam 9:13, Samuel is to "bless" the sacrifice, this probably means that it was his privilege to pronounce the *bᵉrākâ* at mealtime (cf. 1QS 6:4f.; 1QSa 2:17–20; Mark 8:6f.; Luke 9:16).

The texts prove to be rather uninterested in the blessing procedure itself. Only Gen 48:17 alludes to the laying on of hands in the context of the paternal blessing; Lev 9:22 mentions the raising of the hands during the priestly blessing.

3. In association with the praise of God, *brk* plays a role in a particular group of praises and exhortations to praise.

(a) Praises formed with *bārûk* substantially follow a fixed schema: *bārûk*—divine name or appellative (sometimes additional epithets)—a clause giving the reason for praise, often introduced with the relative particle (cf. W. S. Towner, *CBQ* 30 [1968]: 386–99; W. Schottroff, *Der altisr. Fluchspruch* [1969], 163ff.; see III/1c). Such statements of praise are, first, spontaneously expressed in everyday life immediately after the experience of divine assistance (Gen 24:27; 1 Sam 25:32, 39; 1 Kgs 1:48; Ezra 7:27); sometimes they are spoken not by the person who experienced God's deed but by deeply moved observers (Exod 18:10; 2 Chron 2:11; Aram. Dan 3:28, in each case in the mouth of a non-Israelite; Ruth 4:14). The same formula is used in association with some cultic procedures in Gen 9:26; 14:20; 1 Kgs 8:15 = 2 Chron 6:4; 1 Kgs 8:56.

It occurs in Psa 28:6 and 31:22 (a causal clause introduced by *kî;* cf. 1 Sam 23:21) in individual laments, indeed, at the point at which the lament evolves into praise (cf. Gunkel-Begrich 243–47; Westermann, *PLP* 59–64). The statement of praise (with *še-*) functions similarly in a communal song of thanksgiving (Psa 124:6). Psa 68:20 introduces the description of the divine saving act in this manner. Such usages of this statement of praise develop into a doxological formula that occurs primarily at the conclusion of some psalms (66:20, with *ᵓᵃšer;* 68:36, without a causal clause; 135:21). This placement leads to the use of the formula as the conclusion of the first four books of Psa as well, joined secondarily to the respective psalms (41:14; 72:18f.; 89:53; 106:48; cf. Kraus, *Psa,* CC, 1:16ff.).

Psa 106:48 seems to be a revision of 1 Chron 16:36, so that the doxology may have been introduced from Chron into the psalm, which in turn may have become the conclusion of the fourth psalm collection (cf. Rudolph, HAT 21, 128).

The formula begins a psalm only in 144:1 (with a participial continuation). Here, too, it apparently does not function as a call to praise; rather, the psalm begins without prelude (contra Psa 18), directly with the praise of God. Ezek 3:12 is a self-contained exclamation of praise, if the text is original (usually emended to *bᵉrûm,* e.g., Zimmerli, *Ezek,* Herm, 1:94); also Deut 33:20; Zech 11:5.

Third-per. statements of praise primarily address a human forum; the speakers celebrate God's greatness, manifest in the concrete act toward their hearers (cf. e.g., Exod 18:10, "Yahweh is full of blessing, who delivered you"; 1 Sam 25:32, "Blessed be Yahweh, . . . who sent you"; Ruth 4:14, "Blessed be Yahweh, who has not left you without a redeemer"). Prayer style is first used in two late texts, i.e., God is addressed directly, "You are full of blessing, Yahweh" (Psa 119:12; 1 Chron 29:10, in each as an introduction to a prayer or a request).

This usage becomes the most common, then, in the deuterocanonical literature (cf. Dan 3:26, 52 LXX; Tob 3:11; 8:5, 15–17; 11:14, etc.), at Qumran (1QS 11:15; 1QH 5:20;

10:14; 11:27, 29, 32, etc.), and in Jewish prayers (18 Benedictions). Apparently the doxologies constructed in this manner in the oldest portions of the Jewish liturgy and in the latest layers of the OT go back to a common pattern (cf. Towner, op. cit. 397–99).

(b) The pl. impv. of *brk* pi. occasionally occurs as the introit of a hymn: "Praise Yahweh" (Psa 96:2; 100:4; 134:1f.; cf. Judg 5:2, 9) (in addition to the more frequent introductions with →*hll* pi., Psa 113:1; 117:1; 135:1, 3, etc.; → *ydh* hi., Psa 33:2; 105:1; 106:1; 107:1, etc.). The pu. ptcp. with *y*ᵉ*hî* functions similarly in Psa 113:2; Dan 2:20 (Aram.).

The call to praise in Neh 9:5 is independent of the following thanksgiving prayer (cf. 1 Chron 29:20; Psa 68:27, although the pf. should more likely be read here; cf. Kraus, *Psa*, CC, 2:47). Psa 135 repeats it once more at the end (vv 19f.) applied to the various groups within the community. It is then also expanded to call for God's praise by all people (Psa 66:8; 96:2), the entire creation (103:22a), and the powers surrounding the heavenly king (103:20f.).

In songs of the individual, one appropriately calls upon oneself (Psa 103:1f., 22b; 104:1, 35) or declares one's intention in the voluntative (16:7; 26:12; 34:2; 63:5; 145:1f.).

As is true of statements of praise, declarative statements concerning God (Psa 16:7; 26:12; 34:2) seem to be original in contrast to the prayer (63:5; 145:1f.; 26:12 LXX). The supplicant addresses, then, a human audience and declares to it the intention to praise God (Psa 26:12, "I will praise Yahweh in assemblies"). Such declarations occur characteristically at the beginning of individual songs of thanksgiving (34:2, with *ydh* hi., e.g., 9:2; 57:10; 138:1f.), in vows of praise at the end of individual laments (26:12), and in the songs of assurance that have arisen from them (16:7; 63:5). More frequently, the supplicant's concern continuously to praise God comes to expression (Psa 34:2; 63:5; 145:1f.).

V. In Judaism (and in the NT) usage evolves in such a way that reference to the praise of God now predominates. In the NT, 40 of the total of 68 occurrences of *eulogein* and its derivatives concern praise of God. The concept of blessing itself is modified through relation to the Christ event (Acts 3:25f.; Gal 3:8f.; Eph 1:3). The summons to bless directed to people is assigned to the commandment to love the enemy (Luke 6:27f.; Rom 12:14; 1 Pet 3:9; cf. 1 Cor 4:12). The cultic blessing is not mentioned; cf., however, the peace greeting of the disciples (Matt 10:12f.; Luke 10:5f.) and Jesus' blessing (Mark 10:16, blessing the children; Luke 24:50, farewell blessing). Cf. H. W. Beyer, "εὐλογέω," *TDNT* 2:754–65; W. Schenk, *Der Segen im* NT (1967); C. Westermann, *Blessing in the Bible and the Life of the Church* (1978).

C. A. Keller (I-III)/G. Wehmeier (IV-V)

בשׂר *bśr* pi. **to bring a message** → מַלְאָךְ *mal*ʾ*āk*

בָּשָׂר *bāśār* flesh

S 1320; BDB 142a; *HALOT* 1:164a; *TDOT* 2:317–32; *TWOT* 291a; *NIDOTTE* 1414

1. The subst. **baśar-* "flesh, body" may be identified with certainty only in WSem. (*HAL* 156b; P. Fronzaroli, *AANLR* 8/19 [1964]: 170, 253, 266, 277). Whether the root can also be found in the Akk. *bišru* "infant" remains questionable (*AHw* 131a; *CAD* B:270a); cf., however, Pun. *bšr* (also written *bšʾr* and *bšʿr*) "child, offspring" (J. Hoftijzer, "Eine Notiz zum pun. Kinderopfer," *VT* 8 [1958]: 288–92; *DISO* 45). The relationship sometimes suggested to the verb *bśr* pi. "to report, bring a message" is unlikely.

Ug. occurrences are *KTU* 1.4.II.5, "the covering of her body"; 1.24.9, "blood for his flesh"; 1.15.IV.25, V.8, of meat at a meal (cf. *UT* no. 534; *WUS* no. 598).

Other texts contemporary with the OT are only the passages with Aram. *bšr* (= Bibl. Aram. *bᵉśar*) in the sayings of Ahiqar, line 89, "to pour out his blood and consume his flesh," and line 104, "why should wood contend with fire, flesh with the knife, a man with the king?" (Cowley 215f.).

Arab. *bašar* signifies more broadly "human being," *bašarat*, by contrast, "skin" (see 3).

2. In the OT, Hebr. *bāśār* is attested 270x and Aram. *bᵉśar* 3x (Dan 2:11; 4:9; 7:5; Lis. overlooks Gen 9:15a; for detailed statistics according to chronological categories cf. D. Lys, *La chair dans l'Ancien Testament, "Bâsâr"* [1967], 15–19). Hebr. occurrences are distributed as follows:

Gen	33	2 Kgs	6	Psa	16
Exod	14	Isa	17	Job	18
Lev	61	Jer	10	Prov	4
Num	17	Ezek	24	Eccl	5
Deut	13	Hos	1	Lam	1
Judg	6	Joel	1	Dan	2
1 Sam	4	Mic	1	Neh	2
2 Sam	3	Hag	1	1 Chron	1
1 Kgs	4	Zech	4	2 Chron	1
				total	270

3. The beginning point is the numerous passages in which *bāśār* designates the corporeal substance of the human or animal, living or dead body. Within this broad realm the specific referent can vary greatly: flesh as food, as sacrifice, or as an object of P's sacral-medicinal purity prescriptions. Sometimes *bāśār* occurs alongside other parts of the body as a vital component of the corporeal whole: with bones (Job 2:5; *ʿeṣem* 123x, 20x in the meaning "even these"; cf. Dhorme 9f.; L. Delekat, *VT* 14 [1964]: 49–52), with skin and bones (Lam 3:4; *ʿôr* "skin, hide" 99x, 46x in Lev 13), with skin, blood (→ *dām*), and excrement (Num 19:5), with skin, bones, and sinew (Job 10:11; cf. Ezek 37:6, 8).

Otherwise biological relationship is indicated by the expression "(my/your) bone and flesh" (Gen 2:23; 29:14; Judg 9:2; 2 Sam 5:1 = 1 Chron 11:1; 2 Sam

19:13f.; cf. W. Reiser, "Die Verwandtschaftsformel in Gen. 2,23," *TZ* 16 [1960]: 1–4). "(Your/our) flesh" alone sometimes has the same meaning (Gen 37:27; Isa 58:7; Neh 5:5) and twice the cs. phrase *šᵉʾēr bāśār* does (Lev 18:6; 25:49).

The expression "flesh and blood" to describe the person as mortal occurs first in Sir 14:18.

About 50x *bāśār* indicates the body, i.e., the visible flesh of the person or, as an exception, the animal (Job 41:15), the corporal in its totality with emphasis upon the visual and the graphic. This usage always concerns the live body; *bāśār* is never used of the corpse, not even in Ezek 32:5. For all this, *bāśār* is deeply tied to the material and is never used in the sense of "appearance, figure"; *bāśār* is *corpus*, not *figura*. Significantly, the word is used in contrast to various terms for the spiritual life: →*rûaḥ* "spirit" (Gen 6:3; Num 16:22; 27:16; Isa 31:3; Joel 3:1), → *nepeš* "soul" (Gen 9:4; Deut 12:23; Job 14:22), → *lēb* "heart" (Ezek 44:7, 9; Psa 84:3).

The other words for "body," e.g., *gᵉwîyâ* (Ezek 1:11, 23; Dan 10:6), Bibl. Aram. *gᵉšēm* (Dan 3:27f.; 4:30; 5:21; 7:11), readily evolve further into the meaning "being, self" *(gap* Exod 21:3f.; *gᵉwîyâ* Gen 47:18; Neh 9:37; cf. Hebr. *ʿeṣem*, Aram. *garmāʾ*, Akk. *ramānu)* or into the meaning "corpse" *(gᵉwîyâ* Judg 14:8f.; 1 Sam 31:10, 12bis; Nah 3:3bis; Psa 110:6; *gûpâ* 1 Chron 10:12bis; cf. 1 Sam 31:12; *peger* 22x, Aram. *pagrāʾ* and Akk. *pagru* also "body"; cf. D. Neiman, *JBL* 67 [1948]: 55–60, on Lev 26:30 and Ezek 43:7, 9; otherwise *nᵉbēlâ* 48x, → *nbl)*. Cf. Dhorme 7–12; F. Baumgärtel and E. Schweizer, "σῶμα," *TDNT* 7:1044–48.*

Arab. *bašarat* means "skin" (see 1). A slight alteration of perspective becomes apparent in the shift of meaning "body" > "skin." The skin is outwardly visible portion of the body. The semasiological proximity of the two concepts is apparent in a few OT passages in which both meanings are equally possible (Psa 102:6; 119:120; Job 4:15). Other passages clearly distinguish the two concepts (Lev 13:2ff.).

An expansion of meaning toward the abstract occurs in the expression *kol-bāśār* "all flesh," which appears approximately 40x and which can refer either to humanity (e.g., Deut 5:26; Psa 65:3; 145:21) or to all creatures, i.e., people and animals (e.g., Gen 6:17; 9:16f.; Job 34:15; cf. A. R. Hulst, "*Kol-bāśār* in der priesterlichen Fluterzählung," *OTS* 12 [1958]: 28–68).

In a few passages *(mik)kol-bāśār* can be translated "of all kinds, varieties" (esp. in P: Gen 6:19; 7:15; 8:17; 9:16; Num 18:15).

bāśār occurs as a euphemism for penis in Lev 15:2f.; Ezek 16:26; 23:20.

The much less common word *šᵉʾēr* "flesh" is largely synonymous with *bāśār* in profane usage, but is not employed as a theological term, primarily because it has no collective usage (Exod 21:10; Jer 51:35; Mic 3:2f.; Psa 73:26; 78:20, 27; Prov 5:11; 11:17; originally more the inner, bloody flesh; cf. F. Baumgärtel, *TDNT* 7:107f.; in P in the meaning "blood relative": Lev 18:6, 12f.; 20:19; 21:2; 25:49; Num 27:11; in addition to Lev 18:17 *šaʾᵃrâ* txt?; on the Sem. equivalents and their shifts in meaning, cf. Fronzaroli, op. cit. 168, 252f., 266, 277)

4. *bāśār* is theologically significant in passages that express a qualitative assessment. Only as an exception does this usage involve an evaluation of status, as in Ezek 11:19 and 36:26, where the bestowal of a heart of flesh

instead of a heart of stone is an aspect of religious renewal. A negative judgment is more often evident, particularly if the flesh, i.e., humanity, is qualitatively distinguished as mortal and impotent from the divine being as spirit (Gen 6:3, 12; Isa 31:3; 40:6; Jer 17:5; Psa 56:5; 78:39; Job 10:4; 2 Chron 32:8). Cf. also J. L. Helberg, "Communication on the Semasiological Meaning of Basar," *OuTWP* (1959): 23–28 (cf. *ZAW* 72 [1960]: 284); J. Scharbert, *Fleisch, Geist und Seele im Pentateuch* (1966), 13, 25f., 40f., 48–56; Lys, op. cit.

5. In the Qumran texts *bāśār* is a frequent and theologically significant term (cf. H. Huppenbauer, "Bśr 'Fleisch' in den Texten von Qumran," *TZ* 13 [1957]: 298–300; R. E. Murphy, "Bśr in the Qumran Literature," *Sacra Pagina* 2 [1959]: 60–76; R. Meyer, "σάρξ," *TDNT* 7:110–14). A characteristic shift of meaning in relation to the OT usage appears in many passages: flesh involves not only mortality but also sinfulness. The altered connotation appears in expressions such as *rûaḥ bāśār* "spirit of the flesh" (1QH 13:13; 17:25), *b*ᵉ*śar* ʾ*ašmâ* "guilty flesh" (1QM 12:12), *b*ᵉ*śar* ʿ*āwel* "evil flesh" (1QS 11:9).

In rabbinic usage, too, characteristic shifts of meaning in relation to the OT occur; on this and the NT, cf. R. Meyer and E. Schweizer, "σάρξ," *TDNT* 7:115–51; H. Seebass and A. C. Thiselton, "Flesh," *DNTT* 1:671–82.

G. Gerleman

בַּת *bat* **daughter** → בֵּן *bēn*

גאה *g*ʾ*h* **to be high**

S 1342; BDB 144a; *HALOT* 1:168a; *TDOT* 2:344–50; *TWOT* 299; *NIDOTTE* 1448

---

1. The root *g*ʾ*h* (**g*ʾ*w/y*) occurs in NWSem.

Cf. Ug., *KTU* 1.17.VI.44 *gan* "arrogance" (par. *pš*ʿ "sin"; *UT* no. 548; *WUS* no. 613); Pun., *Poen.* 1027 *gune bel* (*DISO* 46 "grandeur of Bel"; Sznycer 144); Syr., *LS* 99f.; Mand., Drower-Macuch 72a, 76a, 89.

The Eg. root *q*ʾ*y* "to be high" is attested in association with things, persons, and gods; the fig. meaning "with a high back = arrogantly" also occurs (cf. Erman-Grapow 5:1ff.).

In addition to the verb in the qal, the adjs. *gē*ʾ, *gē*ʾ*eh*, *ga*ʾᵃ*yôn* "arrogant" and the substs. *gē*ʾ*â* "arrogance," *ga*ʾᵃ*wâ* "height, majesty, pride," *gē*ʾ*ût* "ascension, grandeur, insolence," and *gēwâ* "arrogance, pride" occur in the OT as nominal derivatives, the last term also, perhaps as a Hebr. loanword, in Bibl. Aram. Cf. further the PN *g*ᵉʾ*û*ʾ*ēl* (Num 13:15; see, however, *HAL* 161b).

2. *g*ʾ*h* qal occurs 7x (also in Sir 10:9 in the meaning "to overreach"), *gē*ʾ 1x (Isa 16:6), *gē*ʾ*eh* 8x (excl. Psa 123:4 Q; also in Sir 10:14; 11:30), *ga*ʾᵃ*yôn* 1x

(Psa 123:4 K), *gēʾâ* 1x (Prov 8:13), *gaʾ*ᵃ*wâ* 19x (also in Sir 7:17; 10:6–8; 13:20; 16:8), *gāʾôn* 49x (also Sir 10:12; 48:18), *gēʾût* 8x, *gēwâ* 3x (also 1QS 4:9) and 1x in Bibl. Aram. (Dan 4:34).

Aside from a few cases of *gāʾôn* in Ezek, all occurrences of the root appear in poetical texts (even *gʾh* qal in Lev 26:19; cf. Elliger, HAT 4, 367). The 100 occurrences in the OT are represented most strongly in the prophetic literature (Isa 24x; Jer and Ezek 10x; Zech 3x; Hos, Amos, Nah, and Zeph 2x each; Mic 1x), elsewhere roughly equally in the wisdom literature (Job 11x, Prov 7x) and in hymnody (Psa 15x, also Exod 15:1[bis], 7, 21[bis]; Deut 33:26, 29).

3. All meanings of the root *gʾh* and its various derivatives are grouped around the basic meaning "to be/become high":

(a) The more infrequent concrete meaning occurs in Job 8:11 (papyrus grows aloft); Ezek 47:5 (the water rises in the river); Isa 9:17 (the rising of the smoke is described as *gēʾût* ʿ*āšān*). The archaic style of two psalms, which describe Yahweh's conquest of the powers of chaos in the mythical tradition, suggests the meaning "arrogance, rebellion, impetuosity" even for the discussion of the "raging, foaming" of the sea (*gaʾ*ᵃ*wâ* Psa 46:4; *gēʾût* 89:10; cf. Job 38:11).

Lit. and fig. meanings (G. R. Driver, FS Robinson 59, "raging of the Jordan"; KBL 162, "high trees"; better: Rudolph, HAT 12, 84, "splendor") are even opposed in attempts to explain Jeremiah's depiction of the thicket of Jordan *g*ᵉʾ*ôn hayyardēn* (Jer 12:5; 49:19 = 50:44; cf. Zech 11:3).

(b) Figuratively, the root expresses human pride, arrogance, and presumption. In a positive sense, the land is Israel's *gāʾôn*, "pride" (Psa 47:5; Nah 2:3; cf. Isa 13:19 of Babel); according to Isa 4:2, the fruit of the land contributes to Israel's "pride *(gāʾôn)* and ornamentation *(tipʾeret, → pʾr)*." Most passages should, however, be understood in a negative sense.

P. Humbert ("Démesure et chute dans l'AT," FS Vischer 63ff.) offers a collection of Hebr. synonyms for "pride, arrogance"; worthy of mention are the roots → *gbh*, → *gdl*, → *rûm*, and *yāhîr* "presumptuous, proud" (Hab 2:5; Prov 21:24; cf. J. Blau, *VT* 5 [1955]: 342), *r*ᵉ*ḥab lēb*/*nepeš* "presumptuous" (Psa 101:5; Prov 21:4; 28:25), *sll* hitpo. "to behave high-handedly" (Exod 9:17), *zîd* qal "to be impudent" (Exod 18:11; Jer 50:29), hi. "to act impudently" (Deut 17:13; 18:20; Neh 9:10, 16, 29), *zēd* "cocky, impudent" (Isa 13:11, etc.), *zādôn* "impudence" (Deut 17:12, etc.).

*š*ᵉ*pal rûaḥ* "humble" (Prov 16:19; 29:23) and *šaḥ* ʿ*ênayim* "with downcast eyes" (Job 22:29) may be cited as antonyms, in addition to the verbs *špl* hi. "to abase, humble" (Job 22:29; 40:11; Prov 29:23), *kn*ʿ hi. "to humble" (Job 40:12), *šḥt* hi. "to ruin" (Jer 13:9), *šbr* "to shatter" (Lev 26:19).

(c) Wisdom literature warns against the proud and arrogant attitude in the measured equilibrium of the comparative *ṭôb*- saying (Prov 16:19); it is aware that disaster follows impudence (Prov 16:18); God abases the "pride of the arrogant" (Job 22:29 txt em; cf. Fohrer, KAT 16, 352; cf. Job 40:11f., on which see S. Loffreda, "Raffronto fra un testo ugaritico [2 Aqhat VI, 42–45] e Giobbe 40:9–12," *BeO* 8 [1966]: 103–16), God tears down the house of the proud (Prov 15:25), and abundantly repays the one who "practices arrogance" (Psa 31:24).

The laments of the Psalter often use the root *gʾh,* and its derivatives characterize the → *rāšāʿ*, the "evildoer" (e.g., Psa 36:12; 59:13; 73:6; 94:2; 140:6; nevertheless, the term *gēʾîm* can hardly be regarded as a reference to a specific group, namely the Sadducees, as H. Steiner, *Die Geʾim in den Psalmen* [1925], 22–30, thinks). Psa 10:2 describes the *rāšāʿ* as *gēʾût* (txt em) in terms of high-handedness and self-sufficiency, as one who devises dangerous plans for the destruction of the humble (*ʿānî,* → *ʿnh* II). Characteristic is the "proud self-assurance" of speech (Psa 17:10; cf. 73:9), the "arrogance" with which their lips "speak insolence *(ʿātāq)* against the righteous" (Psa 31:19).

4. (a) Wisdom proposes that the arrogant fall and the humble receive honor (cf. Prov 29:23), challenging people to self-moderation; the prophets use the root theologically to describe the perverse, self-glorifying relationship of people to God. In both Israel (Jer 13:9, 17; Ezek 7:20, 24; 16:49, 56; 24:21, cf. Lev 26:19; Ezek 33:28) and the foreign nations (Isa 13:19; 16:6; cf. Isa 48:29; Ezek 30:6, 18; Zeph 2:10; Zech 9:6; 10:11), God thwarts self-glorification. God will expose as empty any *gāʾôn* that Israel impudently adopts (Amos 6:8; Hos 5:5, "Israel's arrogance testifies openly against it"; cf. 7:10; here arrogance is the final prosecution witness against Israel). According to Isa 2:12 the "day of Yahweh of hosts" consists precisely in the execution of judgment "on all the proud and haughty and on all the lofty and high (following LXX)" (cf. 13:11). "Isaiah does not speak, as wisdom does, about what is good or better, but rather about what Yahweh Sebaoth opposes with his whole being, because of his claim to be the only one who is 'high,' the only one who is lord and king" (Wildberger, *Isa 1–12,* CC, 115).

(b) God's *gʾh* (Exod 15:1, 21), *gāʾôn* (Exod 15:7; Isa 2:10, 19, 21; 24:14; Mic 5:3; Job 40:10), *gaʾᵃwâ* (Psa 68:35), and *gēʾût* (Isa 26:10: Psa 93:1), divine characteristics and predications of majesty, nobility, and kingdom (*hᵃdar gᵉʾōnô* "sublime majesty," Isa 2:10, 19, 21; on the phrase cf. Joüon §141m: "superlative nuance"), contrast with the presumed *gāʾôn* of people, which people can claim for themselves only in foolish arrogance (cf. Job 40:9–11, God's royal robes, Fohrer, KAT 16, 519f.). The substantial correlation of Psa 68:35 (cf. Psa 104); 93:1; and Deut 33:26 (cf. Pun. *gune bel;* see 1) may indicate that this predication deals with concepts originally borrowed from Can. religion (royal god of heaven), although now united with traditions of God's saving acts on Israel's behalf (Exod 15:1, 21).

5. The LXX frequently renders *gʾh* in reference to God with *doxa* or the like; otherwise, it usually translates *hybris* or *hyperēphania,* etc., with a somewhat more negative connotation than MT and accenting the aspect of arrogant action (G. Bertram, *TDNT* 8:300; id., " 'Hochmut' und verwandte Begriffe im griech. und hebr. AT," *WO* III/3 [1964]: 32–43).

On Judaism, the NT, and early Christianity, cf. G. Bertram, "ὕβρις," *TDNT* 8:295–307.

H.-P. Stähli

גאל $g^{\supset}l$ to redeem

S 1350; BDB 145a; *HALOT* 1:169a; *TDOT* 2:350–55; *TWOT* 300; *NIDOTTE* 1457

1. The verb $g^{\supset}l$ occurs only in Hebr. From the OT it enters Samaritan as a loanword (*HAL* 162a) and the language of postbibl. Judaism as an authentic legacy (cf. *TDNT* 4:350f. and 7:987f.).

Regarding the PN *g*ʾ*lyhw* on a seal impression from Beth-zur, cf. *DOTT* 223f.

So far only one occurrence has been identified in the Qumran literature: CD 14:16, where the ptcp. *gō*ʾ*ēl* appears in the meaning "(nearest) relative."

The limitation of the verb to Hebr. contributes to the difficulties in establishing its etymology.

At any rate, it is totally unrelated semantically to the homonymous *g*ʾ*l* ni. "to be made (cultically) unclean" *(HAL* 162f.: a by-form of *g*ʿ*l*; → *ṭm*ʾ*)*. This dissociation should be maintained with Fohrer (KAT 16, 110) among others, against A. R. Johnson ("Primary Meaning of *g*ʾ*l*," *SVT* 1 [1953]: 67–77), who assumes the common basic meaning "to cover" for both *g*ʾ*l* verbs. This meaning would have resulted in the sense "to protect" for the first *g*ʾ*l* and the sense "to soil" for the second. *g*ʾ*l* "to protect" provides a questionable point of departure for the verb under consideration, however, a point of departure totally inappropriate to its actual denotation; cf. also J. Blau, *VT* 6 (1956): 244f. on Job 3:5.

The verb occurs in the qal and the ni.; *g*ᵉʾ*ullâ* (in a nominal formation favored for legal terms; cf. F. Horst, FS Rudolph 153: "the right or obligation of redemption [buying back]") and *g*ᵉʾ*ûlîm* (Isa 63:4; according the L. Köhler, *ZAW* 39 [1921]: 316 and *HAL* 161b: "time, status of the *gō*ʾ*ēl* blood avenger"; on the nominal formation cf. BL 472 and Gulkowitsch 20) are derivative abstract nouns. The PN *yig*ʾ*āl* (impf. form; cf. *IP* 28, 200) also derives from the root.

2. The root *g*ʾ*l* occurs 118x in the OT (with the PN *yig*ʾ*āl* in Num 13:7; 2 Sam 23:36; 1 Chron 3:22 there are 121). The qal ptcp. *gō*ʾ*ēl* (46x) is, except for Gen 48:16 and Psa 103:4, substantivized and will be cataloged separately in the following list (the number in parentheses indicates the number of occurrences of the special combination *gō*ʾ*ēl haddām* "blood avenger"; in Num 35:12 *haddām* should probably be supplied).

	qal	ni.	subst. *gō*ʾ*ēl*	*g*ᵉʾ*ullâ* (*g*ᵉʾ*ûlîm*)	total
Gen	1	–	–	–	1
Exod	2	–	–	–	2
Lev	13	7	2	9	31
Num	–	–	8 (6)	–	8
Deut	–	–	2 (2)	–	2
Josh	–	–	3 (3)	–	3
2 Sam	–	–	1 (1)	–	1
1 Kgs	–	–	1	–	1
Isa	9	1	13	(1)	24
Jer	1	–	1	2	4

Ezek	–	–	–	1	1
Hos	1	–	–	–	1
Mic	1	–	–	–	1
Psa	9	–	2	–	11
Job	1	–	1	–	2
Prov	–	–	1	–	1
Ruth	12	–	9	2	23
Lam	1	–	–	–	1
OT	51	8	44 (12)	14 +1	118

This overview reveals a particular profile: the qal is concentrated in Lev and Ruth, the ni. and *geʾullâ* also in Lev, namely chs. 25 and 27, which are concerned with repurchase and redemption. This circumstance is also associated with the prominence that Ruth assumes in the first column. The distribution of *gōʾēl haddām* may be explained by the fact that the figure of the blood avenger has its place in the asylum laws offered in Num 35, Deut 19, and Josh 20. Regarding *gōʾēl*, 10 of 13 occurrences in Isa belong to Deutero-Isa, the first to assign Yahweh the attributes of a *gōʾēl* of his people.

3. (a) The preceding list also demonstrates that legal literature, in particular, used *gʾl* qal/ni. This phenomenon suggests that the verb has a legal provenance, from which it was adapted in the terminology of the cult and in religiotheological language. As will be shown (see 4), the old, legally stamped meaning remains largely active in this adaptation.

On the understanding of the verb in this sense, cf. O. Procksch, "λύω," *TDNT* 4:328–35; J. J. Stamm, *Erlösen und Vergeben im AT* (1940), 27–45; A. Jepsen, "Die Begriffe des 'Erlösens' im AT," FS Hermann 153–63; N. H. Snaith, "Hebrew Root *gʾl*," *ALUOS* 3 (1961/62): 60–67.

(b) The original sense of *gʾl* and its derivatives *gōʾēl* and *geʾullâ* appears unmistakably in Lev 25. This ch., which belongs to H but which developed in a long process (cf. Elliger, HAT 4, 335ff.), contains regulations aimed at the reestablishment of original conditions in Israel, freed from intrusions. Taking account of only the extensive passages, these regulations include the Sabbath year (vv 1–7) and the year of Jubilee, i.e., the restitution of all property to the original owner every 49 years (vv 8–55). In association with the latter of these regulations but probably originally independent from them (cf. Noth, *Lev*, OTL, 189), a passage concerning the *geʾullâ* occurs in both vv 25–28 (vv 29f.) and vv 47–49 (vv 50–55). The *geʾullâ* in the first passage concerns the property *(ʾaḥuzzâ)*, which an Israelite in material need may be forced to sell. The near relative described as *gōʾēl* exercises the *geʾullâ* by "paying the purchase-price . . . and thus getting back the piece of land that had been sold. This was not in order to retain it himself, but only to return it to the original owner" (Noth, op. cit. 189).

The second passage (vv 47–49) deals with an impoverished Israelite who has had to sell himself to a wealthy patron or neighbor. The *gōʾēl* should redeem *(gʾl)* him. Family members who bear this responsibility are named in vv 48f.: brothers, paternal uncles, cousins, any other blood relative. If an Israelite must sell himself not to a foreigner but to a fellow citizen, the law (vv 39–46) does not call for the *geʾullâ* but for the liberation that will follow anyway in the year of Jubilee. The postulated year of Jubilee competes, in this regard, with the old regulation concerning the manumission after six years of the Hebrew who has fallen into debt slavery (Exod 21:2–6; Deut 15:12ff.).

The *g*ᵉʾ*ullâ* as the right or obligation to buy back lost family land or enslaved persons was not limited to Israel. Babylonian law knows it both for land and for persons, in connection with which the Bab. verb *paṭāru* "to loose, redeem" replaces the Hebr. *g*ʾ*l*. *paṭāru* exceeds *g*ʾ*l* in usage, however, by indicating not only repurchase (by the family), but also redemption in general, e.g., of a slave or a captive; cf. *AHw* 849–51.

(1) Repurchase of land: Laws of Eshnunna §39 = *ANET* 163a; R. Haase, *Die keilschriftlichen Rechtssammlungen in dt. Übersetzung* (1963), 14; the same issue in Old Bab. contracts in M. Schorr, *Urkunden des altbab. Zivil- und Prozessrechts*, VAB 5 (1913), 119. (2) Redemption of persons who have been sold: of free persons see Mid. Assyr. Laws §48 = *ANET* 184b; Haase, op. cit. 107; of slaves see Code of Hammurapi §§119, 281 = *ANET* 171a, 177b; Haase, op. cit. 37, 55; this is also the subject of letter no. 46 in R. Frankena, *Briefe aus dem British Museum*, AbB 2 (1966). (3) The redemption of a captive soldier in the Code of Hammurapi §32 = *ANET* 167b; Haase, op. cit. 27.

The uniqueness of the Israelite *g*ᵉʾ*ullâ* in contrast to the Bab. lies in its relationship to Yahweh. Because the land belongs to him and the Israelites have received it from him as a loan, it may not be sold absolutely and should be subject to the right of repurchase (Lev 25:23f.). And, according to Lev 25:42, an Israelite should not continue to be a slave, because he/she is a descendant of those whom Yahweh freed from Egypt.

(c) The OT finds the *g*ᵉʾ*ullâ* effective in practical life only with respect to land ownership and blood vengeance, i.e., respect for a dead fellow clan member, probably because of the right to freedom after six years that a member of the covenant people enjoys. Jeremiah exercises the *g*ᵉʾ*ullâ* for property (Jer 32:6–15). He acquires land in Anathoth, which his cousin must sell for unspecified reasons. This transaction is a case, then, not of repurchase but of prepurchase; cf. Rudolph, HAT 12, 209. Similarly, according to Ruth 4, Boaz acquires a plot of ground belonging to the deceased Elimelek through the exercise of the *g*ᵉʾ*ullâ*. The wording in Ruth 4:3, "the field that Naomi has sold," seems to presuppose that Boaz repurchases for the family something that has already been transferred to outside hands. Yet the ptcp. *mōk*ᵉ*râ*, "is about to sell," has often been read instead of the pf. *māk*ᵉ*râ*, and, besides, the unemended text also permits the translation "Naomi wants to sell"; cf. Gerleman, BK 18, 35. One cannot, therefore, determine with certainty whether prepurchase or repurchase is described.

(d) Now, according to Ruth 4, Boaz also acquires Ruth, the widow of Mahlon, together with the field "in order to reestablish the name of the deceased on his property" (4:5, 10). Boaz enters into a levirate or in-law marriage with Ruth, who represents Naomi here. Because this is the only case of this nature in the OT, one may not be certain whether the levirate is one of the obligations of the *gō*ʾ*ēl*. In view of the essential relationship of *g*ᵉʾ*ullâ* and levirate—both seek to keep the family whole—it is entirely probable.

The designation of the one who exercised blood vengeance as *gō'ēl haddām* (→ *dām*) indicates that blood vengeance was surely a component of *g^e'ullâ*. He is accordingly the one who seeks (→ *bqš* pi., → *drš*) the shed blood and the murderer to whom it clings and returns it to the community to which it belongs. "This 'return' presupposes that the murdered is indeed, completely dead, but not his blood; rather, it still conceals secret life" (K. Koch, *VT* 12 [1962]: 410).

The broad range of the *gō'ēl*'s responsibilities are indicated by repurchase, blood vengeance, and, in the unique case, levirate. He was the nearest relative responsible in family matters (so Procksch, *TDNT* 4:330.

At times the full meaning of the word could diminish, so that *gō'ēl* would then only mean something like "relative," as in 1 Kgs 16:11; CD 14:16; and probably also Num 5:8.

(e) According to the preceding, *g'l* and its derivatives prove to be family law terms. Koch (op. cit. 410) renders its sense well with "to redeem that which belongs to the family from outside jurisdiction." This rendering encompasses the salvific character of the term, extending beyond the purely legal; the reacquisition of lost family belongings brings liberation and salvation, the renewal of an earlier order, the reestablishment of a lost totality; cf. also Jepsen, op. cit. (see 3a), 159.

4. (a) The salvific element, which always applies to the old legal term, blossoms in religiotheological language. *g'l* here does not accidentally parallel → *yš'* hi. "to save" (Isa 49:26; 60:16; 63:9; Psa 72:13f.; 106:10), → *nṣl* hi. "to save" (Exod 6:6), → *'zr* "to help" (Isa 41:14), → *ḥyh* pi. "to make well" (Psa 119:154), and → *nḥm* pi. "to comfort" (Isa 52:9). The verb → *pdh* "to free, redeem, liberate" stands nearest to *g'l* in this regard. In some of its uses, however, this verb is a neutral commercial law term, which does not include the notion of the reacquisition of that which has been lost (cf. Stamm, op. cit. 7ff.; slightly different, Jepsen, op. cit. 154f.). Although the difference between the two verbs was probably always apparent (see 4f), they still approximate one another, as the usage in Lev 27 (see immediately below) and their par. occurrence show (Hos 13:14; Isa 51:10f. = 35:9f.; Jer 31:11; Psa 69:19).

(b) In religious language, the use in cultic terminology stands alone. It is present in Lev 27, a ch. concerning voluntary gifts and the existent or nonexistent possibility of redeeming them by monetary payment.

g'l is the verb used predominantly in this respect (vv 13, 15, 19f., 28, 31, 33). *pdh*, which occurs together with *g'l* again in v 27 in reference to the redemption of the firstborn of unclean animals, stands alone in v 29, in the prohibition against redeeming a person dedicated to the ban.

Offerings whose redemption is treated in Lev 27 are primarily originally the property of the cult practitioner that he reacquires by payment of the prescribed amount, if permitted. The preference for *g'l* should be understood in this manner. One could determine the reason v 29 uses the neutral *pdh*, foreign to the notion of reacquisition, only if one could establish what this late text means by "ban." If it were, as in earlier times, spoils of war, then *pdh* would indicate that the redeemer had no prior claim to it. If "ban" in v 29 also means Israelite property (as in v 28), which could or must be surrendered, then *pdh* would be used in a broader sense no longer strictly distinguishable from *g*ʾ*l*. This is also true for v 27, where *g*ʾ*l* and *pdh* occur together. The *g*ʾ*l* of the text also reflects an expanded usage in reference to the redemption of a portion of the tithe (v 31) that belongs to Yahweh without question and is removed from any human claim.

(c) If one arranges occurrences from the religiotheological realm according to the groups of people who experience liberation, and considers the time period involved, the following picture emerges:

(1) Deliverance of the *individual:*

(a) In the past: Gen 48:16; Psa 107:2; Lam 3:58;

(b) In the present: Psa 19:15; 69:19; 72:14; 103:4; 119:154; Job 3:5; 19:25; Prov 23:11;

(2) Deliverance of the *people:*

(a) In the past: Exod 6:6; 15:13; Psa 74:2; 77:16; 78:35; 106:10; Isa 51:10; 63:9;

(b) In the future: Hos 13:14; Isa 35:9f.; Jer 31:11; 50:34; Mic 4:10.

Additional Deutero- and Trito-Isa texts: *g*ʾ*l* Isa 43:1; 44:22f.; 48:20; 52:3, 9; 62:12; *gō*ʾ*ēl* Isa 41:14; 43:14; 44:6, 24; 47:4; 48:17; 49:7, 26; 54:5, 8; 59:20; 60:16; 63:16.

This arrangement, which I have used earlier (Stamm, op. cit. 7ff.), has the advantage of extreme clarity, but the disadvantage of too rigid schematization, which forces one to emphasize, more than is appropriate for Hebr., differences in tense and the distinction between individual and community. For these reasons, I now prefer, with Jepsen (op. cit. 158ff.), to discuss first occurrences that directly involve the basic meaning of *g*ʾ*l* and then those in which it is less applicable.

(d) Prov 23:10f. and Jer 50:34 apply to Yahweh the status of the *gō*ʾ*ēl* in a family as the helper of the relative fallen into distress, calling him *gō*ʾ*ēl* as protector of the weak over aginst a mighty opponent. Job (Job 19:25) calls God, the last guardian of his right, his *gō*ʾ*ēl*, which could be paraphrased in Eng. with a term such as "lawyer" or "legal aid." Disappointed by his friends and robbed by God of his rights (Job 19:7ff.; 27:2, 5), Job nevertheless falls back on God, because he is not totally unaware of God's true nature, intent upon delivering (cf. Job 16:18–21).

In accord with a common ancient Near Eastern ideal, the constitutive activities of the *gō*ʾ*ēl* are esp. expected of the king (Psa 72:13f.), who "saves (*y*š^c^ hi.) the life of the poor and redeems their life from oppression and violence (*yig*ʾ*al napšām*)." *g*ʾ*l* here certainly includes, among other concepts, legal aid through which the king reestablishes the rights deprived from the subject who seeks his assistance. With regard to Yahweh, this is also the intention of the request, "Conduct my case and redeem me; preserve my life according to your word" (Psa 119:154), and of the confession, "You, Yahweh, have led the fight for my life, you have saved my life (*gā*ʾ*altā ḥayyāy*)" (Lam 3:58), or, as *g*ʾ*l* can also be translated here, "have reestablished my life" (so Jepsen, op. cit. 160).

One of Job's statements cursing the day of his birth (3:5) preserves the concrete sense of *g*ʾ*l* "to ransom lost property": "darkness and gloom should demand payment of it," i.e., the powers of chaos, which are older than the light, should exercise their old right to that day.

(e) *g*ʾ*l* refers to the liberation from Egypt in the passages mentioned previously (see 4c; Exod 6:6; 15:13; Psa 74:2; 77:16; 78:35; 106:10; Isa 63:9), which recall other acts of deliverance in addition to the initial act. In Isa 51:10 the pass. ptcp. *g*ᵉʾ*ûlîm* indicates those saved at the Reed Sea. But the *p*ᵉ*dûyê yhwh* "those redeemed by Yahweh" in v 11 are those who experience the second, eschatological exodus (on problems concerning the content of the text, cf. Westermann, *Isa 40–66*, OTL, 243). All of these texts, even Exod 15:13, could be dated from the exilic to the post-exilic periods. I call attention to this point for the following reasons: in older times the verbs *yṣ*ʾ hi. "to lead out" and ʿ*lh* hi. "to bring up" were most common for the deliverance from Egypt (cf. Stamm, op. cit. 14f., and P. Humbert, *TZ* 18 [1962]: 357–61). They were joined in Deut (13:6; 15:15; 21:8; 24:18; 7:8; 9:26) by *pdh* "to redeem, liberate." The corresponding use of *g*ʾ*l* depends upon this innovation. This use does not necessarily mean, however, that *g*ʾ*l* had lost its specific sense "to regain something lost" and had become entirely conformed to *pdh*. Although this amalgamation is possible (cf. above 4a, c), one may expect that late documents that associate *g*ʾ*l* with the liberation from Egypt all presuppose the patriarchal tradition, even if they do not mention it. Thus one could also include the patriarchal period in the usage of *g*ʾ*l*, and one could understand the exodus from Egypt as the return of the enslaved to their legitimate lord, as a reestablishment of their freedom.

(f) Deutero-Isaiah proclaimed the return of the Babylonian exiles as a second exodus surpassing the first (cf. von Rad, *Theol.* 2:239), and like the first, the second will be a redemption. Apparently, Deutero-Isaiah appropriated the term introduced by Deut, except he used *g*ʾ*l* rather than *pdh*. The root *pdh* and its derivative *p*ᵉ*dût* "redemption" is certainly not unknown to him, but its two occurrences are rather insignificant (Isa 51:11 = 35:10; 50:2). Consequently, the weight that *g*ʾ*l* must have had for the prophet becomes only the more apparent.

The term appears often in Deutero-Isa (cf. 4c), but variations in usage are limited. Beside the dominant qal, only one unique ni. occurs, in a passage of disputed authenticity, Isa 52:3, "Since you were sold for nought, you will be redeemed without price" (cf. Westermann, *Isa 40–66*, OTL, 247). In addition, this is the only occurrence of an impf. form of the verb. Apart from the similarly infrequent pass. ptcp. *g*ᵉʾ*ûlîm* "the redeemed" (Isa 51:10), only the pf. and the act. ptcp. of the qal occur. The former has its place, on the one hand, in the promise of salvation (Isa 43:1; 44:22) and, on the other, in the eschatological song of praise (44:23; 48:20; 52:9; cf. C. Westermann, *Forschung am AT* [1964], 157ff.). Both genres discuss the immediately imminent, but still future, salvation in the so-called prophetic pf. as though it had already transpired. While the prophet addresses the promise of salvation to the exiled Jews, the worldwide circle of addressees answers the message that reaches them in the song of praise.

As seen by Deutero-Isaiah, this liberation or redemption has the most comprehensive dimension, applying not only to the exiles in Babylon (48:20) and to the wider Diaspora (43:5f.; 49:12, 18, 22f.), but also to the nations. As witnesses of the emancipation by which Yahweh reconstitutes his people, the nations themselves will recognize Yahweh for who he is (41:4f.; 45:6; 49:26; 52:10) and will become aware of the impotence of their idols (41:11; 42:17; 45:24). In view of all this, what is the significance of the prophet's preference for *g'l* as a term for redemption? (On the other verbs of salvation he uses, see 4a.) The significance is most clearly seen in his designation of Yahweh as *gō'ēl*, thus becoming the first to apply this attribute to him (for texts see 4c).

He adopts the epithet *q^edôš yiśrā'ēl* "the holy one of Israel" introduced by First Isaiah and repeatedly adds the new term *gō'ēl* (41:14; 43:14; 48:17; 49:7). The others majestic titles combined with *gō'ēl* are: "King of Israel" (44:6), "the mighty one of Jacob" (49:26), and "maker" (*yōṣēr:* 44:24, "Thus says Yahweh, your redeemer, your maker from the womb onward"). Here terms for making and redeeming have almost become synonymous. They "describe a sweep, a history, God's history with his chosen people" (so Westermann, *Isa 40–66*, OTL, 155). By not only comparing Yahweh's saving activity with the act of an earthly redeemer, but even equating the two through the use of the word *gō'ēl*, Deutero-Isaiah anchors the end of Israel's history in its beginning. Such is the call of Abraham, whose descendants the exiled Jews are and continue to be (41:8; 51:2). Even if their ancestors and they themselves were sold and rejected since the early days because of their apostasy, this separation is not final because there is no bill of divorcement (50:1). Because no such separation exists, the prophet can use the verb *g'l* in order to attest at the same time that no separation exists. For as *gō'ēl* Yahweh does not purchase strange goods; rather, he regains that which has always—since the time of Abraham—belonged to him. Yahweh lays claim to his ancient right to Israel; he actualizes a claim that is his because he has created and chosen this people and he is its king. Only *g'l* shaped by family law and not the neutral *pdh* could serve as a vehicle for this message.

g'l seems to be interpreted in a more narrowly commercial sense in the salvation oracle in Isa 43:1–7, indeed, such that Yahweh offers other lands as a ransom for Israel, i.e., probably that he grants them to the world ruler Cyrus as reparation for the soon-to-be-freed Israel. This reading presumes that one may appeal to vv 3 and 4 in addition to v 2 in order to elucidate v 1, a presumption that is uncertain (cf. Jepsen, op. cit. 161). Even if this assumption is appropriate, the fact remains that in 45:13 the prophet has Cyrus fulfill his mission "without purchase price and without gift."

(g) Following Deutero-Isaiah, Trito-Isaiah also calls Yahweh *gō'ēl*. In Isa 59:20 and 60:16 this designation also occurs in an eschatological context; in 63:16 *gō'ēl* parallels *'āb* "father," but in a broader sense encompassing deliverance from Egypt, salvation in the present, and salvation in the future.

The confession in Psa 19:15 ("Yahweh, my rock and my redeemer") expresses confidence in Yahweh's future protection, and the same is true for the passage already mentioned (4d), Jer 50:34, in view of the deliverance of those enslaved by Babel: "Indeed, their redeemer is strong, Yahweh of hosts is his name."

As we saw (4e), *g^e'ûlîm* in Isa 51:10 means those saved by Yahweh at the Reed Sea. Trito-Isaiah appropriated the expression (62:12), although for him it refers to the members of the people brought home from the Diaspora (cf. v 11). The author of the apocalypse Isa 34–35, imitating Deutero-Isa, uses the word *g*[e]*'ûlîm* in 35:9b, 10a, but once again the redeemed are those who return from the Diaspora on wondrously prepared streets: "There the redeemed will go, the redeemed of Yahweh will return thereon." Return always means the reconstitution of a lost totality and thus is essential to the *g'l* concept. Hence one may say that the old sense of the verb is still alive in the passages just mentioned, perhaps no longer in all its legal connotations, but still such that an essential aspect of *g'l*—the liberating reconstitution of the original—finds unmistakable expression.

(h) According to Jepsen (op. cit. 161), this is no longer the case in the following 8 passages: Gen 48:16; Hos 13:14; Mic 4:10; Jer 31:11; Psa 69:19; 103:4; 106:10; 107:2. With the single exception of Psa 69:19, these passages always associate *g'l* with the prep. *min* "from" and parallel it three times to *pdh* (Hos 13:14; Jer 31:11; Psa 69:19). Both usages indicate that *g'l* here means less the reconstitution of an earlier status than liberation from the might of an opposing power, manifest as a political enemy (Mic 4:10; Jer 31:11; Psa 106:10), as a personal opponent (Psa 69:19), as a situation of need (Gen 48:16; Psa 107:2), as ill-fate (Hos 13:14), and as fatal illness (Psa 103:4).

Another brief word is necessary regarding two of these texts, Psa 106:10 and Gen 48:16. Psa 106:10, "And he redeemed them from the power of the enemy," concerns, according to the context, deliverance from Egypt, so that the passage has already been treated (4e). Because it offers *g'l min* "to redeem from," however, it belongs at the same time in the series of texts above. In Gen 48:16, in the blessing of the dying Jacob (according to E), the words *hammal'āk haggō'ēl 'ōtî mikkol-rā'* should be rendered with Jepsen (op. cit. 161): "The angel, which has protected me from all evil." This is a derived meaning for *g'l*, not the original, as Johnson thinks (cf. 1).

(i) The expanded usage of *g'l* just mentioned also applies to the PN *yig'āl* (see 1 and 2) "he (Yahweh) has redeemed," i.e., he has redeemed the child so named from evil, esp. from sickness. This name should be understood in analogy to the Bab. name *ipṭur-sin* "Sin (the moon god) has undone (the evil)," formed with the verb *paṭāru* (see 3b; cf. Stamm, *AN* 191).

5. In post-OT literature, *g'l* continues to have a threefold usage: in reference to God's saving intervention in general, to the liberation from Egypt, and to the (eschatological) redemption of Israel (cf. *TDNT* 4:350; 7:987f.).

The LXX renders *g'l* either with *lytrousthai* or *rhyesthai* (cf. *TDNT* 4:332; 6:999), but not by *sōzein.*

Exceptions are Isa 44:23, where LXX[A] has *elytrōsato* instead of *ēleēsen,* and Jer 31:11 (LXX 38:11), where the second verb in the parallelism *pdh//g'l* is represented by a form of *exaireisthai (exeilato).*

The LXX offers *ho anchisteuōn* "the one who exercises the right of the nearest relative" for *gō'ēl haddām* "blood avenger." The related subst. *anchisteus/anchisteutēs* "nearest relative" corresponds to the Hebr. *gō'ēl* in 2 Sam 14:11; 1 Kgs 16:11, and the verb *anchisteuein* is used for *g'l* in Ruth. The abstract *g*[e]*'ullâ* "the right (or the duty) of redemption" in Ruth 4:6f. = *anchisteia;* Lev 25:29, 48 = *lytrōsis* (so also Isa 63:4 for *g*[e]*'ûlîm*); Lev 25:31f. = *lytrōtai* "(houses) which are redeemable"; Lev 25:24, 26, 51f. = *lytra.* The renderings in Jer 32:7f.; Ezek 11:15; Job 3:5 are particularly noteworthy.

The NT used both of LXX's verbs, although they lose a great deal of significance in contrast to *sōzein*. The latter occurs 106x, *lytrousthai* only 3x, and *rhyesthai* 16x. The use of *lytrousthai* is supplemented, however, by the derivatives *lytron, lytrōsis*, etc., which will not be considered here (cf. F. Büchsel, "λύω," *TDNT* 4:335–56).

NT usage of *lytrousthai* and *rhyesthai* exhibits a deficiency in comparison to the OT in that the redemption from Egypt is not treated, and a surplus in that Jesus is also the author of salvation in addition to God. This situation is true for all three uses of *lytrousthai* (Luke 24:21; Titus 2:14; 1 Pet 1:18). Their subject is the eschatological salvation brought about by Jesus.

rhyesthai also describes eschatological salvation; it is attributed to God (Matt 6:13; Rom 11:26; Col 1:13) and to Jesus (1 Thess 1:10). Following the OT use of *g'l, rhyesthai* also refers to salvation from the might of opposing powers. These powers include: death (Matt 27:43; Rom 7:24; 2 Cor 1:10), enemies (Luke 1:74; cf. 2 Tim 4:17), disobedient or perverse and evil people (Rom 15:31; 2 Thess 3:2), temptations (2 Pet 2:9), and oppression or persecution (2 Tim 3:11; 4:18). The theme of salvation in the primeval period, so important in the OT, is represented only by the reference to the deliverance of Lot (2 Pet 2:7).

J. J. Stamm

גבה *gbh* to be high

S 1361; BDB 146b; *HALOT* 1:170a; *TDOT* 2:356–60; *TWOT* 305; *NIDOTTE* 1467

---

1. The root *gbh* (with consonantal *h*) "to be high" occurs almost exclusively in Hebr.

gbh "height" in the Siloam tunnel inscription should be mentioned as an extrabibl. occurrence: "And the height of the rock above the head(s) of the miners was 100 cubits" (*ANET* 321b; *KAI* no. 189.5f.).

Aram. uses → *rûm*. The only Aram. occurrences of *gbh* independent of the OT are Aḥ. 107 (Cowley, 216, 233, "A king is like the merciful[?]: even his voice is high") and the Pahlavi ideogram *gbh* (*HAL* 163b).

Cf. also Arab. *jabhat* "forehead"; on the relationship of the roots *gbh* and *gbḥ* "to be bare," cf. P. Fronzaroli, *AANLR* 8/19 (1964): 165, 167 ("rideterminazione espressiva").

In addition to the qal "to be high, elevated, haughty" and hi. "to raise" of the root, the derivatives *gābōah* "high, elevated, haughty," *gōbah* "height, growth, majesty, arrogance," and *gabhût* "arrogance" also occur in the OT.

The adj. occurs 4x in the cs. state in the form *g^ebah*, derived either from **gābēah* or better from *gābōah* (cf. W. Baumgartner, FS Eissfeldt [1958], 31), as well as in the form *g^ebōah* in 1 Sam 16:7 (listed as an inf. in Mandl. 245c).

2. Most of the 94 occurrences of the root (qal 24x, hi. 10x, *gābōah* 41x, *gōbah* 17x, *gabhût* 2x) appear in the Prophets (Ezek 22x, Isa 14x, Jer 7x), in the Psa (7x), and in wisdom literature (Job 8x, Eccl 5x, Prov 4x).

3. All meanings of *gbh* and its derivatives are closely grouped around the basic meaning "to be high."

(a) The qal indicates the growth of a tree (Ezek 31:10, 14), or a branch (Ezek 19:11), the elevation of the heaven above the earth (Isa 55:9 *gbh min* = "to tower above"; Psa 103:11), or of the clouds above people (Job 35:5); Saul towers above all the people by a head (1 Sam 10:23).

A causative hi. meaning "to raise" occurs in 2 Chron 33:14 (wall); Ezek 17:24 (to let a tree grow tall); Jer 49:16 (the nest; cf. Obad 4); Job 5:7 (to fly high, in conjunction with *ʿûp* "to fly"; Job 39:27 without *ʿûp*); Psa 113:5 (to dwell on high, spoken by God); Prov 17:19 (door; according to Gemser, HAT 16, 73, and Ringgren, ATD 16/1, 74, the mouth is meant; cf. Mic 7:5; Psa 141:3; the saying would then be directed at bragging).

The adj. *gābōah* describes objects such as high mountains (Gen 7:19; Isa 30:25; 40:9; 57:7; Jer 3:6; Ezek 17:22; Psa 104:18), hills (1 Kgs 14:23; 2 Kgs 17:10; Jer 2:20; 17:2), gates (Jer 51:58), battlements (Zeph 1:16), towers (Isa 2:15), gallows (Esth 5:14; 7:9), horns (Dan 8:3), trees (Isa 10:33; Ezek 17:24; cf. 31:3 in conjunction with *qômâ:* "tall growth"). It refers to tall people (1 Sam 9:2; 16:7).

The subst. *gōbah* indicates the height, the stature of the trees (Ezek 31:10, 14; Amos 2:9); it serves as a term for measurement (cf. Ezek 40:42, the height of a table, alongside *ʾōrek* "length" and *rōḥab* "breadth"; 41:22 txt em, the height of an altar; 2 Chron 3:4, the height of the hall; 1 Sam 17:4, the height of Goliath; cf. also the Siloam tunnel inscription; see 1). Ezek 41:8 may well be read *gabbâ* "raised pavement" with *BHS* instead of *gōbah;* cf. Gk. *gabbatha* John 19:13; Zimmerli, *Ezek*, Herm, 2:371f.

The more common word for "height" in measurements is *qômâ* (→ *qûm;* Exod 25:10, 23, etc.; 1 Kgs 6–7; 2 Kgs 25:17, etc.; cf. Rudolph, HAT 21, 207, on 2 Chron 4:1).

(b) The following fig. meanings with positive or negative connotations also derive directly from the basic meaning.

Eccl 5:7, "For a loftier one watches over the lofty, and an even loftier one over them" refers to "superiors" (Zimmerli, ATD 16/1, 191: "in view of the multiple layers of the structure of civil offices or of the court, one always observes and spies on the other and seeks to supplant him").

Isa 52:13, which concerns the future exaltation of the servant of God in sharp contrast to his humility (v 14), *gbh* denotes the majesty of God's servant (cf. the par. terms → *rûm* and → *nśʾ*).

In a negative sense *gbh* means the haughty, arrogant attitude of people. In addition to roots that appear individually (cf. Isa 3:16; Ezek 16:50), the following fixed phrases may be mentioned here:

gbh lēb "the heart is proud" (*HAL* 163b: "to have high aspirations"; Ezek 28:2, 5, 17; Psa 131:1; Prov 18:12; 2 Chron 26:16; 32:25). 2 Chron 17:6 is the only passage that discusses the "pride of the heart" in a positive sense ("high-spirited" may be a good translation): Jehoshaphat is "high-spirited" in following Yahweh and therefore removes the high places and Asherahs from Judah;

g^e^bah lēb "high-spirited" (Prov 16:5); *g^e^bah rûaḥ* "haughty" (Prov 7:8); *g^e^bah ᶜênayim* "proud-eyed, haughty, condescending" (Psa 101:5; cf. here the par. term *r^e^ḥab lēbāb* "the broad, arrogant heart," as well as Isa 2:11 *ᶜênê gabhût* "the haughty eyes" and Psa 131:1 *lōᵓ rāmû ᶜênay* "my eyes do not look haughtily");

gōbah lēb "haughtiness" (2 Chron 32:26; cf. Ezek 31:10); *gōbah rûaḥ* "haughtiness" (Prov 16:18); *gōbah ᵓap* "arrogance" (Psa 10:4);

dbr pi. *g^e^bōhâ* "to speak loftily, haughtily" (1 Sam 2:3).

Esp. noteworthy par. terms that appear in the context of *gbh* are the roots → *gᵓh*, → *nśᵓ* and → *rûm* (cf. Isa 2:11f., 17; Jer 13:15, 17; 48:29; Prov 16:18, etc.), *ᶜātāq* "audacity" (1 Sam 2:3), and as antonyms the roots *špl* "to be lowly, humble" (Isa 2:11; 5:15; cf. 10:33; Ezek 17:24; 21:31), *šḥḥ* "to bend down" (Isa 2:17; cf. 5:15), *knᶜ* "to humble oneself" (2 Chron 32:26). It becomes apparent that *gbh* is closely related to *gᵓh, nśᵓ* and *rûm* in the semantic field of arrogance; a distinction in meaning is hardly perceptible; the terms often seem interchangeable.

(c) Wisdom warns against a haughty, arrogant (impudent) attitude in Prov 16:18 (here together with → *gᵓh*); 18:12; Eccl 7:8 (a *ṭôb-* saying with a contrasted *ᵓerek rûaḥ* "patient"); such an arrogant individual is an abomination to God and will not go unpunished, Prov 16:5 (cf. Psa 131:1, the declaration of loyalty of the *ṣaddîq*).

4. The preceding gives rise to the theological usage.

(a) Wisdom is at first concerned more with observations of life than theological notions (see Prov 16:18), although Prov 16:5 admittedly already emphasizes the relationship to God (cf. here the king's vow of loyalty, Psa 101, where the king, as representative of Yahweh's judicial authority in Israel [Kraus, *Psa*, CC, 2:279], expressly addresses himself in v 5 to the *g^e^bah ᶜênayim*). But the following passages characterize human arrogance as the haughty behavior of ignoring God (Jer 13:15; 1 Sam 2:3; Psa 10:4), as the proud attitude of the one who opposes God (Ezek 28:2). Therefore, the exalted will be humbled and the humble exalted (Ezek 21:31; cf. Job 36:6f.; in a metaphor, Ezek 17:22–24); therefore, judgment comes over the *gbh* of the individual (cf. Zeph 3:11f.: the new behavior here is that of the *dal* and *ᶜānî*, the "lowly" and the "humble"; in Jer 49:16 the aerie is a picture of the haughty pride of Edom in its unconquerable mountain fortresses; Ezek 31:10). In Isa 2:12–17 (→ *gᵓh* 4a) the day of Yahweh comes as judgment upon all the exalted and haughty (cf. in 2:12 the roots *gᵓh, rûm, nśᵓ* and, according to the LXX, *gbh* in par.; on 2:17, cf. 2:11; 5:15 is probably a gloss in Isa diction: *ᶜênê g^e^bōhîm* "the eyes of the arrogant"; for the details of the traditiohistorical backgrounds of this passage, see Wildberger, *Isa 1–12*, CC, 111–15).

(b) The theological use of the root in a few passages to indicate God's majesty arises from the meaning "to be exalted, majestic" (cf. Job 40:10, *gōbah* alongside *gāᵓôn* as an attribute of God's dominion), primarily with a view to God's infinite transcendence and incomparability as the absolutely superior (Psa 113:5; cf. Job 22:12; Psa 103:11; Isa 55:9; Job 11:8), whose glance down becomes a helpful act, a bending down to the helpless and poor (cf. Psa 113:5f.).

5. The LXX employs various terms to translate *gbh*, most often *hypsos* and *hypsēlos*, but never *hybris*. The OT usage of *gbh* survives at Qumran (cf. CD 1:15; 2:19), in early Judaism (cf. StrB 2:101ff.), and in the NT (cf. G. Bertram, "ὕψος," *TDNT* 8:602–20).

H.-P. Stähli

גבר *gbr* **to be superior**

S 1396; BDB 149b; *HALOT* 1:175a; *TDOT* 2:367–82; *TWOT* 310; *NIDOTTE* 1504

---

1. The root *gbr* "to be superior, strong" occurs in all branches of the Sem. languages; the subst. in the meaning "man" is limited to NWSem. (P. Fronzaroli, *AANLR* 8/19 [1964]: 245).

Akk. exhibits only the verb *gapāru* "to be superior" and the corresponding verbal adj. *gapru* "superior" (*AHw* 281; on the *b/p* shift, cf. the summary in M. Weippert, *Settlement of the Israelite Tribes in Palestine* [1971], 75–79).

Phoen. demonstrates only the subst. *gbr* "man" (*KAI* no. 24.8; no. 30.2), in Neo-Pun. perhaps *gbrt* "mighty deed(s?)" (*KAI* no. 145.6); similarly, the Mesha stele attests only the substs. *gbr* "man" and *gbrt* "woman" (*KAI* no. 181.16). Ug. exhibits the root only in PNs (cf. Gröndahl 126).

The root plays a large role in Aram., where in addition to the verb (*KAI* no. 223B.19; Fitzmyer, *Sef.* 82f.), the subst. *gbr* "man" (often in the sense of "anyone"), in particular, occurs in a broad distribution since Old Aram. (*DISO* 47; *LS* 102f.; cf. also *gbrth* "his might" in *KAI* no. 214.32).

Eth. *gbr* developed into the general verb "to do, work" (Dillmann 1159–67).

In addition to the qal, the verb occurs in pi., hi., and hitp.; nom. derivatives are *geber*, *g^ebûrâ*, *g^ebîr*, *g^ebîrâ*, and *gibbôr*, in Bibl. Aram. *g^ebar*, *g^ebûrâ*, and *gibbar*.

The PNs *geber* (1 Kgs 4:13–19), a short form of *gabrîʾēl* (Dan 8:16; 9:21; *IP* 190: "God has proven himself strong"; cf. C.-H. Hunzinger, *RGG* 2:1185), and the place-names *gibbar* (Ezra 2:20) and *ʿeṣyôn geber* (*BHH* 1:461f.) must be included.

2. The verb *gbr* occurs 25x in the OT, 17x qal, 3x pi., 2x hi., and 3x hitp. The figures for the nouns are: *geber* 66x (Job 15x, Psa 10x, Jer 9x, Prov 8x), *g^ebûrâ* 61x (Psa 17x, 2 Kgs and Isa 7x), *g^ebîr* 2x (Gen 27:29, 37), *g^ebîrâ* 15x, *gibbôr* 159x (1 Chron 31x, Jer 19x, 2 Sam 16x, Psa and 2 Chron 12x).

In Bibl. Aram. *g^ebar* appears 21x (Dan 17x), *gibbar* 1x (Dan 3:20), and *g^ebûrâ* 2x (Dan 2:20, 23). In all, the word group occurs 352x in the OT in a rather broad pattern of distribution.

3. (a) All semantic nuances of the qal are related to the basic meaning "to be/become superior, strong."

gbr can be used abs., with a comparative *min* (Gen 49:26; 2 Sam 1:23), *ʿal* (2 Sam 11:23) or *b^e* (1 Chron 5:2). Thus Gen 7:18–20, 24 uses *gbr* 4x to express the rising of the flood waters (7:18 par. *rbh* "to become many"). In battle *gbr* signifies "maintaining the upper hand" over the enemy (Exod 17:11; 2 Sam 11:23; Lam 1:16).

The pi. verb should be translated "to make strong" (Zech 10:6, 12; Eccl 10:10 in conjunction with *ḥ^a^yālîm* "to expend might"), the hi. as an inner-trans. (internal) "to show oneself strong" (Psa 12:5; Dan 9:27 txt?), and the hitp. "to show oneself superior" (Isa 42:13; "to behave proudly" Job 15:25; 36:9).

The verb has no regular antonym; the flood narrative uses the verbs *škk* "to recede" (Gen 8:1) and *ḥsr* "to diminish" (8:3, 5) as opposites of *gbr.*

(b) The basic meaning of *g^e^bûrâ*, closely related to the verb, is "superiority, strength, might."

Very often it is "military might" (Isa 3:25; Jer 49:35; Ezek 32:29f.; in combination with *milḥāmâ* "battle": 2 Kgs 18:20 = Isa 36:5; Isa 28:6). The Dtr framework uses *g^e^bûrâ* in the more general sense of "ability" (always in association with *ʿśh* "to do": 1 Kgs 15:23; 16:5, 27; 22:46, etc.). *g^e^bûrâ* can mean the "strength of the stallions" (Psa 147:10; Job 39:19) or fig. the "splendor" of the sun (Judg 5:31).

It has no consistent antonym in the semantic field.

(c) The segholate form *geber* (see H. Kosmala, "The Term *geber* in the OT and in the Scrolls," *SVT* 17 [1969]: 159–69) is primarily attested in later OT literature (Psa, Job, Prov). The basic meaning of the root is curtailed here; *geber* is used as a rule just like → *ʾîš* "man."

Thus *geber* can parallel *ʾîš* (Jer 22:30; Mic 2:2), *zākār* "man" (Jer 30:6), *ʾ^e^nôš* "person" (Job 4:17), or *ʾādām* "person" (Job 14:10). *ʾiššâ* "woman" (Deut 22:5; in the series "men-women-children," Jer 43:6; cf. 44:20) and *n^e^qēbâ* "woman" (Jer 31:22; cf. Rudolph, HAT 12, 198f.) occur as antonyms. Like *ʾîš* (here the distance from the basic meaning of the root becomes esp. apparent), *geber* can even mean "male child" (Job 3:3) or be generalized to the pron. "anyone" (Joel 2:8, etc.; cf. the usage in Aram.; see 1).

(d) The intensive form *gibbôr* conforms closely to the meaning of the root.

gibbôr can be translated adj. as "strong" (1 Sam 14:52 "strong man" alongside *ben-ḥayil;* cf. 2 Sam 17:10; Psa 112:2 progeny; Gen 10:9 "mighty hunter"; Prov 30:30 uses *gibbôr* of an animal).

Accordingly, the basic meaning of the subst. is "strength"; par. terms include *ʾaddîr* "powerful one" (Judg 5:13), *ḥāzāq* "strong one" (Amos 2:14), and *ʿārîṣ* "mighty one" (Isa 49:25). *gibbôr* is the "strong (man)" in contrast to the (weak) woman (Josh 1:14; cf. Jer 48:41; 49:22; 51:30) or simply to the weak (Joel 4:10 *ḥallāš*) or the stumbling (1 Sam 2:4 *kšl*); as a development of this basic meaning *gibbôr* should be translated "tyrant" in Gen 10:8 = 1 Chron 1:10. Wisdom literature can contrast the strong with the wise (Prov 21:22; cf. Jer 9:22).

In most cases *gibbôr* is the "war hero," sometimes in the common phrase *gibbôr ḥayil* (or the pl.). This phrase occurs 4x in Josh and 27x in Chron, for example. In particular, the par. terms that appear in the semantic field unambiguously indicate a military function for the *gibbôr* (phrases such as *ʾîš milḥāmâ*, or the like: Josh 6:2f.; 10:7; 2 Sam 17:8; 2 Kgs 24:16; Isa 3:2; 42:13; Ezek 39:20; Joel 2:7; 4:9; 2 Chron 17:13; *ʾanšê haḥayil:* 2 Kgs 24:16; Isa 5:22; Jer 48:14; Nah 2:4). *gibbôr ḥayil* in a more general sense, however, can also simply mean "capable man" (1 Sam 9:1; 1 Kgs 11:28; 2 Kgs 5:1; 1 Chron 9:13; 26:6). Regarding the *gibbôrê ḥayil* as the social class of the (land-owning) militia, cf. the (somewhat divergent) positions of E. Würthwein, *Der ᶜamm haᵓarez* (1936), 15, 28; J. van der Ploeg, *RB* 50 (1941): 120–25; id., *OTS* 9 (1951): 58f.; de Vaux 1:70; Noth, BK 9, 257.

(e) Closely dependent on the basic meaning of the root, *gᵉbîr* can mean the "lord, master" (only Gen 27:29, 37), before whom servants (v 37) bow (v 29).

The fem. form is *gᵉbîrâ* "lady, mistress" (with the antonym *šipḥâ* "maid" in Gen 16:1ff.; Isa 24:2; Psa 123:2). *gᵉbîrâ* is an honorary title at the royal court either for the queen (1 Kgs 11:19 par. *ᵓiššâ* "wife") or the king's mother (1 Kgs 15:13 par. *ᵓēm* "mother"; cf. Jer. 13:18, etc.). On the office of *gᵉbîrâ*, → *ᵓēm* 4b.

4. (a) The discussion of Yahweh's strength *(gᵉbûrâ)* occurs primarily in the Psa, in various contexts: in descriptive praise of Yahweh's strength (Psa 65:7; 66:7; 89:14; 145:11; cf. Jer 10:6; Job 12:13; 1 Chron 29:11f.; 2 Chron 20:6); in the lament, which questions Yahweh's might (Isa 63:15); in the request for God's might (Psa 54:3; 80:3); in the vow of praise (Psa 21:14; 71:18); and in the historical psalms (Psa 106:8). Outside the Psa, Yahweh's *gᵉbûrâ* is mentioned only 3x, in prophecy: in the announcement of judgment (Isa 33:13; Jer 16:21) and in the announcement of messianic salvation (Isa 11:2).

A whole series of pars. occur in the semantic field of the discussion of Yahweh's *gᵉbûrâ:* *ᶜōz* "strength" (Psa 21:14), *yᵉšûᶜâ* "help" (Psa 80:3), *qinᵓâ* "zeal" (Isa 63:15), *zᵉrôaᶜ* "arm" (Psa 71:18; cf. 89:14), *yād* "hand" (Jer 16:21), *gᵉdullâ* "greatness," *tipᵓeret* "majesty" (1 Chron 29:11), and *kōaḥ* "might" (1 Chron 29:12; 2 Chron 20:6). Although *gᵉbûrâ* and *ḥokmâ* "wisdom" are opposites in Eccl 9:16, they become par. terms in Job 12:13 and Prov 8:14.

(b) Descriptive praises express the greatness and strength of Yahweh's → *ḥesed* "grace" by the verb (in qal; Psa 103:11; 117:2). The contention that people, in contrast to God, are not strong in their own might *(kōaḥ)* and that therefore the godless will become naught (1 Sam 2:9), is a statement of trust. The lamenter's experience that enemies (Psa 12:5, hi.; Lam 1:16) and the godless (Job 21:7) are strong nevertheless and even feel that they are superior to God (*gbr* hitp. in Job 15:25; 36:9) is a harsh contrast.

(c) A variety of contexts use *gibbôr* to express the fact that Yahweh is "strong" (Deut 10:17 = Neh 9:32 par. *gādōl* "great" and *nôrāᵓ* "frightful"; Jer 32:18 par. *gādôl;* cf. Isa 10:21) or a "hero" (Isa 9:5; Jer 20:11; Zeph 3:17).

(d) The Psa occasionally discuss Yahweh's *gᵉbûrôt*. Terms like *tᵉhillâ* "glorious deed" and *niplāᵓôt* "wondrous deeds" (Psa 106:2 in the context of a report of Yahweh's historical acts; cf. Psa 71:16f.; 145:4ff.) occur in the semantic field. Introductions to descriptive psalms of praise (Psa 145:4ff.; 150:2) or expressions of confidence in lament contexts (Psa 20:7; 71:16; cf. 106:2; Deut 3:24) mention such *gᵉbûrôt*, and one may surmise that *gᵉbûrôt* should be understood as "Yahweh's mighty historical acts," by which supplicants do not refer to specific events, but describe and summarize, at once, Yahweh's historical activity.

(e) The reports that the historical books give concerning the holy wars often discuss the fact that Yahweh himself fights against the enemies (*lḥm* ni. Exod 14:14, etc.) and confuses them (*hmm* Josh 10:10, etc.), but the root *gbr* is entirely absent from these reports. By contrast, the root designates Yahweh's military might in the Psa and in prophecy. Thus the entrance liturgy of Psa 24:8 describes Yahweh as *ʿizzûz wᵉgibbôr* "strong one and hero" and in par. as *gibbôr milḥāmâ* "hero in battle"; similarly, the eschatological song of praise in Isa 42:13 has the hitp. verb as well as *gibbôr* (par. *ʾîš milḥāmâ*). The lament in Jer 14:9 ("Why are you like a warrior who cannot help?") and the late historical Psa 78:65 also use *gibbôr.*

(f) In contrast, the term *geber* in the general meaning "man, person" is never used of Yahweh; rather, Yahweh and his activity are distinguished from those of the *geber* (Job 10:5; 22:2; 33:29; Prov 20:24).

5. The LXX translates the word group with a wide variety of terms; the NT too has no uniform correlation to *gbr.* Cf. Kosmala, "The Term *geber* in the OT and in the Scrolls," *SVT* 17 (1969): 167–69, on the post-OT usage of *geber* (esp. at Qumran).

J. Kühlewein

גָּדוֹל *gādôl* **great**

S 1419; BDB 152b; *HALOT* 1:177b; *TDOT* 2:390–416; *TWOT* 315d; *NIDOTTE* 1524

---

1. The root *gdl* "to be great" occurs only in Hebr. and Ug. In accordance with the general susceptibility of qualitative adj. modifiers to innovation, there is no common Sem. designation for "great"; terms for "great" in the other Sem. languages (Akk. *rabû,* Phoen. *ʾdr,* Aram. *rab,* Arab. *kabīr,* Eth. *ʿabīy*) exist with other meanings in Hebr. (→ *rab* "much, many," → *ʾaddîr* "majestic," *kabbîr* "strong, mighty," *ʿbh* "to be thick").

It is doubtful that *gādôl* is associated with the (common Sem.) root *gdl* II "to turn, twist" (Hebr. *gādil* "tassels," Deut 22:12; 1 Kgs 7:17; Akk. *gidlu* "skein"; Aram. *gᵉdîlāʾ* "string," etc.; on Arab. cf. J. Blau, *VT* 5 [1955]: 339); cf. GB 130b; *SNHL* 18f. (M. Dahood, *Bib* 45 [1964]: 397 also suggests *gdl* II unnecessarily in Psa 12:4 and 41:10).

Ug. uses *rb* (→ *rab*) more frequently than *gdl* for "great" (*WUS* no. 632; *UT* no. 562).

In addition to the verb in qal, pi., pu., hi., and hitp., Hebr. exhibits the nom. formations *gādôl* and *gādēl* (verbal adj.) "great," *gōdel* and *gᵉdûllâ (gᵉdûlâ)* "greatness," as well as *migdāl* "tower" (in place-names also *migdōl*), also found in Ug., Moab. (*DISO* 142), Aram. and, as a loanword, in Arab. (Fraenkel 236f.), Copt., and Berber (GB 396a).

The PNs *gᵉdalyâ(hû), yigdalyāhû,* and *giddēl* (a shortened form; cf. *gdwl* in the Elephantine texts, *BMAP* 149) should also be mentioned; textually uncertain are *giddaltî* (1 Chron 25:4, 9; cf. Rudolph, HAT 21, 167f.) and *haggᵉdôlîm* (Neh 11:14; cf. Rudolph, HAT 20, 184).

2. *gdl* occurs 54x in the qal (incl. Esth 9:4, inf. abs., listed in Lis. as an adj.), pi. 25x, pu. 1x, hi. 34x, hitp. 4x. *gādôl* appears 525x (incl. 1 Sam 6:18; excl. Esth 9:4 and Neh 11:14; see above) in the following distribution: Jer 48x, Deut 44x, Ezek 36x, 1 Sam 35x, Gen 33x, Psa 30x, 2 Kgs 29x, Neh and 2 Chron 27x, Josh 26x, 1 Kgs 22x, 2 Sam 18x, Exod and Dan 15x, Isa and Jonah 14x,

Judg 12x, 1 Chron 11x, Zech 10x, Num and Esth 8x, Hag, Job, and Ezra 6x, Mal, Prov, and Eccl 4x, Joel 3x, Lev, Zeph and Nah 2x, Hos, Amos, Mic, and Lam 1x; it does not occur in Obad, Hab, Ruth, or Song Sol. *gādēl* occurs 4x (Gen 26:13; 1 Sam 2:26; Ezek 16:26; 2 Chron 17:12), *gōdel* 13x (Deut 5x), *g*ᵉ*dûllâ* (Esth 6:3 *g*ᵉ*dûlâ*) 12x (1 Chron 4x, Psa and Esth 3x, also 2 Sam 7:21, 23), *migdāl* 49x (excl. 2 Sam 22:51 Q *migdôl* and the place-names).

3. (a) The numerous concrete-dimensional and abstract-figurative usages of *gādôl* "great" in reference to persons and things (cf. e.g., the categorization in *HAL* 170b) largely correspond to those of Eng. "great." The semantic range is somewhat broader because *gādôl* also means "old (the older/oldest)" (cf. *qāṭān*/*qāṭōn* "small" and "young [the younger/youngest]," e.g., in Gen 29:16, "The older was named Leah, the younger Rachel"; 44:12, "He began with the oldest and ended with the youngest"), and "rich, wealthy" (e.g., 2 Sam 19:33; 2 Kgs 4:8), as well as "esteemed, leading" (often substantivized: e.g., sg. Lev 19:15; 2 Sam 3:38; Jer 52:13; pl. 1 Sam 17:14; 2 Sam 7:9; 2 Kgs 10:6; Jer 5:5, etc.); expressions such as *qôl gādôl* "loud voice" (Gen 39:14; Deut 5:22, etc.), *ʾôr gādôl* "bright light" (Isa 9:1), or *ʿôd hayyôm gādôl* "it is still high day" (Gen 29:7) are also somewhat idiomatic. The semantic range may be somewhat more restricted in view of the fact that not *gādôl* but → *rab* "much, many" is used with some terms of volume (e.g., with *r*ᵉ*kûš* "possessions," Gen 13:6; *māqôm* "space," 1 Sam 26:13; *derek* "way," 1 Kgs 19:7; → *t*ᵉ*hôm rabbâ* "the great primeval waters," Gen 7:11; Isa 51:10; Amos 7:4; Psa 36:7).

The normal antonym of *gādôl* in all its meanings is *qāṭān* "small, young, petty" (47x) or *qāṭōn* (54x, occurs only in the masc. sg., assimilated to the nom. formation of *gādôl*; BL 466), cf. e.g., Gen 1:16; Exod 18:22; Deut 25:13f.; 1 Chron 12:15.

ṣāʿîr "small, young, petty" (23x, incl. Dan 8:9, 8x in Gen) does not occur in opposition to *gādôl*, but to *b*ᵉ*kōr*/*b*ᵉ*kîrâ* "firstborn" (Gen 19:31–38; 29:26; 43:33; 48:14; Josh 6:26; 1 Kgs 16:34), *rab* "the elder" (Gen 25:23), *ʾaddîr* "majestic" (Jer 14:13), and *ʿāṣûm* "strong" (Isa 60:22).

The merism "great and small" in the meaning "all," also favored in other languages, occurs quite often (cf. P. Boccaccio, "I termini contrari come espressioni della totalità in Hebraico," *Bib* 33 [1952]: 173–90; A. M. Honeyman, "Merismus in Biblical Hebrew," *JBL* 71 [1952]: 11–18; H. A. Brongers, "Merismus, Synekdoche und Hendiadys in der bibel-hebr. Sprache," *OTS* 14 [1965]: 100–114; on Eg. cf. A. Massart, FS Robert 38–46). Of 32 cases, 25 concern persons, the others animals (Psa 104:25) or (almost always negated) things (Num 22:18; 1 Sam 20:2; 22:15; 25:36; 30:19; 2 Chron 36:18).

The morphology of the usages varies greatly. *qāṭān* (12x; in Esth 1:5, 20; 2 Chron 31:15; 34:30 also in the masc. sg.) occurs along with *qāṭōn* (20x); the sequence of the expressions also varies (24x small-great, 8x great-small). The arrangement *min . . . w*ᵉʿ*ad* "from . . . to" is most frequent (17x; *miqqāṭōn w*ᵉʿ*ad-gādôl*, Gen 19:11; 1 Sam 5:9; 30:2; 2 Kgs 23:2; 25:26; Jer 8:10; 42:1, 8; 44:12; 2 Chron 15:13; with arts. or sufs., 1 Sam 30:19; Jer 6:13; 31:34; *miggādôl w*ᵉʿ*ad qāṭān*, Esth 1:5, 20; 2 Chron 34:30; with sufs., Jonah 3:5); one also finds the simple *w*ᵉ "and" (1 Sam 25:36; 1 Kgs 22:31 = 2 Chron 18:30 txt em; Jer 16:6; Job 3:19; 2 Chron 36:18), *k*ᵉ . . . *k*ᵉ "as . . . so" (Deut 1:17; 1 Chron 25:8; 26:13; 2 Chron 31:15), *ʾô* "or" (Num 22:18; 1 Sam 20:2; 22:15), and *ʿim* "together with" (Psa 104:25; 115:13).

(b) The two substs. *gōdel* and *g^edûllâ* are not simply synonyms. Rather, *gōdel* signifies abstract greatness (of God: Deut 3:24; 5:24; 9:26; 11:2; 32:3; Psa 150:2; of his grace, Num 14:19; of his arm, Psa 79:11; of arrogance of the heart, Isa 9:8; 10:12; of the pharaoh compared to a cedar, Ezek 31:2, 7, 18), and *g^edûllâ/g^edûlâ* means specifically either "high position, honor, majesty" (of God: 1 Chron 29:11; of a person: Psa 71:21; Esth 1:4; 6:3; 10:2) or something "great," a "great deed" (of God: 2 Sam 7:21, 23; cf. 1 Chron 17:19bis, 21, twice in the pl.; Psa 145:3, 6); the latter meaning is expressed in the plural, besides through the substantivized fem. pl. of *gādôl* (*g^edōlôt* "great things, great deeds"; Deut 10:21; Jer 33:3; 45:5; Psa 71:19; 106:21; Job 5:9; 9:10; 37:5; of Elisha, 2 Kgs 8:4; great speech, Psa 12:4; involvement with great things, Psa 131:1).

(c) In principle, the verb acquires no new connotations in comparison to the adjective. *gdl* qal means not only "to *become* great = grow" (of children: Gen 21:8, 20; 25:27; 38:11, 14; Exod 2:10f.; Judg 11:2; 13:24; 1 Sam 2:21; 3:19; 1 Kgs 12:8, 10 = 2 Chron 10:8, 10; 2 Kgs 4:18; Ezek 16:7; Job 31:18 [cf. Fohrer, KAT 16, 423]; Ruth 1:13; of a lamb, 2 Sam 12:3; of a horn, Dan 8:9f.) and "to become great = be well-off" (Gen 24:35; 26:13[bis]; 1 Kgs 10:23 = 2 Chron 9:22; Jer 5:27; Eccl 2:9), but also "to *be* great, prove oneself great" (of God, his might, his name, his deeds: Num 14:17; 2 Sam 7:22, 26 = 1 Chron 17:24; Mal 1:5; Psa 35:27; 40:17 = 70:5; 92:6; 104:1; outcry, Gen 19:13; boasting, Zech 12:7; lament, Zech 12:11; pain, Job 2:13; guilt, Lam 4:6 and Ezra 9:6) and "to be great = be significant, mighty, valuable" (king: Gen 41:40; 2 Sam 5:10 = 1 Chron 11:9; Messiah, Mic 5:3; Mordecai, Esth 9:4; Ephraim and Manasseh, Gen 48:19bis; life, 1 Sam 26:24bis). Verbal clauses here are distinguished from nom. clauses with *gādôl* as predicate (something over 50x) by the fact that the former describe (analytically) an empirically perceived process and do not express (synthetically) a subjective assessment of a phenomenon (cf. the confession formulated as a new perception with a predicate adj. in Isa 12:6, "Great in your midst is the Holy One of Israel," with the verbal statement of confidence that already presupposes the experience of Yahweh's greatness in Mal 1:5, "You will say yourselves: Yahweh proves himself to be great beyond Israel's borders"; cf. *HP* 26, 29–33).

The pi. of *gdl* is mostly factitive "to make great" (Gen 12:2; Num 6:5; Josh 3:7; 4:14; 1 Kgs 1:37, 47; Esth 3:1; 5:11; 10:2; 1 Chron 29:12, 25; 2 Chron 1:1; reflexive in the hitp. "to show oneself great" Ezek 38:23) and "to raise, rear" (2 Kgs 10:6; Isa 1:2; 23:4; 44:14; 49:21; 51:18; Ezek 31:4; Hos 9:12; Jonah 4:10; Dan 1:5; pass. in the pu., Psa 144:12; cf. *HP* 58f.), less frequently declarative "to declare great = praise" (Psa 34:4; 69:31; cf. the PN derived from a psalm quotation in 1 Chron 25:4, 9; cf. *HP* 40–43) or evaluative "to consider great" (Job 7:17; reflexive in the hitp. "to brag" Isa 10:15; Dan 11:36f.).

gdl hi. is either a normal causative "to make something great, to prove oneself great" (Gen 19:19; 1 Sam 12:24; 20:41 txt?; 22:51 K = Psa 18:51 Q; Isa 9:2; 28:29; 42:21; Ezek 24:9; Joel 2:20f.; Amos 8:5; Obad 12; Psa 41:10; 126:2f.; 138:2; Eccl 1:16; 2:4) or an inner-causative "to make oneself great = brag" (Jer 48:26, 42; Ezek 35:13; Zeph 2:8, 10; Psa 35:26; 38:17; 55:13; Job 19:5; Lam

1:9; on the distinction from the hitp. see *HP* 46–49) or "to make oneself become great = become great, wonderful" (Dan 8:4, 8, 11, 25; 1 Chron 22:5).

Again, of the relatively uncommon antonyms *qṭn* qal "to be small" (Gen 32:11; 2 Sam 7:19 = 1 Chron 17:17), hi. "to make small" (Amos 8:5), and *ṣᶜr* qal "to be small, petty" (Jer 30:19; Zech 13:7; Job 14:21), only the former occurs opposite *gdl*.

4. (a) If one surveys passages with *gādôl* in a theological usage, it becomes apparent that the statement "Yahweh is great," etc., occurs primarily in the hymnic texts of the Zion tradition (Psa 48:2 "great is Yahweh and greatly to be praised in the city of our God"; 77:14 "who is as great a god as God"; cf. Kraus, *Psa*, CC, 2:116; 95:3 "for Yahweh is a great God, a great king over all gods"; cf. 47:3 "a great king over all the world"; 96:4 = 1 Chron 16:25 "for great is Yahweh and greatly to be praised, he is more awesome than all the gods"; cf. Psa 145:3; 99:2 "Yahweh is great in Zion, he is exalted over all the nations"; 135:5 "Yahweh is great, our Lord is greater than all gods"; 147:5 "great is our Lord and rich in might"; also a reflection of Jerusalemite theology, Isa 12:6 "great in your midst is the Holy One of Israel"; and, as a hymnic motif in an individual lament, Psa 86:10 "for you are great and you do wonders"). Several passages also make clear that Yahweh's greatness over against the other gods was the original intention (Psa 77:14; 95:3; 96:4; 135:5), easily understandable as an adaptation from pre-Israelite Jerusalemite cult tradition concerning *ᵓēl* → *ᶜelyôn* (cf. the epithets → *ᵓaddîr* and → *rab*, equally at home in Canaan, and also evident in Ug. as divine predications; on the Eg. designation of the divine as *wr* "the great," see S. Morenz, *Äg. Religion* [1960], 156f.). At the same time, Yahweh's greatness may be related to the nations of the world, often in conjunction with the royal title (Psa 47:3; 86:9f.; 99:2; cf. also Jer 10:6f. "you are great and great is your name in might"; Mal 1:14 "I am a great king"; Ezek 38:23 "I will prove myself to be great and holy before the eyes of many nations," with *gdl* hitp.), or stated without any particular referent (Psa 48:2; 145:3; 147:5; cf. also Psa 104:1 "Yahweh, my God, how great you are," with *gdl* qal).

But divine predications could also be formed with *gādôl* or with *gdl* qal in other contexts, such as confessional statements (Exod 18:11, Jethro: "now I know that Yahweh is greater than all gods"; 2 Sam 7:22, David: "therefore, you are great, my Lord Yahweh"; 2 Chron 2:4, Solomon: "and the house that I will build must be great; for our God is greater than all gods") and statements of confidence in prayers of lament and supplication (Psa 35:27; 40:17 = 70:5; cf. Mal 1:5; each of these passages with *gdl* qal). A further tradition complex is recognizable in the Dtn series of divine epithets (Deut 7:21 "Yahweh . . . , a great and awesome God"; 10:17 "the great, strong, and awesome God"), which are particularly popular in the diction of the post-exilic communal prayer (Jer 32:18; Neh 1:5; 8:6; 9:32; cf. 4:8; Dan 9:4; all passages with *gādôl*).

Since the Dtn period, God's "greatness" is also discussed in the abstract (*gōdel* Deut 3:24; 5:24; 9:26; 11:2; 32:3; Psa 150:2; *gᵉdullâ* 1 Chron 29:11 in a long series of similar expressions); the PNs *gᵉdalyâ(hû)* and *yigdalyāhû* ("God is great") had already come into use somewhat earlier (Zeph 1:1 or Jer 38:1).

The book of Job expresses God's greatness (in contrast to that of people or the creation) not by *gdl* but by *rbh* qal (Job 33:12 "God is greater than any human") and by *śaggîʾ* "exalted" (36:26 "see, God is exalted, we know him not"; cf. also 37:23 *śaggîʾ kōaḥ* "great in power"); *ʾēl kabbîr* "mighty God" in 36:5 is probably a textual error.

The messianic king, as representative and instrument, also receives the predicate "great" in Mic 5:3, "For now he will be great (*gdl* qal) to the ends of the earth."

(b) The numerous passages that speak of the greatness of the divine character, manifestation, or activity should be distinguished from divine predications. Noteworthy here are esp. the name of God (→ *šēm; gādôl:* Josh 7:9; 1 Sam 12:22; 1 Kgs 8:42 = 2 Chron 6:32; Jer 10:6; 44:26; Ezek 36:23; Mal 1:11; Psa 76:2; 99:3; *gdl* qal: 2 Sam 7:26 = 1 Chron 17:24; *gdl* pi.: Psa 34:4; 69:31; *gdl* hi.: Psa 138:2 txt?) and the day of Yahweh (→ *yôm;* Jer 30:7; Joel 2:11; 3:4; Zeph 1:4; Mal 3:23; cf. Hos 2:2 "the day of Jezreel.")

Further entities of this type associated with *gādôl* are *ʾap* "wrath" (Deut 29:23, 27), *zᵉrôaᶜ* "arm, might" (Exod 15:16; cf. Psa 79:11 with *gōdel*), *ḥēmâ* "anger" (2 Kgs 22:13 = 2 Chron 34:21; Jer 36:7), *ḥesed* "grace" (1 Kgs 3:6 = 2 Chron 1:8; Psa 57:11 = 108:5; 86:13; 145:8; cf. Num 14:19 with *gōdel;* Gen 19:19 with *gdl* hi.), *yᵉšûᶜôt* "salvation" (2 Sam 22:51 = Psa 18:51 with *gdl* hi.), *kābôd* "glory" (Psa 21:6; 138:5), *kōaḥ* "strength" (Exod 32:11; Jer 27:5; 32:17; Nah 1:3, etc.; Num 14:17 with *gdl* qal), *nᵉqāmôt* "vengeance" (Ezek 25:17), *ᶜēṣâ* "counsel" (Jer 32:19), *raḥᵃmîm* "mercy" (Isa 54:7, otherwise with → *rab*), and *tôrâ* "instruction" (Isa 42:21 with *gdl* hi.).

Particularly popular in Dtn-Dtr literature and later in connection with the exodus tradition (cf. Exod 14:31 J, "the great demonstration of might" with → *yād*) are expressions with *gādôl* that discuss great deeds, signs, wonders, etc., in the early history of the people (Deut 4:32, 34, 36f.; 6:22; 7:19; 9:29; 11:7; 26:8; 29:2; 34:12; Josh 24:17; Judg 2:7; 2 Kgs 17:36; Jer 32:21; Neh 1:10; cf. in P Exod 6:6 and 7:4; in reference to a phenomenon in Samuel's time, 1 Sam 12:16).

Finally, expressions that appear in rather varied contexts for the great deeds of Yahweh should also be mentioned (*gᵉdûllâ:* 2 Sam 7:21, 23; cf. 1 Chron 17:19bis, 21; Psa 145:3, 6; *gᵉdōlôt:* Deut 10:21; Jer 33:3; 45:5; Psa 71:19; 106:21; Job 5:9; 9:10; 37:5; *gdl* hi.: 1 Sam 12:24; Joel 2:21; Psa 126:2f.).

(c) In the great majority of passages, *gādôl* is thus a thoroughly positive term. This significance is no less true for its application to the people Israel, which, according to the patriarchal promises, is to become a "great people (→ *gôy*)" (Gen 12:2; 17:20; 18:18; 21:18; 46:3; Deut 26:5; cf. also Exod 32:10; Num 14:12; Deut 4:6–8; with → *rab,* Gen 50:20; Exod 1:9). In contrast, negative connotations, which treat human arrogance (with *gᵉdōlôt* Psa 12:4; with *gōdel* Isa 9:8; 10:12; with *gdl* hitp. Isa 10:15; Dan 11:36f.; with *gdl* hi. see the passages cited in 3c), are relatively rare for the root *gdl* (in contrast e.g., to → *gʾh,* → *gbh*).

To some degree as a corrective for the overestimation of human greatness, several passages in the OT emphasize the smallest or youngest, or the smallness and low position of a family or a people (Benjamin, Gideon, Saul, David, Bethlehem-Ephrathah, even Israel). On these "statements of insignificance or humility" (with *qāṭōn* Gen 42:13, 15, 20, 32, 34; 43:29; 44:26; 1 Sam 15:17; Isa 60:22; with *qāṭān* Gen 44:20; 1 Sam 16:11; 17:14; with *ṣāᶜîr* Gen 43:33; Judg 6:15; 1 Sam 9:21; Isa 60:22; Mic 5:1 txt em; Psa 68:28;

with *m*^e^*ᶜaṭ* Deut 7:7 "not because you were more numerous than all nations did Yahweh incline to you and choose you, for you are the smallest among all the peoples, but because Yahweh loved you"), see O. Bächli, "Die Erwählung des Geringen im AT," *TZ* 22 (1966): 385–95.

5. In the language of Qumran, which hardly progresses beyond OT usage, a new word *gwdl* for "thumb" appears (1QM 5:13; cf. *qōṭen* "little finger" in 1 Kgs 12:10 = 2 Chron 10:10).

On the LXX, intertestamental literature, and the NT, see W. Grundmann, "μέγας," *TDNT* 4:529–44; O. Michel, "μικρός," *TDNT* 4:648–59.

E. Jenni

גּוֹי *gôy* **people** → עַם *ᶜam*

גור *gûr* **to sojourn**

S 1481; BDB 157b; *HALOT* 1:184a; *TDOT* 2:439–49; *TWOT* 330; *NIDOTTE* 1591

גֵּר *gēr* **sojourner**

S 1616; BDB 158a; *HALOT* 1:201a; *TDOT* 2:439–49; *TWOT* 330a; *NIDOTTE* 1731

---

1. The root *gûr,* certainly attested in the meaning "to sojourn" only in NWSem., occurs outside Hebr. almost exclusively as a subst. "guest, protégé, client."

Akk. *gurru,* associated with *gēr* in *CAD* G:140b, is explained differently in *AHw* 287a.

The Ug. occurrences from *KTU* 1.19.III.47; 1.140.35 are very uncertain (*WUS* nos. 690f.; *UT* no. 567; Gray, *Legacy* 122, 243).

Phoen.-Pun. *gr* means "protégé, client" *(KAI* no. 37A.16, B.10; a frequent element in PNs, Harris 92f.; cf. Stamm, *AN* 264, on *ubārum),* as does Moab. *gr* in *KAI* no. 181.16f., where a fem. can be also be inferred (*KAI* 2:176).

Because the Old Aram. *gûr* "to be exiled" (so *DISO* 49 following Dupont-Sommer) should be disregarded (thus, with some difference, Fitzmyer, *Sef.* 91; *KAI* 2:263; K. R. Veenhof, *BO* 20 [1963]: 142–44, followed by R. Degen, *Altaram. Grammatik* [1969], 19, 71), Aram. examples begin with Nab. and Palm. *gr* "client" (*DISO* 53). Later Aram. dialects develop the divergent meaning *gûr* "to commit adultery" (*gayyôrāʾ* "adulterer").

SSem. equivalents adduced (namely Arab. *jār* "neighbor"; cf. Eth. *gôr*) contribute nothing to the elucidation of the Hebr. root.

The verb *gûr* (qal and hitpo.) "to sojourn," the subst. *gēr* "foreigner, protégé," and the derivative abstract formations *gērût* (Jer 41:17 in a place-name; according to Alt, *KS* [1959], 3:358f. "guest's fief") and *m*^e^*gûrîm* "strangerhood" occur in Hebr.

2. After the exclusion of the homonyms *gûr* II "to attack" and *gûr* III "to be afraid," Lis. 319f. lists 81 occurrences of *gûr* qal (incl. Judg 5:17; Isa 54:15b; Jer 13x, Lev 11x) and 3 of the hitp. (1 Kgs 17:20; Jer 30:23 txt?; Hos 7:14 txt?). Although *gûr* is already attested before the exile (Gen 12:10; 19:9; 20:1, etc.), the focus of the usage lies in the exilic and post-exilic literature (in H, Lev 17–26, 10x; in Jer 42–50, 12x).

gēr occurs 92x in MT (Deut 22x, Lev 21x, Exod 12x, Num 11x, Ezek 5x, Psa 4x), *m*[e]*gûrîm* 11x (excl. the sg. form in Psa 55:16; Gen 6x and Exod 1x, all passages in P; further Ezek 20:38; Psa 119:54; Job 18:19; Lam 2:22), *gērût* 1x.

The term *gēr* has evidently been used since early times (Covenant Code 6x, 2 Sam 1:13), but it apparently came into frequent usage only toward the end of the state of Judah (de Vaux 1:75) or after the exile. This phenomenon can be adequately explained in terms of events of the period (population loss, emigration, economic difficulties) and theological motifs (the community's concerns for its unity in distinction from the environment, achieved, in part, by the integration of the "sojourner in your gates"; thus the weight that the legal texts of priestly origin place on this problem; cf. Elliger, HAT 4, 227).

3. (a) The *gēr* is distinguished from the foreigner in general, the *nokrî* or → *zār*, in that he/she is the stranger who has settled, who has established himself/herself for a particular period in the land and to whom a special status is granted. The *tôšāb* "inhabitant," discussed in post-exilic priestly texts in particular (14x, 8x in Lev), often parallels the *gēr* (Gen 23:4; Lev 25:23, 35, etc.). The social status of the *tôšāb* is comparable, if not identical, with that of the *gēr*. The Spartan *perioikos* or the Athenian *metoikos* would be comparable to the *gēr*.

The *gēr*, alone or in a group, has left his/her homeland as a result of political, economic, or other circumstances and seeks protection in another community, as Abraham did in Hebron (Gen 23:4), Moses in Midian (Exod 2:22 = 18:3), the Bethlehemite Elimelech and his family in Moab (Ruth 1:1), an Ephraimite in Benjaminite territory (Judg 19:16), and even as the Israelites in Egypt (Exod 22:20 = 23:9 = Lev 19:34 = Deut 10:19; Lev 25:23). The relationship between the landless Levites and the *gērîm* also bears comparison: Judg 17:7ff.; 19:1; Deut 14:29; 26:11–13, etc.

The *gēr* does not enjoy the full rights of an Israelite; e.g., he/she possesses no land (according to Ezek 47:22 this limitation will be revoked in the Israel of the future). The *gēr* is usually the servant of an Israelite, who is lord and patron (Deut 24:14). As a rule, the *gēr* is poor (cf., however, Lev 25:47) and is as a result numbered among the economically weak who, like widows and orphans, can lay claim to aid.

They have the right to glean (Lev 19:10; 23:22; Deut 24:19–21, etc.); they stand under divine protection (Deut 10:18; Psa 146:9; Mal 3:5); the Israelites should love them as they love themselves (Lev 19:34; Deut 10:19), bearing in mind their own sojourn in Egypt (Exod 22:20, etc.); they take care not to oppress the *gēr* (so already in the Covenant Code, Exod 22:20–23; 23:9), who enjoys largely the same rights as their own citizens (participation in the tithe, Deut 14:29; Sabbath year, Lev 25:6; cities of refuge, Num 35:15). According to Lev 20:2; 24:16, 22; Deut 1:16, Israelite and *gēr* are subject to the same law; in short, in daily life no distinction between *gērîm* and Israelites existed (de Vaux 1:75).

(b) From a religious perspective the same prescriptions are valid for Israelites and *gērîm* (Exod 12:49; Num 15:15f.): the *gēr* too must keep the Sabbath (Exod 20:10 = Deut 5:14), the fasts of the Day of Atonement (Lev 16:29), and the Passover (Num 9:14, etc.), on the condition that he is circumcised (Exod 12:48). He can sacrifice (Lev 17:8; 22:18; Num 15:15f., etc.) and participate in the festivals (Deut 16:11, 14). He is by all means obligated to observe purity regulations (Lev 17:8–16; 18:26, etc.; cf. Lev 17:15 in contrast to Deut 14:21). Thus the *gēr* is more or less equal to the Israelite even in this area.

Consequently, the LXX translation of the Hebr. term primarily with *prosēlytos* and understanding of the *gēr* as a proselyte in the technical sense, i.e., as one who, through an act of initiation (circumcision), has identified himself with Judaism (so also Mid. Hebr. *gēr* and Aram. *gîyā/ôrāʾ*; cf. *DISO* 53; see 5 below), is not surprising at all. In the LXX *prosēlytos* occurs 77x, *paroikos* 11x (Gen 15:13; 23:4, etc., i.e., when the specific understanding of the term as a proselyte is excluded), *xenos* 1x (Job 31:32), and *g(e)iōros* 2x (Exod 12:19; Isa 14:1).

(c) As the sources indicate, the status of the *gēr* evolved over time. The legal texts suggest an increasingly pronounced tendency to assimilate the *gēr* to the Israelites, esp. in religious contexts (the technical term for the native full citizen is *ʾezrāḥ*, 17x, juxtaposed with the *gēr* in Exod, Lev, Num, Josh 8:33; Ezek 47:22; in addition to Lev 23:42 and Psa 37:35 txt em). Originally a foreigner who settled in Israel or in one of the tribes and as such was placed under Yahweh's protection (Covenant Code), the *gēr* already merits special treatment in Deut alongside the widow and the orphan, indeed, on the basis of a salvation-historical concept: Israel itself was once *gēr*. Finally, the priestly tradition practically makes the stranger a member of the community by imposing precise requirements upon him.

Regarding the history of the term and its background, cf. A. Bertholet, *Die Stellung der Israeliten und der Juden zu den Fremden* (1896); E. Neufeld, *HUCA* 26 (1955): 391–94; P. Grelot, *VT* 6 (1956): 177f.; de Vaux 1:74f.; F. Horst, *RGG* 2:1125f. with bibliog.; K. G. Kuhn, *TDNT* 6:727–44; Th. M. Horner, "Changing Concepts of the 'Stranger' in the OT," *ATR* 42 (1960): 49–53; L. M. Muntingh, "Die Begrip *gēr* in die OT," *NedGTT* 3 (1962): 534–58.

4. The following viewpoints are theologically significant:

(a) Yahweh himself cares for the sojourner in Israel. Israel's God is at the same time its patron and commands his people not only not to oppress the sojourner but even to love him/her (Lev 19:33f.; Deut 10:19; → *ʾhb* IV/1).

(b) Deut in particular (Exod 22:20b; 23:9b are secondary, Lev 19:34b is a development of Deut 10:19) draws a connection between the ethical requirement with reference to the *gēr* and Israel's sojourn in Egypt.

(c) In addition, however, a few passages also treat Israel (like formerly its ancestor Abraham as a type, Gen 23:4) as *gēr* (and *tôšāb*) in Canaan, in Yahweh's land (Lev 25:23 "the land is mine, but you are strangers and sojourners with me"; Psa 39:13 "for I am a guest with you, a sojourner like all my fathers"; 119:19 "I am a guest on earth"; 1 Chron 29:15 "for we are guests and strangers before you like all our fathers"). On these (spiritualized) concepts and their traditio-critical origins—among other things, the asylum function of the sanctuary also plays a role here (cf. Psa 15:1 with *gûr;* also the Phoen. theophoric proper names formed with *gēr*)—cf. K. L. Schmidt, "Israels Stellung zu den Fremdlingen und Beisassen und Israels Wissen um Seine Fremdling- und Beisassenschaft," *Judaica* 1 (1945): 269–96; K. L. and M. A. Schmidt, *TDNT* 5:846–48; H. Wildberger, *EvT* 16 (1956): 417–20.

5. In the Hellenistic era the religious aspect of the term *gēr* underwent increased accentuation. *gēr* no longer indicated just the settled foreigner, but the pagan accepted into the Jewish community, the proselyte (in both Judaism and the NT distinguished from the *sebomenos,* the "God-fearer"; cf. Acts 13:50, etc.). Cf. K. G. Kuhn, "προσήλυτος," *TDNT* 6:727–44; K. L. Schmidt, M. A. Schmidt, and R. Meyer, "πάροικος," *TDNT* 5:841–853; W. Grundmann, "δῆμος: παρεπίδημος," *TDNT* 2:64f.

R. Martin-Achard

גּוֹרָל *gôrāl* **lot**

S 1486; BDB 174a; *HALOT* 1:185a; *TDOT* 2:450–56; *TWOT* 381a; *NIDOTTE* 1598

---

1. *gôrāl* "lot" is attested only in Hebr. and may be said, with a degree of certainty, to be related to Arab. *jarwal* "pebble" (*HAL* 195a).

2. *gôrāl* occurs 77x in the Hebr. Bible (excl. Prov 19:19 K; read Q *gdl*), mostly in late texts (lacking in Gen, Exod, Deut, Sam, Kgs, Amos, Hos, the authentic passages of Isa, etc.), in accordance with its sacral-legal primary meaning predominantly in priestly contexts (Lev 16:8–10 5x, Num 7x, Josh 14–21 26x, 1 Chron 13x, the remaining books 3x or less).

It remains questionable whether *gôrāl* should be read for *gādôl* and *gilyôn gôrāl* should be translated "common tablet" in Isa 8:1, with K. Galling, *ZDPV* 56 (1933): 213.

3. (a) In a concrete meaning, *gôrāl* indicates the lot cast in order to make particular decisions (in Lev 16:8–10 for the selection of the rams for Yahweh and Azazel, in Judg 20:9 for the attack on Gibeah, for the distribution of the spoils in Obad 11, of people in Nah 3:10, of the nation in Joel 4:3, of clothing in Psa 22:19 [cf. Mark 15:24 pars.], for the cessation of hostilities in Prov 18:18, etc. [more examples in *HAL* 178a; J. Lindblom, "Lot-Casting in the OT," *VT* 12 [1962]: 164–66).

The hypothesized technique of casting lots (like the precise meaning of Urim and Thummim and the ephod) remains unclear even today (cf. A. Musil, *Arabia Petraea* [1908], 3:293f.; Dalman, *AuS* 2:43f.; StrB 2:596f.; R. Press, *ZAW* 51 [1933]: 227–31; *BHH* 2:1103; Lindblom, op. cit. 164–78). One should possibly assume various techniques for various places, times, and contexts. Particular indicators with reference to *gôrāl* result from Prov 16:33, according to which the lot is shaken in the lap, as well as from the verbs that *gôrāl* can serve as subj. or obj. (*ʿlh* "to come up," *yṣʾ* "to come out," *hyh lᵉ* and *npl ʿl/lᵉ* "to fall upon," or *ṭûl* hi., *ydd, yrh, npl* hi., *ntn, šlk* hi. "to cast").

pûr (only in Esth) and *qsm/qesem* should be mentioned as semantically related.

Esth 3:7 and 9:24 use *gôrāl* as a gloss or translation of *pûr* (used with *npl* hi. "to cast"; Akk. *pūru* "lot"; cf. L. Dürr, *OLZ* 38 [1935]: 297; J. Lewy, *Revue Hittite et Asianique* 5 [1939]: 117–24), and 9:26 derives the name of the Purim festival (*pûrîm* also in 9:28f., 31f.) from it (cf. e.g., Ringgren, ATD 16/2, 115f.; Bardtke, KAT 17/5, 243ff. with bibliog.; *BHH* 3:1532).

According to KBL 844f., *qsm* means "to inquire of the lot oracle, practice divination" (20x); *qesem* "lot oracle" (11x) and *miqsām* "inquiry of the lot oracle" belong to this root. Wildberger (*Isa 1–12*, CC, 99, 105f. on Isa 2:6 txt em) argues for a somewhat broader meaning "to divine."

(b) According to Num 26:55f.; 33:54; 34:13; 36:2f.; Josh 14:2, etc., territory was to be alloted to the individual Israelite tribes during the conquest by means of the lot. Alt even suggests that every seven years a new lottery took place (*EOTHR* 128n.119; cf. also id., *KS* [1959], 3:373–81 on Mic 2:1–5).

Subsequently, the allotment of a tribe or a family can be metonymically described as *gôrāl* (Josh 15:1; cf. 16:1; 17:1, 14, 17; Judg 1:3, etc.). *gôrāl* thus becomes a par. term for *naḥ^alâ* "inheritance" (→ *nḥl*), *ḥēleq* "portion" (→ *ḥlq*), *ḥebel* "allotment," *y^eruššâ* "possession" (→ *yrš*), *ʾ^aḥuzzâ* "property" (→ *ʾḥz*), → *s^egullâ* "possession," *miqneh* "acquisition" (→ *qnh*), → *ʾereṣ* "land," etc.

The absence of the term in Deut may well be due to the fact that Deut is not interested in individual tribal portions but only in the land as a whole (cf. von Rad, *Gottesvolk* 43).

(c) Like *naḥ^alâ*, *ḥēleq*, and *ḥebel*, *gôrāl* is also used figuratively and generally means, then, "portion, fate, destiny."

The transition from the proper to the fig. meaning may be demonstrated more readily for *ḥēleq* and *naḥ^alâ* than for *gôrāl*. Num 18:20 may serve as one example among many: "Yahweh said to Aaron: You shall receive no inheritance *(nḥl)* in your land and you shall have no portion *(ḥēleq)* of it; I am your portion *(ḥēleq)* and your inheritance *(naḥ^alâ)* among the Israelites."

The most important passages for the fig. usage are Isa 17:14 (par. *ḥēleq*); 34:17 (par. *ḥlq* pi.); 57:6 (par. *ḥēleq*); Jer 13:25 (par. *m^enāt* "portion"; cf. Wagner no. 175); Psa 16:5f. (par. *m^enāt*, *ḥēleq*, and *ḥebel*); perhaps Psa 125:3; Dan 12:13, "You will arise to your lot at the end of days."

On the whole problem, cf. J. T. E. Renner, "A Study of the Word Gôrāl in the OT" (diss., Heidelberg, 1958).

4. To the degree that the casting of lots in the understanding of the OT, as for antiquity in general, may be considered a request for divine judgment, all usages of *gôrāl* can be describe as theological. The fig. usage makes this concept clear by the fact that Yahweh expressly determines the lot and fate of people or even is their lot himself. One passage does not assume the otherwise automatic identification of decision by lot and divine judgment (it may even be called into question): Prov 16:33, "The lot is cast in the lap, but all judgment *(mišpāṭ)* comes from Yahweh."

5. At Qumran the term underwent a further semantic transformation. It simultaneously indicates: (a) a decision or a conclusion, (b) a rank or office within the community, (c) a party or adherents, (d) the fate coming to pass

(as requital), and (e) (in 1QM) even a military formation (cf. F. Nötscher, *Zur theologischen Terminologie der Qumran-Texte* [1956], 169–73).

The NT follows LXX usage, which translates *gôrāl* in the majority of cases (62x) with *klēros*, for which the fig. meaning predominates in the NT. Cf. W. Foerster and J. Herrmann, "κλῆρος," *TDNT* 3:758–85.

H. H. Schmid

גיל *gîl* to rejoice

S 1523; BDB 162a; *HALOT* 1:189b; *TDOT* 2:469–75; *TWOT* 346; *NIDOTTE* 1635

---

1. *gîl* "to rejoice" also occurs outside Hebr. in Ug., where in *KTU* 1.16.I.15, II.37 the par. *šmḫ* "to be happy" (Hebr. → *śmḥ*) seems to assure the meaning.

Regarding the suggested connection with Arab. *jāla* "to revolve, wander about," cf. P. Humbert, "Laetari et exultare dans le vocabulaire religieux de l'AT," *RHPR* 22 (1942): 213 = *Opuscules d'un hébraïsant* (1958), 144; contrast L. Kopf, *VT* 9 (1959): 249f. (Arab. *jll*). Each of the SSem. verbs adduced for the meaning of *gîl* in the OT is unproductive (cf. still *HAL* 182).

Hebr. forms the verbal nouns *gîl* and *gîlâ* in addition to the verb (qal). On the PN *ʾabîgayil*, cf. J. J. Stamm, FS Baumgartner 316.

2. The verb occurs 45x (Psa 19x [2:11 may be disregarded due to emendation], Isa 11x, Min. Pr. 8x, Prov 5x, in addition to Song Sol 1:4 and 1 Chron 16:31 [= Psa 96:11], the subst. *gîl* 8x (Psa 3x, Prophets 4x, Job 3:22 txt?), and *gîlâ* 2x (Isa 35:2; 65:18).

The assignment of Psa 43:4 to *gîl* I "youth(?)" or *gîl* II "joy" is disputed (*HAL* 182a).

3. (a) The word group occurs almost exclusively, then, in the prophetic books and in the Psa; a great portion of the prophetic texts, however, contain psalm forms. Thus *gîl* belongs in the context of the cult; it has a firm place in the process of the praise of God. It occurs only rarely in profane contexts (Isa 9:2b; 16:10 = Jer 48:33; Hab 1:15; Psa 45:16; Prov 2:14; 23:24f.; 24:17; Song Sol 1:4). Isa 16:10 = Jer 48:33; Hos 9:1; and 10:5 use the word in the context of the prophetic accusation.

śmḥ "to be happy" most often (over 30x) parallels *gîl;* it is followed by *śûś/śîś* "to be happy," *rnn* "to rejoice," *rûaʿ* hi. "to cry out," *ʿlz* "to exult," etc.; cf. the list in Humbert, op. cit. 206, 137f.

The resultant picture indicates that *gîl* belongs in the semantic field indicated by Eng. "joy." This semantic field is much more richly developed in Hebr. than in modern languages because in Hebr. joy does not primarily mean a feeling, an emotion, or an attitude, but joy visibly expressed, i.e., a congregational act. Now, because options for the verbal and gestural expression of joy are highly varied, one has difficulty precisely translating many Hebr. terms. The rendering of *gîl* with "to rejoice" or "to jubilate" is only an approximate, rough translation. Because *gîl* parallels *śmḥ* in more than half its occurrences, the broader sense of the word, even if not the precise nuance, is firmly established.

Like *śmḥ*, *gîl* can express joy in the profane realm: at a wedding (Psa 45:16 subst.; cf. Song Sol 1:4), the joy of parents in their children (Prov 23:24f.), joy at the division of plunder, joy at harvest, joy at gloating, etc. (Isa 9:2b; 16:10 = Jer 48:33; Hab 1:15; Prov 2:14; 24:17). One cannot, however, distinguish sharply between the profane and the cultic usage; in Joel 2:23 joy for the rain is simultaneously "joy for Yahweh." The usage of the word still gives clear evidence of a phase in which profane event and holy event were not differentiated.

(b) Subjects of *gîl* are (1) people: an individual (Isa 61:10; Hab 3:18; Psa 9:15; 13:6; 16:9; 31:8; 35:9; 43:4 txt?; 51:10; Prov 23:24f.; 24:17), the nation (Psa 14:7 = 53:7; 48:12, etc.), the nations (Isa 25:9; cf. 66:10), the poor and the righteous (Isa 29:19; Psa 32:11), enemies (Psa 13:5; cf. Hab 1:15), evil (Prov 2:14), idol priests (Hos 10:5), and the king (Psa 21:2); (2) nature: the earth (Isa 49:13; Psa 96:11 = 1 Chron 16:31; Psa 97:1), steppe and desert (Isa 35:1f.), and hill (Psa 65:13 with *gîlâ*); (3) God (Isa 65:19; Zeph 3:17).

People are thus predominantly the subject of the verb. In this respect the people or the individual are usually intended in contrast to God. Because God's praise always has the tendency to broaden itself, the circle of the joyous is also broadened to include creation. God "rejoices" in two late texts.

The (intrans.) verb is generally used absolutely. Otherwise it is often constructed with b^e (usually in reference to God, e.g., Psa 118:24, or his deed, e.g., Psa 9:15), also twice with *ʿal* (Hos 10:5; Zeph 3:7); cf. Humbert, op. cit. 205, 137.

4. (a) The vast majority of passages refer to praising God. The impv. cry of praise is issued in the context of the call to praise: Psa 32:11, "Be happy over Yahweh, and rejoice, O righteous"; similarly Isa 65:18; 66:10; Joel 2:21, 23; Zech 9:9. Psa 149:1f. extends the impv. cry of praise in a juss.: "Sing to Yahweh a new song . . . , may Israel rejoice in its creator, may the sons of Zion rejoice over their king"; juss. also occur in Isa 35:1f.; Psa 96:11 = 1 Chron 16:31; Psa 97:1. A call to praise in the 1st per. (voluntative or cohortative) occurs in Psa 118:24, "This is the day which Yahweh has made, let us rejoice and be happy over it"; similarly in Isa 25:9; Psa 31:8. The call to praise in the "eschatological song of praise" is a prophetic variation (Isa 49:13; 61:10; 66:11; Zech 9:9). Praise or joy is a consequence of God's action: Psa 9:15, "That I may tell . . . , (that) I may rejoice over your aid"; cf. Isa 29:19; 41:16; Zech 10:7; Psa 14:7 = 53:7; 16:9; 21:2; 48:12; 51:10; 65:13; 89:17; 97:8; with the subst. Isa 9:2a txt em; Psa 43:4 txt?; the joy of Yahweh corresponds to this praise in Isa 65:19; Zeph 3:17. *gîl* occurs in the vow to praise in Psa 35:9, "But I will rejoice over Yahweh and be happy over his aid," in addition to Hab 3:18; Psa 13:6.

The motif "so that my enemies may not rejoice" occurs in prayer in Psa 13:5. The disappearance of happiness and joy (from the house of Yahweh) is mourned in the lament (Joel 1:16) and announced in the judgment oracle (Isa 16:10 = Jer 48:33).

In all these groups the basic procedure is the same: the happy, joyous reaction to an event, in most passages to a saving or liberating act of God

(Psa 9:15; 35:9). An act of God in the history of the people or of an individual is usually intended, but history includes God's creative activity (Joel 2:21, 23). The fact that passages termed "profane" also have essentially the same intention should be understood on this basis; even parents' happiness in their children (Prov 23:24f.) presupposes an act of God and is, so seen, joy over an act of God.

(b) The contrast to the two Hos passages in which *gîl* is modified negatively, is, then, all the more pronounced: 9:1, "Do not rejoice, Israel! Do not exult (read *ʾal-tāgēl* for *ʾel-gîl*) like the nations! For you are unfaithful to your God" (cf. the translation of Wolff, *Hos*, Herm, 149), and 10:5, "They rejoice over it because of its glory" (txt?). Wolff (op. cit. 153) says of 9:1: "In the Old Testament the word-pair ניל־שׂמח ("rejoice-exult") occurs for the first time in Hosea. The expression is at the same time evidence for the originally Dionysian character of the Canaanite fertility cult." It may be assumed with certainty that *gîl* also occurred in the Canaanite fertility cults, and it is directly attested by 10:5, if the text is in order. One may not conclude from this, however, that the procedure intended by *gîl* or the term *gîl* itself belonged originally to "the Dionysian character of the Canaanite fertility cult" (cf. Wolff, ibid.). Jubilation as an expression of joy, esp. in the cult, is one of the most widely known phenomenon common to religions. In Hos 9:1 (just as in Amos 5:23), however, *Israel's* joy and exultation in *its* worship is rejected; not because it had its origins in the Canaanite fertility cult, but because it is not in response to the activity of Israel's God: "for you are unfaithful to your God."

5. The LXX usually renders *gîl* by *agalliaomai*, less often by *chairō*. Qumran (cf. Kuhn, *Konk.* 44c) and the NT continue the OT usage. Cf. R. Bultmann, "ἀγαλλιάομαι," *TDNT* 1:19–21.

C. Westermann

גלה *glh* to uncover

S 1540; BDB 162b; *HALOT* 1:191b; *TDOT* 2:476–88; *TWOT* 350; *NIDOTTE* 1655

---

*1. Hebr. *glh* (trans.) meaning "to uncover" has primarily NWSem. counterparts (DISO 50; *HAL* 183b; also Arab. *jalā* "to make/become clear"): Phoen. in the Ahiram inscription (*KAI* no. 1.2), *wygl ʾrn zn* ". . . shall uncover this sarcophagus" (*ANET* 661b); Imp. Aram. in Aḥ. 141, "Reveal not *(ʾl tgly)* thy *[secrets]* before thy [fri]ends" (*ANET* 429b); and in Cowley no. 37.8, "if we were to appear *[glyn ʾnpyn]* before . . . ," as well as in later Aram. (cf. e.g., *LS* 115f.).

A second (intrans.) meaning occurs in Ug., which offers a verb of motion (M. H. Pope, *El in the Ugaritic Texts* [1955], 64; *WUS* no. 652, *gly* "to proceed toward"; *UT* no. 579, "to leave"), also in Hebr. and in later Aram. "to go forth, to go into exile" (as an Aram. loanword also in Akk. *galû;* cf. *AHw* 275b), as well as in Arab. (*jalā* "to emigrate").

The relationship of the two meanings, as usually understood (GB 139f.; *HAL* 183f.; Pope, op. cit.), can be pictured in terms of a regular elliptical omission of the obj. "land" resulting in the meaning "to go forth, to emigrate = to lay (the land) bare." In view of the questionable nature of this derivation, it is probably preferable to leave the etymology issue open and to assume two different verbs for semasiological purposes (cf. Mandl. 262f.; Zorell 151f.): a trans. *glh* I "to uncover" (see 4) and an intrans. *glh* II "to go forth, to be led into exile" (see 3).

glh occurs in the OT in all seven stems (as do only *bq*ᶜ "to divide," → *ḥlh* "to be weak, sick," → *yd*ᶜ "to know," → *yld* "to bear," and → *pqd* "to visit"); with the division into two verbs, the qal, ni., pi., pu., and hitp. remain for *glh* I "to uncover," and qal, hi., and ho. (Isa 38:12 ni. is textually uncertain) remain for *glh* II "to go forth." Of the noms., *gillāyôn* "tablet" (Isa 8:1; on Isa 3:23 see *HAL* 185b) may be assigned to *glh* I; *gôlâ* "exiles; exile" and *gālût* "deportation; deportees" (each with a secondary abstract or concrete meaning, resp.) belong to *glh* II.

glh I pe. "to reveal" and *glh* II ha. "to take into exile," as well as the subst. *gālû* "deportation," occur in Bibl. Aram.

Whether the PN *yoglî* (Num 34:22) should be derived from *glh* I remains uncertain (cf. *IP* 244).

2. The verb occurs in Hebr. 187x (Mandl. mentions Jer 52:29 in some MSS and editions, as well), in Aram. 9x. The distribution of the verb stems is as follows: qal 50x ("to uncover" 21x, "to go forth" 29x, if, contrary to Mandl., Prov 27:25 should be assigned to *glh* II), ni. 32x (Isa 8x, 1 Sam 6x, Ezek 5x, 2 Sam 4x), pi. 56x (excl. Psa 119:22, which, contrary to Lis., belongs to *gll* pi.; Lev 24x, Isa 6x), pu. 2x, hitp. 2x, hi. 38x (Jer 13x, 2 Kgs 12x), ho. 7x; Aram. pe. 7x (Dan), ha. 2x (Ezra). As for the two verbal roots, *glh* I occurs 112x (in addition to 7x Aram.) and *glh* II 75x (incl. Isa 38:12 ni.; as well as 2x Aram.).

gôlâ occurs 42x (Ezra 12x, Ezek 11x, Jer 10x), *gālût* 15x (Jer 5x, Ezek 3x), Aram. *gālû* 4x.

3. Ezek 12:3(bis), where the prophet receives the commission "go forth," and the lament in 1 Sam 4:21f. "the glory has departed from Israel" demonstrate the basic meaning of *glh* II. The same or a similar meaning occurs in Isa 24:11; 38:12 txt? (ni.); Hos 10:5; Job 20:28 (par. *ngr* ni. "to flow, to pour out"); Prov 27:25 (par. *ʾsp* ni. "to be assembled"); Lam 1:3. In the remaining passages, the qal means "to be led into exile" (20x): Judg 18:30(?); 2 Sam 15:19; 2 Kgs 17:23 (par. *sûr* hi. "to remove"); 24:14; 25:21; Isa 5:13; 49:21 (par. *sûr* "to turn aside"); Jer 1:3; 52:27; Ezek 39:23; Amos 1:5; 5:5(bis); 6:7(bis); 7:11(bis), 17(bis); Mic 1:16. There are also 39 hi. passages with the meaning "to lead away (into exile)" and 7 ho. passages (pass., in meaning similar to the qal). The verb has acquired a special place in the prophetic announcement of judgment in Amos (1:5; 5:5, 27; 6:7; 7:11, 17) and Jer (13:19; 20:4; 22:12; 27:20); this announcement of judgment occurs only once in the early

period of Isaiah's preaching (5:13). Most passages occur—in a variety of contexts—in narratives, once even in the sufferer's lament (Lam 1:3).

Notably, only a few, mostly prophetic texts describe Yahweh as the one who takes Israel (Judah) into exile: Jer 29:4, 7, 14; Ezek 39:28; Amos 5:27; Lam 4:22; 1 Chron 5:41 (other nations: 2 Kgs 17:11); the subj. of the verb is usually the nation that takes Israel into exile or its ruler. The notion is certainly firmly established in the prophetic announcement of judgment that the exile is Yahweh's judgment; still, the whole weight of a concrete political event, which resists thorough theologization, characterizes the process described by *glh*. Only once and relatively late is Yahweh's activity identified with a political event in an explicitly conceptual manner: "Yahweh by the hand of Nebuchadnezzar" (1 Chron 5:41). In contrast, cf. e.g., Ezekiel's discussion of the exile; he primarily employs the thoroughly unpolitical verbs *pûṣ* hi. and *zrh* "to disperse" (*glh* qal/hi. only in Ezek 39:23, 28; cf. 12:3), and here Yahweh is regularly the subj. (5:10, 12; 11:16; 12:14f.; 20:23; 22:15; 36:19).

The fact that Yahweh, the God of Israel, took his own people into exile makes sense in the context of history, at the beginning of which stood the promise of and guidance into the land; Yahweh's judgment consists of his removal of the gift of the land from the people who turned away from him despite every warning (cf. the parallelism of the expulsion of the nations in the conquest and the expulsion of Israel in 2 Kgs 17:11 [Dtr], similarly Deut 7:22; 8:19f.).

Remarkably, *glh* does not occur in this usage in the Pentateuch, nor in Deut, where expulsion from the land is an important and emphasized threat in the event of disobedience (instead, *ʾbd mēʿal hāʾāreṣ*, "to disappear from the land," Deut 4:26; 11:17; cf. 8:19f.; *pûṣ* hi. "to scatter," 4:27; 28:64). The fact that *glh* "to go forth," which could also refer to the old and widespread practice of the deportation of an individual (2 Sam 15:19), became specialized to mean "to be taken into exile" only when deportations of whole population groups as a means of conquest entered Israelite history, contributed to this usage; in this regard, one should remember the mass deportations and resettlement of the Neo-Assyr. Empire, and of the Urartians (Wolff, *Amos*, Herm, 149–52). 8th-cent. prophecy (esp. Amos) adopted the verb only in this specialized meaning, although it did not gain universal popularity, as Deut demonstrates; only in Dtr diction does it become the dominant term for exile. This assumption is supported by the fact that the noms. *gôlâ* and *gālût* "exile, exiles" occur only in the prophets of judgment and in later historical books.

One can detect another process with respect to *šbh* "to lead out as captives": *šbh* originally indicated the plundering of captives (esp. of women and children) on military campaigns (Gen 34:29; 1 Sam 30:2ff., etc.); after the deportation of Samaria an expansion of the basic meaning appears (Obad 11), so that exile can also be indicated by *šbh* (1 Kgs 8:46ff.; Jer 13:17; Ezek 6:9).

4. (a) *glh* I qal "to uncover" refers primarily to the organs of perception: "to uncover = open" the ear (a human subj.: 1 Sam 20:2, 12f.; 22:8bis, 17; Ruth 4:4; divine subj.: 1 Sam 9:15; 2 Sam 7:27 = 1 Chron 17:25; Job 33:16; 36:10, 15); "to expose = open" the eye (Num 24:4, 16; cf. pi. Num 22:31 and

Psa 119:18). *glh* is also used for the publication of a document (Esth 3:14; 8:13), the pass. ptcp. *gālûy* for the open (as opposed to the sealed) bill of sale (Jer 32:11, 14). Otherwise, *sôd* "secret" is the only obj. of *glh* qal (Amos 3:7; Prov 20:19; see also Prov 11:13 and 25:9 with *glh* pi.; cf. *HP* 202f.).

(b) The ni. envisions action with respect to the subj. itself; the translation can be either pass., "to be uncovered" (nakedness: Exod 20:26; Isa 47:3; Ezek 16:36, 57 txt em; 23:29; skirt: Jer 13:22; foundations: 2 Sam 22:16 = Psa 18:16 par. *rʾh* ni. "to become visible"; Ezek 13:14; cf. Mic 1:6 pi.; guilt, evil: Ezek 21:29; Hos 7:1; Prov 26:26; "to become known" Isa 23:1; "to be revealed" Dan 10:1 [a word]) or reflexive, "to expose oneself" (3x in 2 Sam 6:20), "to show oneself, reveal" (people: 1 Sam 14:8, 11; gates of death: Job 38:17 par. *rʾh* ni.; God: Gen 35:6; 1 Sam 2:27bis; 3:21; Isa 22:14; his arm: Isa 53:1; his majesty: Isa 40:5; his righteousness: Isa 56:1; his word: 1 Sam 3:7). The impv. in Isa 49:9 can be understood as a tolerative, "let yourself be revealed = come into the light." The plur. ptcp. *hanniglôt* refers to the Sinai revelation and should not be translated "what is revealed," but (nonresultantly) "what has been revealed (is valid for us and our children forever)."

(c) The pi. always indicates the disclosure of something normally hidden ("to disclose"; cf. *HP* 202f.). It parallels the qal to a degree: to "open" eyes (Num 22:31; Psa 119:18 alongside *nbṭ* hi. "to view"), "to make known, publish, reveal" (Jer 11:20; 20:12; 33:6; Psa 98:2), "to divulge" (Isa 16:3; Prov 11:13; 25:9). Other meanings are: "to discover, find" something hidden (Jer 49:10; Job 12:22 par. *yṣʾ* hi. *lāʾôr* "to bring to light"; Mic 1:6 foundations), "to uncover, accuse, punish" guilt (Job 20:27; Lam 2:14; 4:22 par. *pqd* "to visit"; Isa 26:21 bloodguilt). The chief use of the pi. refers, however, to the forbidden sexual realm (40x of the uncovering of private parts or of that which covers them: skirt, veil, cover in Deut 23:1; 27:20; Isa 22:8; 47:2[bis]; 57:8 txt em; Nah 3:5; Job 41:5; Ruth 3:4, 7). 24 passages in this group occur in Lev 18 and 20. They are legal prescriptions treating forbidden sexual relations; "to uncover the shame" here is primarily an expression for engagement in sexual intercourse. In many passages it has the meaning "to rape."

These passages are significant for the meaning of the verb *glh* as a whole in that the verb in them has a negative tone in the ear of the Israelite: with the obj. *ʿerwâ* "shame, nakedness," *glh* was something forbidden, something that one must avoid. This connotation is associated with the Israelite concept that clothing is essential to being human; it is a gift of the creator (Gen 3:21), and disrobing harms human worth.

Besides Lev 18 and 20, prophetic accusations charging Israel with faithlessness toward Yahweh (Isa 57:8; Ezek 23:18[bis]; cf. Ezek 16:36, 57 ni.) and related announcements of judgment use *glh* pi. in the manner under discussion: Israel will be violated by its lovers (Hos 2:12; Nah 3:5; Ezek 16:37; 22:10; 23:10; cf. Jer 13:22 ni.; against Babel Isa 47:2[bis]).

The pu. ptcp. means "open, uncovered" (Prov 27:5, a reprimand; Nah 2:8 txt?), the hitp. means "to uncover oneself" (Gen 9:21, Noah; Prov 18:2, "heart").

(d) Relatively few passages have God as the subj. of *glh* I; thus its proper usage is in the realm of profane events. At any rate, one cannot see this verb as a theological term; rather, the Hebrews heard in it a thoroughly this-worldly process that could occasionally—but only rarely—be used to describe an act of God, primarily in two groups of texts: (1) just as a human being can be said to expose (open) someone's ear, so can God; and (2) just as a person can appear to someone else, so God can appear (reveal himself) to someone.

(1) The revelation in 1 Sam 9:15, "But Yahweh had . . . exposed the ear of Samuel," is a divine instruction to the mediator concerning the anointing of the king. The expression "to open the ear" occurs in the same context in Isa 22:14, "But Yahweh of hosts has revealed himself to my ear"; the clause replaces the messenger formula and is the only passage of this nature in the pre-exilic writing prophets. In 2 Sam 7:27 = 1 Chron 17:25 David prays: "You have uncovered the ear of your servant." Here, however, it is not a direct revelation but one mediated by the prophet. Three passages in Job (33:16; 36:10, 15; all in the discourses of Elihu) refer to God's revelation to a normal person; in 33:16 it takes place by means of a dream or a night vision, in 36:10, 15 it is God's warning or reprimand that no longer comes as a direct revelation but through difficulties. Here, then—already in the OT!—the word "to reveal" no longer has transcendental character; it means something that anyone can experience, even in the normal events of life.

(2) In Gen 35:7 the phrase "for there God revealed himself to him" refers back to the theophany in Gen 28. The passage shows that the verb can describe a theophany; it does so, however, only in this passage, never in the narrative of a theophany. The word occurs 3x in the narrative of Samuel's childhood. A man of God reminds Eli: "Thus says Yahweh: I did indeed reveal myself to the house of your father when they were still in Egypt" (1 Sam 2:27); and then 1 Sam 3:21 says: "Yahweh revealed himself to Samuel" (cf. also 1 Sam 3:7 "the word of Yahweh had not yet been revealed to him"). Here then *glh* indicates explicitly a verbal revelation in prophetic fashion. This reference also appears in Amos 3:7 in the programmatic phrase: "Yahweh does nothing . . . without disclosing (revealing) his decision to his servants, the prophets." The phrase is not spoken by Amos; rather, it is a later reflection concerning the activity of the prophets. The passages in 1 Sam 2 and 3 (as well as 9:15), together with Amos 3:7, demonstrate that the verb *glh* can serve, *subsequently,* in reflection from a distance, to describe the prophetic reception of the word. But even this sense appears only in a very small group of texts (incl. also the late passage Dan 10:1). It thus becomes even more obvious that, like the theophanies, the prophetic reception of the word per se is *not* indicated in the OT by *glh.*

Passages from the Balaam pericope describe the seer as "with downcast and uncovered eyes" (Num 24:4, 16; cf. 22:31). Here the verb *glh* describes a specific process of revelation: the eyes of the seer are opened so that he sees something that he otherwise could not see and that only he sees. Only here does the verb *glh* belong integrally to the process of the seer's vision; here an original locus for the verb *glh* in a "revelation" process can be unmistakably recognized in the description of the vision of the seer (cf. H. Haag, " 'Offenbaren' in die hebräischen Bibel," *TZ* 16 [1960]: 251–58; further

W. Zimmerli, "'Offenbarung' im AT," *EvT* 22 [1962]: 15–31 with bibliog.; R. Schnackenburg, "Zum Offenbarungsgedanken in der Bibel," *BZ* 7 [1963]: 2–22).

The concluding phrase of Deut 29:28, "The hidden remains with Yahweh, our God, but what is revealed (apparent) is valid for us and our children for ever," implies that the word of God, God's commandments and promises, are openly accessible. The verb *glh*, with God as subj., points to this free accessibility of God's word for the Israelites.

In Isa 40:5 ". . . and the glory of God will be revealed," the word has the sense "will be recognizable, perceptible," as the continuation demonstrates: ". . . and all flesh will see." This text indicates not a specific process of revelation but God's activity in history: the glory of Yahweh will be recognizable in his act of deliverance for Israel. The verb functions similarly in Isa 56:1. The question in Isa 53:1: "And to whom will the arm of Yahweh be revealed?" means: To whom has the activity of Yahweh become clear? In all three passages, therefore, *glh* refers to God's activity in history.

(e) If one surveys passages with God as the subj. of *glh*, one discovers that *glh* in the OT has not become a term for revelation. No fixed, frequent, and clearly defined usage can be demonstrated. *glh* can indicate God's appearance or self-revelation in discourse or in action, but this meaning only rarely occurs and overwhelmingly in retrospect. The verb is so minimally tied to specific revelation processes that it can also indicate, in addition to verbal revelation to the prophets (only rarely) or an appearance of the divine (only Gen 35:7), God's activity in history and in an individual's destiny. The expression of these extremely varied types of God's self-revelation with one verb—still rarely used for these purposes—also indirectly demonstrates that Israel saw these various possibilities for revelation as relatively close together, and one could not play the one against the other. It ought also to be observed that the verb *glh* in this meaning did not produce a nom. formation.

5. The two distinct groups of meaning are also mirrored in the LXX renderings: *glh* II is predominantly translated by *apoikizein*, followed by *metoikizein* and the corresponding derivatives. *aichmalōteuein*, etc., also occur, corresponding more to the Hebr. *šbh*, although even in Hebr. some overlappings are already apparent. The basic meaning still stands behind the translation *aperchesthai*.

The overwhelmingly predominant rendering of *glh* I is *apokalyptein;* it corresponds precisely to the Hebr. verb in the sexual realm as well as in reference to the sense organs. Occasionally, however, other verbs of removal (i.e., *ektithēmi*) or of perception *(epiphainein, phaneroun)* could also be used. The LXX too, then, did not yet understand *glh* as a special term for "to reveal."

The situation has already changed at Qumran. The traditional usages of *glh* I also occur here (*glh* II occurs only as a citation of Amos 5:27 in CD 7:14f.): "to open" the ear (1QH 1:21; 6:4; 18:4f.; CD 2:2; etc.), the heart (1QH 12:34; 18:24), the eyes (1QH 18:19; CD 2:14). Yet a specific technical usage also appears: the revelation of the eschaton contained in the Torah and the Prophets that must be made known through study of the Scriptures *(drš)* and exegesis (*pešer;* 1QS 1:9; 5:9, 12; 8:1, 15f.; 9:13, 19; cf. 1QpHab 11:1; 1QH

5:12; CD 3:13; 15:13; cf. D. Lührmann, *Das Offenbarungsverständnis bei Paulus und in paulinischen Gemeinden* [1965], 84–87, with bibliog.).

On the NT see, in addition to Lührmann, A. Oepke, "καλύπτω," *TDNT* 3:556–92. No relationship between the OT usage of *glh* and the NT concept of revelation, which shifts the focus from the process of revelation to that which has been revealed (the content of revelation), can be identified, but the parallelism continues on into the NT as an indication of the saving activity of God and of the apocalyptic vision of a particular individual (Rom 3:21; 1 Cor 14:6); cf. Lührmann, op. cit. An essential distinction between the usage of *glh* in the OT and the NT concept of revelation lies in the fact that the strict association of revelation and faith is entirely absent here; in the OT *glh* indicates a self-disclosure of God that can be experienced.

C. Westermann/R. Albertz

גמל *gml* **to do, show**

S 1580; BDB 168a; *HALOT* 1:197a; *TDOT* 3:23–33; *TWOT* 360; *NIDOTTE* 1694

---

1. The root *gml* may only be certainly and originally identified in Akk., Hebr., and Arab.; but the meanings diverge sharply.

Akk. has *gamālu* "to treat cordially, to spare, to save" (*AHw* 275f.; *CAD* G:21–23) and numerous derivatives, particularly *gimillu* "cordial (less often, negative) requital" (*AHw* 288f.) and *gitmālu* "to complete" (*AHw* 294; although *CAD* G:110f. separates it from *gamālu* on account of the divergent meaning).

Jew. Aram., Sam., and Mid. Hebr. occurrences (*HAL* 189a) are purely bibl. usages and consequently offer no independent information.

In Arab. two different terms appear: *jamala* "to gather" and *jamula* "to be pretty" (with derivatives, e.g., *jumlat* "totality, sum"). On the problem of etymology, cf. L. Kopf, *VT* 8 (1958): 168f.

One should probably posit some connection to the root *gmr* (attested in Akk., Ug., Hebr., Aram., etc.).

Hebr. has only the qal in the meaning "to be at an end, bring to an end" (Psa 7:10; 12:2; 57:3; 77:9; 138:8; cf. Bibl. Aram. *g*[e]*mîr* "filled out" in Ezra 7:12). M. Dahood ("The Root GMR in the Psalms," *TS* 14 [1953]: 595–97; *Bib* 45 [1964]: 400) suggests the meaning "to avenge" for Psa 7:10; 57:3; 138:8 (followed by *HAL* 190a "to retaliate, avenge") corresponding to Ug. *gmr* (*WUS* no. 664; *UT* no. 592) and combines *gmr/gml;* cf. O. Loretz, "Das hebr. Verbum GMR," *BZ* 5 (1961): 261–63. The LXX translation of Psa 57:3, where *euergetēsas* renders *gōmēr,* demonstrates that the root *gmr* could be understood in the sense of the meaning of *gml.*

The OT uses only the ni. ("to be weaned") in addition to the qal; nom. derivatives are: *g*[e]*mûl* and *g*[e]*mûlâ* "deed, requital," and *tagmûl* "good deed"; the PNs *gāmûl, g*[e]*mallî,* and *gamlîʾēl* should also be included (*IP* 182).

2. The verb *gml* qal occurs 34x (23x in the meaning "to do, show," 11x "to wean, mature"), *gml* ni. "to be weaned," 3x (Gen 21:8bis; 1 Sam 1:22). *g*[e]*mûl*

occurs 19x (pl. only Psa 103:2), *g^emûlâ* 3x (sg. 2 Sam 19:37, pl. Isa 59:18 and Jer 51:56), *tagmûl* 1x (Psa 116:12, pl., with an Aram. suf.). Of the total of 60 occurrences of the word group, 15 are in Psa, 12 in Isa, 6 in 1 Sam, and 5 in Prov.

3. It is difficult to accept a basic meaning valid for all derivatives. The meaning "to execute, do (to the end, to completion), complete" most probably underlies the subsequent development (cf. GB 144a "to complete" with reference to the Arab. *kml* "to be complete," etc.). From here it can evolve, on the one hand, into the meaning "to do," either good (1 Sam 24:18a; Prov 11:17; 31:12) or evil (Gen 50:15, 17; Deut 32:6; 1 Sam 24:18b; Isa 3:9; Psa 7:5; 137:8; Prov 3:30; 2 Chron 20:11), which occasionally assumes the nuance of "requital, repayment" (2 Sam 19:37). Cf. also the double meaning in Akk. *turru gimilla* (*AHw* 289a; see 1). Only through it can a relationship that has become uneven be rebalanced and brought to perfection (cf. e.g., Psa 7:5). Thus *gml* can be used in conjunction with *šlm* pi. "to requite" (Joel 4:4; Psa 137:8). On the other hand, the meanings "to perfect (a child) = wean" (1 Sam 1:23f.; 1 Kgs 11:20; Isa 11:8; 28:9; Hos 1:8; Psa 131:2) and "to ripen" (Num 17:23, almonds on Aaron's staff; Isa 18:5, grapes) can develop from the starting point assumed above.

The subst. *g^emûl* occurs only in the sense of repayment and requital (Isa 3:11; Prov 12:14; 2 Chron 32:25) or of the doing of good or evil (Joel 4:4, 7; similarly *g^emûlâ* 2 Sam 19:37), which can revisit the agent (Judg 9:16; Obad 15; Psa 28:4; 94:2; Lam 3:64). Like the verb, *g^emûl* can be used in conjunction with the root *šlm* (Isa 59:18; 66:6; Jer 51:6; Joel 4:4; Psa 137:8; Prov 19:17; with *šûb* hi. "to requite" Joel 4:4, 7; Psa 28:4; 94:2; Prov 12:14; Lam 3:64).

4. Derivatives of the root *gml* also describe God's relationship to people (2 Sam 22:21 = Psa 18:21) and vice versa (Joel 4:4). The examples particularly emphasize God's action for good (Isa 63:7; Psa 13:6; 103:10; 116:7; 119:17; 142:8), although they do not suggest a specific connotation. The subst. indicates divine deeds (Psa 103:2) requiring corresponding human behavior (Isa 35:4). It is often associated with *šlm* pi. (see 3; Isa 59:18 has *g^emûlâ* too; 66:6), indicating the original meaning "to complete, repay (in order to bring to a conclusion)" (esp. in Prov 19:17). Thus God can even be called *ʾēl g^emūlôt* "God of requital" (Jer 51:56, against Babel, par. "he will repay them" with → *šlm* pi.).

5. *gml* occurs in the documents from Qumran in the meaning "to do"; *g^emûl* also occurs (Kuhn, *Konk.* 45f.; also *GCDS* 104). The LXX uses *antapodidōmi*, etc., most frequently, among numerous other translations, thereby taking into account, however, only the meaning "to do, requite"; cf. F. Büchsel, *TDNT* 2:169, on this term in the NT.

G. Sauer

גער $g^{c}r$ to scold

S 1605; BDB 172a; *HALOT* 1:199b; *TDOT* 3:49–53; *TWOT* 370; *NIDOTTE* 1721

1. The verb $g^{c}r$ "to scold" occurs in the OT only in the qal; two fem. substs. derive from it: $g^{e\,c}\bar{a}r\hat{a}$ and *mig*^{c}*eret* (*HAL* 192a, KBL 494a with suppl. 164). The root also occurs in Ug. (*UT* no. 606; *WUS* no. 681; Gröndahl 125) and in other related languages (Aram., Arab., Eth., sometimes for the sounds made by cattle and horses; cf. Ug. *KTU* 1.72.27), but is lacking in Akk. (cf. *HAL* 192a).

2. The verb is attested in the OT 14x, the subst. $g^{e\,c}\bar{a}r\hat{a}$ 15x, the subst. *mig*^{c}*eret* 1x (Deut 28:20).

Mal 2:3 should surely be emended with Horst (HAT 14, 266), *HAL*, and others to *gōdēa*^{c}; the emendation of $g^{c}r$ for rg^{c} in Isa 51:15; Jer 31:35, suggested by H. Gunkel, *Schöpfung und Chaos* (1896), 94n.8, has not gained acceptance.

Prov 13:8 should be emended with Gemser, HAT 16, 48 (contra F. M. Seely, "Note on $g^{c}rh$ with Especial Reference to Proverbs 13:8," *Bible Translator* 19 [1959]: 20f.); the second $g^{e\,c}\bar{a}r\hat{a}$ in Isa 30:17 is stricken by many exegetes (e.g., O. Procksch, *Jesaja*, KAT, 1:394).

3. According to P. Joüon ("*gā*^{c}*ar* et $g^{e\,c}\bar{a}r\bar{a}h$," *Bib* 6 [1925]: 318ff.; and Seely, op. cit. 20f.), the basic meaning of $g^{c}r$ is "to cry aloud, scream at" (cf. also A. A. Macintosh, "A Consideration of Hebrew $g^{c}r$," *VT* 19 [1969]: 471–79). Of the many verbs with the meaning "to cry" (see KBL suppl. 73; → *ṣ*^{c}*q*), it is distinguished by its limitation to "to cry out scoldingly, scold." The concept of scolding has the basic meaning in German, too, of "to raise commotion about something" (Kluge 643). Scolding or reviling is "a sterilized and domesticated form of cursing or exorcising" (*BFPS* 68; van der Leeuw 2:408f.); it seeks "to tear someone down." The stem $g^{c}r$ occurs in Psa 119:21 and Deut 28:20 alongside forms of → ʾ*rr*. Many passages attest to the destructive effect of $g^{c}r$ (J. Pedersen, *Der Eid bei den Semiten* [1914], 82; Seely, op. cit. 20f.); for this reason the rendering "to threaten" (so *HAL* and others) is not recommended (*BFPS* 65f.: "threatening" primarily means a gesture, leaves open the question of the realization of that which is threatened, and usually has a qualified or conditional character—all of this does not apply to $g^{c}r$; cf. Joüon, op. cit. 320). Gen 37:10 demonstrates the "destructive" character of the $g^{c}r$ through the report of the words of the reprimand. The wisdom examples in Prov 13:1; 17:10; Eccl 7:5 should be understood in the same sense. The subj. of $g^{c}r$ in these cases is the father or the wisdom teacher. When in Ugaritic Baal scolds the gods on account of their cowardice (*KTU* 1.2.I.24), or Anat scolds Baal on account of his overzealousness in the battle with Yamm (1.2.IV.28), when the captain of the temple guard does not scold Jeremiah in Jer 29:27, and when the servants of Boaz do not scold Ruth in Ruth 2:16, in each case the scolding was meant to hinder something (Gunkel, op. cit. 59n.2). In Isa 30:17, $g^{c}r$ describes a military action; it cannot, however, easily concern the "battle cry of the Assyrians" (B. Duhm, *Jesaia*, HKAT [1968^{5}], 221; J. Jeremias, *Theophanie* [1965], 33n.2, considers this the basic

meaning); rather, it concerns the reprimand at the beginning of the battle (cf. Gunkel, op. cit. 113), as we know it from Homer's *Iliad* (e.g., 17.11f.; cf. 1 Sam 17:41ff.; Enuma Elish IV:76ff.). In Hebrew the battle cry is called *t^e^rû^c^â* or *ṣeraḥ*. The point in Isa 30:17 would then be: the Israelites already flee at the reprimand.

The use of $g^{c}r$ (almost always) with b^{e} (= an inimical "against"; BrSynt §106h) and of $g^{ec}\bar{a}r\hat{a}$ with *min* in conjunction with verbs with a pass. meaning (e.g., Psa 18:16; 76:7; 80:17) or with "to flee" (Isa 30:17; Psa 104:7) corresponds to the characteristic just mentioned.

4. The specifically theological usage connects primarily with the reprimand in battle. The $g^{c}r$ often occurs in connection with Yahweh's struggle with chaos (Psa 104:7; Job 26:11; Nah 1:4; Psa 68:31; 106:9; 18:16 [= 2 Sam 22:16]; Isa 50:2; cf. Gunkel, op. cit. 68, 106, 111; Jeremias, op. cit. 20, 31ff., 67f., 90ff., 146; it must be maintained against Ph. Reymond, "L'Eau, sa vie, et sa signification dans l'AT," *SVT* 6 [1958]: 188f., that the chaos struggle and thus the $g^{c}r$ do not originally belong to the creation concept; cf. Westermann, *Gen*, CC, 1:31). The effects of the $g^{c}r$ are: the sea, the water, the $t^{e}h\hat{o}m$, the Reed Sea flee, recede, or dry up, the pillars of heaven sway. $g^{c}r$ stands parallel to God's "wrath" (*za^c^am*, → *^ap*, → *ḥēmâ*, Nah 1:4ff.) or to rg^{c} "to agitate," *mḥṣ* "to strike down," *ḥll* po. "to bore through" (Job 26:11). $g^{c}r$ occurs together with the chaos struggle motif in epiphanies (Westermann, *PLP* 93ff.). $g^{c}r$ in Yahweh's struggle with the nations (Isa 17:13; Psa 9:6; Isa 66:15, a world judgment epiphany; Psa 80:17; 76:7 at the Reed Sea) and with the spirits of Belial (1QM 14:10) may also be associated with the chaos struggle motif. Where Israel is the obj. of a divine reprimand (Isa 51:20; 54:9), the concept of Yahweh as a warrior also probably stands in the background. In Mal 3:11 Yahweh's reprimand is supposed to hinder the locust plague (Horst, HAT 14, 273); in Zech 3:2 Yahweh reprimands the Satan for opposing a majestic act of Yahweh (Horst, BK 16, 13f.).

5. Qumran follows the theological usage of the OT. On the LXX and the NT, cf. E. Stauffer, "ἐπιτιμάω," *TDNT* 2:623–27; Joüon, op. cit. 320f.; H. Hanse, "λοιδορέω," *TDNT* 4:293f.; H. C. Kee, *NTS* 14 (1967): 232–46.

G. Liedke

גֵּר *gēr* **sojourner** → גור *gûr*

דבק *dbq* to hang on

S 1692; BDB 179b; *HALOT* 1:209a; *TDOT* 3:79–84; *TWOT* 398; *NIDOTTE* 1815

1. The root *dbq* occurs only in Hebr., Aram., and Arab. (apparently adapted from Aram.; Fraenkel 120f.); cf. Eth. *ṭbq.*

The verb appears in the qal, pu., hi. (normal causative "to make stick" and inner-trans. or internal "to make oneself stick, overtake"), and ho.; additionally, there are a verbal adj. *dābēq* "adhering, attached" and a subst. *debeq* "solder" (Isa 41:7), "appendage" (1 Kgs 22:34 = 2 Chron 18:33).

Extrabibl. occurrences contemporary with the OT are only Aram. pe. in the Elephantine Papyri (5th cent. BCE; *DISO* 54), used in contracts concerning the borders around plots of ground, sections of buildings, etc. (e.g., *BMAP* 9.9 *ʿlyʾ lh byt qnḥnty dbq lh ʾgr bʾgr* "in the upper portion thereof the house of Q. borders on it, wall to wall"); also in 1QapGen in the meaning "to reach" (usually stereotypically, e.g., 21:1 *ʿd dy dbqt lbyt ʾl* "until I arrive at Bethel").

2. The OT exhibits the word group 60x in Hebr. and 1x in Aram. in a normal distribution (*dbq* qal 39x, pu. 2x, hi. 12x, ho. 1x; Aram. pe. 1x; Hebr. *dābēq* 3x, *debeq* 3x).

3. All meanings cluster tightly around the basic meaning "to be close by"; only the most important are mentioned here:

(a) In the objective realm the (neutrally inflected) qal expresses the circumstance of "hanging on, sticking to, hugging to, bordering on," with the verb construed intrans. with the preps. *bᵉ*, *lᵉ*, *ʾel*, *ʿim*, and *ʾaḥᵃrê*, except in Gen 19:19. Causative hi. "to cause to hang on" with *bᵉ or ʾel* belongs in this category.

(b) Of persons, the qal means "to hang on, hold fast to, hold on to (willingly)," etc.; the (inner-trans.) hi. "to cause oneself to be close by" signifies "reaching, overtaking, following" in military contexts (with an obj. or with *ʾaḥᵃrê*).

Aram. pe. also has the meanings "to reach" and "to follow" to a degree (1QapGen, Christ. Pal., and Syr.); regarding the transition in meaning, cf. *dbq* with *ʾaḥᵃrê* in Jer 42:16.

(c) *ḥšq* qal "to hang on (in love)" (8x) is the verb most clearly related semantically. It is used to describe a relationship between man and woman (Gen 34:8; Deut 21:11), human and God (Psa 91:14), and God and human (Deut 7:7; 10:15), as well as more generally in the meaning "to have desire (for an activity)" (1 Kgs 9:19 = 2 Chron 8:6, with the corresponding subst. *ḥēšeq* "lust, desire," 1 Kgs 9:1, 19; 2 Chron 8:6). *ḥšq* pi. "to bind" (Exod 38:28, plus the pu. Exod 27:17; 38:17, and *ḥiššūq* "[binding =] wheel spoke," 1 Kgs 7:33) and *ḥāšûq* "binding" (8x in Exod 27:10f.; 36:38; 38:10–19) have acquired a technical, mechanical meaning.

(d) *ʿzb* "to leave" (Gen 2:24; Ruth 1:14, 16), *sûr* "to turn aside" (2 Kgs 3:3; 18:6), and *ʿlh mēʾaḥᵃrê* "to fall away from" (2 Sam 20:2) can be cited as antonyms to *dbq* "to hang on to."